Indian Paintings

The Collection of the Dresden
Kupferstich-Kabinett

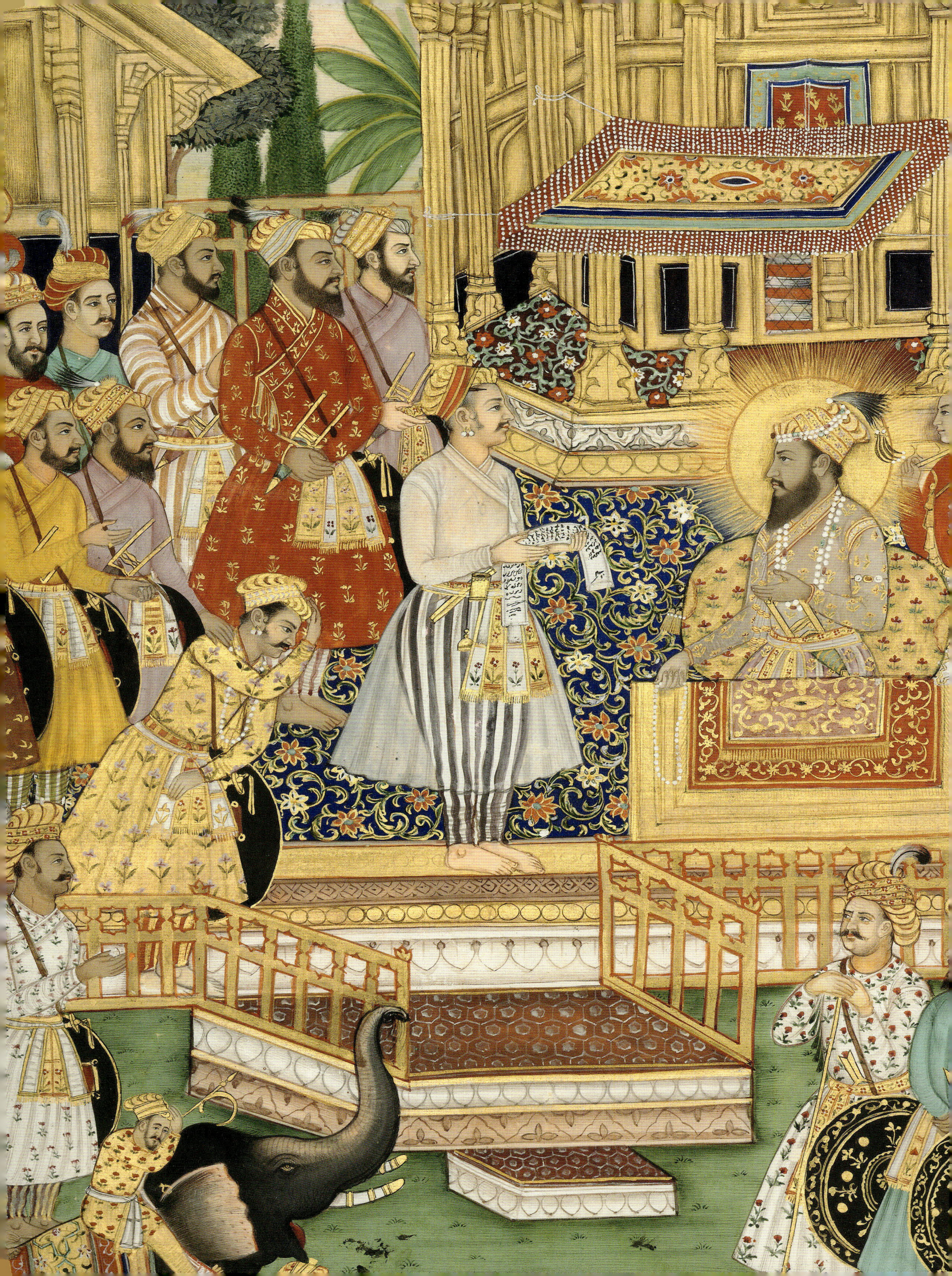

Indian Paintings

The Collection of the Dresden Kupferstich-Kabinett

EDITED BY
STAATLICHE KUNSTSAMMLUNGEN DRESDEN
PETRA KUHLMANN-HODICK

SANDSTEIN VERLAG

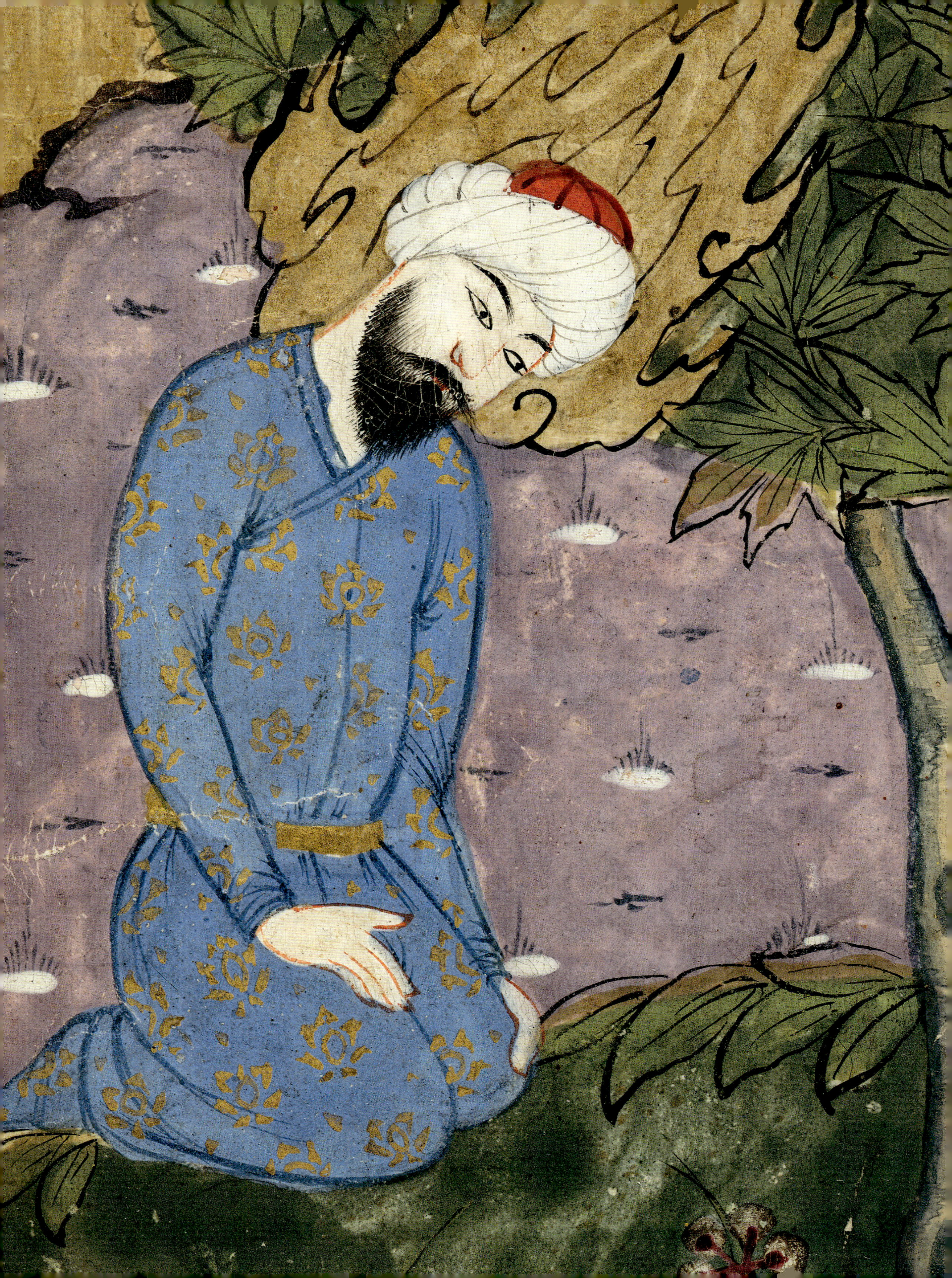

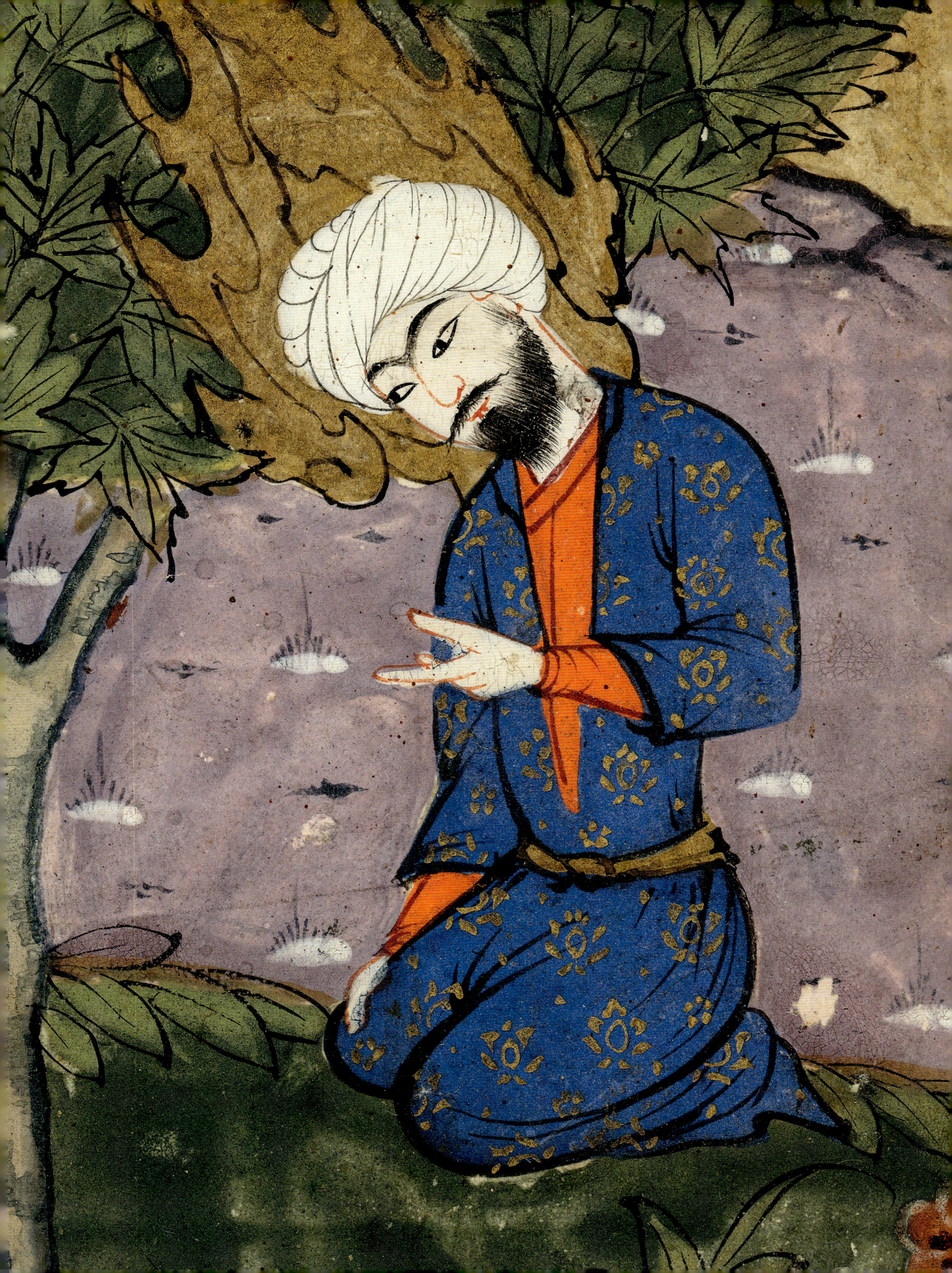

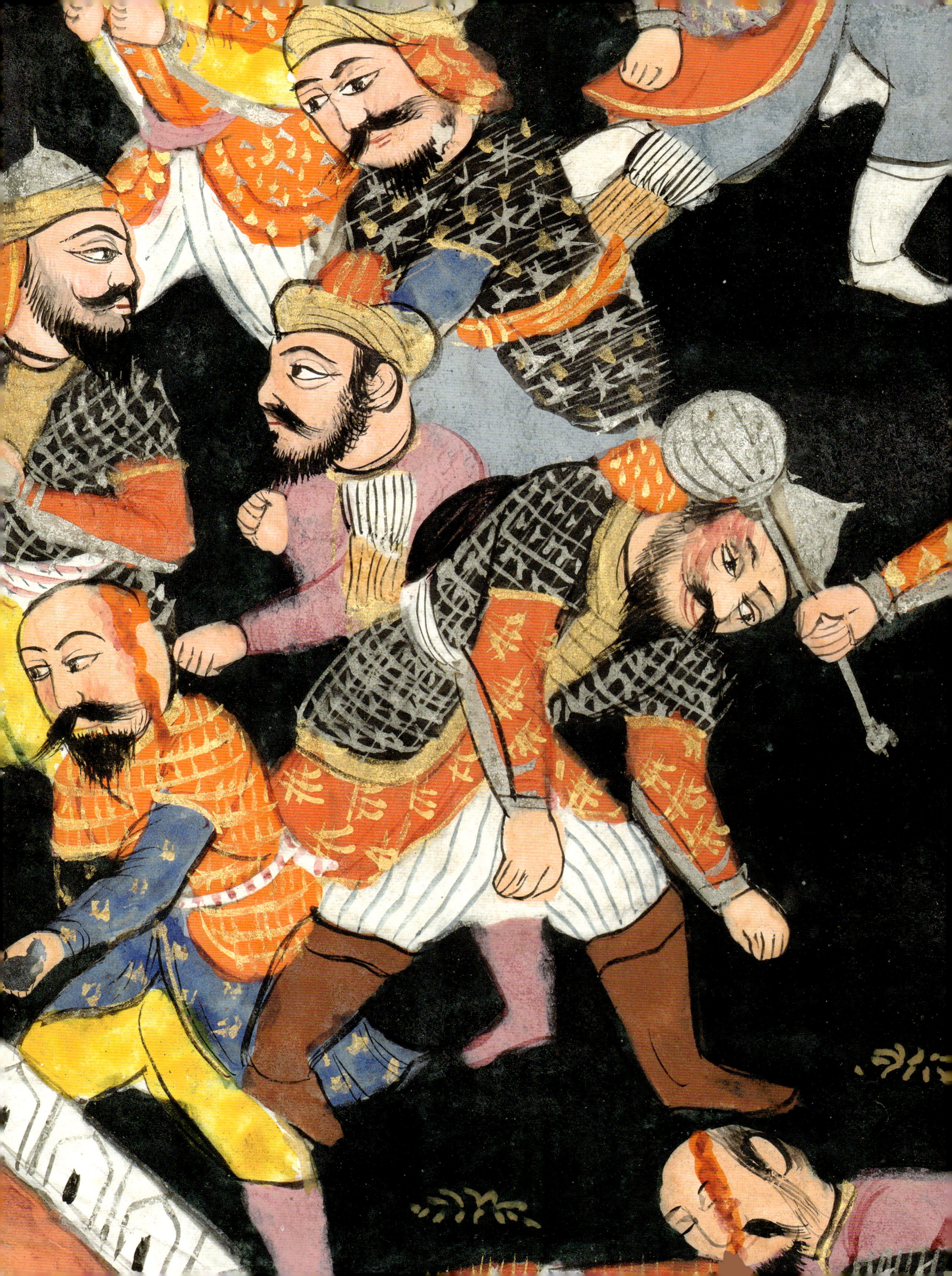

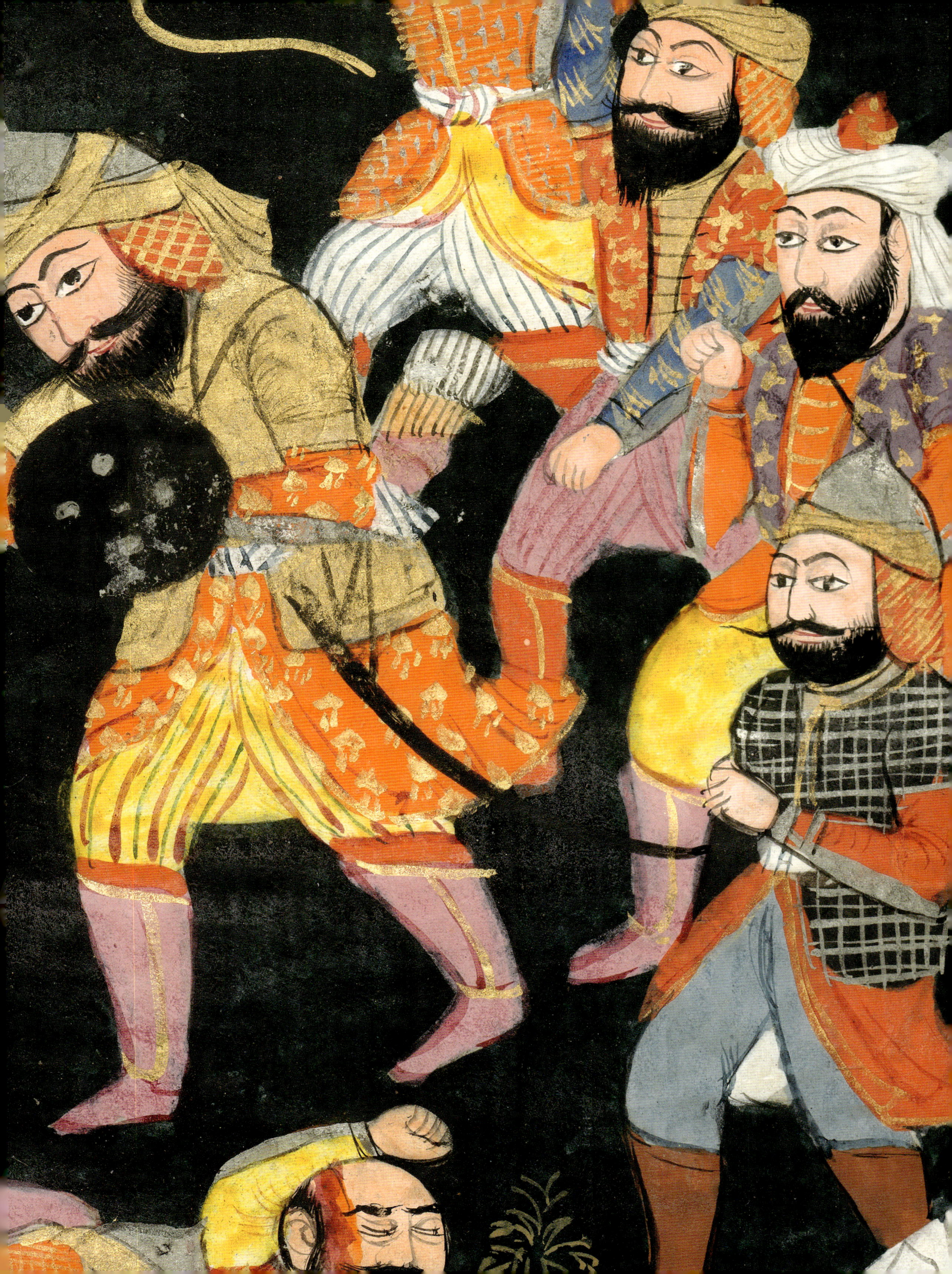

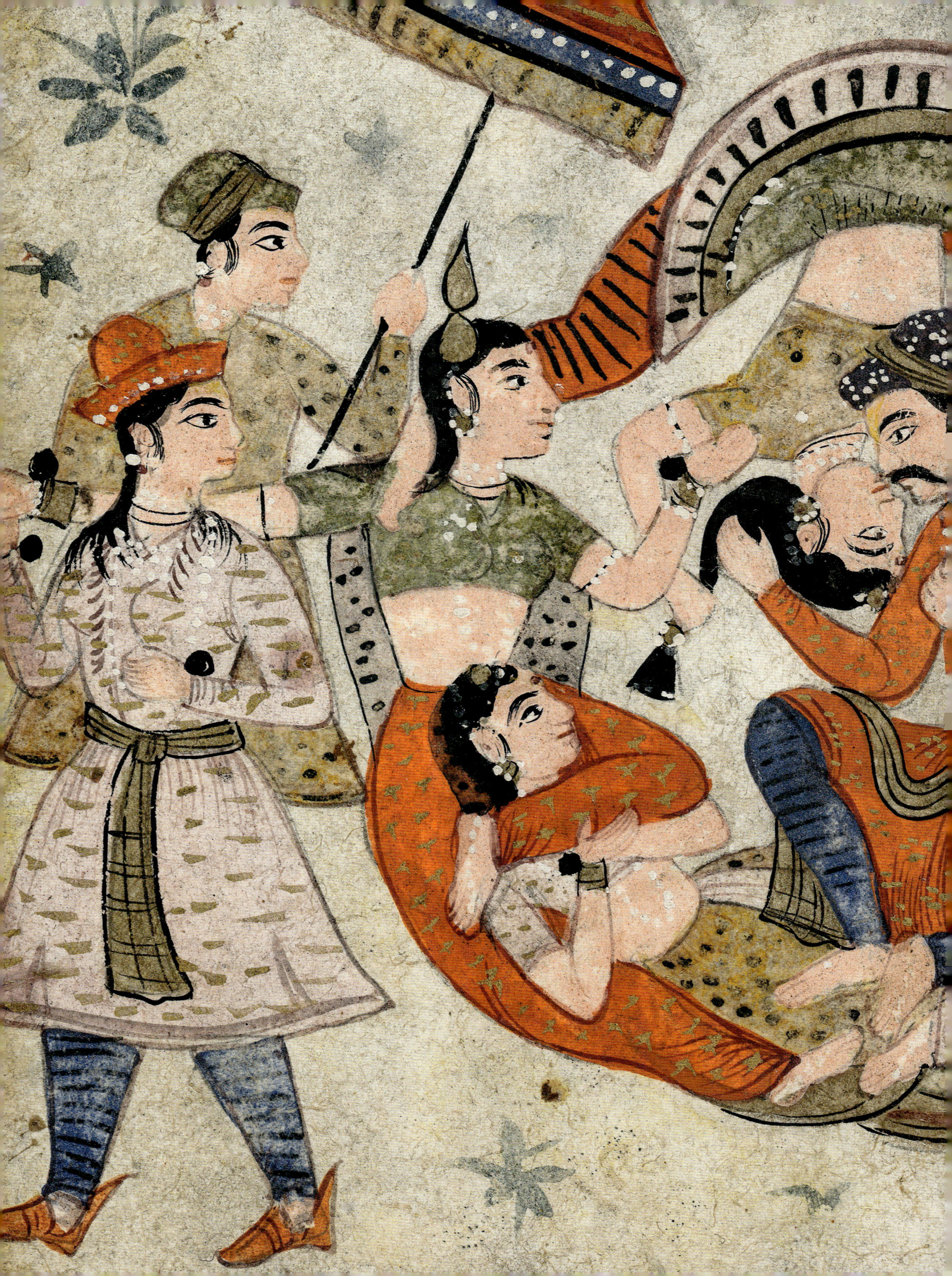

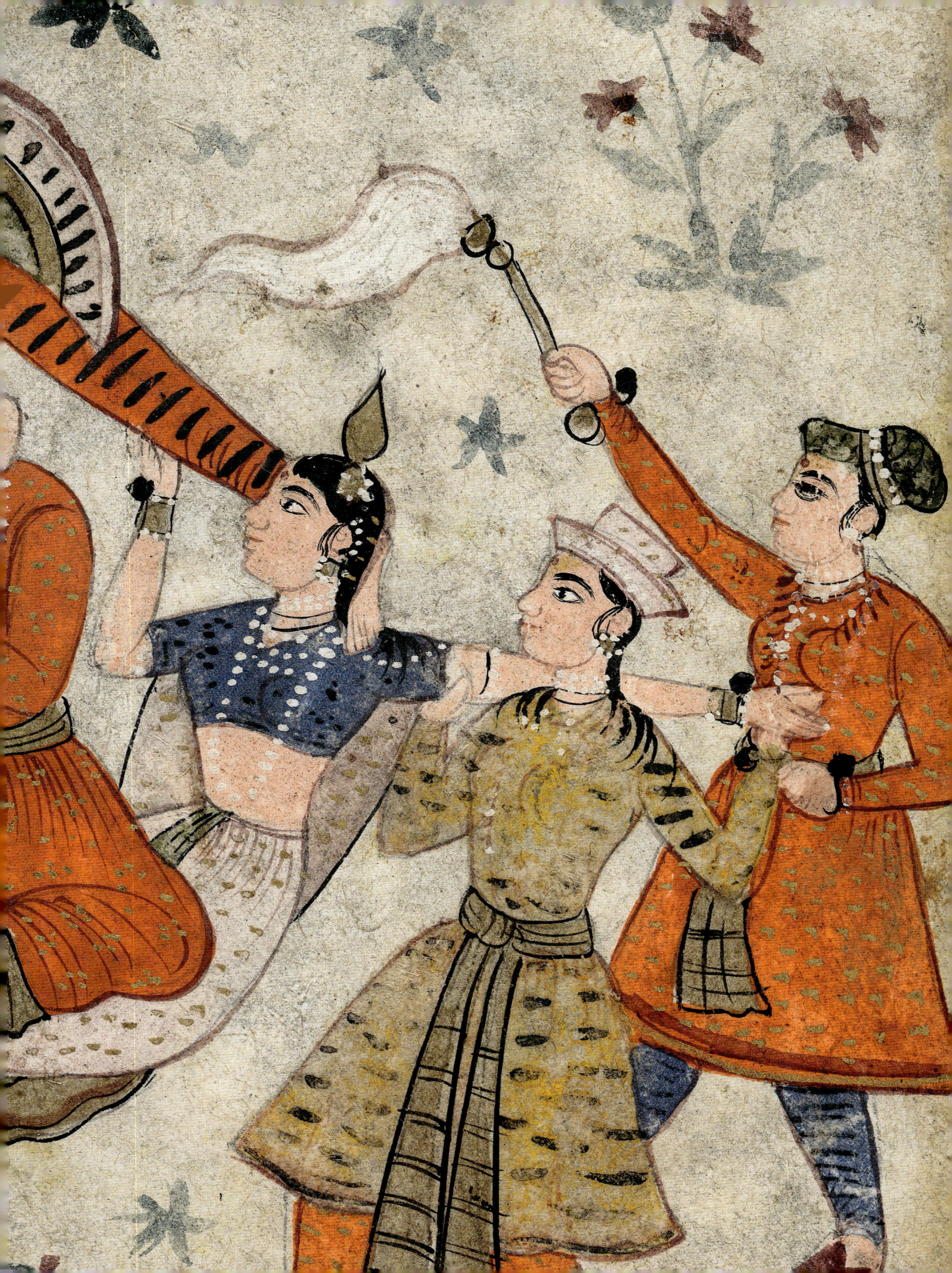

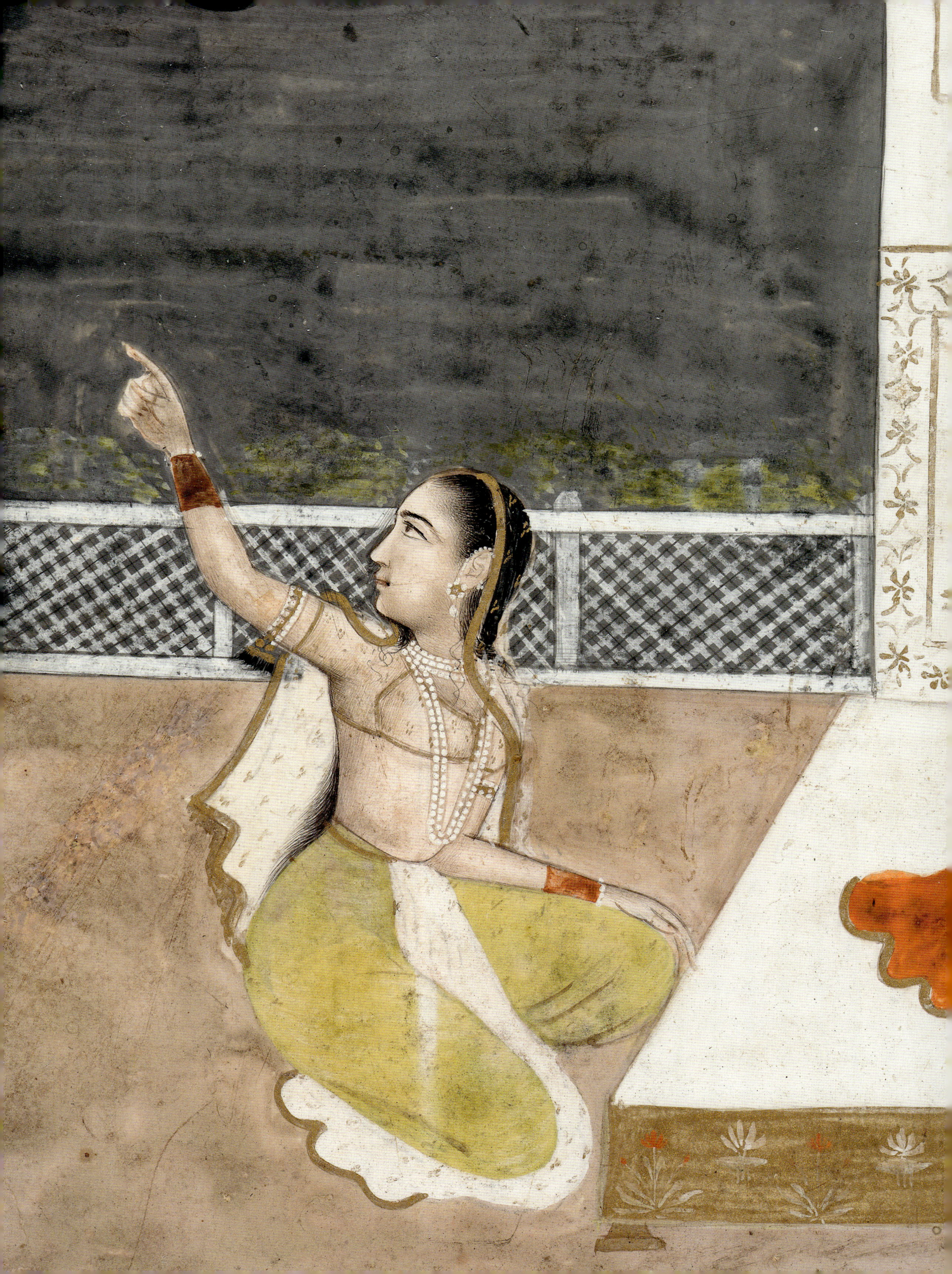

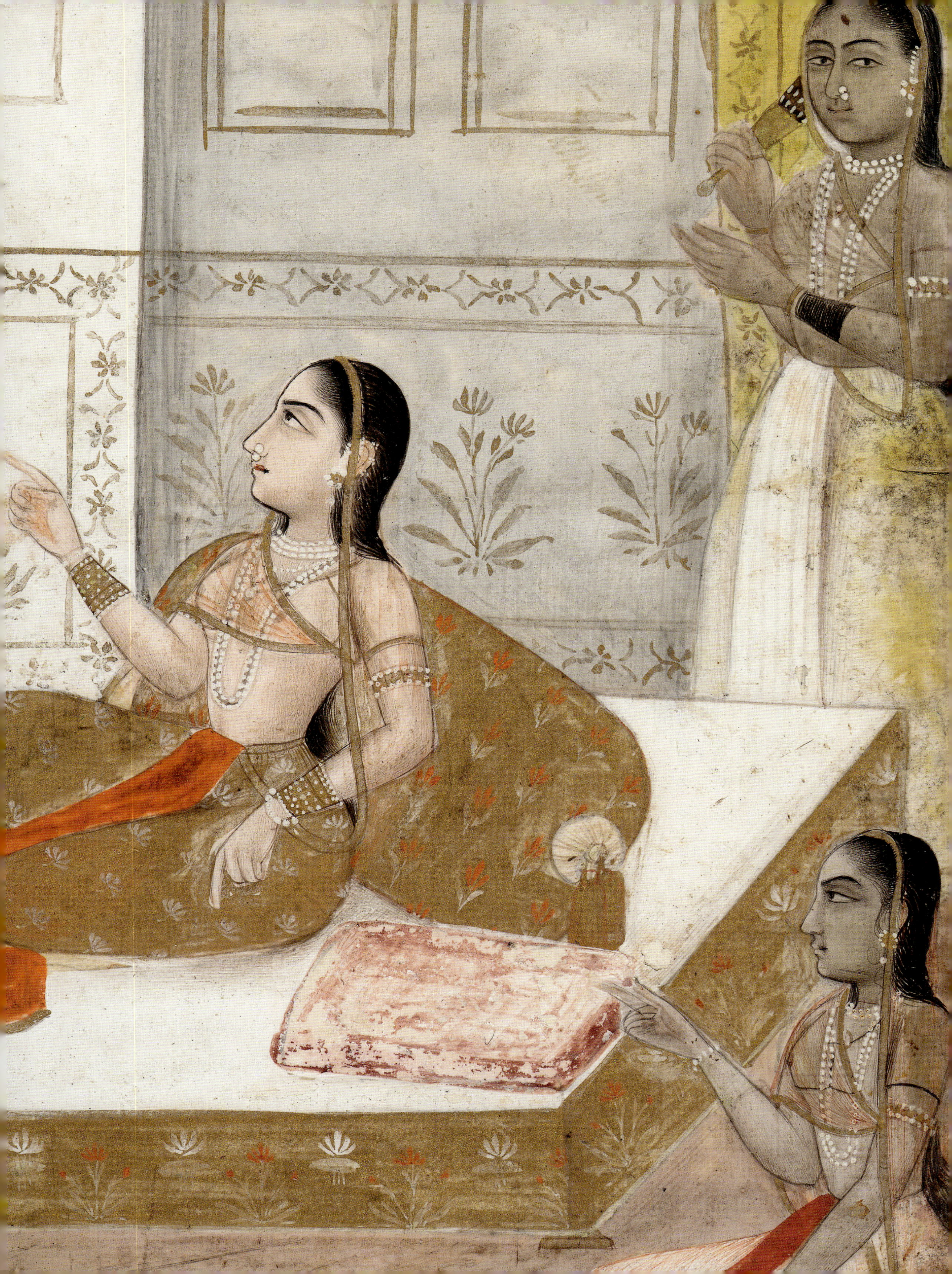

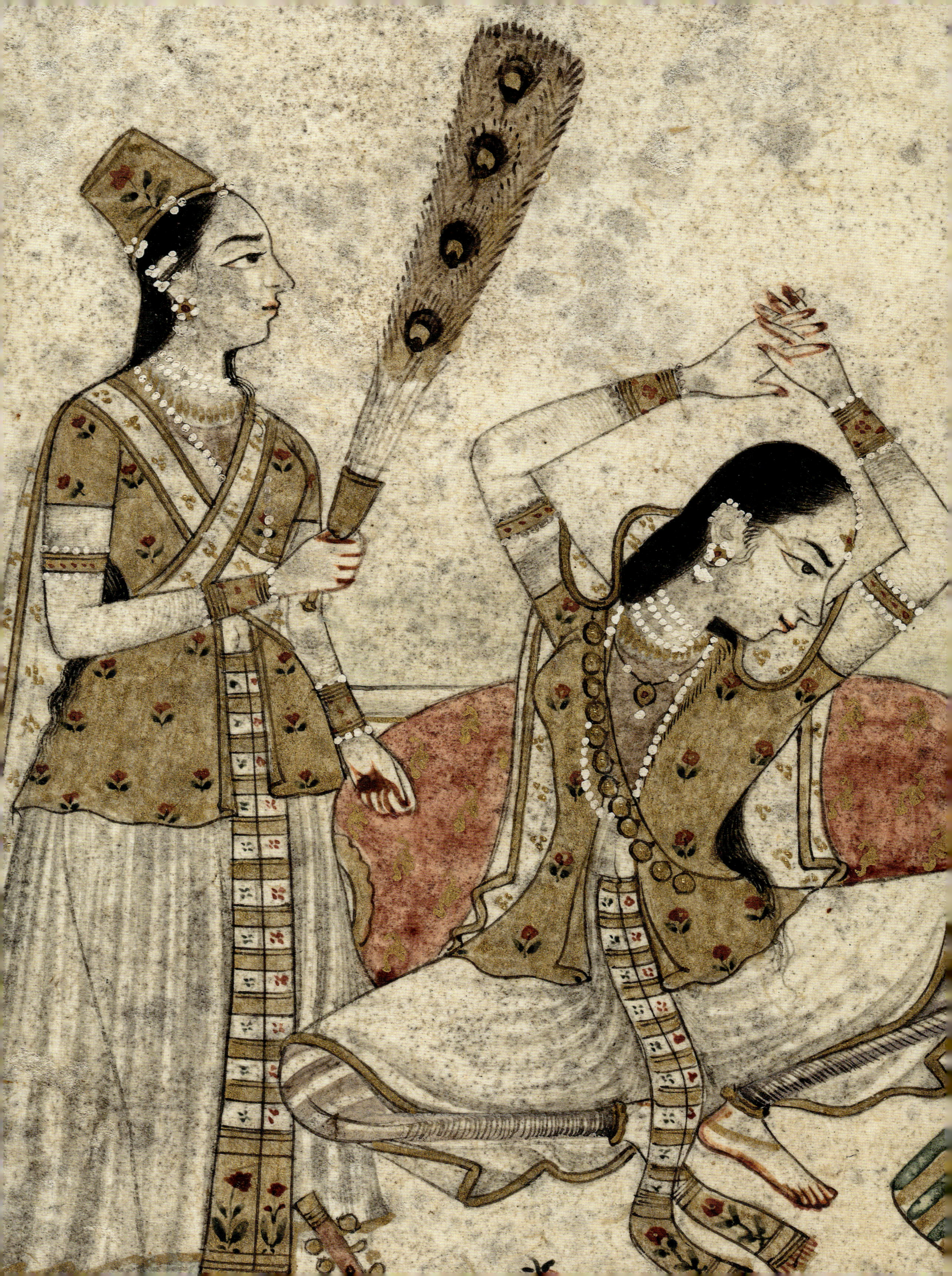

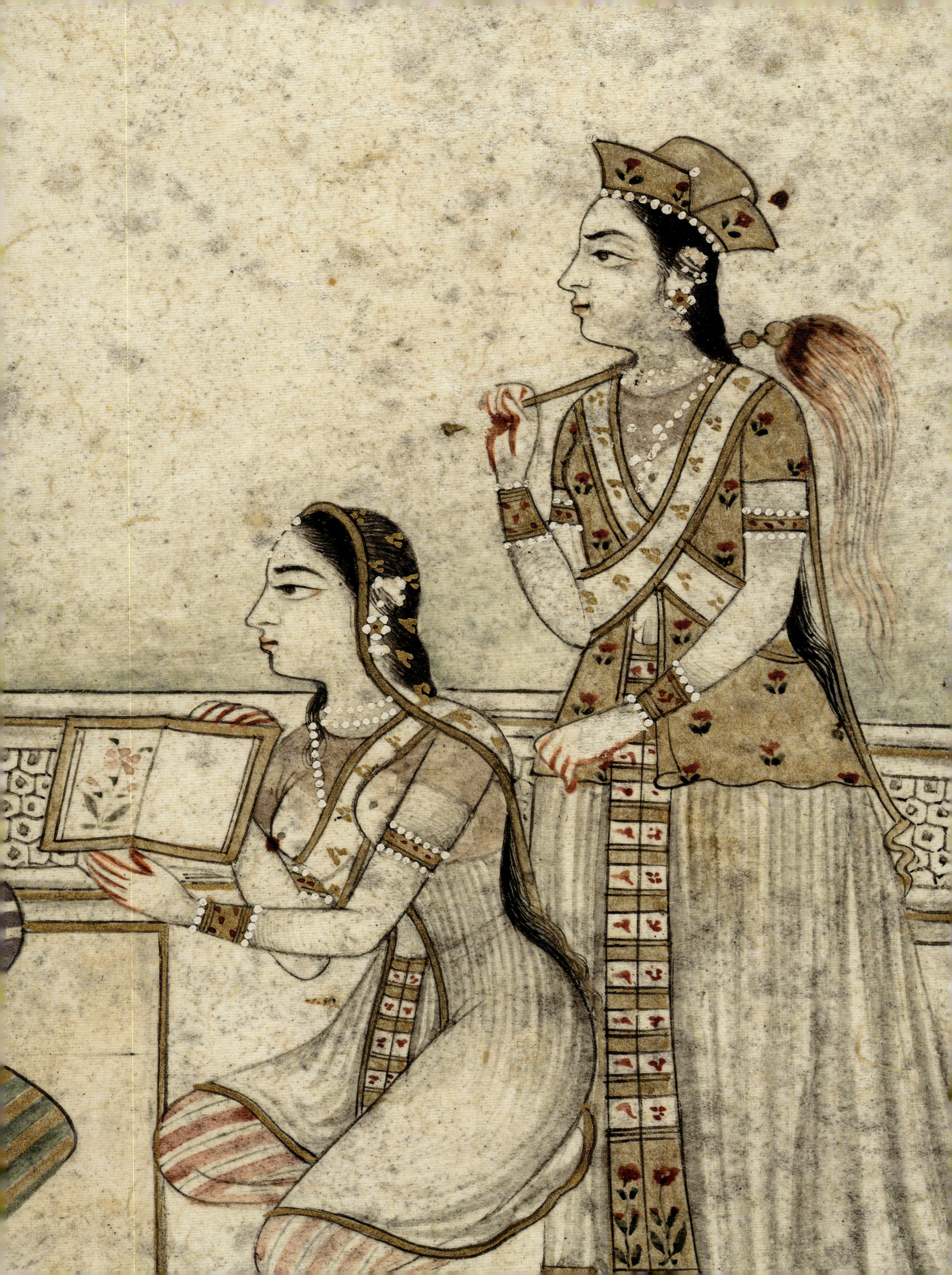

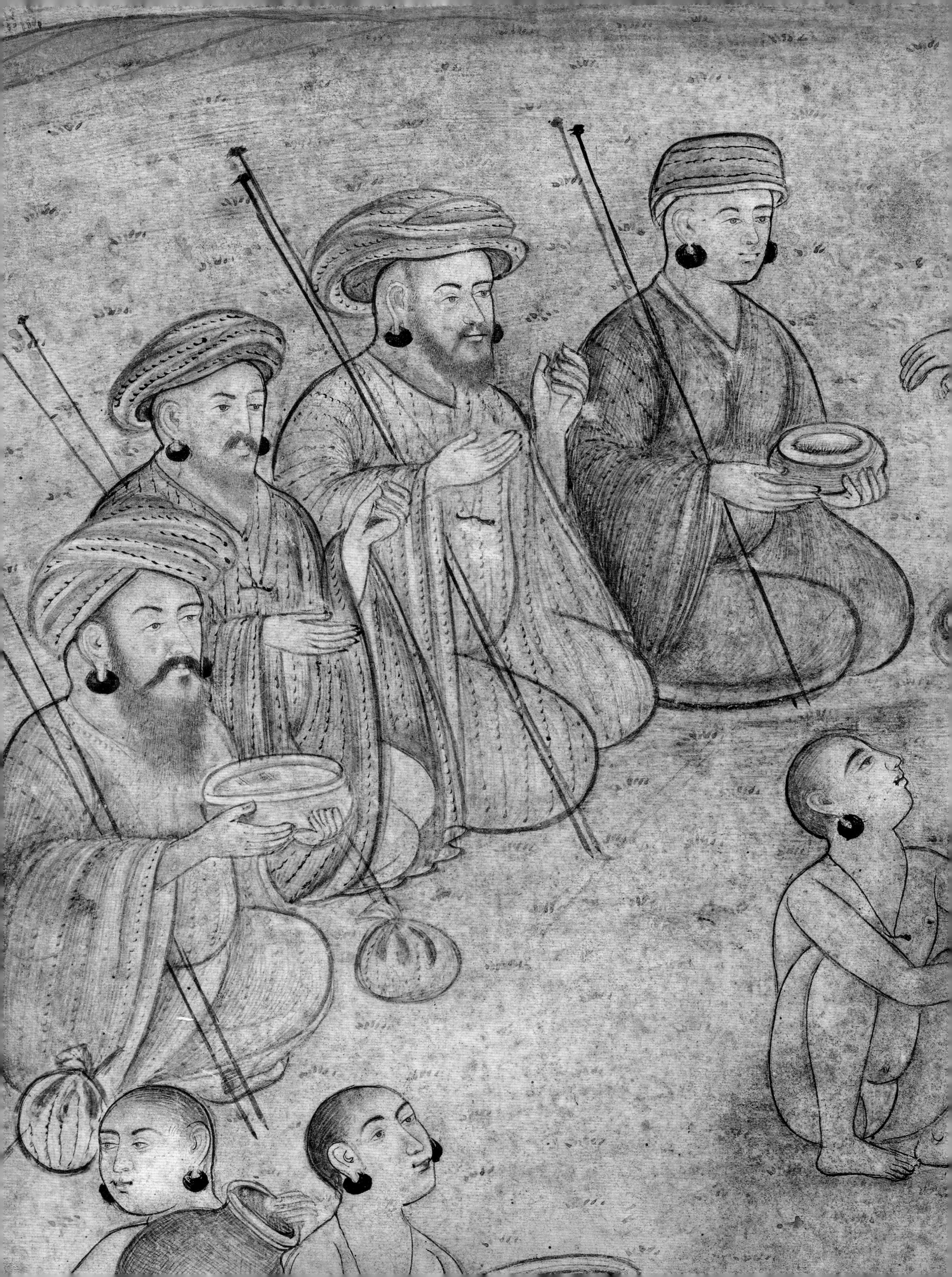

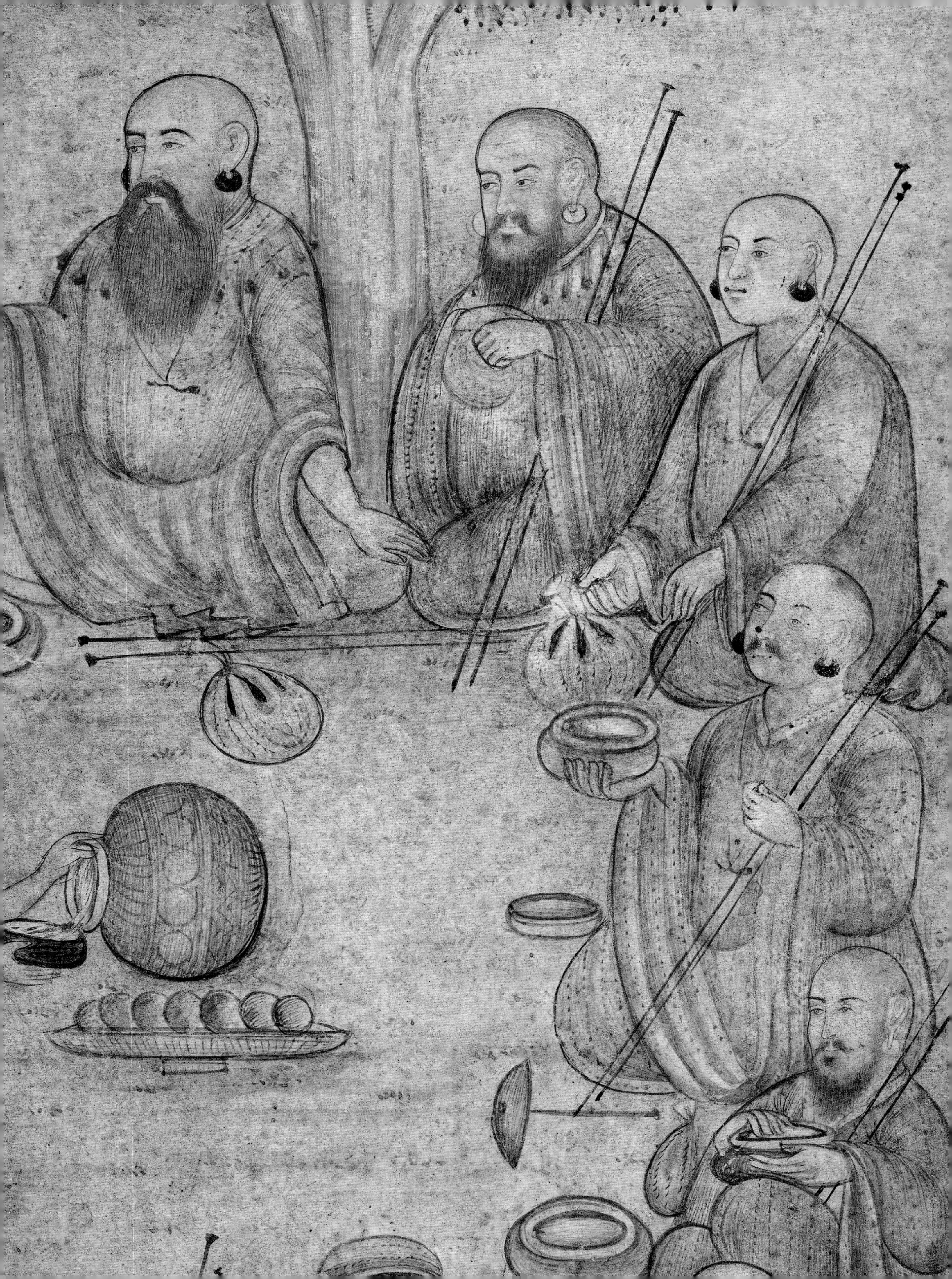

Contents

Catalogue

PETRA KUHLMANN-HODICK AND NEHA BERLIA WITH CONTRIBUTIONS BY CORDULA BISCHOFF, CLAUS-PETER HAASE, NEDIM SÖMNEZ, AND ANDREW TOPSFIELD

Appendices

Foreword

The Kupferstich-Kabinett of the Staatliche Kunstsammlungen Dresden (SKD) preserves a collection of more than half a million prints, drawings, and photographs. Its vast holdings of works on paper also include a significant number of miniatures from India and the Near East. These paintings were acquired during two campaigns: the first group arrived during the Baroque era, before 1738, when the works were included in the Kupferstich-Kabinett's first inventory. The second group, which once formed the collection of the philosopher and Indologist August Wilhelm Schlegel, came as a gift during the Romantic period. As collections of prints and drawings in Western museums rarely have such holdings, it is not surprising that the Indian miniatures in Dresden remained relatively unknown to scholars until earlier this year, when our exhibition "Stories in Miniatures" highlighted the collection. The accompanying catalogue includes not only the Dresden works on view during the exhibition but also loans of prints and drawings as well as complementary decorative arts objects.

The present scholarly catalogue illustrates our entire holdings of Indian miniatures, including an important illuminated Shāhnāma that entered the collection in 2016. We are most grateful to Roland Steffan and Hans-Jörg Schwabl for this generous gift. Moreover, it is thanks to the expertise and unflagging scholarly support of Roland Steffan that the Kupferstich-Kabinett felt confident enough to embark on the adventure of producing this collection catalogue.

We could not have done so without the help of our colleagues at the Chhatrapati Shivaji Maharaj Vastu Sangrahalaya (CSMVS) in Mumbai, especially Sabyasachi Mukherjee, Vandana Prapanna, and Anupam Sah. We are also indebted to many colleagues and friends for sharing their knowledge and expertise with us, especially Claudia Bamberg (Marburg), Thomas Bürger (Dresden), Ludwig von Habighorst (Coblenz), Oliver Hahn (Berlin), Anna Martin (Marburg), Roger Paulin (Cambridge), Pauline Lungsingh Scheurleer (Amsterdam), Robert Skelton (London), Ursula Weekes (London), and Friederike Weis (Berlin).

I am most grateful to all the authors, particularly my colleagues Neha Berlia and Olaf Simon for their unfailing commitment. I would also like to thank Désirée Noffke for her tremendous help with many aspects of the text; Pamela Barr for her skillful copyediting; Christoph Nöthlings for his translations; and Sandstein Verlag Dresden. The SKD and the entire team of the Kupferstich-Kabinett lent their support to make this demanding project happen, especially Andreas Diesend, Katrin Kruppa, Antonella Meloni, Gudula Metze, and Anna Caroline Schleicher.

This catalogue was made possible by the generous funding of the Museum and Research Foundation and Embassy of India, Berlin. The study of the Indian miniature paintings was an important focus of their project "Europe—World." The International Music and Art Foundation gave crucial help. We could not have wished for more patient and loyal friends in this complex undertaking. I would also like to thank Francesca Galloway and Sam Fogg for their additional help.

I reserve my warmest personal thanks for Petra Kuhlmann-Hodick, Senior Curator of nineteenth-century prints and drawings. As the catalogue's editor and moving spirit, she has undertaken this project with remarkable commitment over several years, opening our collection for scholars and the public far beyond Dresden and Europe. Collection catalogues are adding further momentum to the study of museum holdings, and it is my hope that this volume will facilitate the scholarly community's engagement with the Kupferstich-Kabinett's extraordinary holdings.

Stephanie Buck
Director, Kupferstich-Kabinett

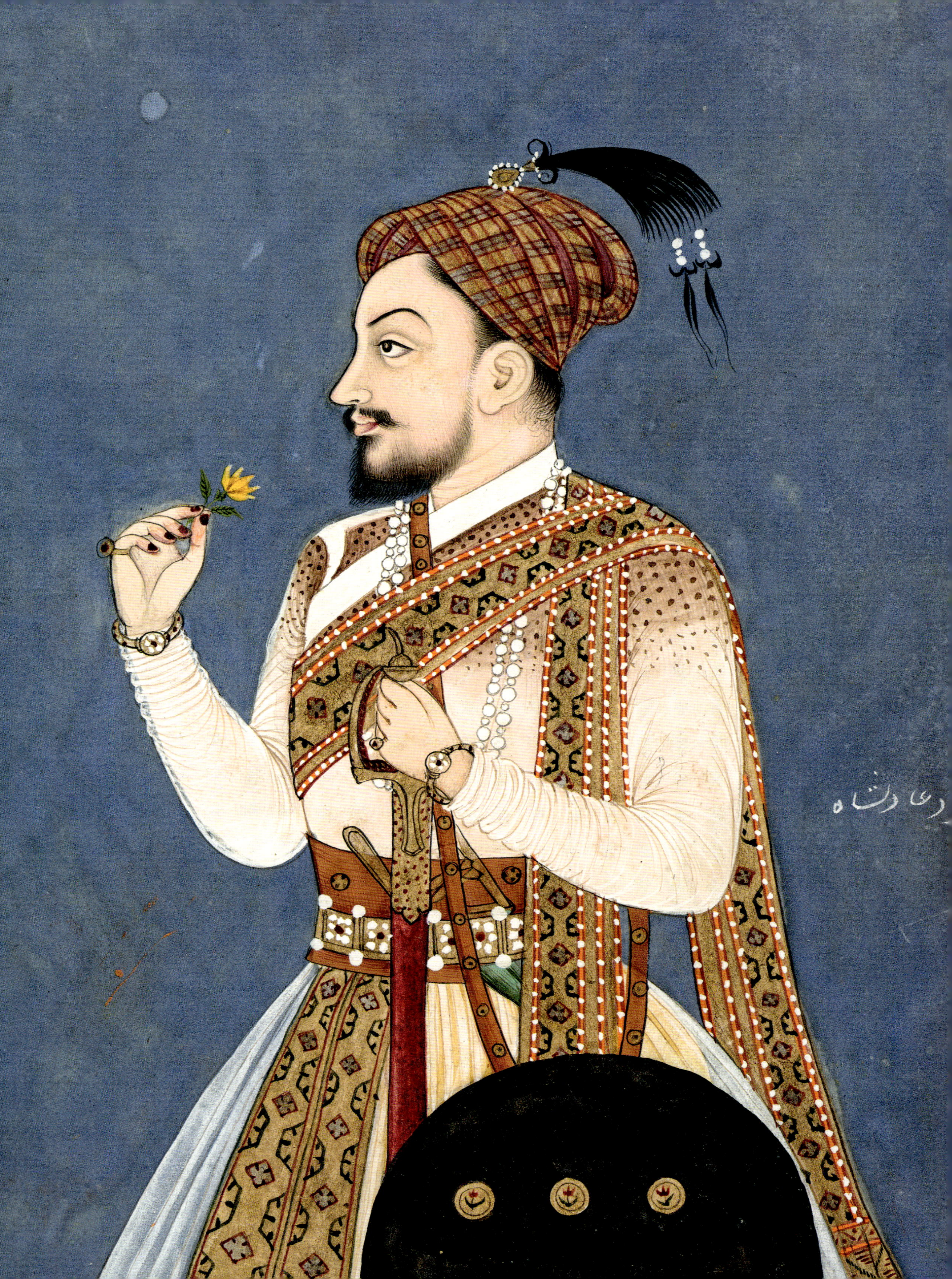

PETRA KUHLMANN-HODICK

Introduction

During the more than fifty years of Aurangzēb's reign (r. 1658–1707), the Mughal Empire reached its greatest extent in the Indian subcontinent. Jadunath Sarkar, who wrote the first biography of the ruler based on historical sources, begins his story with an event from the life of the young prince. For the biographer, the most remarkable incident in Aurangzēb's childhood was his demonstration of courage. On May 28, 1633, during an elephant race on the banks of the Yamuna River, just outside Agra Fort, an elephant attacked the child right in front of his own father. While his brothers fled, he confronted the raging animal until help came. His father, Shāh Jahān, rewarded the courageous boy by giving him his weight in gold.[1]

Aurangzēb's power reached its zenith with the conquest of Golconda in 1687 and the annexation of the Deccan. At about the same time, during the reign of Augustus the Strong (fig. 2), the Baroque period began to blossom at the Dresden court. Two famous travellers to India—the doctor François Bernier, who served at the Agra court at the beginning of Aurangzēb's reign, and Jean-Baptiste Tavernier, King Louis XIV's jeweller, brought their knowledge of Indian customs, religions, cultures, and political developments to Europe in detailed reports.[2] Their vivid descriptions of the annual weighing ceremony celebrated on the occasion of Aurangzēb's birthday (fig. 3) inspired the workshop of court goldsmith Johann Melchior Dinglinger to produce one of its most famous works, the *Throne of the Great Mughal Aurangzēb* (fig. 4).[3] Saxon perceptions of the Indian court associated with the name Aurangzēb evoked images of unbelievable riches and a grand display of splendour as a demonstration of political power.

During the Renaissance and the Baroque periods, books and prints of costumes were assembled in the European courts as demonstrations of political power and court culture. A collection of this kind, useful for documentary purposes and to serve as a source for preparing opulent festivities, was assembled in Saxony. This electoral *Kunstkammer*, established in 1560, housed important volumes of prints of Turkish costumes.[4] The increase in celebrations under Augustus the Strong led to a demand for new costumes, providing sartorial ideas for the hundreds of guests attending the events who dressed as representatives from every corner of the earth, with the king himself leading the way, appearing as a "Sultān" or an "African."[5] In 1709, two years after the death of Aurangzēb, when Augustus purchased Dinglinger's *Throne of the Great Mughal Aurangzēb*—one of the most elaborate and expensive handcrafted masterpieces of his time—thus shifting the focus towards India, Saxony was in a rather desolate state following the first defeats in the war against the Swedes. The Saxon ruler was forced to give up the Polish crown in 1706 and would regain it only in 1710.

fig. 1
Cat. 1 | Ca 112/8
Muḥammad ʿĀdil Shāh (r. 1627–1656) (detail)
Golconda (Deccan), 1668–1689
Watercolour and gold, 32.1 × 18.7 cm, image 23.8 × 10.9 cm

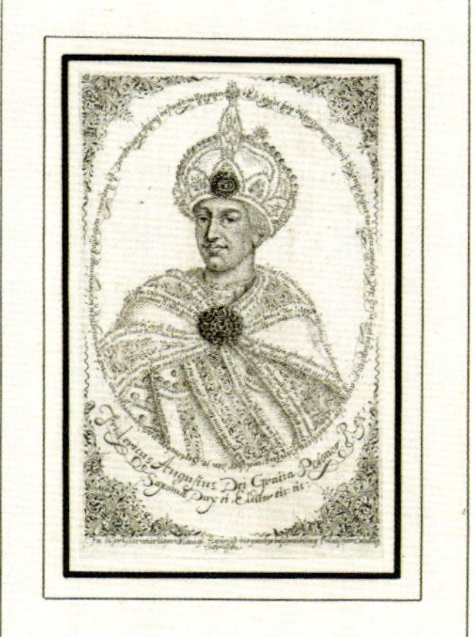

fig. 2
Johann Michael Püchler the Younger (German, 1679–1709)
Augustus II, King of Poland and Elector of Saxony (Augustus the Strong; r. 1694–1733)
c. 1697
Engraving, 10 × 6 cm
Kupferstich-Kabinett, SKD, inv. no. A 2017-23

Acquisitions of Indian Paintings before 1738

Among the Indian works at the Kupferstich-Kabinett, there is only one portrait album, Ca 112 (cat. 1), which may have become part of the Dresden collection prior to the *Throne of the Great Mughal Aurangzēb*. The endpaper is inscribed, "dies Buch ist ganz von hohen Werth, d. 23. Dec. 1689" (This book is of very high value, the 23 Dec. 1689). Although this inscription does not securely place the volume in Dresden at this time, it certainly was in Germany or was owned by a German.[6] The album contains forty-six posthumous portraits with captions in *nasta'līq* depicting the Mughal emperors from Akbar to Aurangzēb and the rulers and nobles of the ʿĀdil Shāhī dynasty up to the young Shāh ʿAbbās, who ruled Golconda until 1629 (fig. 1). Even though the employees in Dinglinger's workshop could have seen the album when they began work on the *Throne of the Great Mughal Aurangzēb* in 1702, there is no evidence of direct imitation. This pictorial world draws largely on contemporary illustrated travelogues and includes Turkish and Japanese motifs and chinoiserie. In contrast to Ottoman and Chinese works in the electoral *Kunstkammer*, for which there is a documented history of their use, the same cannot be said for the Indian works.

Four albums with depictions of rulers and princes represent the main collection of Indian art acquired for the Dresden Kupferstich-Kabinett at the beginning of the eighteenth century. These acquisitions can be traced to the early years of the museum, established in 1720, which built its collections upon the electoral *Kunstkammer*.[7] The Indian works initially belonged in the group of Eastern works on paper, in particular Chinese and Chinese style prints that were acquired on a large scale. The oldest inventory of the museum, documented in 1738 by the first director, Johann Heinrich von Heucher (1677–1746),[8] records these acquisitions under the category "La Chine."[9] Judging by the notes in the volumes and the labels attached to them, these items were probably not classified as "Sinica" and "Indica" until the nineteenth century. In addition to the four portrait albums, the "Indica" collection also includes depictions of Indian rulers, a set of *ganjīfa* playing cards, two Ottoman volumes of costumed figures,[10] and an album with medallion portraits based on Indian models but presumably produced by European artists.[11]

The works in the Heucher Inventory are given brief descriptions. They are designated as "Indica" on the works themselves[12] and also in the catalogue cards begun in 1906 which record the organisation of the sketchbooks and volumes of drawings according to "Ca" numbers.

An album with portraits of Mughal rulers and regents of Golconda, assembled and bound in Europe about 1700 and mounted in simple Indian paper frames, is recorded under number 11 as "39 Japanese portraits of men, from head to feet, in Maroquin rouge doré in folio" (cat. 2).[13]

Number 12 (cat. 1) contains portraits executed in the same style but with more elaborate frames and is described as "24 folios of the like, which, except for the first are painted on both sides, in Marcoquin rouge d'oré. Placed in a leather bag. Folio."[14]

Number 20 (cat. 3) is an album with "179 Mughal portraits."[15] Like Ca 112, it was bound at the place of manufacture. On the verso, the portraits are inscribed, somewhat awkwardly, in *devanāgarī*, presumably by local workshop employees, with the names of the sitters. There are paintings pasted on the interior and the exterior of the lacquered covers. Both miniatures on the exterior show the same scene of women making music. The miniature on the front pastedown shows a woman opening a book; on the rear endpaper, the same woman is shown closing the book.[16] This poetic, allegorical framing of a book about the history of India, which traces the ruling dynasties of Hindustan back to the age of legends and consists entirely of "illustrated names," is thus given a programmatic character.

According to Heucher, the fourth portrait album, listed in the inventory as number 29 (cat. 4), represents the "House of Tamerlane."[17] Sixty-two portraits, apparently from various series, were pasted into the album, which was bound in Europe. Many of the paintings are executed in the *nīmqalam* (half-pen) style comparable to those in Ca 113; others are similar to earlier paintings produced in Golconda, with a more opaque application of paint. They document the

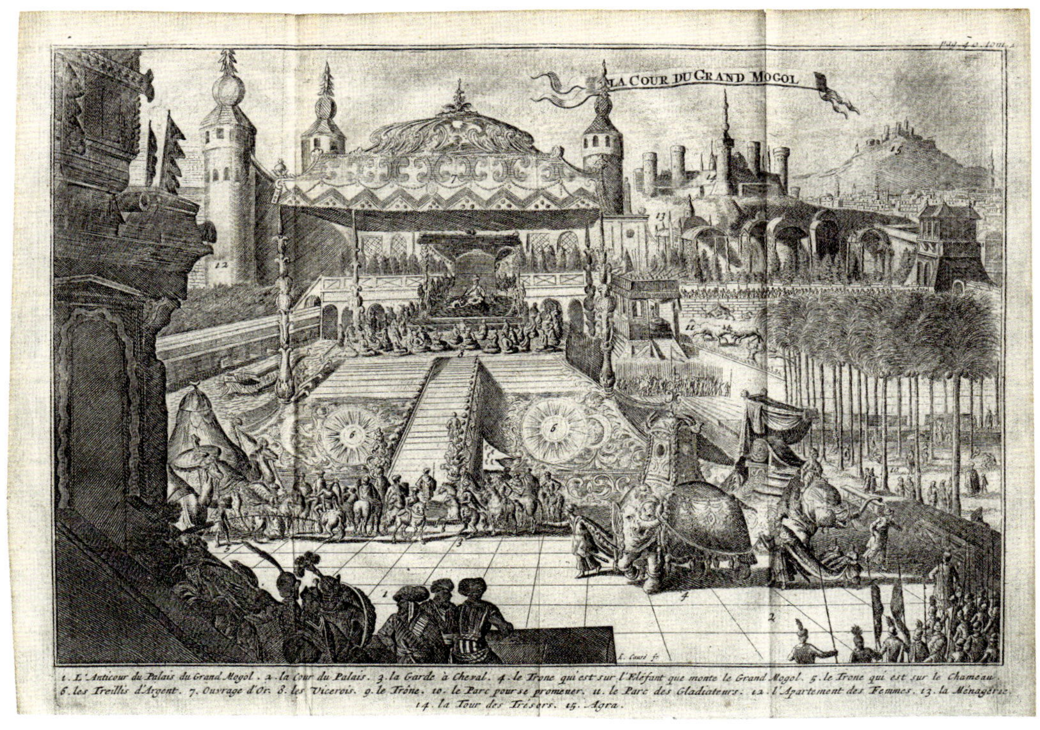

fig. 3
The Great Mughal's Court
Etching, 20.8 × 29.4 cm
From François Bernier, *Voyages … contenaent la description des ètats du Grand Mogol …*, Amsterdam 1714, vol. 2, p. 40
Sächsiche Landesbibliothek – Staats- und Universitätsbibliothek Dresden, sig. Geogr.C.906-1,2

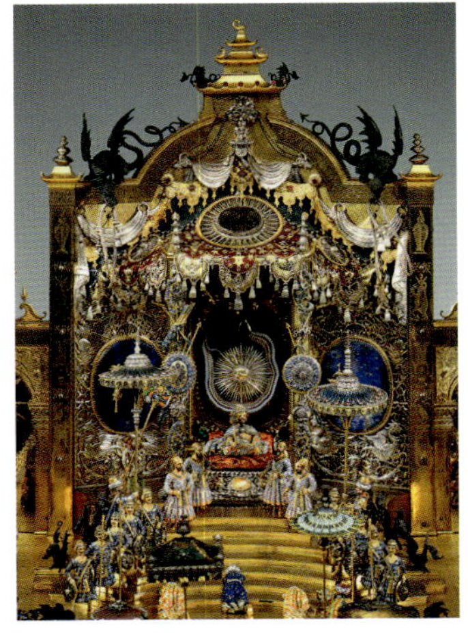

fig. 4
The Throne of the Great Mughal Aurangzēb
Johann Melchior Dinglinger and workshop (Dresden), c. 1701–1708
Goldwork and enamel, 58 × 142 × 114 cm
Grünes Gewölbe (Green Vault), Staatliche Kunstsammlungen Dresden, inv. no. VIII 204

portraits common in the Deccan at the beginning of the eighteenth century, with all the stylistic variations and developments. In addition to notes in *nasta'līq* and *devanāgarī*, the similarly assembled album Ca 111 features descriptions of the figures in Dutch.[18] On the basis of the handwriting, the inscriptions can be dated to the time the volume was assembled. According to the descriptions, the ten portraits of women at the end of the volume were added later.

A set of portraits of Indian rulers in medallions is designated as Japanese in the Heucher Inventory, number 17: "18 miniature portraits of Japanese kings mounted on a small board" (cat. 5).[19] Under number 3 (cat. 6–7), other Indian works are listed as "2 beautiful Chinese paintings—under glass and in a gilt frame."[20] Under number 30 (cat. 88) we find "1 Chinese Almanac."[21] Number 32 (cat. 89) is described as "13 portraits from the Great Mughal's court, a small blue booklet bound with golden decorated paper."[22] The volume itself, however, is labelled "Japanese miniature portraits."

The categorisation of Indian works as Japanese or Chinese was not atypical for the period. For dealers and collectors who usually brought the works with them as members of the East India Company, making them accessible to a European clientele, 'Oriental' and Asian rarities were of equal interest. They were often acquired together from one source and not necessarily recorded precisely. Even in contemporary travelogues, there are frequent summaries, mixtures, and mistakes—most of all when using visual depictions, which usually draw on the models from the countries visited.[23]

These errors are, however, counterbalanced by the great interest reflected in widely printed and illustrated reports and in the booming art market. Important private collections of Asian works on paper, including Indian paintings, had begun in the Netherlands by the mid-seventeenth century. For instance, it is well known that Rembrandt owned a large collection of portraits of Indian princes, which he copied.[24]

For contemporary collectors it was apparently more important to associate the pictures with historic names than to achieve a definitive attribution of the works that came to Europe from India. After being assembled on a single sheet and mounted on a wooden board, the eighteen

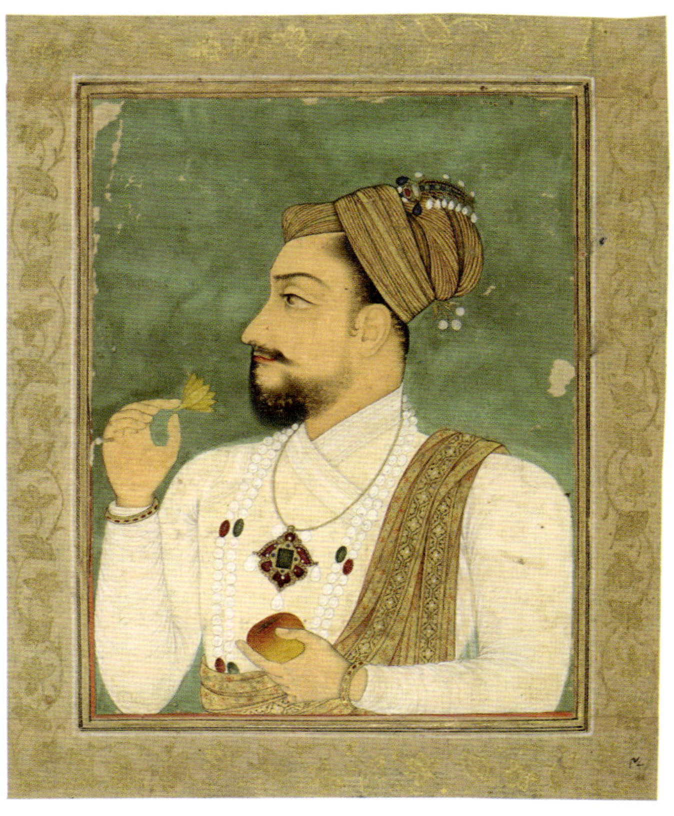

fig. 5
Muḥammad ʿĀdil Shāh (r. 1627–1656)
Deccan (Bijapur), c. 1645
Watercolour and gold, 15.5 × 11.7 cm
The British Museum, London,
inv. no. 1937,0410,0.4

medallion portraits of rulers (cat. 5), for instance, were given small labels that were inscribed in Dutch in silver—in other words, before they joined the collection in Dresden. Portraits were also compiled into sets or albums at their place of manufacture and inscribed in *devanāgarī* or *nastaʿlīq*, such as the two portrait cycles in the Dresden collection (cat. 1 and 3) that were bound in albums in India.

A odd hybrid can be found under the inventory number Ca 115 (cat. 89) labelled "Indica VIII."[25] The small notebook, decorated with Japanese seals and bronze varnished papers, depicts members of the Japanese court. The inscriptions, in French, specify their rank and wages. The medallion portraits were pasted on the pages opposite the text, following Indian models, and labelled on the verso with fragments of Japanese writing or seals.

While the volume with Turkish figures and decorative papers, which had become part of the Saxon Art Chamber in 1582 and was later included in the "Indica" collection, turned out to be the *Album amicorum of Elector Augustus of Saxony* (cat. 90), actual Indian works were acquired for the most part during the 1720s, during the last years of the elector's reign. A large group of these Indian works, together with additional Chinese volumes, was acquired for the Dresden court in 1728 at the auction of Nicolaas Witsen's estate in Amsterdam. They can be attributed on the basis of the numbers from the auction catalogue recorded in the Heucher Inventory as well as on the basis of their descriptions.[26] This auction of one of the most extensive and significant Dutch collections of the time forms an important nucleus of European collections of Indian art from Aurangzēb's reign. Many of the pieces that ultimately became part of museum's collections previously had been in royal or private ownership.[27]

The continuing interest in Indian art in Dresden is evident in two *darbār* scenes with Shāh Jahān and Aurangzēb (cat. 6–7), described as "Chinese paintings," that were acquired for Augustus the Strong during an African expedition (1731–1733) and included, among the treasures in the Kupferstich-Kabinett.

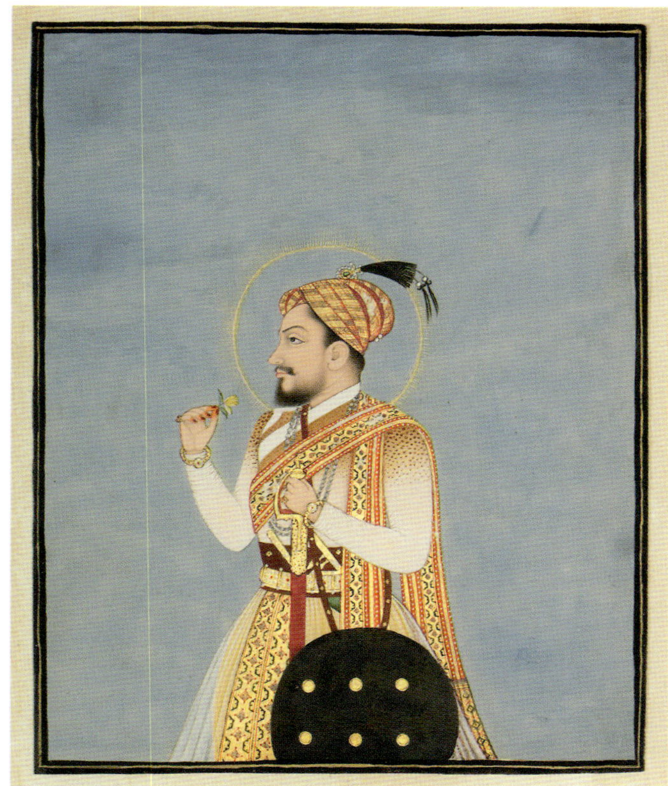

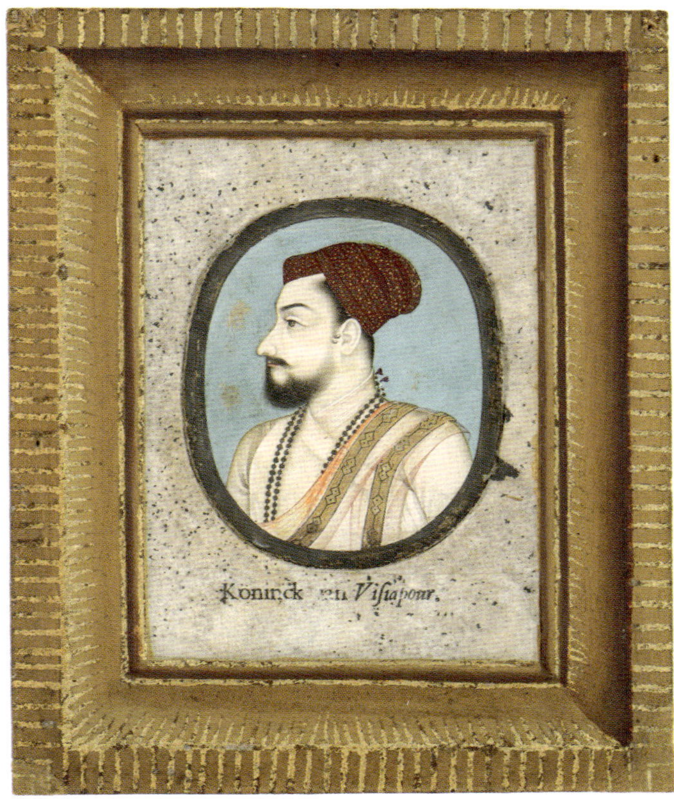

fig. 6
Muḥammad ʿĀdil Shāh (r. 1627–1656)
Deccani Mughal (Hyderabad), c. 1700
Album from the Liechtenstein Princely Collections, no. 25
Watercolour and gold, album 31 × 23 × 4 cm, image 23.8 × 10.9 cm
Courtesy of Francesca Galloway, London, and Sam Fogg, London

fig. 7
Cat. 8 | Ca 121/7
Muḥammad ʿĀdil Shāh (r. 1627–1656)
Bijapur (Deccan), mid-17th century
Watercolour, gold, and silver, painted frame 17.2 × 14 cm, image 11.3 × 8.3 cm, medallion 8.1 × 6.8 cm

The Schlegel Collection

In 1848 the Dresden Kupferstich-Kabinett received a gift of Indian paintings formerly owned by August Wilhelm Schlegel (cat. 8–85).[28] When the author's estate came up for sale at the Bonn branch of Johann Matthias Heberle's Cologne auction house in 1845, the announcement included a set of works listed as "Peintures orientales" and a "collection of 95 subtly executed Indian paintings of different sizes up to the largest folio in book-shaped portfolios. A highly important collection that will be auctioned off first as a whole and then separately."[29] Several of Schlegel's 'Oriental' manuscripts were sold to the Königliche Bibliothek in Berlin and are today preserved in the Staatsbibliothek Berlin.[30] Apparently, however, there were no successful bids for the entire corpus of Indian paintings and only a few individual sheets were sold. The majority of the collection thus remained in the possession of the painter Augusta von Buttlar (1796–1857), one of Schlegel's three nieces designated as principal heirs.[31] Augusta, then residing in Dresden, was the obvious choice: she had been in close contact with Schlegel, who had firmly supported her training as an artist—a rather unusual career for a woman in those days—in Dresden and Munich. He had also encouraged her other interests, putting her in touch with customers and promoting her travels to England and France. Augusta von Buttlar's interest in Indian art is documented by two of her drawings that copy Indian miniatures.[32] She became a widow in 1841 and lost her two daughters in 1830 and 1844, respectively. When she left Dresden for Brixen in 1848, she bequeathed seventy-eight works from this part of her uncle's India collection to the museum:[33] eight portfolios, covered in marbleed paper on the exterior and lined with green paper on the interior, with leather spines reminiscent of books.[34] The gold-embossed lettering designates the content as Indian paintings. A green leather label that was added later indicates in French that the donation, originating from Schlegel's collection, was made by Augusta von Buttlar in 1848.

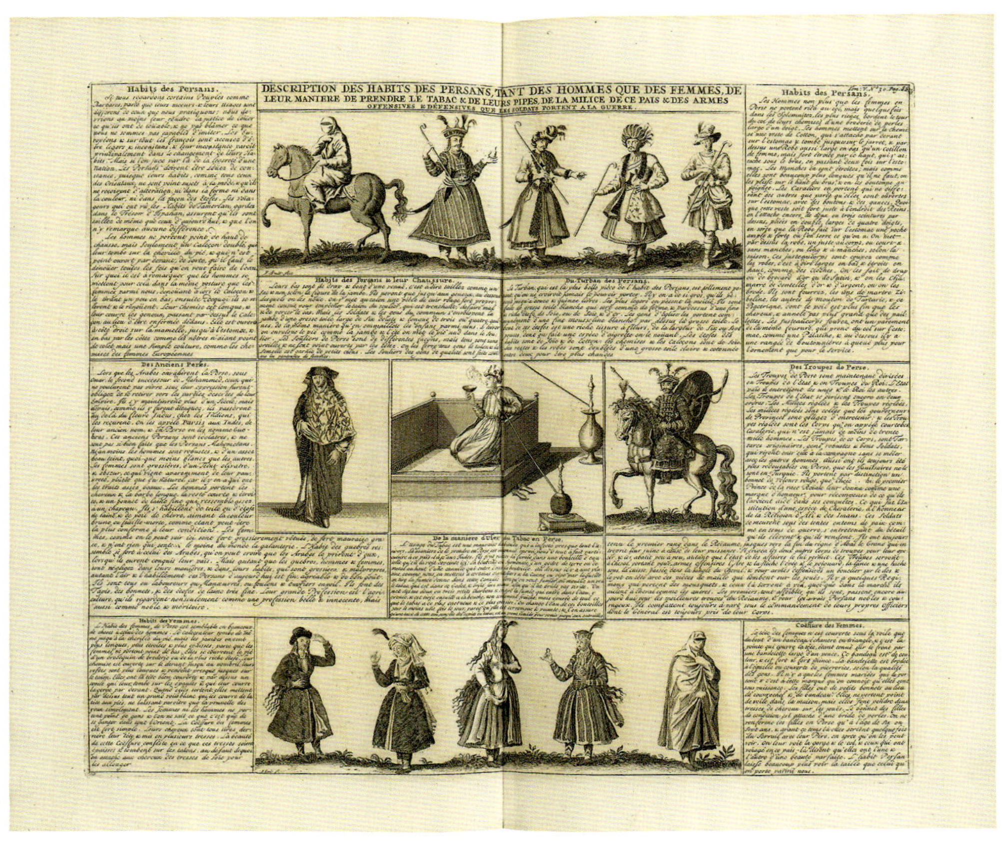

fig. 8
Description des Habits des Persans
From Henri Chatelain, *Atlas historique* (Amsterdam 1719), vol. 5, no. 30, p. 86
Etching and engraving, 45.8 × 62 cm
Sächsiche Landesbibliothek – Staats- und Universitätsbibliothek Dresden, sig. Geogr.A.73.5

With Friedrich Schlegel (his brother), Friedrich Tieck, and Novalis, August Wilhelm Schlegel belonged to the circle of writers and philosophers whose writings had initiated the early Romantic movement in Jena and Dresden about 1800. The ideas of this movement triggered the enthusiasm for India shared by the Schlegel brothers.[35]

August Wilhelm Schlegel (1767–1845), known mainly for literary criticism and translations of Shakespeare, was one of the founding fathers of Bonn University in 1819. Schlegel was primarily interested in the cultural history of India in general and in translations of early Sanskrit epics. At Bonn University, he introduced Indology as a field of study and in the 1820s published a Latin edition of important Sanskrit literature along with his student Christian Lassen.[36] Schlegel wrote the scholarly work "Indische Bibliothek" for his fellow scholars and the two articles in the "Berliner Kalender" for the general public.[37]

Editions of Indian literature, which Schlegel used for his research, had been published since the early eighteenth century in the Netherlands, France, and, a bit later, in England, where colonial interest and trade relations existed and where those returning from India to Europe brought with them their impressions. Schlegel intensively studied the famous Arabian collection of fairy tales *One Thousand and One Nights*,[38] and the literary traditions of Persia and India that lay behind it. In 1791 Georg Forster's German translation of Kālidāsa's tale *Śakuntalā* was published.[39] Herder and Goethe as well as the Schlegel Brothers and the German Romantics were deeply impressed by the story.[40]

Schlegel's extensive correspondence bears witness to European scholarly dialogue within the nascent discipline of Indology.[41] However, unlike his British and French colleagues, neither he nor his younger brother, Friedrich, had ever travelled to India. Nevertheless, a personal event had sparked the brothers' interest in India. In 1789 their oldest brother, Karl, had died from a tropical disease in Madras, where he served as cartographer in the Hanoverian army fighting for the British Crown under George III.[42] In a letter written to August Wilhelm from Fort St. George

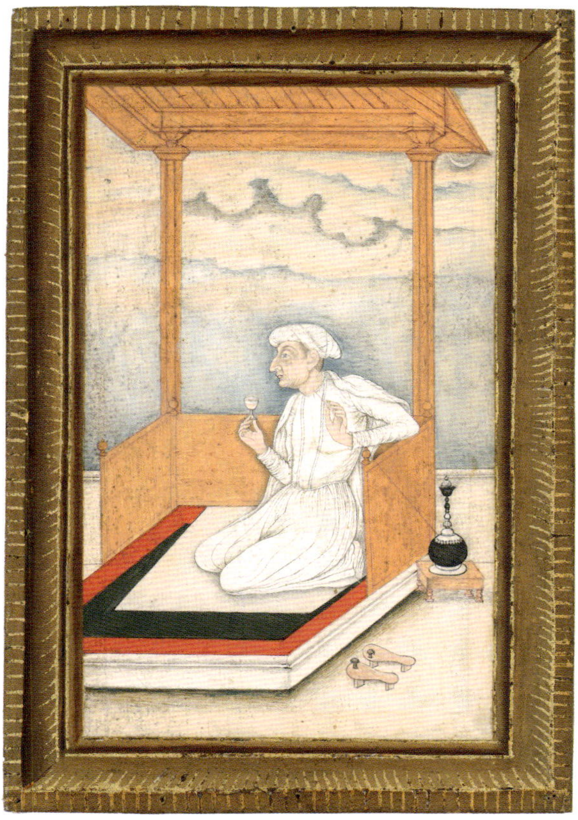
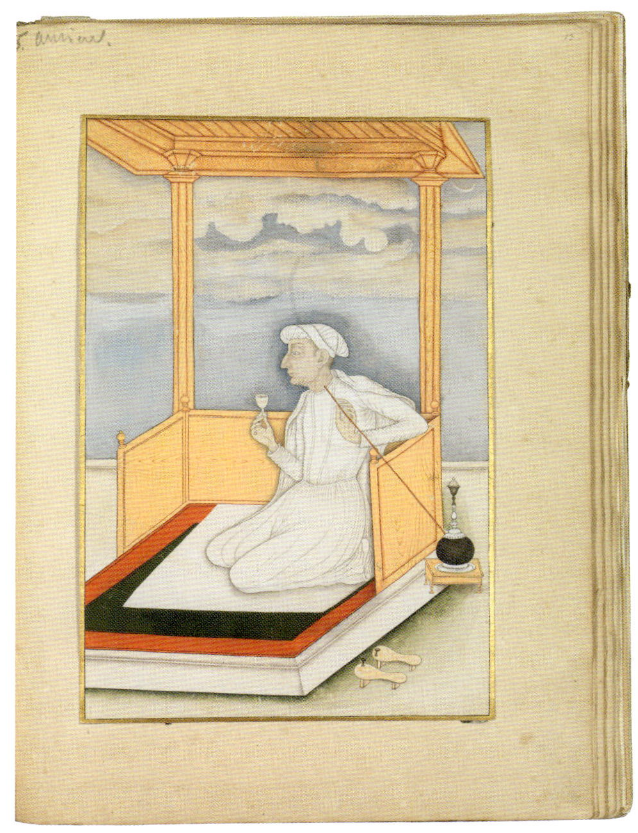

fig. 9
Cat. 32 | Ca 121/8
Neknām Khān (d. 1672)
Deccan, late 17th – early 18th century
Watercolour, painted frame
30.1 × 20.7 cm, image 24.4 × 14.8 cm

Fig. 10
Neknām Khān (d. 1672)
Deccani Mughal (Hyderabad), c. 1700
Album from the Liechtenstein Princely Collections, no. 15
Watercolour and gold, album 31 × 23 × 4 cm
Courtesy of Francesca Galloway, London, and Sam Fogg, London

on February 1, 1784, Karl gives a moving account of a Brahmin's funeral that certainly inspired his brother's enthusiasm for Indian culture.[43]

Compared to the previously acquired part of the Indian collection, the Schlegel Collection comprises a larger variety of items. Next to the portraits of Mughal princes and their dynastic ancestors, dignitaries, and courtiers, there are pictures of courtly audiences and processions as well as portraits of women in a courtly setting, musicians, and lovers. Further, the collection contains several portraits of ascetics and literary illustrations—it is these, if any, that can be related to Schlegel's editorial and linguistic preoccupation with India. In addition to the characteristic miniatures produced in the Deccani workshops under the influence of Mughal painting in the early eighteenth century, several works in the collection can be attributed to contemporary provincial Mughal schools. Some of the pictures, executed in a more popular and narrative style, are inspired by Persian models and combine the influences of different schools.

Undoubtedly, it was not only Schlegel's general interest in art and cultural history but also his passion as a collector that motivated him to purchase these works. His apartments in Bonn had both an Indian and a Chinese room.[44] Schlegel was constantly seeking to acquire Indian works for his collection. In Germany, however, unlike in colonising countries such as England and France, such works were rather difficult to obtain, and legend has it that Schlegel proudly showed the gems of his collection to guests and even took them along on his travels.[45]

Schlegel was consulted as an expert in art and India in many ways but in turn sought the advice of colleagues for his own acquisitions. For the collection today preserved in Dresden, he asked the Bonn archaeologist Wilhelm of Dorow for assistance.[46] Luise Rosalie von Sinclair, a cousin of the famous writer Isaac von Sinclair (1775–1815), who was himself a friend of the poet Friedrich Hölderlin and a diplomat at the court of Hessen-Homburg, advertised a collection of Indian paintings for sale in 1821. In the advertisement, she honestly pointed out that some illustrations of Indian court ceremonies and a series of portraits had been affected by moisture.[47]

Schlegel, who had no opportunity to examine the collection himself, asked Dorow to verify the authenticity of the works and to assess whether the price of three hundred florins was adequate.[48] Later, he enquired closely about the origin of the works. However, the only thing Mrs. Sinclair was able to tell Dorow was that the collection came into her possession with a property she had purchased in France. According to her, the former owner of the property, Marc Antoine Chartraire de Montigny, had acquired the Indian paintings from the collection of King Louis XVI, who in turn had received them as a diplomatic gift from the *sultān* of Mysore, Tipū Sāhib.[49]

If no one provided misleading information intended to improve sales prospects, the alleged donation could have been made at the 1788 reception of the Indian ambassador at Versailles.[50] Sultān Tipū Sāhib had managed to win France as his ally in the decades-long war against the British. A huge number of soldiers serving in the same volunteer regiment as Karl Schlegel had been killed during the Third Mysore War, which the British and their allies—Hyderabad, Travancore, and the Marātha Empire—won in 1799.[51]

Even though there is, as yet, no evidence that Schlegel's miniature collection actually originated in Mysore and passed through the hands of the French court,[52] the alleged origin of the consignment (and the seventy-eight sheets preserved in Dresden) is plausible if one looks at the works themselves. The paintings, and especially the mounting cardboards, are badly affected by the moisture damage mentioned in Mrs. Sinclair's sales announcement. Painted and gold-decorated frames were added to combine them into an ensemble. The frames are attached like Indian paper frames; the decoration, however, imitates European wooden frames of circa 1800. Even thorough technical investigations have not been able to clarify the origin of these frames, and no comparable examples have been found yet.[53] They probably were attached after the miniatures had been damaged by moisture—that is, prior to their acquisition by Schlegel. In view of their skilful yet somewhat crude execution, the likelihood that they were added at the French court or at de Montigny's estate is remote. It is also questionable whether paper frames of this kind were used at Tipū Sāhib's court or manufactured for diplomatic gifts. The most likely—but unproven—theory is that they were produced in India for a European customer. Thus, some of the mysteries concerning the history of the Schlegel Collection at the Dresden Kupferstich-Kabinett remain unresolved.

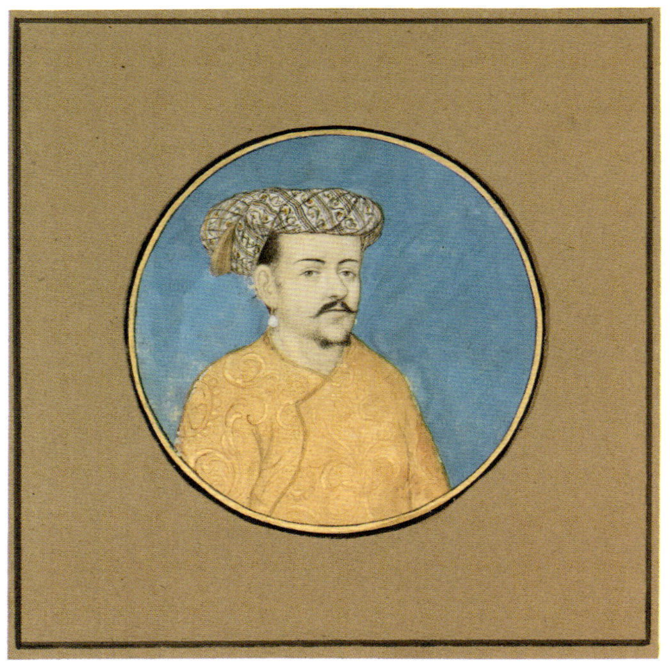

Fig. 11
Unidentyfied nobleman
Deccani Mughal (Hyderabad), c. 1700
Album from the Liechtenstein Princely Collections, no. 30
Watercolour and gold, album 31 × 23 × 4 cm
Courtesy of Francesca Galloway, London, and Sam Fogg, London

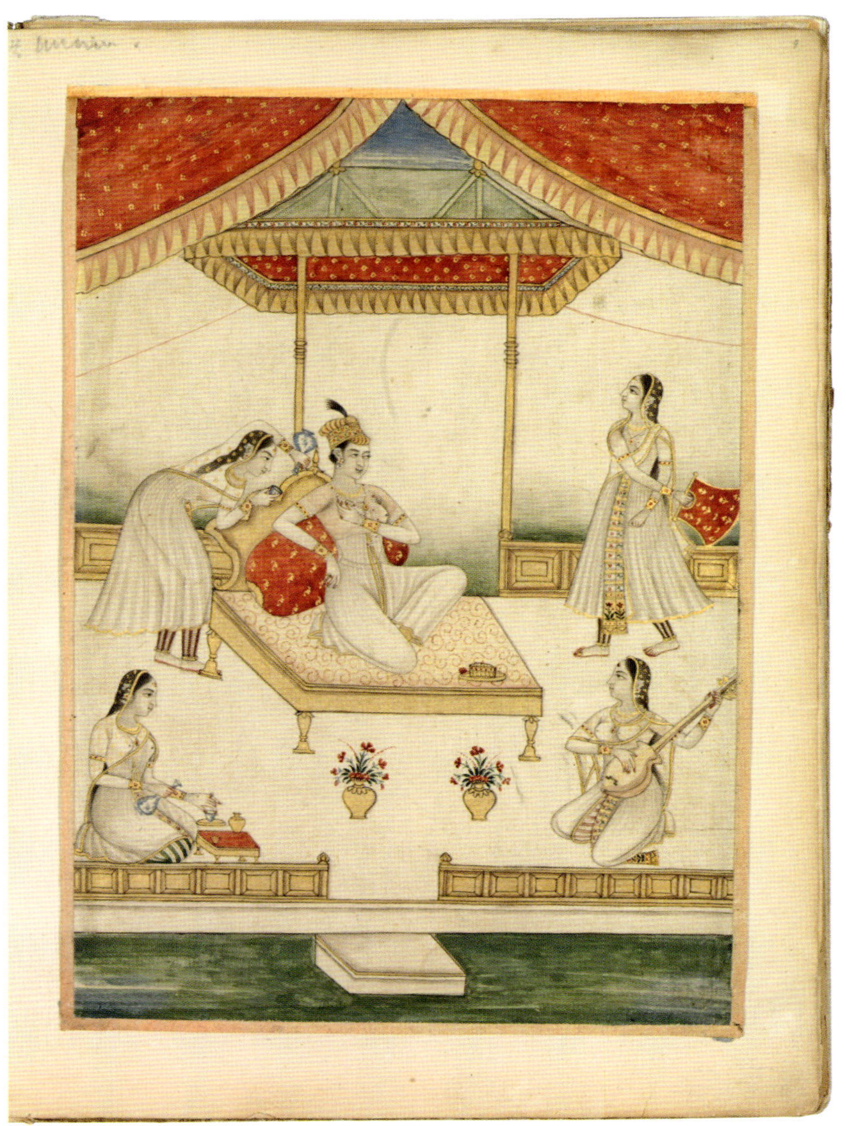

Fig. 12
A princess in the zenāna (Rāzia Sultāna?)
Deccani Mughal (Hyderabad), c. 1700
Album from the Liechtenstein Princely Collections, no. 4
Watercolour and gold, album 31 × 23 × 4 cm
Courtesy of Francesca Galloway, London, and Sam Fogg, London

Similarities

Even though it did not enter the collections of the Kupferstich-Kabinett until more than one hundred years later, the overwhelming majority of the Schlegel Collection can be traced to the same schools of painting as the Indian collection acquired during the Baroque period—namely, the Deccan school that emerged during the late seventeenth and early eighteenth centuries under the influence of the Mughal style. There are numerous correspondences with not only individual works and groups of works from the two consignments but also, more broadly, with other European collections of Indian art. For example, many of the Indian paintings preserved in Dresden are comparable to individual works and groups of works at the Bibliothèque Nationale in Paris, the British Museum and the Victoria & Albert Museum in London, the Rijksmuseum in Amsterdam, the Nationaal Museum van Wereldculturen in Leiden, the Hermitage in St. Petersburg, and the Museum of Islamic Art and the Museum of Asian Art in Berlin. Particularly strong parallels with the Dresden holdings—that is, with both the early portrait albums and the Schlegel Collection—can be found in the decoration of the Millionenzimmer at Schönbrunn Castle, Vienna, and in two albums formerly belonging to the same collection and now preserved in the Österreichische Nationalbibliothek.[54]

An album from the Princely Collections in Liechtenstein, now in the possession of Francesca Galloway, London, and Sam Fogg, London, offers a small but particularly interesting compilation.[55] Losty in his essay on the album refers to the French inscriptions on sheets to support his assumption that the collection was compiled in the early eighteenth century by a representative of the French East India Company operating—just like the British and Dutch companies—a regional office in Hyderabad, the capital of Golconda. The reference to the French market is noteworthy with regard to the alleged French origin of the Schlegel Collection.

The Liechtenstein Album contains several versions of portraits in the style of the famous Golconda sets found in the early Dresden albums.[56] Two almost identical portraits of Murād Bakhsh offer a vivid example of the serial production of such sheets and their subsequent compilation into sets. Variations and similarities between different portraits become apparent when comparing the portrait made from life of Muḥammad ʿĀdil Shāh in the British Museum (fig. 5) with his posthumous portraits in the former Liechtenstein Album (fig. 6) as well as in the Schlegel Collection (fig. 7) and in album Ca 112 (fig. 1) in Dresden.[57]

The goal of the collaborative manufacture of works and the practice of repetition in painting was not the invention of original motifs but the fidelity to a model—that is, to an accurate rendering that was true to both the known image of the sitter and a given typology. The artist's imagination instead found expression in elaborate details, elegant lines, subtle colour combinations, barely noticeable shades in the flesh tones, the rendering of fabrics in decorative colours, and the playful variation in the design of attributes.

The dissemination of motifs is also reflected in the illustration of travelogues. Chatelain in his *Atlas historique*, for example, used the figure of the *huqqā*-smoking Neknām Khān to illustrate Persian customs (fig. 8), which is found in both London and Dresden (figs. 9–10). Also included in the Liechtenstein Album is a medallion portrait made by a European hand (fig. 11) in the style of Dresden album Ca 115 (cat. 89), which also belongs to the consignment purchased before 1738. Most comparable to the holdings of the Schlegel Collection are the *zenāna* scenes in the *nīmqalam* style. One painting takes up the same central figure (fig. 12) that is used for a composition in the Schlegel Collection and in a portrait of Rāzia Sultāna in Ca 113.[58] The painting style of these *nīmqalam* paintings is related to many works in the Schlegel Collection and to those in albums Ca 111 (cat. 4) and Ca 113 (cat. 3) that are part of the previously acquired Dresden holdings. In contrast to the works from the Golconda portrait albums, which are entirely painted in opaque watercolour, this type of painting is limited to a few colours and leaves large areas of paper in reserve; the drawing is elaborated with wash and accentuated with smaller areas in colour and gold. Losty described this technique as "white style." To his mind, the economic demands of the labour required were a significant factor in the development of Hyderabad painting in the early eighteenth century.[59] The same environment in the Deccan produced different manifestations of Mughal style painting well into the eighteenth century: court scenes and portraits of rulers and ascetics belong just as much to the repertoire of models used for European travelogues as do the *rāgiṇī* and *zenāna* pictures.

The Schlegel Collection also includes individual representations of subjects familiar from historical, religious, and poetic literature that remind us that this imaginary world originated with manuscript illustrations. The recent donation of a manuscript of the *Shāhnāma*, the Persian epic written around A. D. 1000 by Firdausī, with one hundred illustrations in the Kashmir style of the early nineteenth century (cat. 86), is a particularly meaningful addition to the Dresden Kupferstich-Kabinett. The Dresden collection has thus been supplemented with a preeminent example of the ongoing tradition of Persian and Indian storytelling and illustration that was extremely important for the development of Indian painting itself and at the same time a main source of inspiration for Romantic poetry.

Notes | 1 Sarkar 1925, p. 1. | 2 See Dresden 2017, cat. 90 and 91. See Tavernier 1676; Tavernier 1681; and Tavernier 1925. See Bernier 1699; and Bernier 1670–1671. | 3 See Syndram 2017. | 4 See Dresden/Bonn 1995, pp. 103–6; 227–78; see also cat. 90, Ca 114. | 5 Dresden 2000, pp. 68–9, 161–2. | 6 A repeatedly revised list of the sitters that was added to album Ca 112 suggests that the volume was studied in the mid-nineteenth century. According to the inscription, it can be attributed to Edward Gardner, a Bengal-based London politician, Indologist, and one of the founding fathers of the Royal Asiatic Society of Bengal. | 7 For the early history of the Kupferstich-Kabinett and acquisitions of this time, see Melzer 2010. | 8 The Kupferstich-Kabinett was founded in 1720 in the course of establishing special collections at the Saxon Court. Augustus the Strong entrusted his personal physician, Johann Heinrich von Heucher, with the arrangement and establishment of the collection. | 9 See Dresden 2017, cat. 1, pp. 123–4. Heucher's inventory from 1738, sig. Cat. 1, is entitled "Consignation en detail de tous les Tomes d'Estampes qui Se trouvent dans les Bureaux du Salon d'Estampes de Sa Maj[esté] Le Roi de Pol[ogne] Elect[eur] de Saxe". It records the elements of the collection in drawers ("Repositoires") in a total of 22 collection cabinets ("Bureaux"), organised according to schools, themes, artists and techniques. | 10 See cat. 5, 88, 90, 91. | 11 Cat. 89. Two Japanese maps, on the other hand, belong to the "Sinica", which are the object of a comprehensive research project currently being conducted under the direction of Cordula Bischoff. | 12 In addition to its written entry, the information was recorded on pre-produced adhesive labels with a blue border. | 13 "39. Japanische Portraits von Mannspersonen, von Kopff bis auf die Füsse, en Maroquin rouge d'oré in Folio" (Ca 110). | 14 "24. Blat dergleichen, davon die Blätter, das erste ausgenommen, auf beyden Seiten bemahlt, en Maroquin rouge d'oré. Steckt in einem ledernen Beutel. Folio" (Ca 112, "Indica IV"). | 15 "179. Mogolische Portraits. n. 6." (Ca 113, "Indica III"). | 16 See p. 83, fig. 1–4. | 17 "1. Tom [Band] Das Geschlecht der Tamerlans, nebst inliegender Verzeichnung, in roth mit Gold verziert Saffian gebunden. n. 8." (Ca 111, "Indica II"). | 18 See Appendices, pp. 142–3. | 19 "18. Kleine Portraits en Migniature, von Japanischen Kaysern, auf ein Brethgen gezogen." (Ca 116, "Indica VII"). | 20 "2. schöne chinesische Gemählde. – unter Glas in vergoldten Rähmen." (Ca 125; additional collection marks on the works may have been lost when they were remounted in 1910). See also Schnitzer 2010, p. 55. | 21 "1. Chinesischer Almanach n. 11" (Ca 127). | 22 "13. Portraits, des grossen Mogols Hoff, klein Büchlein in blau mit Gold verziert Papier gebunden" (Ca 115, "Indica VIII"). | 23 See Dresden 2017, pp. 226–9. For the European reception of Indian art, see Forberg 2017. | 24 See references in Dresden 2017, cat. 88, pp. 222–3. | 25 The indication can be found on a small label with a blue border; on the first front page is written "Japanisch VIII." | 26 For cat. 2, Ca 111, see Amsterdam 1728, p. 10, no. 8; for cat. 3, Ca 113, see ibid., p. 10, no. 6; for cat. 91, Ca 126, see ibid., p. 12, R.; for cat. 88, Ca 127, see ibid., p. 11, no. 11. However, the Heucher Inventory does not record all numbers from the 1728 Amsterdam auction catalogue. Ca 115, for instance, might be identical with Amsterdam in 1728, p. 11, no. 19: "Een Boek met Tekeningen, zynde de Wapens, Titels en Inkomsten der Japanse Vorsten en Grooten." (A Book with Drawings of Weapons, Titles and Revenues of the Japanese Sovereigns and Nobles). In addition to the Indian holdings, also Ca 129, Ca 132, Ca 157, Ca 161, Ca 162, Ca 163 and Ca 222 are from the Witsen auction; and so are three volumes in the Sächsische Landesbibliothek – Staats- und Universitätsbibliothek, Mscr Dresd. B 64, 65, and 66. | 27 See Lungsingh Scheurleer 2017. | 28 See Dresden 2017, cat. 6, pp. 232–4. | 29 "Sammlung von 95 fein ausgeführten indischen Malereien von verschiedenen Größen bis zum größten Folio in buchförmigen Mappen. Eine höchst wichtige Sammlung, die zuerst im Ganzen und dann vereinzelt ausgesetzt werden soll." Heberle 1845, p. 117. | 30 See Dresden 2017, cat. 102–3, pp. 235–7. | 31 Dresden 2017, pp. 132–6; and 238–41. See Schlegel's will of March 27, 1845, and the certificate of inheritance for Augusta von Buttlar in the archives of Bonn Universitätsbibliothek, sig. urn:nbn:de:hbz:5:1-51261, p. 3 and urn:nbn:- de:hbz:5:1-51348. Schlegel's three nieces—the other two were Wilhelmine and Amalie Schlegel—were appointed equal heirs. For Augusta von Buttlar, see also Enzinger 1967; and Ho 2013. | 32 See Dresden 2017, cat. 104, pp. 238–41. | 33 Ibid., p. 239. | 34 The portfolios were probably commissioned by Schlegel himself; their design is similar to the book bindings in his library. | 35 For Friedrich Schlegel, see Tzoref-Ashkenazi 2009; for Schlegel's essay, "On the Language and the Wisdom of the Indians," see ibid., pp. 140–46. For August Wilhelm Schlegel and India, see Paulin 2016, pp. 478–515. | 36 For their correspondance, see Schlegel/Lassen 1914. See Dresden 2017, cat. 98–100, pp. 232–7. See Schlegel Bhagavad Gita 1832, Schlegel Ramayana 1829, *Hitopadesa* 1829. For Schlegel's Indology, see also Rocher/Rocher 2012. | 37 Schlegel Indische Bibliothek 1820–1830; Schlegel. Hauptbeziehungen 1/1828 and 2/1830. | 38 First published between 1704 and 1708 in Antoine Galland's French translation, *Les Mille et une nuit*; see Dresden 2017, p. 233. See also Schlegel's letter to John G. Lockhart, dated January 17, 1826, in Schlegel Briefe, 1930, vol. 1, p. 633, as well as his elaborate letter to Jacob Grimm on the subject of the *Hitopadeśa* and the nature of the Indian fable, dated June 3, 1833, in Schlegel Briefe, 1930, vol. 1, p. 506. | 39 Forster 1791. See also cat. 75. | 40 Dresden 2017, cat. 97, p. 233. | 41 See Paulin 2017; and Hanneder 2017. Schlegel's correspondence was digitally edited by a joint project between the Sächsiche Landesbibliothek – Staats- und Universitätsbibliothek Dresden, where a large part of Schlegel's literary estate is preserved, and the Universities of Marburg and Trier. | 42 See Paulin 2016, pp. 24–6. As of 1689, Madras was the base of the British East India Company. | 43 Sächsische Landesbibliothek – Staats- und Universitätsbibliothek Dresden, sig. Mscr.Dresd.e.90, XIX, vol. 22, no. 3; see Dresden 2017, p. 232. | 44 See Czapla/Schankweiler 2012, p. 35. For Schlegel's collection, see Dresden 2017, pp. 234–7. | 45 See Hanneder 2017, p. 92; and Dresden 2017, cat. 6, pp. 132–4, cat. 102–3, pp. 235–6. | 46 See Dresden 2017, pp. 95, 132–4. | 47 See Sächsiche Landesbibliothek – Staats- und Universitätsbibliothek Dresden, Mscr.Dresd.e.90, L, vol. 6e, no. 8. Luise Rosalie von Sinclair advertised the consignment on a number of occasions. A second copy with the same advertisement is preserved at the Hessisches Landesarchiv Darmstadt, sig. C 12 no. 43, f. 9, no. 16. | 48 Letter of March 31, 1821, Stadtarchiv Bonn, sig. SN 19–58. | 49 See Luise Rosalie von Sinclair's letter of July 6, 1821, Sächsische Landesbibliothek – Staats- und Universitätsbibliothek Dresden, sig. Mscr.Dresd.e.90, XIX, vol. 25, no. 66. In the letter, she offers Schlegel another eight sheets from the same consignment that she had initially withheld because they were even more affected by moisture damage. On the verso of the mounting cardboards, there is an old numbering up to 112, which suggests that the collection had originally been larger. Some cardboards, which lack any numbering, were exchanged before World War II. Instead, they show Russian numbering that was added when the holdings were taken to the Soviet Union in 1945; see Dresden 2017, pp. 133–4. | 50 See the report on the course of the events, "Les Indiens ou Tipou Sultan 1788," published in 1788. For the reception at Versailles, see pp. 190–5. See also François Barrière's introduction to Campan 1823, p. XXVII. | 51 Tipū Sāhib was killed in 1799, when British troops under Warren Hastings stormed the capital, Shrirangapattana. Hastings brought the substantial spoils of war he had seized in India home to London; see Jaffer 1999. | 52 It has never been proven whether paintings from the Deccan were taken to Mysore, travelling by way of the provinces of Sultān Haider 'Alī and his son Tipū Sāhib. | 53 See p. 39. | 54 Examples in cat. 3 (Ca 113) and 4 (Ca 111) and mainly cat. 7, 9, 32, 39, and 48. They can be found in numerous European collections. The number of works in this style in the Österreichische Nationalbibliothek and the Schönbrunn Castle is particularly significant for comparison with the Dresden collection; see Dresden 2017, cat. 28, 32, 33, 85–7, pp. 220–1. For Schönbrunn, see Duda 1984; Duda 1991; Duda 1997; Koch 2004; and Strzygowski 1923. | 55 Losty 2012, pp. 62–75, no. 25. | 56 For further works open to comparison, see Losty 2012, p. 62. | 57 See Dresden 2017, cat. 23–4, pp. 165–6. | 58 Cat. 61, Ca 119/7; and cat. 3, Ca 113/130, p. 85, fig. 6. | 59 Losty 2012, p. 62. For works of this type, see Lungsingh Scheurleer 2017.

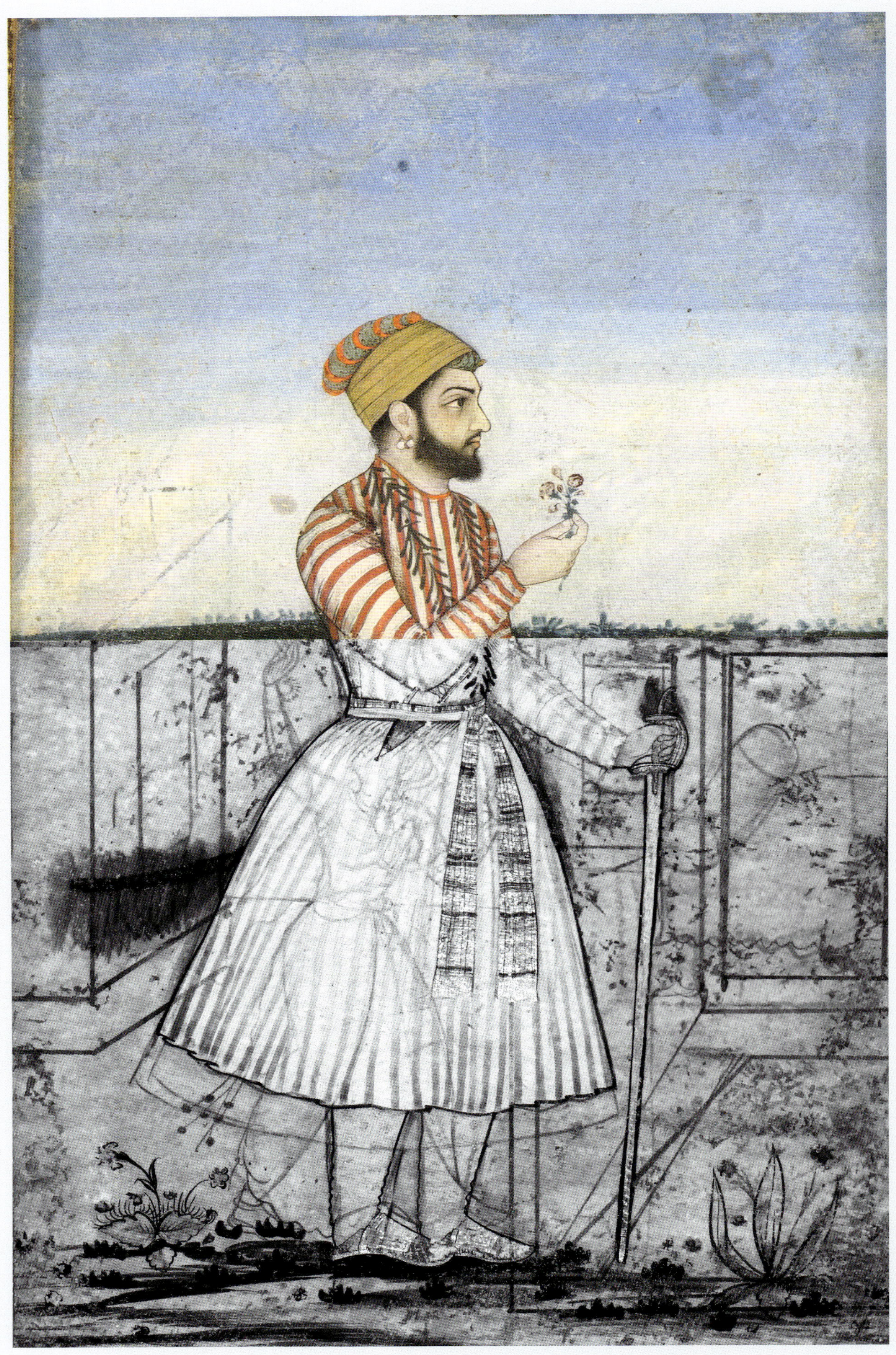

OLAF SIMON

Research and Restoration

The Technical Investigation and Conservation of the Indian Paintings at the Dresden Kupferstich-Kabinett[1]

In 1821 August Wilhelm Schlegel wrote to Hofrat Wilhelm Dorow from Bonn, who advised him in the acquisition of his collection of Indian miniatures: "In my opinion, we should purchase the collection provided that the pictures have not been entirely destroyed by moisture. Indian art may be less expensive in England, but in mainland Europe you have to be satisfied with what chance throws in your way."[2] Surprisingly, Schlegel never personally examined the collection before purchasing it, even though he must have been aware of its compromised condition.

The seventy-eight Indian miniatures, stored as loose sheets in eight boxes, were donated by Schlegel's niece Augusta von Buttlar in 1848 and have remained at the Kupferstich-Kabinett Dresden. The sheets were damaged by mould, which, among other things, might account for the scant attention given to them after they entered the collection some 160 years ago. They came to mind only in 2012, when a delegation of Indian restorers visited Dresden. Along with some 350 Indian paintings preserved in four albums from the collection of Augustus the Strong, they became the starting point for a two-year interdisciplinary research project that began in 2015. In addition to art-historical issues, the main focus was the technical examination and conservation of the miniatures.

Cooperation with institutional partners such as the Bundesanstalt für Materialforschung und -prüfung Berlin (BAM; Federal Institute for Materials Research and Testing Berlin), Papiertechnische Stiftung Heidenau (Paper Technology Foundation Heidenau), Hochschule für Bildende Künste Dresden (Dresden Academy of Fine Arts), Technische Universität Dresden (Technical University of Dresden), Institut für Holztechnologie Dresden (Dresden Institute of Wood Technology), and Carsten Wintermann (papierrestaurierungdresden) served to answer a variety of technological questions. Methods used included radiation diagnostics, digital infrared reflectography (IRR), ultraviolet radiation (UV), digital radiography, and scientific methods such as X-ray fluorescence analysis (XRF), Raman spectroscopy, and spectrophotometry (VIS).

The actual restoration, however, could not have been conducted without the expertise of our colleagues from India. A concept for the conservation and restoration of the objects was developed and implemented in cooperation with restorers from the Chhatrapati Shivaji Maharaj Vastu Sangrahalaya (CSMVS) in Mumbai. The results of the Kupferstich-Kabinett's first cooperation with an Indian institution are presented in this article.

cat. 78 | Ca 121/6
Portrait of a Deccani nobleman
showing the digital infrared reflectograph which reveals the underdrawing: Kakubhā rāgiṇī
Deccan, 18th century
Watercolour and gold, painted frame
26.3 × 18.9 cm, image 20.2 × 13.2 cm
(see figs. 3a and b)

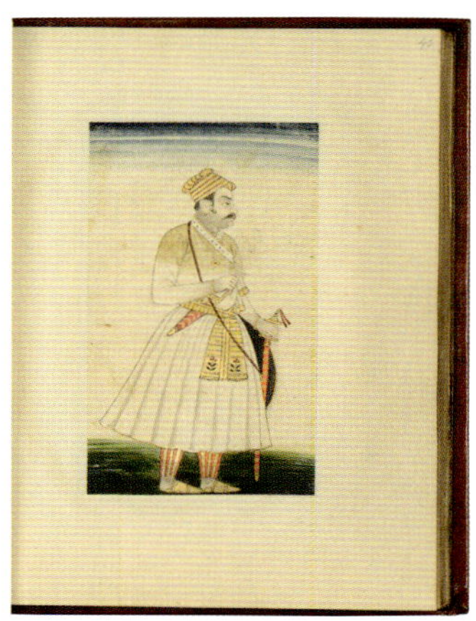

Fig. 1a
Cat. 4 | Ca 111/43 (fol. 39)
Sukh Singh
Deccani Mughal, late 17th – early 18th century
Watercolour and gold, 16.6 × 9.9 cm

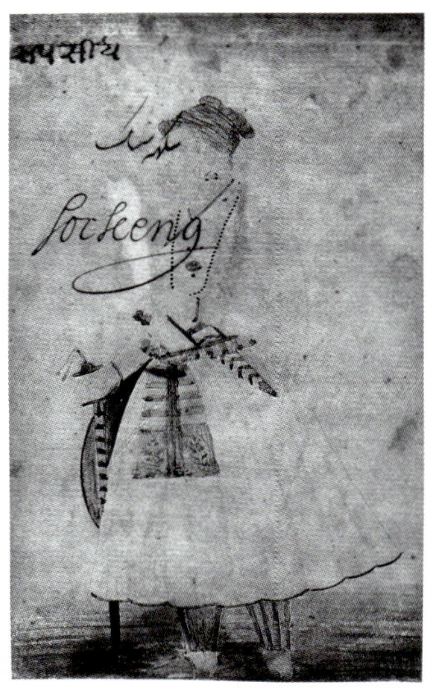

Fig. 1b
Inscriptions on verso seen via transmitted light in *nāgari*: S[…]ingh; in *nasta'līq*: Sukhah Singh; and in Dutch: Sockeng

The Indian Paintings at the Dresden Kupferstich-Kabinett: A Hybrid

The painting method used for the Indian miniatures is similar to the European gouache technique.[3] The support consists of a special paper called *wasli*. It is made by bonding two or more sheets of thin paper that are then burnished with a polishing stone to produce a smooth, glossy texture. The making of a painting began by outlining the composition in red or black. As these outlines shone through the subsequently applied layer of chalk or white lead, the contours could be drawn in black ink. The different pictorial planes, from the background to the foreground, were then created in corresponding colours. The pigments of each newly applied layer were condensed by turning the paper over and smoothing it, from the back, with a polishing stone (*agate*) or a Kauri snail (Latin: *cypraea tigris*). The enamel-like gloss characteristic of miniatures—the key difference between them and Western watercolours—was created using this process. The painting was completed by adding details such as contours and shadows, physiognomic features, and jewellery with a very fine brush made of a single squirrel hair.

The manufacture of Indian miniature paintings traditionally involved a number of participants. The master painter (*musawwir*, *ustād*) was responsible for the overall composition and the execution of the artistically more demanding elements; several subordinate painters (*shāgird*) employed in his workshop (*tasvīrkhāna*) took care of the simpler parts. In addition there was an assembler and a paper manufacturer (*wasligar*), who provided the miniature with a more or less elaborate paper frame. At times, a special painter (*naqshanavī*) added artistic ornaments to the frame. Calligraphers (*khusnavīs*) often added magnificently executed religious or lyrical texts on the verso of the mounted miniatures.

In the context of investigating the studios of court painters appointed to Mughal rulers such as Akbar, Jahāngīr, and Shāh Jahān, art-historical research has in recent decades identified a number of artists and their workshops. In general, however, Indian miniatures were rarely signed, especially if they were not commissioned by the court and manufactured for lesser nobles or the European market, which is probably the case with the Kupferstich-Kabinett's Indian collection.[4]

From a technical point of view, the two consignments of early eighteenth- and nineteenth-century miniatures preserved in Dresden are of a hybrid character indicative of the underlying cultural exchange that took place between India and Europe.

Indian miniatures were usually provided with a broad paper frame so that they could be either bound into albums or protected when the sheets were held when viewed.[5] These frames come in lavishly ornamented and simple monochromatic versions. The sheets from the Schlegel Collection, on the other hand, were completely pasted on larger, sometimes five-ply cardboard of different formats. The protruding edges were then decorated with a painted frame, whose design is reminiscent of European wooden picture frames of the classicist era. Cavettos, common about 1800, with their specific depth were imitated using a brown resin containing colour and gold.[6] Numerous nail holes on all four sides of the illuminated frames suggest that a former owner had affixed the miniatures to a wall.[7] In the Indian context, this form of mounting is rather unusual. It could therefore have been either manufactured in India for a European collector or the European market or produced in Europe right away. In a paper analysis examining their material composition, the cover papers, added later to protect the miniatures, were discovered to be of Indian origin, leading to the hypothesis that they were likely made in India.[8]

In conformity with the traditional form of preserving Indian paintings at Mughal courts between the sixteenth and eighteenth centuries, however, the miniatures from Augustus the Strong's collection are mounted in albums. Two albums have an Oriental binding (cat. 1 and 3) characterised by a lack of protruding edges; instead, the fore-edge is often covered with a flap.[9] Conversely, the other two albums (cat. 2 and 4) have European bindings; in two of them, the watermarks in endpapers and interleaving sheets suggest that they are of Dutch or English manufacture.[10] The gold embossed geometric patterns on the front and back covers of these albums, however, have a somewhat orientalising look for the European eye; here, too, the form of presentation combines Indian and European styles, thus raising questions about makers, clients, and trade routes.

Technical Investigations: Inscriptions, Signatures, Pigments

A variety of technical methods is available for tracing the provenance and dissemination of works of art. One of the simplest is examining the works in reflected light, raking light, or transmitted light. Initially used to analyse condition and to locate and document damage, these methods also reveal underdrawings and inscriptions that have been overpainted that may provide information about manufacturing processes or clues as to origin. When examined in transmitted light in connection with digital post-processing, writings in *nastaʿlīq*, *nāgarī* and Dutch, were found on roughly thirty miniatures—both those pasted into albums and those mounted on paper backings. These inscriptions, mostly mentioning the sitter, in different languages provide evidence of the number of hands through which the works may have passed (figs. 1a and b). For those miniatures from Augustus the Strong's collection that are mounted in albums, a custom-made "light wedge" was used during the examination to protect the pages of the book.

Using digital infrared reflectography, it was possible to visualize inscriptions that had been painted over, and, in individual cases, obtain information on workshop practices.[11] Under the dark blue of the sky at the upper left of the *Baṅgālī rāgiṇī*, for example, a line written in a local *nastaʿlīq* script was found that described the subject matter as "night time conversation with a cheetah" (figs. 2a and 2b). The inscription probably was to be painted over by an artist after completing the picture.

Infrared radiation can be used to make certain colours or underlying layers transparent. In *Portrait of a Deccani Nobleman*, for instance, a completely different first composition became visible that had been painted over. Originally the artist had sketched in black ink a scene from the *Kakubhā rāgiṇī* showing a young woman frightened by the cry of a peacock sitting on a roof (figs. 3a and b).

In the miniature *A Visit to a Shrine*,[12] an underdrawing with sketches of figures drawn in different directions, which was subsequently painted over with a completely different scene, can be detected with infrared reflectography and, in parts, with the naked eye. This discovery supports the assumption that artists re-used papers for the manufacture of *wasli*.[13] The ink lines, visible in transmitted light, bear no relation to the actual subject matter and might be indicative

Fig. 2a
Cat. 59 | Ca 122/14
Baṅgālī rāgiṇī
Hyderabad, early 18th century
Watercolour and gold, painted frame
28 × 19.5 cm, image 21.3 × 13.1 cm

Fig. 2b
Digital infrared reflectograph (detail)

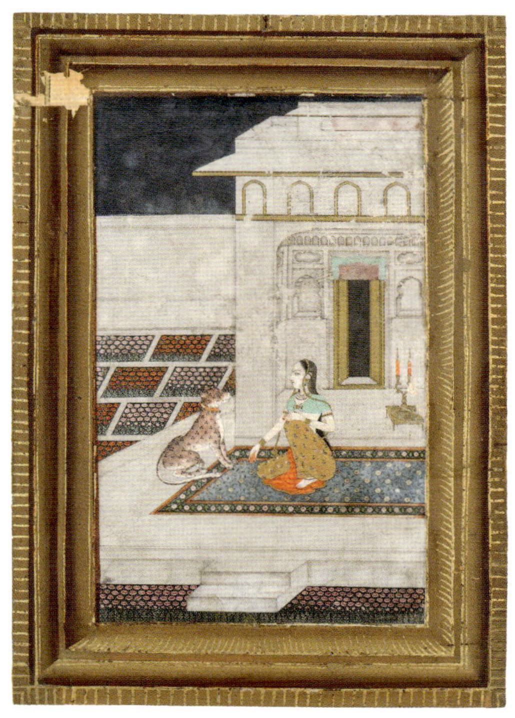

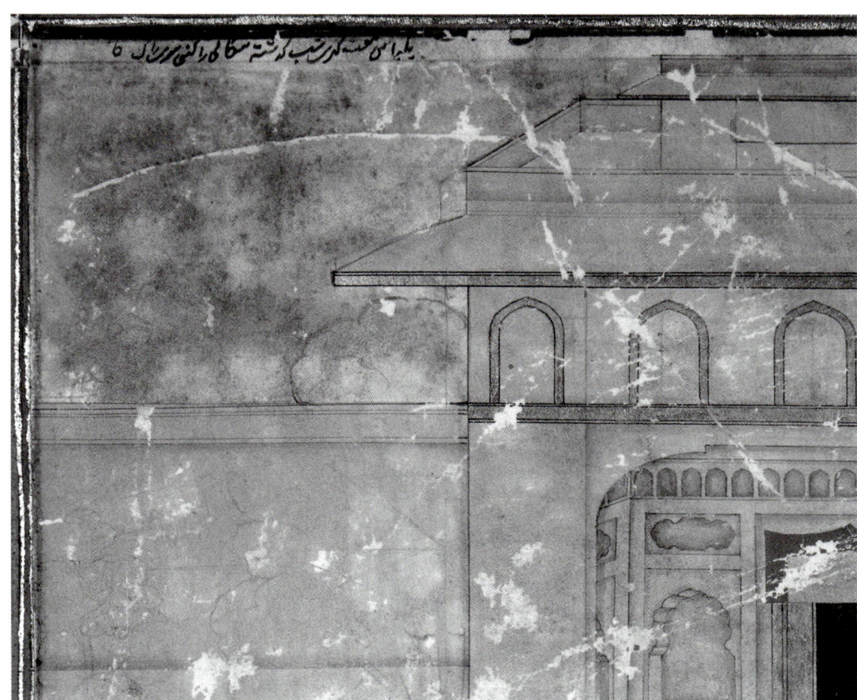

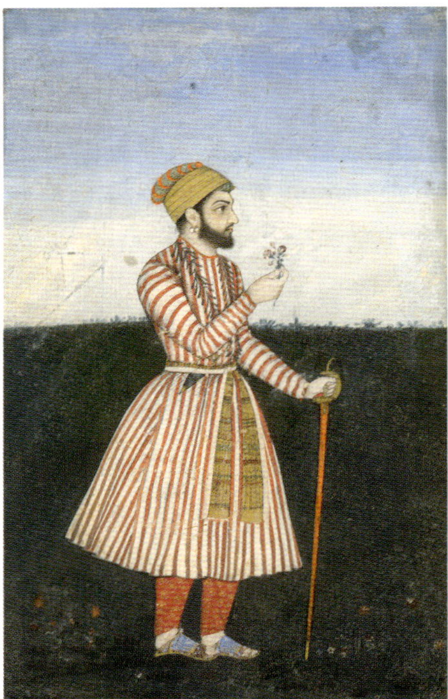

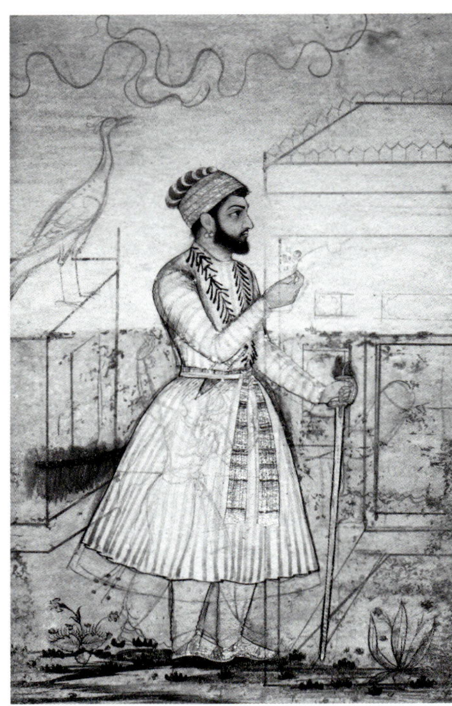

Fig. 3a
Cat. 78 | Ca 121/6
Portrait of a Deccani nobleman
Underdrawing: Kakubhā rāgiṇī
Deccan, 18th century
Watercolour and gold, painted frame
26.3 × 18.9 cm, image 20.2 × 13.2 cm

Fig. 3b
Digital infrared reflectograph

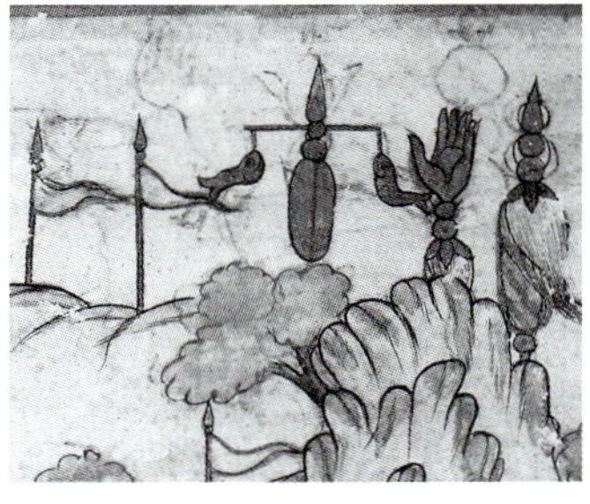

Fig. 4
Cat. 48 | Ca 118/2
Jahāngīr hunting
Deccani Mughal, early 18th century
Watercolour, gold, and silver [?],
painted frame 33.7 × 45.1 cm,
image 26.9 × 37.9 cm
Digital infrared reflectograph (detail)

of foolscap and waste paper being used in a different layer of the *wasli*. Presumably, paper was too precious to simply dispose of discarded drawings or a degree of pragmatism prevailed in the workshop responsible for reusing such sheets.

Preparatory drawings containing carbon material, made visible with infrared reflectography, are less obvious. In a hunting scene with Jahāngīr (cat. 48),[14] only small corrections are detectable, where the arrangement of lances and spears in the group of figures at the upper right was slightly changed (fig. 4). A variation of this motif, preserved in the Millionenzimmer at Schönbrunn Castle in Vienna, provides a starting point for examining, with stylistic and scientific methods, the practice of copying.[15]

Technical investigations often involve unexpected discoveries. Originally, *Shāh Jahān's Court in a Procession*[16] was examined in order to determine to what extent the painted brown frame covered parts of the miniature. Due to the density of the ochre, the observation in the infrared range obtained no results. Relying on the support of the Hochschule für Bildende Künste Dresden, we resorted to digital radiography in order to penetrate all the painted layers of the picture.[17] The pigments containing heavy metals such as white lead or cinnabar are especially visible in the X-ray. This method, well established in painting restoration, is a novelty in the examination of Indian miniatures. With it, it was possible to show that the painter of the frame had generously painted over the miniature at the edges. In addition, a fundamental change in the composition of the scene was detected. The central figure of Shāh Jahān, now shown on an elephant riding to the left, was originally designed as a man on a horse riding to the right (figs. 5a and b). The reasons for this change remain unclear. It might have been occasioned by a new request from the customer or by the workshop practice of reusing papers.

Material analysis can provide important information for the purposes of dating works of art, particularly in cases when archival sources are scanty or not available at all. In the case of a sheet with eighteen portraits of Mughal rulers from Tīmūr to Rafī' ud-Darajāt (cat. 5), dendrochronological investigation of the wooden board to which it was mounted provided a terminus post quem for its creation. The so-called Heucher Inventory of the Dresden Kupferstich-Kabinett, drawn up in 1738 and thus the earliest source to mention the Indian collection from the time of Augustus the Strong, incorrectly identifies the series as "18 small miniature portraits of Japanese

Fig. 5a
Cat. 49 | Ca 119/9
Shāh Jahān's court in a procession
Deccani Mughal, late 17th–
early 18th century
Watercolour and gold, painted frame
41.8 × 28.9 cm, image 35.2 × 22.5 cm

Fig. 5b
Digital radiograph

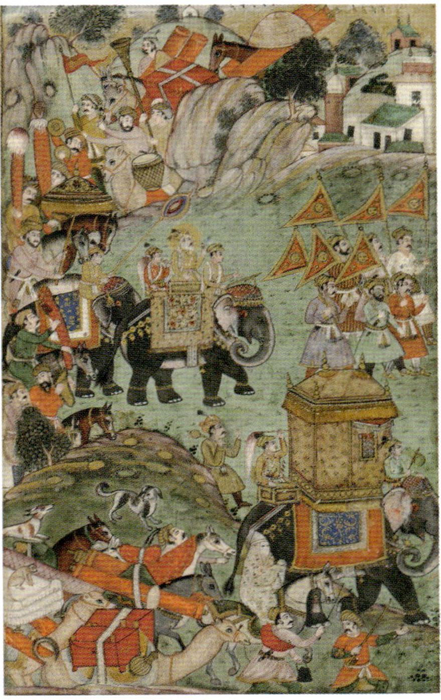

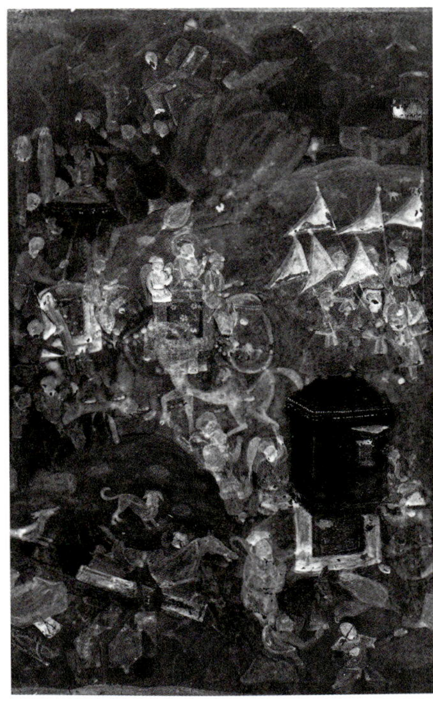

emperors mounted on a small board."[18] This raises the question whether the extant board of about 34 × 22.3 × 0.9 cm is identical with the mentioned "small board" or a later replacement.[19] The portraits themselves were cut out and pasted onto a paper of European origin. The names of the rulers portrayed were noted in Dutch under the respective pictures. The wood onto which the paper was mounted was identified as European oak. The dendrochronology of the board established that the last remaining annual ring of the section examined grew in 1665, suggesting that the support is precisely the "small board" described in the inventory.

The use of European materials for the mounting suggests that the portraits were mounted by Dutch traders in India using imported materials or that they were mounted at a later date in the Netherlands. Whether the wooden board was used as a decorative element in a wainscoting or mounted in a frame is beyond reconstruction. The presumed authenticity of the mount was, however, taken into consideration for the conservation treatment. Instead of removing the paper and mounting it on acid-free cardboard, the original state was preserved as testimony to the methods used for dealing with works of art in the eighteenth century.

Colour as a distinguishing feature of Indian painting gave rise to further radiological examinations. Until recently, the knowledge of pigments and dyes was based on historical literature and visual identification. Non-destructive examination methods developed in recent years have made the exact chemical identification of colours possible. In cooperation with the BAM, forty-four miniatures were examined with VIS spectroscopy; twenty-four were also examined using micro-XRF. For the first time, a high-resolution micro-XRF scanner enabling the measurement and imaging of element distributions on a larger surface was used in this context.[20]

The identification confirmed the Indian origin of mineral pigments and organic dyes such as indigo, lapis lazuli, smalt, copper green, Indian yellow, ochre, cinnabar, red lead, lac dye, gold, and silver. Typically European colours such as blue azurite and yellow auripigment were not discovered. As the data collected on the Baroque collection were entered before 1738, they allowed a temporal comparison with the sheets in the Schlegel Collection. The colour measurements confirmed the hypothesis, formed on the basis of stylistic similarity, that some of the miniatures, such as the portrait of Abū Sa'īd or 'Omar Shaikh (cat. 24), originated from the same region or workshop.[21] Here, as with other miniatures in both collections, the green used in the foreground was made from indigo and Indian yellow. The turning of this green into blue, observed in some of the miniatures and probably caused by a reduction of the pigments in the Indian yellow due to water damage (fig. 6), provided helpful insights for the conservator's damage assessment.

Radiation diagnostic findings on the distribution and processing of pigments in the various sectors of the pictures served as interpretation aids for art-historical evaluation. Lapis lazuli, for instance, is often used as a pure blue pigment to enhance the brilliance of a particular detail such as the carpet in the *Darbār of Aurangzēb* (cat. 6), whereas indigo was often mixed with other pigments.

As a side effect, as it were, these investigations produced even further discoveries. The miniature *Khiẓr and Moses* (cat. 85) was XRF-scanned to make a Persian inscription of several lines of a *Qur'ān* text on the verso more legible; it had previously been detected in transmitted light but was covered by a solidly pasted cardboard. However, as the text was probably written with an ink containing carbon, not detectable by RFA, the investigation did not yield any results. Yet another line of non-visible writing, part of a longer text on the verso, was detected in the analysis of the gold pigment used for the nimbus of flames surrounding the two prophets and for other areas. The use of gold pigment within the text has an almost programmatic ring in the context of the scientific methods used here to detect something hidden under the surface (figs. 7a, b, and c).[22]

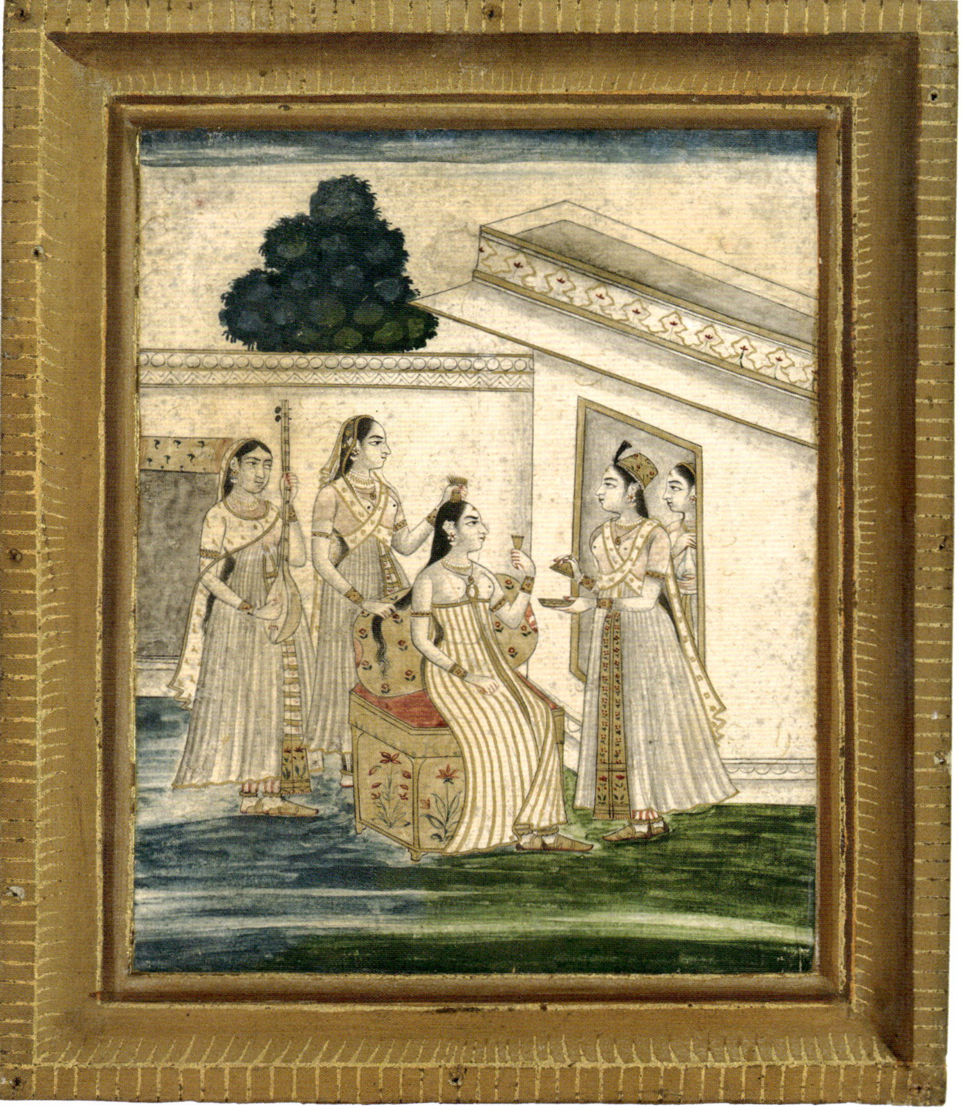

Fig. 6
Cat. 62 | Ca 122/3
Women in a terrace garden
Hyderabad, early 18th century
Watercolour and gold, painted frame
23.6 × 19.7 cm, image 17.9 × 14.2 cm

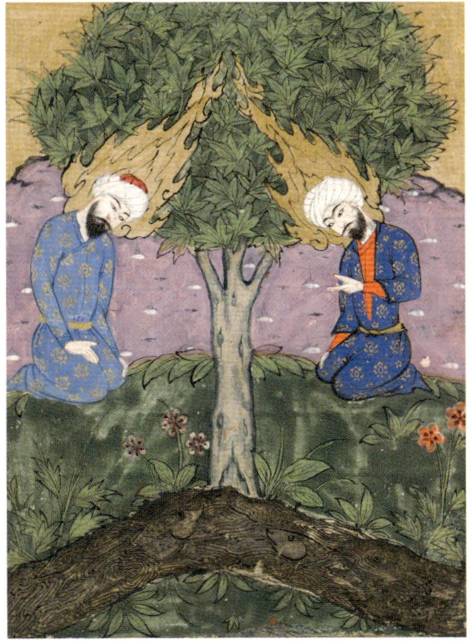

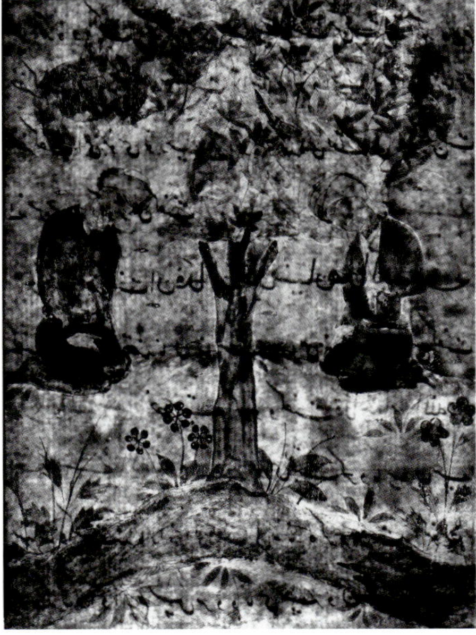

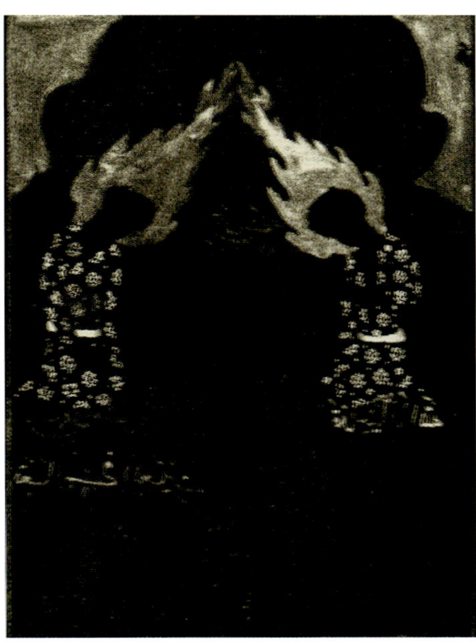

Fig. 7a
Cat. 85 | Ca 121/12
Khiẓr and Moses
Deccan, late 17th – early 18th century
Watercolour, gold, and silver, painted frame 22.3 × 17.7 cm, image 16.7 × 12.2 cm

Fig. 7b
Backlit image showing lines of text on the verso

Fig. 7c
X-ray fluorescence showing the distribution of gold

The Restoration of the Indian Miniatures

The restoration campaign carried out with restorers from the CSMVS in Mumbai focused on the seventy-eight miniatures from the Schlegel Collection.[23] The fear of destruction by moisture, which Schlegel had expressed in his letter to Dorow, probably referred to the considerable mould damage on almost all the sheets. Where fungal colonies are active, they endanger not only the work of art itself but also, by flying spores, human beings in close proximity. A microbiological examination was therefore conducted by the Institut für Holztechnologie Dresden prior to any further restoration measures. The six samples taken directly from the original were infested with Cladosporium species germination trials were negative, indicating a very old infestation. In addition, some structural changes in the fungal spores were observed;[24] a reactivation of the existing mycelia could thus be ruled out. A territorial limitation was not feasible because Cladosporia are widespread and occur in almost all climatic zones. It thus remained unclear whether the mould was of European or Asian origin.

The mould in the affected miniatures is located between individual layers of cardboard. In its active phase, it had left dark dots and larger spots on the front page. As a result of the moisture, the miniatures had become detached from the cardboard support and had begun to form bubbles (figs. 8a and b). Further damage included discolourations and colour losses, blackening of white lead, scratches, insect damage, and warping and flaws in the cardboard frames (figs. 8–11). All these damages suggest that the collection was not kept in a cabinet but was shown unprotected on a wall.

The objective of the restoration measures was to improve the conservation status of the works without changing the form of their mounting, which significantly restricted the scope of action. The only experimental deviation from this concept was undertaken with *Darbār of Jahāngīr* (figs. 8a and b). This badly preserved miniature was removed from the backing paper to gain more in-depth insight into the special structure of the mount and to sample material for fibre analysis. At the same time, it was possible to test this method's efficiency in reducing mould spots. Partial bleaching experiments with hydrogen peroxide on a low-pressure table failed to produce aesthetically convincing results that would justify such a complex treatment.[25]

A different surface cleaning concept was therefore developed that helped soften the irreversible stains and thus improved the overall appearance. Impurities on the top paint layer such as insect faeces or wax stains were mechanically removed with a scalpel; other contaminants were

Fig. 8a
Cat. 47 | Ca 119/8
Darbār of Jahāngīr (III)
Deccani Mughal, late 17th – early 18th century
Watercolour and gold, painted frame
36.6 × 29.2 cm, image 29.6 × 22.2 cm
Photograph in raking light taken prior to restoration

Fig. 8b
Photograph taken after restoration

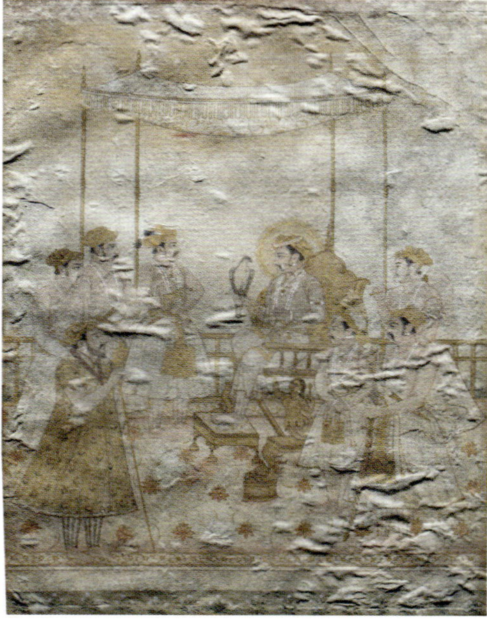

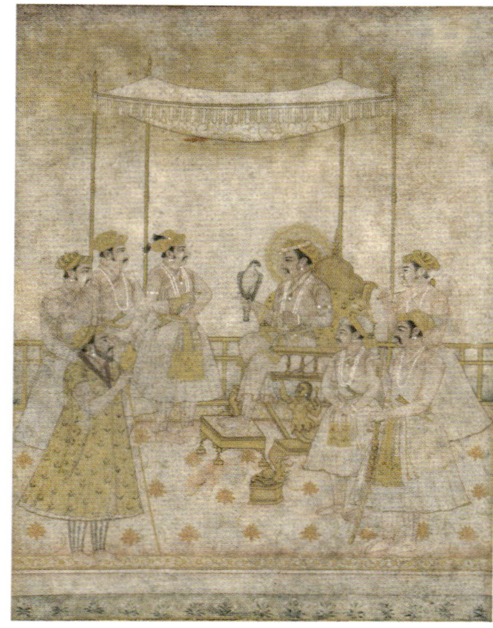

Fig. 9a
Cat. 53 | Ca 122/11
Yogī
Mughal, late 17th century
Watercolour and gold, painted frame
28.5 × 19.2 cm, image 21.7 × 12.5 cm
Photograph taken prior to restoration

Fig. 9b
Photograph taken after restoration

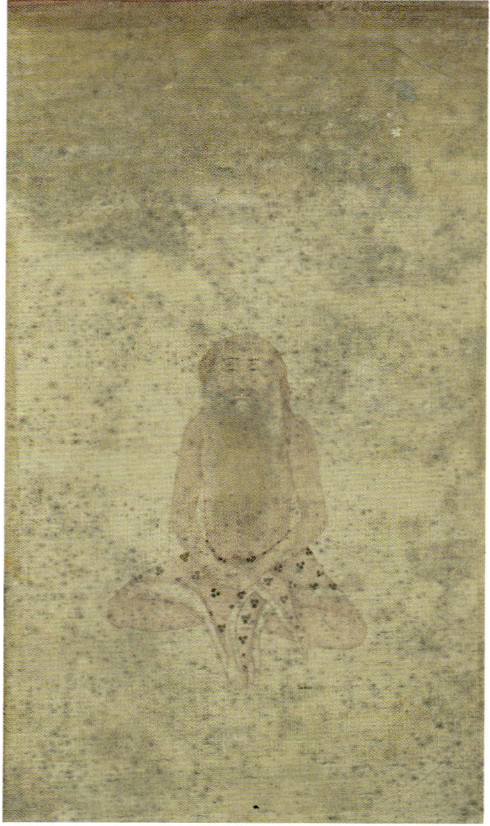

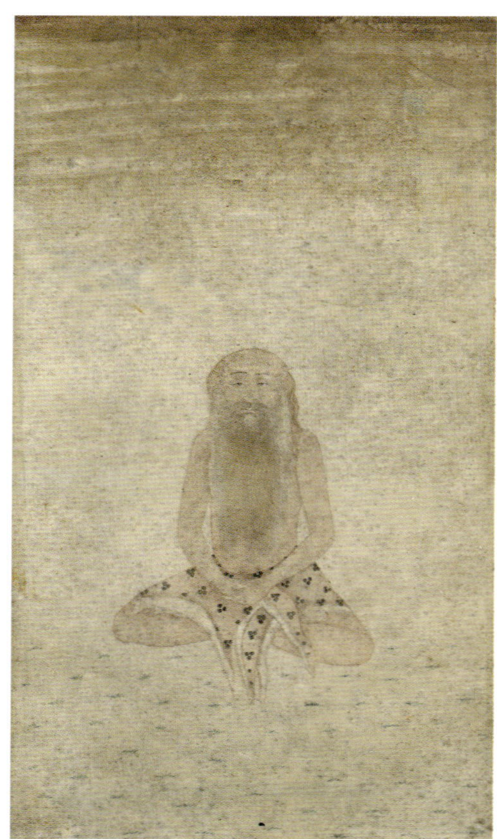

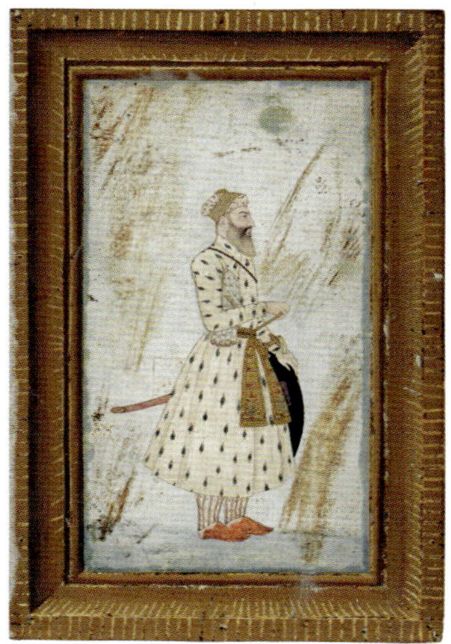
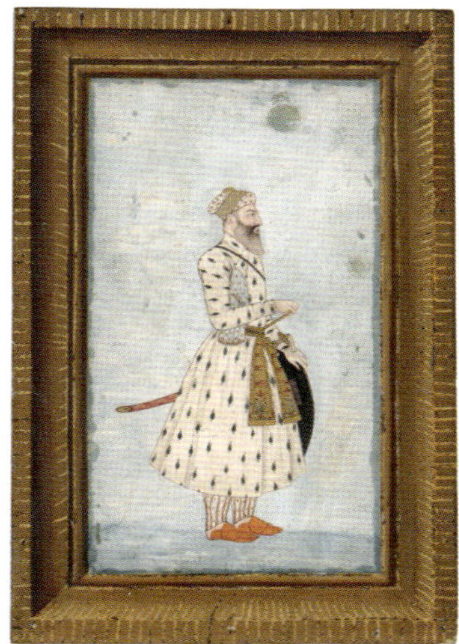
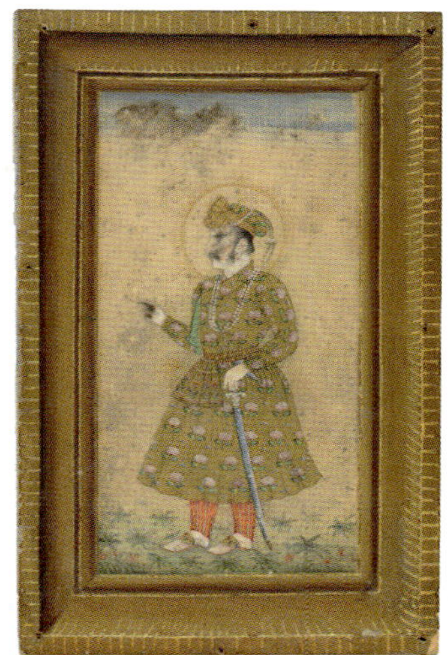
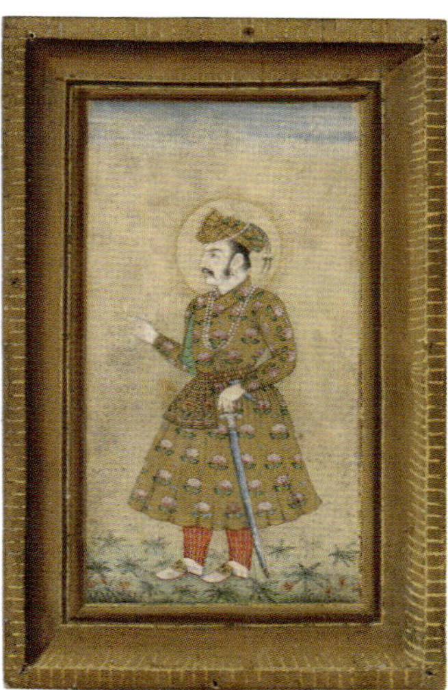

Fig. 10a
Cat. 121/3 | Ca 121/3
Bahādur Khān Chaghatai
Deccani Mughal, late 17th – early 18th century
Watercolour and gold, painted frame
25.7 × 17.3 cm, image 20.3 × 11.7 cm
Photograph taken prior to restoration

Fig. 10b
Photograph taken after restoration

Fig. 11a
Cat. 21 | Ca 123/8
Jahāngīr (r. 1605 – 1627)
Deccani Mughal, late 17th century
Watercolour and gold, painted frame
24.9 × 15.8 cm, image 18.7 × 9.8 cm
Photograph taken prior to restoration

Fig. 11b
Photograph taken after restoration

reduced with cotton swabs soaked in alcohol or synthetic saliva. Particularly dark mould stains were partially treated with a solution of hydrogen peroxide, acetone, and ammonia, resulting in a slight brightening (figs. 9a and 9b). The uneven background in some of the paintings, caused by mould and insect damage, was smoothed using visually acceptable watercolour retouching. Following a recommendation from our Indian colleagues, the solidifying agent EHEC was used to consolidate flaking paint layers.[26] An ultrasonic atomiser and the consolidant Klucel G were used for to fix powdering paint layers. Where warping and bubble formation could not be entirely eliminated, they were at least reduced with various humidification and clamping methods.

The reconstructive approach pursued, together with art historians, in the restoration of the Schlegel Collection is also the result of a new development in scientific conservation research that puts the maintenance of historical preservation and presentation forms on a par with the requirements of the restoration treatment. Less than one hundred years ago, Percy Brown, an English art historian who specialised in Indian art, recommended that miniatures be removed from the albums into which they had been pasted and mounted individually in order to protect them.[27] It is still unclear how such issues will be dealt with in the future, especially if one takes digital strategies into account.

Notes | 1 This essay is based on the cooperation with Anupam Sah, Head Conservator at the Restoration Department of CSMVS Mumbai, Oliver Hahn, Head of the Department of Art and Cultural Analysis, and Ira Rabin, both of them Federal Institute for Materials Research and Testing Berlin (BAM), as well as Carsten Wintermann, Papierrestaurierung, Dresden. For the German version of this text see Simon 2017. | 2 Letter from Paris, dated March 31, 1821, Stadtarchiv Bonn, sig. SN 19–58. See also Dresden 2017, p. 132. | 3 See Chandra 1949; Ohri 2001; and Beach/Goswamy/Fischer 2011, pp. 793–8. | 4 See Lunsingh Scheurleer 2017. | 5 See Brown 1975, p. 22. | 6 The cavetto, particularly common in Mannerist and Neoclassical frames, is a concave moulding running at a right angle to the frame. | 7 In cat. 80, Ca 120/7, for instance, there was a nail hole still containing the head of a metal nail. | 8 The fibre analysis of the cover paper was conducted by the Papiertechnische Stiftung Heidenau. Hemp was identified as a fibre by infrared spectroscopic measurement and morphological determination. | 9 See Beach/Carswell/Petherbridge 1981; and Haldane 1983. | 10 Cat. 2, Ca 110; and Cat. 4, Ca 111. | 11 The IRR analysis was conducted by Carsten Wintermann, Papierrestaurierung Dresden, with the help of two 1000-watt halogen lamps. The spectral range between 1000 and 1300 nm, which is invisible to the human eye, was visualised by an infrared-sensitive camera (digital camera and infrared filter RG 1000). | 12 Ca 111/64 (fol. 60). | 13 See Agrawal 1984, p. 140; and Gupta, 2006, p. 5. | 14 See p. 156–7. | 15 Work meeting with Karin Troschke, Schönbrunn Castle, Vienna, November 5, 2014. In the 1980 and 1990s Karin Troschke directed the restoration of the miniatures preserved in the Millionenzimmer. | 16 Cat. 49, Ca. 119/9. | 17 X-ray tube Eresco 42 MF4 from GE Sensing & Inspection Technologies GmbH, X-rayed on image plates of the IPU 43 type (43 × 35 cm) then scanned with CRxFlex. The investigation was conducted by Kerstin Riße, Hochschule für Bildende Künste Dresden. | 18 Heucher Inventory 1738, sig. Cat. 1, p. 156, no. 17. | 19 The investigation was conducted by Björn Günther, expert in wood protection. | 20 The investigations were carried out by Ira Rabin, BAM. See Appendices, *Pigment and Dye Analysis*, pp. 252–4. | 21 Cat. 4, Ca 111/52 (fol. 48) and cat. 13, Ca 124/2. | 22 See Hahn/Rabin 2017, pp. 69–71. | 23 Under the joint guidance of Anupam Sah, head conservator in Mumbai, and Olaf Simon, two conservators from the CSMVS, Omkar Kadu and Lalit Pathak, worked at this task during a six-week stay. This work was continued by freelance restorer Irina Kreipe. | 24 Although it is not documented, it seems probable that the miniatures were treated with gamma rays between 1960 and 1985—a method then used at the Kupferstich-Kabinett for the treatment of fungal infections. | 25 See the documentation of the restoration available at the Kupferstich-Kabinett. | 26 EHEC = water soluble ethyl hydroxyethyl cellulose. | 27 See Brown 1975, p. 28.

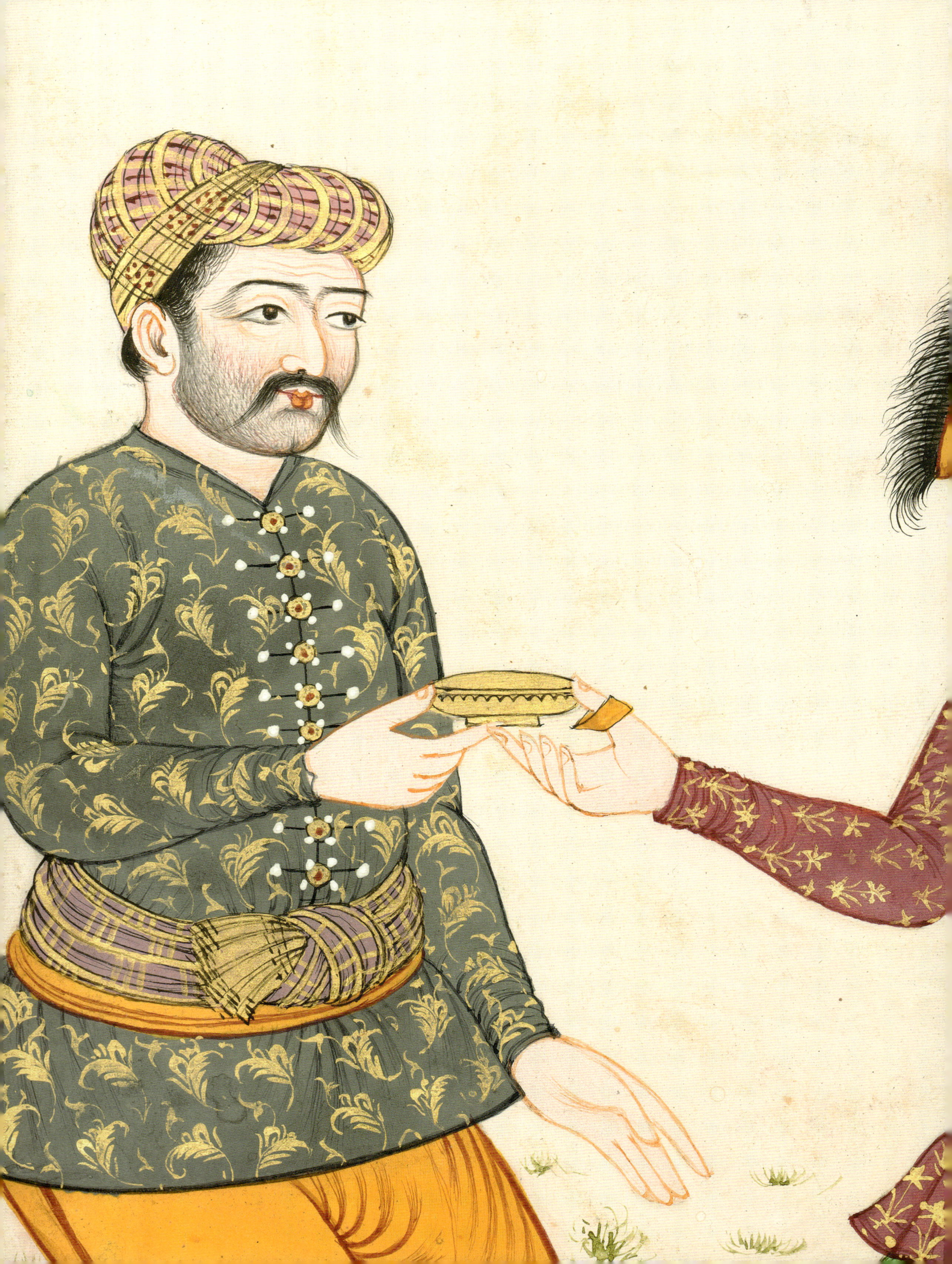

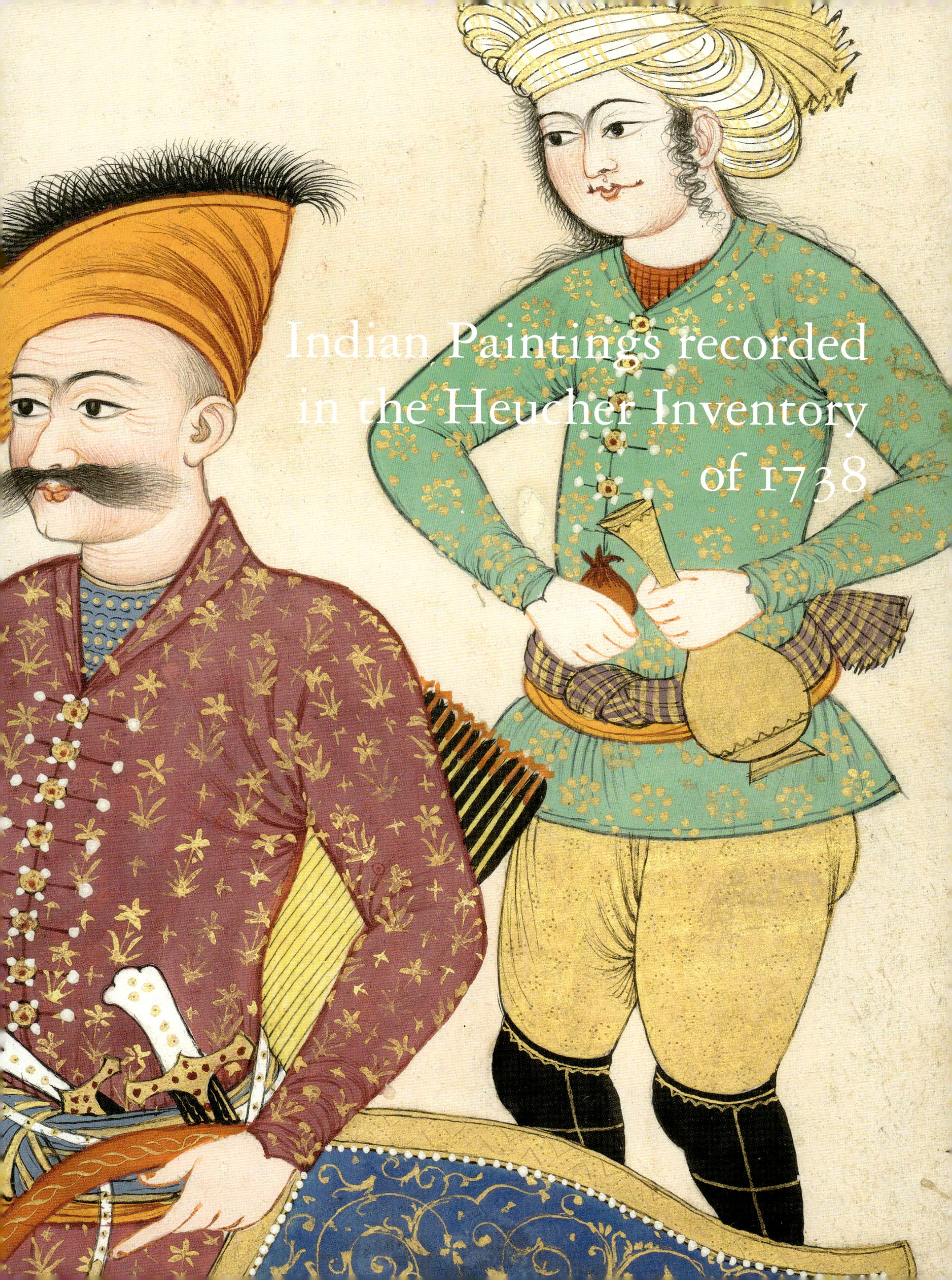

Indian Paintings recorded in the Heucher Inventory of 1738

Cat. 1–4
Four Portrait Albums of Indian Rulers

Note to the Reader

The systematic catalogue of the Dresden Kupferstich-Kabinett lists the Indian works in the collection acquired before 1738 as described in the Heucher Inventory (cat. 1–7), followed by the Indian paintings from the Schlegel Collection donated in 1848 (cat. 8–85), and illustrations from a recently donated copy of the *Shāhnāma* illustrated in Kashmirian style (cat. 86). It goes on to describe three Indian paintings pasted into an album with texts and artworks of various origins—European, Japanese, and Chinese—deriving from a number of sources (cat. 87) and an incomplete set of Indian playing cards (cat. 88). Finally, there are a number of works, possibly of European or Ottoman origin, categorised as "Indica", probably during the nineteenth century (cat. 89–91).

The inventory number is provided in the caption following the catalogue number.

Inscriptions on the verso are provided in the captions or listed in the appendices.

The medium referred to as "watercolour" includes different types of ink and of opaque and lavish watercolour, and many of the works show a mixture of these mediums. Gold and silver pigments are listed separately. All paintings from the Schlegel Collection have frames painted on paper in brown watercolour and gold. The indication of the medium is referring to the painting itself only.

If a portrait could not be clearly assigned to a person, the supposed name is followed by a question mark in square brackets.

Authors (Catalogue and Appendices):

NB Neha Berlia
CB Cordula Bischoff
CPH Claus Peter Haase
OH Oliver Hahn
PKH Petra Kuhlmann-Hodick
IR Ira Rabin
NS Nedim Sönmez
AT Andrew Topsfield

The opulent lands of the Great Mughals attracted a wide array of Europeans to India seeking economic opportunities. Beginning with the presence of the Portuguese in the sixteenth century, along with some Germans and Italians,[1] the European presence in India expanded vastly over the late sixteenth and seventeenth centuries.[2]

Art objects as well as written and painted materials became popular ways of representing India. Manuscripts and paintings began to arrive in Europe, mainly in the Netherlands, via the factors of the Dutch East India Company, for royalty and aristocrats as well as scholars and shareholders in the company.[3] The Indian painting albums in the Kupferstich-Kabinett (Ca 110–Ca 113) that can be broadly categorised as Deccani Mughal in style consist largely of individual portraits of Indian rulers and of their officers and noblemen. These join the corpus of known portrait albums of similar style and period in other European collections,[4] often reflecting upon the close relationship that existed between collectors, painters, and engravers. Ca 112 demonstrates how European travellers and collectors shared their works with engravers, thus becoming a part of history in their famous published travelogues.

During the reign of Aurangzēb (r. 1658–1707), artists from the Mughal imperial atelier became increasingly desperate for work, as his rule brought about a precipitous decline in imperial patronage of illustrated manuscripts and *muraqqa'*. The closing of ateliers led to the dismissal of master painters and their assistants, who established their own workshops[5] and sought new patrons—not only among noblemen and the rich[6] but also among Europeans.[7] The craftsmanship of these artists who had worked in the service of the kings[8] now suffered, as they quickly produced multiple works of mediocre quality to meet the demand.[9] Indian art now travelled as a part of the ongoing Indo-European trade.

James Frazer (1713–1754), a collector and an official of the East India Company in Surat, wrote to the English novelist John Cleland (1709–1789) regarding the sale of Persian manuscripts and portraits in his possession.[10] Frazer inquires if any of Cleland's friends in London would be interested in buying them and says that he already has an offer from a gentleman called Mons. Martin[11] and could easily send them to France if there were a lack of interest. This exchange demonstrates the lively market for these manuscripts, not only in Amsterdam but in England and France as well.[12]

The Dresden portrait albums that are similar to the type of portraits produced in Golconda in the 1660s for European audience can be grouped into four standard types. The first type includes rulers from Tīmūr (r. 1370–1405) until Aurangzēb, sometimes extending as far as the Emperor Farrukh Sīyar (r. 1713–1719).[13] The second type includes about 179 kings and queens of India from Rājā Yudhiṣṭhira until Aurangzēb.[14] The third type includes the Mughal rulers from Akbar until Aurangzēb, portraits of rulers of Golconda, mostly ʿAbdullāh Qutb Shāh (r. 1626–1672), Abū'l Hasan Qutb Shāh (r. 1672–1686), and the Bijapur rulers Muḥammad ʿĀdil Shāh (r. 1627–1656) and ʿAlī ʿĀdil Shāh II (r. 1656–1672). Sometimes there are a few portraits of their dignitaries and of Safavid rulers such as ʿAbbās I (r. 1588–1629), ʿAbbās II (r. 1642–1666), and Sulaimān (r. 1666–1694).[15] And the fourth type includes a selection from the previous three categories along with other loose sheets, probably remnants of other albums that were dispersed.[16]

The four albums of Indian portraits that are now in Dresden, when compared to other albums around Europe, bear witness to the Indian workshop production in the eighteenth century.[17] NB

Notes | 1 Subrahmanyam 2017, p. 16. | 2 The Dutch established factories at Masulipatnam and Nizampatnam in 1606 and at Pulicat in 1621; the English East India Company established theirs at Masulipatnam and Negapattam in 1611 and at Pulicat in 1621. | 3 Subrahmanyam 2017, p. 31. | 4 Bibliothèque Nationale de France, Paris, Smith-Lesouëf 232 and 233; British Museum, London, inv. nos. 1974 6-17 02, 1974 6-17 04, and 1974 6-17 011; Witsen Album, Rijksmuseum, Amsterdam, inv. no. RP-T-00-3186; Staatliche Museen zu Berlin, Museum für Asiatische Kunst, inv. no. MIK 1 5066-68 68 and some folios in MIK I 5004; and the collections of Count Abate Giovanni Antonio Baldini and Simon Schijnvoet reproduced in Chatelain 1719 and Valentijn 1726. | 5 Lunsingh Scheurleer/Kruijtzer 2005, p. 52. | 6 Michell/Zebrowski 1999, p. 157. | 7 For example, the Dutch East India Company ambassador Johannas Bacherus commissioned "Camping with the Mughal Emperor" in 1687 from a Golconda artist. See Lunsingh Scheurleer/Kruijtzer 2005, p. 52. | 8 De Bruin 1737, p. 220. | 9 Bernier 1699, p. 190. | 10 Ms. Top Oxon. B. 43 in MS. Frazer 277, Bodleian Library, Oxford. The Frazer collection at the Bodleian comprises original manuscripts and copies. Proficient in Sanskrit and surrounded by Brahmins, Frazer, who translated the *Śāstras*, knew his collection was highly valued abroad. | 11 Martin had received a letter at Surat from Pondicherry (capital of French India in 1664), five years before, advising him to procure Persian manuscripts, especially those brought into India by the Afghans as per the orders from the Royal Academy of Sciences and was offering Frazer double the costs for his collection. | 12 In this concern the Vatican Barberini album is mentioned as one of the earliest examples from the period between the reigns of Mughal emperors Jahāngīr (r. 1605–1627) and Shāh Jahān (r. 1628–1658) and is typical of albums of portraits in seventeenth-century European collections. See Subrahmanyam 2017, p. 133; also Kurz 1967. A later album in Dresden, Ca 111 (cat. 4), is one example for a compilation of artworks by a collector to form an album of Indian paintings; the unique subject of Ca 113 (cat. 3), resonates upon the popularity and demand of Indian artworks with historical evidence amongst Europeans for at least two more copies of this album belonged to famous collectors along with the discovery of two other similar albums in London and Bodleian. | 13 See cat. 5 (Ca 116); see also Nationaalmuseum van Wereldculturen Leiden, inv. nos. 360–7346–360–7363, and the collections of Count Giovanni Antonio Baldini (1654–1725) and Simon Schijnvoet reproduced in Chatelain 1719 and Valentijn 1726, respectively. | 14 Cat. 3 (Ca 113); cf. Victoria & Albert Museum, London, inv. no. IM9–1912; and Bodleian Library, Oxford, MS. Ind. Misc. d. 3. | 15 Cat. 1 and 2 (Ca 112, Ca 110); cf. Bibliothèque Nationale de France, Paris, Smith-Lesouëf 232 and 233; British Museum, London, inv. nos. 1974 6-17 04 and 1974 6-17 011; Musée Guimet, Paris, inv. no. 35.491, 35.492; Witsen Album, Rijksmuseum, Amsterdam, inv. no. RP-T-00-3186. | 16 Cat. 4 (Ca 111); cf. British Museum, London, inv. no. 1974 6-17 02; Rijksmuseum, Amsterdam, Canter Visscher album, inv. nos. NG-008-60-1 to NG-2008-60-28; inv. no. NG-2008-60; Österreichische Nationalbibliothek, Vienna, Min. 44 and Min. 64; Staatliche Museen zu Berlin, Museum für Asiatische Kunst, inv. no. MIK 1 5066-68 and some folios in MIK I 5004; Staatsbibliothek zu Berlin, Orientabteilung, Libri pict. A91. | 17 See Appendices, pp. 242–51.

Cat. 1 | Ca 112

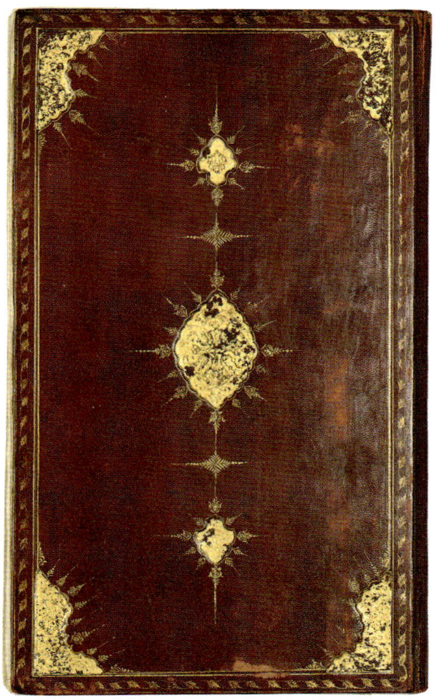

Fig. 1
Ca 112
Cover, right

Album with forty-six portraits of Persian, Mughal and Deccani kings and noblemen
Golconda (Deccan), 1668–1689
Album with 55 fols., 32.2 × 18.8 × 1.5 cm, Persian style morocco binding, embossed with gold
46 images on 24 fols., watercolour and gold, borders with framing lines in black ink and gold on sprinkled ground, inscribed on recto in *nasta'līq* with the name of the sitter, one page with empty frame design, verso of no. 46 empty
32 endpapers and separating pages, inscribed on left endpaper in German: "Dieses Buch ist ganz von hohen werth / d. 23 Dec. 1689."
Two added loose leaves with lists of names, written in ink, one list with a note in English, "By the Hon[ora]ble Edward Gardner. Late one of the Political Residents in Bengal"; corrections in graphite and blue pencil
References: Melzer 2010, pp. 292–3; Dresden 2013, p. 111; Dresden 2017, cat. 10, pp. 143–7

Assembled along with other albums of Indian paintings and an incomplete set of playing cards, Ca 112 (fig. 1) formed part of the rich collection of Augustus the Strong (r. 1694–1733).[1] The album contains two handwritten lists of the names of the rulers portrayed, one of them along with a note referring to Edward Gardner.[2] The album is mentioned in the 1738 inventory of Johann Heinrich Heucher as "24 Blat[3] dergleichen,[4] 17 davon die Blätter, das erste ausgenommen auf beyden Seiten bemahlt, en Marcoquin rouge d'oré. Steckt in einem ledernen Beutel. Folio"[5] (24 folios of the like, which, except for the first are painted on both sides, in morocco rouge d'oré. Placed in a leather bag). The album consists of forty-six portraits, each separated by a sheet of Indian paper: forty standing, four seated, one double, and one group. Reading from right to left, as the book is in its original Islamic binding, the portraits of the rulers are grouped by dynasty, with the first being a portrait of the third Mughal emperor of India, Akbar (r. 1556–1605), and the last a group portrait of the fifth *shāh* of the Safavid dynasty in Iran, Shāh 'Abbās I (r. 1588–1629), and Mīrzā Barkhurdār, the ambassador of the Mughal Emperor Jahāngīr (r. 1605–1627).[6] The album represents the rulers of four dynasties—Mughals, Qutb Shāhīs of Golconda, 'Ādil Shāhīs of Bijapur, and Safavids—along with Hindu *rājās* and other dignitaries and high-ranking personages belonging to these dynastic courts.[7]

Executed with great uniformity, these miniatures are mounted on album leaves with a floral border executed in gold against a sprinkled background. In the margins are arabesque designs similar to the kind found on monuments of the time of Shāh Jahān (r. 1628–1658). Painted in watercolour and lavishly decorated with gold, most of the portraits on facing pages seem to be in dialogue, as in the visual representations known as *sawāl-u jawāb*, or question and answer (figs. 4a and 4b). The exceptions are the portrayals of Safavid men and of Aurangzēb and Murād Bakhsh, two sons of Shāh Jahān, who but look away from each other (Ca 112/41 and 42). In light of the history between these two brothers, who conspired to remove their elder brothers, Dārā and Shujā', in the war of succession, and the episode of Aurangzēb convicting Murād of killing a fellow officer and hence executing him in 1661, it is reasonable to assume that the artist or artists made this compositional change deliberately.

Paintings occupy the central position on each page accompanied by *nasta'līq* inscriptions in the glowing tinted backgrounds, which have minimal representations of sky and ground. The stamped binding in dark red leather—probably goat skin—showcases the impressed decoration of inlaid and gilded medallions (see fig. 1). Although in good condition, the text is extruding from the case due to shrinkage over time.

A similar album of forty-eight portraits (fig. 2)[8] is known to have belonged to Count Giovanni Antonio Baldini (1654–1725), as described by Antonio Vallisnieri of Padua in the *Giornale dei letterati d'Italia* (1722). Vallisnieri catalogued Baldini's collection (now dispersed) with Baldini's assistance.[9] This album includes an inscription in Italian on the front page, apparently in Baldini's hand: "It contains forty-seven portraits[10] in miniature of the princes of Mogol that were collected during a voyage in the year 1690 in Persia and Oriental India by the Dutch painter Mr. Claudio Le Brun.[11] The burgomaster of Amsterdam, Witsen, had said portraits copied, and I saw the copies in his house in 1714"[12] (fig. 3).

The collection of Nicolaas Witsen (1641–1717), the burgomaster of Amsterdam and the director of the Dutch East India Company from 1693 onwards, was sold upon his death. It is clear from Baldini's statement that an album similar to the one in Paris belonged to Witsen, as confirmed by the mention of such a set in the auction catalogue of Witsen's collection, Amsterdam, March 30, 1728, no. 9: "Een ditto Boek met 46 Mogolse Portraiten, zynde heele Stand-beeldjes van de Grooste des Ryks" (A similar book with 46 Mogul portraits of full-length figures of the greatest of the empire).[13]

A detailed comparison between the Dresden and the Baldini albums, which probably were made side by side, provides an opportunity to look closely into the art of reproduction and the market for Indian miniature paintings among Europeans in the late seventeenth and early eighteenth centuries. Although a full discussion is beyond the scope here several observations can be made while studying the two albums.

The portraits in Ca 112 are grouped by dynasty. Within these groups are carefully ordered portraits of the dignitaries of each dynasty either facing each other or their ruler. For example, folio Ca 112/7 depicting Ikhlās Khān (d. 1656), the military commander who became the governor of a province on the border with Golconda during the reign of Muḥammad ʿĀdil Shāh (r. 1627–1656) of the ʿĀdil Shāhi dynasty of Bijapur (1490–1686) is shown facing Muḥammad ʿĀdil Shāh. Another example is the depiction of Shāh Rājū (Ca 112/15), the *pīr,* or spiritual guide, of Sultān Abū'l Hasan (r. 1672–1687), the eighth *sultān* of the Qutb Shāhī dynasty of Golconda (1496–1687), who is shown facing Sultān Abū'l Hasan (Ca 112/16). This system of relating portraits is occasionally absent in the Baldini set.[14] One reason could be that the folios were mixed up during binding or that the binder did not recognize the figures portrayed. That could not have happened with Ca 112, as all the portraits are inscribed with the names of the sitters.

In the Baldini album, the depictions of Sultān Bahādur Shāh I (r. 1707–1712; folio 233–3v) and Bābur (r. 1526–1530; folio 233–4r) on facing pages are rather suspicious. Although the style of painting is similar to that of the other folios, the settings of these two portraits are more elaborate, with added elements such as carpets and cushions. Bābur, who is not depicted in Ca 112, is shown surrounded by manuscripts, and Bahādur Shāh I is relaxing in front of a fountain. At the turn of the seventeenth century, many artists left the imperial atelier where they had produced works according to the wishes of the emperor, and began to produce works, sometimes multiple copies, for the market and thus had more independence. For the latter, the main aim was to sell, and they did not confine themselves to the aesthetics of courtly art. With the aim of luring customers or fulfilling demand, folios could easily be altered, added to, or reduced, as may have been the case here.

The physiognomic significance of the portraits in Baldini's album was noted by the Bolognese Baroque painter Carlo Cignani (1628–1719)[15] and by Vallisnieri. In the inscription on the front cover of Smith-Lesouëf 233, Baldini stated, "Signore Carlo Cignani, having attentively considered the portraits of this book in the month of November 1716 said that almost all the heads could have been done by Titian or Tintoretto." Commenting further, Vallisnieri stated, "The complexions of the faces are fine, lively, and correctly drawn."[16] While the faces are indeed finely rendered, those in the Dresden album were executed using a different technique, as can be seen by comparing the depictions of Mīrzā Nāsir in both albums (Ca 112/14 and fig. 6). Apart from the differences in brushstroke, the artist of the Dresden image characterized Mīrzā Nāsir as a thin man with lines of wisdom on his forehead, a prominent Adam's apple, protruding collar bones, and a turban almost superficially balanced on his head. The Baldini artist elaborated on his old age through the wrinkles around his eyes but kept the attributes to a minimum. The portraits in the Baldini album are executed using firmer lines than those in Dresden, and the rulers have haloes, which are often absent in the Dresden set. In the depiction of Neknām Khān[17] in the Dresden album (Ca 112/20), the artist tried his hand at hatching, which envelops Neknām Khān's face and body. These differences establish the fact that there was more than one artist or even two different groups of artists in either same or different workshops involved in making these two similar sets of portraits.

By putting an end to historical painting in 1668 and shifting the Mughal capital to Aurangabad in 1681, soon after conquering the Deccan sultanates of Bijapur and Gol-

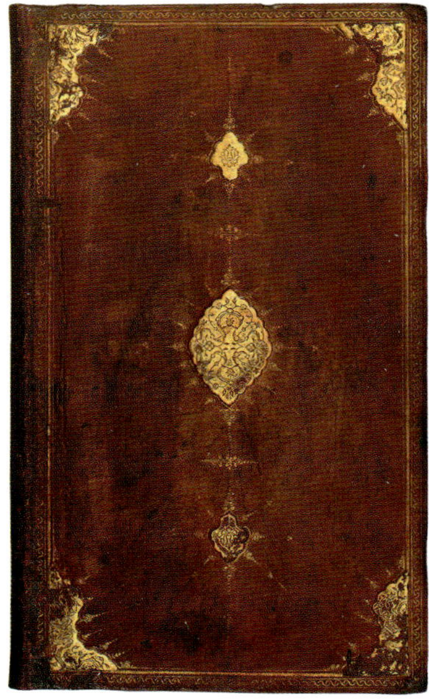

Fig. 2
Recueil de portraits de rois et de ministres des royaumes musulmans de l'Inde
(Album of portraits of muslim kings and royle ministers of india)
Golconda (Deccan), c. 1700
Album with 25 fols., 32 × 19 × 2 cm
BnF, Paris, Département des Manuscrits
Smith-Lesouëf Album 233
Cover, left

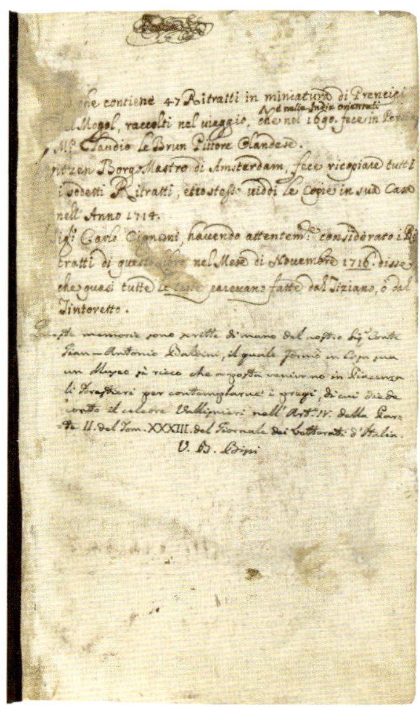

[illegible] che contiene 47 Ritratti in miniatura di Prencipi [illegible] Mogol, raccolti nel viaggio, che nel 1690. fece in [illegible]
[illegible] Claudio Le Brun Pittore Olandese.
[illegible] Borgomastro di Amsterdam, fece ricopiare tutti i sodetti Ritratti, et io stesso viddi le Copie in sua Casa nell'Anno 1714.
[illegible] Carlo Cignani, havendo attentem.te considerato i Ritratti di questo [illegible] nel Mese di Novembre 1716. disse che quasi tutte le [illegible] parevano fatte dal Tiziano, ò dal Tintoretto.

Fig. 3
Endpaper, left
BnF, Paris, Département des Manuscrits, Smith-Lesouëf Album 233/page de garde recto

Fig. 4a
Ca 112/27
Sultān Muḥammad Qūlī Shāh
(r. 1580 – 1612)

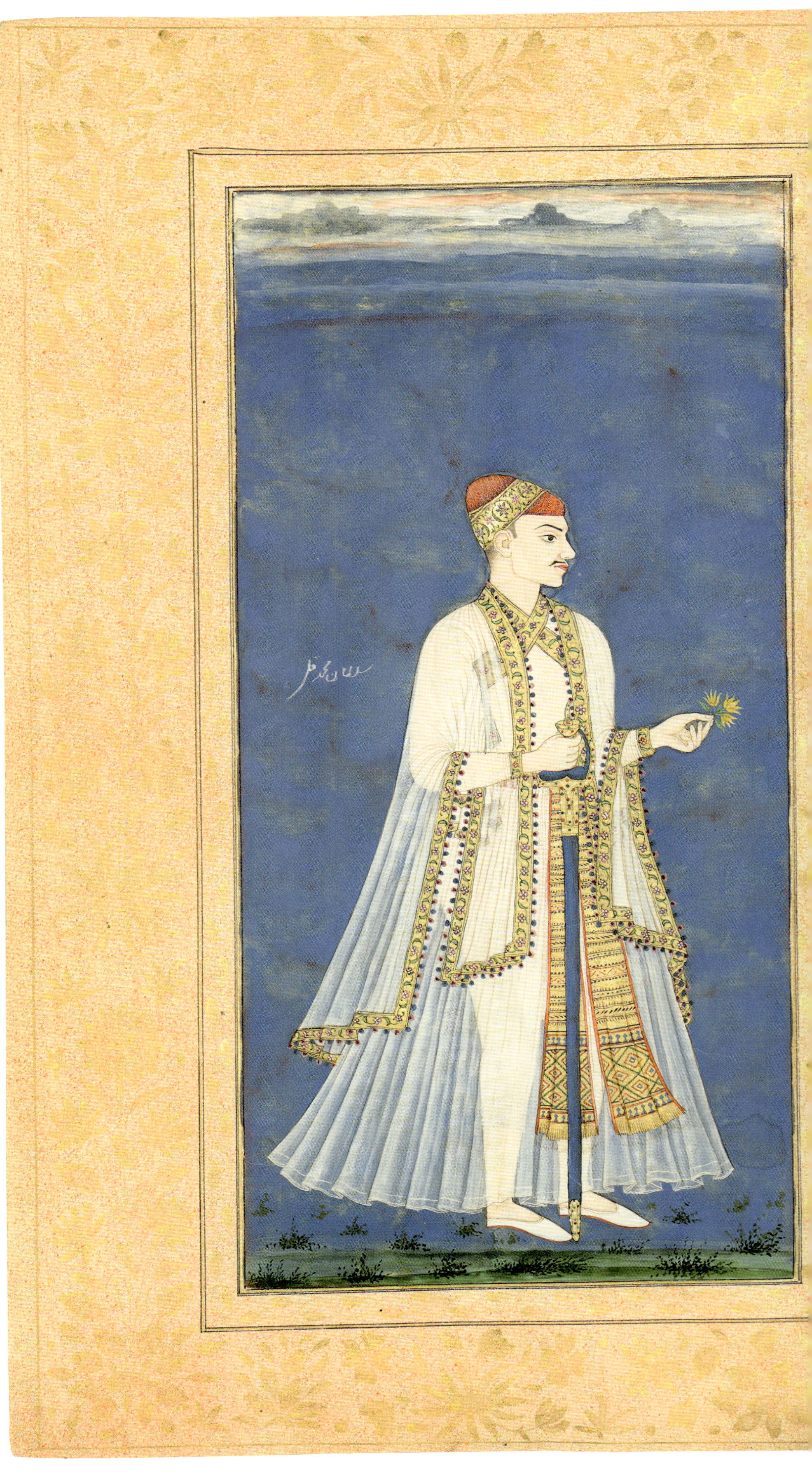

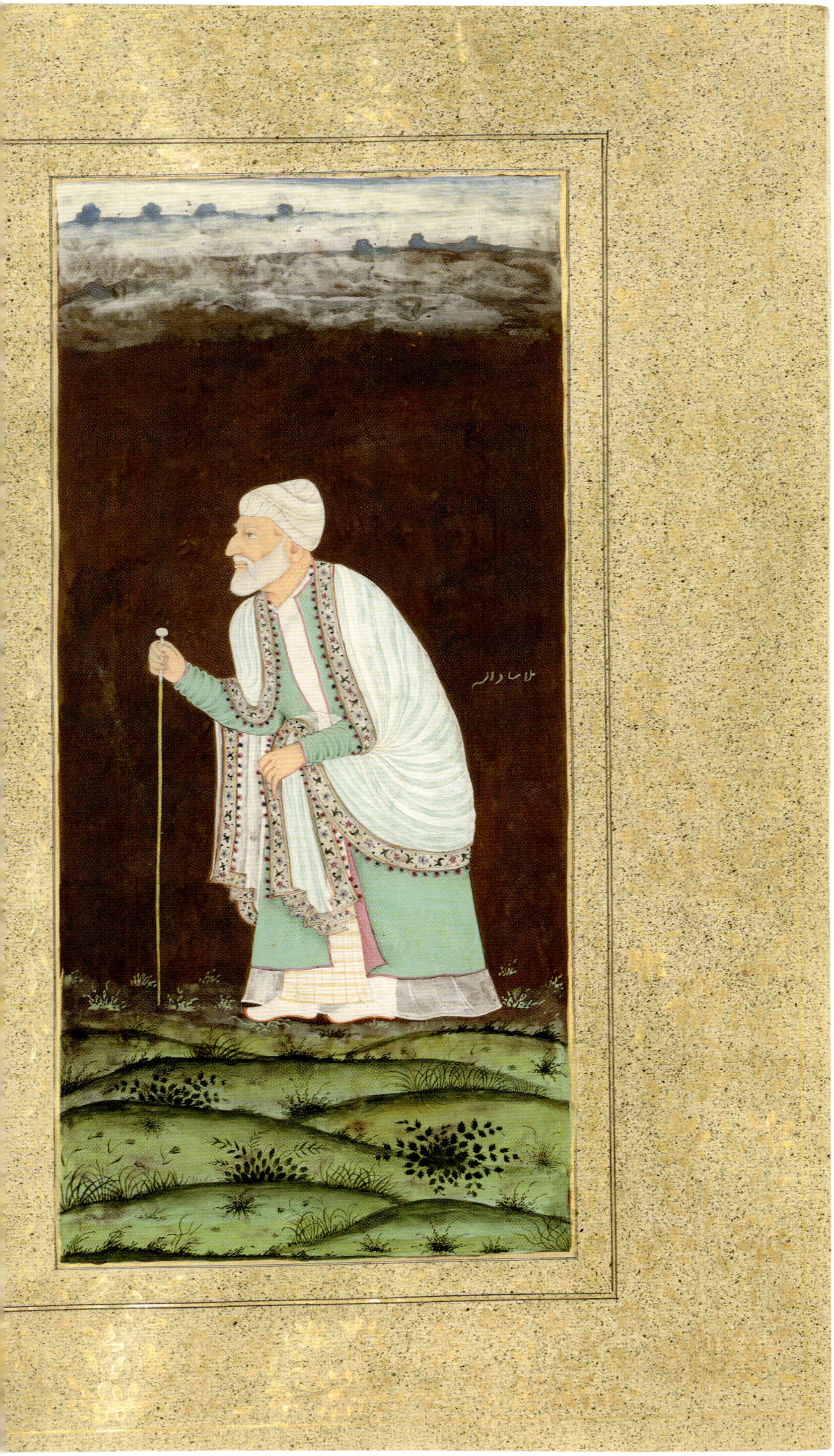

Fig. 4b
Ca 112/28
Mullāh Sādullāh

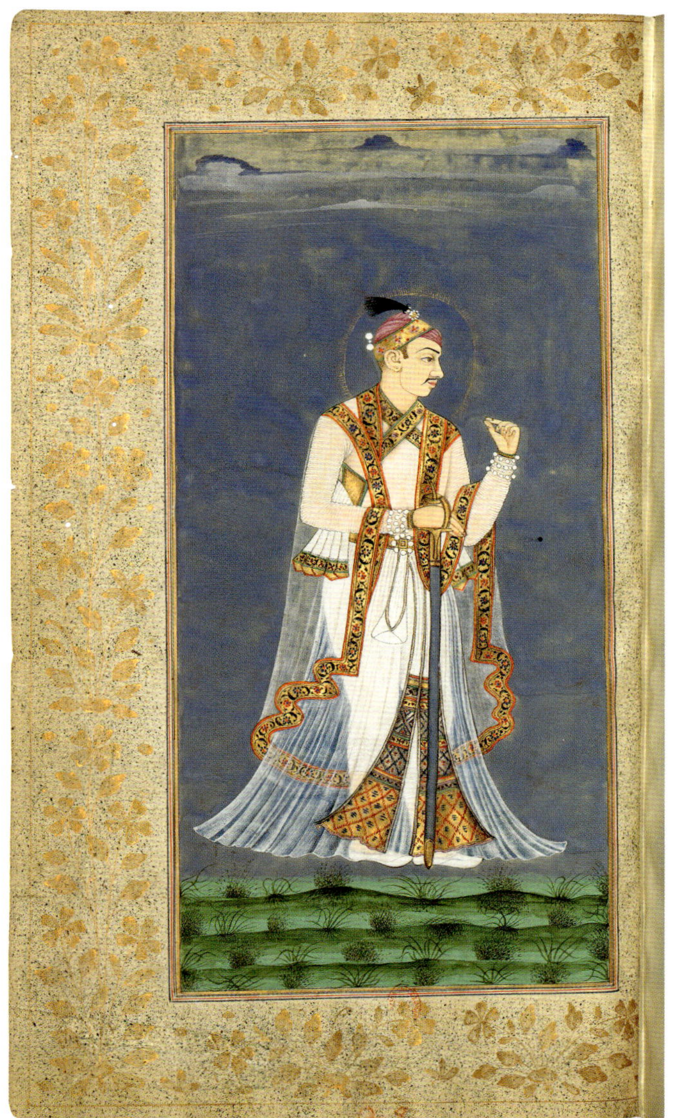

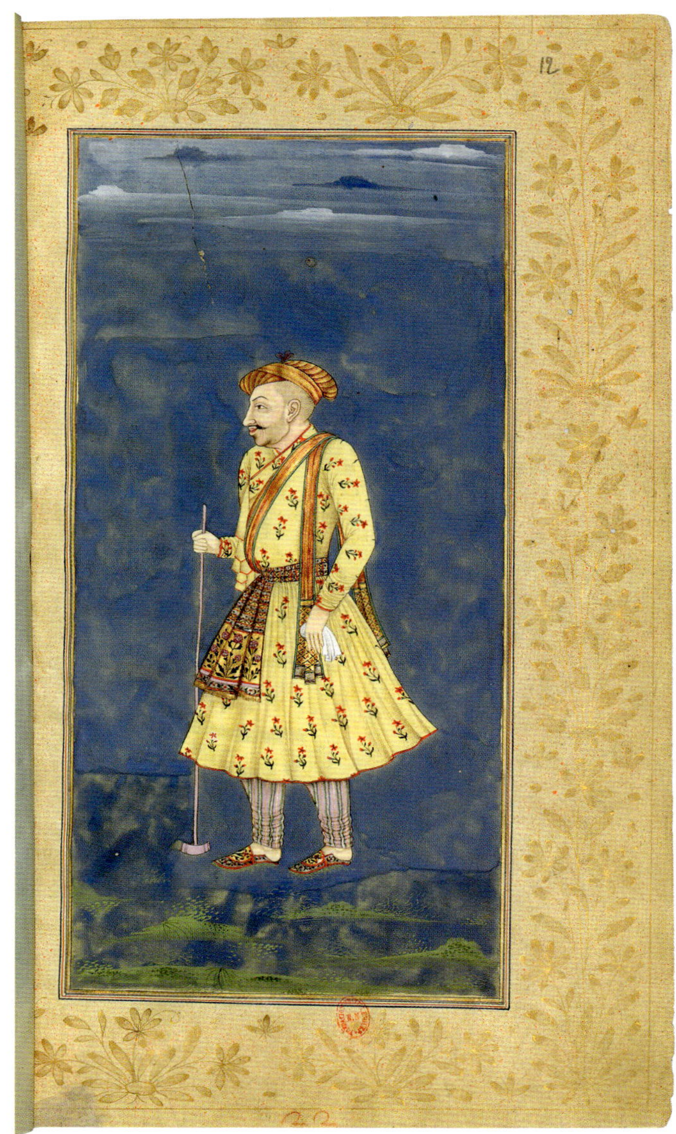

Fig. 5
Sultān Muḥammad Qūlī Shāh (r. 1580–1612)
Golconda (Deccan), c. 1700
Watercolour and gold, 31.6 × 18.2 cm
Bibliotheque nationale de France (BnF), Paris, Département des Manuscrits, Smith-Lesouëf Album 233/15v

Fig. 6
Mīrzā Nāsir
Golconda (Deccan), c. 1700
Watercolour and gold, 31.6 × 18.2 cm
Bibliothèque nationale de France (BnF), Paris, Département des Manuscrits, Smith-Lesouëf Album 233/12r

conda in 1686 and 1687, respectively, Aurangzēb brought about a wave of cultural integration and further dissipated the courtly art in the Deccan. Several artists from the imperial ateliers who were trained in both Mughal and Deccani styles were now left without a fixed income. These artists were no longer compelled to maintain, let alone enhance, their usual high standard of work. While in both albums the artists attained an impeccable standard in the execution of the facial features, the costumes tell a different story. One clearly can sense the involvement of trained Deccani artists in the Dresden album from the manner in which the folds of the garments have been perfectly mastered compared to those in the Baldini set (figs. 4a and 5).

Having established that both Witsen and Baldini owned a book of forty-six[18] Indian portraits, the puzzling question is if Ca 112 is the same one that belonged to Witsen. Two albums (Ca 161 and Ca 222)[19] with paintings of animals in Batavia[20] were signed and inscribed by Witsen in Dutch.[21] These two books are also mentioned in the 1728

Witsen auction catalogue[22] and in the 1738 Heucher Inventory[23] with the same reference number. One could thus conclude that they are the same books acquired by Augustus the Strong at the 1728 Witsen auction. Upon further investigation into the Heucher Inventory and the auction catalogue of 1728, one indeed discovers that apart from the above-mentioned albums, several Chinese and Japanese artworks[24] were bought at this sale as were other Indian albums that have similar descriptions.[25]

Ca 112, which is similar to the Paris set in content, size (31.6 × 18.2 cm), and format, also has the same dark red leather binding embossed with gold as Ca 112 (32.1 × 18.7 cm). The latter is inscribed in ink in German at the lower left of the frontispiece: "Dieses Buch ist ganz von hohen werth / d. 23 Dec. 1689" (This book is of very high value / the 23 Dec. 1689). This proves that the album was owned by a German by 1689 and hence could not have any association with the sale of Witsen's collection.

Therefore, having established that Ca 112 is not the same book mentioned in the Witsen auction catalogue, we turn our attention towards its date of production, which might be established based on one painting in the album. The inscription on folio Ca 112/2 reads, "Shāh Sulaimān" representing Safī Mīrzā (r. 1666–1694),[26] the eldest son of Shāh 'Abbās II, who came to the throne in 1666 with the title Safī II followed by a second coronation in 1668 at which he received the title of Shāh Sulaimān.[27] Since the inscription in *nasta'līq* assigns him this title, it cannot have been executed earlier than 1668, thus providing us with a confirmed dating of 1668–1689 for this album, in its original binding.

The series of portraits in the Baldini and the Dresden albums belong to the third type of portrait albums.[28] With a probable dating of about 1660–1680, these two albums, along with Witsen's now-lost set, testify to the enormous popularity of such portraits among European collectors and might have marked the prototype for other sets that were produced and collected by Europeans at the turn of the seventeenth century. NB

Notes | 1 See pp. 21–4. | 2 See p. 31, note 6. | 3 The album contains 24 folios with a total of 46 images. | 4 Referring to the entry no. 11 in the same inventory list. See cat. 2. | 5 Heucher Inventory 1738, sig. Cat. 1, p. 156, no. 12. | 6 See Robinson 1972. | 7 See Appendices, p. 242–5. | 8 Bibliothèque Nationale de France, Paris, Smith-Lesouëf 233, described as "Recueil de portraits de rois et de ministres des royaumes muslmans de l'Inde, fin du 17e siècle." See URL http://gallica.bnf.fr/ark:/12148/btv1b52506689l/f1.image.r=Smith-Lesou%C3%ABf%20233 (8. 11. 2017). | 9 Vallisnieri 1722, p. 133–4, no. 24. | 10 As noted in the inscription by Baldini, who counts forty-seven folios in the Paris album. | 11 Cornelis de Bruyn (c. 1652–1727), Dutch artist, traveler, and author of *Travels into Muscovy, Persia, and part of the East- Indies*, see De Bruin 1737, 2 vols. (London: A. Bettesworth, 1737). | 12 Baldini's comment is followed by another by U. B. Bissi (also in Italian): "These memories are written by the hand of our Sg. Conte Gian-Antonio Baldini, who formed such a rich museum in his house in Piacenza, visited by foreigners who came to see these valuable, that the celebrated Vallisnieri gives credit to them in article 4 of the card of *Giornale de' letterati d'Italia* 33, no. 2 (1722)." | 13 Amsterdam 1728, p. 11; see also Lunsingh Scheurleer 1996, p. 204, no. 15. | 14 To name a few, Shāh Rājū (folio 233/22v) is shown facing Murād Bakhsh (233/23r), the youngest son of Shāh Jahān; Abū'l Hasan Qutb Shāh (233/3r) is shown facing the bow bearer of Shāh 'Abbās I (233/2v), and the portrait of Shāh 'Abbās I with Khān 'Ālam (233/22r) is on the facing page with a portrait of Sultān Muḥammad (d. 1676), the eldest son of Mughal Emperor Aurangzēb (233/21v). | 15 For more on Cignani, see Fabbri 1991. | 16 Vallisnieri 1722, p. 274. | 17 *Wazīr* of Sultān 'Abdullāh, who served as the military leader of Karnatak after Mīr Jumla. | 18 The Paris album includes forty-eight portraits but two folios (fol. 10r, which depicts Akbar with a falcon, an attendant, and a goat; and folio 10v, a blank page at rightvue 23—folio 10rvue 23—folio 10r) were no doubt added later, as they differ in both style and composition and in the quality of paper. In addition, if these were removed folios 9v and 11r depict the same portraits as seen facing each other in the Dresden album Ca 112. | 19 Heucher Inventory 1738, sig. Cat. 1, p. 4. | 20 Inscribed on verso in French: "No. 3. / Animaux, Poissons / Fleurs et Fruits de / la Chine." | 21 Ca 161, "Dese vissen vogels beesten / en insecten etc sij / voor mij in japan daen / maken. [...] N. Witsen" (These fishes, birds, animals, and insects were made for me in Japan, N. Witsen); and Ca 222, "Dit gedierte beeste en / gevogels etc sȳ[n] voor / mij op batavia afgetekent / N. Witsen" (These wild animals and birds etc. were copied for me in Batavia, N. Witsen). | 22 In Witsen's auction catalogue, part 3, "Artificialia", no. 2, under the heading "Eenige Indiaansche kruydboeken en andere" (A few Indian herbals and others): "Een ditto [= groot] Boek met vogels, Landgedierten en Insecten, in Japan met Couleuren na 't Leven getekent." (A large book with birds, land animals, and insects, painted in Japan in colours after life.) And "Artificialia", no. 5: "Een Boek met Dieren, Vogels, Vissen en Insecten, op Batavia na 't leeven Geschildert" (A Book of Animals, Birds, Fish, and Insects, painted on Batavia after life). | 23 Heucher Inventory, sig. Cat. 1, p. 4. See Amsterdam 1728, p. 13, nos. 2 and 5. | 24 Non-Indian artworks acquired from Witsen's sale in 1728 are Dresden, inv. nos. Ca 126, Ca 128, Ca 132, Ca 157 a, b, Ca 162, Ca 163, and probably Ca 150 and Ca 134. | 25 Confirmed Indian painting albums acquired from the Witsen's collection sale auction in 1728 are Dresden, inv. nos. Ca 113, Ca 111, Ca 127, and probably Ca 110, Ca 114, and Ca 116. | 26 The correct depiction of Shāh Sulaimān is seen in Ca 112/3 and has been confused with Ca 112/2 depicting Shāh 'Abbās II (r. 1642–1666). | 27 Roemer 1986, pp. 288–304. | 28 See pp. 44–5.

Ca 112/1
Shāh 'Abbās I (r. 1588–1629)
26 × 13 cm
Inscribed recto (*nasta'līq*):
Shāh 'Abbās-i buzurg
(Shāh 'Abbās the Great)

Ca 112/2
Shāh 'Abbās II (r. 1642–1666)
24.3 × 11.8 cm
Inscribed recto (*nasta'līq*):
Shāh Sulaymān

Ca 112/3
Safī II (r. 1666–1694)
24.4 × 11.8 cm
Inscribed recto (*nasta'līq*):
Shāh 'Abbās

Ca 112/4
The bow bearer of Shāh 'Abbās I ('Ālam Khān [?])
24.2 × 11.7 cm
Inscribed recto (*nasta'līq*):
Kamānbardār-i Shāh 'Abbās
(Bow bearer of Shāh 'Abbās)

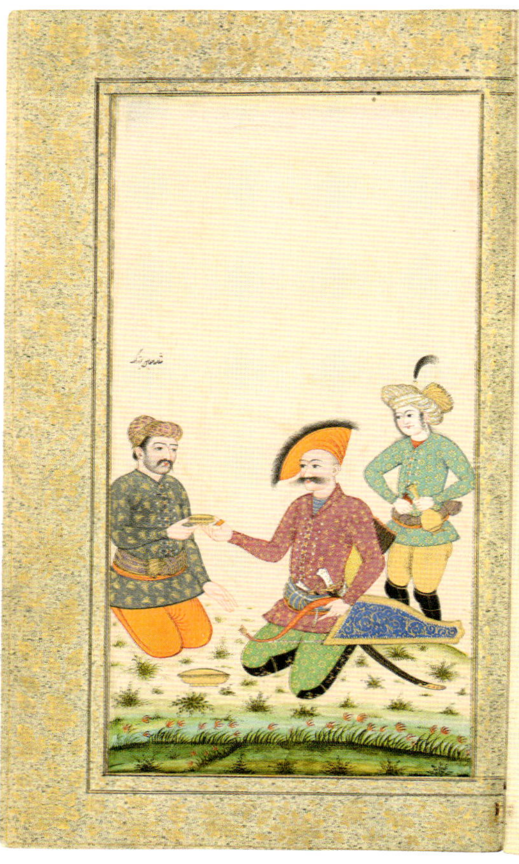

Ca 112/1

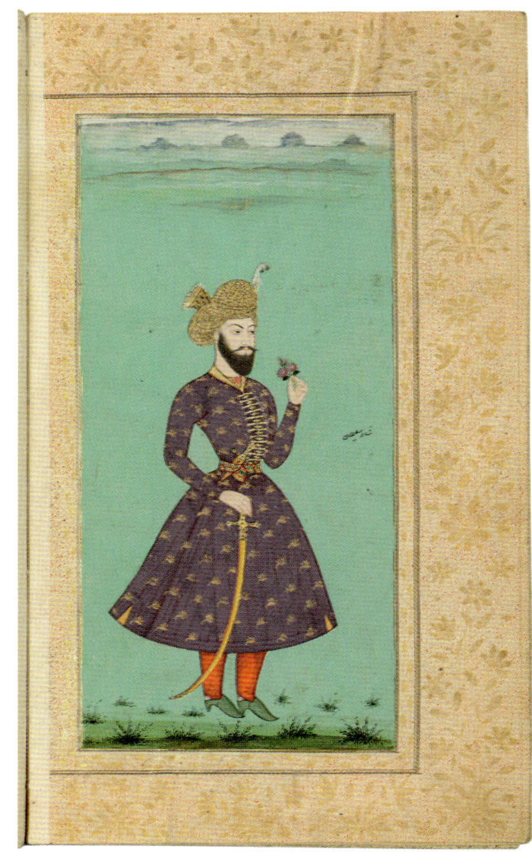

Ca 112/2

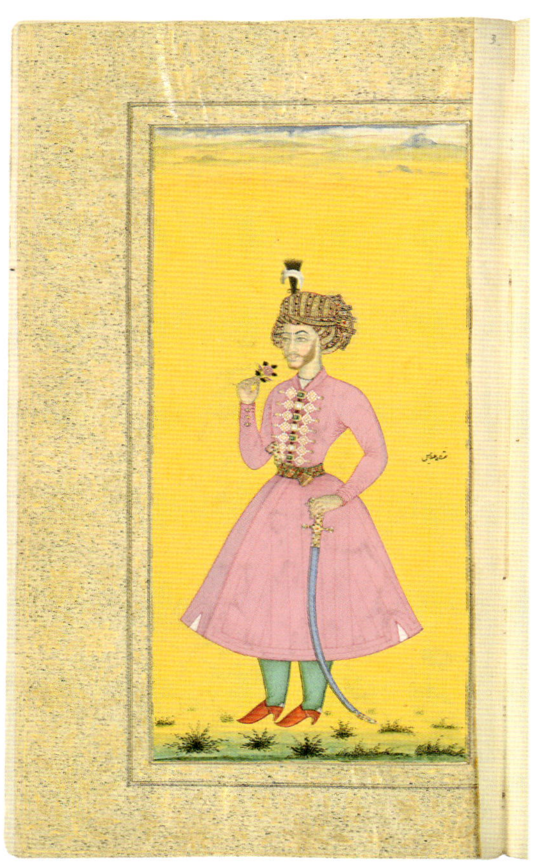

Ca 112/3

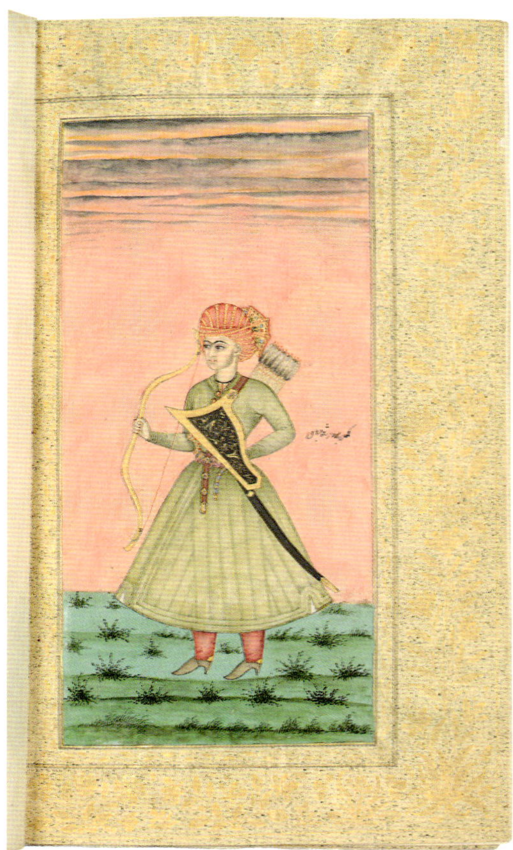

Ca 112/4

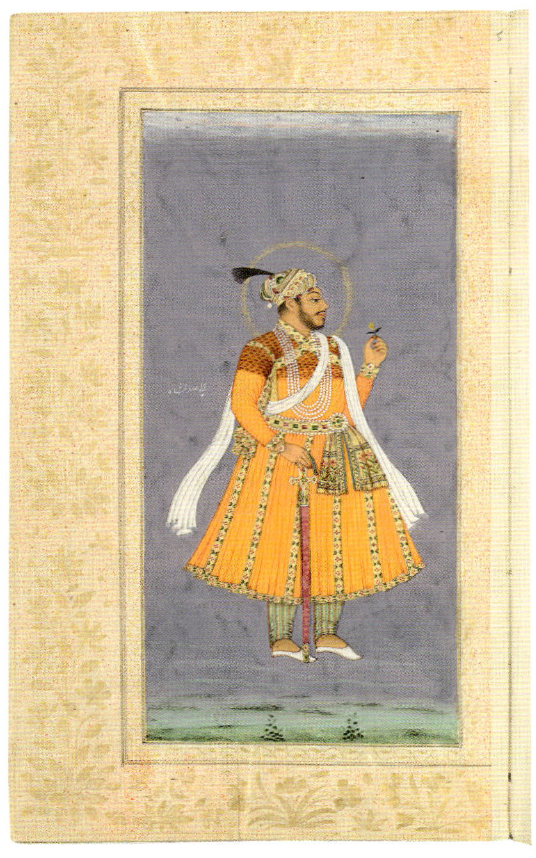

Ca 112/5

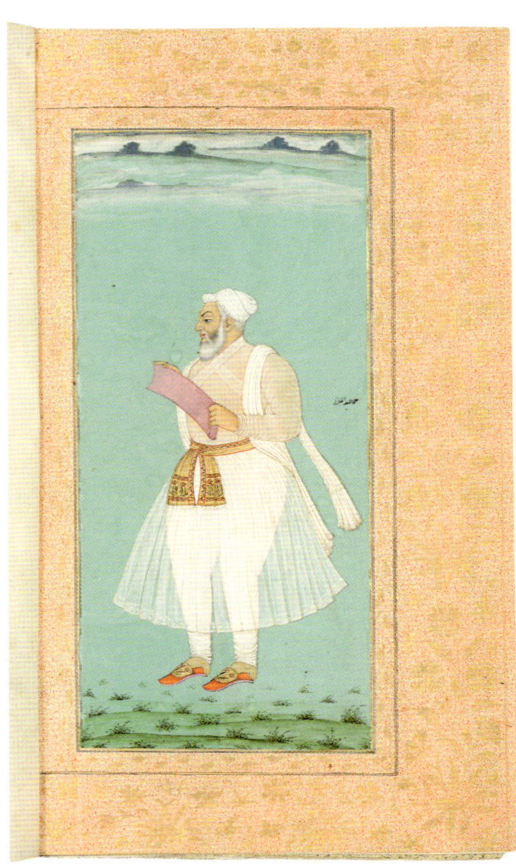

Ca 112/6

Ca 112/5
'Alī 'Ādil Shāh II (r. 1656–1672)
24.5 × 11.7 cm
Inscribed recto (*nasta'līq*):
'Alī 'Ādil Shāh

Ca 112/6
Mullāh 'Abdul Mali
23.8 × 11 cm
Inscribed recto (*nasta'līq*):
Mullā 'Abd al-Mali [?]

Ca 112/7
Ikhlās Khān (d. 1656)
23.9 × 11 cm
Inscribed recto (*nasta'līq*):
Ikhlāṣ Khān

Ca 112/8
Muḥammad 'Ādil Shāh (r. 1627–1656)
23.8 × 10.9 cm
Inscribed recto (*nasta'līq*):
Maḥmūd 'Ādil Shāh

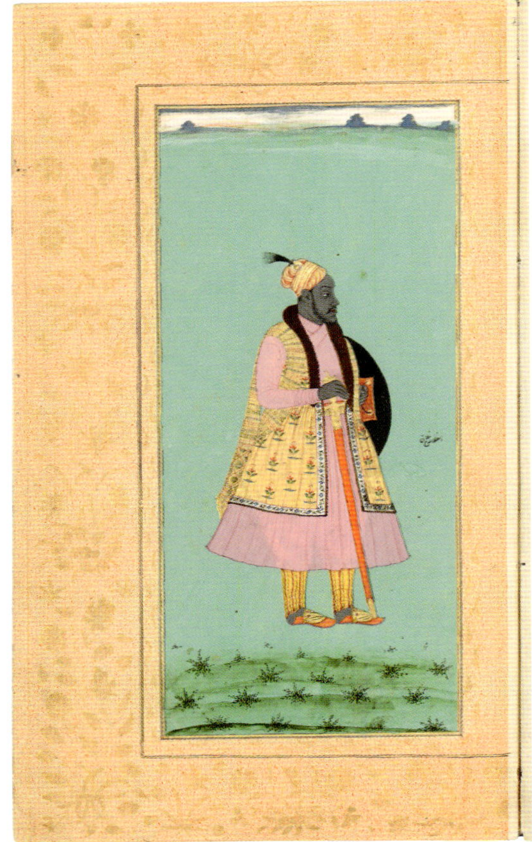

Ca 112/7

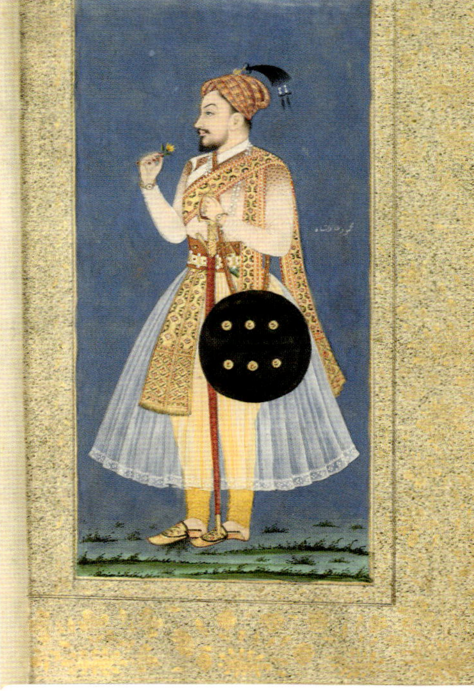

Ca 112/8

Ca 112/9
Mūsā Khān
23.9 × 11 cm
Inscribed recto (*nasta'līq*):
Mūsā Khān

Ca 112/10
Ahmad Khān
23.7 × 10.9 cm
Inscribed recto (*nasta'līq*):
Aḥmad Khān

Ca 112/11
Husain Shāh
23.8 × 10.8 cm
Inscribed recto (*nasta'līq*):
Ḥusayn Khān

Ca 112/12
Hasan Khān
23.9 × 11 cm
Inscribed recto (*nasta'līq*):
Ḥasan Khān

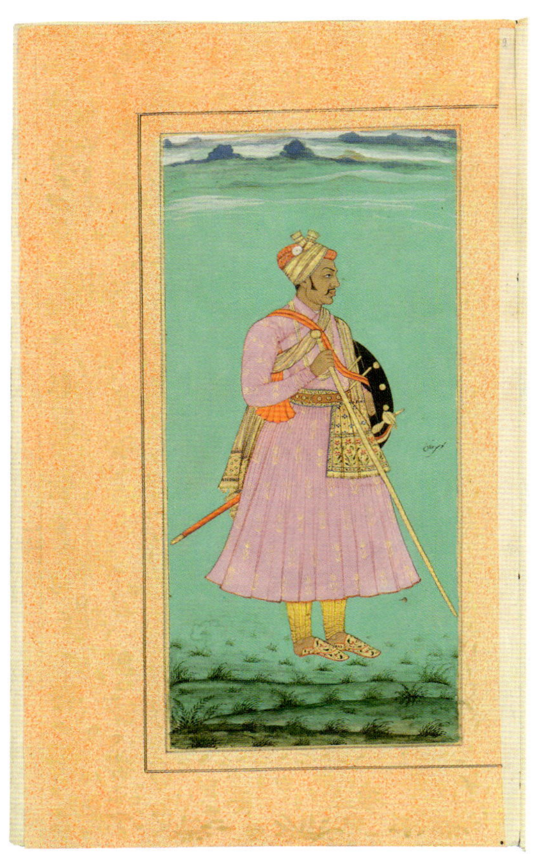

Ca 112/9

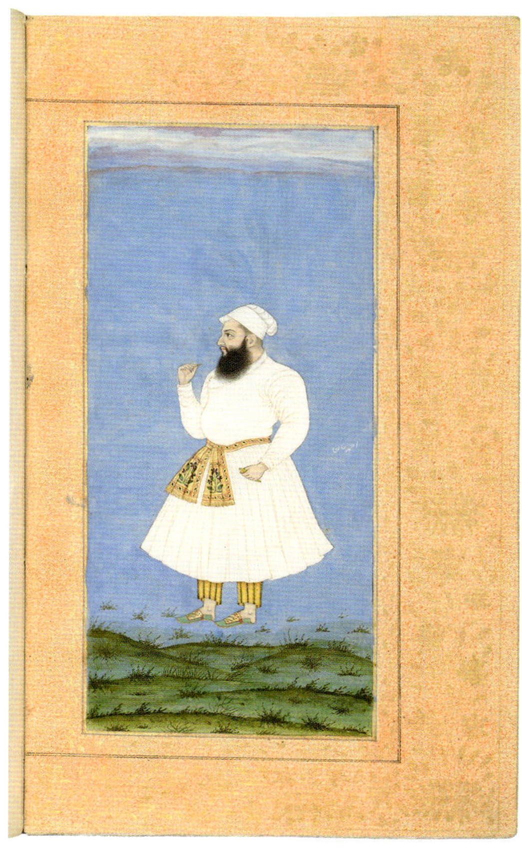

Ca 112/10

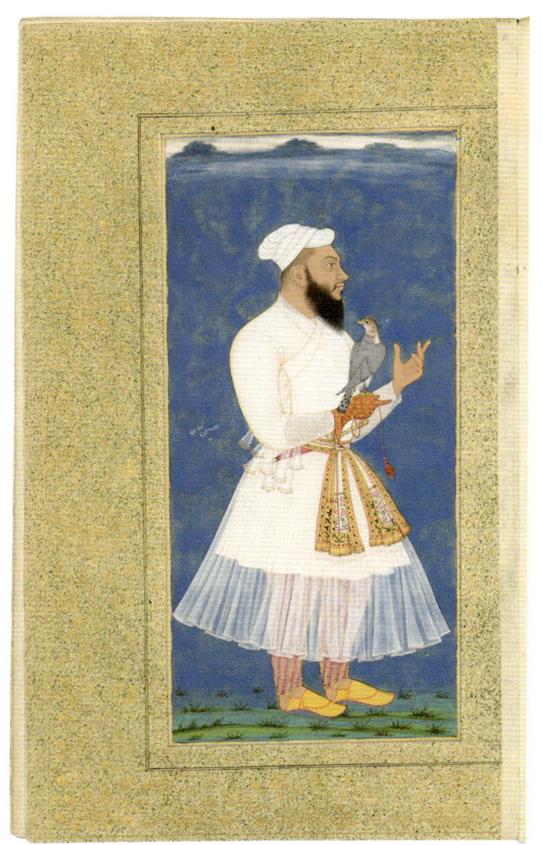

Ca 112/11

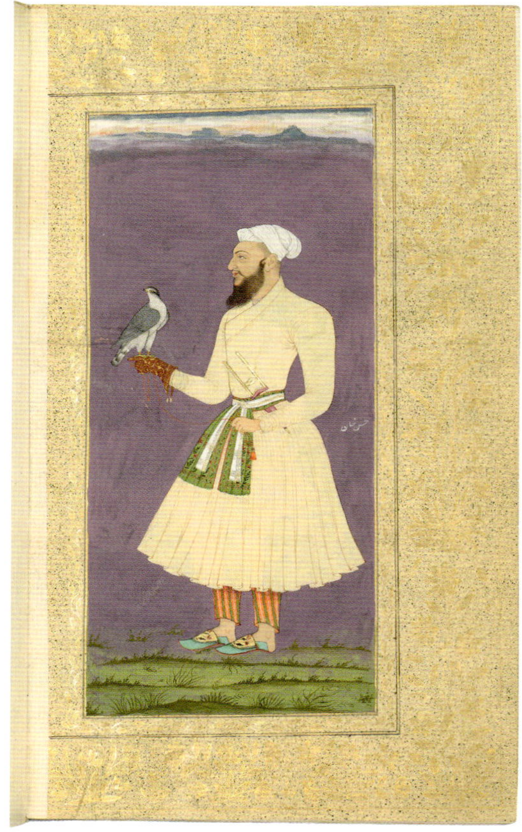

Ca 112/12

Ca 112/13
Sharzah Khān
23.9 × 11 cm
Inscribed recto (*nasta'līq*):
Šarzah Khān

Ca 112/14
Mīrzā Nāsir
23.8 × 11 cm
Inscribed recto (*nasta'līq*):
Mīrzā Nāṣir

Ca 112/15
Shāh Rājū
23.9 × 11 cm
Inscribed recto (*nasta'līq*):
Shāh Rājū

Ca 112/16
Abū'l Hasan Qutb Shāh (r. 1672–1687)
23.9 × 11.1 cm
Inscribed recto (*nasta'līq*):
Sulṭān 'Abd al-Ḥasan Quṭb Shāh

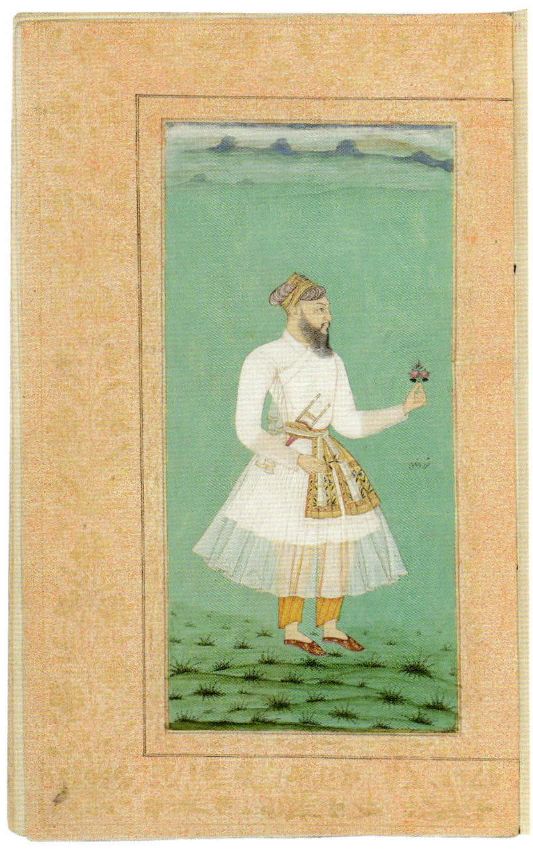

Ca 112/13

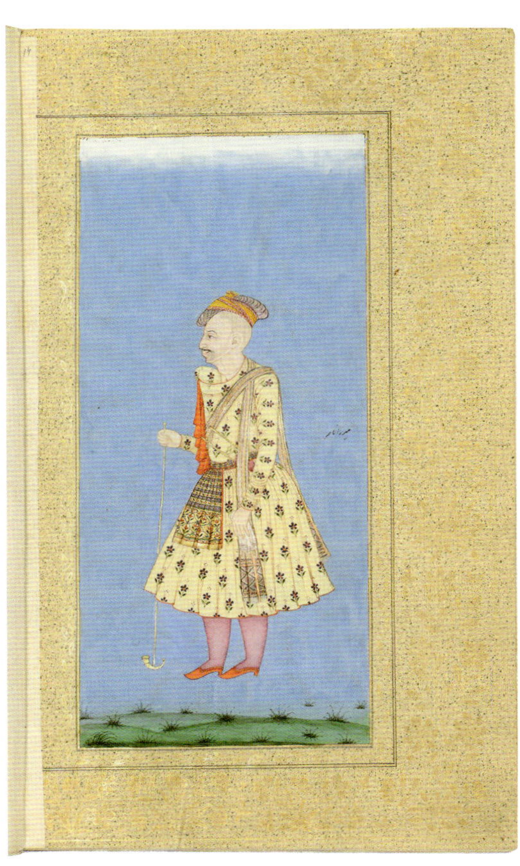

Ca 112/14

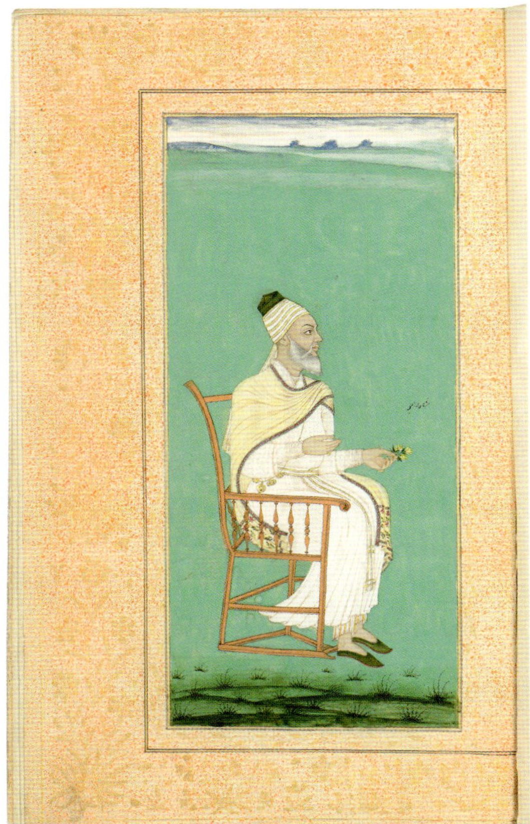

Ca 112/15

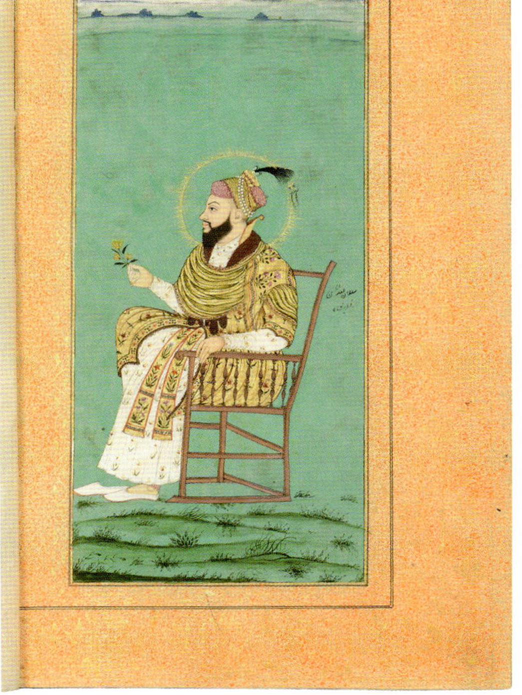

Ca 112/16

Ca 112/17
Mullāh 'Abd al-Samad
24 × 11 cm
Inscribed recto (*nasta'līq*):
'Abd al-Ṣamad

Ca 112/18
Sayyid Muḥammad 'Alī
23.8 × 11 cm
Inscribed recto (*nasta'līq*):
Sayyid Muḥammad 'Alī

Ca 112/19
Khayrāt Khān (d. 1655)
23.8 × 11 cm
Inscribed recto (*nasta'līq*):
Khayrāt Khān

Ca 112/20
Neknām Khān (d. 1672)
24.3 × 11.8 cm
Inscribed recto (*nasta'līq*):
Nīknām Khān

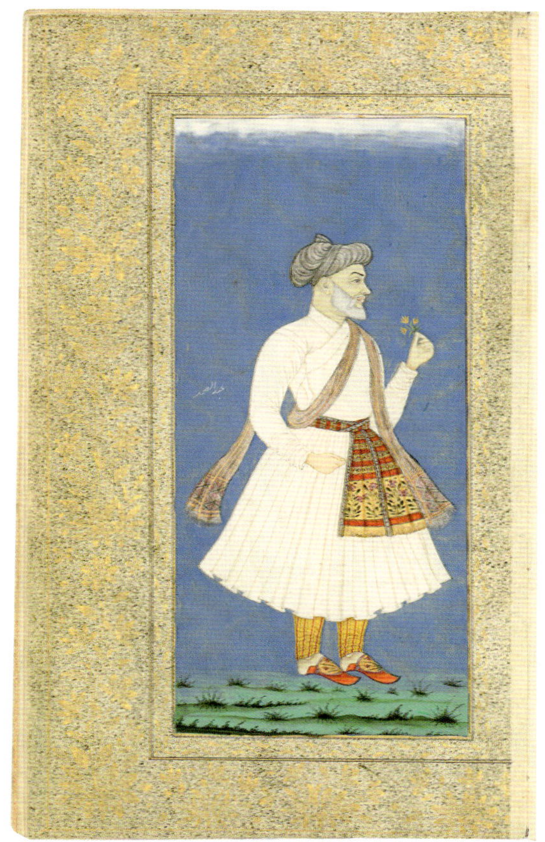

Ca 112/17

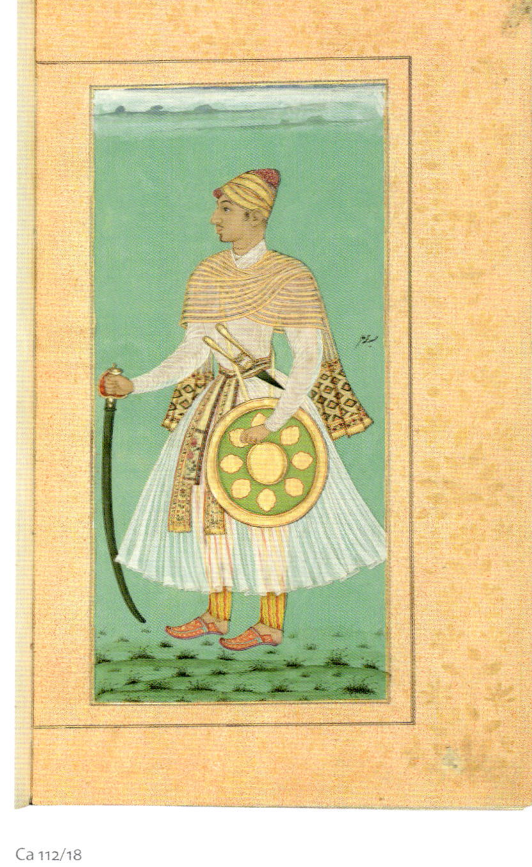

Ca 112/18

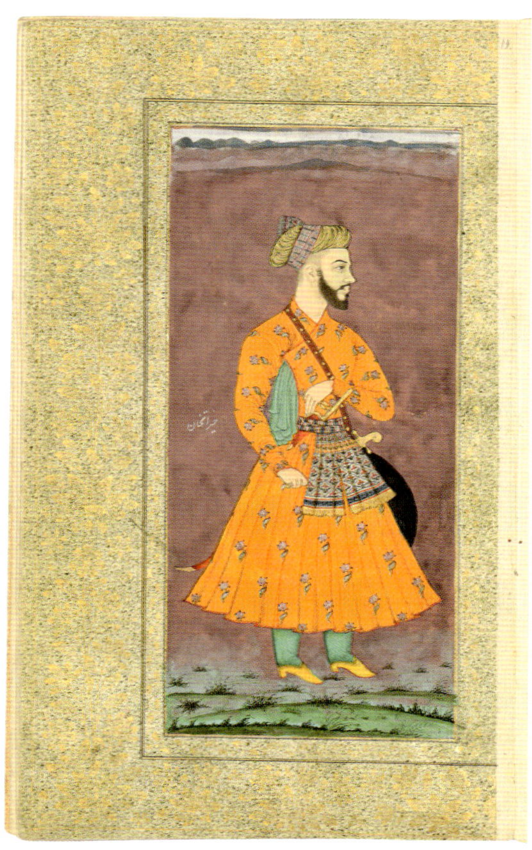

Ca 112/19

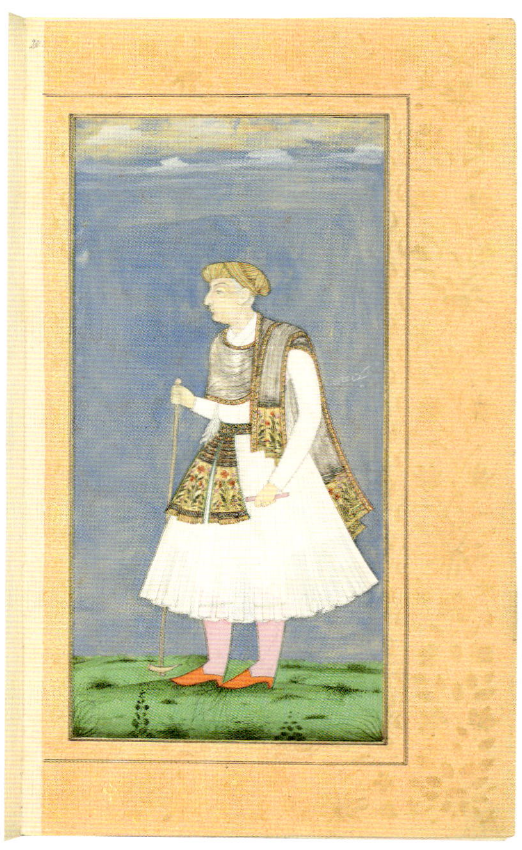

Ca 112/20

Ca 112/21
'Abd al-Ja'far Beg
24.4 × 11.9 cm
Inscribed recto (*nasta'līq*):
Jabbār Bayg

Ca 112/22
Shāh Mīrzā
24.5 × 11.9 cm
Inscribed recto (*nasta'līq*):
Shāh Mīrzā

Ca 112/23
Muḥammad Sayyid Muzaffar
24.5 × 11.9 cm
Inscribed recto (*nasta'līq*):
Sayyid Muẓaffar

Ca 112/24
'Abdullāh Qutb Shāh
(r. 1626–1672)
24.4 × 11.9 cm
Inscribed recto (*nasta'līq*):
Quṭb Shāh

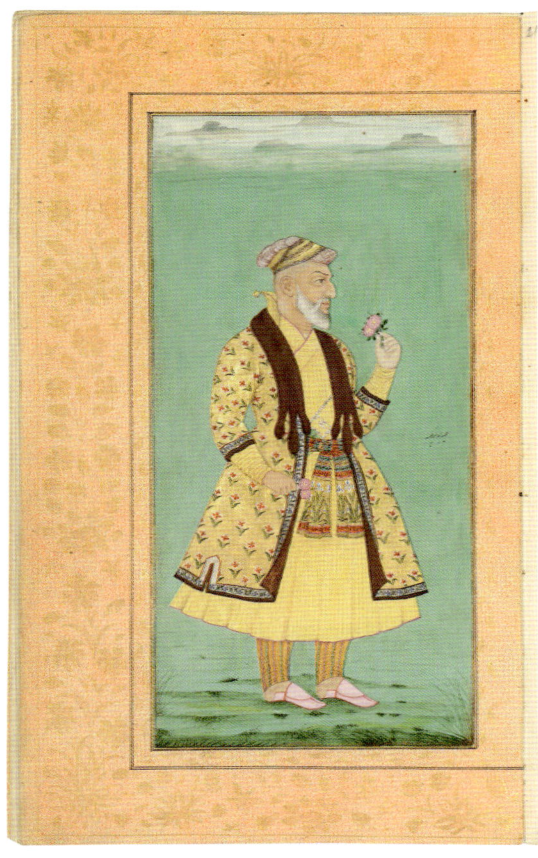

Ca 112/21

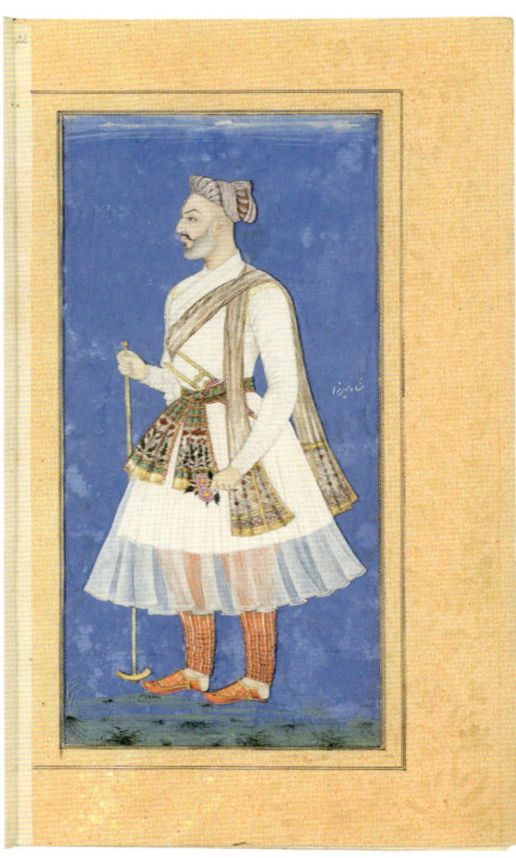

Ca 112/22

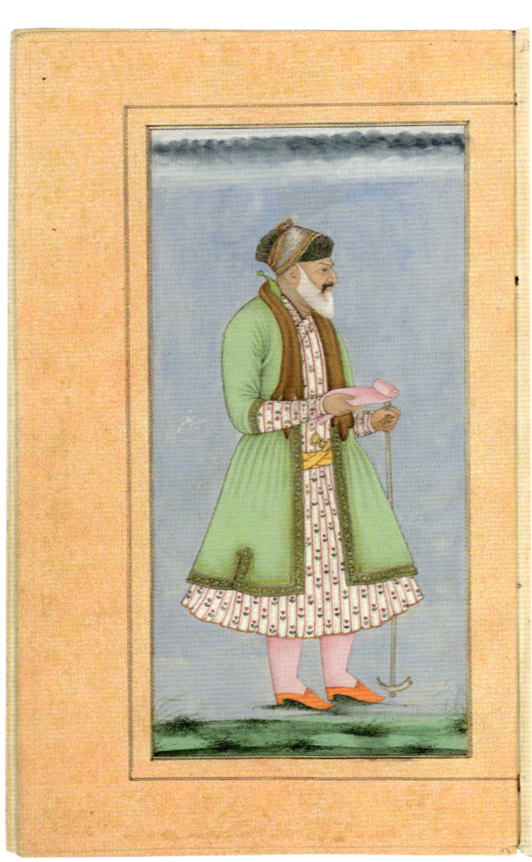

Ca 112/23

Ca 112/24

Ca 112/25
'Abdullāh Qutb Shāh (r. 1626–1672)
24.5 × 11.7 cm
Inscribed recto (*nasta'līq*): 'Abd Allāh Quṭb Shāh

Ca 112/26
Ibn-i Khātūn
24.4 × 11.9 cm
Inscribed recto (*nasta'līq*): Shaikh Muḥammad Khātūn

Ca 112/27
Sultān Muḥammad Qūlī Shāh (r. 1580–1612)
24.6 × 11.9 cm
Inscribed recto (*nasta'līq*): Sulṭān Muḥammad Qūlī

Ca 112/28
Mullāh Sādullāh
23.9 × 11 cm
Inscribed recto (*nasta'līq*): Mullā Ṣādallāh [?]

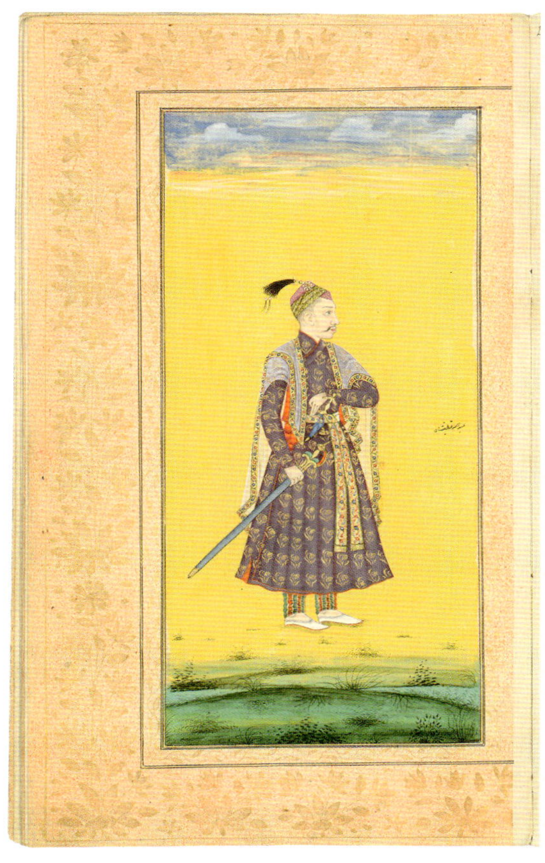

Ca 112/25

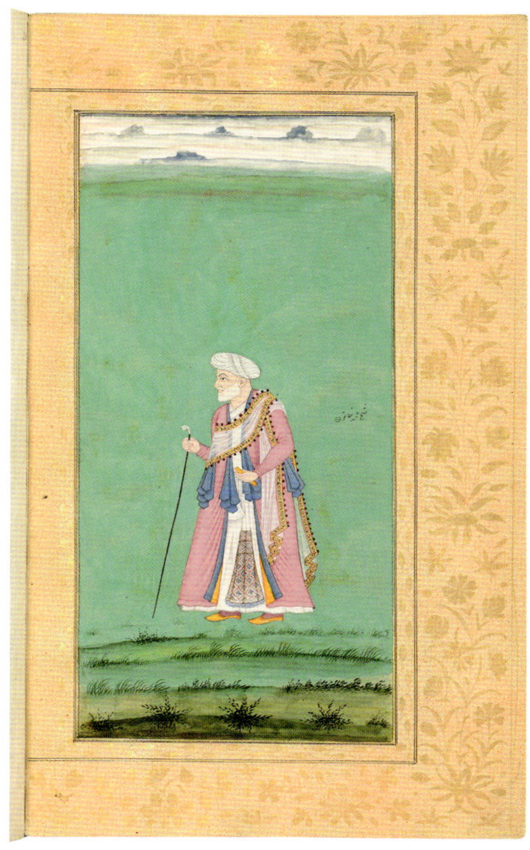

Ca 112/26

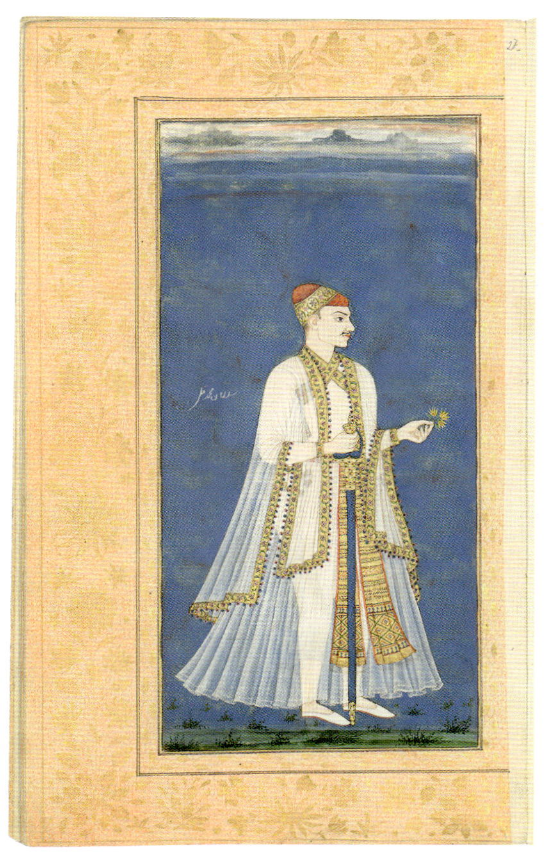

Ca 112/27

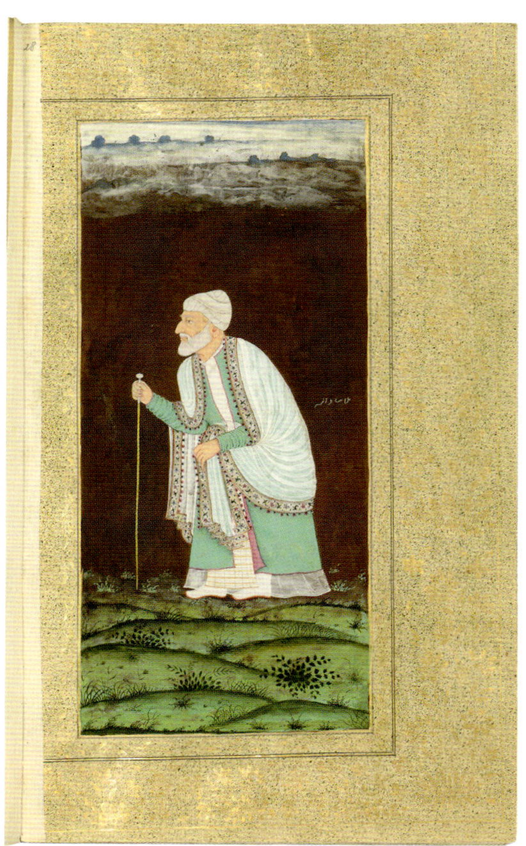

Ca 112/28

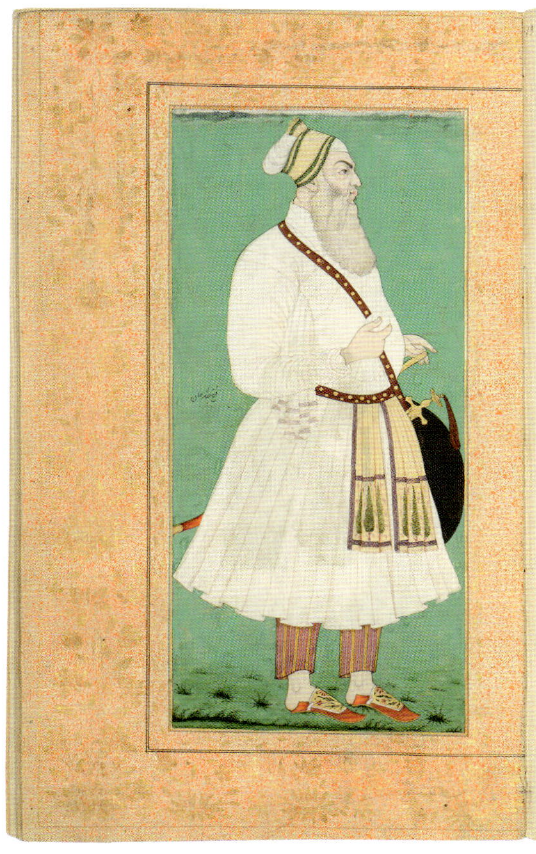

Ca 112/29

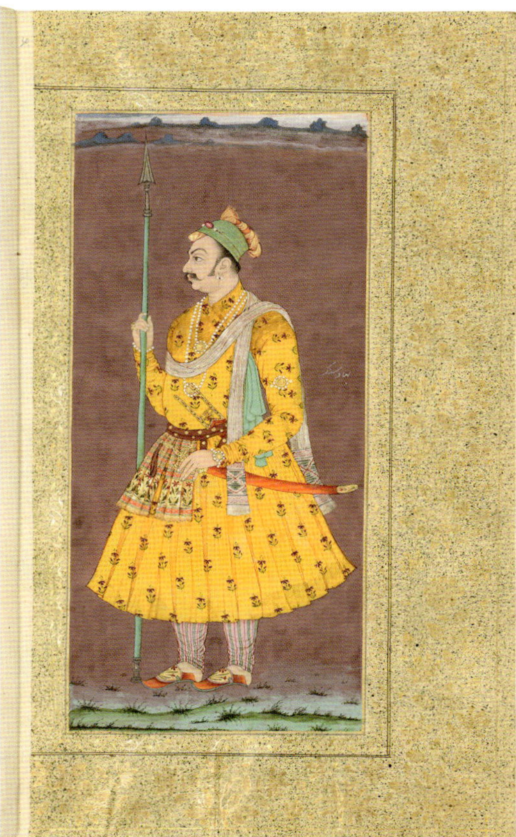

Ca 112/30

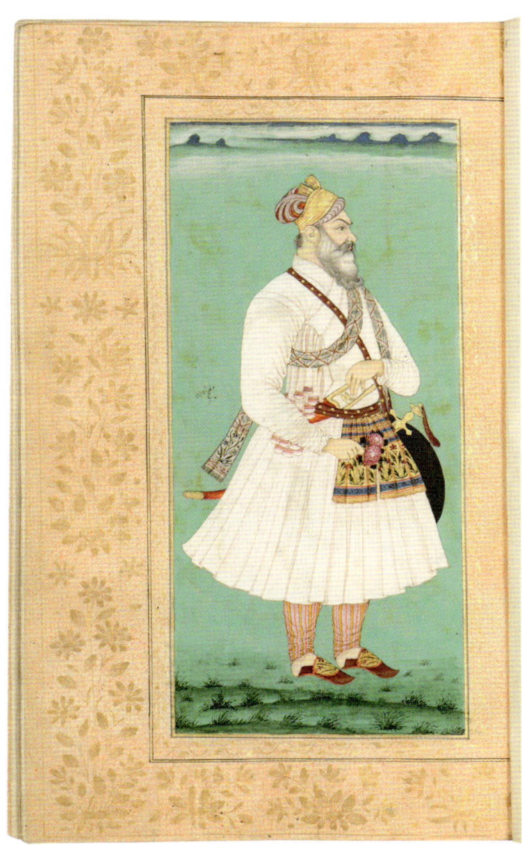

Ca 112/31

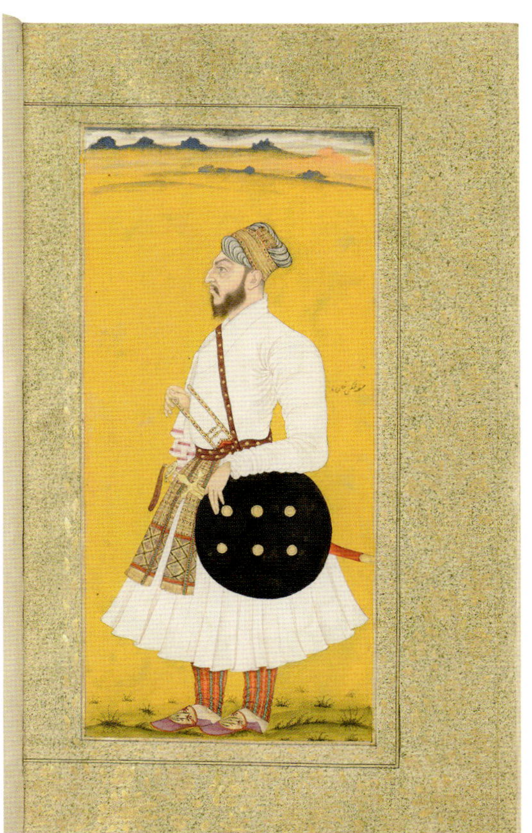

Ca 112/32

Ca 112/29
Fath Jang Khān
24 × 11 cm
Inscribed recto (*nasta'līq*):
Fatḥ Jang Khān

Ca 112/30
Bhao Sīngh (d. 1678) [?]
23.9 × 11 cm
Inscribed recto (*nasta'līq*):
Bhao Sīngh

Ca 112/31
Mīrzā Qilich Khān
24 × 11 cm
Inscribed recto (*nasta'līq*):
Īlīch Khān

Ca 112/32
Safshikan Khān
23.8 × 10.9 cm
Inscribed recto (*nasta'līq*):
Safshikan Khān

Ca 112/33
Mān Sīngh I
(r. 1589–1614) [?]
23.8×10.9 cm
Inscribed recto (*nasta'līq*):
Mān Sīngh

Ca 112/34
Karan Sīngh
(d. 1666–1667) [?]
23.7×10.9 cm
Inscribed recto (*nasta'līq*):
Rājā Karan

Ca 112/35
Mīrzā Ahmad
23.8×10.8 cm
Inscribed recto (*nasta'līq*):
Mīrzā Aḥmad

Ca 112/36
Mullāh Rauhā
23.8×10.8 cm
Inscribed recto (*nasta'līq*):
Mullā Rūḥā

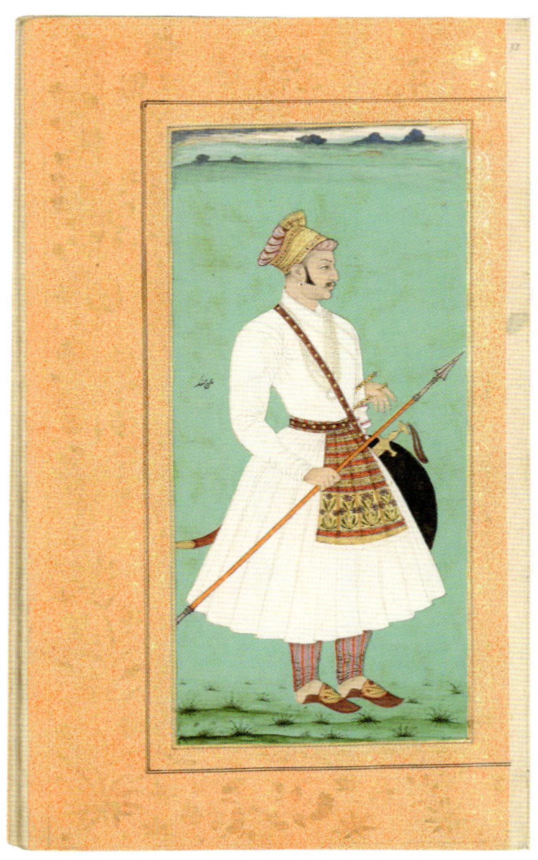

Ca 112/33

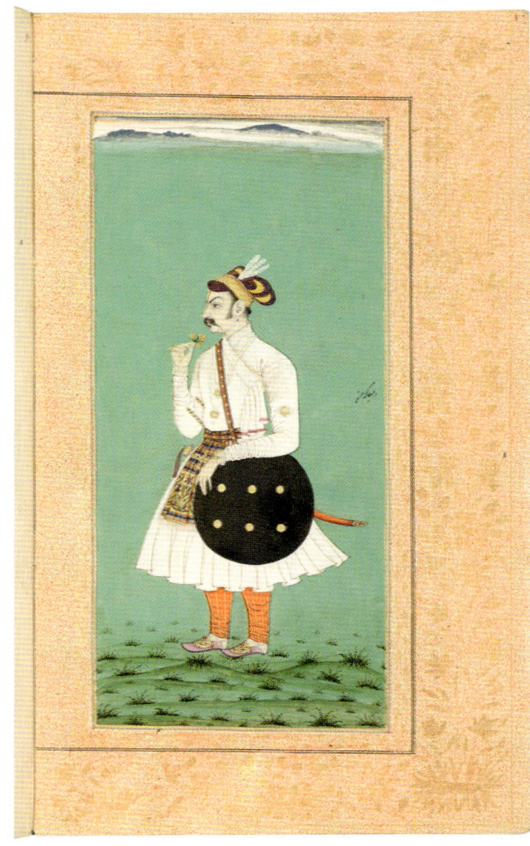

Ca 112/34

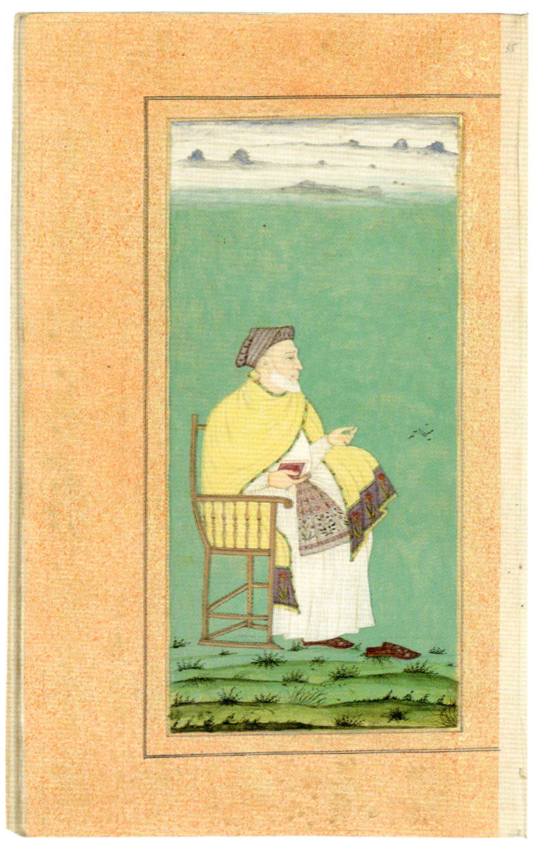

Ca 112/35

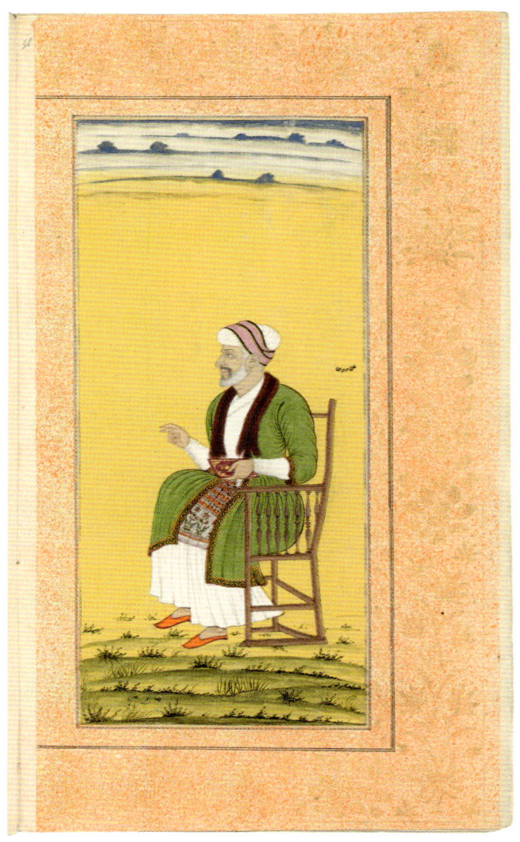

Ca 112/36

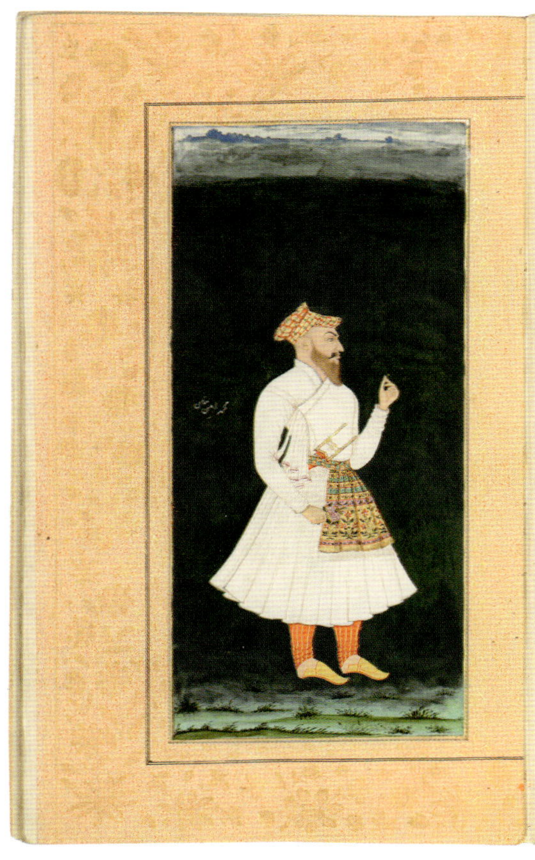

Ca 112/37

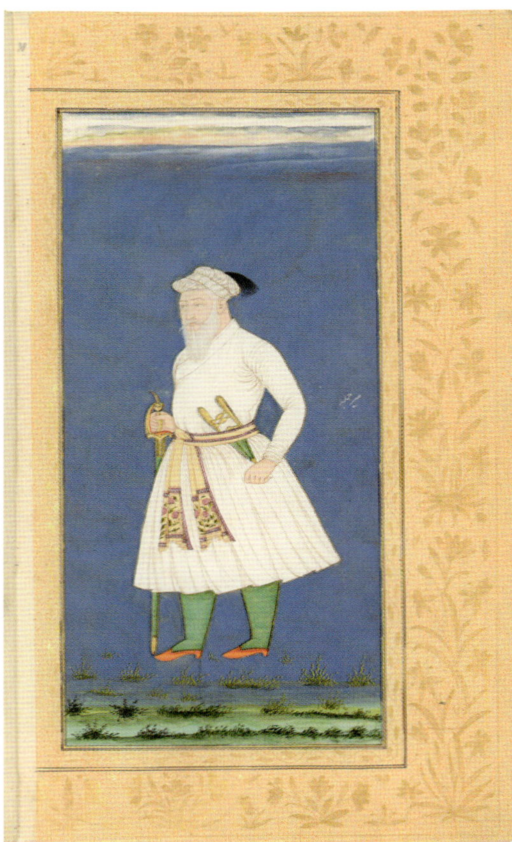

Ca 112/38

Ca 112/37
Muḥammad Amīn Khān Turānī
23.8 × 10.9 cm
Inscribed recto (*nastaʿlīq*):
Muḥammad Amīn Khān

Ca 112/38
Mīr Jumla II (1591–1663)
24.5 × 11.8 cm
Inscribed recto (*nastaʿlīq*):
Mīr Jumlah

Ca 112/39
Muḥammad Sultān (1639–1676)
24.5 × 11.9 cm
Inscribed recto (*nastaʿlīq*):
Sulṭān Maḥmūd

Ca 112/40
Bahādur Shāh I (r. 1707–1712)
24.3 × 11.9
Inscribed recto (*nastaʿlīq*):
Sulṭān Muʿaẓẓam

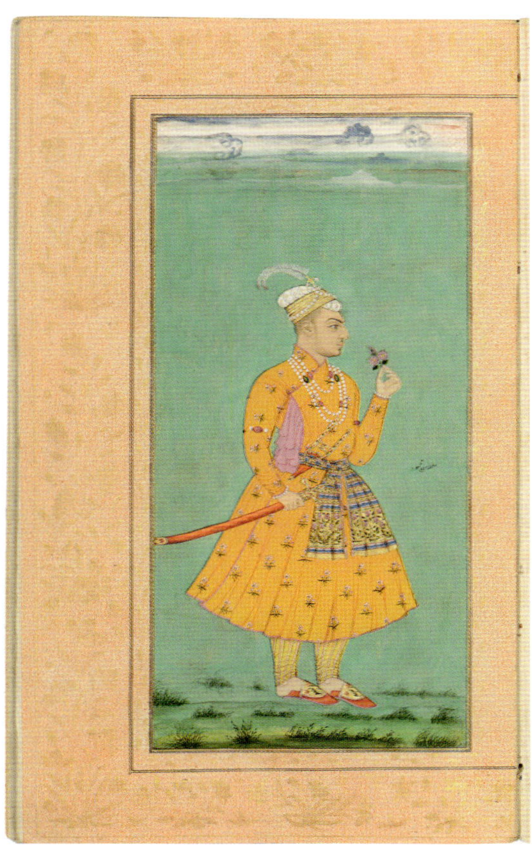

Ca 112/39

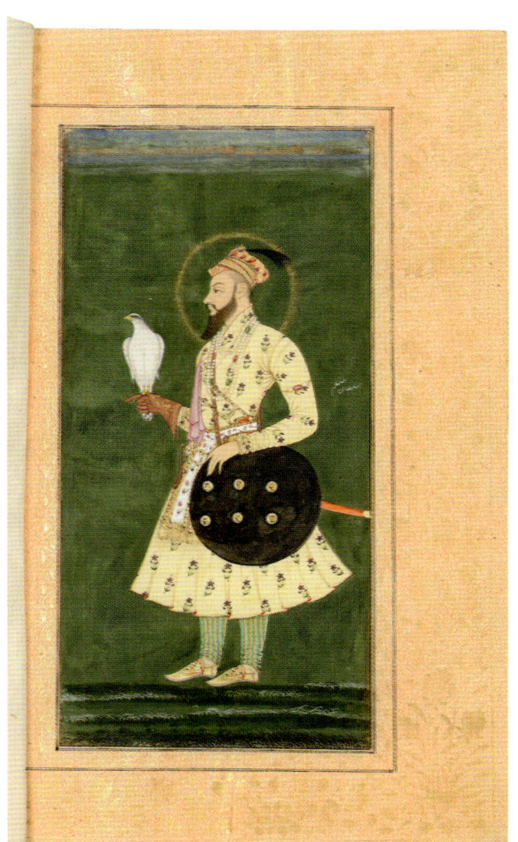

Ca 112/40

Ca 112/41
Aurangzēb (r. 1658–1707)
24.5 × 11.9 cm
Inscribed recto (*nastaʿlīq*):
Awrangzīb

Ca 112/42
Murād Bakhsh (1624–1661)
24.5 × 11.8 cm
Inscribed recto (*nastaʿlīq*):
Murād Bakhsh

Ca 112/43
Shāh Jahān (r. 1628–1658)
24.6 × 11.9 cm
Inscribed recto (*nastaʿlīq*):
Shāh Jahān

Ca 112/44
Double portrait of Dārā Shikōh (1615–1659) and Shāh Shujāʿ (1616–1661)
24.4 × 11.9 cm
Inscribed recto (*nastaʿlīq*):
Dārā Shujāʿ

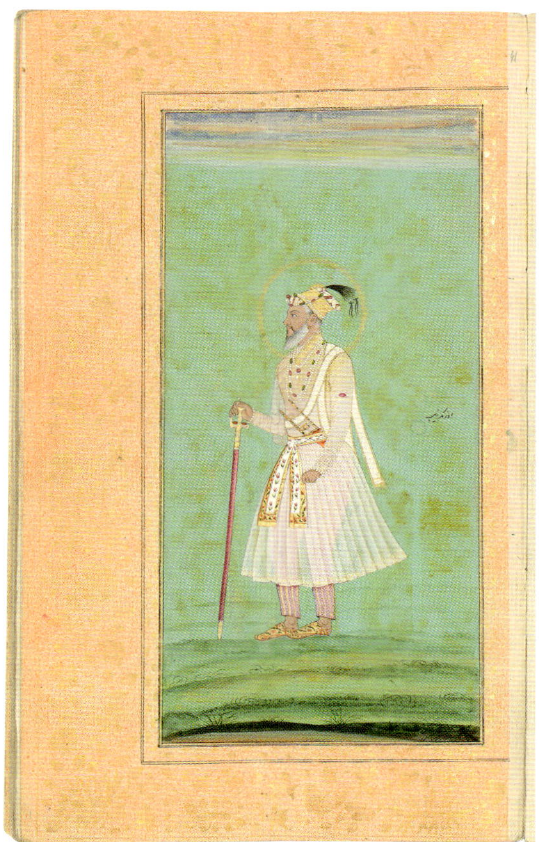

Ca 112/41

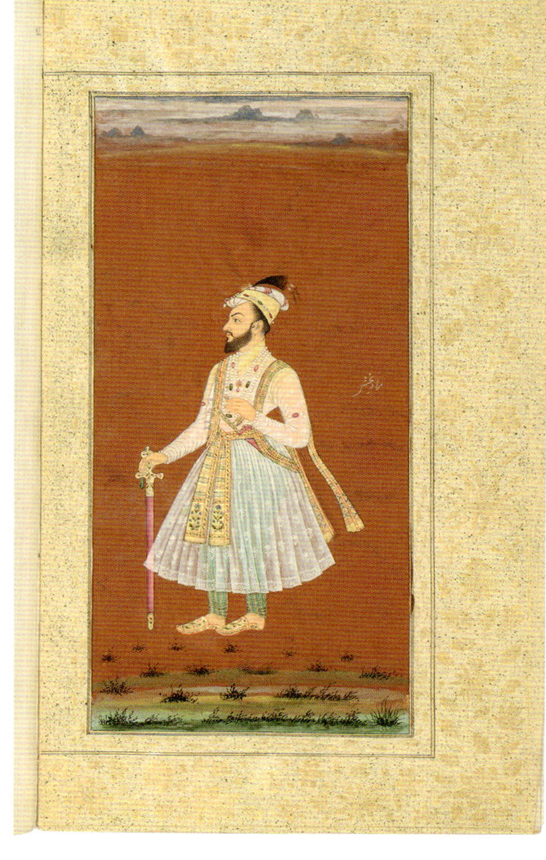

Ca 112/42

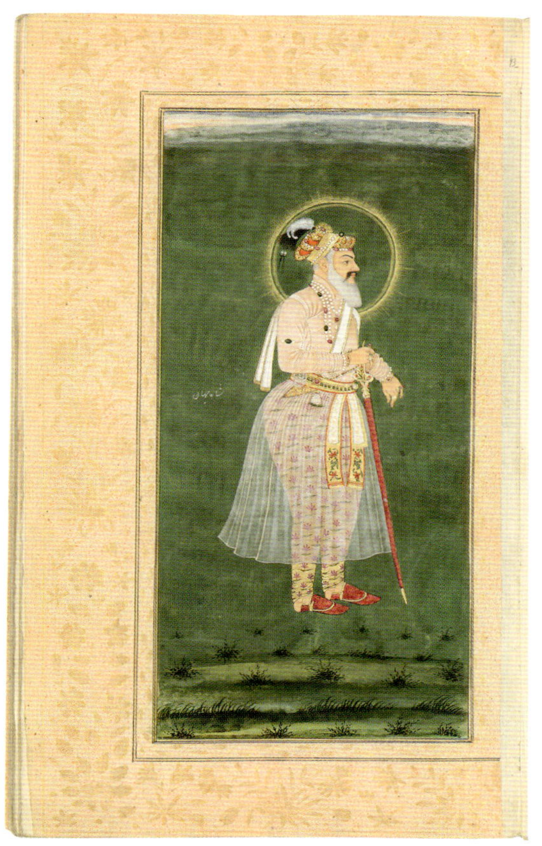

Ca 112/43

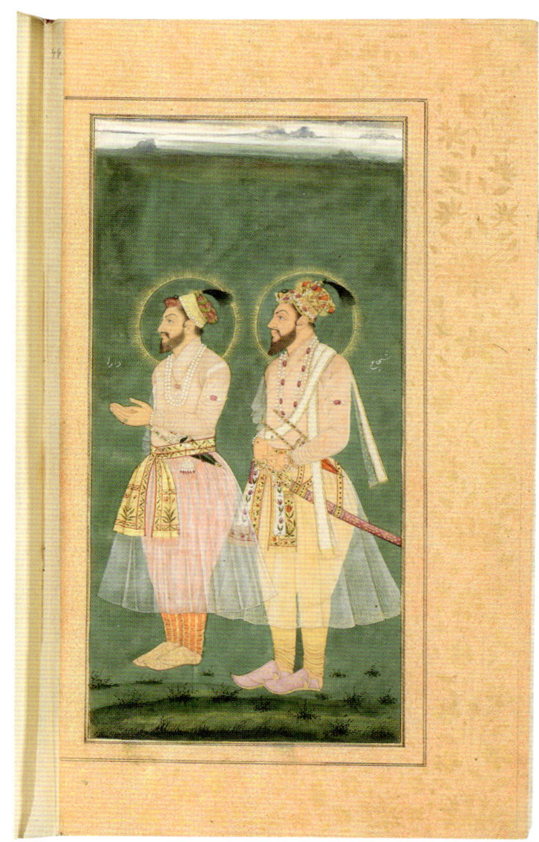

Ca 112/44

Ca 112/45

Jahāngīr (r. 1605–1627)

24.5×11.8 cm

Inscribed recto (*nasta'līq*):

Jahāngīr

Ca 112/46

Akbar (r. 1556–1605)

24.4×11.9 cm

Inscribed recto (*nasta'līq*):

Akbar

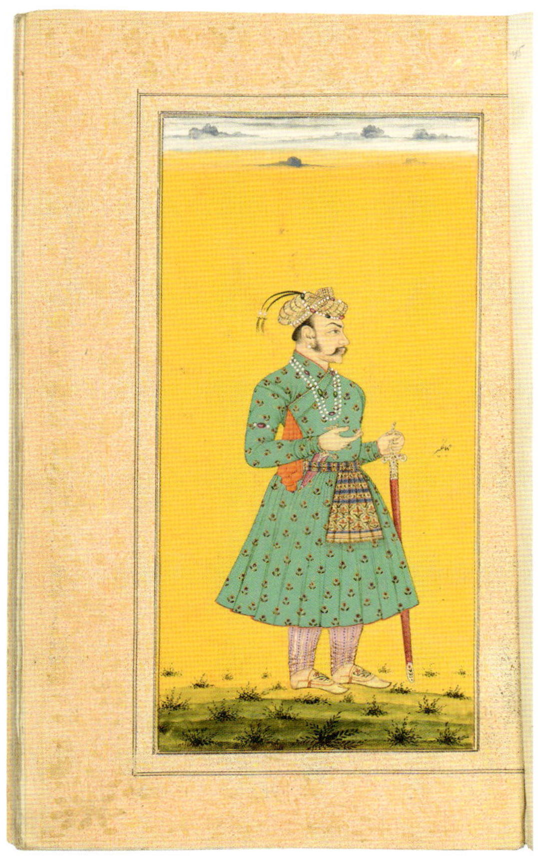

Ca 112/45

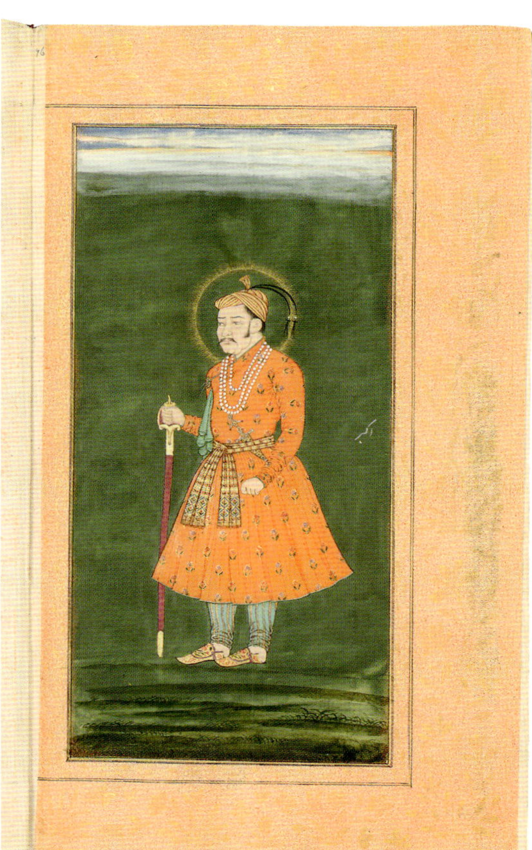

Ca 112/46

Cat. 2 | Ca 110

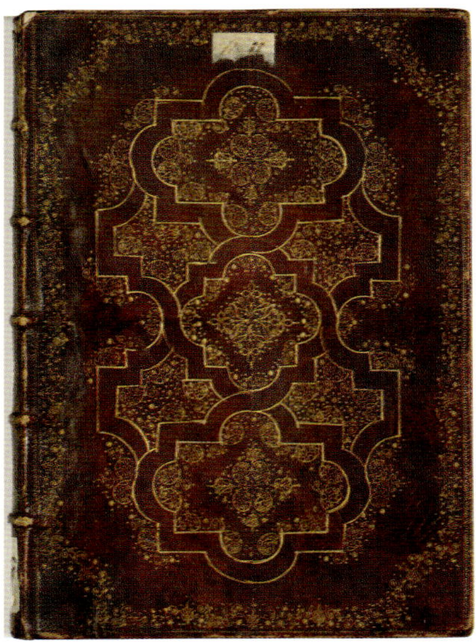

Fig. 1
Cover, left

Album with thirty-nine portraits of Indian kings and noblemen
Golconda (Deccan), late 17th–early 18th century
Album with 84 fols., 29.5 × 21.1 × 2.7 cm, European morocco leather binding with gold stippling
39 painted fols., watercolour and gold, light orange-brown paper borders attached with framing lines in silver, black ink, and white and green watercolour
45 endpapers and separating pages, marbled endpapers
Reference: Dresden 2017, cat. 12, pp. 148–151

The paintings in Ca 110 belong to the third type of portrait albums found in late seventeenth-century European collections. The album is bound in European leather, with stippled tooling (*décoration aux fers pointillés*), and has marbled endpapers similar to those in Ca 111 (fig. 1).[1] Ca 110 contains portraits of rulers and their generals and ministers, which may be placed into rough groupings. It begins with the great Mughal rulers from Akbar (r. 1542–1605) to Aurangzēb (r. 1658–1707), including the four sons of Shāh Jahān (r. 1627–1658) and the first two sons of Aurangzēb. The second group contains representations of the last two *sultāns* of the Golconda dynasty—ʿAbdullāh Qutb Shāh (r. 1626–1672) and Abū'l Hasan Qutb Shāh (r. 1672–1687)—and of the seventh and eight *sultāns* of the Bijapur dynasty, Muḥammad ʿĀdil Shāh (r. 1627–1656) and ʿAlī ʿĀdil Shāh II (r. 1656–1672). In the third category are representations of the great Marātha warrior Śivājī Bhonsle (r. 1627–1680), who led a series of raids on Mughal territories in the Deccan[2] and is included only selectively in other portrait albums: one at the Bibliothèque Nationale de France, Paris, and the other at the Rijksmuseum, Amsterdam.[3]

Unlike many Indian portrait albums found in European collections, Ca 110 also depicts the sons of the Mughal rulers Shāh Jahān and Aurangzēb. Departing from the practice of documenting the lineage and legitimacy of a dynasty by recording the features of its rulers and their ancestors, this album instead focuses on courtly figures from 1626 onwards. Most of these portrait studies of leading Deccani and Mughal political figures portray dignitaries employed under Aurangzēb and ʿAbdullāh Qutb Shāh who also may have served their successors and sometimes even shifted their political allegiance, moving from the Deccan to Mughal courts with the heightened Mughal presence in the Deccan and the eventual fall of Bijapur and Golconda in 1686 and 1687, respectively.

One representation (Ca 110/13) shows Muḥammad Saʿīd Mīr Jumla (1591–1663). Born to a poor oil merchant in Isfahan, he escaped the hard living conditions in Persia and began his career as a clerk working for a diamond merchant in Golconda in the 1630s. He served as the *sar-i daftar shāhī* (keeper of royal records) in 1635–1636, during the reign of ʿAbdullāh Qutb, and his zeal and loyal conduct rapidly gained him undisputed authority in affairs of state. The *sultān* was greatly impressed by him and appointed him to the position of *mīr jumla* (minister general) in 1643. By 1647 Muḥammad Saʿīd Mīr Jumla had conquered territories in eastern Karnatak and begun to regard himself as ruler, which ultimately led to his estrangement from the *sultān*.[4] ʿAbdullāh Qutb Shāh grew suspicions of his victorious minister general and made an unsuccessful attempt to murder him in 1653, after which Mīr Jumla never returned back to his service. Aurangzēb persuaded Shāh Jahān to send an imperial petition for him to join the Mughals, which he did from 1656 onwards. A remarkable personality in the seventeenth-century history of India, "Mīr Jumla was to Aurangzēb what Aristotle was to Alexander."[5]

These portraits of Deccani and Mughal princes, intended for Dutch and English audiences, were made in the Deccani style of Golconda, the chief port of entry for trade with the European East India Company. Europeans, principally the Dutch and the English and a little later the French, proved to be a ready clientele for the many artists in the city whose work had been disrupted by the wars with the Mughals and the final takeover in 1687. Images comparable to those in Ca 110 that highlight the sons of the Mughal rulers Shāh Jahān and Aurangzēb are found in albums sets now in leading museums.[6] Of the four sons of Shāh Jahān—Dārā Shikōh, Shāh Shujāʿ, Aurangzēb, and Murād—the depiction of Murād in these three albums clearly points towards a similar format and palette (Ca 110/5 and figs. 2 and 3).

While the representation of a particular person was fixed, the order and inscriptions accompanying the images varied. When it comes to these albums, which were acquired by connoisseurs worldwide, the attributions frequently prove to be false. The inscriptions have often been translated into the language of Europeans who added them. For

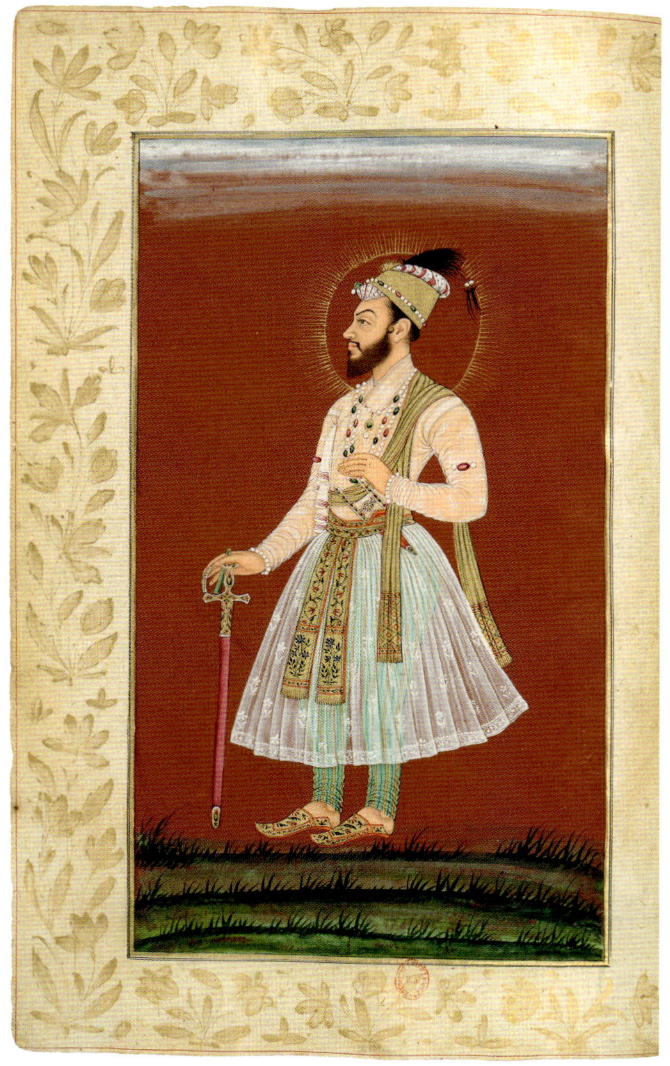

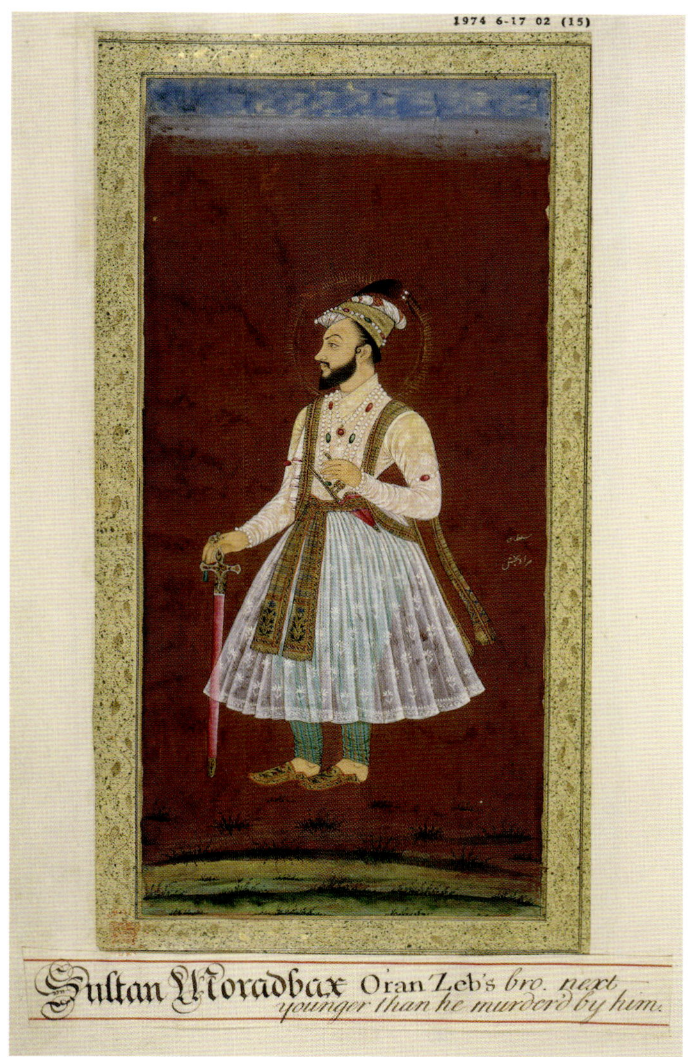

Fig. 2
Murād Bakhsh (1624–1661)
Golconda (Deccan), c. 1668
Watercolour and gold, c. 30 × 20 cm
BnF, Paris, Département des Manuscrits, Smith-Lesouëf Album 232/6v

Fig. 3
Murād Bakhsh (1624–1661)
Golconda (Deccan), c. 1668 – late 17th century
Watercolour and gold, 26.3 × 13.7 cm
The British Museum, London, inv. no. 1974,0617,0.2.15

example, in Smith-Lesouëf 232, where the images have been inscribed in *nasta'līq* and Dutch on the pages facing the portraits, the names are listed in ascending order, going from the eldest to the youngest son of Shāh Jahān (i.e., Dārā, Shujāʿ, Aurangzēb, and Murād) while the corresponding representations have a different order. In this case, the European inscriber might have known about the family depicted but was unable to correctly identify the sitters, since he probably had no personal knowledge of them.

The dating of imperial artworks is often based on the way the latest ruler is represented in a particular album. The older the ruler appears, the more recent the artwork. For instance, the representation of the young black-bearded Bahādur Shāh I (r. 1707–1712) in Ca 110 might point to a late seventeenth to early eighteenth century date (fig. 4). This dating is, however, only tentative, as the last ruler, Aurangzēb, is depicted as a young man with his contemporary Deccani kings, who are shown in their later years. In an album in London,[7] this measure is taken to another level by the inclusion of a young-looking Aurangzēb (similar to Ca 110/6) along with an older Aurangzēb a few portraits later.

What can be more definite for dating such album portraits with multiple copies are aspects such as written records, watermarks, paper, and binding. These indicators help in assigning a place/date for the collection of the artworks in these albums. Ca 110

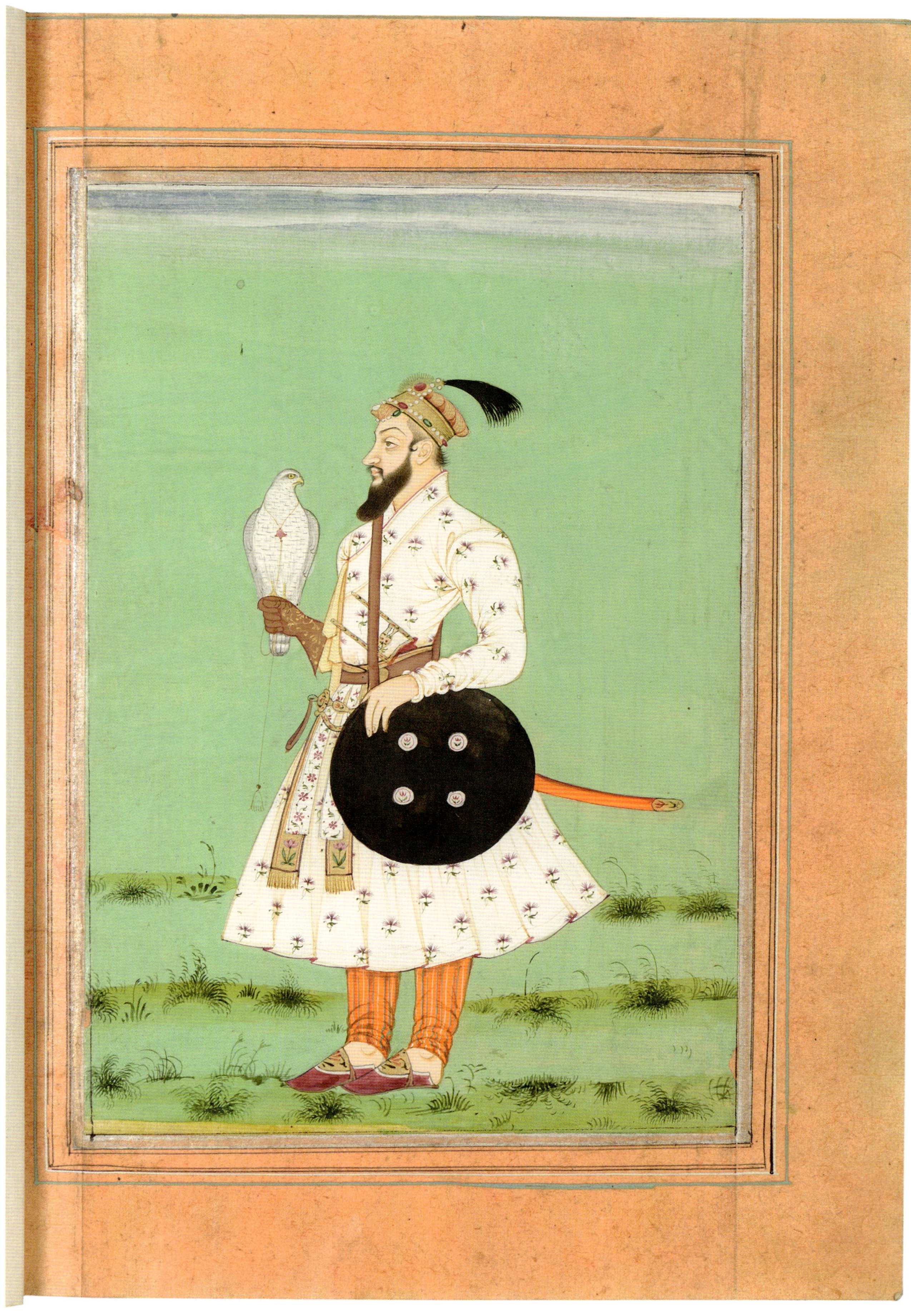

Ca 110/9

is mentioned in the Heucher Inventory as item no. 11: "39 Japanische Portraits von Mannspersonen, von Kopff bis auf die Füße, en Maroquin rouge d'ore in Folio"[8] (39 Japanese portraits of men, from head to feet, in moroccan rouge doré in folio). The mention of Japanese figures instead of Indian and a slight counting error comes as no surprise in such old records. In the Witsen album, which has forty-nine loose leaves with Indian portrait miniatures, there is also an incorrect inscription: "Portraits from life of Chinese and Tarter emperors on heavy Chinese appear most artistically painted in watercolour with gold and silver."[9]

A similar album is mentioned in the auction catalogue of Nicolaas Witsen, from whose collection several works were purchased for Dresden.[10] Item no. 12 lists "Een kasje waarin 35. Portraiten der Koningen van Golconda, Visiapour, Indostan en andere"[11] (A box with 35 portraits of rulers from Golconda, Bijapur, Hindustan, and elsewhere). However, since there is no reference number in the Heucher Inventory, unlike most of the other verifiable acquisitions from Witsen's collection, it can be assumed that these are not necessarily the same albums.[12]

In Ca 110 a "posthorn" watermark (fig. 5) comparable to those dated to 1665, Leiden[13] and 1699–1700, London[14] occurs almost twenty-one times on the European laid paper protecting the painted folios and pasted on the marbled doublures and endpapers. A similar watermark is found in the British Museum album,[15] though the initials at the bottom of the two watermarks differ, being "LVG" in the British Museum album and "WR" in Ca 110. The cover of Ca 110, which is decorated with a pattern of ribbons executed in a stippled tooling technique (see fig. 1), points to a possible origin in late seventeenth-to early eighteenth-century England.[16] While it is true that French paper makers made paper for the Dutch market, mainly during the seventeenth century, using various watermarks and makers initials, and that Amsterdam began to export paper to England and elsewhere in the beginning of the century, papers with the horn mark and the name "L.V. Gerrevink" were also imported by the English markets.[17] Thus it is possible that these images were bound together in England. NB

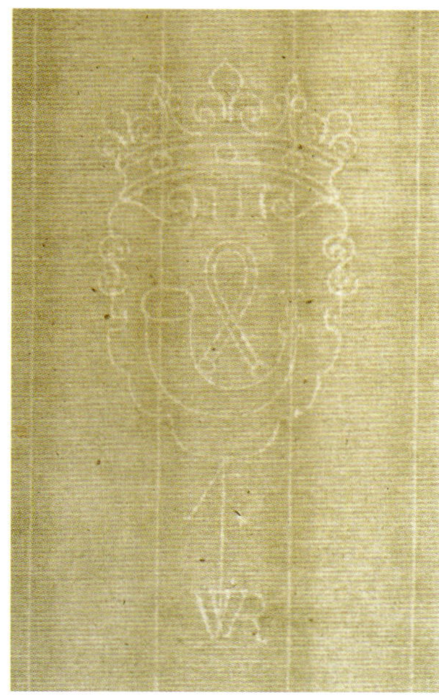

Fig. 5
Ca 110
A "posthorn" watermark

Notes | 1 I would like to thank Kristine Rose Beers, senior conservator at the Chester Beatty Library, Dublin, for help with the description of the binding. | 2 On Śivājī Bhonsle, see Berlia 2017, p. 115. | 3 Bibliothèque Nationale de France, Paris, Smith-Lesouëf 232/20v; and Witsen Album, Rijksmuseum, Amsterdam, inv. nos. RP-T-00-3186, RP-T-00-3186-46. | 4 Sarkar 1979, pp. 10–42. | 5 Ibid., p. 360. | 6 The British Museum, London, inv. nos. 1974 6-17 02 and 1974 6-17 04; Witsen Album, Rijksmuseum, Amsterdam, inv. no. RP-T-00-3186; and Bibliothèque Nationale de France, Paris, Smith-Lesouëf 232–3. | 7 British Museum, London, inv. no. 1974 6-17 02, folios 9 and 18. | 8 Heucher Inventory 1738, sig. Cat. 1, p. 156, no. 11. | 9 Also listed in the Witsen Catalogue, Amsterdam 1728, p. 11, no. 10 as, "Een dito Boek met omtrent de 50 Portraiten, beginnende met den Grooten Tamerlaan, Mogolse, Persiaansche en andere Grooten, zeer konstig met Goud en Couleuren geschildert, als mede de verduyste Naamen der Zelve" (A large book with about 50 portraits, starting with the great Tamerlane, Mogolian, Persian, and other great rulers, painted mostly with gold and other colours, along with their names). See also Lunsingh Scheurleer 1996, p. 204, no. 15. | 10 See cat. 1, p. 51. | 11 Amsterdam 1728; see also Lunsingh Scheurleer 1996, p. 204, no. 15. | 12 For the corresponding numbers in the Heucher Inventory and the Witsen sale catalogue and information on other albums acquired for Dresden from the Witsen sale, see p. 51. | 13 See Heawood 1950, no. 2722. | 14 See ibid., no. 2728. This information was kindly provided by Pauline Lunsingh Scheurleer in consultation with Eric Hinterding, curator of the Print Room, Rijksmuseum, Amsterdam. | 15 British Museum, London, inv. no. 1974,06-17.04. | 16 This observation was kindly provided by Mr. Rens Top, Keeper, Bookbinding Collection, Koninklijke Bibliotheek, The Hague. | 17 See Heawood 1950, p. 27.

Fig. 4
Cat. 2 | Ca 110/9
Bahādur Shāh I (r. 1707–1712)

Ca 110/1
Akbar (r. 1556–1605)
20.8 × 14 cm

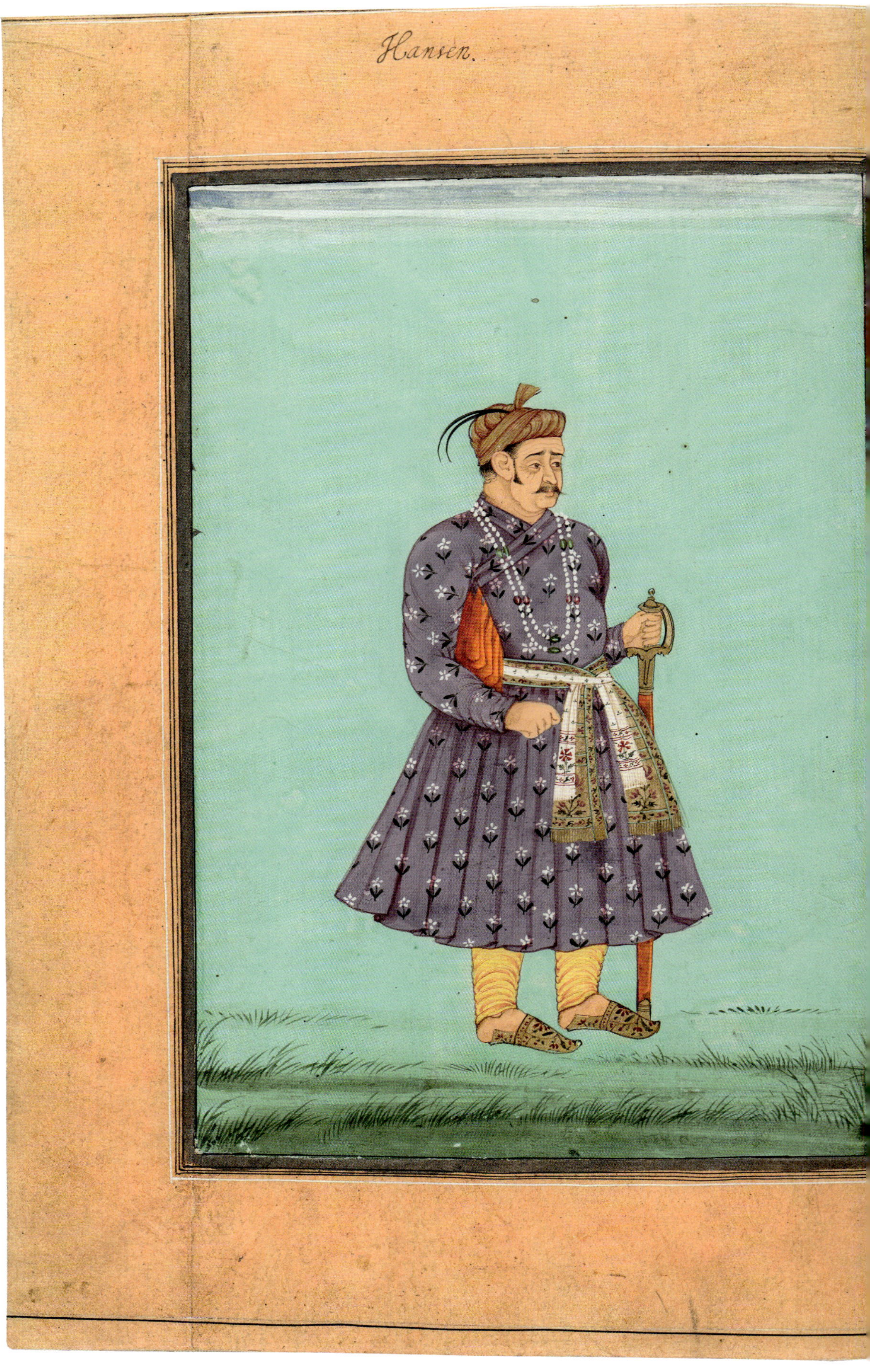

Ca 110/1

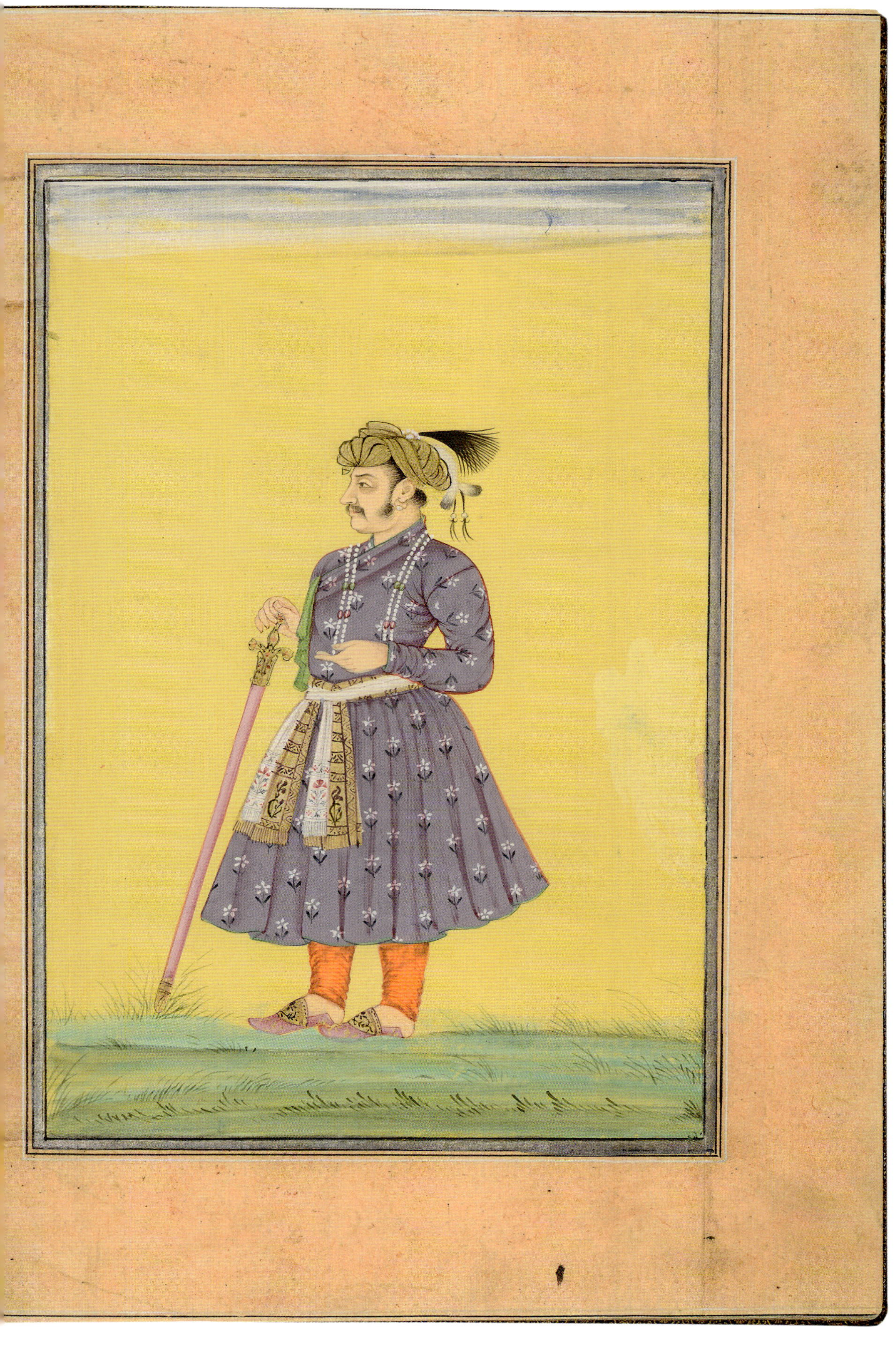

Ca 110/2
Jahāngīr (r. 1605–1627)
21.1 × 14.1 cm

Ca 110/2

Ca 110/3
Shāh Jahān (r. 1628–1658)
23.1 × 15.4 cm

Ca 110/4
Dārā Shikōh (1615–1659)
23.4 × 15 cm

Ca 110/5
Murād Bakhsh (1624–1661)
21.1 × 14.3 cm

Ca 110/6
Aurangzēb (r. 1658–1707)
21.3 × 14.2 cm

Ca 110/7
Shāh Shujāʿ (1616–1661)
22.1 × 14.2 cm

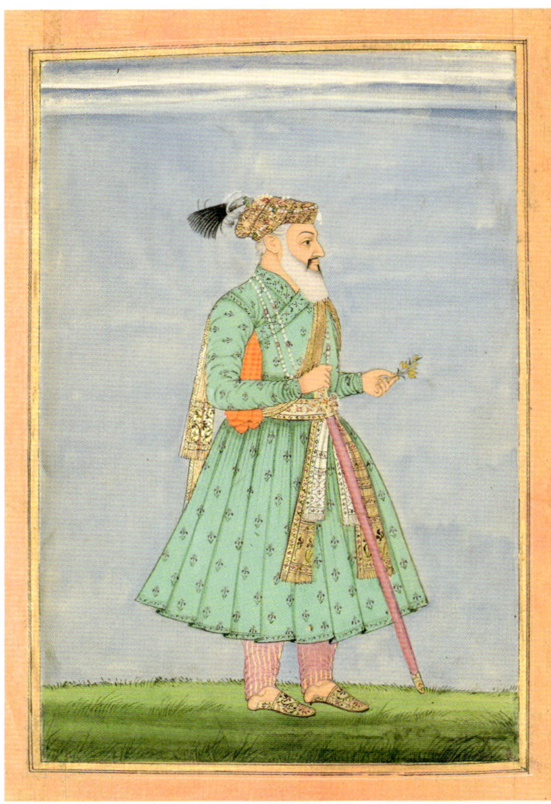

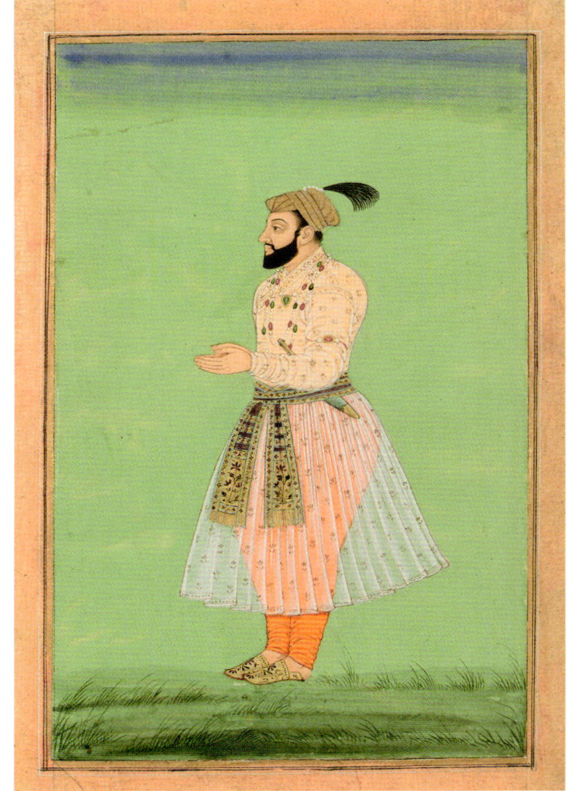

Ca 110/3

Ca 110/4

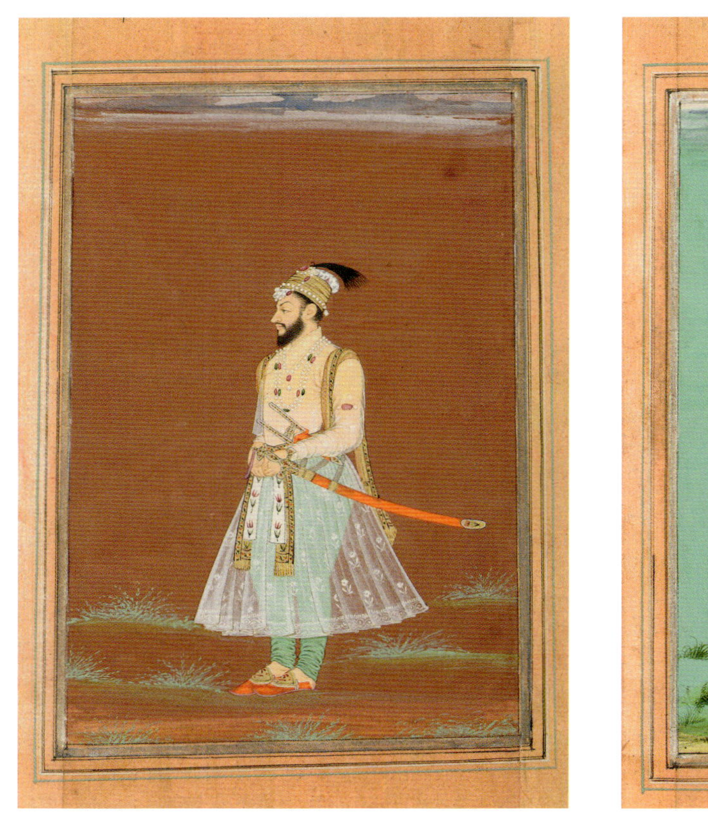

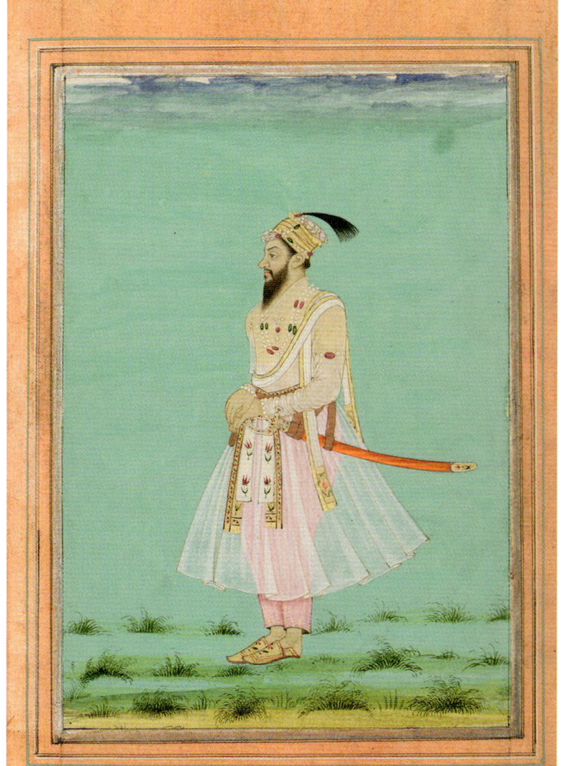

Ca 110/5

Ca 110/6

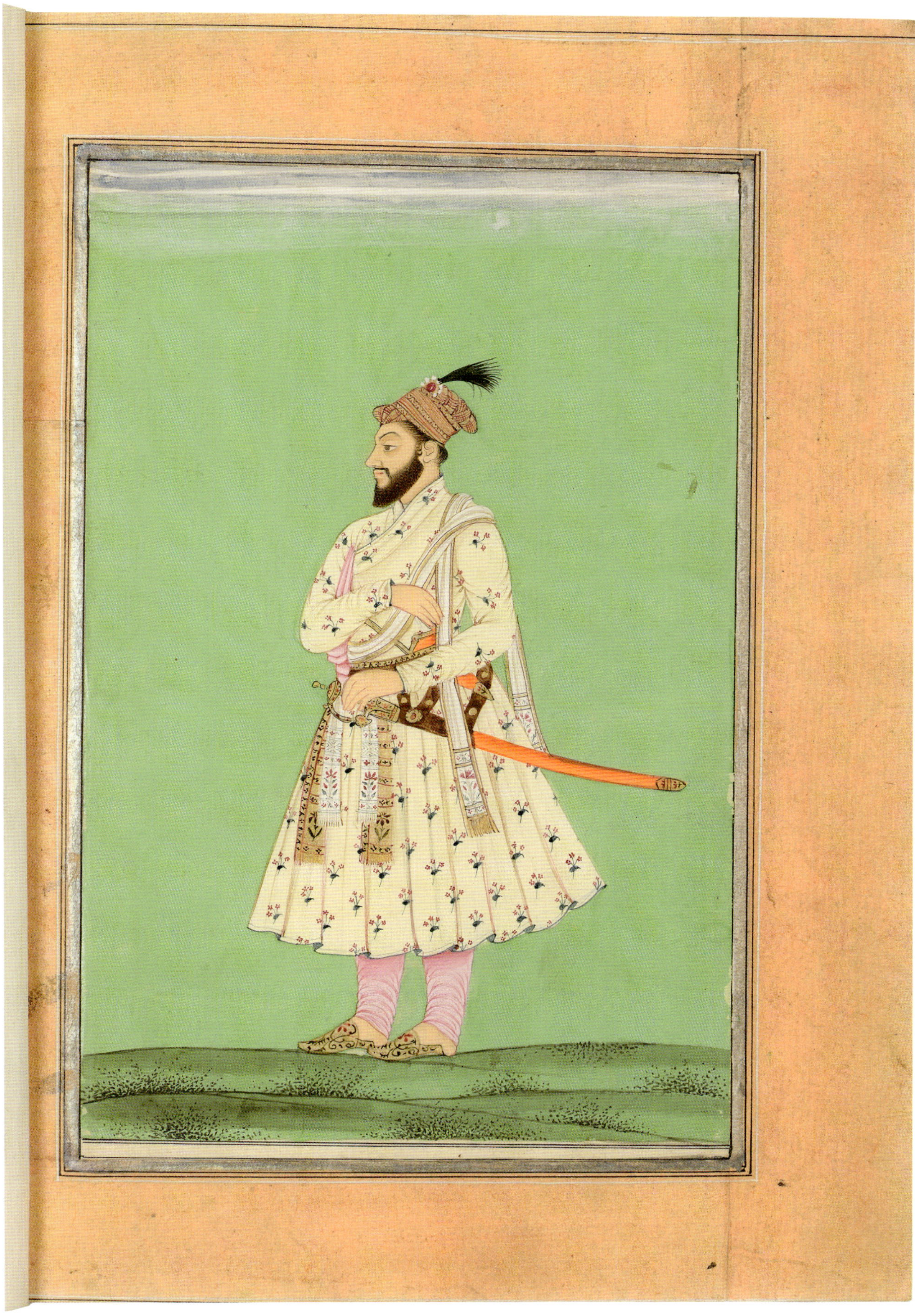

Ca 110/7

Ca 110/8
Muḥammad Sultān
(1639–1676)
22.3 × 14.2 cm

Ca 110/9
Bahādur Shāh I
(r. 1707–1712)
21.2 × 14.2 cm

Ca 110/10
Mīrzā Qilich Khān
22.3 × 17.2 cm

Ca 110/11
Bhao Sīngh (d. 1678) [?]
23.4 × 14.3 cm

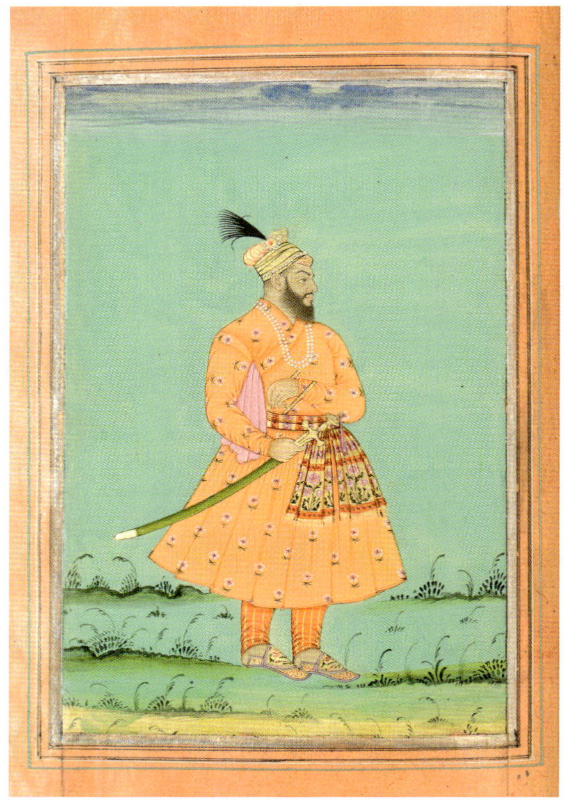

Ca 110/8

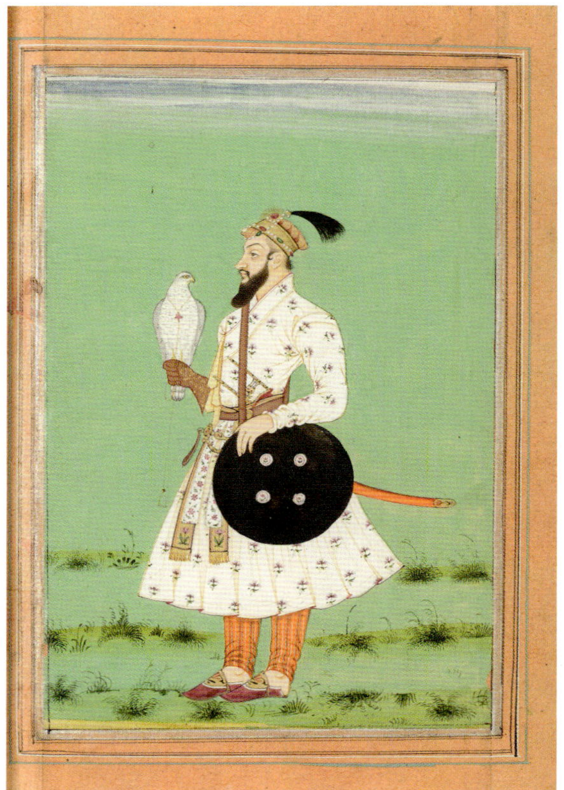

Ca 110/9

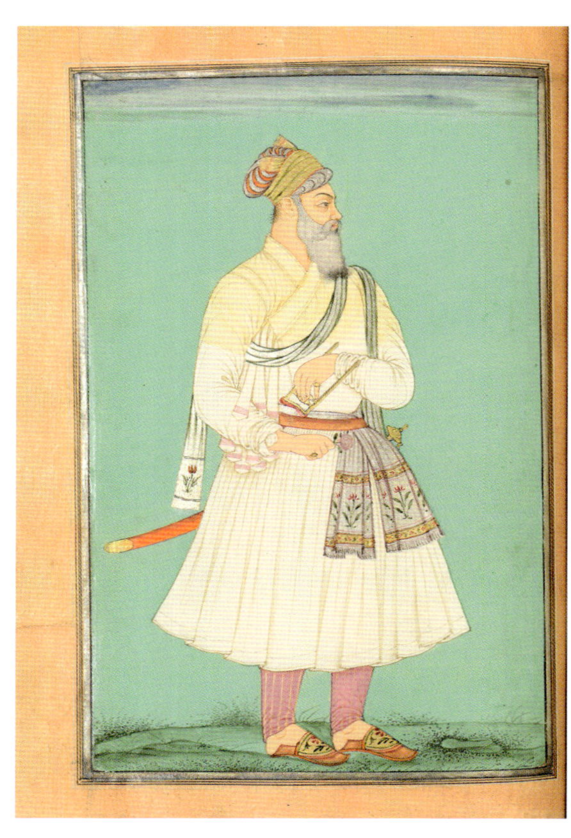

Ca 110/10

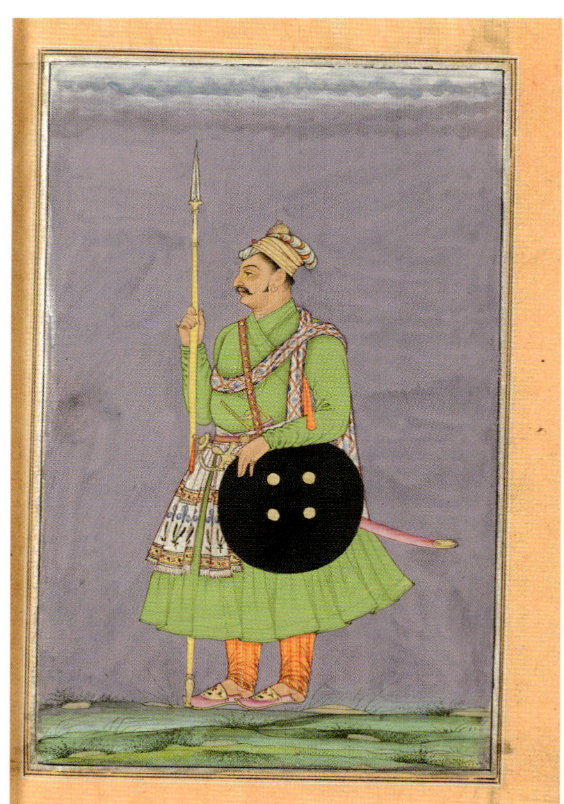

Ca 110/11

Ca 110/12
Muḥammad Amīn Khān Turānī
22 × 14.2 cm

Ca 110/13
Mīr Jumla II (1591 – 1663)
22 × 14.5 cm

Ca 110/14
Mān Sīngh I (r. 1589 – 1614) [?]
22.1 × 14.2 cm

Ca 110/15
Karan Sīngh (d. 1666 – 1667) [?]
22.4 × 15.2 cm

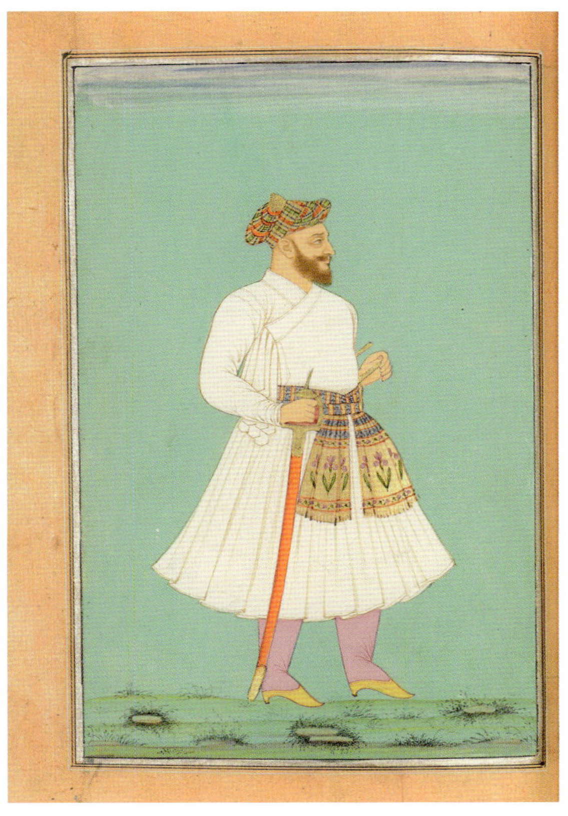

Ca 110/12

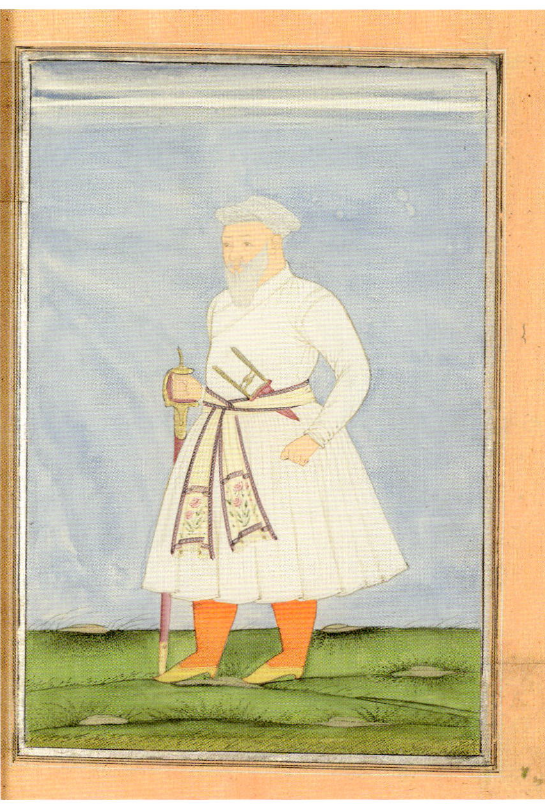

Ca 110/13

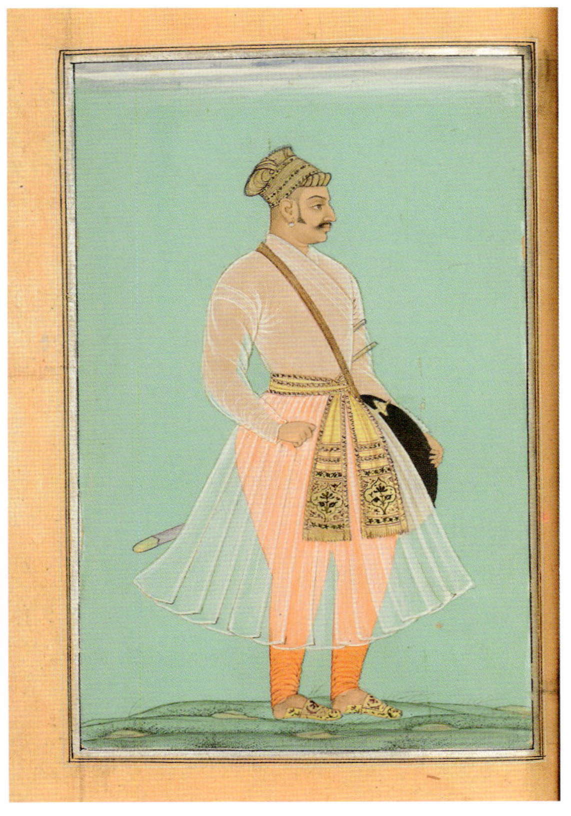

Ca 110/14

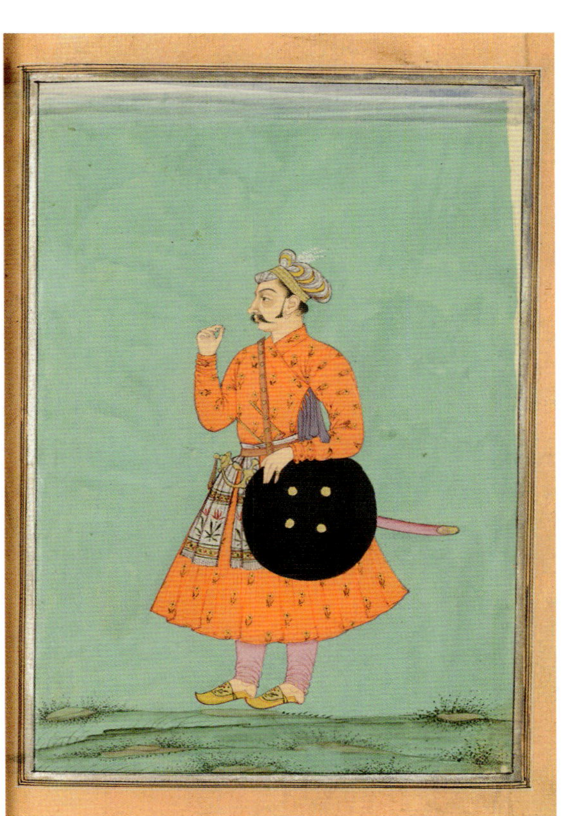

Ca 110/15

Ca 110/16
Fath Jang Khān
23.4 × 15.3 cm

Ca 110/17
Safshikan Khān
23.3 × 15 cm

Ca 110/18
'Abdullāh Qutb Shāh
(r. 1626–1672)
23 × 14.2 cm

Ca 110/19
Ibn-i Khātūn
21.5 × 14.3 cm

Ca 110/20
Mullāh Sādullāh
22 × 14.2 cm

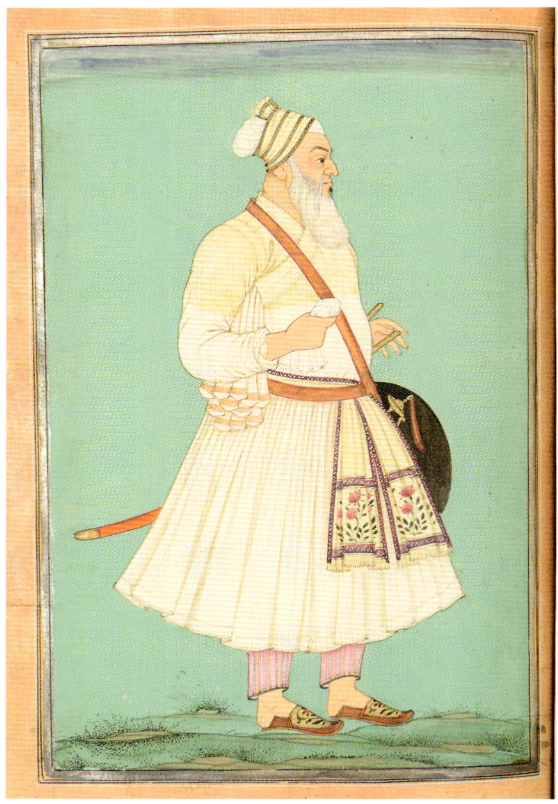

Ca 110/16

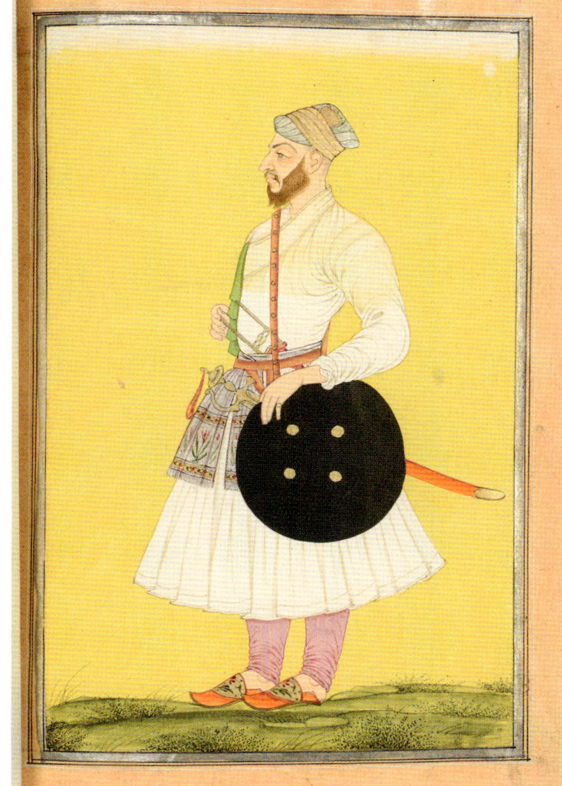

Ca 110/17

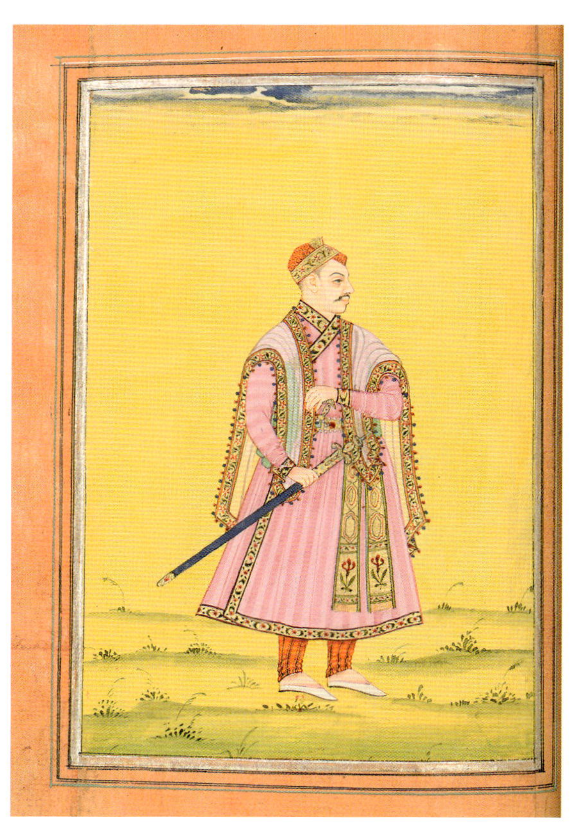

Ca 110/18

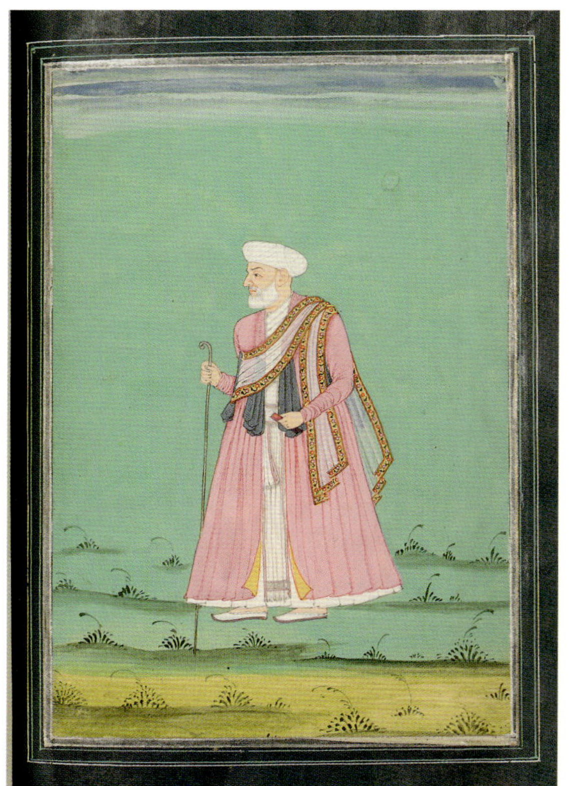

Ca 110/19

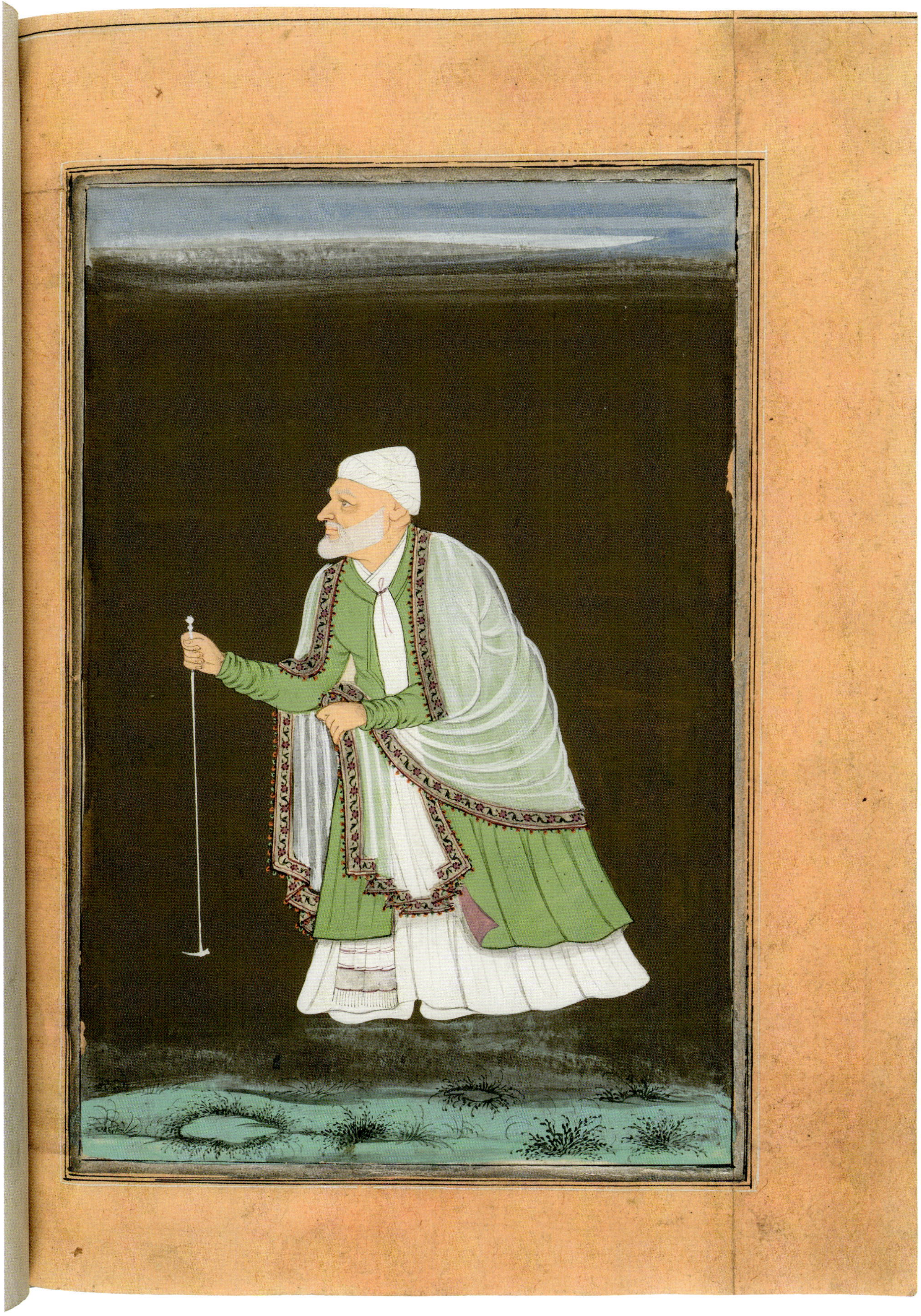

Ca 110/20

Ca 110/21
Muḥammad Sayyid Muzzafar
22.4 × 14.2 cm

Ca 110/22
ʻAbdullāh Qutb Shāh (r. 1626–1672)
21.9 × 14.2 cm

Ca 110/23
Mīrzā Ahmad [?]
22.2 × 14.2 cm

Ca 110/24
Mullāh Rauhā
21.9 × 14.2 cm

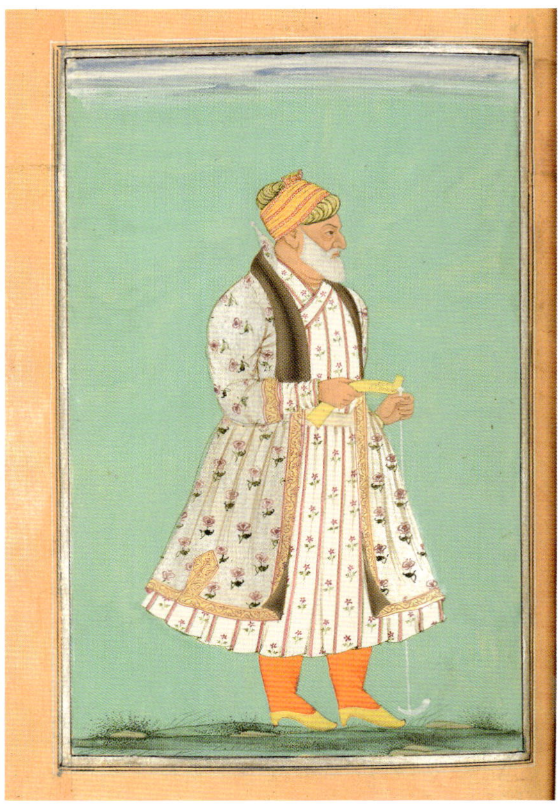

Ca 110/21

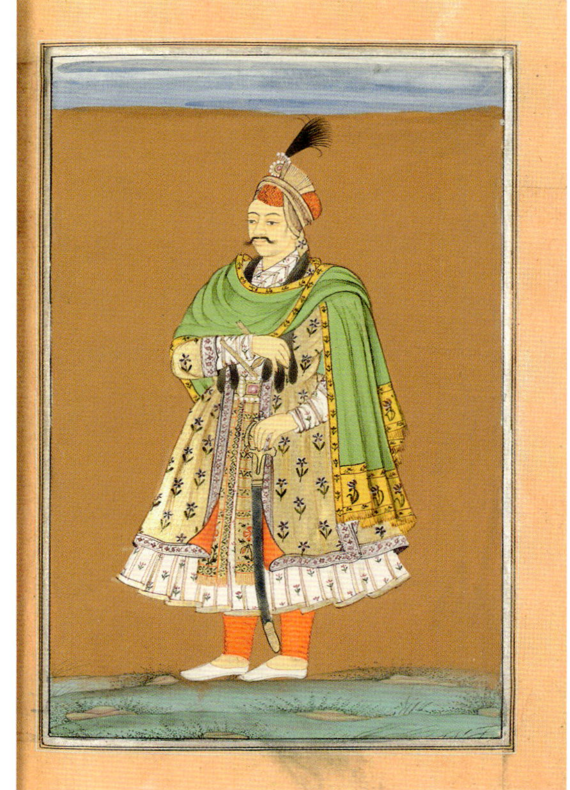

Ca 110/22

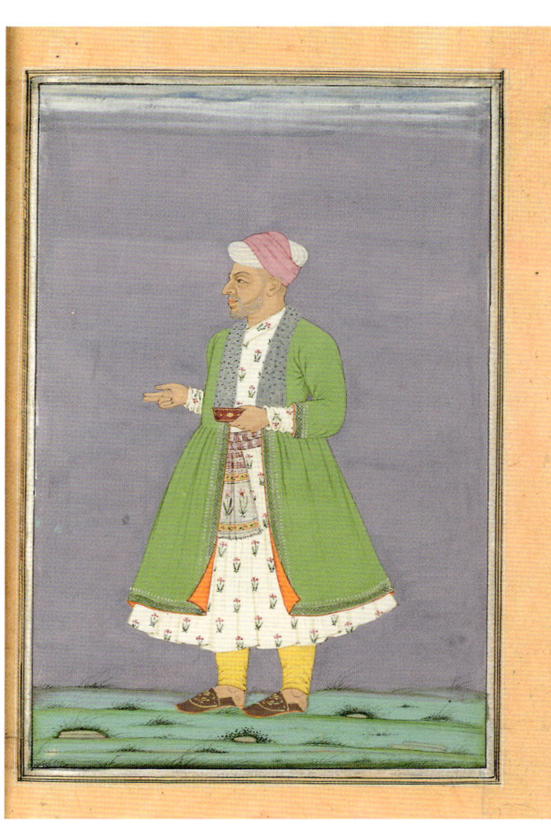

Ca 110/23

Ca 110/24

Ca 110/25
'Abd al-Ja'far Beg
22.2 × 14.1 cm

Ca 110/26
Neknām Khān (d. 1672)
22.1 × 14.1 cm

Ca 110/27
Hasan Khān
22.2 × 14.2 cm

Ca 110/28
Shāh Mīrzā
21.9 × 15.3 cm

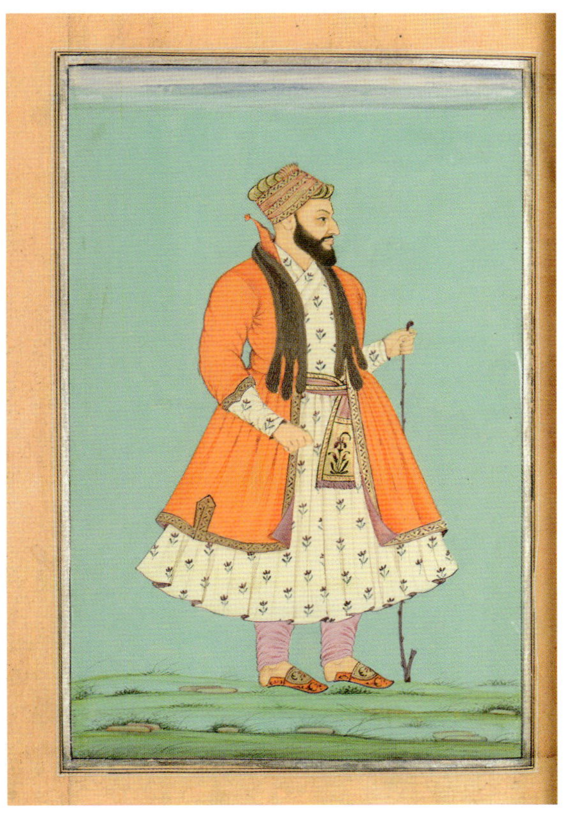

Ca 110/25

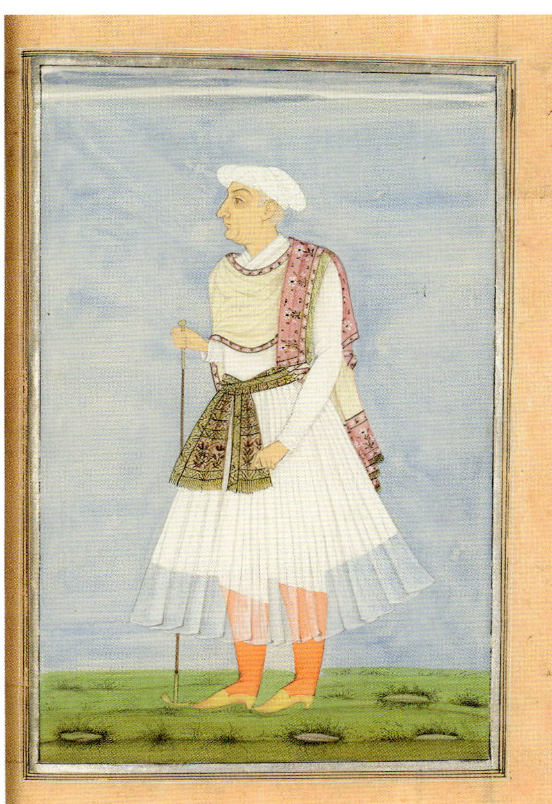

Ca 110/26

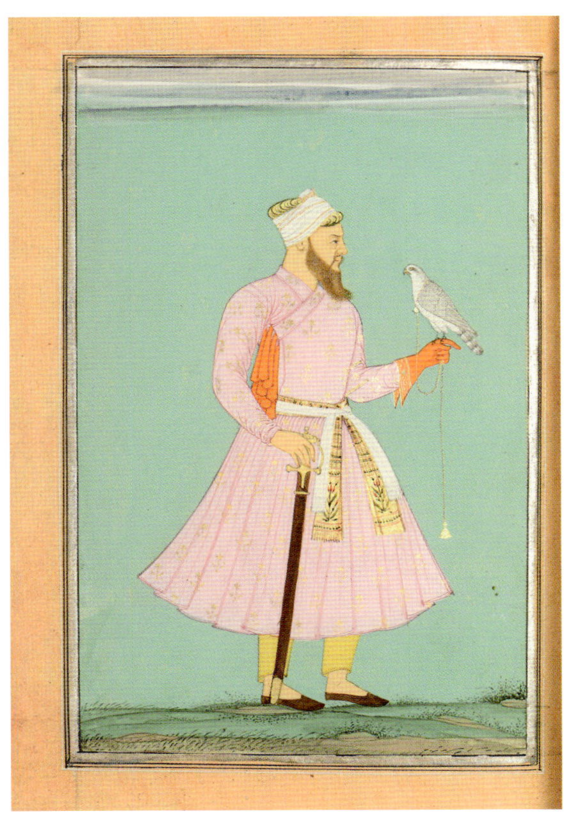

Ca 110/27

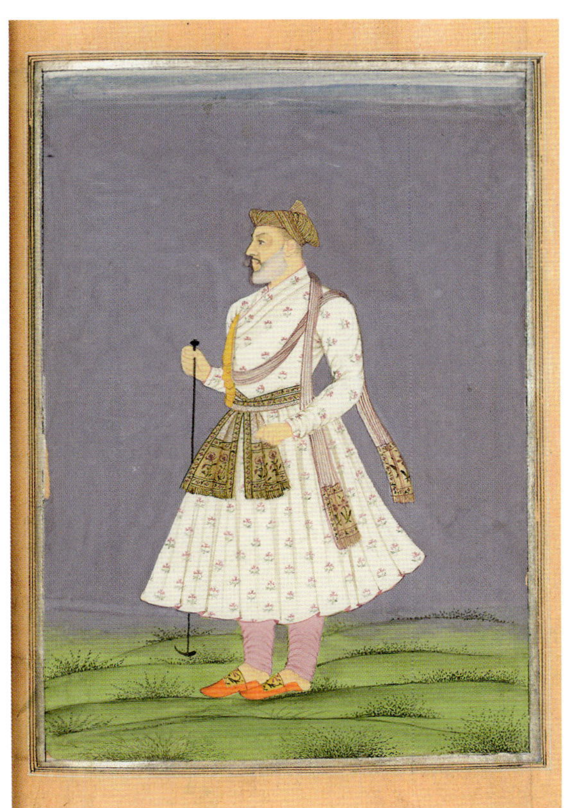

Ca 110/28

Ca 110/29
Mullāh ʻAbd al-Samad
22.1 × 14.2 cm

Ca 110/30
ʻAbd al-Jaʻfar Beg
21.3 × 14.4 cm

Ca 110/31
Mūsā Khān
22 × 14.1 cm

Ca 110/32
Mīrzā Nāsir
21.7 × 14.3 cm

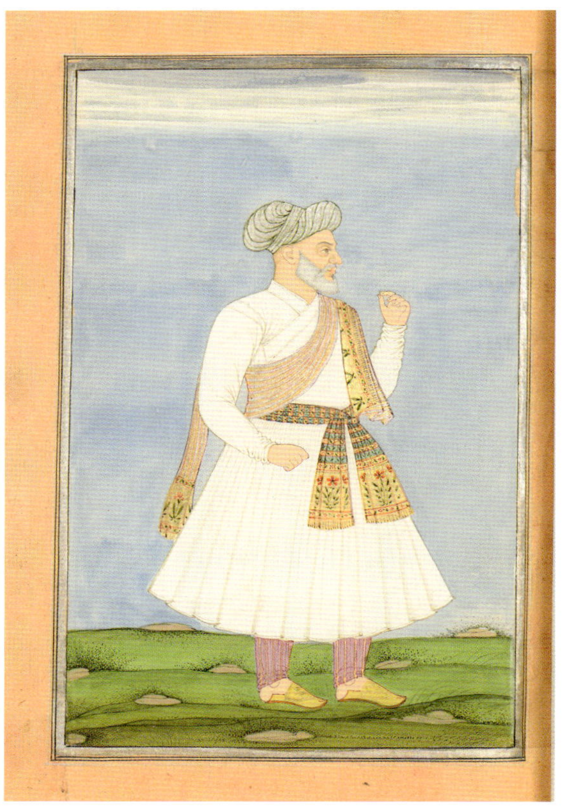

Ca 110/29

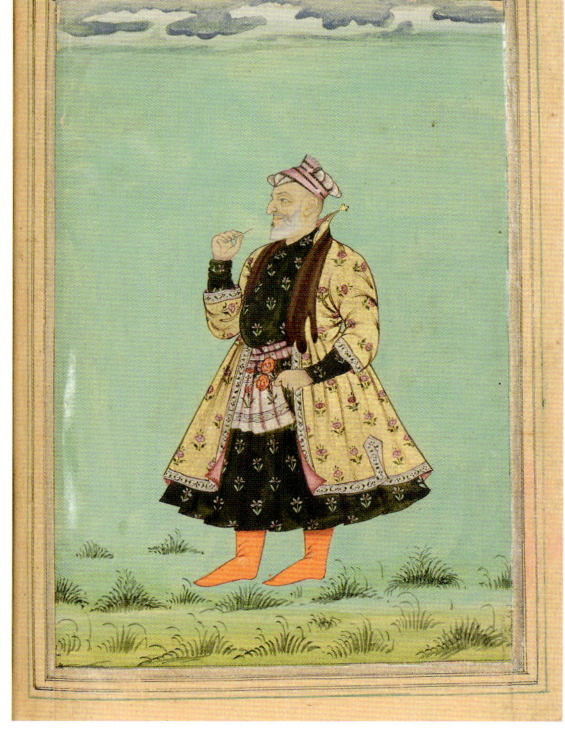

Ca 110/30

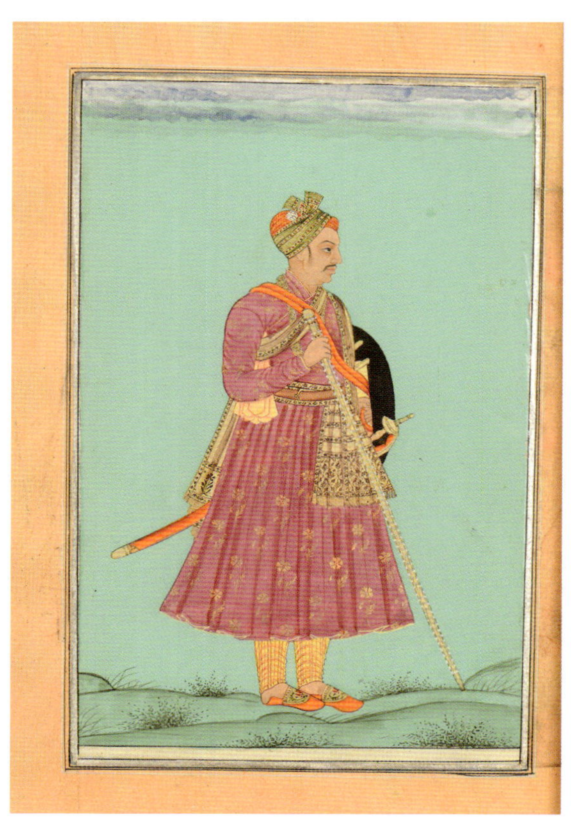

Ca 110/31

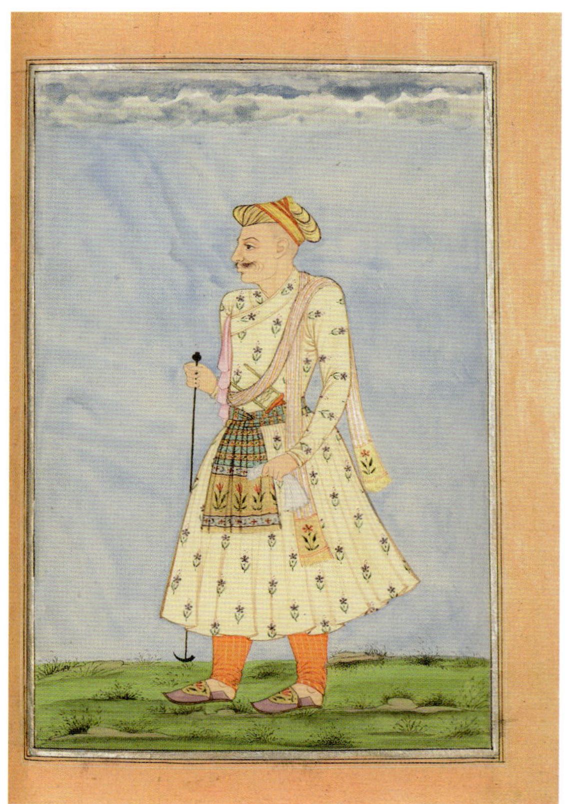

Ca 110/32

Ca 110/33
Abū'l Hasan Qutb Shāh (r. 1672–1687)
23.8 × 15.3 cm

Ca 110/34
Muḥammad Ibrāhīm (d. 1688–1689)
21.6 × 14.2 cm

Ca 110/35
Mādanna Paṇḍit (d. 1685)
22 × 14.2 cm

Ca 110/36
Śivājī (r. 1674–1680)
22 × 14.2 cm

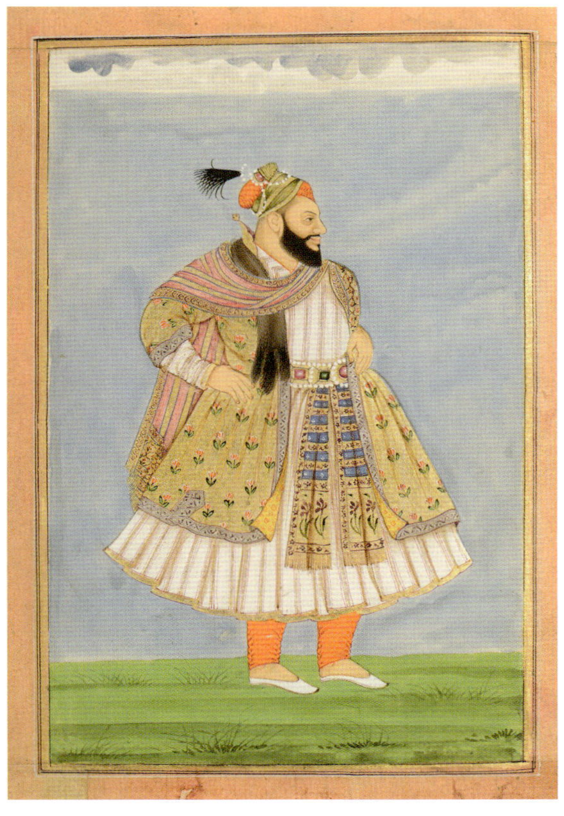

Ca 110/33

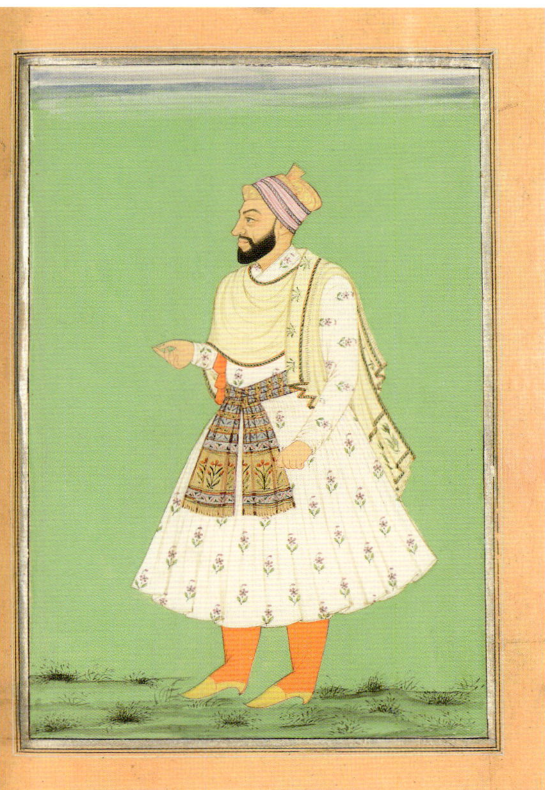

Ca 110/34

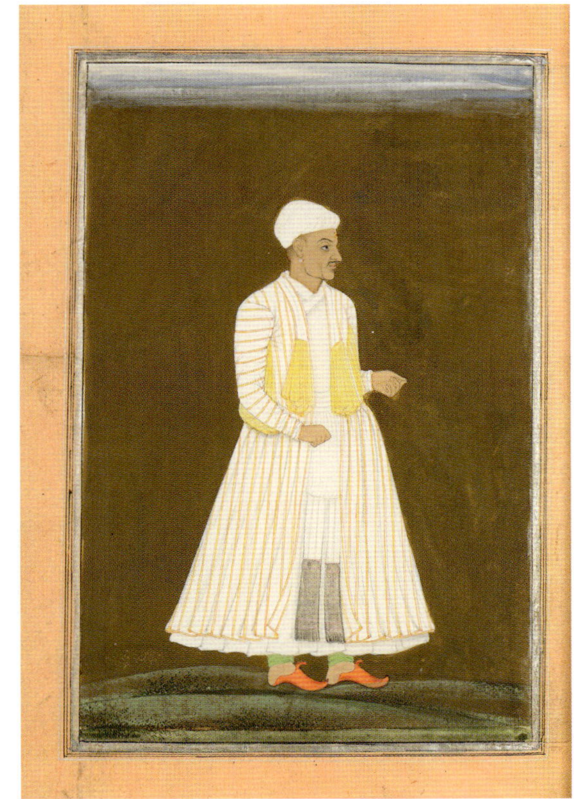

Ca 110/35

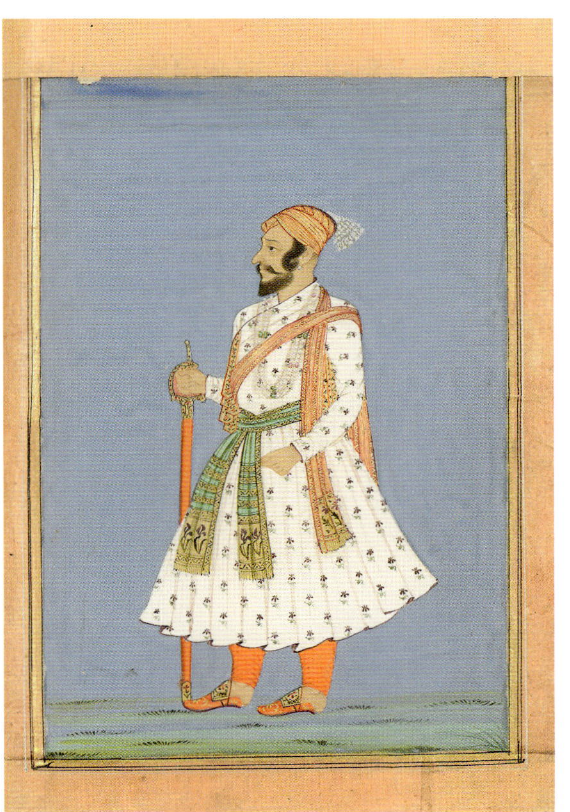

Ca 110/36

Ca 110/37
Ikhlās Khān (d. 1656)
21.9 × 14.3 cm

Ca 110/38
Muḥammad ʿÂdil Shāh (r. 1627–1656)
21.7 × 14.8 cm

Ca 110/39v
Verso showing paper strips pasted to form the borders of the painting on fol. 39r

Ca 110
Marbled endpaper

Ca 110/39
ʿAlī ʿÂdil Shāh II (r. 1656–1672)
19.4 × 12.3 cm

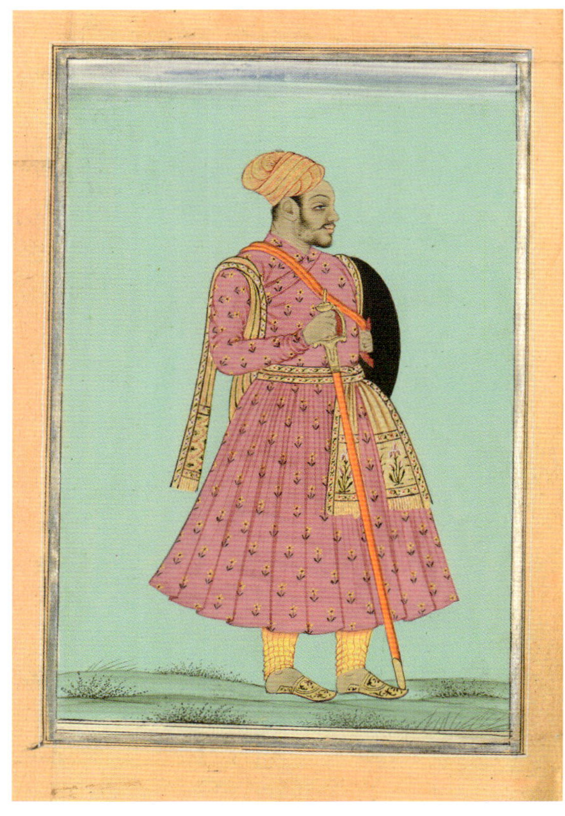

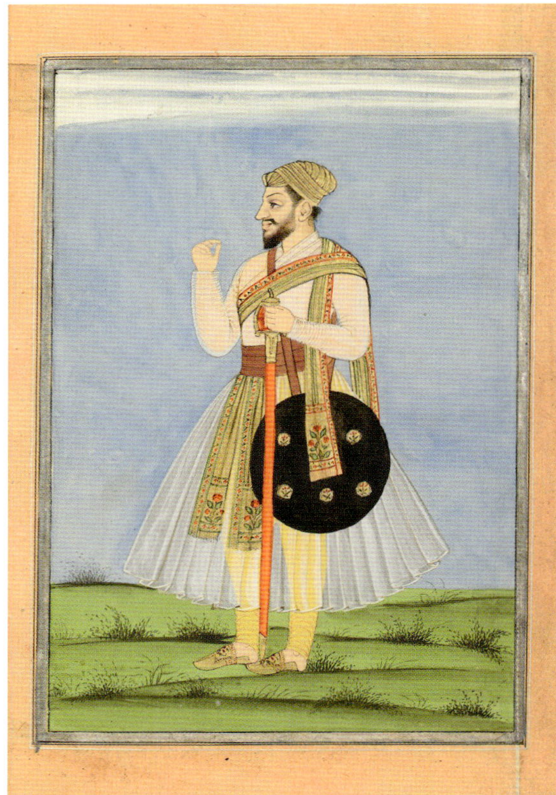

Ca 110/37

Ca 110/38

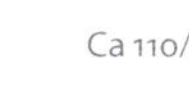

Ca 110/39v

Ca 110, Marbled endpaper

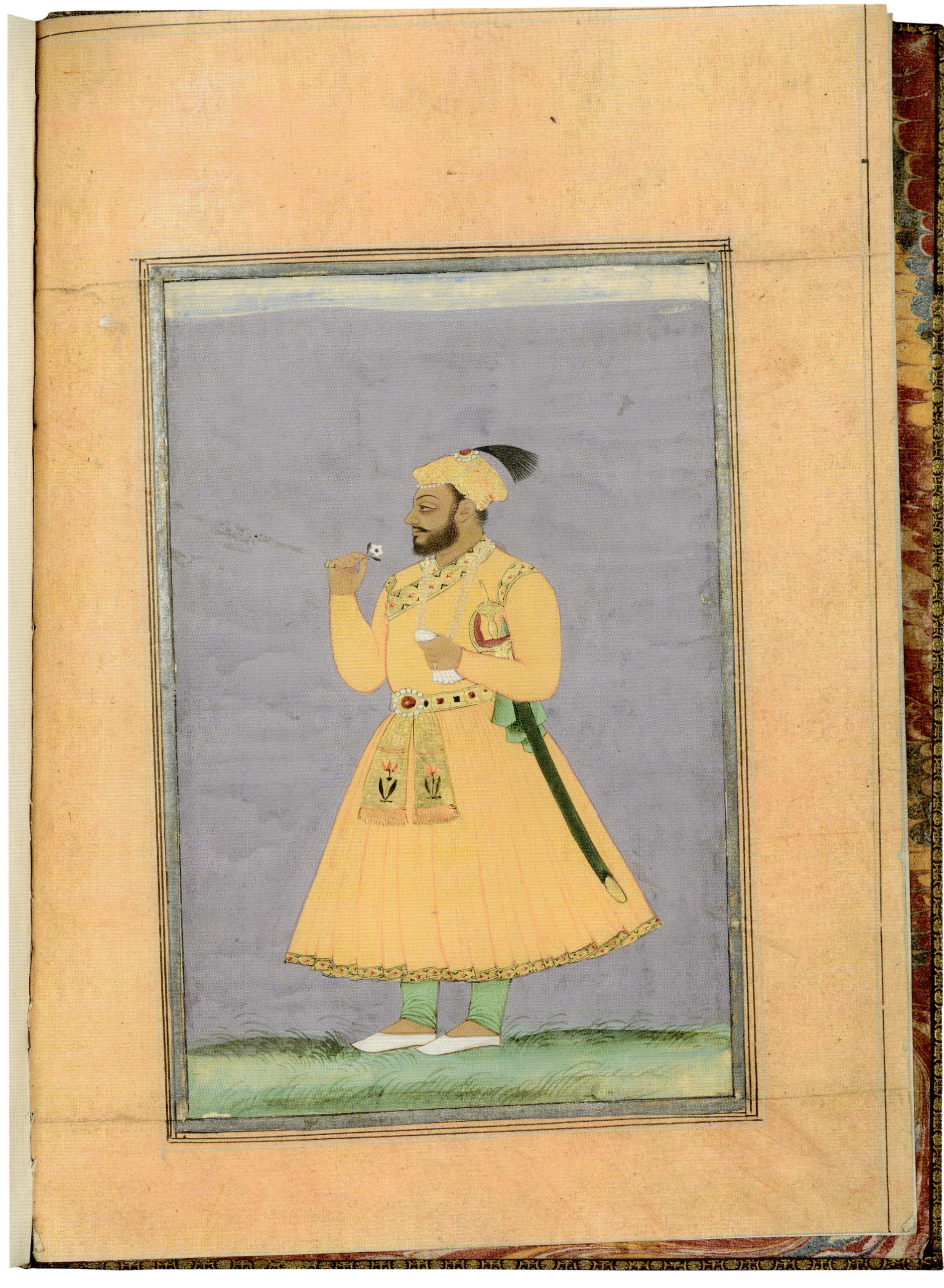

Ca 110/39

Cat. 3 | Ca 113

Album with 179 portraits of rulers from Rājā Yudhiṣṭhira to Aurangzēb
Deccani Mughal, c. 1680–1710
Album with 182 fols., Indian binding, 21.7 × 16.5 × c. 7.5 cm
Cover boards outside and inside decorated with watercolour paintings on paper, pasted on textile
179 single portraits, watercolour and gold, light rose paper borders attached, inscribed on verso in *devanāgarī*
Reference: Dresden 2017, cat. 19, pp. 158–61

Album Ca 113 consists of 48 standing and 76 seated portraits of Hindu rulers and 24 standing and 31 seated portraits of Muslim rulers of India, beginning on folio 125. The first portrait is of Rājā Yudhiṣṭhira (Ca 113/1), the eldest of the Pāṇḍavas from the Sanskrit epic *Mahābhārata,* and the last is of the aging Mughal Emperor Aurangzēb (r. 1658–1707). Astonishingly and rather delightfully portrayed are two Indian empresses, Rāṇī Prabhāvatī (d. 1303; fig. 5) and Rāzia Sultāna (r. 1236–1240; fig. 6). These paintings are mounted on album leaves without margins or a decorative outer border. They show a minimalistic approach towards any form of embellishment, which allows the viewer to focus on the subject. Painted in watercolour with a lavish use of gold, the sitters, both standing and seated, are seen in profile against a plain background, with a few horizontal brushstrokes of blue and green, symbolic of sky and ground. Each portrait occupies the central position on the page, composed using a simplified design of gold and accents of red, indigo, and Indian yellow for the costumes and accompanying props. The folios are to be viewed from right to left and begin with the name of the ruler in *nāgarī* script, a vernacular Sanskrit,[1] with a number at left.

The binding of the folios to protect them and for ease of viewing required the skills of numerous artists and craftsmen working together.[2] The album has typical chevron-patterned Islamic endbands, which were left undisturbed during the last restoration, and the spine shows signs of a modern backing. The boards are adorned with paintings on both sides that have a thin layer of varnish—perhaps an unfinished example of Islamic lacquer style in which the painting is varnished with various layers.[3] The outside of the front and back cover are decorated with a version of the same colourful scene of a princess listening to music on a pavilion surrounded by a hilly green background with trees and a small hut that is traversed by a stream sprinkled with red lotuses (figs. 1–2). The inside of the cover shows an allegory in the form of two painted images. The image at the beginning on the right-hand side shows a seated woman with an open book and an attendant with a *morchal* (peacock feather fan) in hand; continuing to the left, the same woman is shown holding a closed book, implying the end (figs. 3–4). The pale background is reminiscent of the recently published *Pair of Book Covers,* in leather, from the Deccan of about 1700.[4] Another example of Indian lacquer binding, in leather, made in the Persian style, can be seen in an album in the British Museum, *Hindu and Persian Miniatures and Penmanship.*[5] Depicting several episodes of a hunt, this album tells a story in successive actions. Perhaps Ca 113 was also intended to be in a similar lacquer binding but was never finished.

Comparable albums from the Victoria & Albert Museum, London, and the Bodleian Library, Oxford

Two other books of miniature paintings of Indian rulers are comparable to Ca 113. The first is in the Victoria & Albert Museum, London, and the other is in the Bodleian Library, Oxford.[6]

The V&A album, now in fragile condition, consists of 177[7] portraits on Indian paper in an eighteenth-century binding, with fly leaves of European paper. The album reads from right to left, with the first image being of Yudhiṣṭhira (fig. 7) and the last of Aurangzēb. The inscriptions on the folios state the name of the ruler portrayed and the duration of their reign (years, months, and days) in both *nasta'līq* (on top, in accordance with the *Hijra* calendar of Islam) and in English on bottom up to folio 12; from there to the end, there are only *nasta'līq* inscriptions. Inscriptions providing the same information are also found on the verso in *nāgarī.* The portraits are mostly in greens and reds with a slight use of gold and an outer frame in indigo. While the standing figures are shown with a plain background marked with blue and green brushstrokes indicating

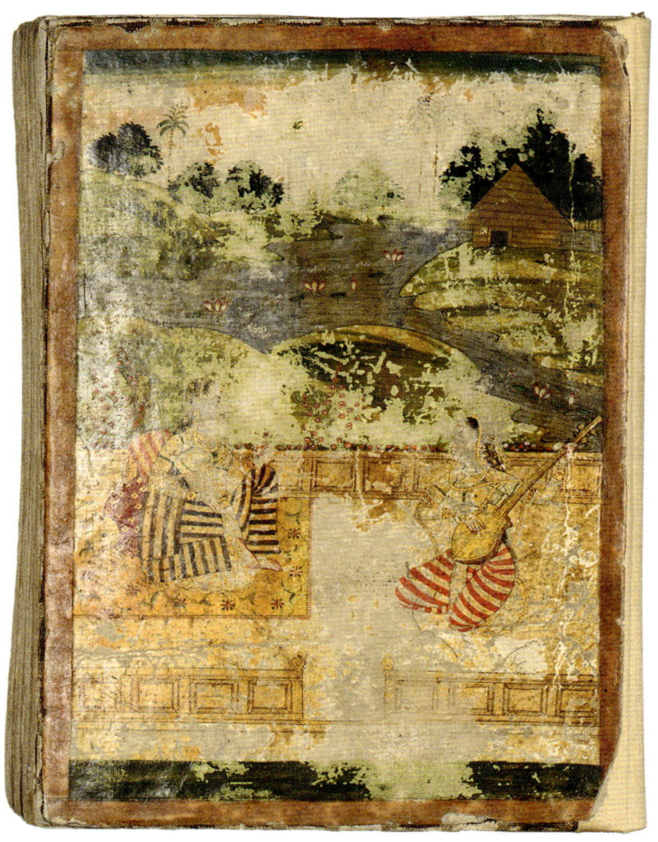

Fig. 1
Painting on back cover

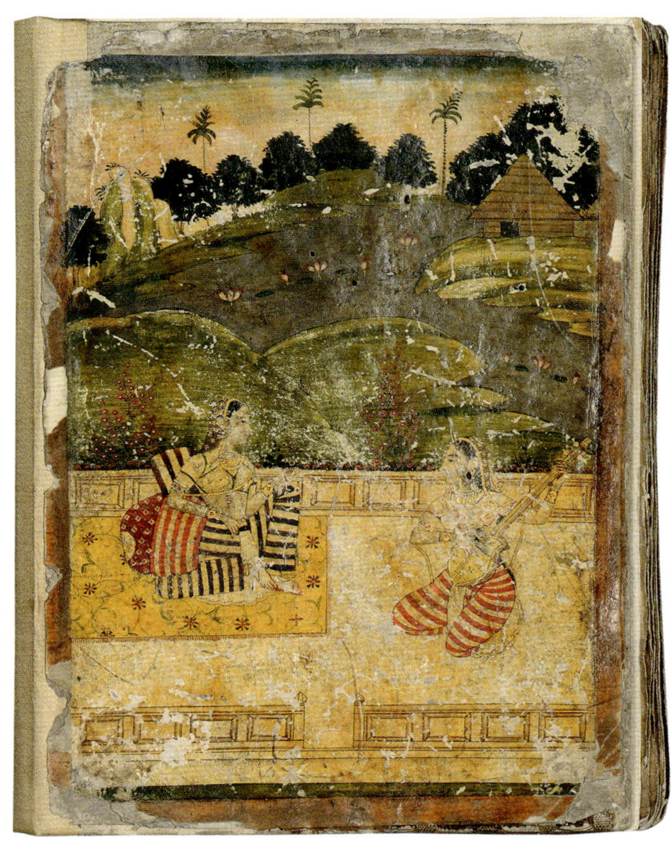

Fig. 2
Painting on front cover

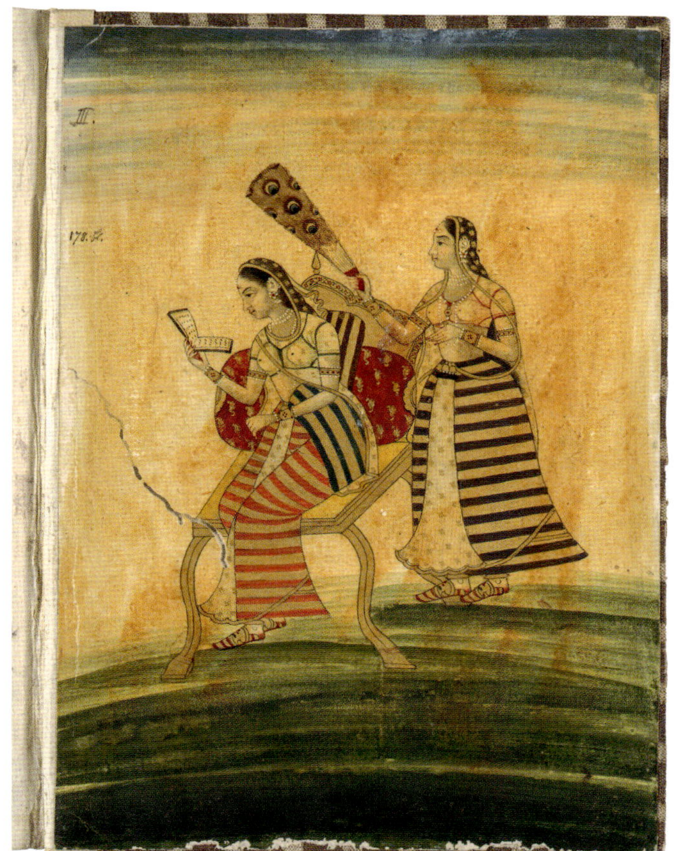

Fig. 3
Painting on back pastedown

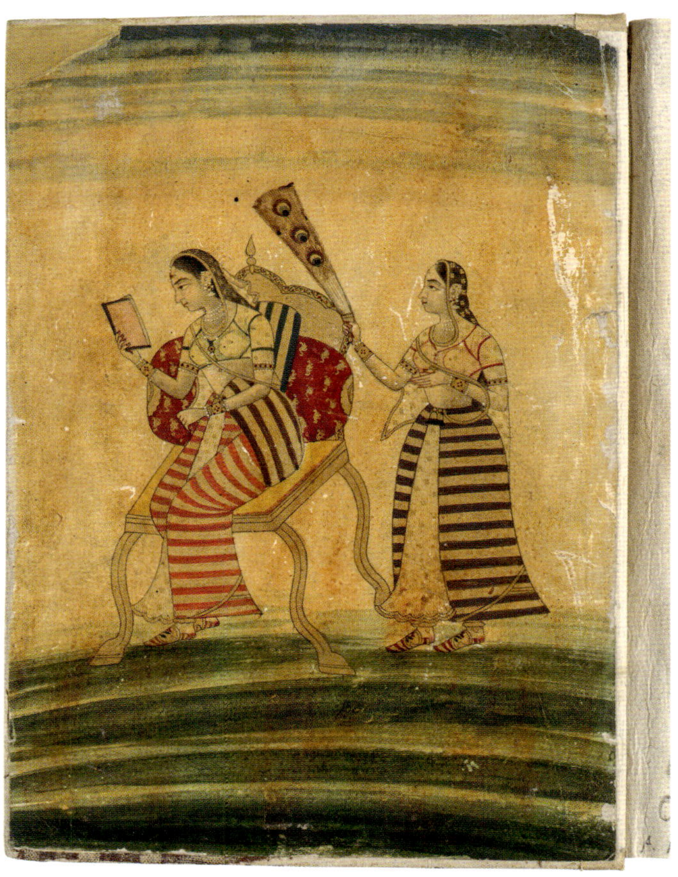

Fig. 4
Painting on front pastedown

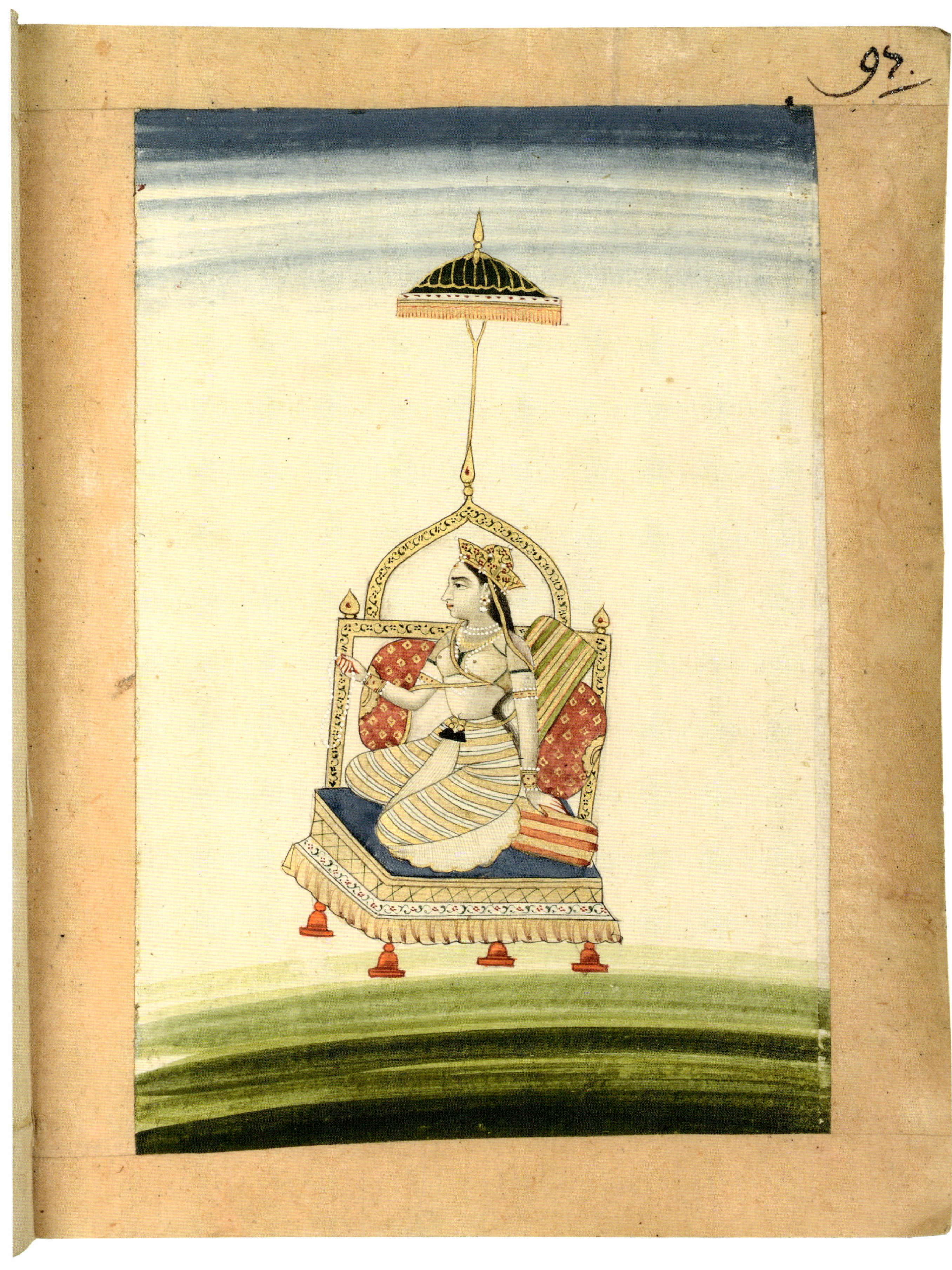

Fig. 5
Cat. 3 | Ca. 113/97
Rāṇī Prabhāvatī (d. 1303)

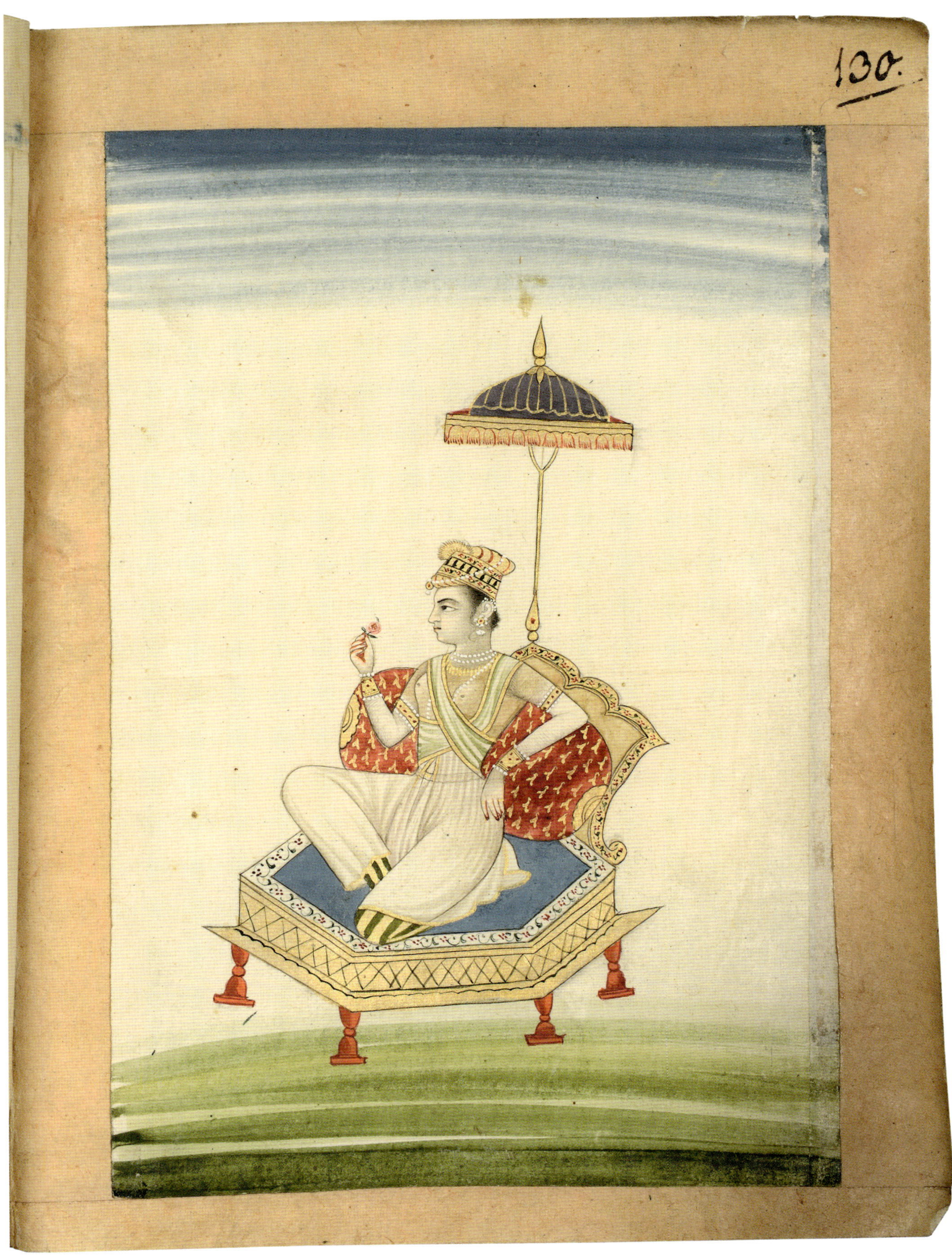

Fig. 6
Cat. 3 | Ca 113/130
Rāzia Sultāna (r. 1236–1240)

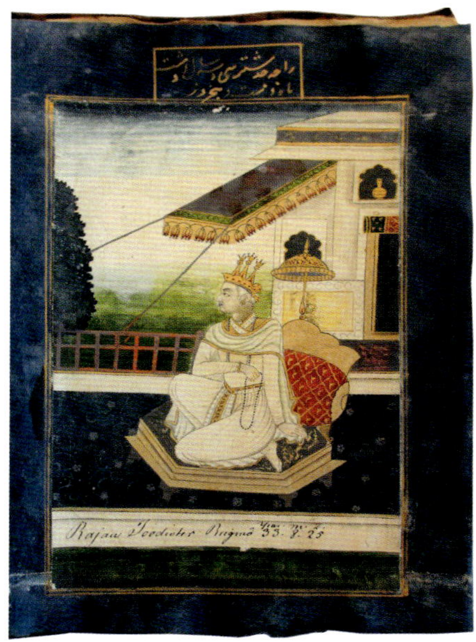

Fig. 7
Rājā Yudhiṣṭhira
Deccani Mughal, c. 1700s
Watercolour and gold, c. 18 × 11 cm
Inscribed at top centre in *nasta'līq*; and at bottom in English; verso in *nāgarī*
Victoria & Albert Museum, London, inv. no. I.M. 9-1912, fol. 1

sky and ground, the sitters are on red cushions or on a throne set against architectural pavilions and awnings with a floral arabesque carpet.

Aurangzēb's total reign is correctly given as fifty years, one month, and twenty-eight days—an indication that the set was produced after 1707, the year of the emperor's death. The end leaf bears the inscription "Lawrence Sulivan/1759," as the book was formerly in the possession of this director (1713–1786) of the East India Company.[8] This set is also mentioned in the file for the Earl and Countess of Carnwath, who are noted as having given the album to the museum in 1911. In this file, a note from the director Stanley Clarke reads, "This leather bound book (silver clasps) containing 177 illuminated tempera drawings of Rājput and Mughal rulers is probably from Kangra (or Chamba) in the Punjab, 18th century."[9]

Despite the convenient provenance, it is difficult to believe that this album was made in the hills of Punjab, Kangra, or even Chamba, especially because of the probable dating of its production.[10] On the other hand, it is possible that the other copy or copies of this set travelled with the first exodus of artists from Delhi to Basohli in 1680–1690, during the reign of Aurangzēb, whose puritanical zeal had dampened art activity in Delhi and even beyond in the hill states in Punjab and Jammu, where it could have been acquired.[11]

The Bodleian album contains 176 portraits[12] of Indian rulers on Indian paper, in a modern binding. The album reads from left to right, with the first image being of Rājā Yudhiṣṭhira (fig. 8) and the last of Aurangzēb. They are numbered from 1 to 178, though numbers 51 and 85 are missing, probably as the result of an accident during rebinding. The gold lettering, leather, and end bands are suggestive of a recent reconstruction, possibly even twentieth century.[13]

A letter attached to the Bodleian manuscript states that the set was procured by a "Banyan Merchant, Broker to the Dutch at Surat,"[14] who, upon his visit to the present residence of the great Mughal, took copies from the collection of original paintings preserved at the court.[15] If the great Mughal referred to here were Aurangzēb, it can be postulated that the earliest copies were made before 1681, when he moved his capital and residence to Aurangabad. With the death of this broker, the collection fell into an English gentleman's hands, even though Mīrzā Ghulām Muḥammad wanted to acquire it as a gift for the Marāthas.[16] The Banya merchant is probably Dayarām Ruidās, upon whose death in 1732 the album came into the hands of Tēg Beg Khān[17] through a Mughal general, camped with an army before the town of Surat, in return for a bribe, usually in the form of gifts, that he paid him in order to avoid too much scrutiny, as he was far from being on good terms with the court.[18] Tēg Beg Khān then presented the album to James Frazer (1712–1754), a collector of Oriental manuscripts and an East India Company official in Surat (1730–1740), who gave it to John Cleland (1710–1789),[19] who in turn sent it to the poet Alexander Pope,[20] who gave it to the Bodleian Library in 1737.[21]

Count Abate Giovanni Antonio Baldini (1654–1725) and the Collection of Nicolaas Witsen (1641–1717)

When Vasco da Gama arrived at Calicut in 1498, beginning the presence of Europeans in India,[22] interest in artefacts was primarily ethnographical rather than aesthetic, as still can be seen from the well-known collection of the German Jesuit Athanasius Kircher (1602–1680).[23] Information was dispersed from India through the medium of letters, travel narratives, and other printed literature that not only presented a picture of this other world in words but also through printed images, often belonging to private European collections.[24] One such important collection of manuscripts representing an interest in ethnography and the history of the Orient belonged to Count Abate Giovanni Antonio Baldini.[25] The fifth volume of the *Atlas historique* published by Henri Abraham Chatelain at Amsterdam in 1719 includes several Indian miniatures collected by Baldini and engraved by Bernard Picart, a French painter, as illustrations for an account of the Mughal Empire.[26]

Born in Piacenza, Italy, Baldini was in Amsterdam from 1712 to 1715 as an envoy of the duke of Parma to the peace conference in Utrecht, where he assembled a large collection of rarities. Now dispersed, Baldini's collection was catalogued by the famous Paduan naturalist Antonio Vallisnieri in his 1722 *Giornale dei letterati d'Italia.*[27] Item twenty-three in the catalogue is a book of fine miniatures on parchment brought from the East Indies containing 178 full-length figures of kings and queens who ruled in Indies for 4,753 years from Yudhiṣṭhira until 1702 when this book was made.[28] Vallisnieri writes that the book includes "on each portrait the duration of the government of the one portrayed, in Portuguese. The full-length portraits are 8 ¾ inches tall and represent all the kings who ruled for many centuries in the province of Kashmir."[29]

In a supplementary article of 1726 that Vallisnieri published in the form of a letter to P. D. Piercaterino Zeno,[30] he provided a chronological list of the rulers in Baldini's set along with the duration of their reign and an outline of the twenty-three[31] families. This list of Baldini's set gives Aurangzēb's total reign as forty-six years,[32] and accordingly this album can be dated about 1704. Vallisnieri owed this information to Nicolaas Witsen, director of the Dutch East India Company from 1693 onwards, and a well-known collector of ethnographic rarities who owned an almost identical book.[33]

While Vallisnieri was cataloguing Baldini's collection, he was in close contact with Witsen and either had a chance to look at the set owned by Witsen or received a detailed description of it. He wrote that the total years of rule represented in Witsen's album, which is said to be exactly the same as that of Baldini, is 4,909—that is, 156 more than the first calculation from Baldini's album.[34] However, he mentions that the difference is not a concern, as it is due to the addition of some non-Mughal kings in Witsen's book and other minor calculations of which Witsen was convinced after his discussion with Gottfried Wilhelm Leibniz (1646–1716) of the Royal Society, where he himself became a fellow in 1689.[35] This suggests that Witsen had the book in his possession when he visited London in 1689.

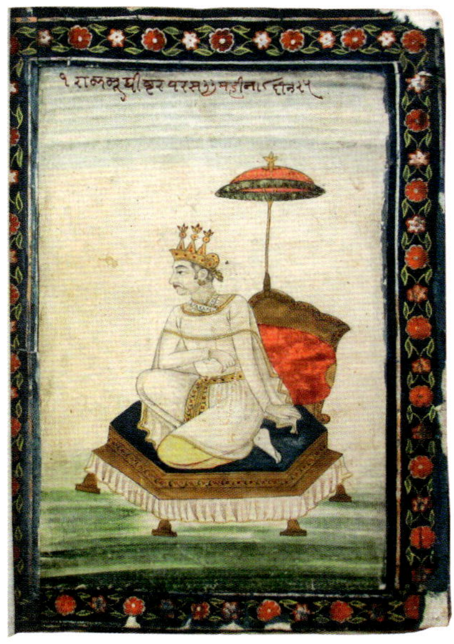

Fig. 8
Rājā Yudhiṣṭhira
Deccani Mughal, c. 1680s
Watercolour and gold, c. 18 × 11 cm
Inscribed at top in *nāgarī* and verso in *nāgarī* and English
Bodleian Library, Oxford, MS. Ind. Misc. d. 3, fol. 1

Origins and dating of Ca 113

Witsen's collection was sold at auction in Amsterdam on March 30, 1728, after his death.[36] In the sales catalogue, lot six is described as "Een Boek met 179 Mogolse Portraiten, zynde de voornaamste groote van't Hof, zeer konstig geschilderd" (A book with 179 Mogul portraits of the great men of the court, painted very artistically).[37]

Ca 113 is similar in content and form to the Baldini and Witsen sets. Could it be from a now-dispersed album that belonged to one of these collectors? While the possibility of Ca 113 having belonged to Baldini is negated by the fact that Ca 113 has 179 portraits while Baldini's album had 178, a connection with Witsen's collection is established through other Indian miniature painting albums and non-Indian albums that were acquired for the Saxon Court at the Witsen auction.[38] The number of portraits in Witsen's set, 179, matches Ca 113. What confirms the fact that the same set belonged to Witsen is the mention of "n. 6" in the Heucher Inventory, where item 20 reads, "179 Mogolische Portraits. n. 6." This is the same numbering found in the 1728 Witsen auction catalogue. There is, however, one significant difference between Baldini's and Witsen's sets and Ca 113, as mentioned by Vallisnieri—the duration of the reigns in both of their sets is entirely missing in Ca 113. In this case, the only possibility is that Witsen owned more than one such album. Therefore, although Ca 113 did belong to Witsen and is the same album that was sold at his auction, it is not the same set mentioned by Vallisnieri. There is no probability of an error in cataloguing by Vallisnieri, as he not only records that both Baldini's and Witsen's sets were inscribed with the years of reign on the rulers' portraits, and he also provides the difference between the total years of rule as 256 years ([sic] correct difference 156 years). The fact that the duration of government along with the names of the rulers are not inscribed in Ca 113 whereas it apparently existed in the Witsen's set mentioned by Vallisnieri therefore suggests that he might have had another copy or copies of this 179 Indian miniature portrait sets as was the case with other parts of his collections.[39]

What remains to be deduced is the possible timeline within which the Dresden set could have been produced. The V&A set correctly states Aurangzēb's total reign as fifty years (on the portrait and on the verso),[40] a certain indication of the production of this set after 1707, the year of the emperor's death. According to letters found with the Bodleian album, it could date as early as 1681, thereby proving that similar sets might have been in production as early as Ca 113. In Baldini's set Aurangzēb's total reign is given incorrectly as forty six years, resulting in a dating of 1704 for the set. Therefore, Ca 113 ending with a portrait of the white bearded Aurangzēb, can be dated about 1680s–1710.

Standard series of ruler's portraits collected at turn of the seventeeth century ran from Tīmūr to Aurangzēb, sometimes even up to Farrukh Sīyar.[41] Far more extensive Ca 113, belonging to the 'second type', represents the kings and queens of twenty-two families that are said to have ruled in India since legendary times surely was much sought after. While some of the known sets might have been commissioned by Dayarām Ruidās after the original in the Mughal Palace,[42] it is possible that others continued to be copied, as in the case of the V&A album, which dates after the death of Aurangzēb. Of the five sets of some 179 portraits of Indian rulers, the Bodleian set was acquired in Surat and the V&A set from the Punjab Hills. This suggests that artworks were not confined to their place of production or even produced in a specific city at that time. In the environment within which these sets were made, the artist who produced an earlier copy might have continued to produce another one or two as he travelled, looking for a buyer. Or a set might have been made by a different artist who had witnessed, or contributed to, the production of an earlier set. These sets of portraits, once owned by well-known collectors and now in important public collections, become a window through which we can look at the spectacular process of reproduction, exchange, and collection of Mughal and related art that found its way to Europe in increasing numbers beginning in the mid-seventeenth century. NB

Notes | 1 Information regarding the script and the language inscribed in Ca 113 as well as the Bodleian Manuscript (MS. Ind. Misc. d. 3) was kindly provided by Dr. Camillo A. Formigatti, John Clay Sanskrit Librarian, Bodleian Library, Oxford. | 2 Wright 2008, p. 42. | 3 I would like to thank Kristine Rose Beers, senior conservator at the Chester Beatty Library, Dublin, for help with the description of the binding. | 4 Haidar/Sardar 2015, cat. 58, p. 138. | 5 British Museum, London, inv. no. 1974,0617,0.10. For image see URL: www.britishmuseum.org/research/collection_online/collection_object_details.aspx?objectId=3398867&partId=1&searchText=+Hindu+and+Persian+Miniatures+and+Penmanship&page=1 (8. 11. 2017). | 6 Inv. nos. IM9-1912 and MS. Ind. Misc. d. 3. | 7 The number of portraits in (inv. no. IM9-1912) is incorrectly listed as 178 in Lightbown 1969, p. 278; and Lunsingh Scheurleer 1996, p. 174. | 8 As published in Brooke 1964, pp. 508–9. Lawrence Sulivan (c. 1713–1786) served as assistant to the governor of Bengal in 1740, till he took a seat on the Bombay Council in 1751 and was elected director of the East India Company in 1755. | 9 My gratitude to Anita Nathwani, Assistant Curator, South and South East Asia, Victoria & Albert Museum, for sharing this information mentioned in 1886–1946 archive of V&A (Ref. MA, 1, C 491), in the nominal file for the Earl and Countess of Carnwath who is noted as depositing the album to the museum. | 10 The earliest works from Kangra date from about 1750 onwards; see Randhawa 1960, p. 34. | 11 See ibid. | 12 The number of portraits in MS. Ind. Misc. d. 3 is incorrectly listed as 158 in Topsfield 2008, p. 10. | 13 Information provided by Kristine Rose Beers, Senior Conservator, Chester Beatty Library, Dublin. | 14 Surat was the principal Indian port at the turn of the eighteenth century; the Dutch and the English had been there for a century and become part of the traditional structure of trade. Trade was conducted by arrangement with merchants who needed the help of a broker whose job it was to put the customer in touch with the seller—no matter what the transaction, the foreign traders needed them more than the local ones. The Head of Customs in Surat and Cambay (*mutasaddī*) was a direct imperial appointee and had agents at the imperial court; see Das Gupta 1979, p. 25. Surat's decline was simultaneous with the weakening and collapse of the three great Mughal empires after Aurangzēb's death. Markets were poor, squabbling families of merchants having ruined them before the fast-declining city. After the death in 1726 of Rakṣikadās Kissendās, from the clan of Kissendās Sunderdās, broker to the Dutch at Surat in 1660s, the family of Ruidās replaced the Kissendās as broker to the East India Company in Surat; ibid., pp. 170–4. Two brothers, Dayarām and Ruderām, became brokers to the Dutch. Dayarām was mortally wounded on July 15, 1732, during a revolt of the Surat merchants against the governor Zohrab Khān; ibid., pp. 226–7. On July 22, 1732, the English and the Dutch approached Tēg Beg Khān (d. 1746). With the military support provided by the Marātha commander Deojī Rāo, Tēg Beg Khān announced the cessation of hostilities, and the twenty-seven-day war in Surat was over on July 29, 1732, with him assuming the governorship on August 10, 1732. He remained governor until his death in 1746, ibid., pp. 224–9. Dismissing the designation of *mutasaddi*, Tēg Beg Khān instead styled himself as the *nawāb*. (Satish Chandra describes the term *nawāb* as a title of rank, such as viceroy or governor); see Medieval India, part II, Delhi, 1999, p. 533. The administration of the town became a family affair, with his brother Begler Beg Khān as the *qilādār* (commander of the castle) and his brother Mīrzā Ghulām Muḥammad, later styled as Safdār Khān, charged with managing financial and administrative affairs. (*Surat District Gazetteer*); see Ahmedabad 1962, pp. 141–4. | 15 Similar mention is made in Vallisnieri 1722, p. 130, where he writes that the originals were in the royal palace of Agra. | 16 MS. Ind. misc. d. 3, Bodleian, p. marked as "v" on top. | 17 See Das Gupta 1979, pp. 220–1. He writes that even though Tēg Beg Khān's governorship in Surat lasted only a few months (1728–1729), it was followed by a growth in power and status from 1732 onwards. | 18 Cleland to Mr. Everard, top right (in pencil) as "1", pp. 1–2. | 19 John Cleland was an East India Company official who lived in Bombay from 1728 to 1740. His father, William Cleland, was a friend of Alexander Pope, and is sometimes addressed in his literary works. | 20 Alexander Pope (1688–1744) was born in London. He was a precocious poet, and his works such as the translation of the *Illiad* (1715–1720) and the *Odyssey* (1725–1726) are well known. In 1717 his works confirmed his position as the major living English poet. Many of his original translations are now in the Bodleian Library. | 21 Cleland to Mr. Everard. Ms. Ind. misc. d. 3, Bodleian, p. 2. | 22 See Falk/Archer 1981. | 23 See Kircher 1667. | 24 See Tavernier 1681; and Bernier 1699. | 25 Count Giovanni Antonio Baldini's (1654–1725) biography, written by Marchese Ubertino Landi (1687–1760) in 1726, describes the enthusiasm with which he collected Indian and Far Eastern objects. | 26 Chatelain 1726. The plates after Baldini's miniatures are found following pp. 100, 114, and 116. For other Indian miniatures, see Valentijn 1726, which includes plates from the collection of the Amsterdam architect Simon Schijnvoet (1652–1727) after page 264. | 27 Vallisnieri 1722, pp. 130–3. Part of Baldini's catalogue was translated and reproduced in Lightbown 1969. | 28 See ibid; and Lightbown 1969, p. 278. | 29 Ibid. | 30 Vallisnieri 1726, pp. 337–76. | 31 Lightbown 1969, p. 278 lists twenty-two families, though there are twenty-three in the original list. | 32 Vallisnieri 1726, p. 345. | 33 Vallisnieri 1722, pp. 131–3. | 34 Ibid., p. 132, incorrectly calculates 256 years of difference. | 35 Vallisnieri 1722, pp. 132–3. Gottfried Wilhelm Leibniz (1646–1716) was a German polymath and philosopher who travelled in 1673 to London, where he met members of the Royal Society and introduced his calculating machine. As a collector interested in arts and sciences, Witsen is known to have maintained contacts with German scholars and might also have met Leibniz. | 36 Peters 2010. | 37 Amsterdam 1728, p. 10. | 38 Ibid. | 39 Peters 1994, pp. 1–49. | 40 A comparison of the inscription on the portrait with the one on the verso was necessary, as in the Bodleian set; discrepancies have been noticed between the two. This could be due to the addition of the inscriptions on the verso either by a different hand or when it arrived in a certain hand. While finding similar inscriptions on the portrait confirms that the images were painted and inscribed at the same time. | 41 Subrahmanyam 2012, p. 201. | 42 See note 14–5. | 43–52 See Huntington 1984, p. 37, 61–64, 93; referring to pp. 102–6.

* Folios counted from right to left but shown here from left to right. Sitters mentioned on verso in *devanāgarī* which could not be related to a historical or legendary name are titled as "Unidentified". See also Appendices, p. 246–51.

Ca 113/1
Rājā Yudhiṣṭhira
18.1 × 11.9 cm
Verso inscr. (Sanskrit): rājā judhiṣṭara

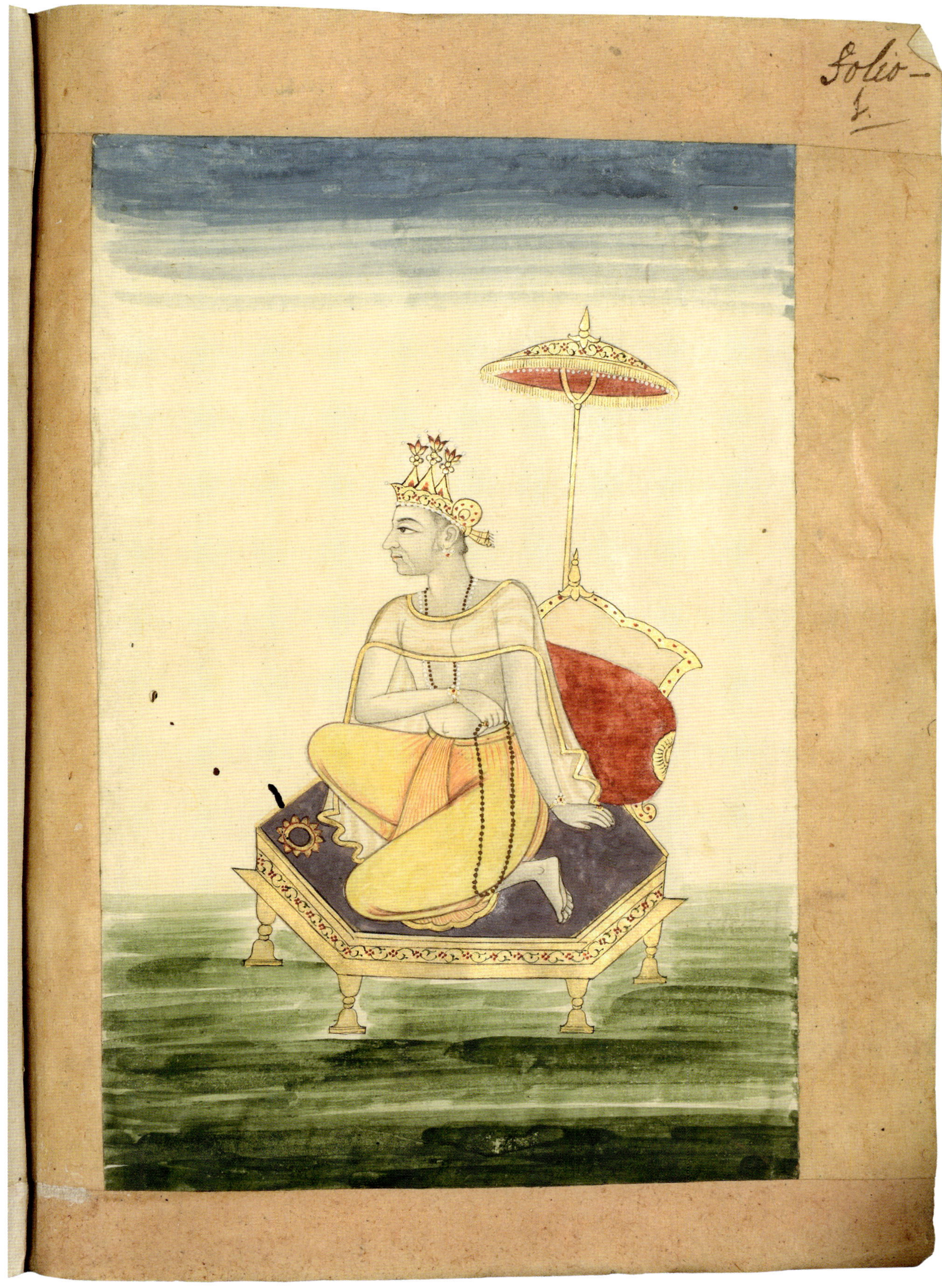

Ca 113/1

Ca 113/2
Parikṣit II
18.4 × 11.5 cm
Inscribed verso (*devanāgarī*): parīchata

Ca 113/3
Janamejaya III
18.9 × 11.5 cm
Inscribed verso (*devanāgarī*): janmejaya

Ca 113/4
Aśvatthāman
18.9 × 11.4 cm
Inscribed verso (*devanāgarī*): asvamedhā

Ca 113/5
Unidentified
18.7 × 11.6 cm
Inscribed verso (*devanāgarī*): rājā ādhīna

Ca 113/6
Unidentified
18.9 × 11.9 cm
Inscribed verso (*devanāgarī*): maṇjalāpa

Ca 113/7
Unidentified
19.2 × 11.7 cm
Inscribed verso (*devanāgarī*): chatraratha

Ca 113/8
Unidentified
18.3 × 11.7 cm
Inscribed verso (*devanāgarī*): dīpapāla

Ca 113/9
Unidentified
18.3 × 11.7 cm
Inscribed verso (*devanāgarī*): ugrasaina

Ca 113/10
Unidentified
18 × 11.6 cm
Inscribed verso (*devanāgarī*): sūrasaina

Ca 113/11
Unidentified
17.6 × 11.9 cm
Inscribed verso (*devanāgarī*): śrīpata

Ca 113/12
Unidentified
17.7 × 11.6 cm
Inscribed verso (*devanāgarī*): *anajaya*

Ca 113/13
Unidentified
18.4 × 12 cm
Inscribed verso (*devanāgarī*): rājā sarajaga

Ca 113/14
Unidentified
17.7 × 11.9 cm
Inscribed verso (*devanāgarī*): suṣitapāla

Ca 113/15
Unidentified
18.1 × 11.5 cm
Inscribed verso (*devanāgarī*): harada-urāma

Ca 113/16
Unidentified
18.6 × 12 cm
Inscribed verso (*devanāgarī*): sūrajaratha

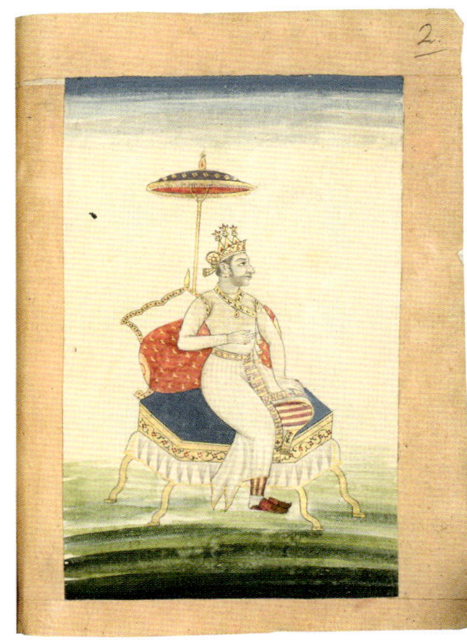

Ca 113/2

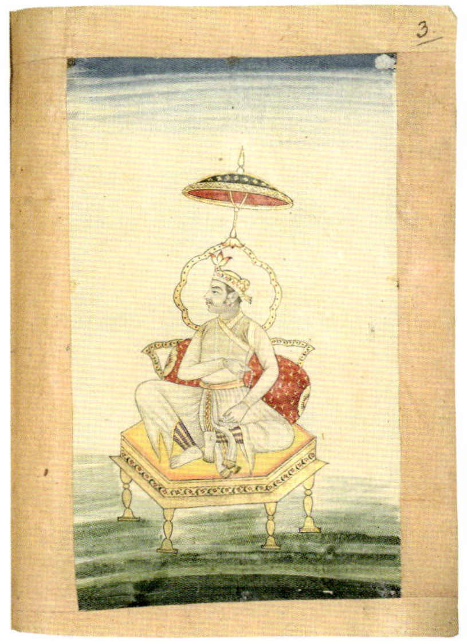

Ca 113/3

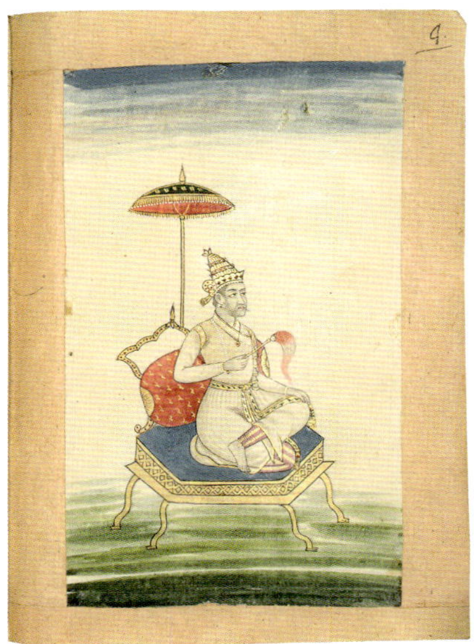

Ca 113/4

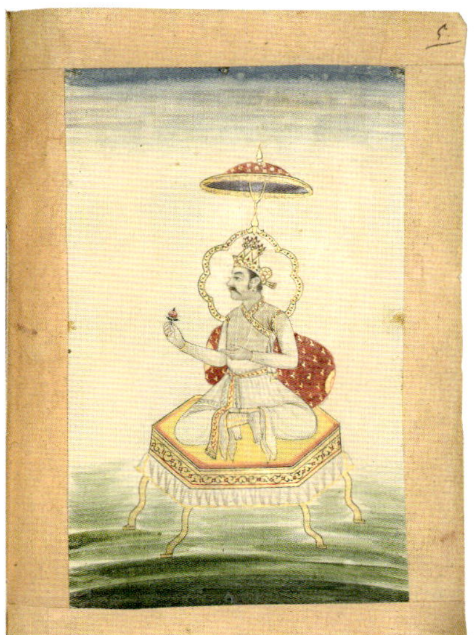

Ca 113/5

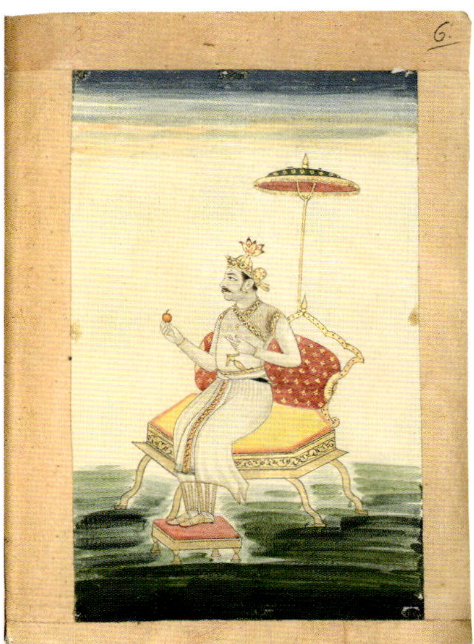

Ca 113/6

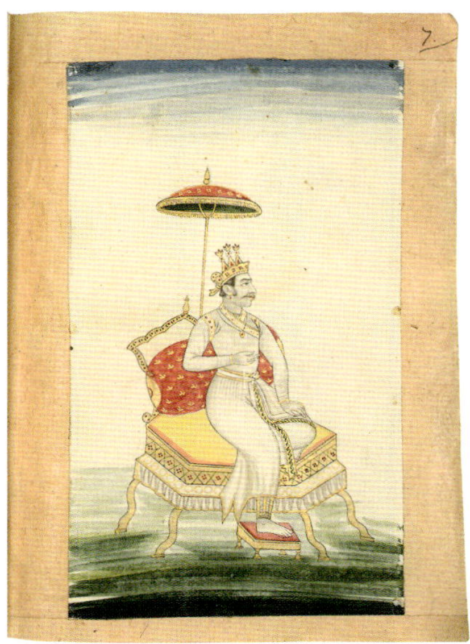

Ca 113/7

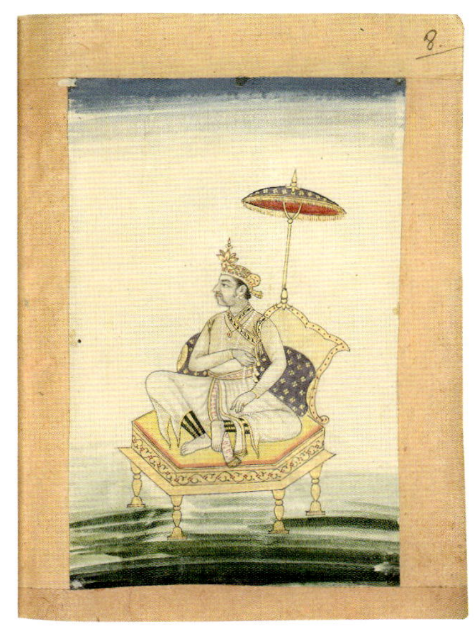

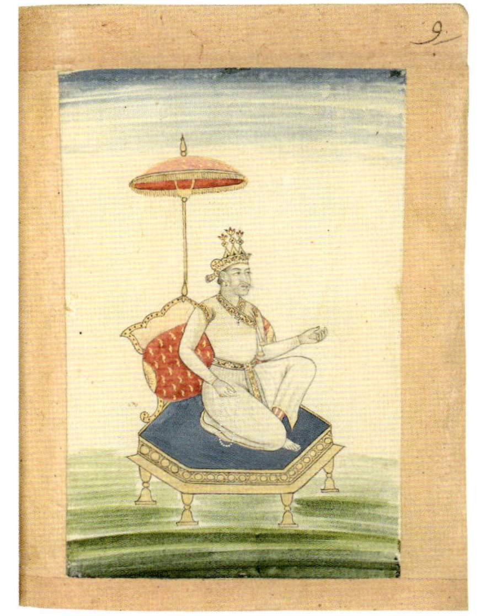

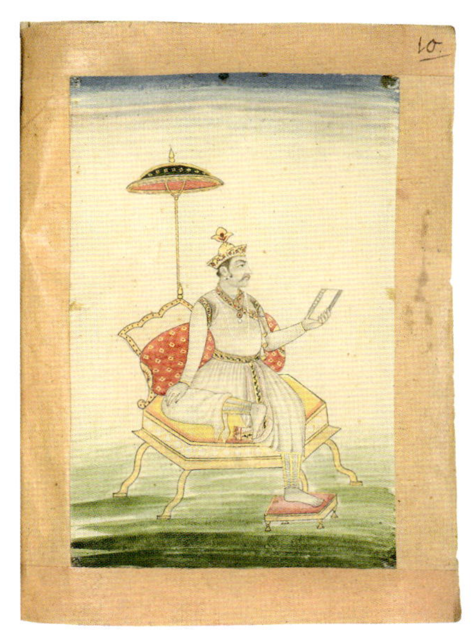

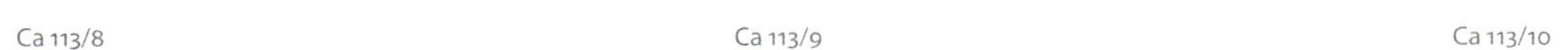

Ca 113/8

Ca 113/9

Ca 113/10

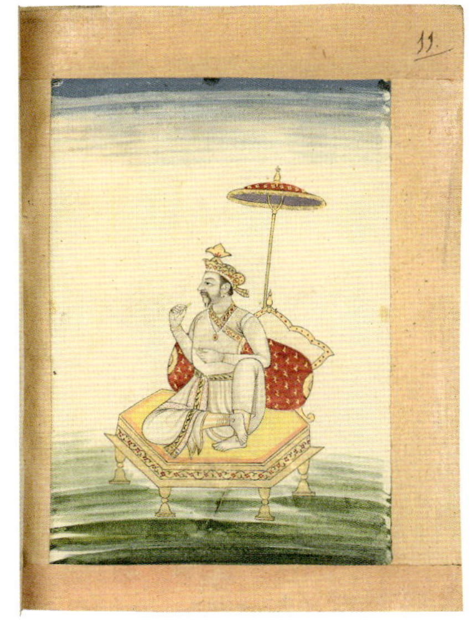

Ca 113/11

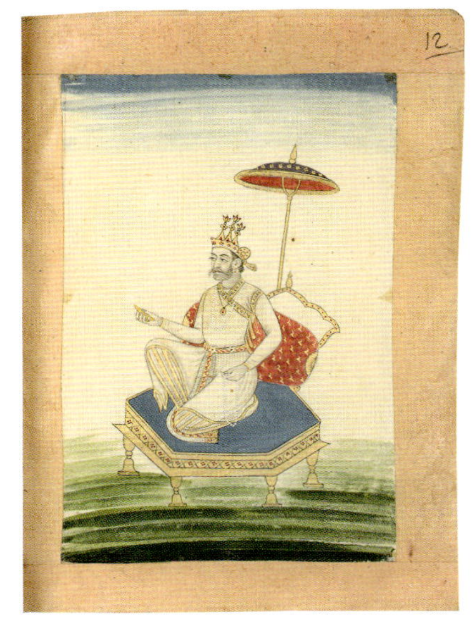

Ca 113/12

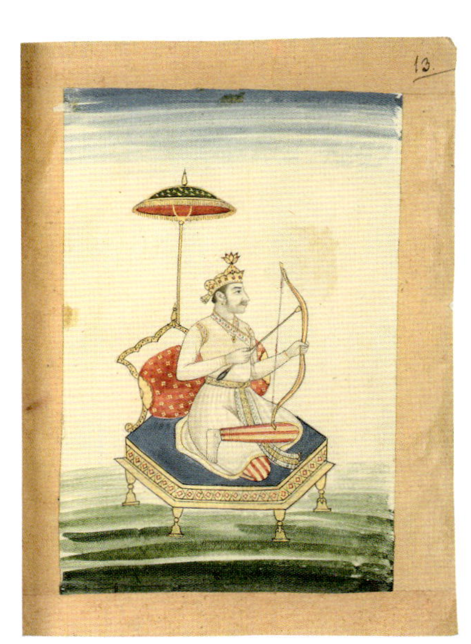

Ca 113/13

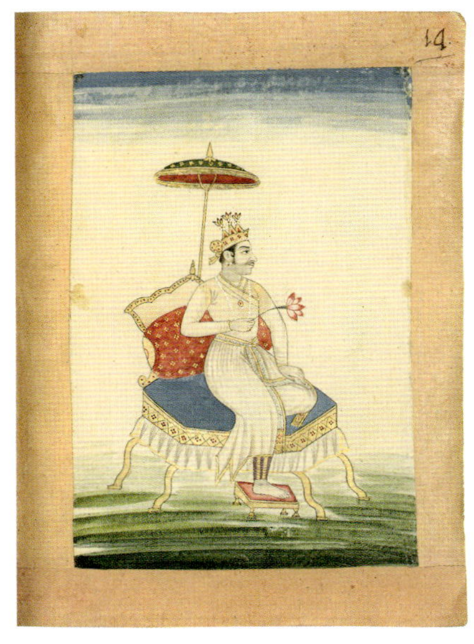

Ca 113/14

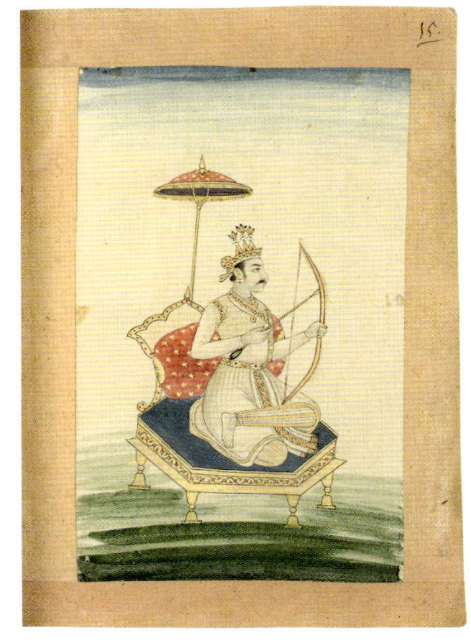

Ca 113/15

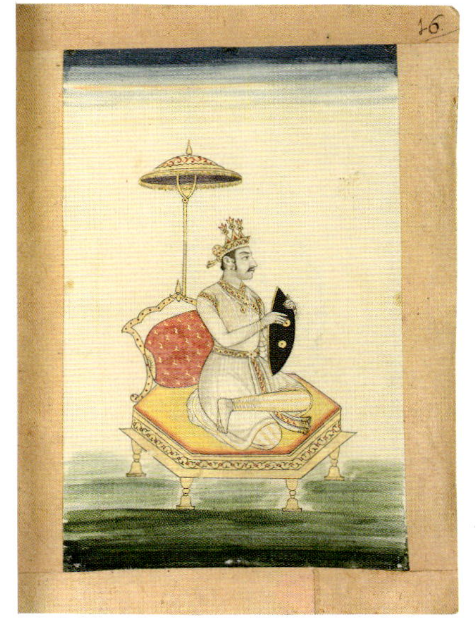

Ca 113/16

Ca 113/17
Unidentified
18.7 × 11.8 cm
Inscribed verso (*devanāgarī*): lokapāla

Ca 113/18
Rājā Śāntanu
18 × 11.8 cm
Inscribed verso (*devanāgarī*): rājā sutana

Ca 113/19
Unidentified
18 × 11.8 cm
Inscribed verso (*devanāgarī*): mādhavasaina

Ca 113/20
Unidentified
18.2 × 11.7 cm
Inscribed verso (*devanāgarī*): subhabhañjana

Ca 113/21
Bhīṣma
18.2 × 11.8 cm
Inscribed verso (*devanāgarī*): bhīṣama

Ca 113/22
Bharata
18.2 × 11.7 cm
Inscribed verso (*devanāgarī*): bhartha

Ca 113/23
Unidentified
18.2 × 11.6 cm
Inscribed verso (*devanāgarī*): rājā pūrana

Ca 113/24
Unidentified
18.2 × 11.6 cm
Inscribed verso (*devanāgarī*): rājā adalī

Ca 113/25
Unidentified
18.1 × 11.9 cm
Inscribed verso (*devanāgarī*): rājā dhannīdhara

Ca 113/26
Unidentified
18 × 11.8 cm
Inscribed verso (*devanāgarī*): ḍhaṇḍhapāla

Ca 113/27
Unidentified
19.1 × 11.8 cm
Inscribed verso (*devanāgarī*): rājā durvalarāi

Ca 113/28
Unidentified
17.9 × 11.7 cm
Inscribed verso (*devanāgarī*): sīrīnāga

Ca 113/29
Unidentified
18.4 × 11.7 cm
Inscribed verso (*devanāgarī*): rājā ṣema

Ca 113/30
Unidentified
18.6 × 11.9 cm
Inscribed verso (*devanāgarī*): laṣamana

Ca 113/31
Unidentified
18.3 × 12 cm
Inscribed verso (*devanāgarī*): visnusaravā

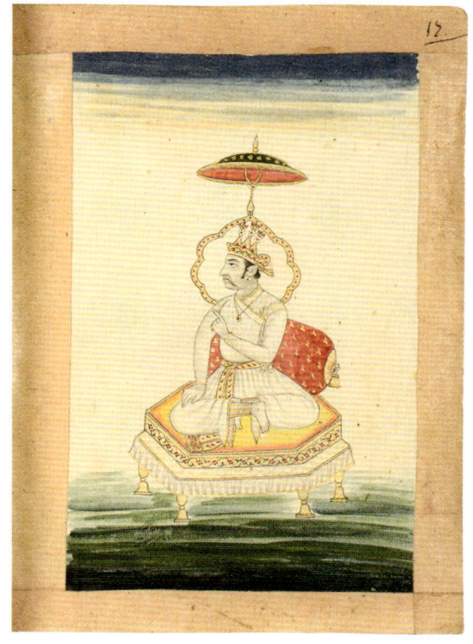

Ca 113/17

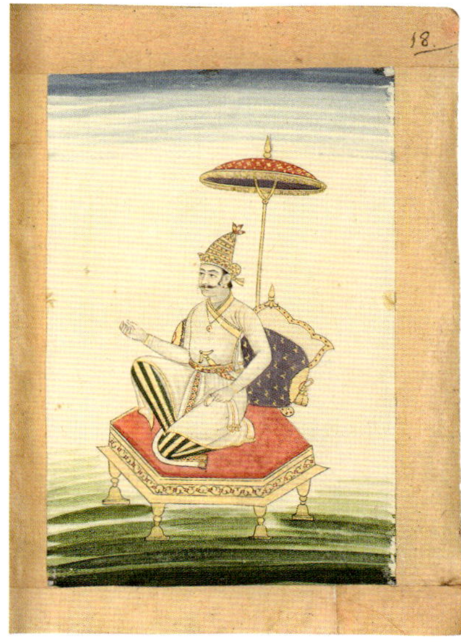

Ca 113/18

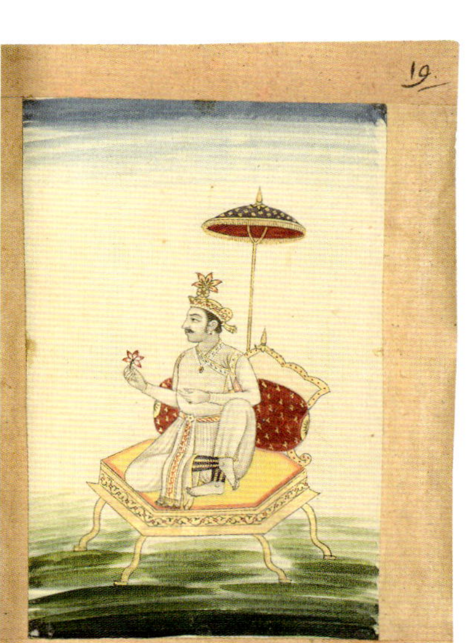

Ca 113/19

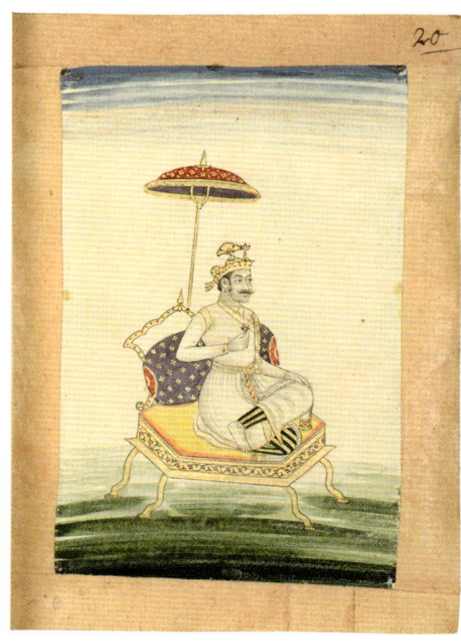

Ca 113/20

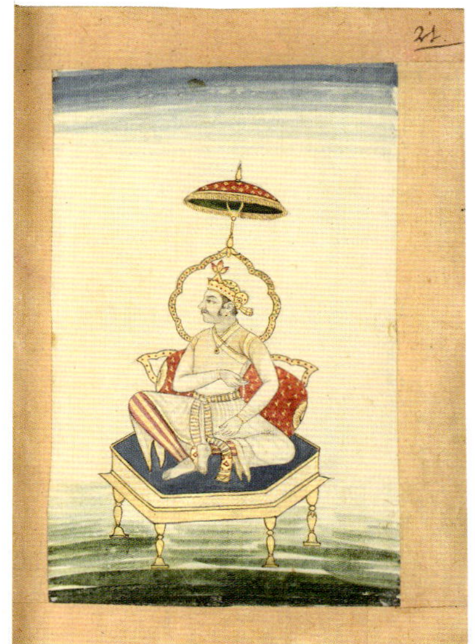

Ca 113/21

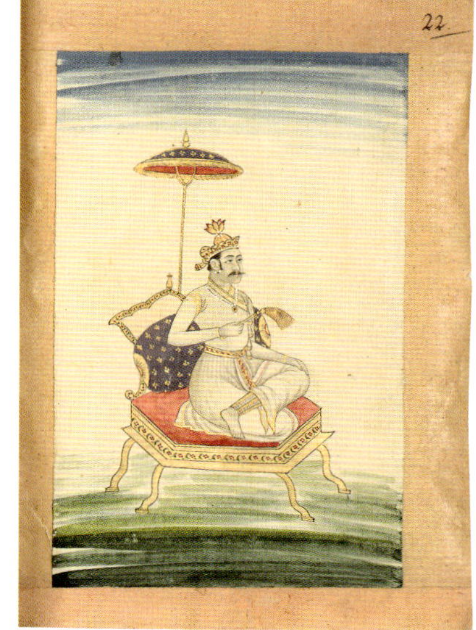

Ca 113/22

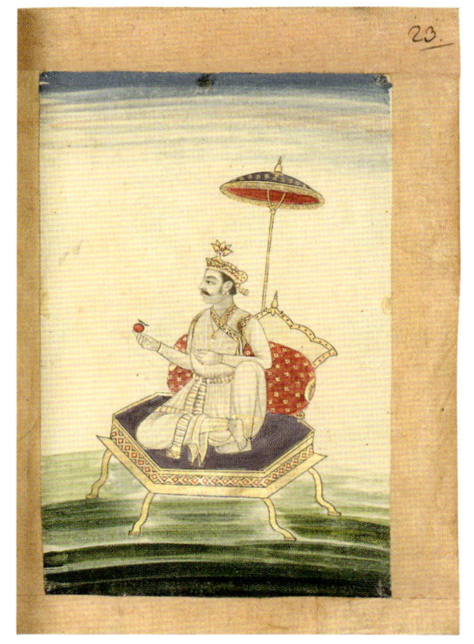

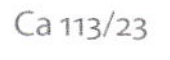
Ca 113/23

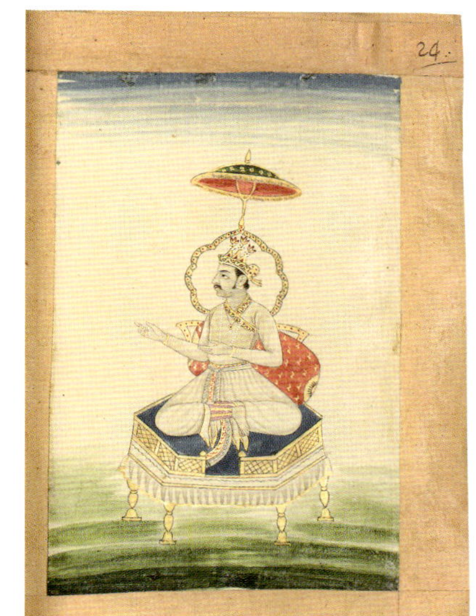

Ca 113/24

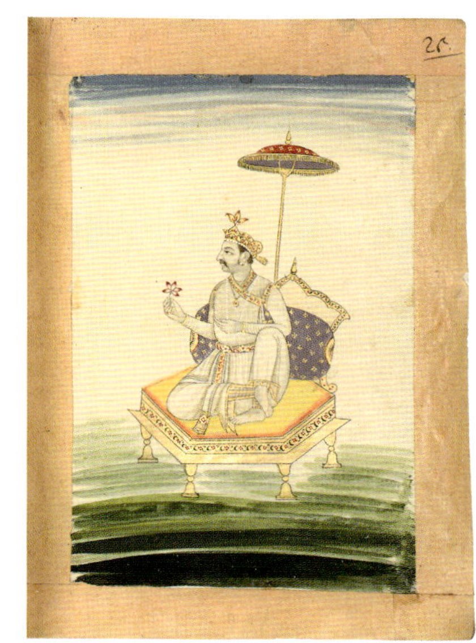

Ca 113/25

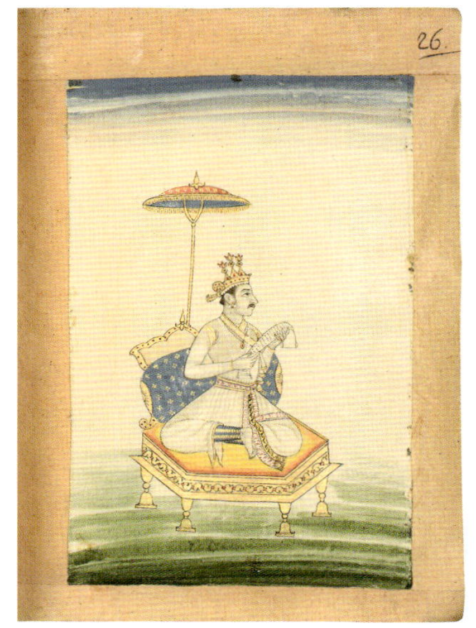

Ca 113/26

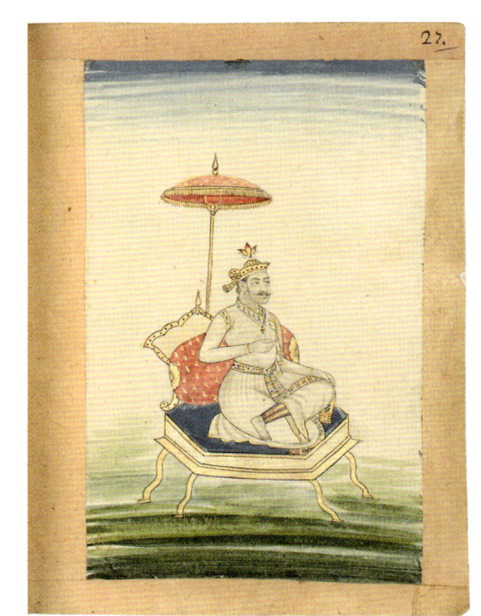

Ca 113/27

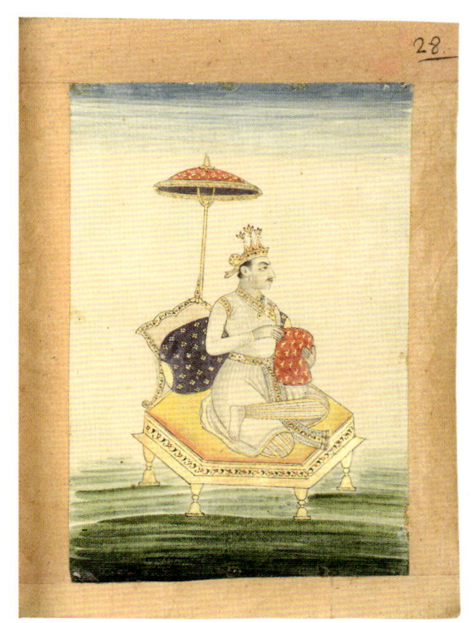

Ca 113/28

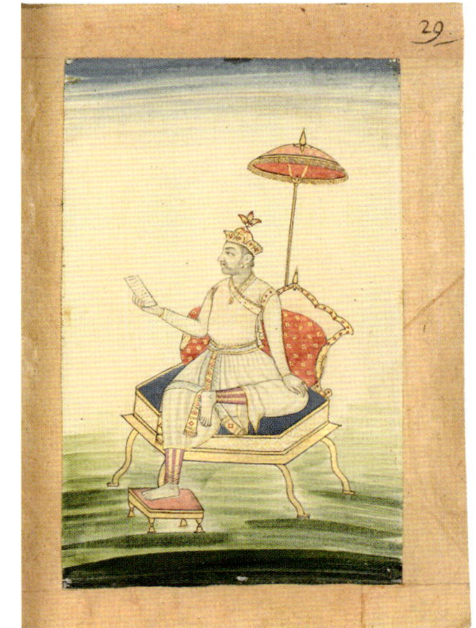

Ca 113/29

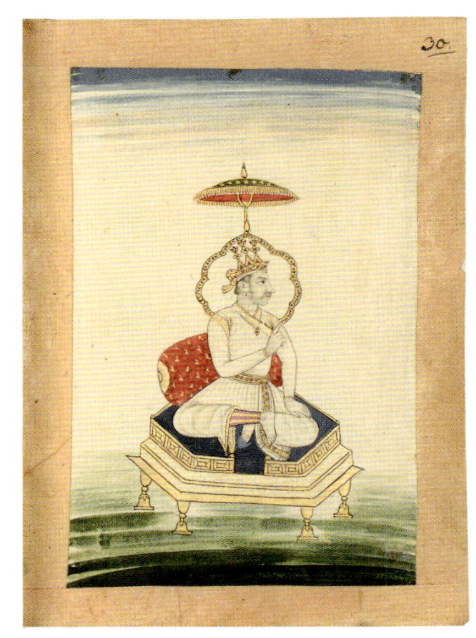

Ca 113/30

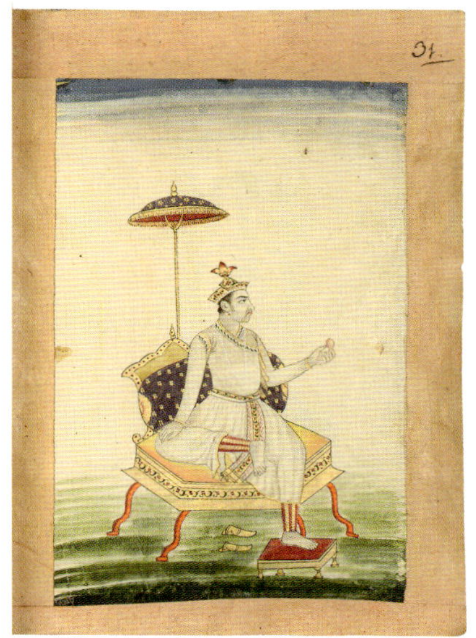

Ca 113/31

Ca 113/32
Unidentified
19.1 × 11.7 cm
Inscribed verso (*devanāgarī*): sūrajasaina

Ca 113/33
Unidentified
17.7 × 11.7 cm
Inscribed verso (*devanāgarī*): vīrasāha

Ca 113/34
Unidentified
18.2 × 11.7 cm
Inscribed verso (*devanāgarī*): tavaisāha

Ca 113/35
Unidentified
18 × 11.7 cm
Inscribed verso (*devanāgarī*): vīrajīta

Ca 113/36
Unidentified
17.6 × 12 cm
Inscribed verso (*devanāgarī*): duratha

Ca 113/37
Unidentified
17.7 × 12 cm
Inscribed verso (*devanāgarī*): siddhapāla

Ca 113/38
Unidentified
17.7 × 11.5 cm
Inscribed verso (*devanāgarī*): rājā punīta

Ca 113/39
Unidentified
17.7 × 11.9 cm
Inscribed verso (*devanāgarī*): rājā vijai

Ca 113/40
Unidentified
17.8 × 11.4 cm
Inscribed verso (*devanāgarī*): amarajodha

Ca 113/41
Unidentified
18.2 × 11.6 cm
Inscribed verso (*devanāgarī*): amīpāla

Ca 113/42
Unidentified
18.2 × 12.1 cm
Inscribed verso (*devanāgarī*): rājā sarohī

Ca 113/43
Unidentified
17.9 × 11.7 cm
Inscribed verso (*devanāgarī*): rājā padāratha

Ca 113/44
Unidentified
18.1 × 11.8 cm
Inscribed verso (*devanāgarī*): paravalasaina

Ca 113/45
Unidentified
18 × 11.8 cm
Inscribed verso (*devanāgarī*): rājā sarapā

Ca 113/46
Unidentified
18.4 × 11.8 cm
Inscribed verso (*devanāgarī*): rājā jurātasuṣa

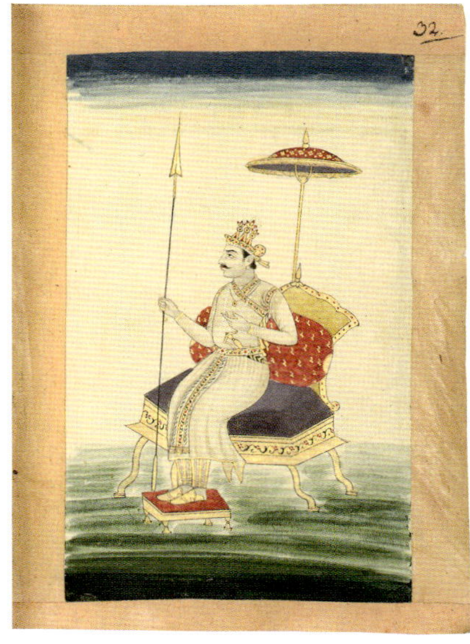

Ca 113/32

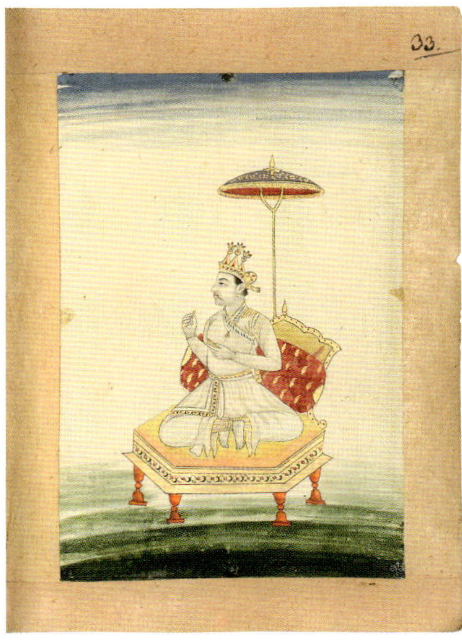

Ca 113/33

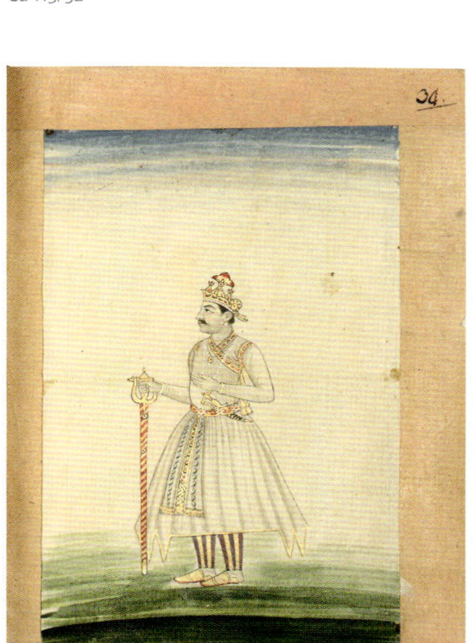

Ca 113/34

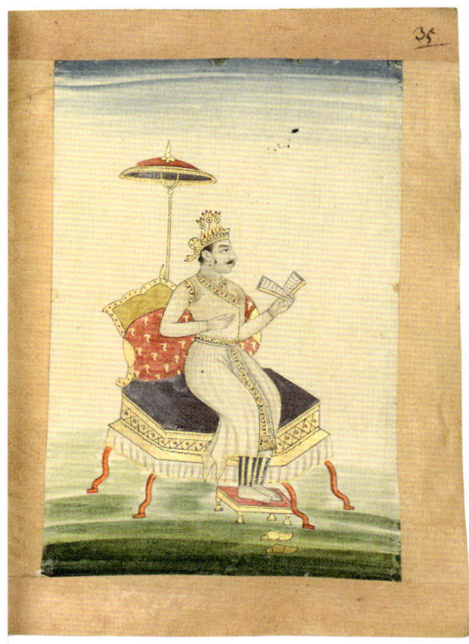
Ca 113/35

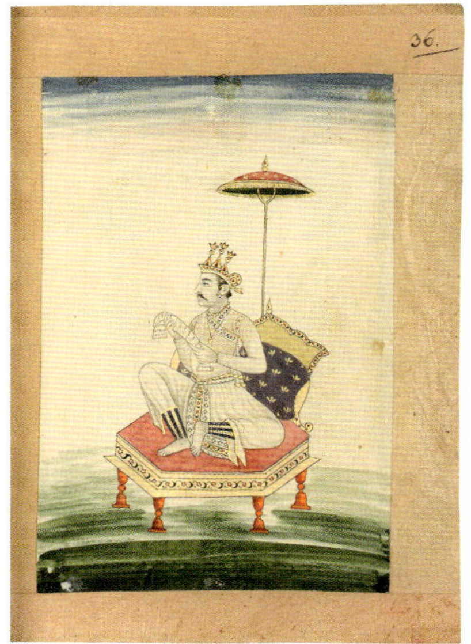

Ca 113/36

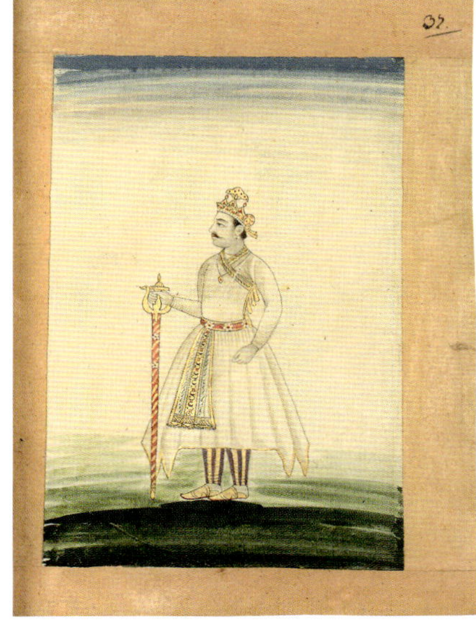
Ca 113/37

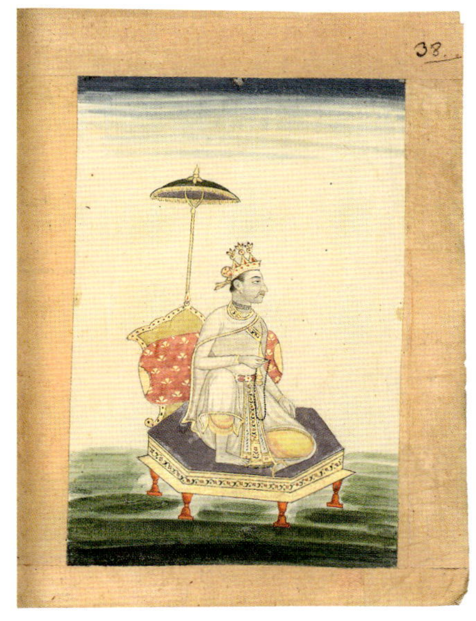

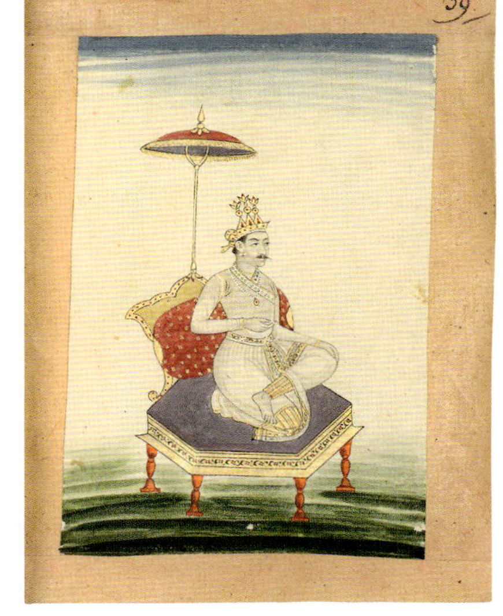

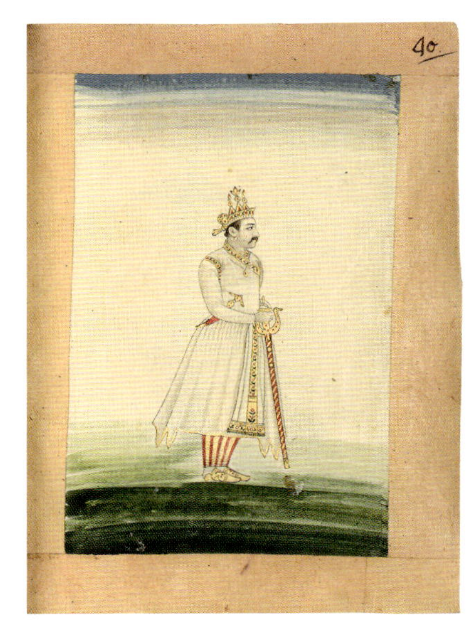

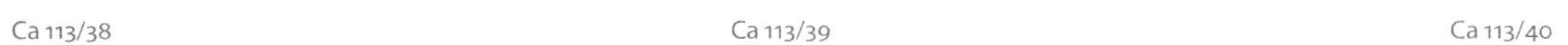

Ca 113/38

Ca 113/39

Ca 113/40

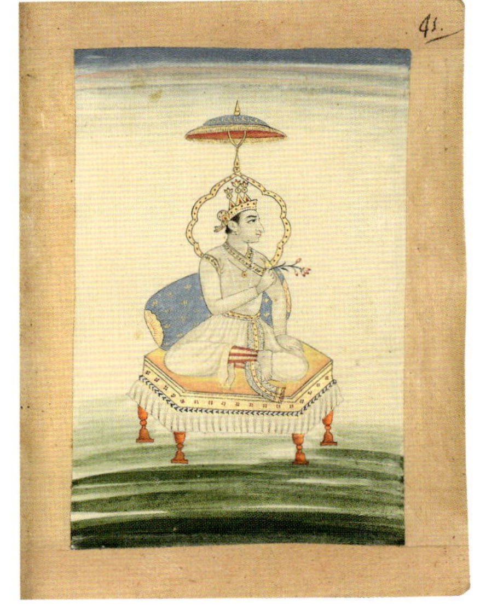

Ca 113/41

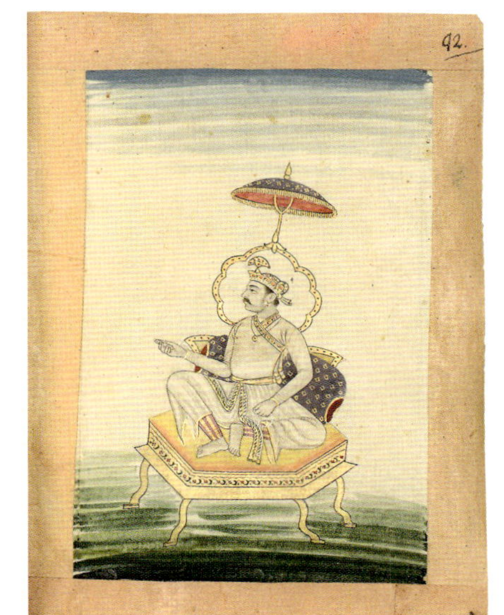

Ca 113/42

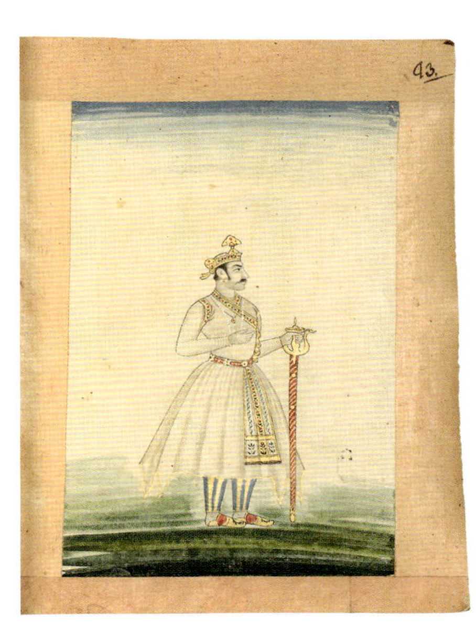

Ca 113/43

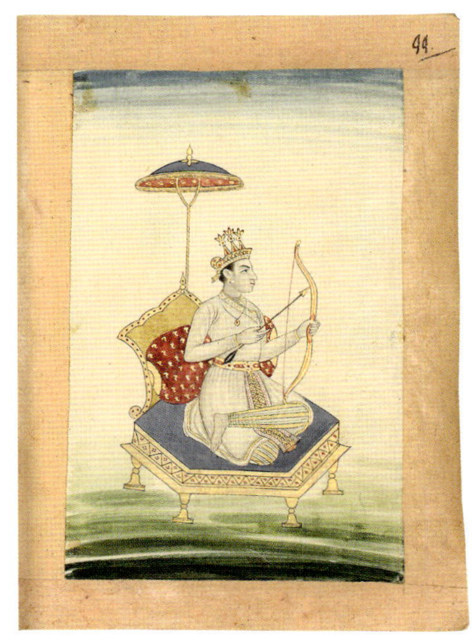

Ca 113/44

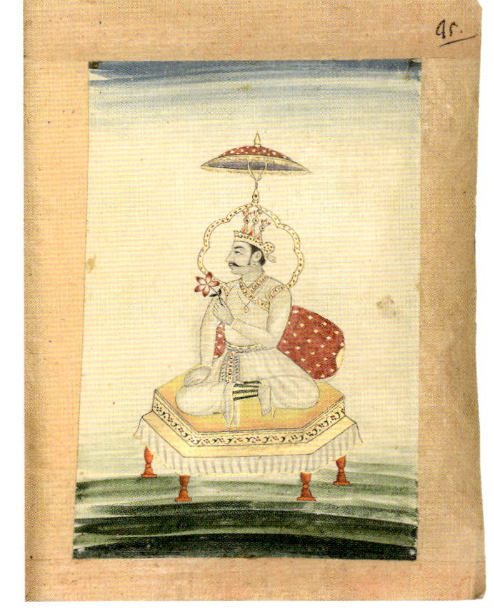

Ca 113/45

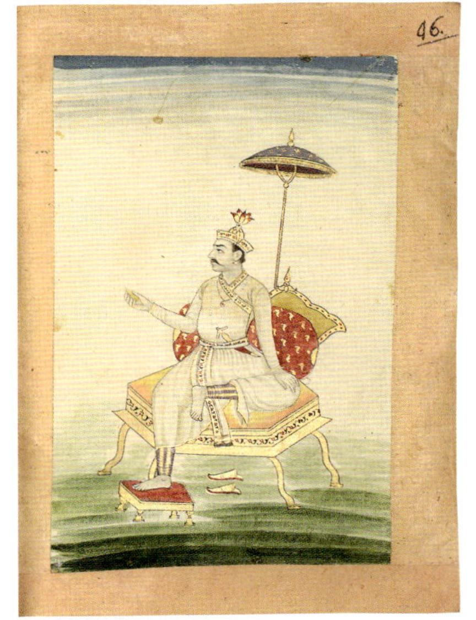

Ca 113/46

Ca 113/47
Unidentified
18 × 12.2 cm
Inscribed verso (*devanāgarī*): saraghana

Ca 113/48
Unidentified
18.2 × 11.7 cm
Inscribed verso (*devanāgarī*): dhanapata

Ca 113/49
Unidentified
18.6 × 12.3 cm
Inscribed verso (*devanāgarī*): mahāvala

Ca 113/50
Unidentified
18.7 × 11.5 cm
Inscribed verso (*devanāgarī*): sātadatta

Ca 113/51
Unidentified
18.2 × 11.8 cm
Inscribed verso (*devanāgarī*): chatrasaina

Ca 113/52
Unidentified
18.2 × 12.4 cm
Inscribed verso (*devanāgarī*): suṣadāna [?]

Ca 113/53
Unidentified
18.2 × 11.8 cm
Inscribed verso (*devanāgarī*): jātavala

Ca 113/54
Unidentified
18.2 × 11.8 cm
Inscribed verso (*devanāgarī*): rājā mahālaṣa

Ca 113/55
Unidentified
19 × 11.8 cm
Inscribed verso (*devanāgarī*): kālagana

Ca 113/56
Unidentified
18.4 × 12.3 cm
Inscribed verso (*devanāgarī*): sarabharā

Ca 113/57
Unidentified
18.8 × 11.8 cm
Inscribed verso (*devanāgarī*): jīvanasaina

Ca 113/58
Unidentified
18.8 × 11.8 cm
Inscribed verso (*devanāgarī*): harajaga

Ca 113/59
Unidentified
18.8 × 11.8 cm
Inscribed verso (*devanāgarī*): vīrasaina

Ca 113/60
Unidentified
18.8 × 12.5 cm
Inscribed verso (*devanāgarī*): udhanta

Ca 113/61
Unidentified
18.3 × 11.9 cm
Inscribed verso (*devanāgarī*): rājā dhadhara

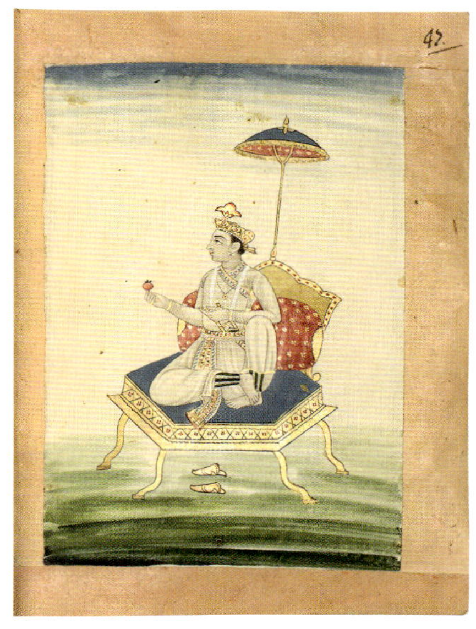

Ca 113/47

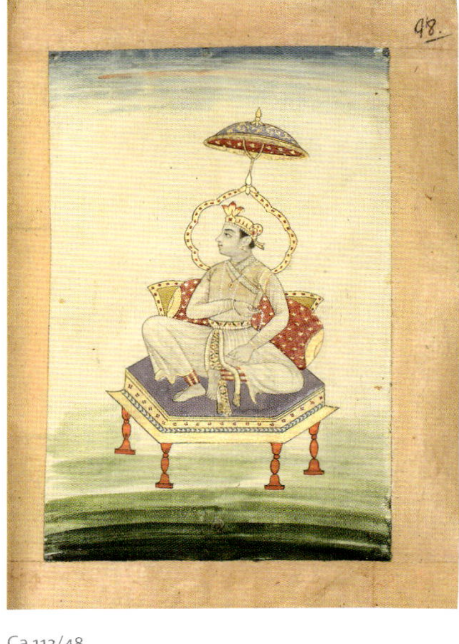

Ca 113/48

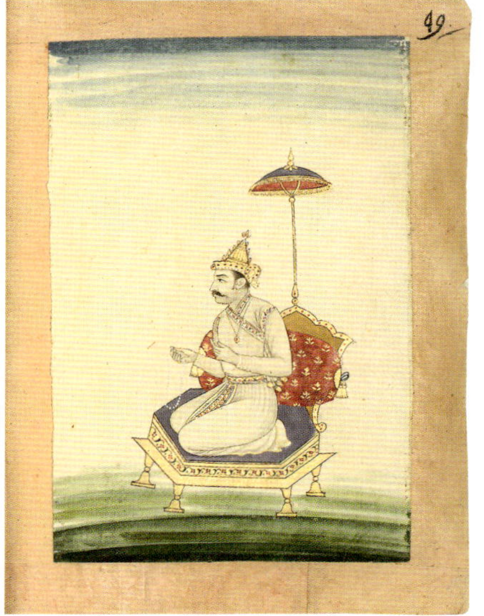

Ca 113/49

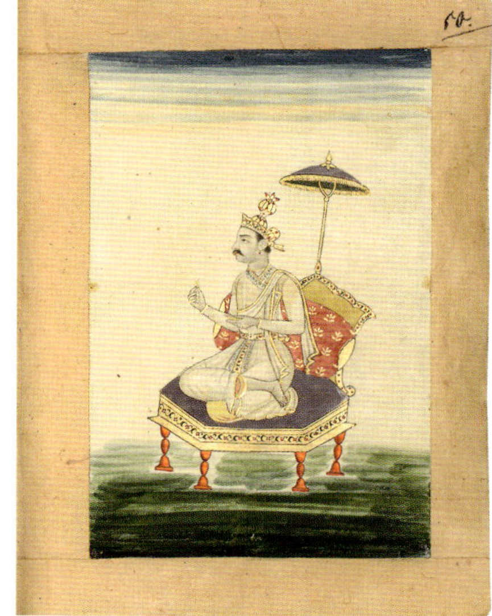

Ca 113/50

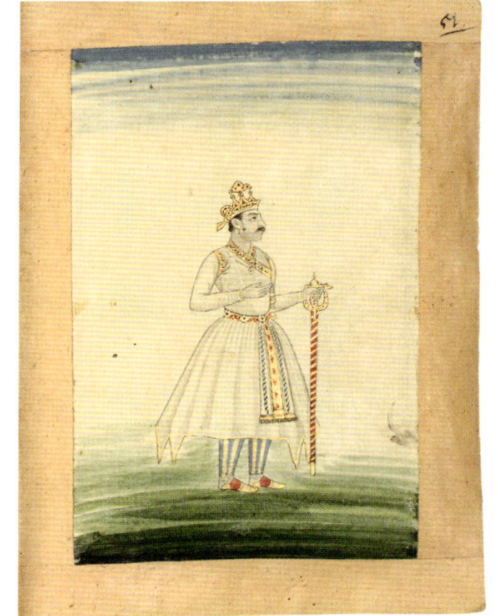
Ca 113/51

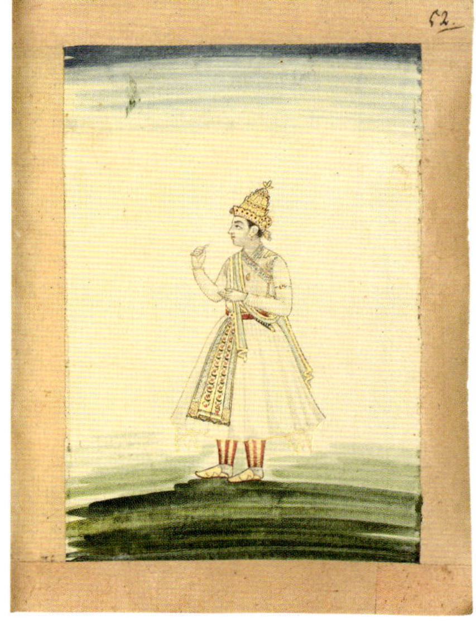

Ca 113/52

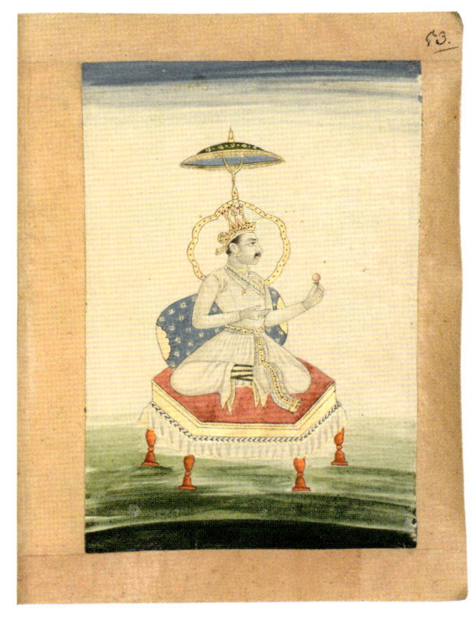

Ca 113/53

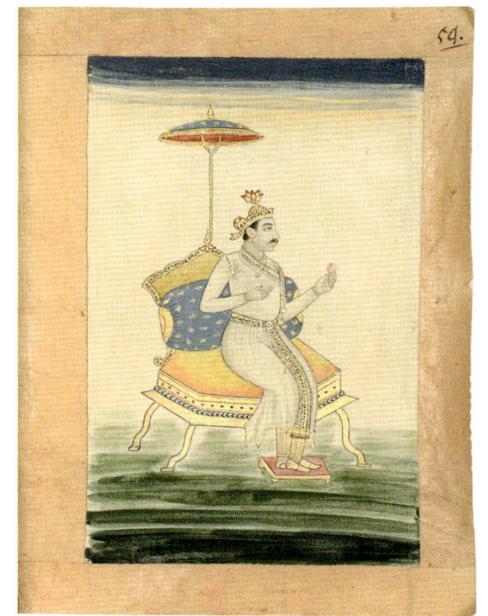

Ca 113/54

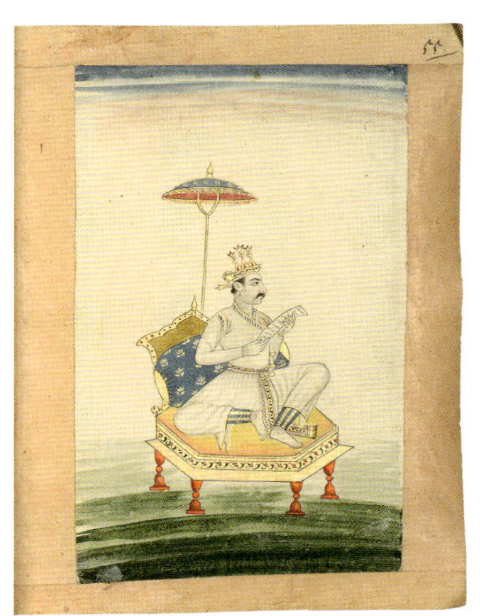

Ca 113/55

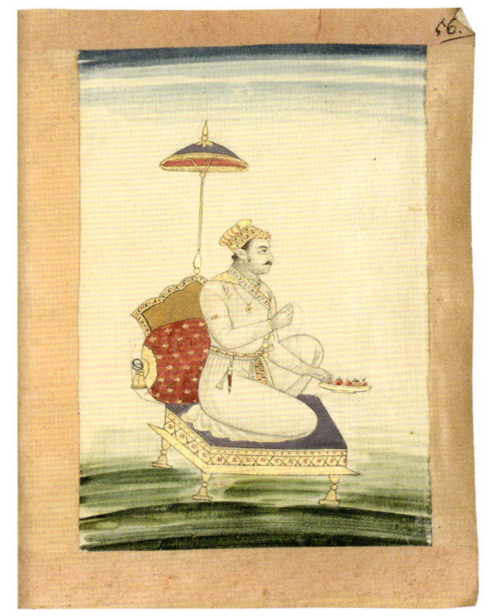

Ca 113/56

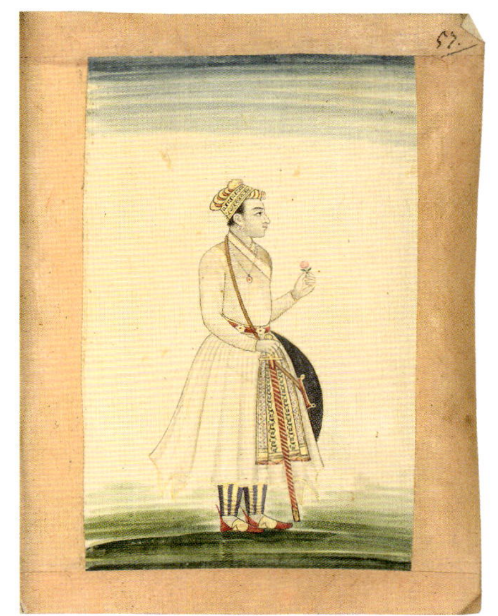

Ca 113/57

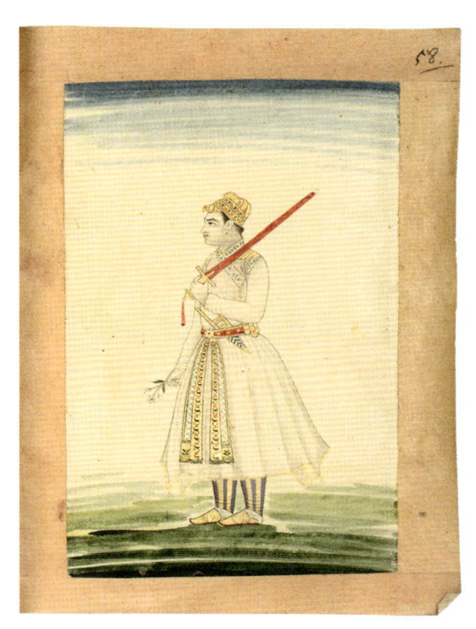

Ca 113/58

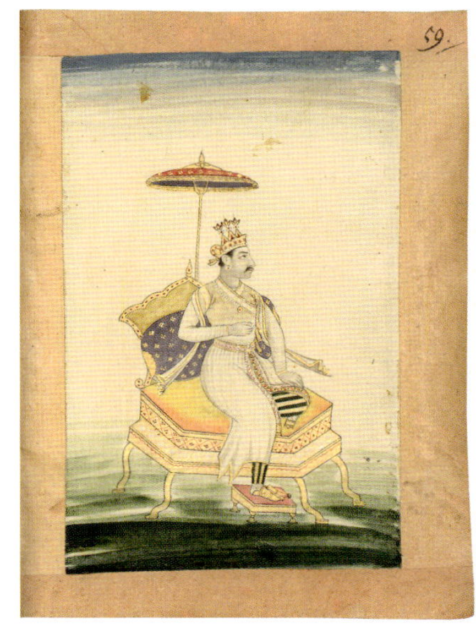

Ca 113/59

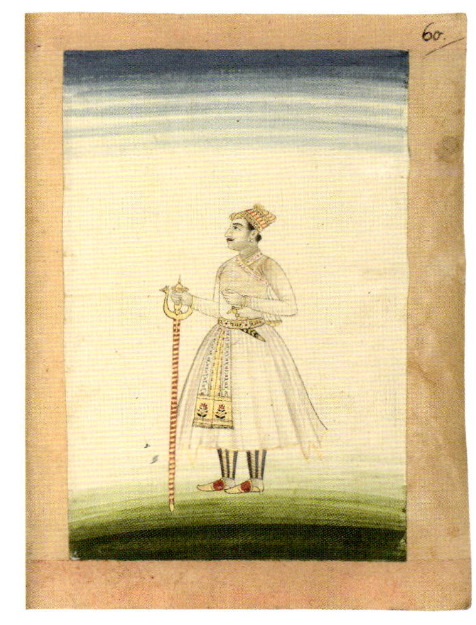

Ca 113/60

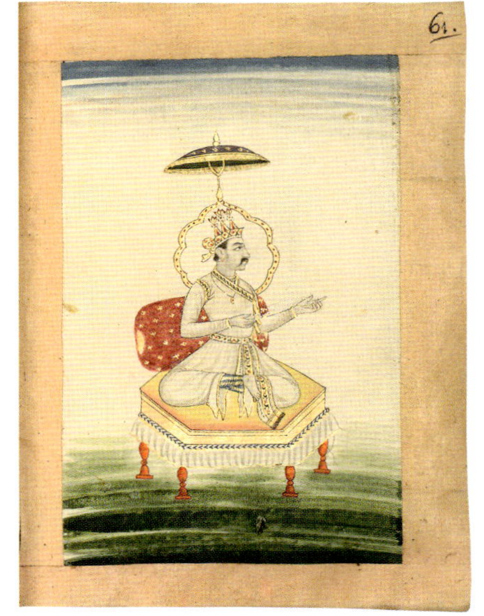

Ca 113/61

Ca 113/62
Unidentified
18 × 11.6 cm
Inscribed verso (*devanāgarī*): rājā sainadhuja

Ca 113/63
Unidentified
18.1 × 11.9 cm
Inscribed verso (*devanāgarī*): venīgaṇgārājā

Ca 113/64
Unidentified
18.6 × 11.5 cm
Inscribed verso (*devanāgarī*): rājā mahājodhā

Ca 113/65
Unidentified
17.9 × 11.9 cm
Inscribed verso (*devanāgarī*): haranātha

Ca 113/66
Unidentified
18.2 × 11.8 cm
Inscribed verso (*devanāgarī*): jīvanarāi

Ca 113/67
Unidentified
19 × 11.8 cm
Inscribed verso (*devanāgarī*): udaisaina

Ca 113/68
Unidentified
17.8 × 11.9 cm
Inscribed verso (*devanāgarī*): ananda jala

Ca 113/69
Unidentified
18.6 × 11.8 cm
Inscribed verso (*devanāgarī*): rājapāla

Ca 113/70
Unidentified
18.8 × 11.8 cm
Inscribed verso (*devanāgarī*): rājā sakavanta

Ca 113/71
Vikramāditya I/II (r. c. 654–80; r. c. 733–742/746)
18.4 × 11.5 cm
Inscribed verso (*devanāgarī*): rājā vikramājīta/
Vira vikramājīta

Ca 113/72
Unidentified
18.4 × 11.5 cm
Inscribed verso (*devanāgarī*): sundarapāla jogī

Ca 113/73
Unidentified
18.6 × 12.1 cm
Inscribed verso (*devanāgarī*): chatrapāla

Ca 113/74
Unidentified
18.6 × 12.2 cm
Inscribed verso (*devanāgarī*): sālabāhana

Ca 113/75
Unidentified
18.6 × 12 cm
Inscribed verso (*devanāgarī*): hasapāla jogī

Ca 113/76
Unidentified
18.1 × 12.1 cm
Inscribed verso (*devanāgarī*): suṣapāla

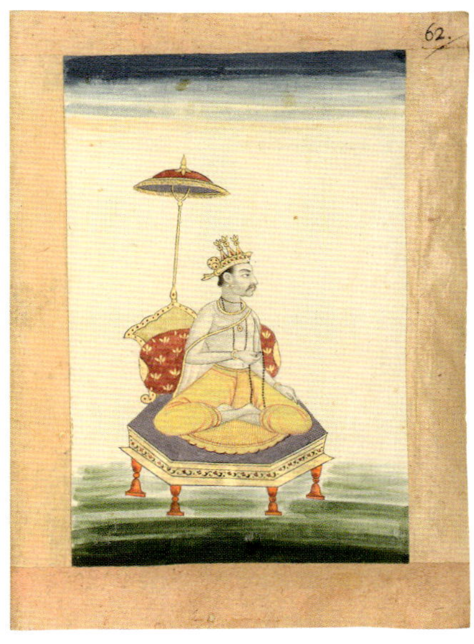

Ca 113/62

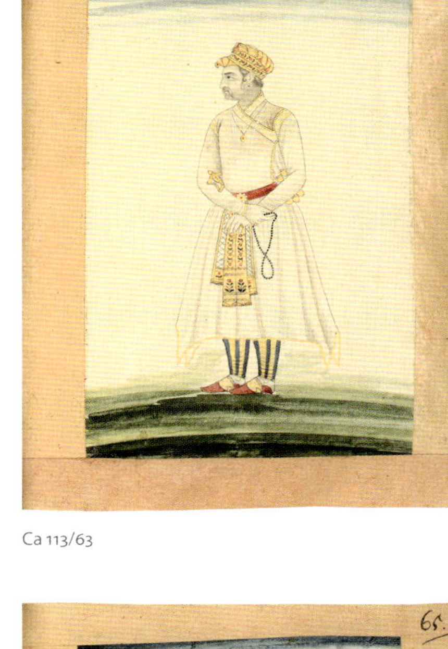

Ca 113/63

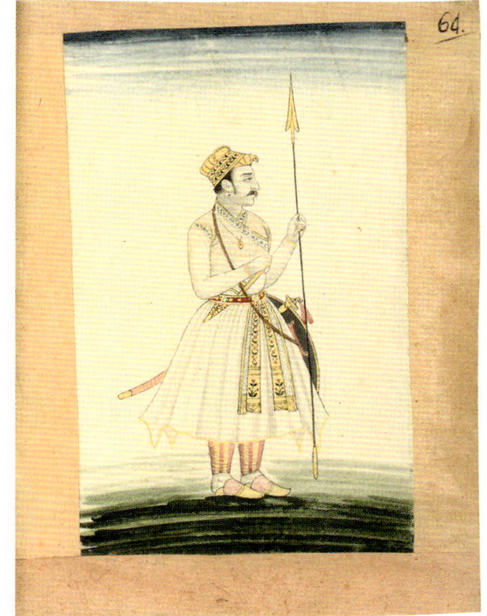

Ca 113/64

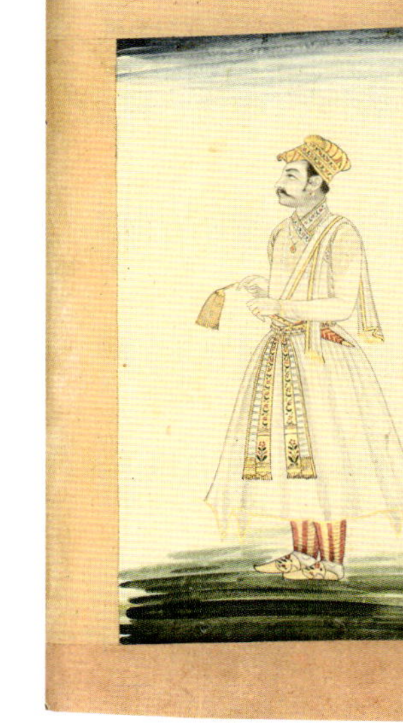

Ca 113/65

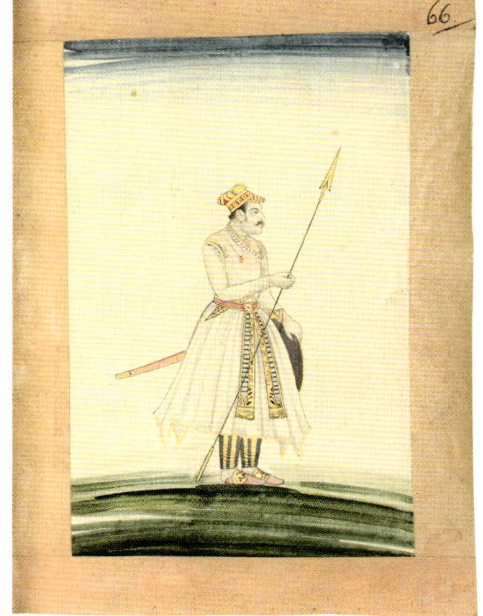

Ca 113/66

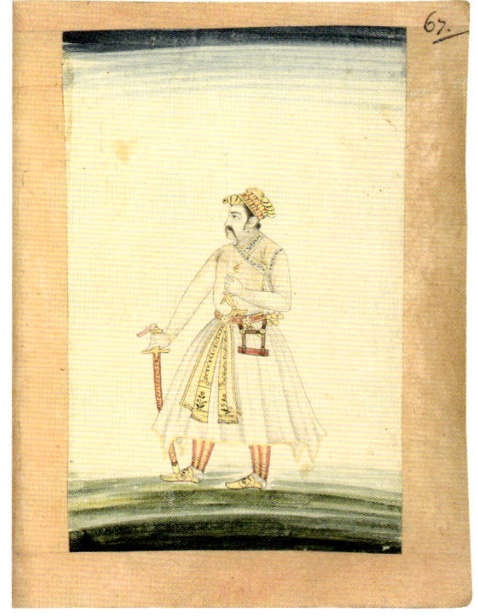

Ca 113/67

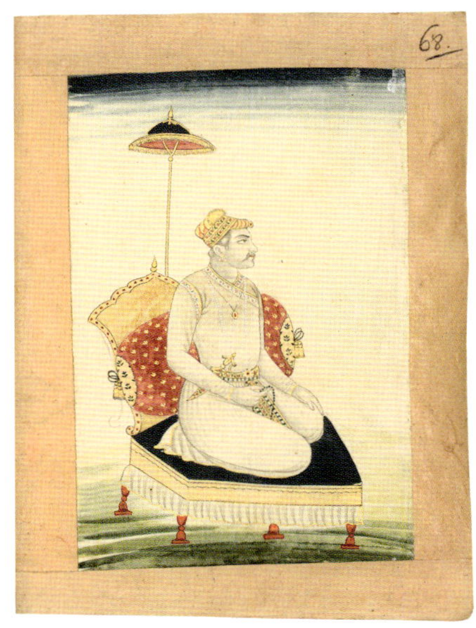

Ca 113/68

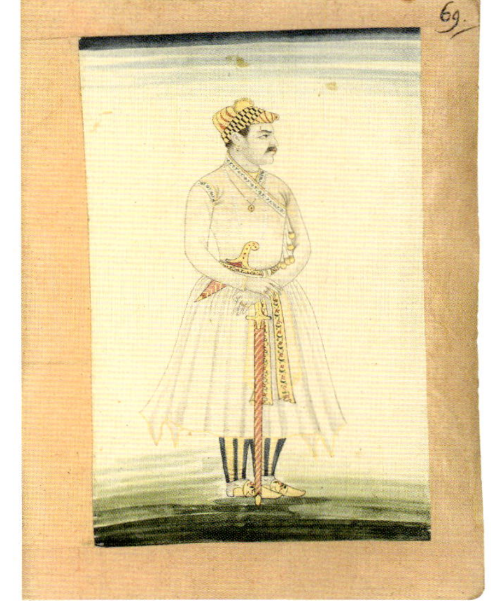

Ca 113/69

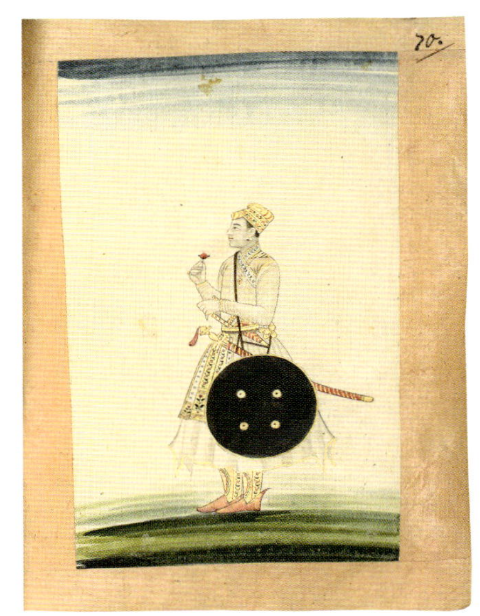

Ca 113/70

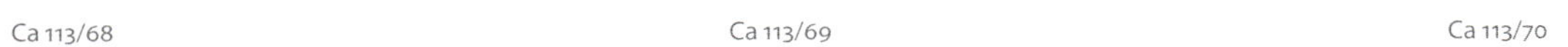

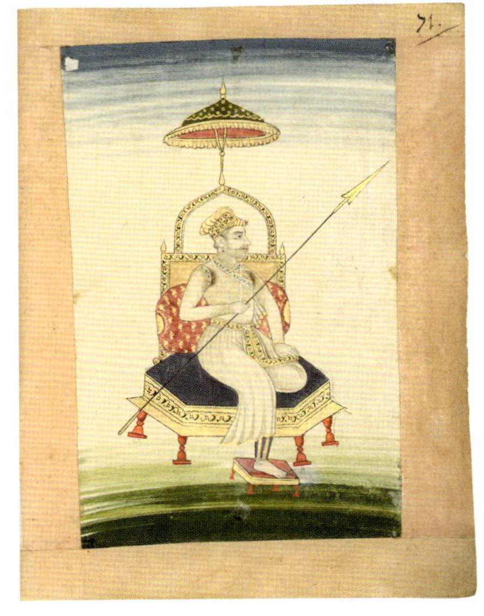

Ca 113/71

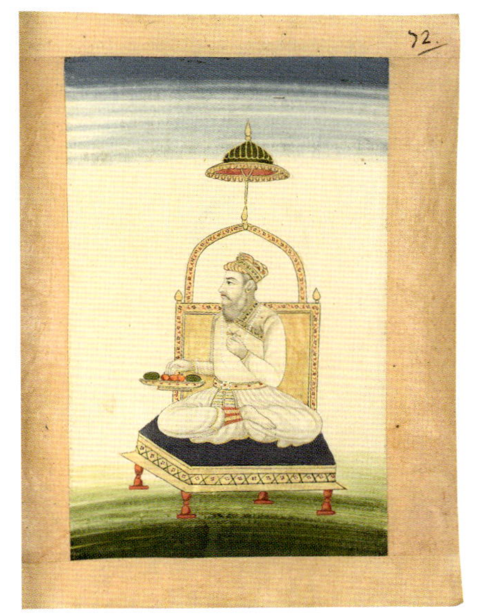

Ca 113/72

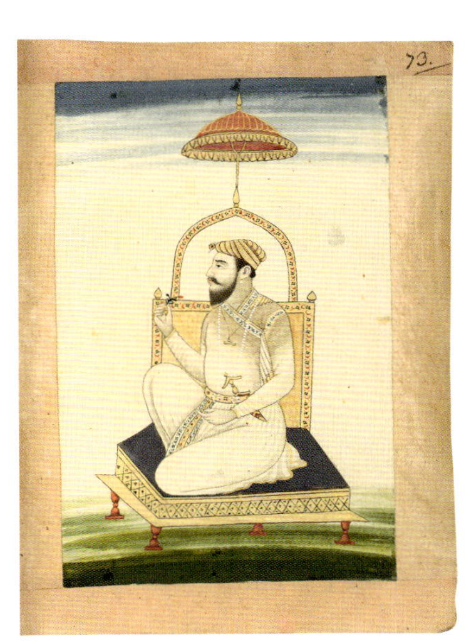

Ca 113/73

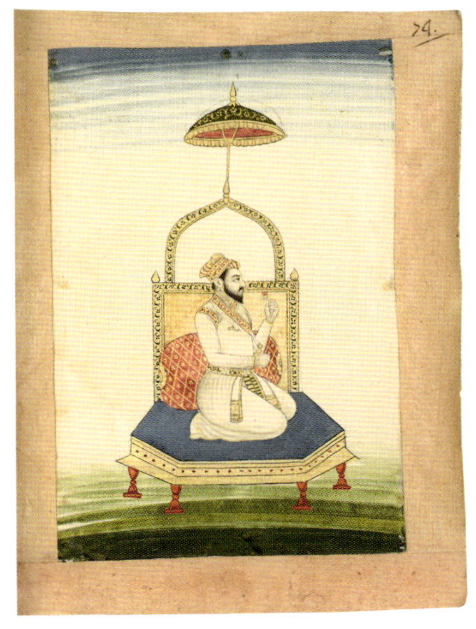

Ca 113/74

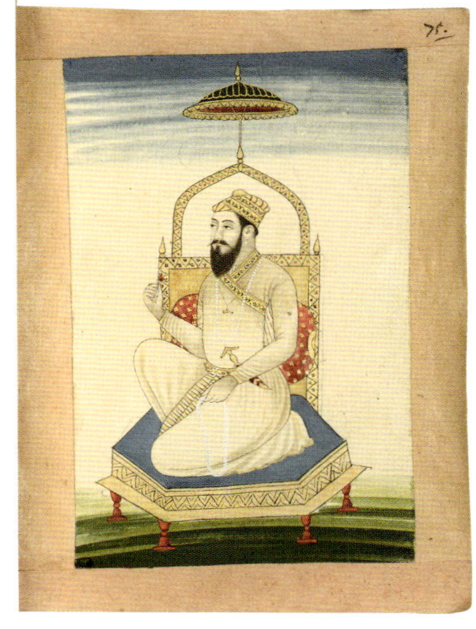

Ca 113/75

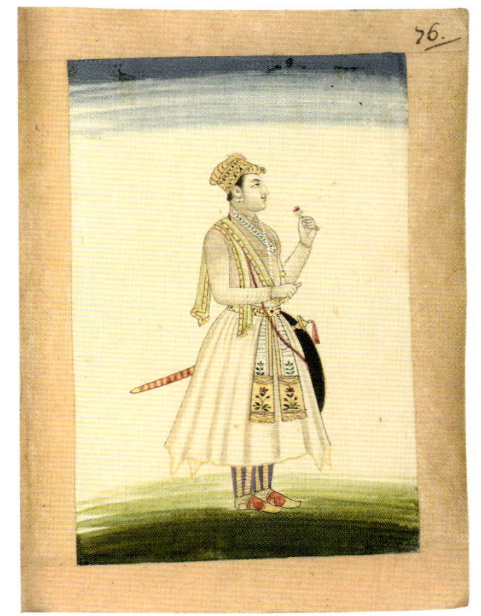

Ca 113/76

Ca 113/77
Śūrapāla I/II (r. c. 865–73; r. c. 1086–1087)[43]
18.5 × 11.8 cm
Inscribed verso (*devanāgarī*): subhapāla

Ca 113/78
Unidentified
18.9 × 12 cm
Inscribed verso (*devanāgarī*): gaṇgapāla

Ca 113/79
Govindāpāla (Gopāla) (r. c. 1176–1180)[44]
18.9 × 12 cm
Inscribed verso (*devanāgarī*): govindapāla

Ca 113/80
Unidentified
18.3 × 11.8 cm
Inscribed verso (*devanāgarī*): amrāpāla

Ca 113/81
Unidentified
18.3 × 11.9 cm
Inscribed verso (*devanāgarī*): valīpāla

Ca 113/82
Mahīpalā I/II (r. c. 992–1042; r. c. 1085–1086)[45]
18.7 × 12 cm
Inscribed verso (*devanāgarī*): mahīpāla

Ca 113/83
Unidentified
18.1 × 11.9 cm
Inscribed verso (*devanāgarī*): harapāla

Ca 113/84
Unidentified
18.7 × 11.9 cm
Inscribed verso (*devanāgarī*): bhīmapāla

Ca 113/85
Madanapāla (r. c. 1158–1176)[46]
18.7 × 12 cm
Inscribed verso (*devanāgarī*): madanapāla

Ca 113/86
Unidentified
18.5 × 11.7 cm
Inscribed verso (*devanāgarī*): karmapāla

Ca 113/87
Vigrahapāla I/II/III (r. c. 873–5; r. c. 987–92; r. c. 1058–1085)[47]
18 × 12.1 cm
Inscribed verso (*devanāgarī*): bikramapāla

Ca 113/88
Unidentified
18.4 × 12.2 cm
Inscribed verso (*devanāgarī*): malūkacanda

Ca 113/89
Vikramacandra [?]
18.6 × 12.2 cm
Inscribed verso (*devanāgarī*): vikramacanda

Ca 113/90
Unidentified
18.5 × 11.7 cm
Inscribed verso (*devanāgarī*): kātalacanda

Ca 113/91
Unidentified
18.9 × 11.9 cm
Inscribed verso (*devanāgarī*): rāmacanda

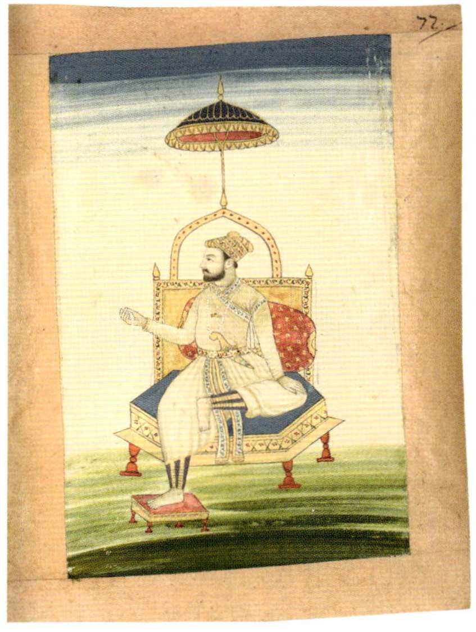

Ca 113/77

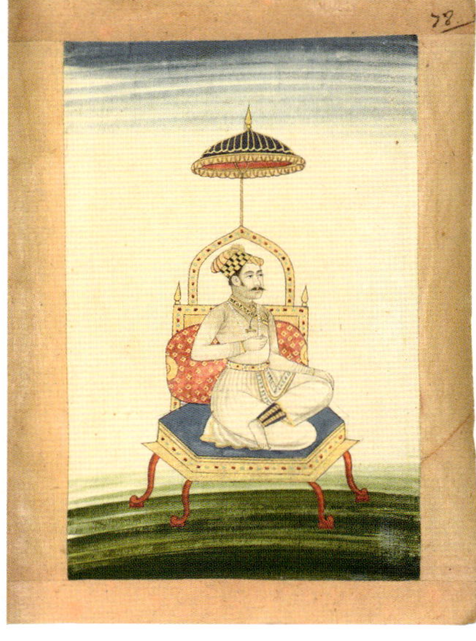

Ca 113/78

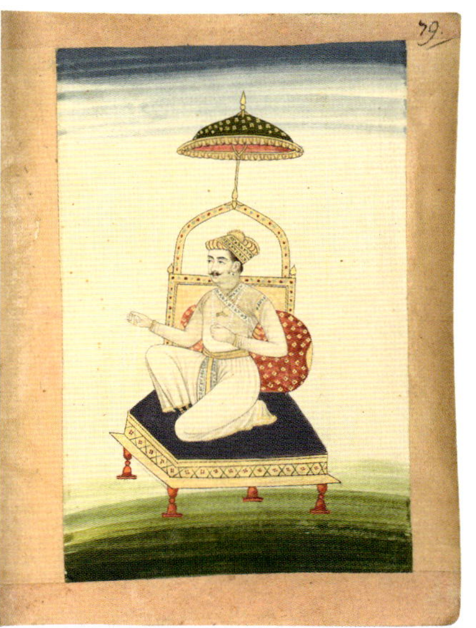

Ca 113/79

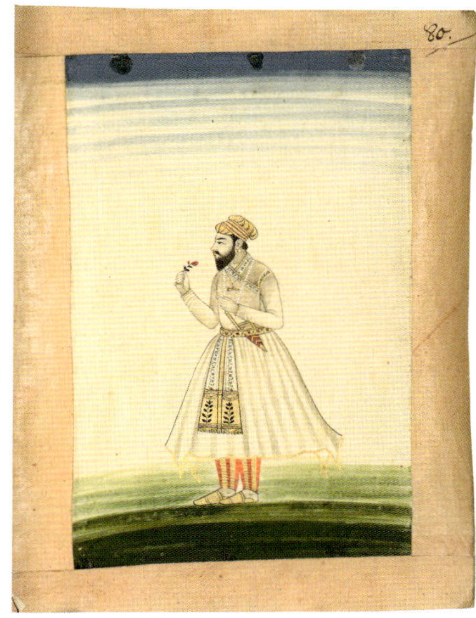

Ca 113/80

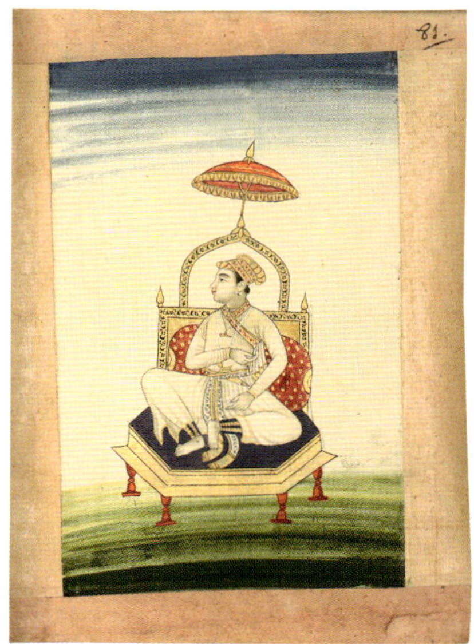

Ca 113/81

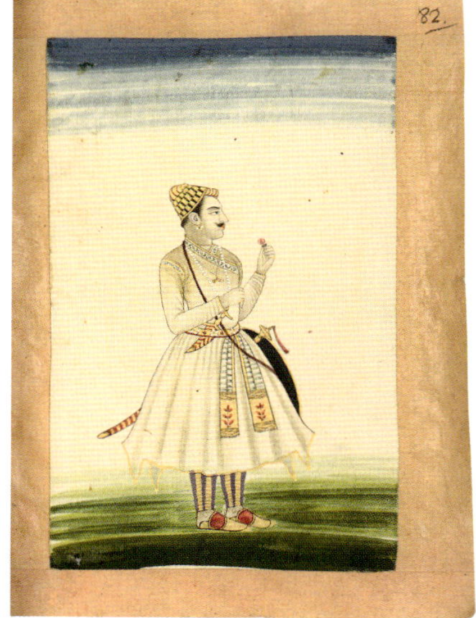

Ca 113/82

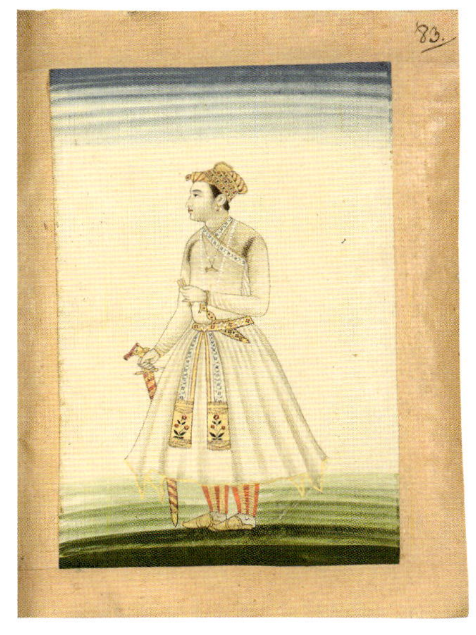

Ca 113/83

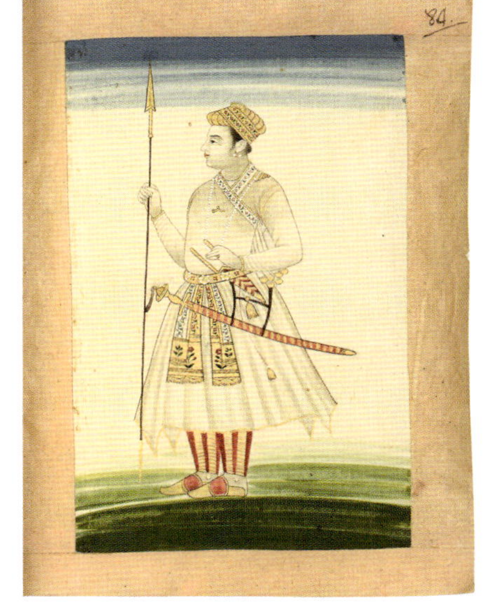

Ca 113/84

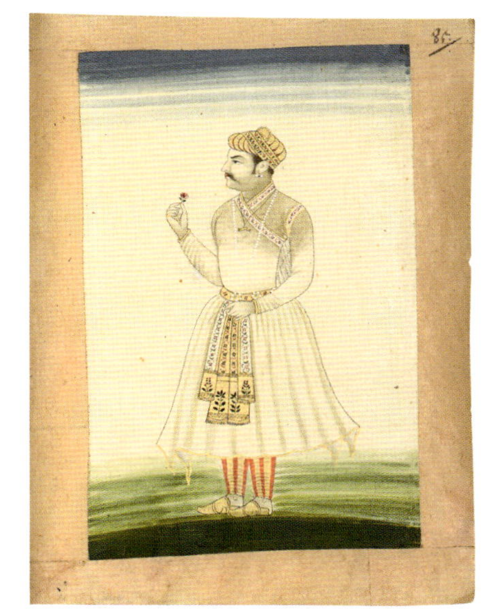

Ca 113/85

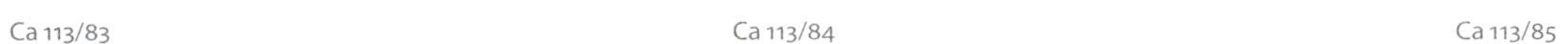

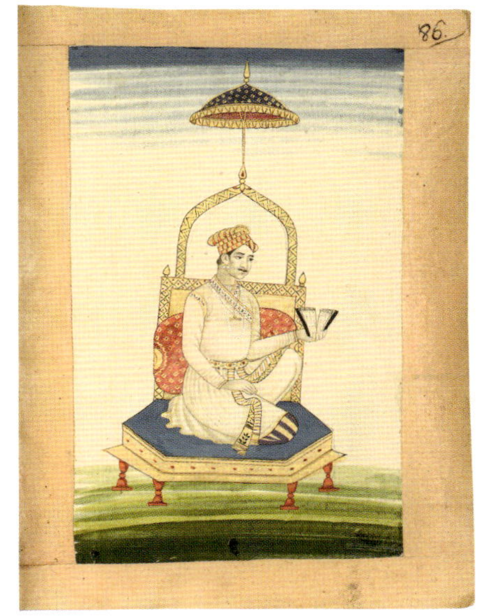

Ca 113/86

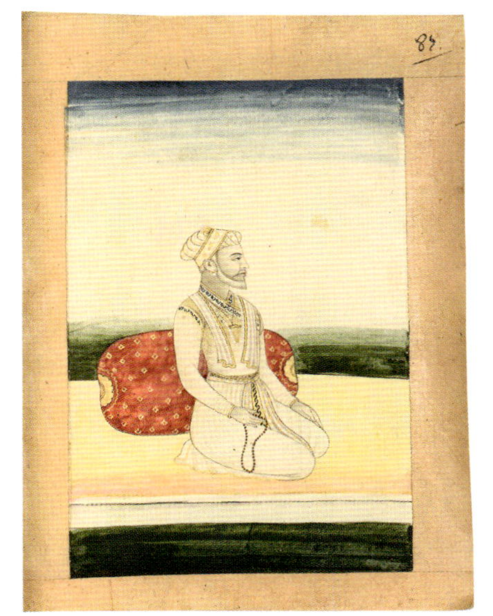

Ca 113/87

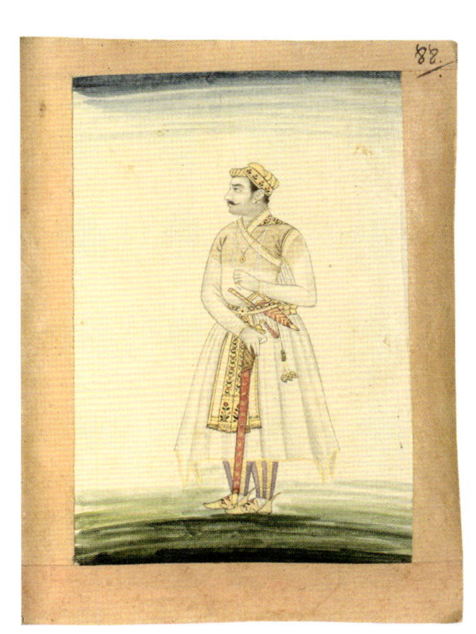

Ca 113/88

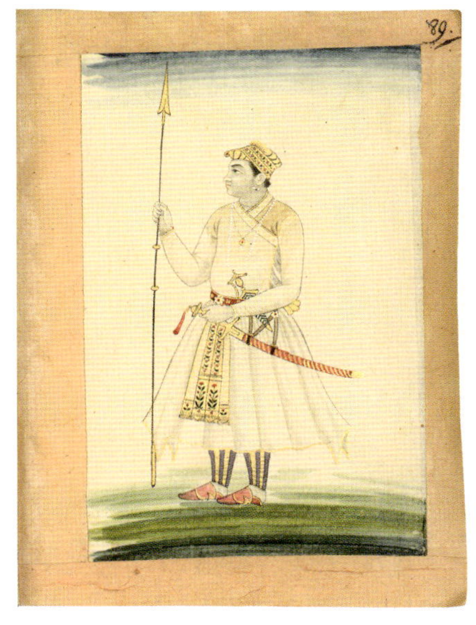

Ca 113/89

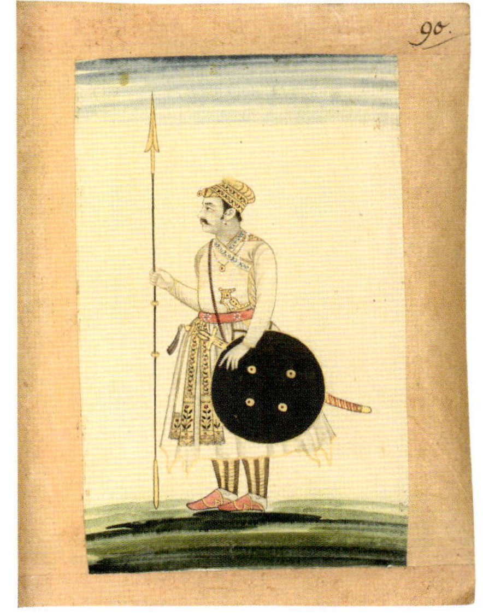

Ca 113/90

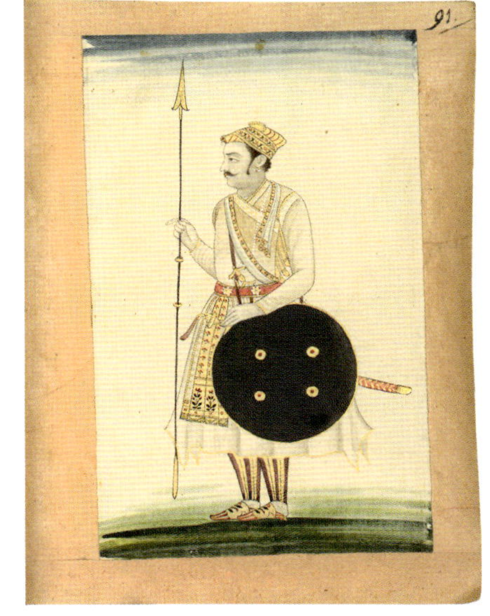

Ca 113/91

Ca 113/92
Unidentified
19 × 12.1 cm
Inscribed verso (*devanāgarī*): dhanīcanda

Ca 113/93
Kalyāṇacandra (r. c. 955–85/975–1000)[48]
19.1 × 12.1 cm
Inscribed verso (*devanāgarī*): kalyānaca(n)da

Ca 113/94
Unidentified
19 × 12 cm
Inscribed verso (*devanāgarī*): bhīmacanda

Ca 113/95
Laḍahacandra (r. c. 985–1010/1000–1020)[49]
18.3 × 12.5 cm
Inscribed verso (*devanāgarī*): lohacanda

Ca 113/96
Govindacandra (r. c. 1010–1035/1020–1045)[50]
18.3 × 12.5 cm
Inscribed verso (*devanāgarī*): govi(n)daca(n)da

Ca 113/97
Rāṇī Prabhāvatī (d. 1303)
18.7 × 12.2 cm
Inscribed verso (*devanāgarī*): rānī parabhāvatī

Ca 113/98
Unidentified
18.4 × 12 cm
Inscribed verso (*devanāgarī*): haravarama jogī

Ca 113/99
Unidentified
18.8 × 11.2 cm
Inscribed verso (*devanāgarī*): govindavarama jogī

Ca 113/100
Gopālavarma (r. 902–4)
18.6 × 12.1 cm
Inscribed verso (*devanāgarī*): gopālavarama

Ca 113/101
Unidentified
18.5 × 11.6 cm
Inscribed verso (*devanāgarī*): mahānātha j(o)g(ī)

Ca 113/102
Unidentified
18.4 × 12.3 cm
Inscribed verso (*devanāgarī*): rājā mahīsena vaṅgālī

Ca 113/103
Vallālasena (r. c. 1158/60 – c. 1178/9)[51]
18.7 × 11.8 cm
Inscribed verso (*devanāgarī*): vilāvalasaina

Ca 113/104
Unidentified
18.4 × 11.8 cm
Inscribed verso (*devanāgarī*): raghūsaina

Ca 113/105
Unidentified
18.5 × 11.4 cm
Inscribed verso (*devanāgarī*): mādhos(ai)na

Ca 113/106
Unidentified
18.1 × 11.7 cm
Inscribed verso (*devanāgarī*): sūrasaina

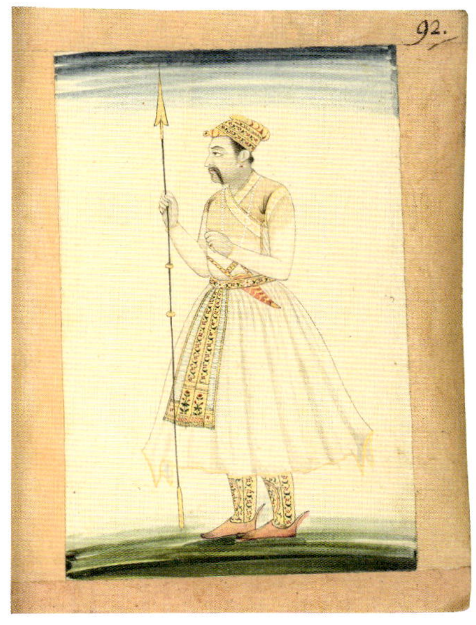

Ca 113/92

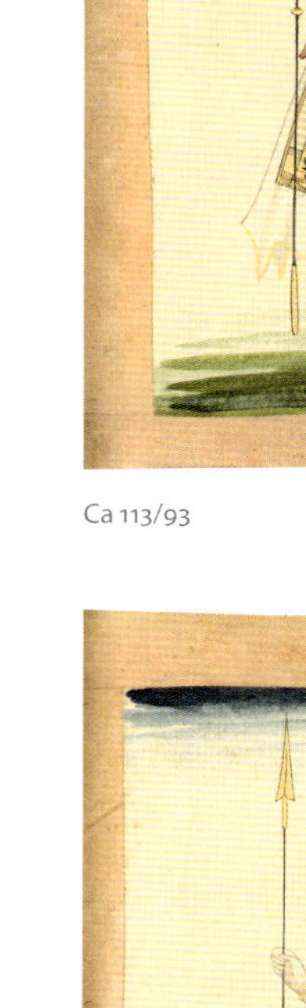

Ca 113/93

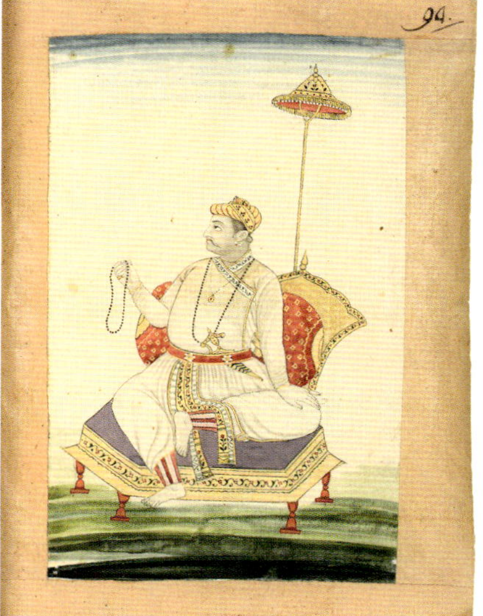

Ca 113/94

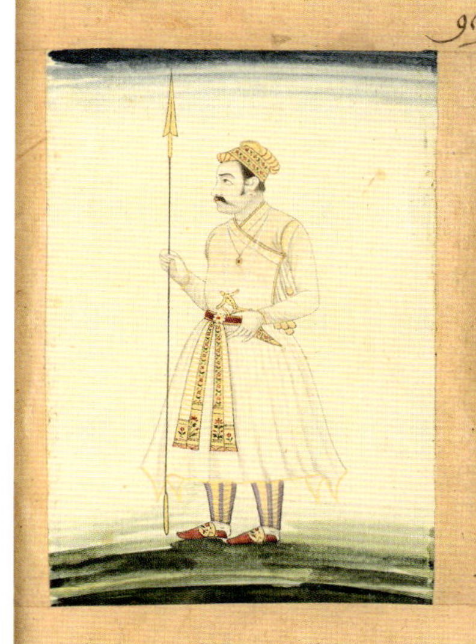
Ca 113/95

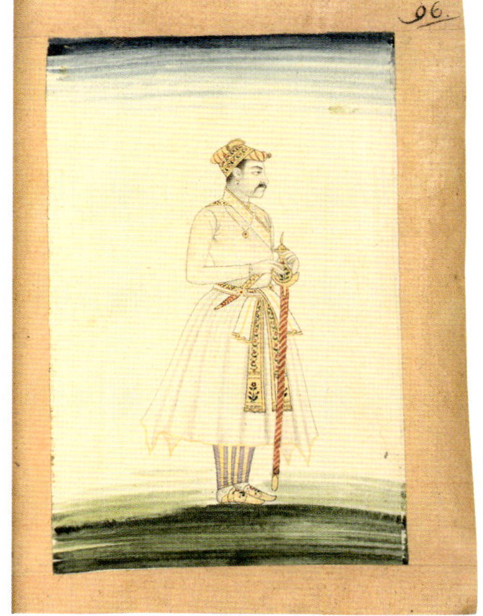

Ca 113/96

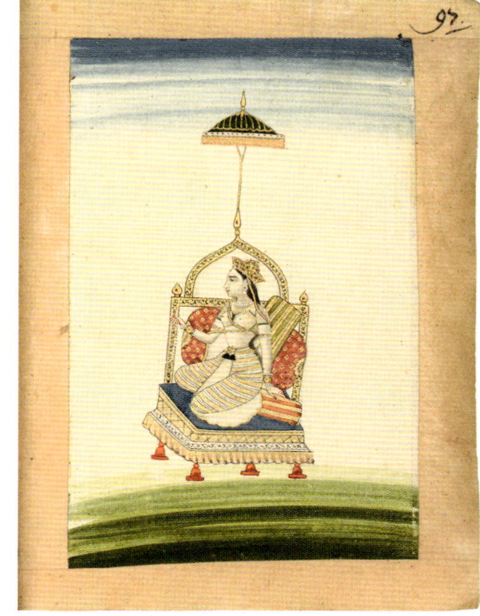
Ca 113/97

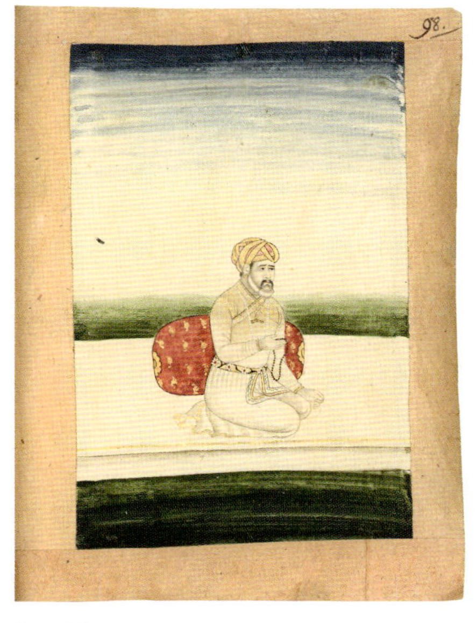

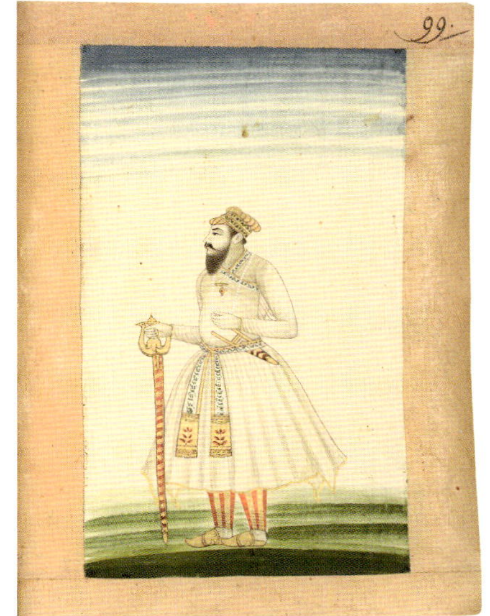

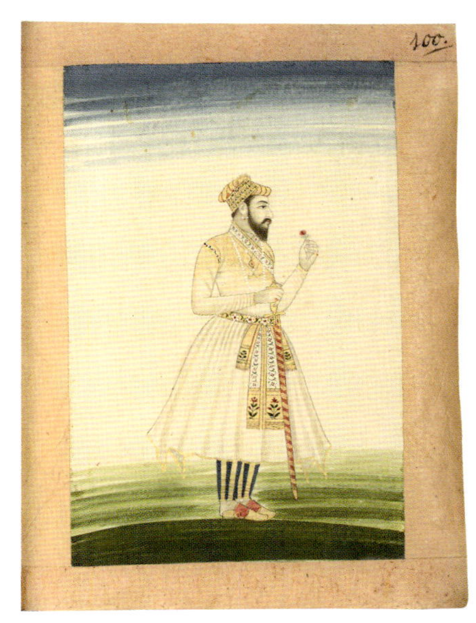

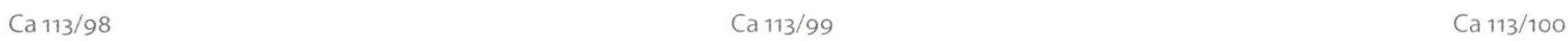

Ca 113/98

Ca 113/99

Ca 113/100

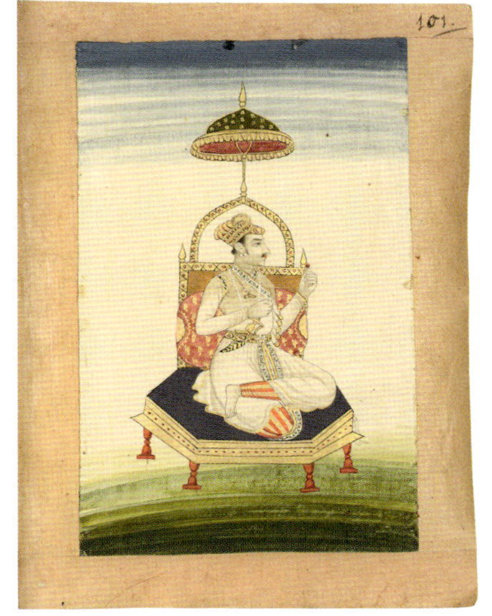

Ca 113/101

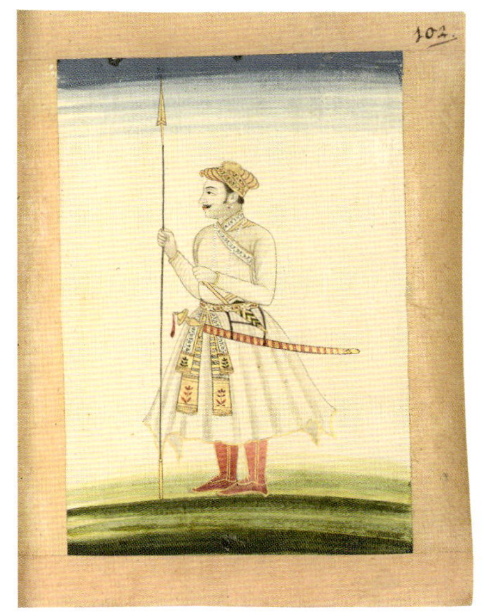

Ca 113/102

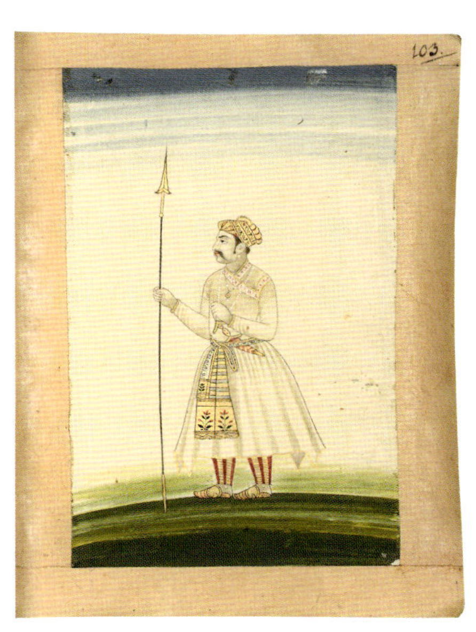

Ca 113/103

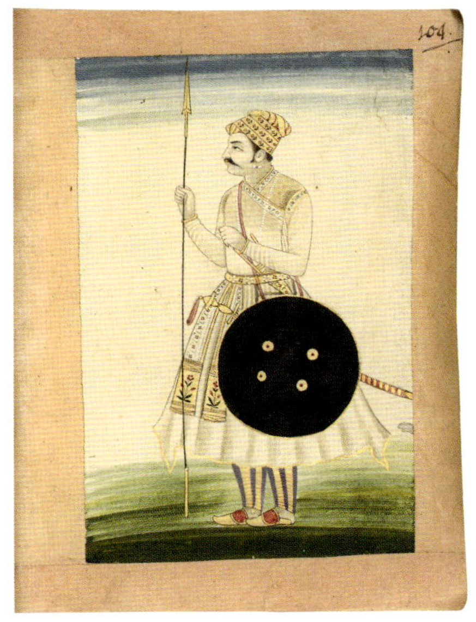

Ca 113/104

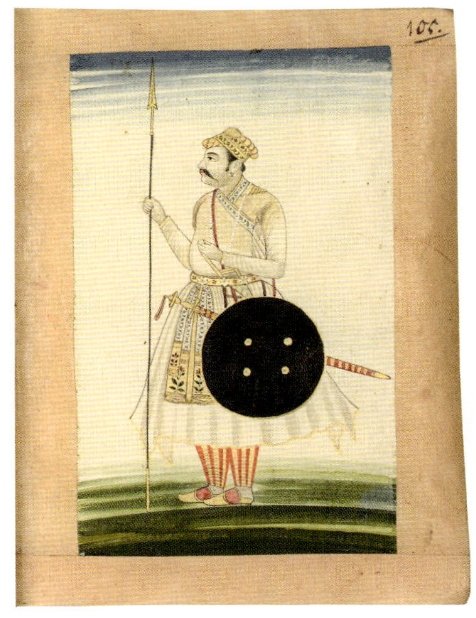

Ca 113/105

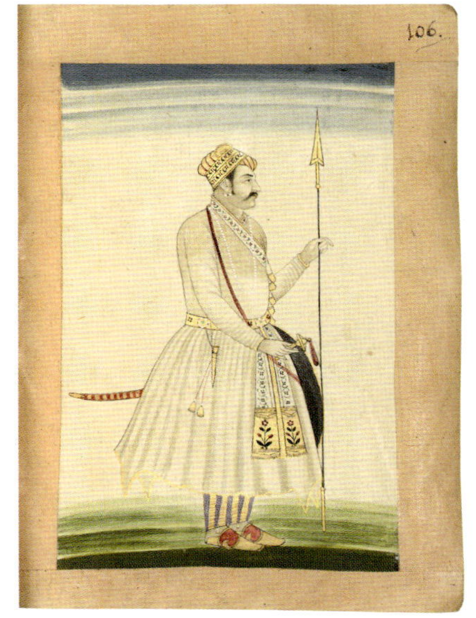

Ca 113/106

Ca 113/107
Unidentified
18.7 × 12.2 cm
Inscribed verso (*devanāgarī*): bhīmasaina

Ca 113/108
Unidentified
18.5 × 12.3 cm
Inscribed verso (*devanāgarī*): kātagasaina

Ca 113/109
Unidentified
18.2 × 12.1 cm
Inscribed verso (*devanāgarī*): harīsaina

Ca 113/110
Unidentified
18.9 × 12.1 cm
Inscribed verso (*devanāgarī*): ṣemasaina

Ca 113/111
Unidentified
17.8 × 12.6 cm
Inscribed verso (*devanāgarī*): narāinasaina

Ca 113/112
Lakṣmaṇasena (r. c. 1178/9 – 1206)[52]
18.7 × 12.5 cm
Inscribed verso (*devanāgarī*): laṣamīsaina

Ca 113/113
Unidentified
18.9 × 12.4 cm
Inscribed verso (*devanāgarī*): damodarasaina

Ca 113/114
Unidentified
18.2 × 12.1 cm
Inscribed verso (*devanāgarī*): dīpasiṇgha

Ca 113/115
Unidentified
18.6 × 12.1 cm
Inscribed verso (*devanāgarī*): rājā anasi(n)gha

Ca 113/116
Unidentified
18.5 × 11.4 cm
Inscribed verso (*devanāgarī*): rājāsi(ṇ)gha

Ca 113/117
Vīra Narasiṁha
18.6 × 12.2 cm
Inscribed verso (*devanāgarī*): vīrasiṇgha

Ca 113/118
Harihara I/II
18.6 × 11.8 cm
Inscribed verso (*devanāgarī*): harasiṇgha

Ca 113/119
Unidentified
18.1 × 12.2 cm
Inscribed verso (*devanāgarī*): jīvanasiṇgha

Ca 113/120
Prithvīrāj Chauhān III (Rāi Pithora) (r. 1178 – 1192)
18.8 × 12.3 cm
Inscribed verso (*devanāgarī*): rājā pithaura

Ca 113/121
Unidentified
18.2 × 12.5 cm
Inscribed verso (*devanāgarī*): haṭhīmala

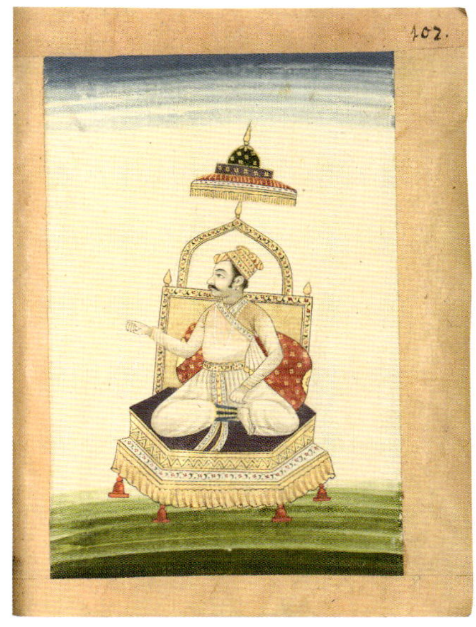
Ca 113/107

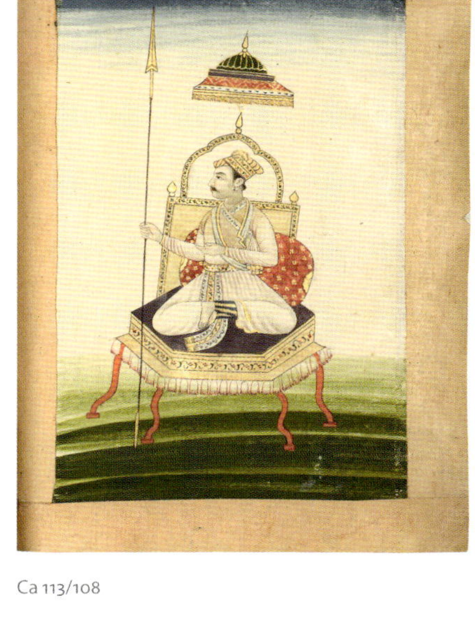
Ca 113/108

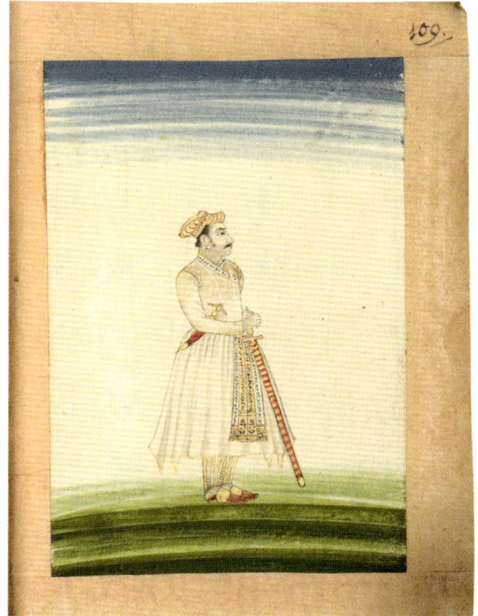
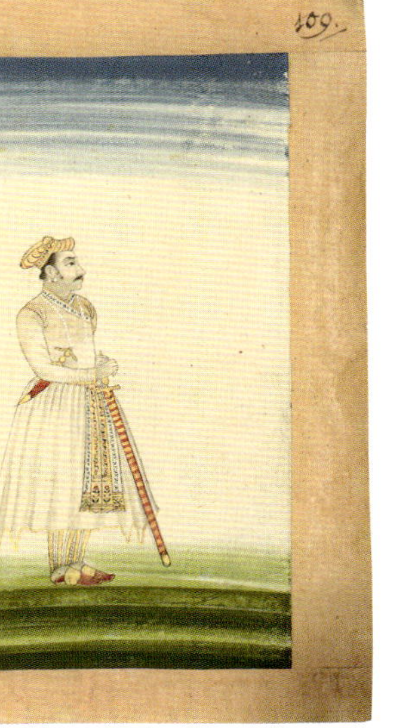
Ca 113/109

Ca 113/110

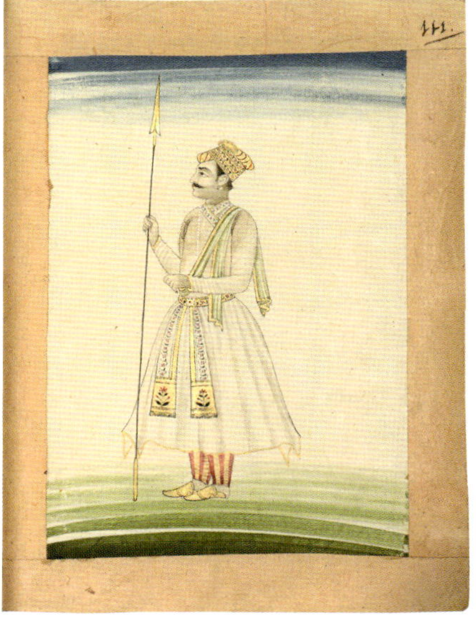
Ca 113/111

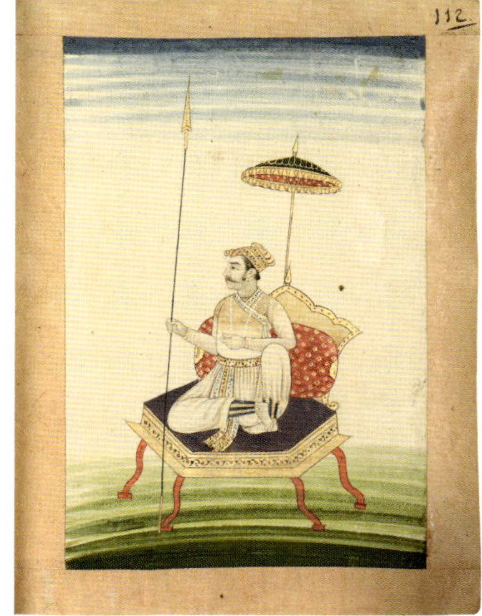
Ca 113/112

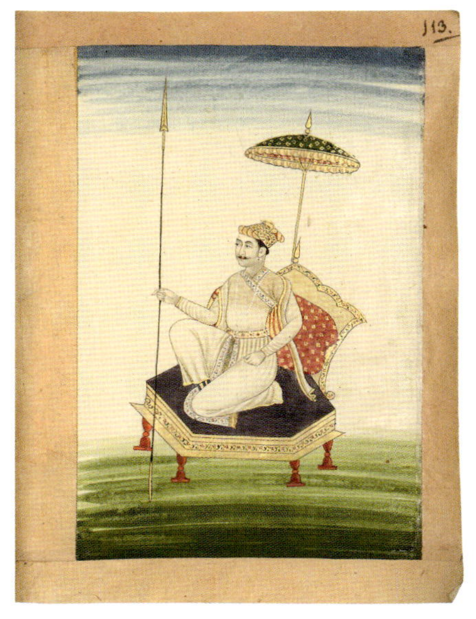

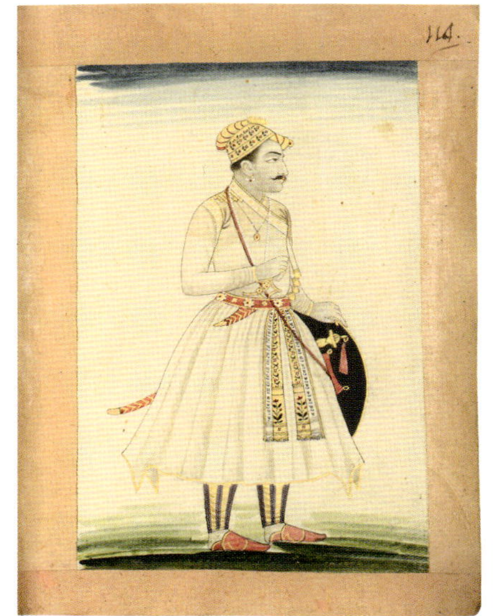

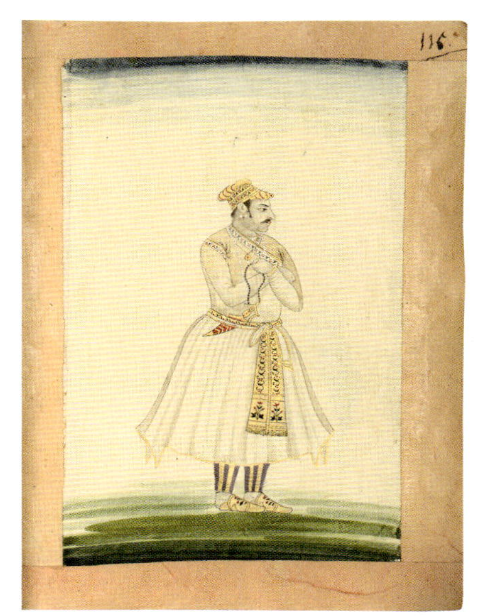

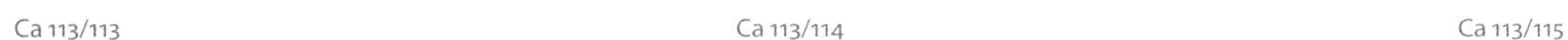

Ca 113/113

Ca 113/114

Ca 113/115

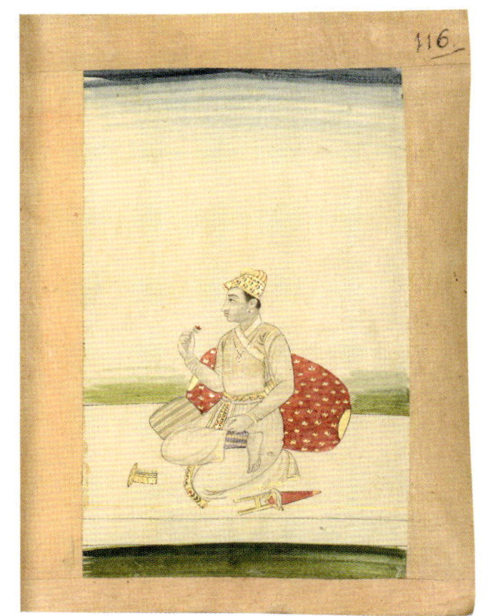

Ca 113/116

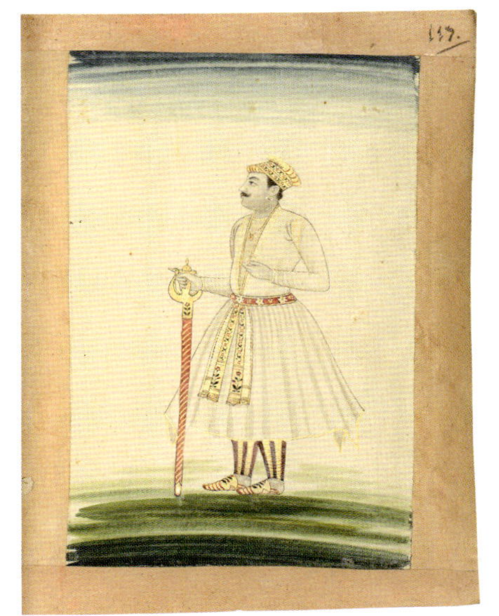

Ca 113/117

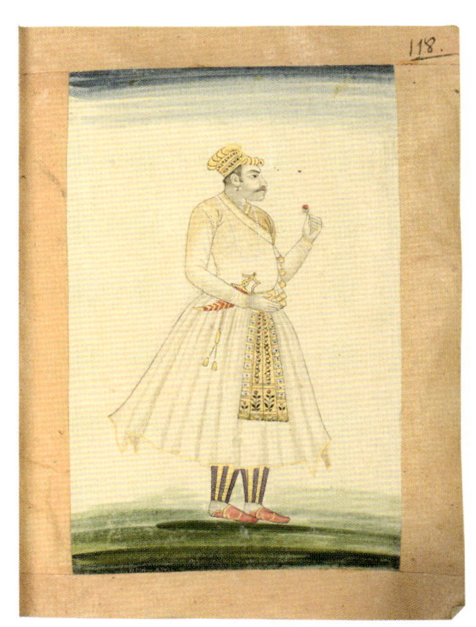

Ca 113/118

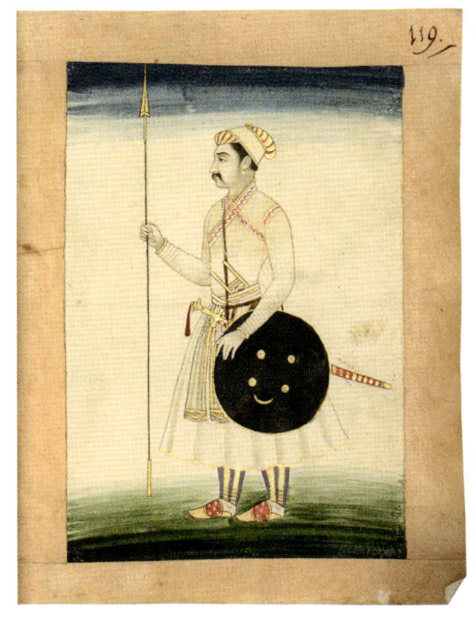

Ca 113/119

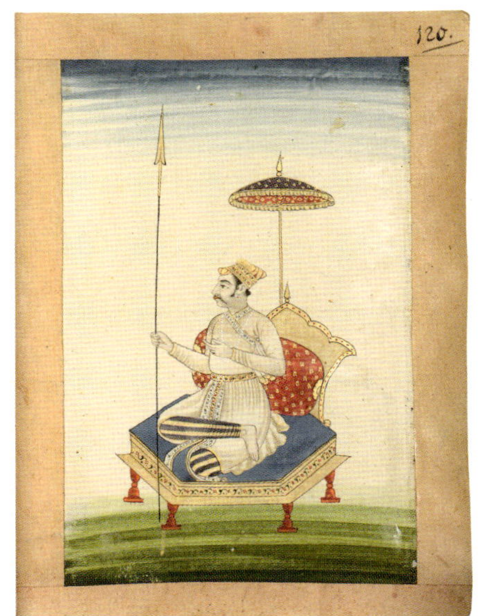

Ca 113/120

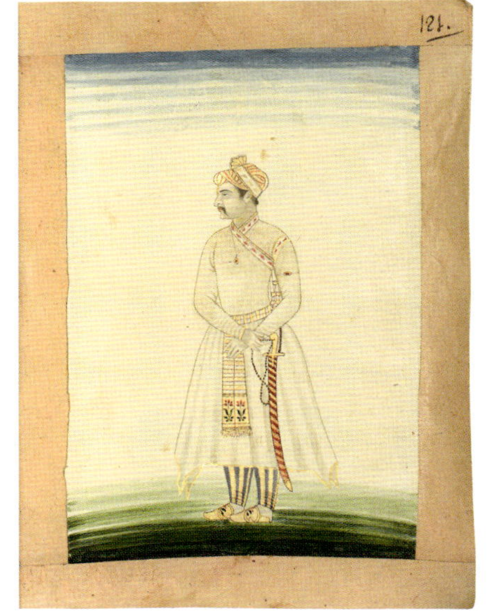

Ca 113/121

Ca 113/122
Unidentified
18.7 × 12.6 cm
Inscribed verso (*devanāgarī*): durjanamadanna

Ca 113/123
Unidentified
18.9 × 12.5 cm
Inscribed verso (*devanāgarī*): udaimadanna

Ca 113/124
Unidentified
18.6 × 12.5 cm
Inscribed verso (*devanāgarī*): lachīmadanna

Ca 113/125
Sultān Sahab ud-Dīn Ghōrī (r. 1173–1202)
17.9 × 11.8 cm
Inscribed verso (*devanāgarī*): sulatāna sahāvadī gorī

Ca 113/126
Sultān Rukn ud-Dīn (r. 1236)
18 × 11.7 cm
Inscribed verso (*devanāgarī*): sulatāna rukanudī

Ca 113/127
Sultān Shams ud-Dīn Īltutmish (r. 1211–1236)
18 × 12.1 cm
Inscribed verso (*devanāgarī*): sulatāna samsuddī

Ca 113/128
Sultān Qutb ud-Dīn Aibak (r. 1206–1210)
18.3 × 12.1 cm
Inscribed verso (*devanāgarī*): sulatāna kutabadī

Ca 113/129
Unidentified
18.7 × 12 cm
Inscribed verso (*devanāgarī*): sulatāna sahāvadī

Ca 113/130
Rāziyyat ud-Dīn Sultāna (Bībī Rāje) (r. 1236–1240)
18.9 × 12.6 cm
Inscribed verso (*devanāgarī*): vivī rāje

Ca 113/131
Sultān Nāsir ud-Dīn Mahmūd (r. 1246–1266)
18.4 × 11.9 cm
Inscribed verso (*devanāgarī*): sulatāna nas(ī)radīna

Ca 113/132
Sultān Ghiyās ud-Dīn Balban (r. 1266–1287)
18.5 × 12.1 cm
Inscribed verso (*devanāgarī*): sulatāna gayāsudīna

Ca 113/133
Shāh Husain
18.7 × 12.1 cm
Inscribed verso (*devanāgarī*): śāha hus(ai)na

Ca 113/134
Jalāl ud-Dīn Fīrōz Shāh Khiljī (r. 1290–1296)
18.3 × 12.1 cm
Inscribed verso (*devanāgarī*): śāha jalāladīna

Ca 113/135
Unidentified
18.3 × 12 cm
Inscribed verso (*devanāgarī*): śāha duladula

Ca 113/136
Shāh Sanjar (r. 1118–1157)
18.3 × 12 cm
Inscribed verso (*devanāgarī*): śāha ṣañjara

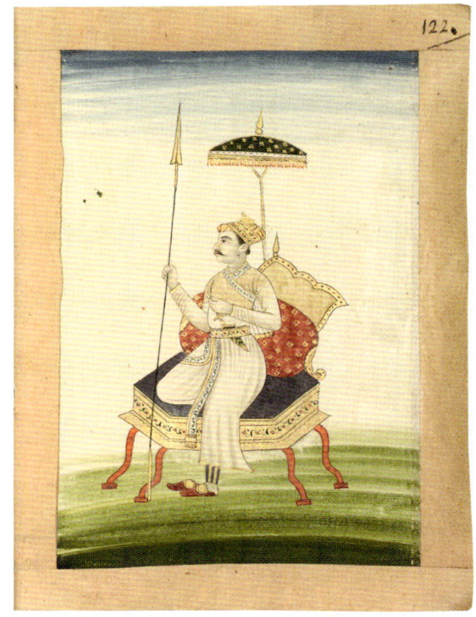

Ca 113/122

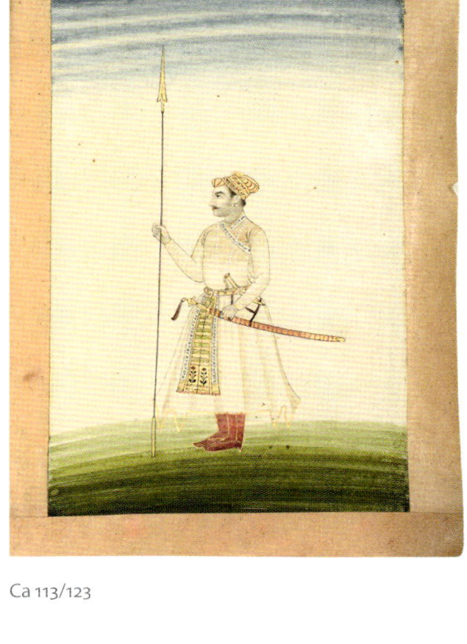

Ca 113/123

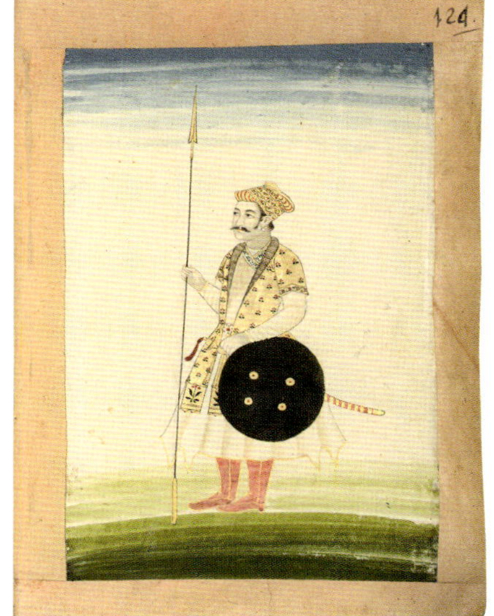

Ca 113/124

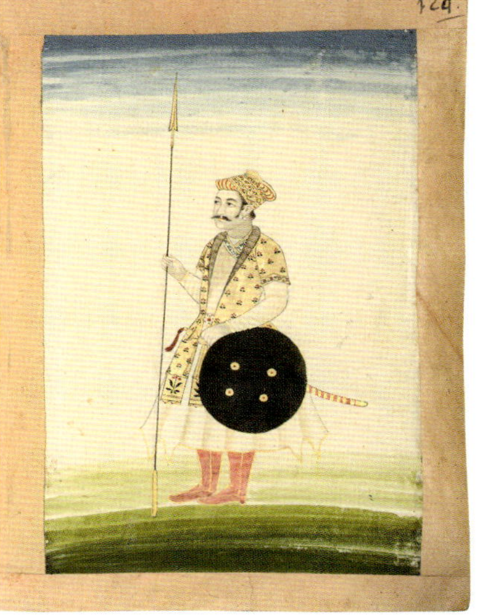

Ca 113/125

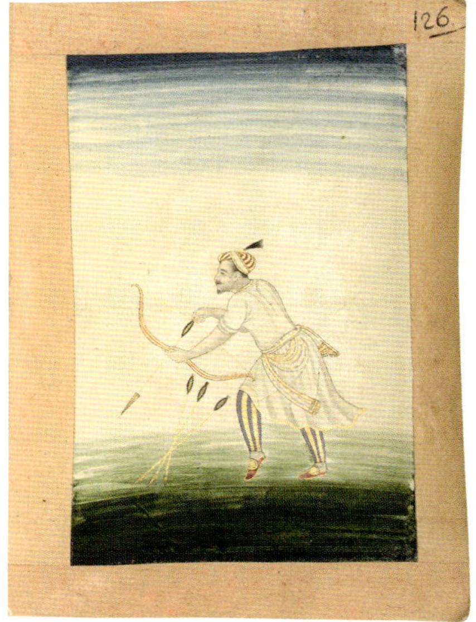

Ca 113/126

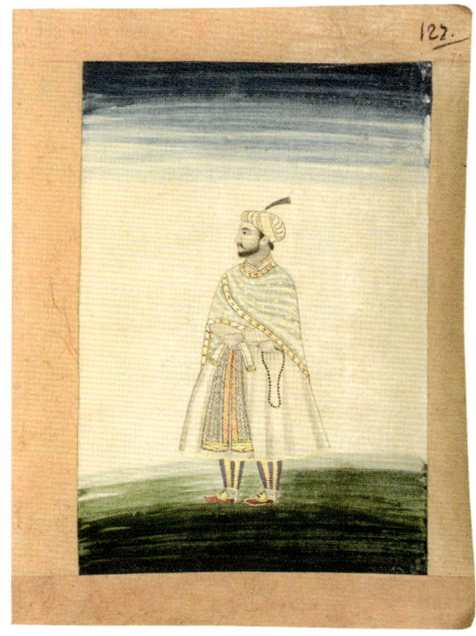

Ca 113/127

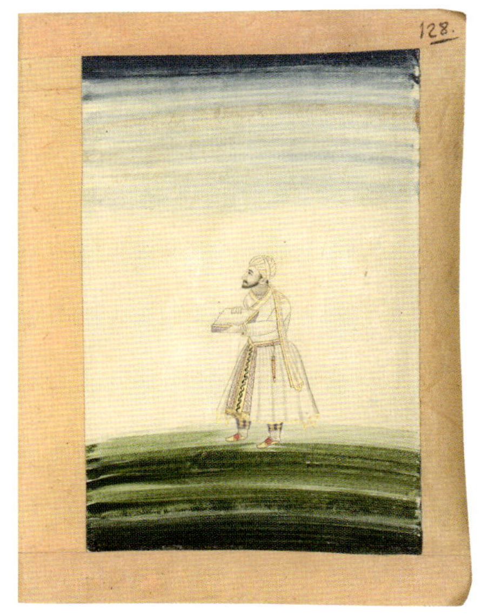

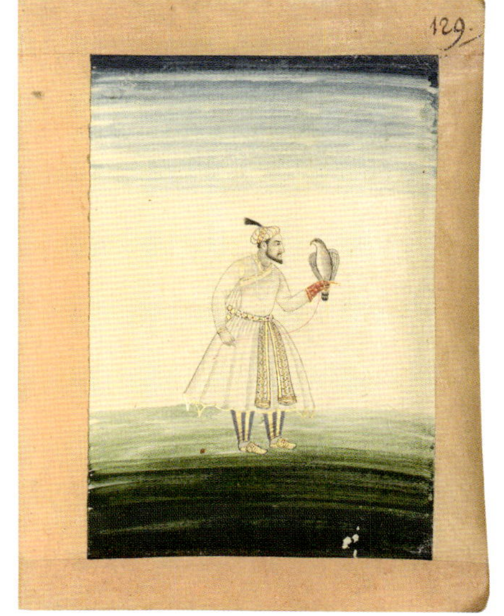

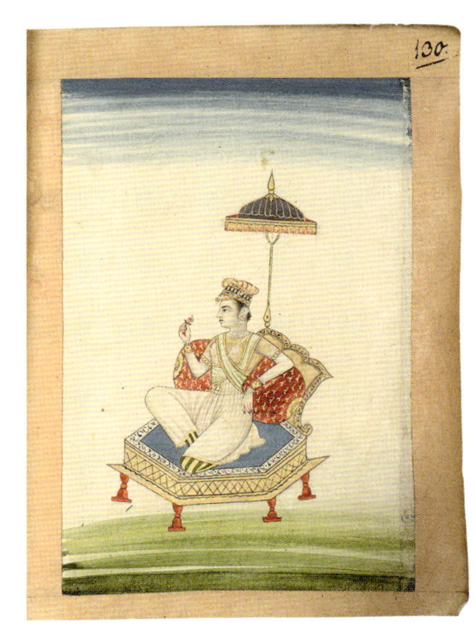

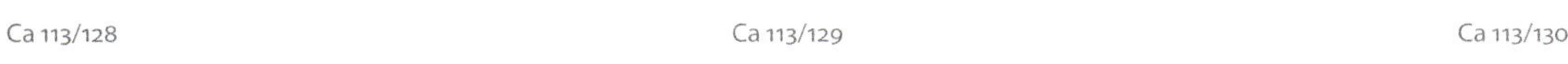

Ca 113/128

Ca 113/129

Ca 113/130

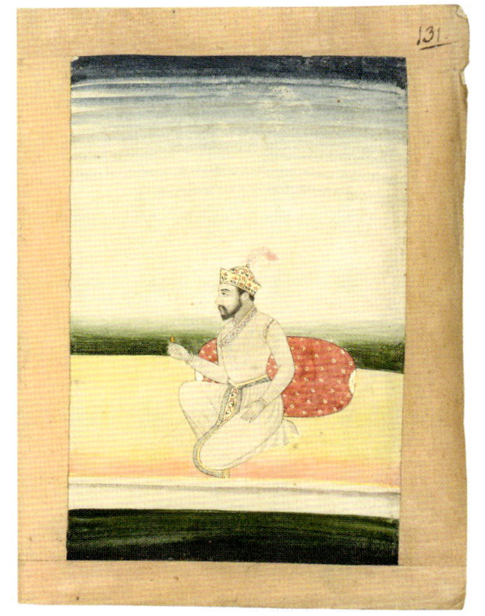

Ca 113/131

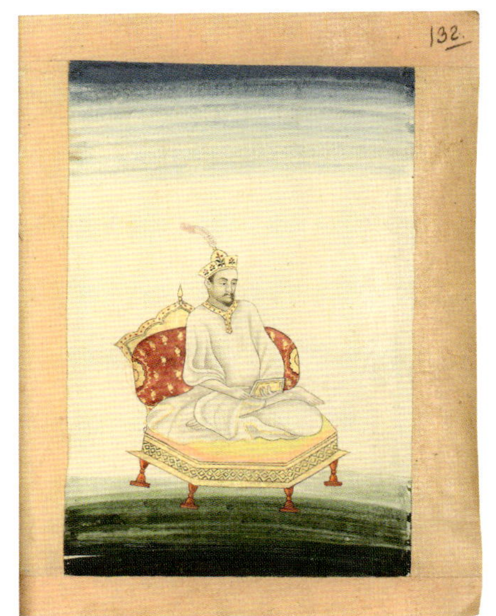

Ca 113/132

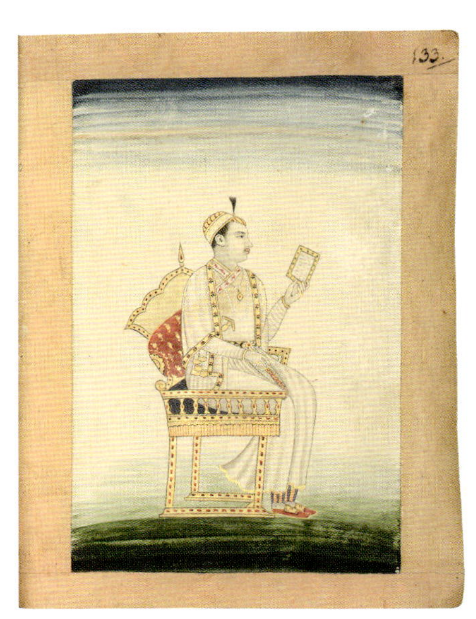

Ca 113/133

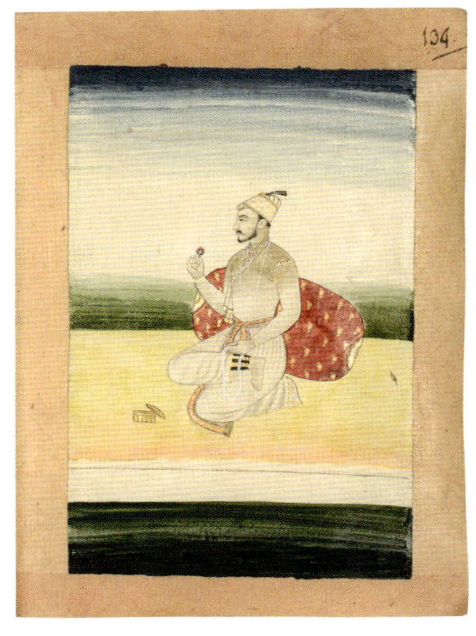

Ca 113/134

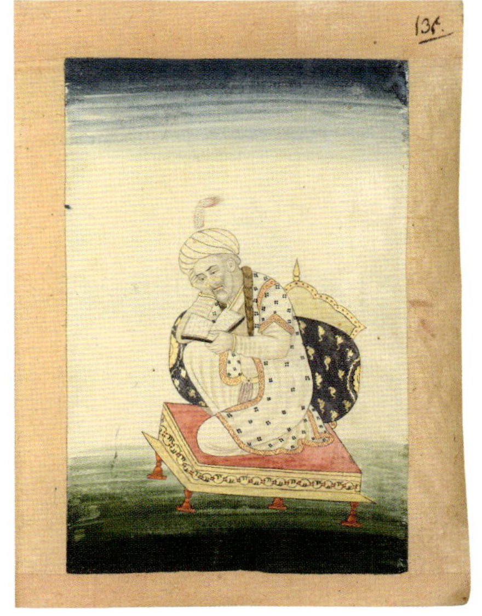

Ca 113/135

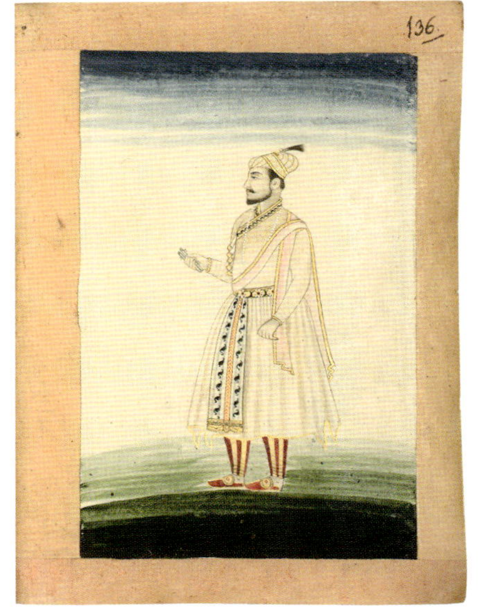

Ca 113/136

Ca 113/137
Shams ud-Dīn
18.5 × 11.9 cm
Inscribed verso (*devanāgarī*): samasudīna

Ca 113/138
Shāh 'Alā' ud-Dīn 'Omar Khiljī (r. 1296–1316)
18.5 × 12.1 cm
Inscribed verso (*devanāgarī*): śāha alāvadīna

Ca 113/139
Qutb ud-Dīn Mubārak Shāh (r. 1316–1320)
18.6 × 11.9 cm
Inscribed verso (*devanāgarī*): kutavadīna

Ca 113/140
Shāh Ghiyās ud-Dīn Tughluq I (r. 1320–1325)
18.5 × 11.9 cm
Inscribed verso (*devanāgarī*): śāha gayāsudīna

Ca 113/141
Unidentified
18.4 × 12 cm
Inscribed verso (*devanāgarī*): śāha saramasta

Ca 113/142
Unidentified
19 × 12.5 cm
Inscribed verso (*devanāgarī*): śāha ṣālaka

Ca 113/143
Unidentified
18.4 × 12 cm
Inscribed verso (*devanāgarī*): śāha mahammada alāvadīna

Ca 113/144
Sultān Fīrōz Shāh Tughluq (r. 1351–1388)
18.8 × 12.2 cm
Inscribed verso (*devanāgarī*): sulatāna perośāha

Ca 113/145
Sultān Muḥammad Tughluq [?]
17.9 × 11.7 cm
Inscribed verso (*devanāgarī*): sulatāna mahammada

Ca 113/146
Sultān Ahmad (Mahmūd) Bāyqarā (r. c. 1458–1511)
18.7 × 12.1 cm
Inscribed verso (*devanāgarī*):
sulatāna ahamadavāīpāva

Ca 113/147
Unidentified
17.9 × 11.5 cm
Inscribed verso (*devanāgarī*): kutabaśāha

Ca 113/148
Unidentified
18 × 11.8 cm
Inscribed verso (*devanāgarī*): lākanaśāha

Ca 113/149
Unidentified
18 × 11.7 cm
Inscribed verso (*devanāgarī*): nūrasāha gorī

Ca 113/150
Unidentified
18.3 × 12.1 cm
Inscribed verso (*devanāgarī*): … [illegible] jāumapati

Ca 113/151
Sultān Mahmūd Ghaznavī (971–1030)
18.2 × 11.9 cm
Inscribed verso (*devanāgarī*):
sulatāna mahamūda gajanavī

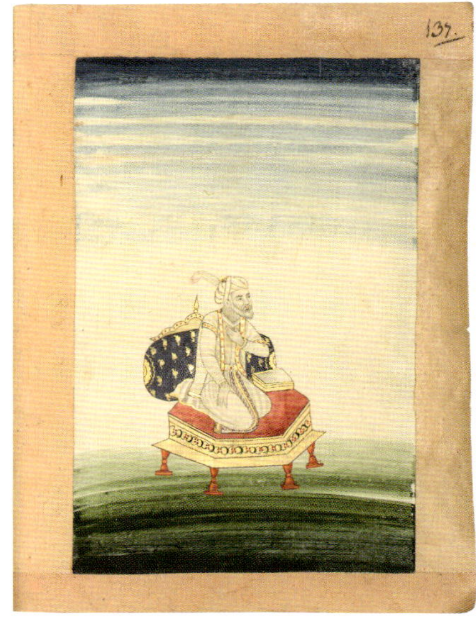

Ca 113/137

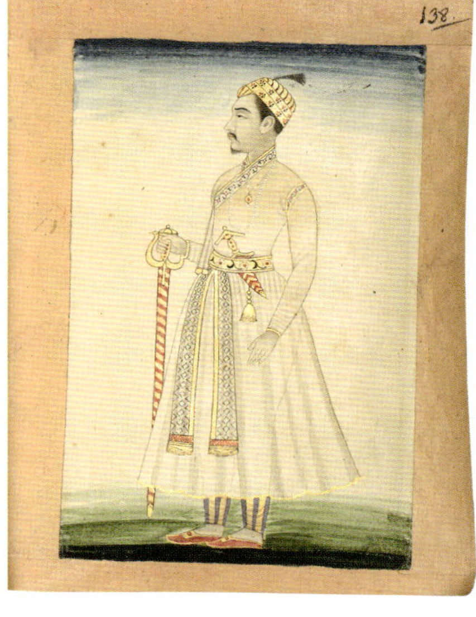

Ca 113/138

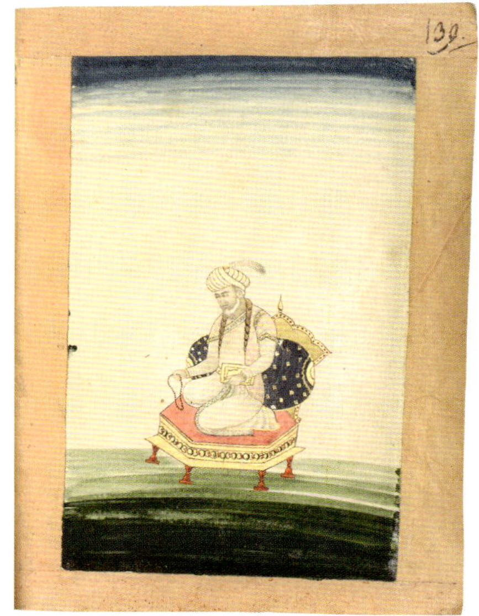

Ca 113/139

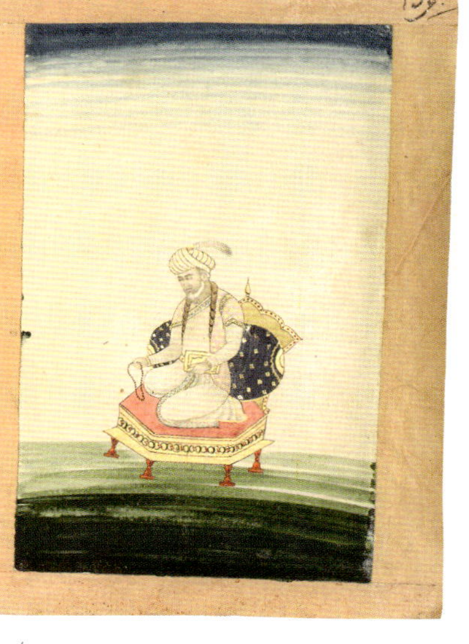

Ca 113/140

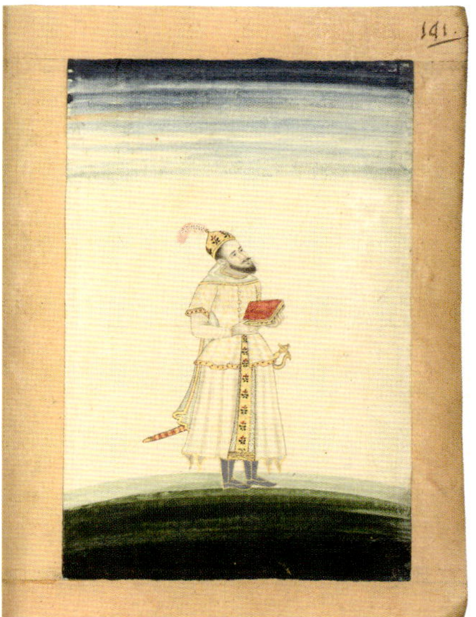

Ca 113/141

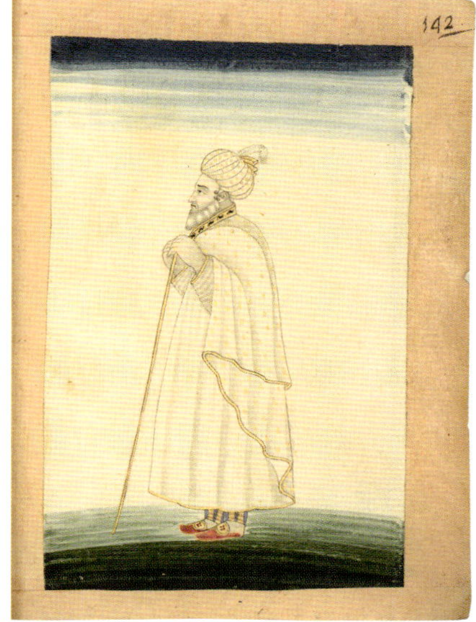

Ca 113/142

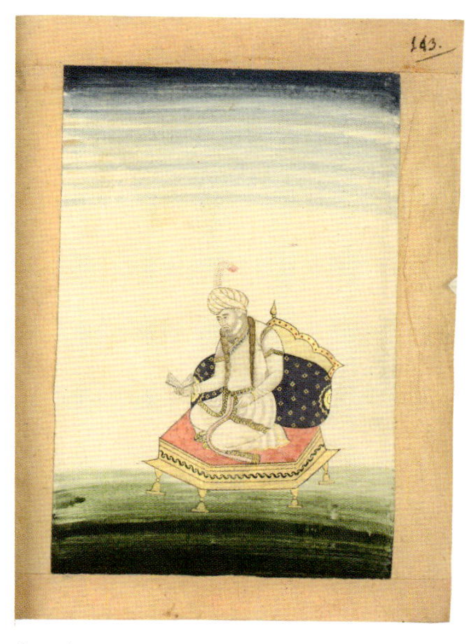

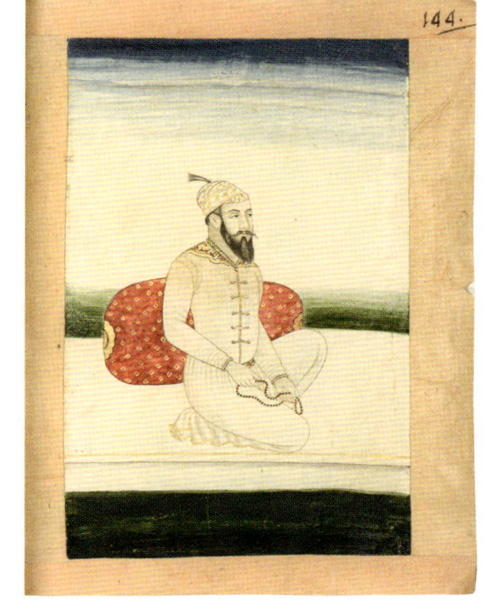

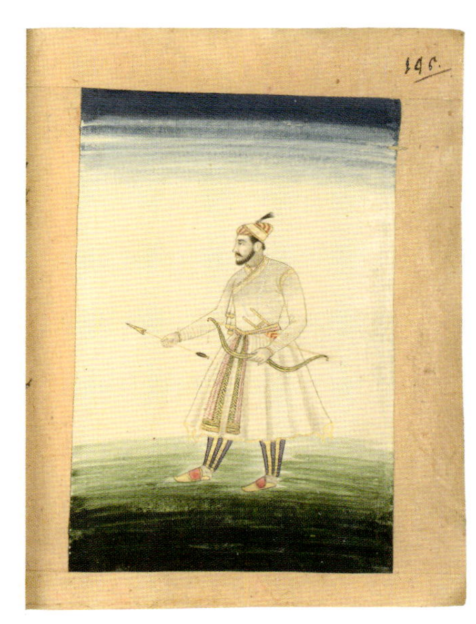

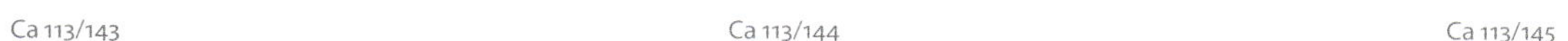

Ca 113/143

Ca 113/144

Ca 113/145

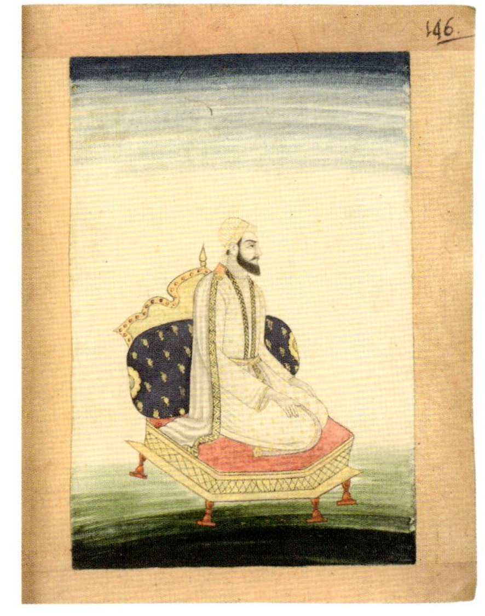

Ca 113/146

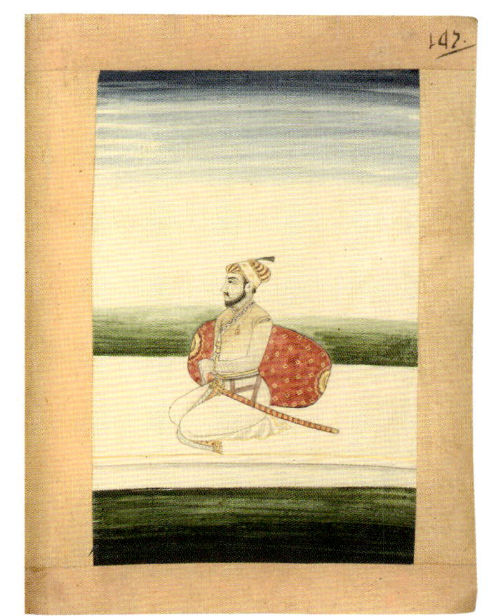

Ca 113/147

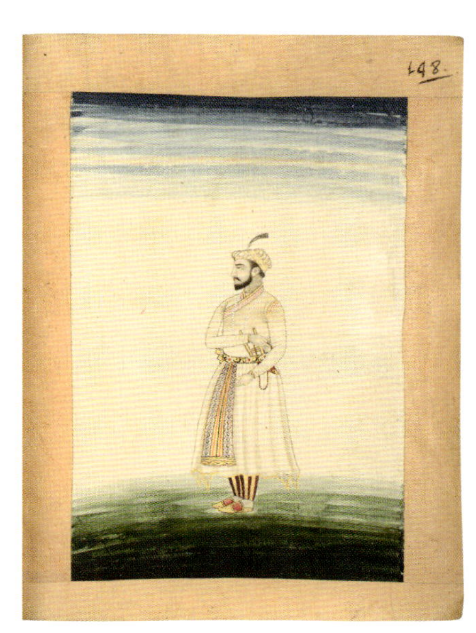

Ca 113/148

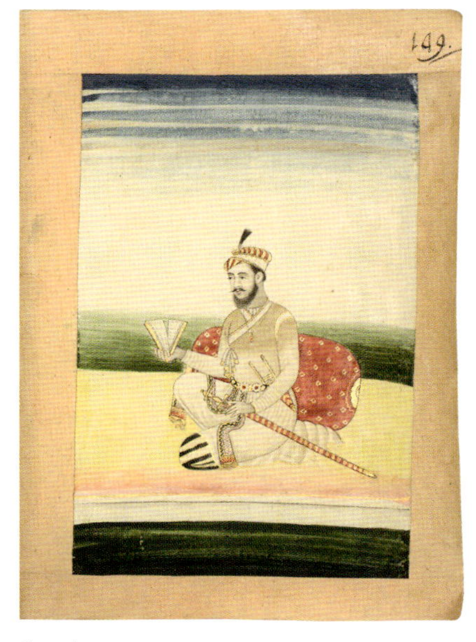

Ca 113/149

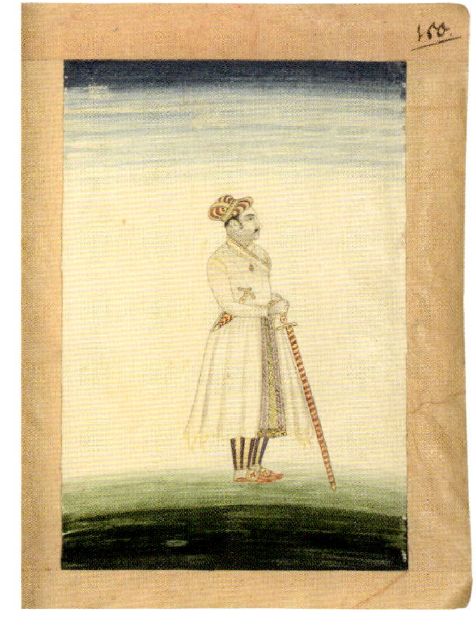

Ca 113/150

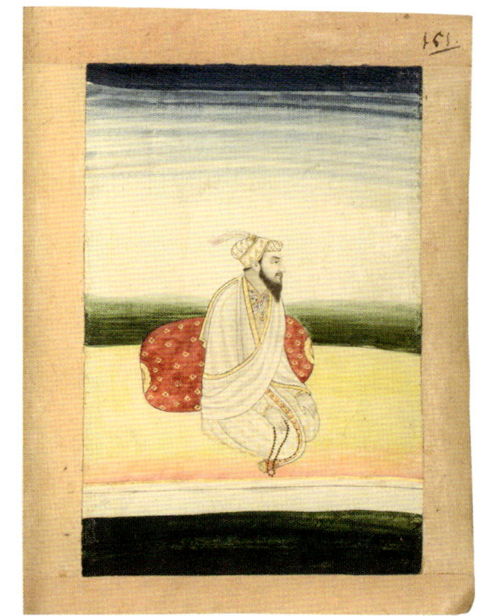

Ca 113/151

Ca 113/152
Shihāb ud-Daula Masūd (r. 1030–1041)
18.4 × 12.1 cm
Inscribed verso (*devanāgarī*): (ś)āha maulā

Ca 113/153
Unidentified
18.1 × 12 cm
Inscribed verso (*devanāgarī*): śāha ṭoḍā

Ca 113/154
Shāh Mubārak (r. 1421–1434)
18.1 × 11.7 cm
Inscribed verso (*devanāgarī*): sāha muvāraka

Ca 113/155
Unidentified
18.6 × 11.5 cm
Inscribed verso (*devanāgarī*): madhūsāha

Ca 113/156
Unidentified
18.7 × 11.8 cm
Inscribed verso (*devanāgarī*): sulatāna hamī sāha

Ca 113/157
Tīmūr Gurgān (r. 1370–1405)
18 × 11.6 cm
Inscribed verso (*devanāgarī*): taimūra

Ca 113/158
Shāh Muḥammad (r. 1578–1588)
18.2 × 11.6 cm
Inscribed verso (*devanāgarī*): śāha mahammada

Ca 113/159
Sultān Muḥammad (d. c. 1411)
18.2 × 11.6 cm
Inscribed verso (*devanāgarī*): sulatāna mahammada

Ca 113/160
Abū Sa'īd (r. c. 1451–1469)
17.9 × 11.8 cm
Inscribed verso (*devanāgarī*): abū saida

Ca 113/161
Mīrān Shāh (c. 1367–1408)
18.8 × 11.6 cm
Inscribed verso (*devanāgarī*): mīrā saida

Ca 113/162
'Omar Shaikh (r. 1469–1494)
18.4 × 11.3 cm
Inscribed verso (*devanāgarī*): umara śāha

Ca 113/163
Shāh 'Alā' ud-Dīn (r. 1445–1451)
18.6 × 12.2 cm
Inscribed verso (*devanāgarī*): śāha alāvadīna

Ca 113/164
Sultān Husain Bāyqarā (r. 1469–1506)
17.8 × 12 cm
Inscribed verso (*devanāgarī*): śāha husaina

Ca 113/165
Unidentified
18.4 × 12 cm
Inscribed verso (*devanāgarī*): śāha vajīl

Ca 113/166
Shāh Sikandar Lōdī (r. 1489–1517)
18 × 12.3 cm
Inscribed verso (*devanāgarī*): śāha sikandara

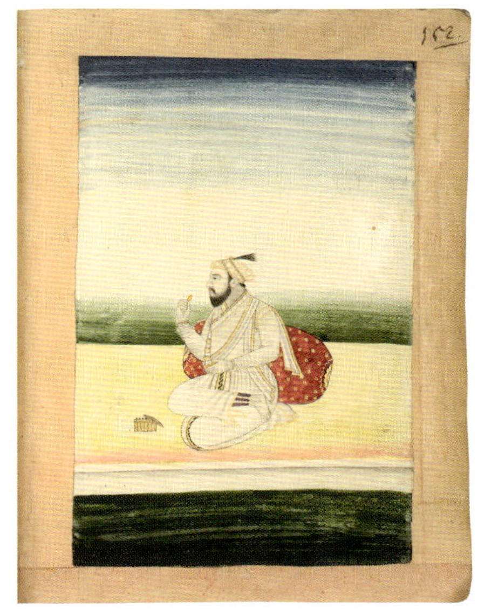

Ca 113/152

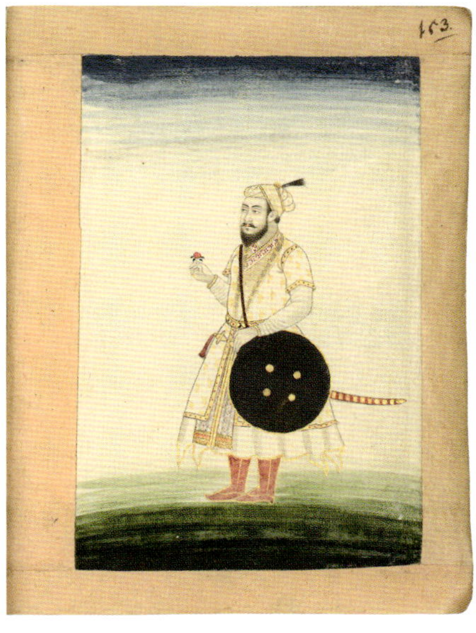

Ca 113/153

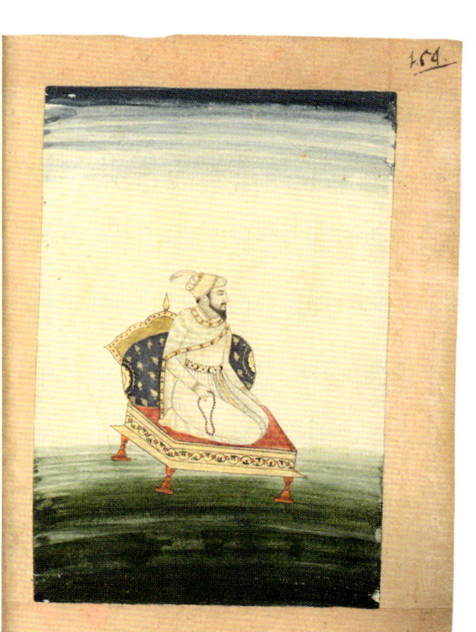

Ca 113/154

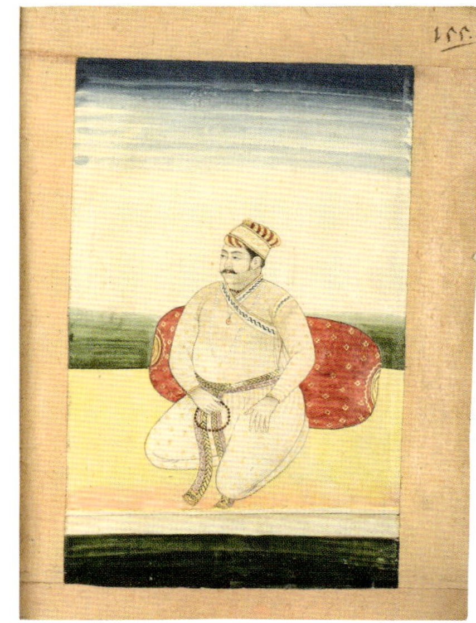

Ca 113/155

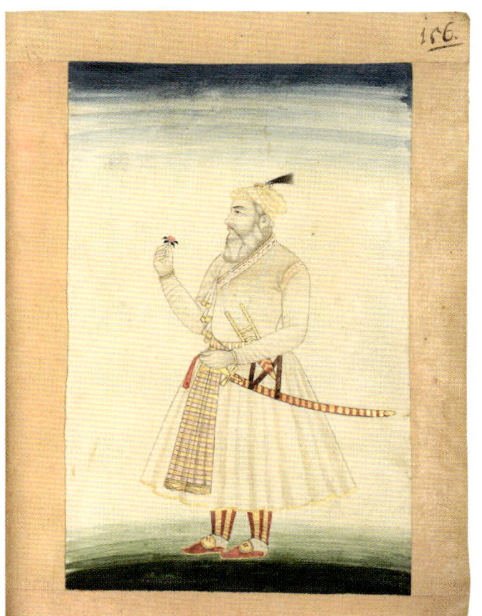

Ca 113/156

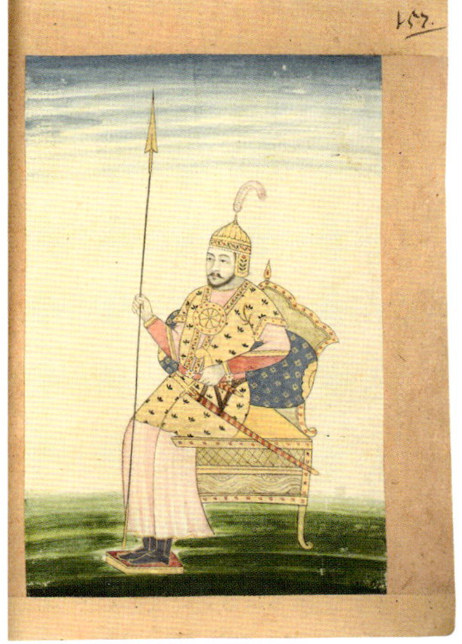

Ca 113/157

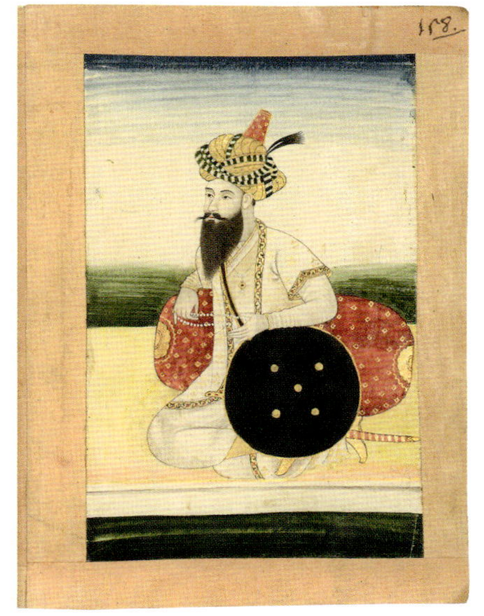

Ca 113/158

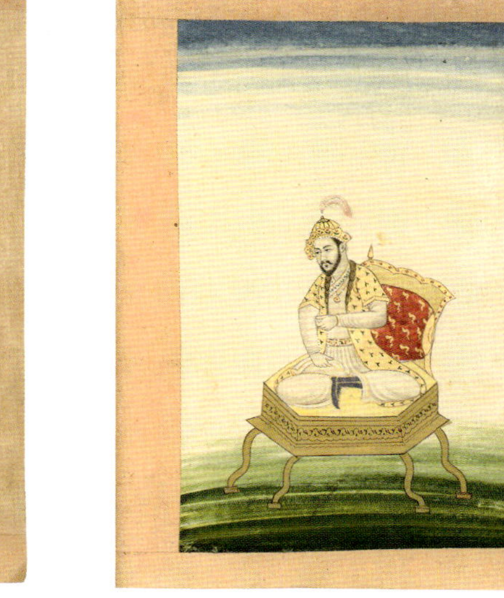

Ca 113/159

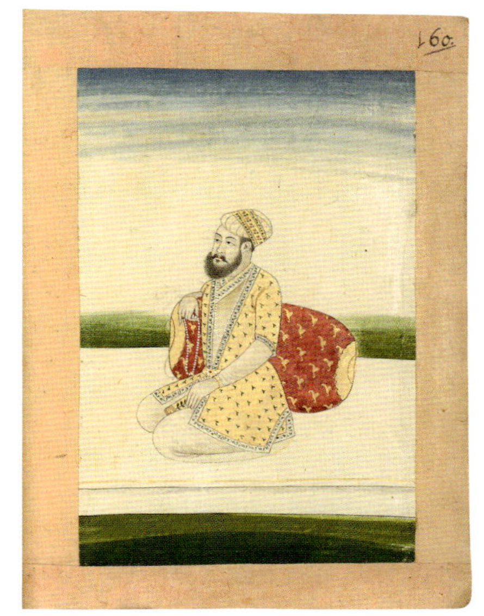

Ca 113/160

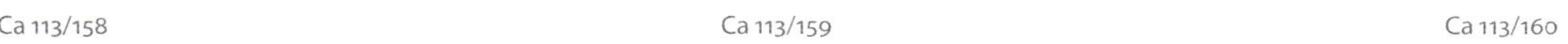

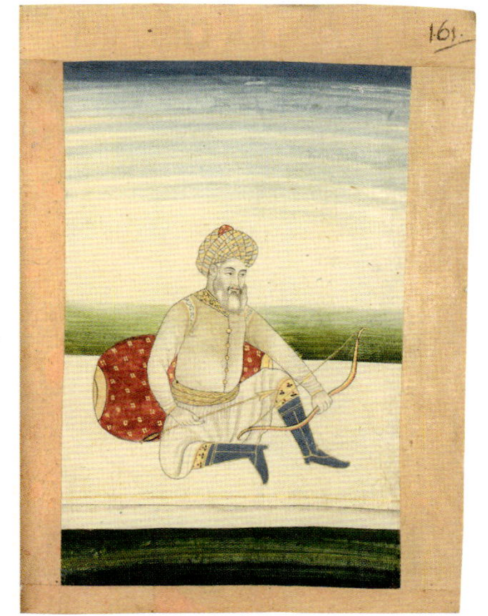

Ca 113/161

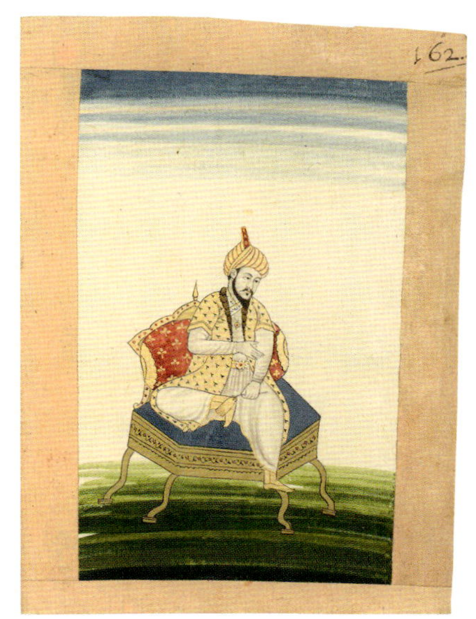

Ca 113/162

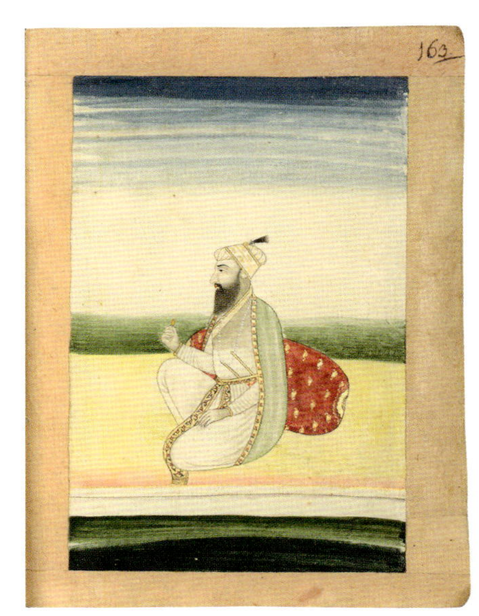

Ca 113/163

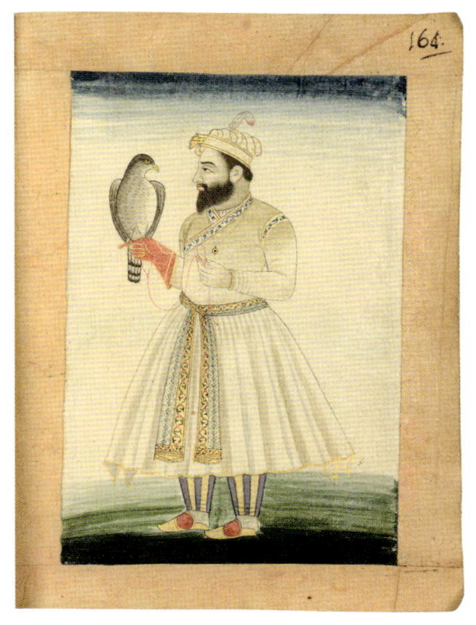

Ca 113/164

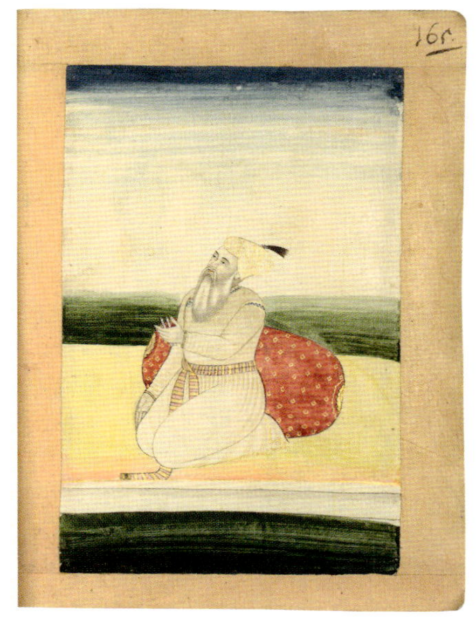

Ca 113/165

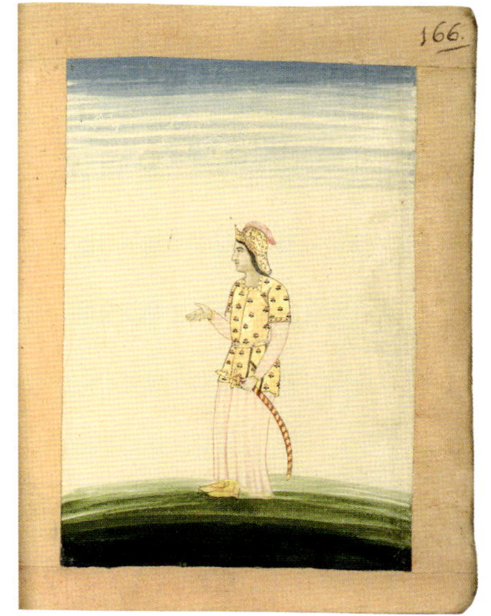

Ca 113/166

Ca 113/167
Shāh Ibrāhīm Lōdī (r. 1517–1526)
18.3 × 11.9 cm
Inscribed verso (*devanāgarī*): śāha ibarāhīma

Ca 113/168
Bābur (r. 1526–1530)
18.6 × 11.3 cm
Inscribed verso (*devanāgarī*): bābara

Ca 113/169
Shēr Shāh Sūrī (r. 1540–1545)
18.1 × 11.7 cm
Inscribed verso (*devanāgarī*): serasāha

Ca 113/170
Salīm (Islām) Shāh Sūrī (r. 1545–1554)
18 × 11.6 cm
Inscribed verso (*devanāgarī*): salemasāha

Ca 113/171
Fīrōz Shāh Sūrī (r. 1554)
18.6 × 12.2 cm
Inscribed verso (*devanāgarī*): saro sāha sakā

Ca 113/172
Muḥammad Khān (ʻAdlī) ʻĀdil Shāh Sūrī (r. 1554–1555)
17.9 × 11.9 cm
Inscribed verso (*devanāgarī*):
mahamada ṣāna adalī

Ca 113/173
Ibrāhīm Shāh Sūrī (r. 1555)
18.5 × 12 cm
Inscribed verso (*devanāgarī*): śāha ibarāhīma

Ca 113/174
Sikandar Shāh Sūrī (r. 1555)
18 × 12.1 cm
Inscribed verso (*devanāgarī*): śāha sikandara

Ca 113/175
Humāyūn (r. 1530–1540, 1555–1556)
16.9 × 11.8 cm
Inscribed verso (*devanāgarī*): humāūn

Ca 113/176
Akbar (r. 1556–1605)
18.4 × 11.2 cm
Inscribed verso (*devanāgarī*): akavara

Ca 113/177
Jahāngīr (r. 1605–1627)
18.1 × 11 cm
Inscribed verso (*devanāgarī*): jahāgira

Ca 113/178
Shāh Jahān (r. 1628–1658)
19.1 × 12.1 cm
Inscribed verso (*devanāgarī*): sāhi jahā

Ca 113/179
Aurangzēb (r. 1658–1707)
18.7 × 12.1 cm
Inscribed verso (*devanāgarī*): auragajeba

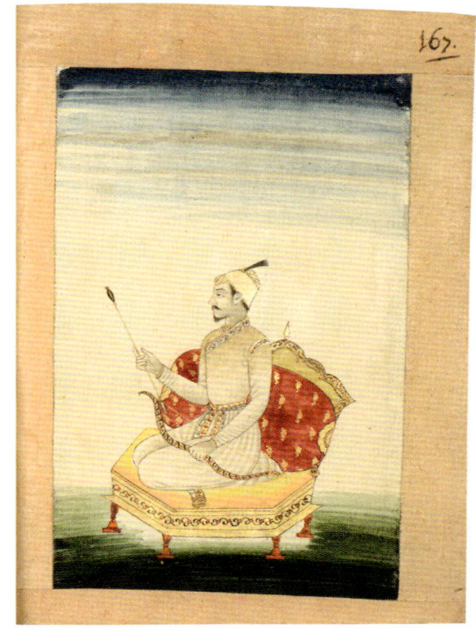

Ca 113/167

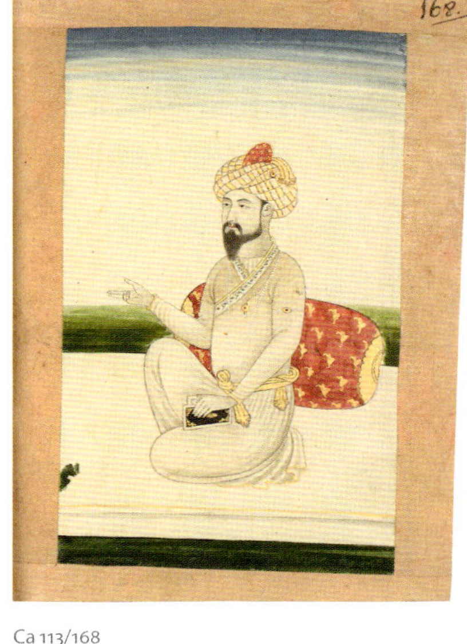

Ca 113/168

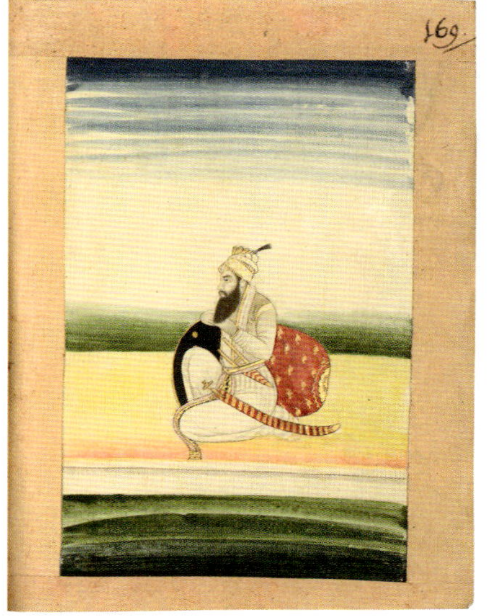

Ca 113/169

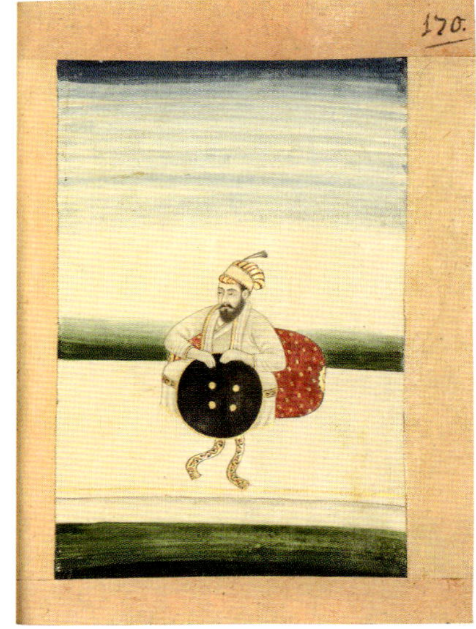

Ca 113/170

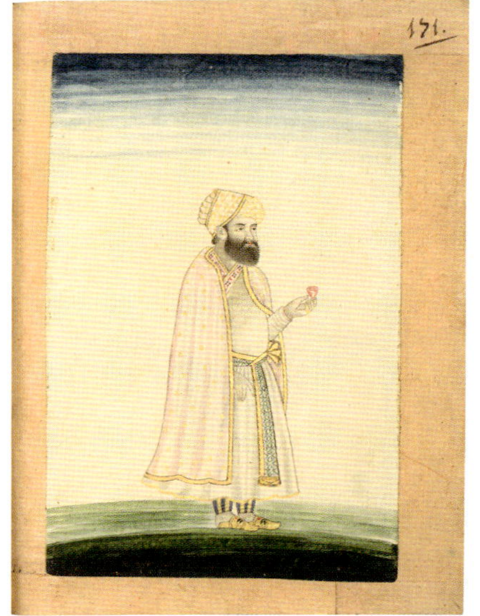

Ca 113/171

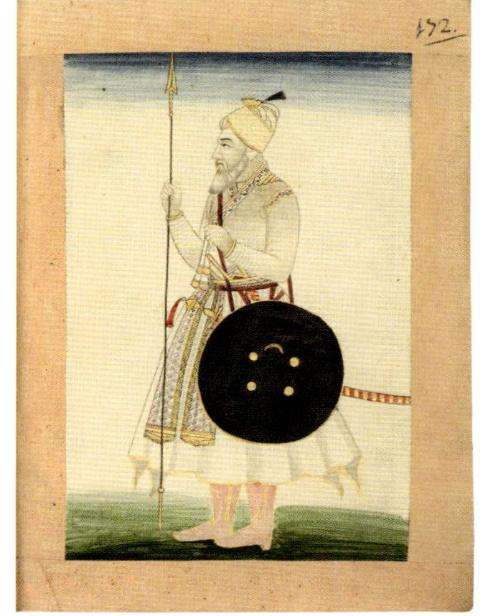

Ca 113/172

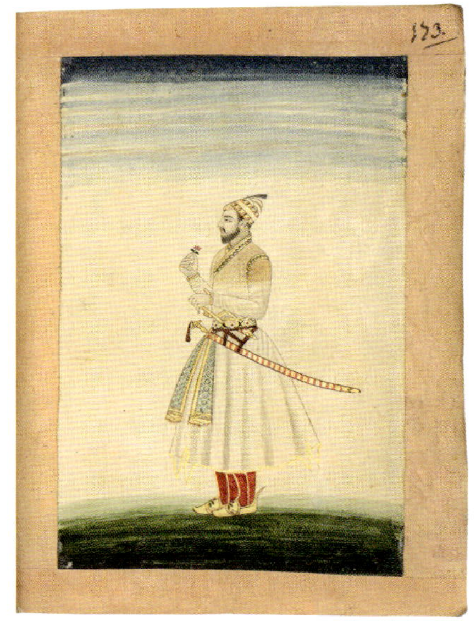

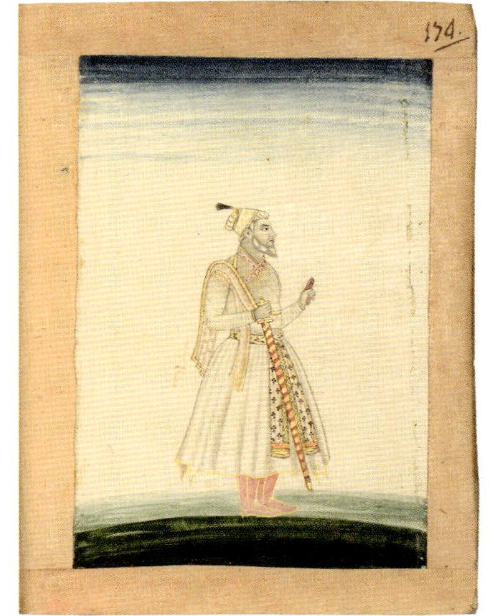

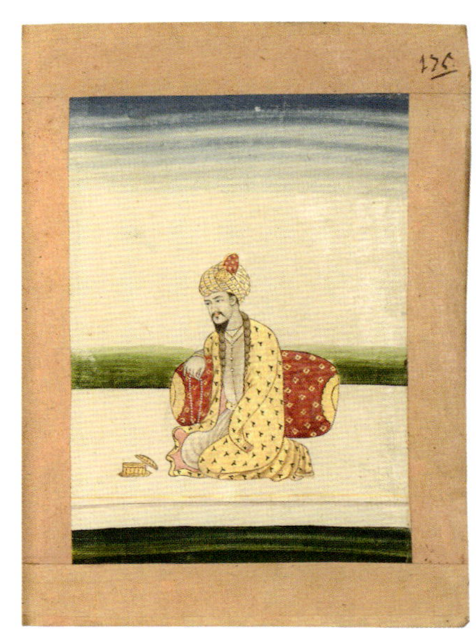

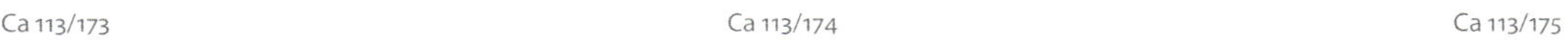

Ca 113/173

Ca 113/174

Ca 113/175

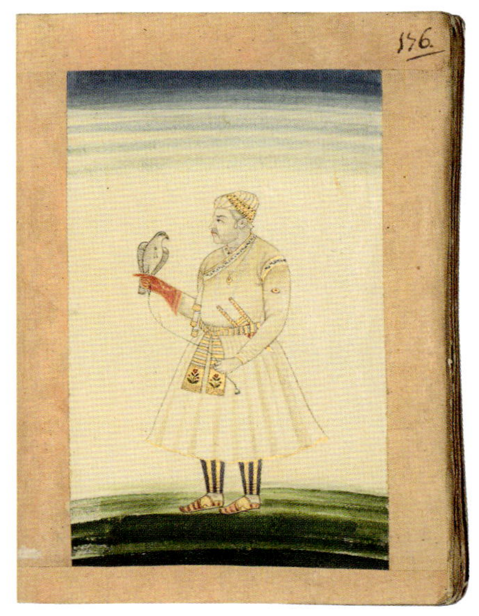

Ca 113/176

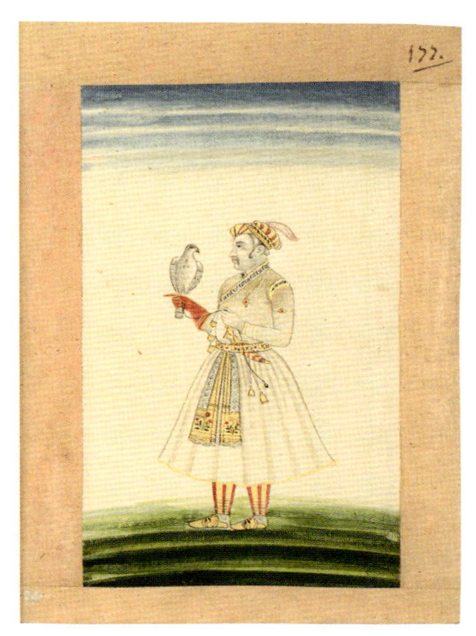

Ca 113/177

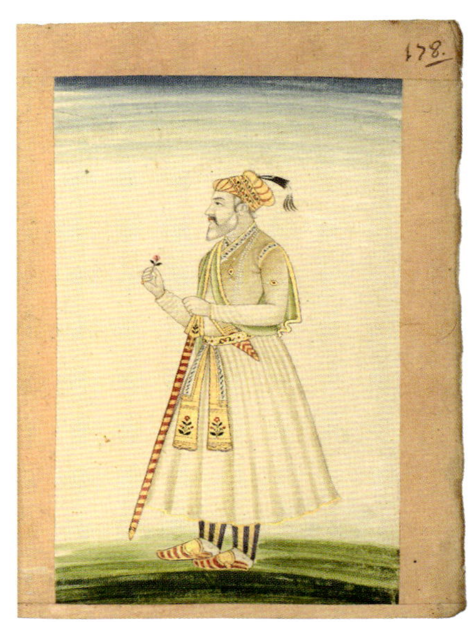

Ca 113/178

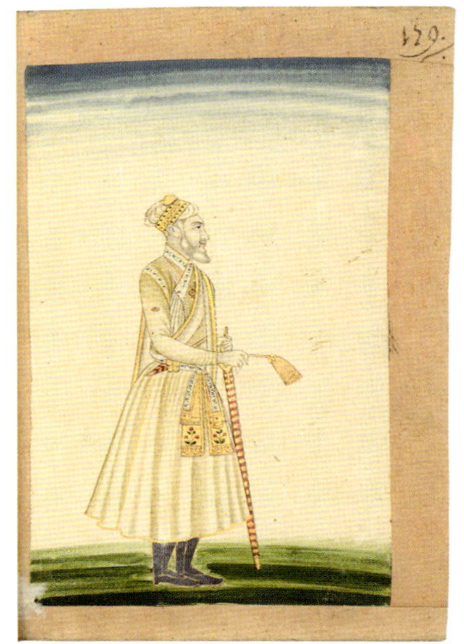

Ca 113/179

Cat. 4 | Ca 111

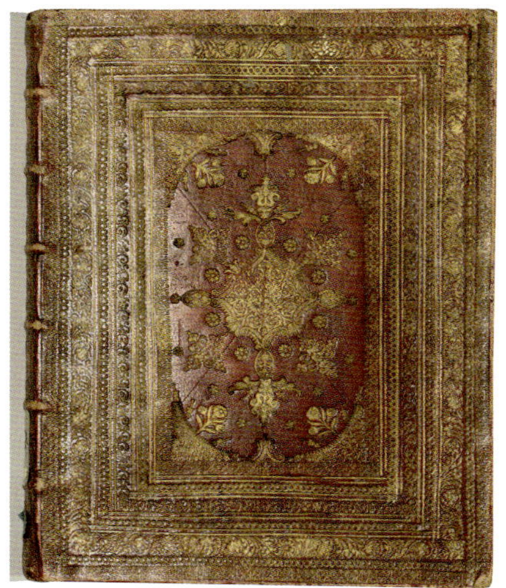

Fig. 1
Cat. 4 | Ca 111
Cover, left

Album with seventy-two portraits of Indian kings, noblemen and women
Deccani Mughal, late 17th – early 18th century
Album with 122 fols., European morocco leather binding, embossed with gold, 26.9 × 21.6 × c. 2.7 cm
72 images on 69 fols., pasted on the recto, watercolour and gold
One added loose leave with list of rulers nos. 1 to 62 in black ink, marbled pastedown, 28 empty fols.
References: Dresden 2017, cat. 18, pp. 155–6; Lunsingh Scheurleer 2017, p. 56

Album Ca 111 contains seventy-two Indian miniature portraits on Indian paper assembled in an eighteenth-century European style binding, with full leather covering, raised end bands, gold tooling, and marbled endpapers (fig. 1).[1] This album belongs to the fourth type.[2] It begins with visual genealogy of the Mughals in a set of twelve medallion busts from Tīmūr (r. 1370–1405) to Bahādur Shāh I (r. 1707–1712), cut and pasted onto the first two pages (Ca 111/1–12, fols. 7 and 8). An identification of the next four rulers—Mīrān Shāh (r. c. 1367–1408), Sultān Muḥammad (d. c. 1411), Abū Sa'īd (r. c. 1451–1469), and 'Omar Shaikh (r. 1469–1494)[3]—is difficult since their representations are very similar and have been inscribed differently in various collections[4] and are fundamentally distinguished by their costumes or gestures.

Sultān Muḥammad (Ca 111/18, fol. 14),[5] son of Mīrān Shāh, is shown in three-quarter profile, a technique frequently used to represent the Persian ancestors of the Mughal emperors who ruled in India. This image, incorrectly inscribed "Mīrān Shāh" in *devanāgarī*, is the most elaborate, showing him seated on a floral arabesque carpet, leaning on a bolster, and holding a bow and arrow. His image appears three more times in this album with different inscriptions. The first time (Ca 111/2, fol. 7) he is correctly listed as Sultān Muḥammad, the second (Ca 111/54, fol. 50) as "'Omar Shaikh", and the third (Ca 111/60, fol. 56) is inscribed "Abū Sa'īd" in *devanāgarī* and *nasta'līq*. This portrait is an example par excellence of the confusion surrounding the identification of the forefathers of the Mughals, which were copied, reproduced,[6] and inscribed in late-seventeenth and eighteenth-century artworks by both Indian artists and collectors.

The middle pages of the album contain representations of the Mughals from Bābur (r. 1526–1530) to Jahāndār Shāh (r. 1712–1713) along with depictions of the Hindu *rājās* and other high-ranking members of the court. These can be broadly divided into two types according to stylistic characteristics. In the first, the subjects are dressed in brightly coloured clothes with firm outlines, hard whitened faces, and a golden halo (fols. 9–23; fol. 30; fols. 34–7; fols. 43–6; fol. 49; fol. 50; fols. 52–4, and fol. 58). In the second, the artist used the *nīmqalam* (half-pen) technique, maintaining a high degree of finish, particularly in the treatment of faces, which are sensitively and carefully rendered with the use of slight shading for contours (fols. 24–9; fols. 31–3; fols. 38–42; fols. 47–8; fol. 51; and fols. 55–7). There are several stylistically related portrait albums of the second type in Dresden[7] and in other European collections. While the first type in Ca 111 compares closely to the album in Nationaalmuseum van Wereldculturen, Leiden[8] (Ca 111/47 [fol. 43] and fig. 2); the second type is comparable to paintings in: Schönbrunn Castle (fig. 3) and Österreichische Nationalbibliothek in Vienna; Liechtenstein Album in London along with reproductions in travelogues from Chatelain, 1719 and Valentijn, 1726 (figs. 4–5).[9] All these paintings show similarities to the Mughal style practiced in the Deccan by artists of various levels of skill creating works of art for a European audience.

While the majority of the Indian paintings in the Witsen album can be dated stylistically to the period between the reigns of Aurangzēb (r. 1658–1707) and Bahādur Shāh I (r. 1707–1712), the album Ca 111 was assembled about 1712 in Amsterdam. This dating is based on a sheet of paper attached to the album that lists the names of the people represented spelled in a phonetic Dutch[10] with watermarks that are comparable to the "Arms of Amsterdam" watermark and a Dutch contramark "AC" dated 1711[11] and another "coat of arms" dated 1720.[12] Although the paper used for this list is not the same as the endpapers of the album, there exists another watermark on these endpapers that is comparable to the Dutch Strasburg Lily watermark of 1625.[13]

Most portraits in Ca 111 are accompanied by inscriptions either in *devanāgarī*, *nast'alīq*, or Dutch and sometimes a combination of two or even all three.[14] The presence of Dutch inscriptions further suggests that these portraits were acquired by a

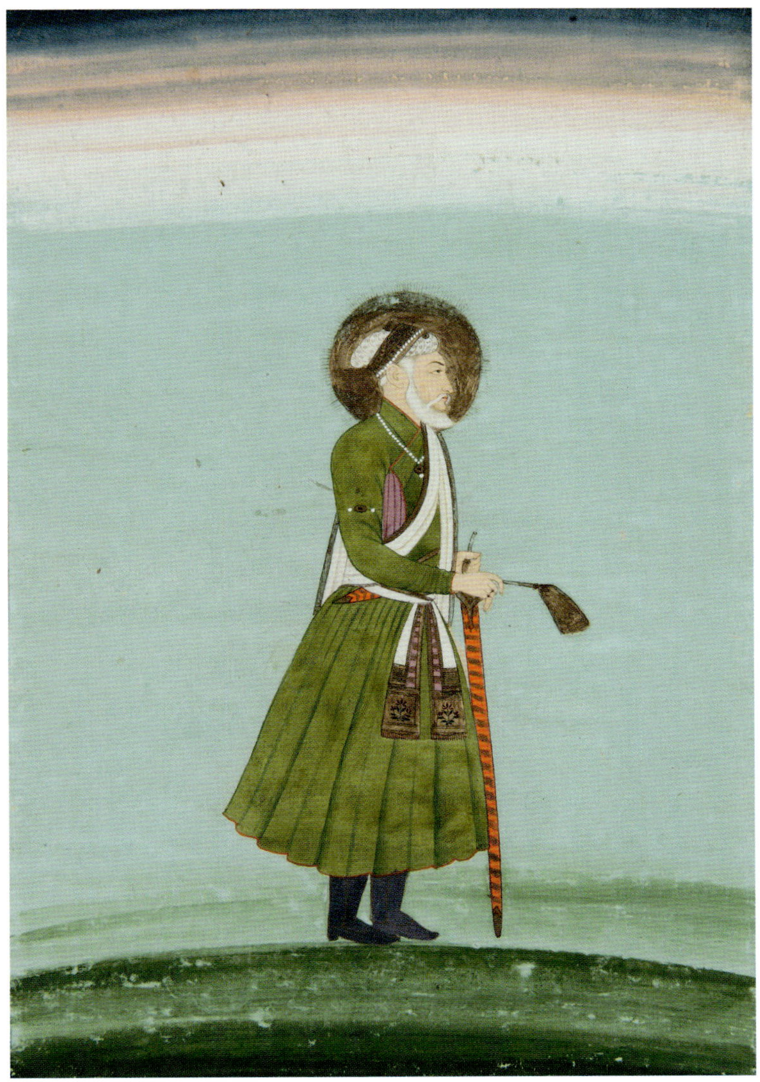

Fig. 2
Aurangzēb (r. 1658–1707)
Deccani Mughal, early 18th century
Watercolour and gold, 23 × 15.7 cm
Nationaalmuseum van Wereldculturen, Leiden (transferred from the Cabinet of Rarities, The Hague, 1883), inv. no. RV-360-990

Dutchman, who might have translated the inscriptions before putting the miniatures together as a set. Finally, the depiction of the last ruling emperor is Jahāndār Shāh (r. 1712–1713), thereby confirming the date of circa 1712 for assembly.

As deduced from the watermarks and the Dutch inscriptions, this album, like many others in the Dresden collection, was apparently in the possession of Nicolaas Witsen. After his death, his collection was sold (Amsterdam, March 30, 1728).[15] Lot 8 in the sale catalogue is "Een Boek met in de 60 stuks Portraiten, zynde het geslagt van den grooten Tamerlaan en deszelfs Nakomelingen, benevens de voornaamste Grooten des Ryks, in een Marokyne band" (A book with sixty portraits, depicting the great Tīmūr and his descendants, in addition to the greatest of the empire, in a morocco album).[16] The same album is mentioned in the Heucher Inventory in Dresden item 29: "Das Geschlecht der Tamerlans, nebst inliegender Verzeichnung, in roth mit Gold verziert Saffian gebunden. n. 8."[17] (The dynasty of the Timurids, a list included, bound in Saffiano decorated in red and gold.). Noting the similarity of these records and the mention of number eight in both, it is beyond doubt that Ca 111 was also in the Witsen collection.

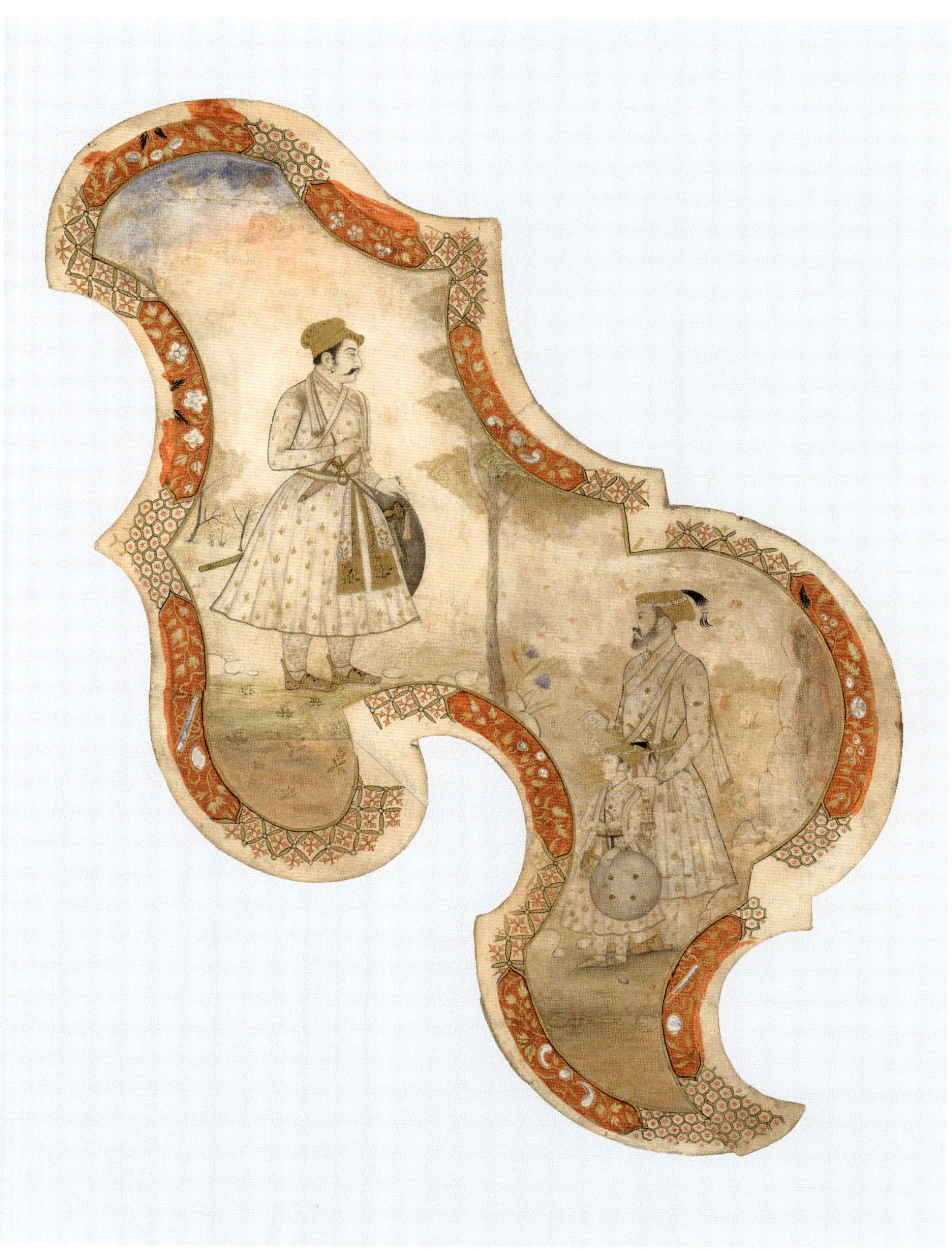

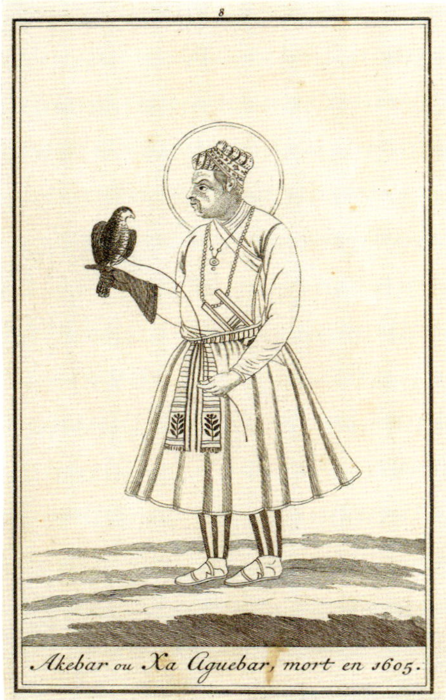

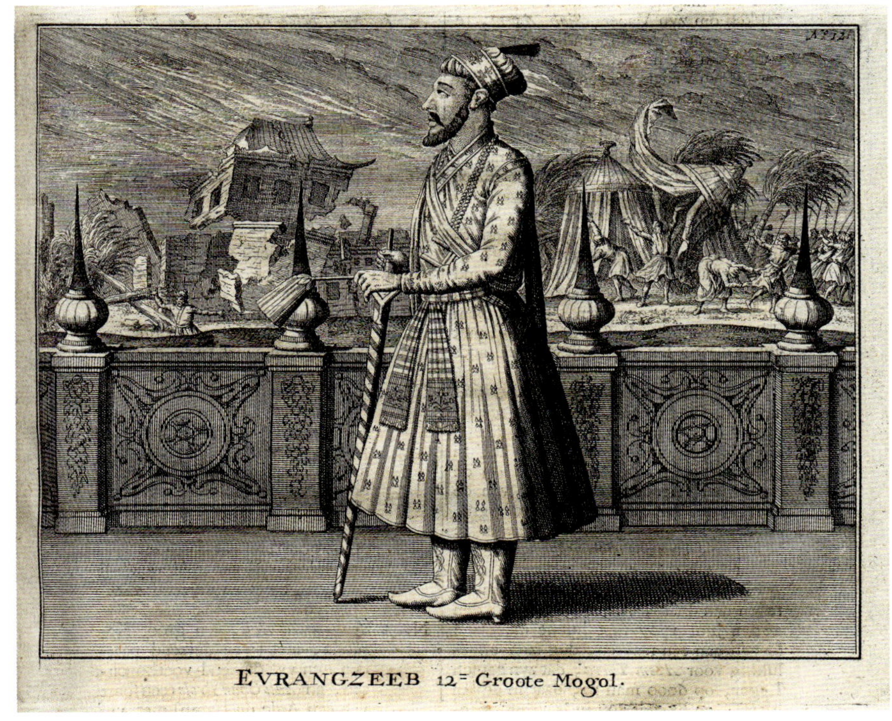

The last ten works subsequently added to the album (fols. 59–68)[18] are depictions of women. Folio 66, dating to the eighteenth century, is titled "A female devotee" and depicts a kneeling saint. She wears a *tilak* (a mark on the forehead) and Indian garments and recalls the eighth-century Iraqi Muslim saint Rābiʿa of Basra (c. 714–801), who was revered as an exemplary ascetic.[19] Other images of women in this album, perhaps royalty, are so finely rendered that they are comparable to the courtly paintings one finds in northern India in the early seventeenth century. These pictures, which differ in size from most of the images in the album, show a delicate rendering of facial features with attention paid to details and finish that is more typical of Mughal style. NB

Notes | 1 Information courtesy of Kristine Rose Beers. | 2 See pp. 44–5. | 3 Berlia 2017, p. 155. | 4 Rijksmuseum, Amsterdam, Canter Visscher album, inv. nos. NG-2008-60-2, 4, 5, and 13; Nationaalmuseum van Wereldculturen Leiden, inv. no. 360-7346 to 51; Ca 116 and Ca 113; Victoria & Albert Museum, London, inv. no. IM9-1912; Bodleian Library, Oxford, MS. Ind. Misc. d. 3. See Chatelain 1719; and Valentijn 1726. | 5 The portrait corresponds to other illustrations of Sultān Muḥammad as seen in the *Atlas Historique*; Chatelain 1719, p. 110, no. 3. | 6 Valentijn 1725, pl. 3, p. 176. | 7 See cat. 3 (Ca 113) and cat. 16 (Ca 124/4). | 8 Nationaalmuseum van Wereldculturen, Leiden (transferred from the Cabinet of Rarities, The Hague, 1883), inv. no. 360-99. | 9 Schönbrunn Castle, Vienna, inv. no. SKB 2648; Liechtenstein Album; see also Losty 2012, cat. 25, p. 71, no. 8; Österreichische Nationalbibliothek, Vienna, sig. Cod. Min. 44, no. 32 (fol. 17). | 10 See Appendices, pp. 240–1. | 11 Churchill 1935, no. 46. This info was kindly provided by Pauline Lunsingh Scheurleer in consultation with Eric Hinterding, curator Print Room, Rijksmuseum Amsterdam. | 12 Heawood 1950, no. 417. | 13 Ibid., no. 401. | 14 These inscriptions are now hidden as the sheets were pasted into the album and could be made visible by using transmitted light. See pp. 34–5, figs. 1a and 1b. | 15 See Amsterdam 1738, p. 10. | 16 Amsterdam 1728, p. 10. | 17 Heucher Inventory 1738, sig. Cat. 1, p. 157, no. 29. | 18 These are not mentioned in the inventory of 1738, p. 157, no. 29, or in the contemporary list attached to the volume. | 19 This information was kindly provided by Ursula Weekes.

◄ Fig. 3
Shāh Jahān with Young Dārā Shikōh
Mughal, late 17th century
Watercolour and gold, 45 × 35 cm
Schönbrunn Castle, Vienna,
inv. no. SKB 2637

Fig. 4
Bernard Picart (1673–1733)
Akbar (r. 1556–1605)
Etching and engraving, image 10.5 × 16.6 cm
Single sheet cut out from: Henri Chatelain, *Atlas Historique* (Amsterdam 1719), vol. 5, no. 37, p. 110, fig. 8
Kupferstich-Kabinett, Staatliche Kunstsammlungen Dresden,
inv. no. Ca 1980-26 (24)

Fig. 5
Aurangzēb (r. 1658–1707)
Etching in: François Valentijn, *Oud en Nieuw Oost-Indien* (Dordrecht 1726), part 4.2, p. 275, pl. 12
Sächsische Landesbibliothek – Staats- und Universitätsbibliothek Dresden,
sig. Hist.Asiae.88-4,2

Ca 111/1 to 12 (fol. 7 and 8)
Twelve Medallion Portraits of the Grand Mughals
Early 18th century

Ca 111/1
Tīmūr (r. 1370–1405)
5.1 × 4.3 cm

Ca 111/2
Mīrān Shāh (d. 1408)
5.6 × 4.9 cm

Ca 111/3
Sultān Muḥammad (d. c. 1411)
5 × 4.3 cm

Ca 111/4
Abū Sa'īd (d. 1469) or 'Omar Shaikh (d. 1494)
5.3 × 4.5 cm

Ca 111/5
Abū Sa'īd (d. 1469) or 'Omar Shaikh (d. 1494)
5.3 × 4.6 cm

Ca 111/6
Bābur (r. 1526–1530)
5.3 × 5.6 cm

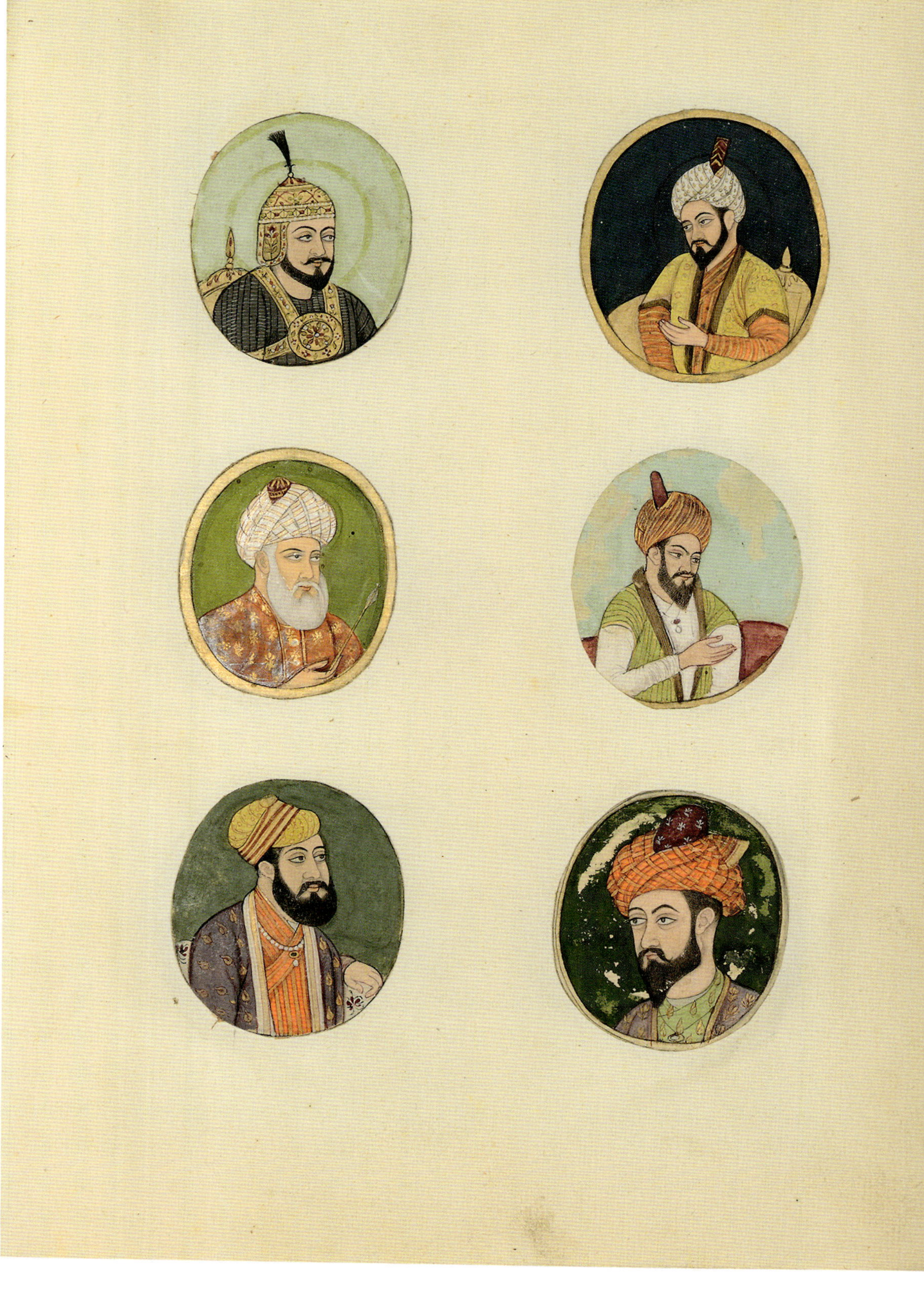

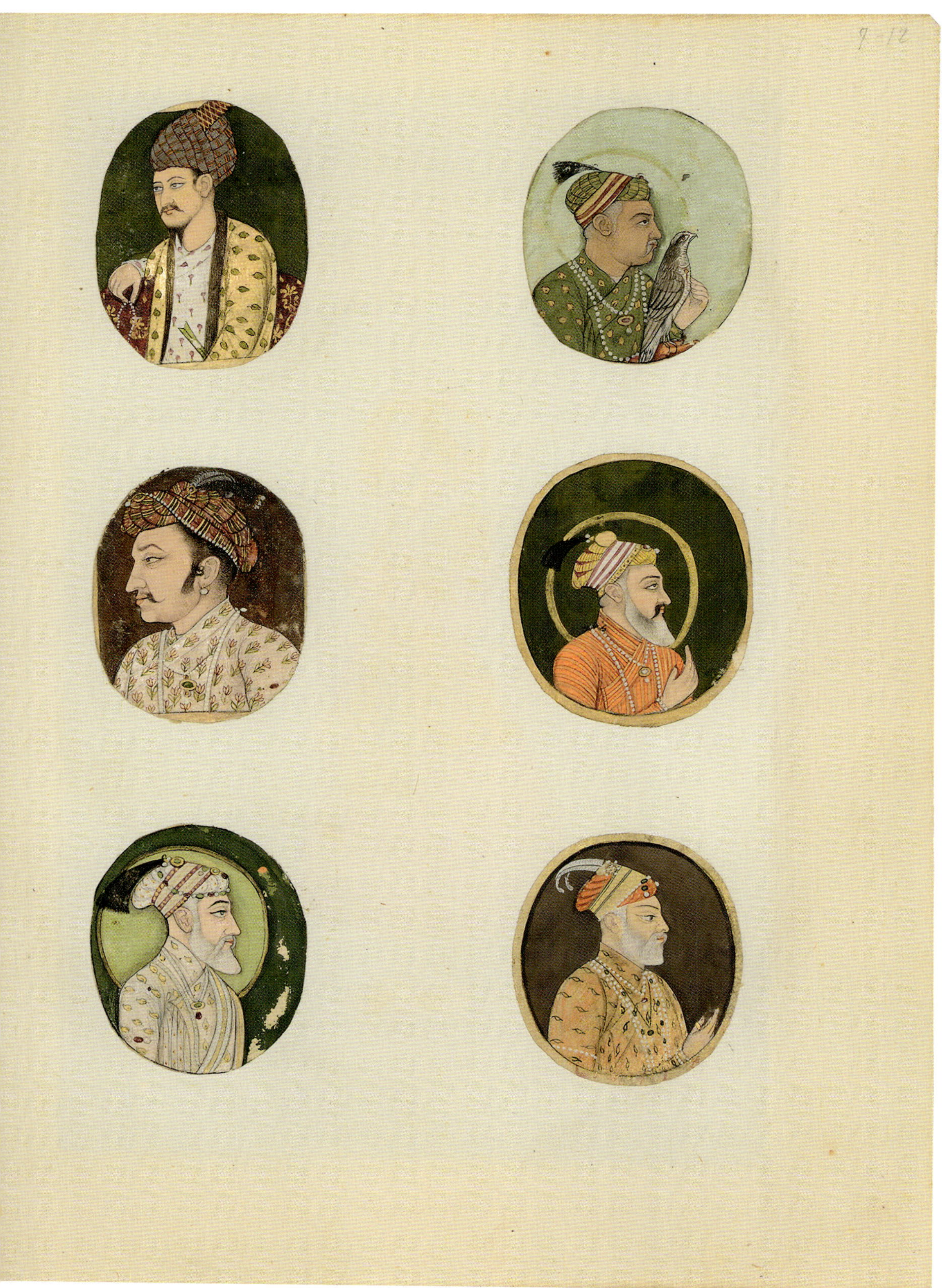

Ca 111/7
Humāyūn
(r. 1530–1540, 1555–1556)
5.5 × 4.2 cm

Ca 111/8
Akbar (r. 1556–1605)
5.1 × 4.5 cm

Ca 111/9
Jahāngīr (r. 1605–1627)
5.1 × 4.2 cm

Ca 111/10
Shāh Jahān (r. 1628–1658)
5.5 × 4.7 cm

Ca 111/11
Aurangzēb (r. 1658–1707)
5 × 4.3 cm

Ca 111/12
Bahādur Shāh I (r. 1707–1712)
5.1 × 4.5 cm

Ca 111/13 (fol. 9)
Shāh Jahān (r. 1628–1658)
21.4 × 13.9 cm

Ca 111/14 (fol. 10)
Parvīz (1589–1626)
21.1 × 11.5 cm

Ca 111/15 (fol. 11)
Khusrau (1587–1622) [?]
20.8 × 13.9 cm

Ca 111/16 (fol. 12)
'Azīm-ush-Shān (1664–1712)
21.5 × 14 cm

Ca 111/17 (fol. 13)
Rājā Todar Māl (d. 1589)
20.1 × 11.9 cm

Ca 111/18 (fol. 14)
Sultān Muḥammad (d. c. 1411)
20.3 × 11.8 cm

Ca 111/19 (fol. 15)
Shahriyār (r. Nov 1627–Jan 1628) [?]
21.3 × 11.3 cm

Ca 111/20 (fol. 16)
Shāh Shujā' (1616–1661)
21.4 × 14 cm

Ca 111/21 (fol. 17)
Daniyāl (1572–1604)
21.3 × 14.4 cm

Ca 111/22 (fol. 18)
Muḥammad A'zam Shāh (r. 1707)
20.3 × 11.8 cm

Ca 111/23 (fol. 19)
Jahāndār Shāh (r. 1712–1713)
21.5 × 14.1 cm

Ca 111/24 (fol. 20)
Murād Bakhsh (1624–1661)
21.9 × 13.7 cm

Ca 111/25 (fol. 21)
Bahādur Shāh I (r. 1707–1712)
21.3 × 14.1 cm

Ca 111/26 (fol. 22)
Muḥammad A'zam Shāh (r. 1707)
21.6 × 14.1 cm

Ca 111/27 (fol. 23)
Rānā Rāj Sīngh (r. 1652–1680) / Rām Sīngh (d. 1658)
22 × 15.9 cm

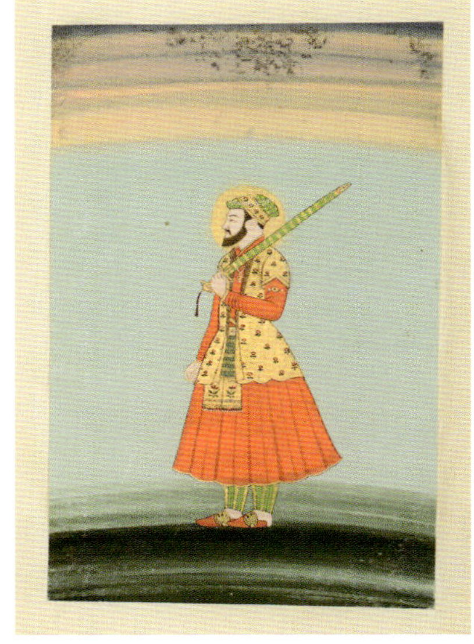

Ca 111/13 (fol. 9)

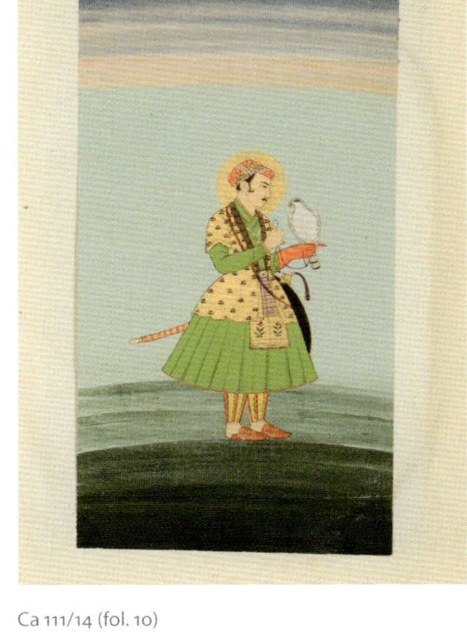

Ca 111/14 (fol. 10)

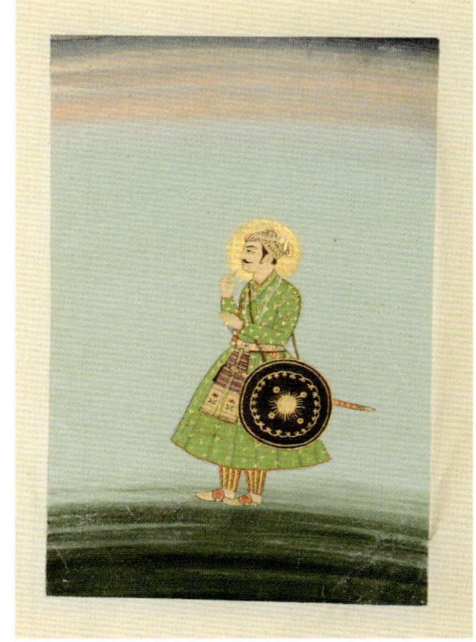

Ca 111/15 (fol. 11)

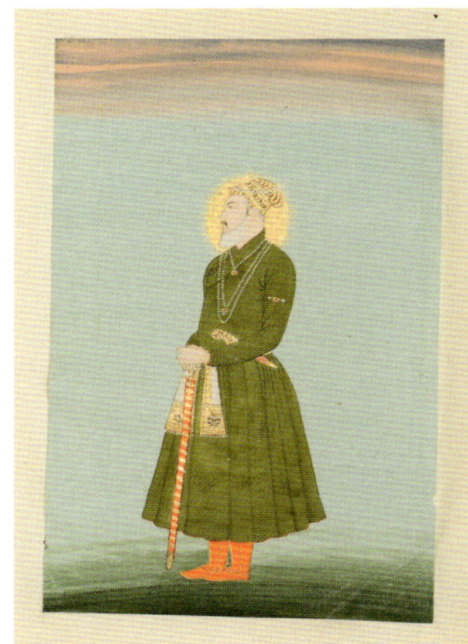

Ca 111/16 (fol. 12)

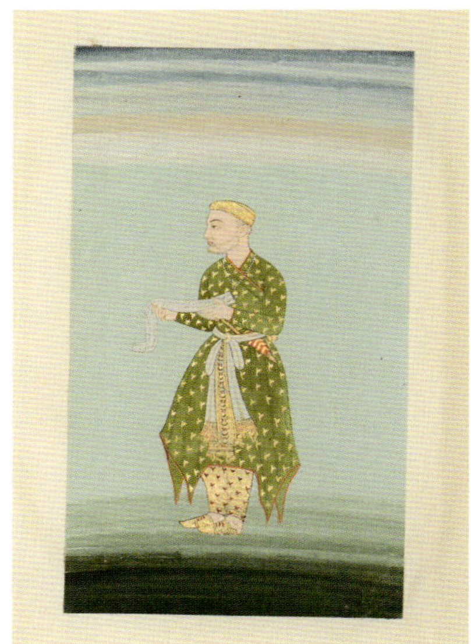

Ca 111/17 (fol. 13)

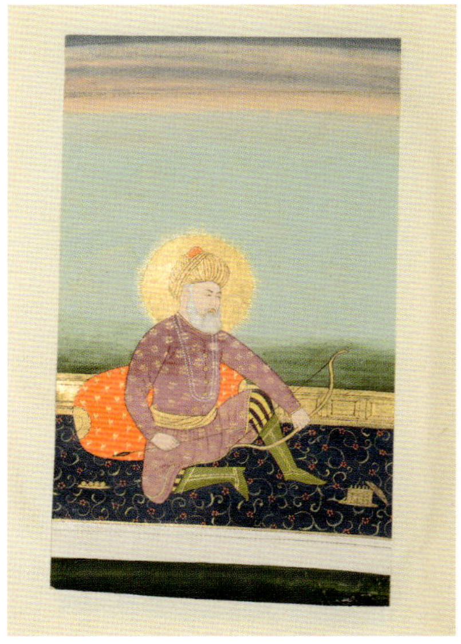

Ca 111/18 (fol. 14)

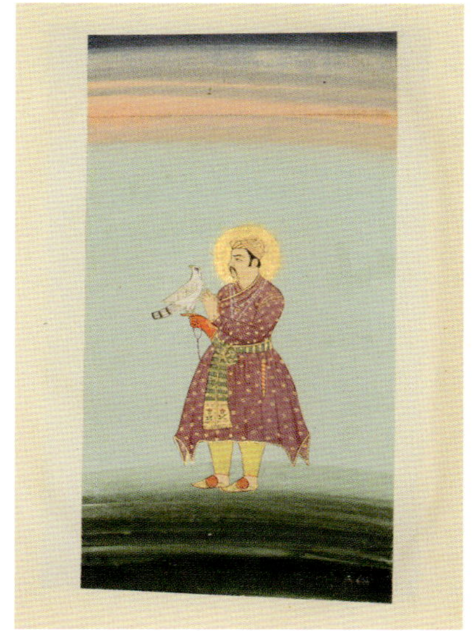

Ca 111/19 (fol. 15)

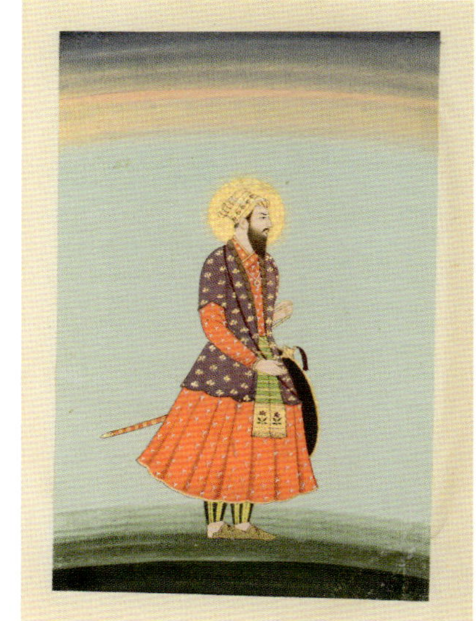

Ca 111/20 (fol. 16)

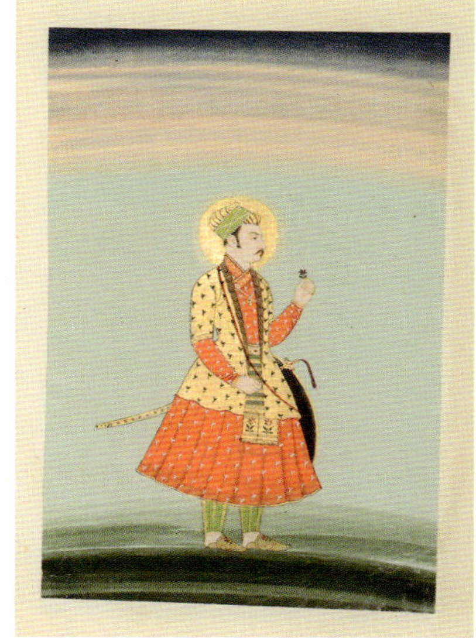

Ca 111/21 (fol. 17)

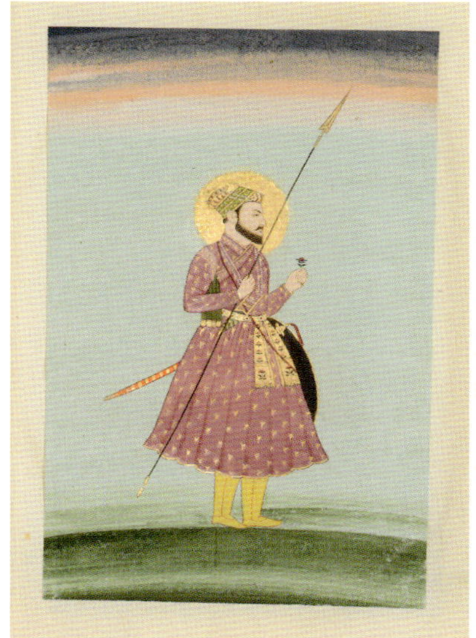

Ca 111/22 (fol. 18)

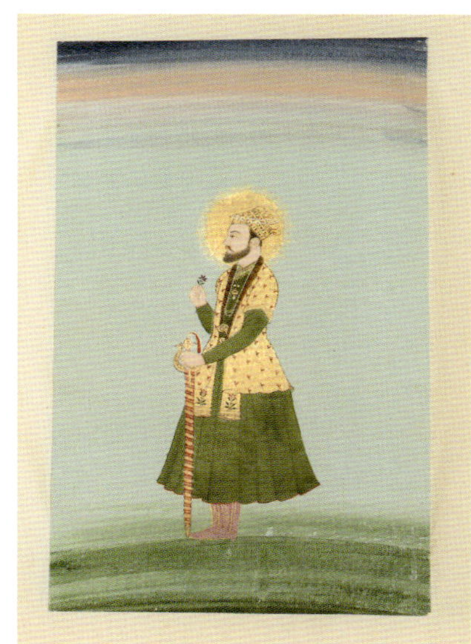

Ca 111/23 (fol. 19)

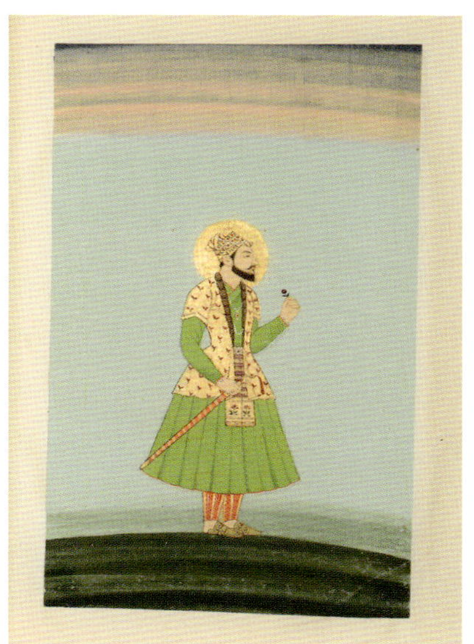

Ca 111/24 (fol. 20)

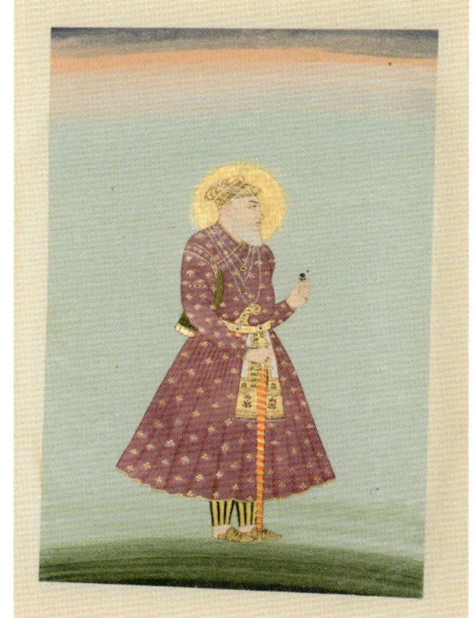

Ca 111/25 (fol. 21)

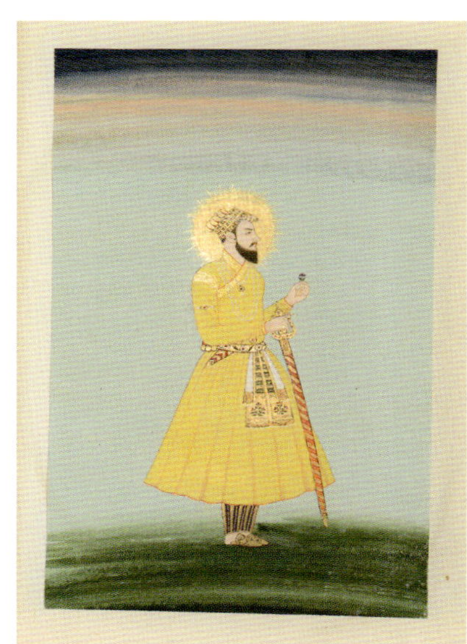

Ca 111/26 (fol. 22)

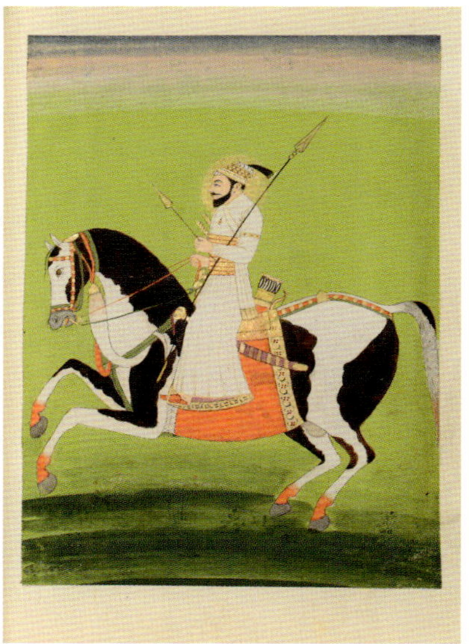

Ca 111/27 (fol. 31)

Ca 111/28 (fol. 24)
Gaj Sīngh (r. 1618–1638)
17 × 10.6 cm

Ca 111/29 (fol. 25)
Diler Khān (d. 1683)
16.4 × 10.3 cm

Ca 111/30 (fol. 26)
Chatra Sal Rāo (d. 1658)
16.7 × 10.4 cm

Ca 111/31 (fol. 27)
Vīr [?] Sīngh
16 × 10.3 cm

Ca 111/32 (fol. 28)
Jahāngīr (r. 1605–1627)
16.5 × 10.1 cm

Ca 111/33 (fol. 29)
Sādullāh Khān (1589–1656)
15.5 × 10.3 cm

Ca 111/34 (fol. 30)
Akbar (r. 1556–1605) [?]
15.8 × 10.4 cm

Ca 111/35 (fol. 31)
Sūr Sīngh
16.2 × 10.6 cm

Ca 111/36 (fol. 32)
Ja'far Khān (d. 1670)
15.9 × 9.5 cm

Ca 111/37 (fol. 33)
Akbar (r. 1556–1605)
16.9 × 10.4 cm

Ca 111/38 (fol. 34)
Bahādur Shāh I (r. 1707–1712)
16.9 × 11.6 cm

Ca 111/39 (fol. 35)
Aurangzēb (r. 1658–1707)
17.1 × 10.6 cm

Ca 111/40 (fol. 36)
Dārā Shikōh (1615–1659)
18.4 × 10.5 cm

Ca 111/41 (fol. 37)
Jahāngīr (r. 1605–1627)
16.7 × 11.8 cm

Ca 111/42 (fol. 38)
Mān Sīngh I (r. 1589–1614) [?]
16.5 × 10.3 cm

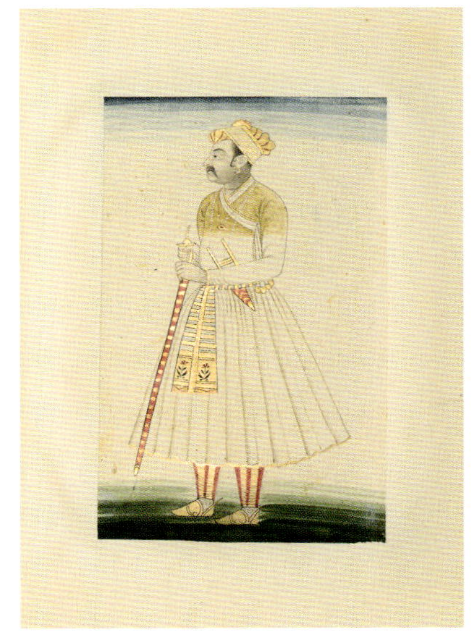
Ca 111/28 (fol. 24)

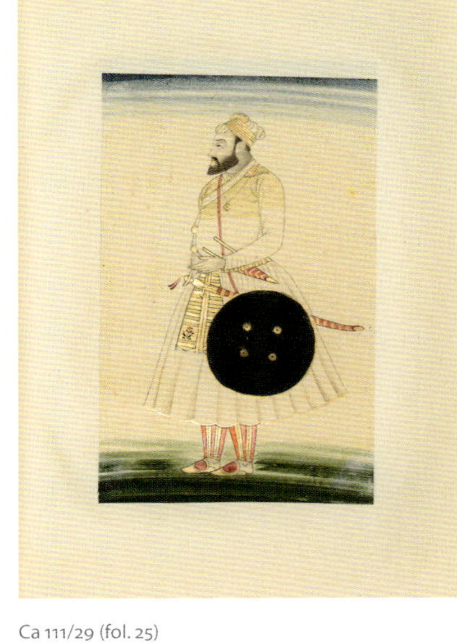
Ca 111/29 (fol. 25)

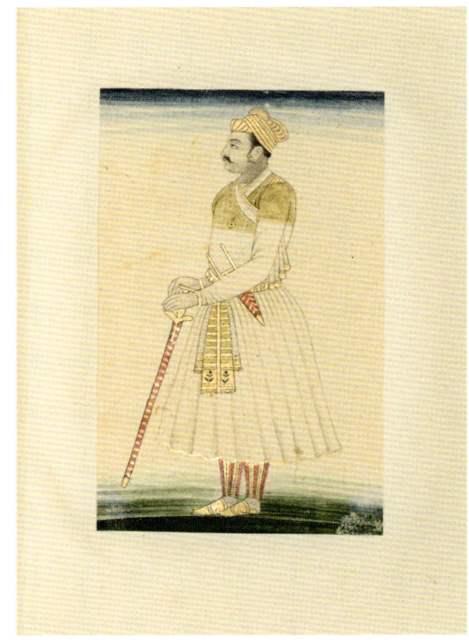
Ca 111/30 (fol. 26)

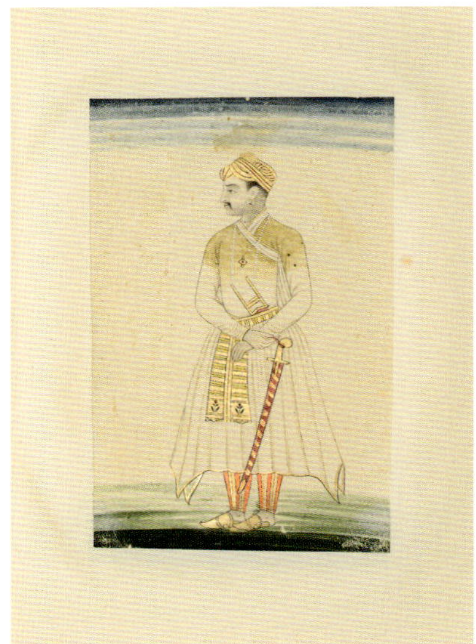
Ca 111/31 (fol. 27)

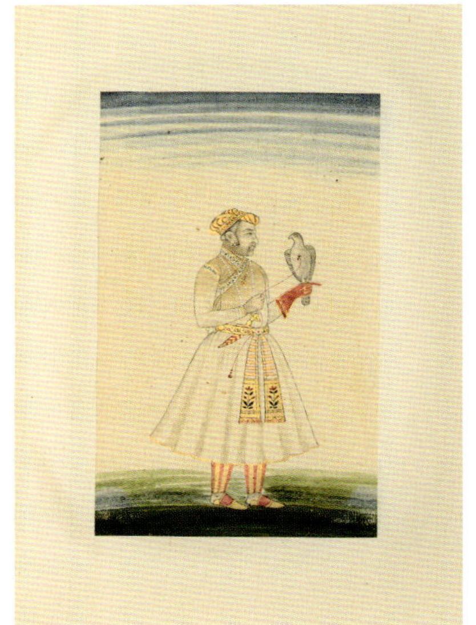
Ca 111/32 (fol. 28)

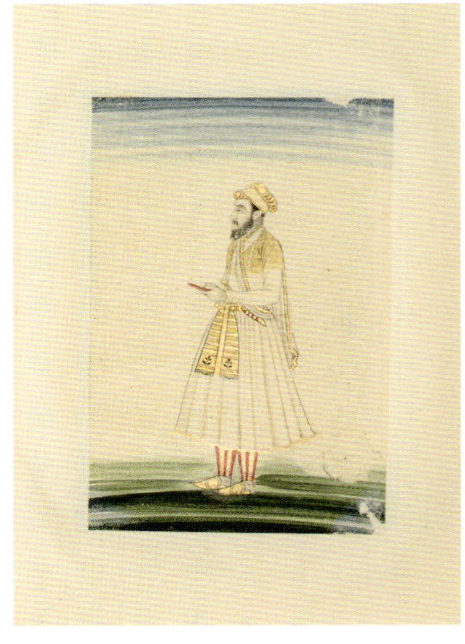
Ca 111/33 (fol. 29)

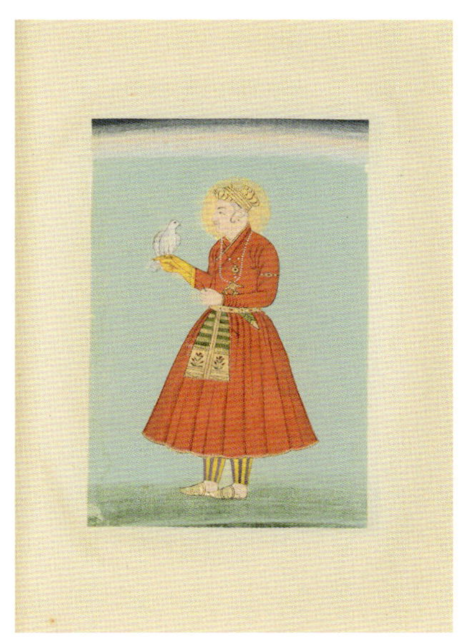

Ca 111/34 (fol. 30)

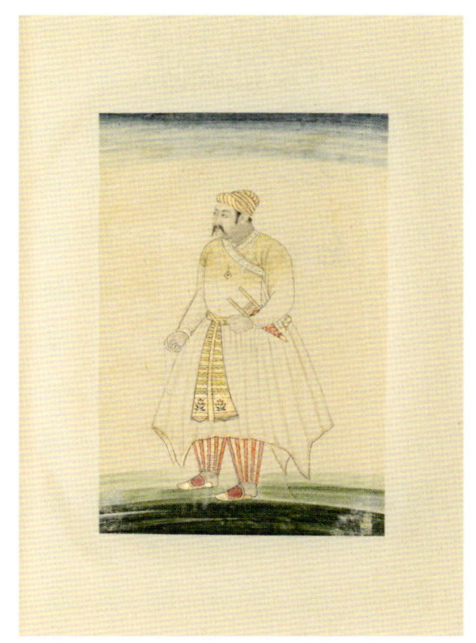

Ca 111/35 (fol. 31)

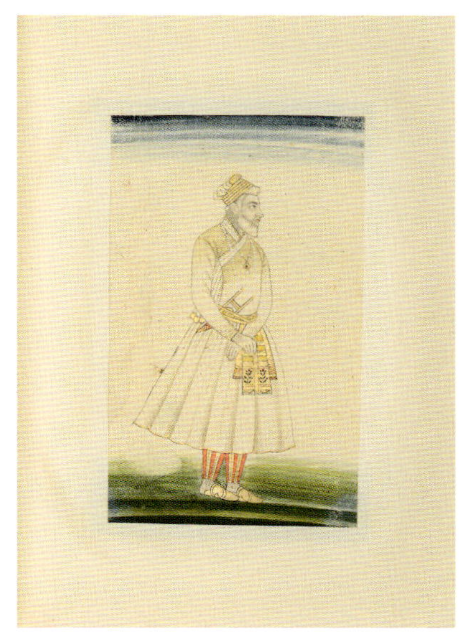

Ca 111/36 (fol. 32)

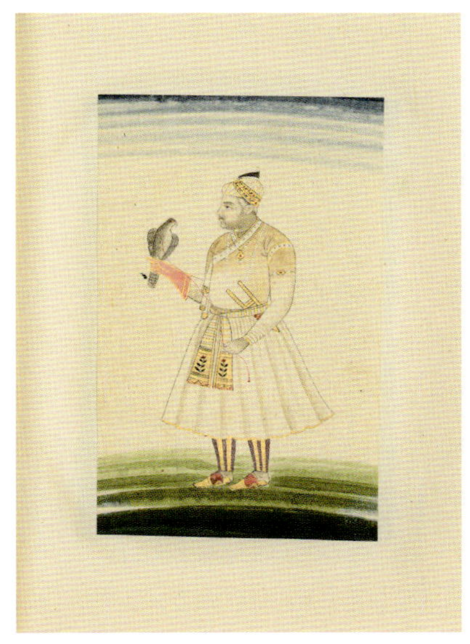

Ca 111/37 (fol. 33)

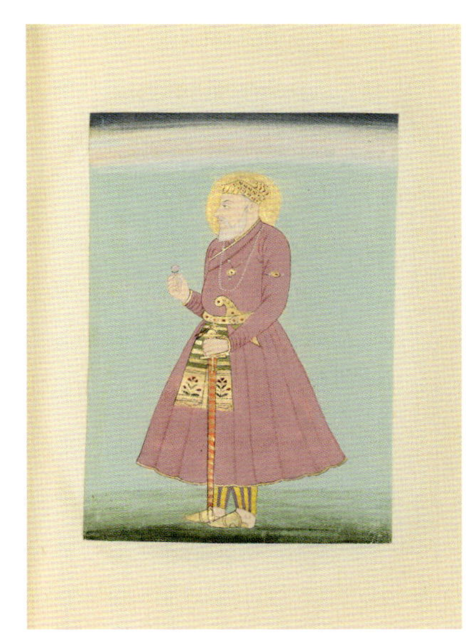

Ca 111/38 (fol. 34)

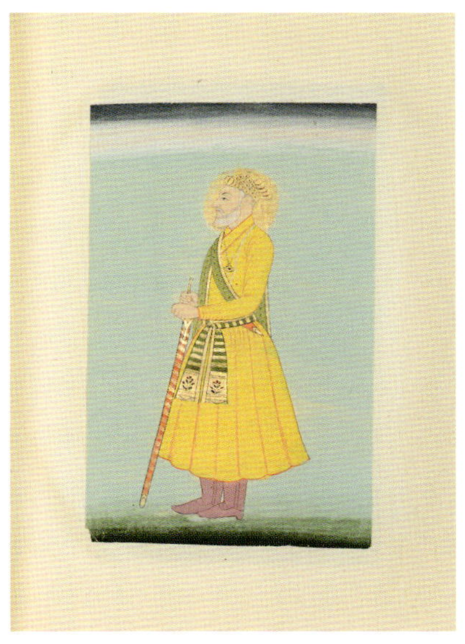

Ca 111/39 (fol. 35)

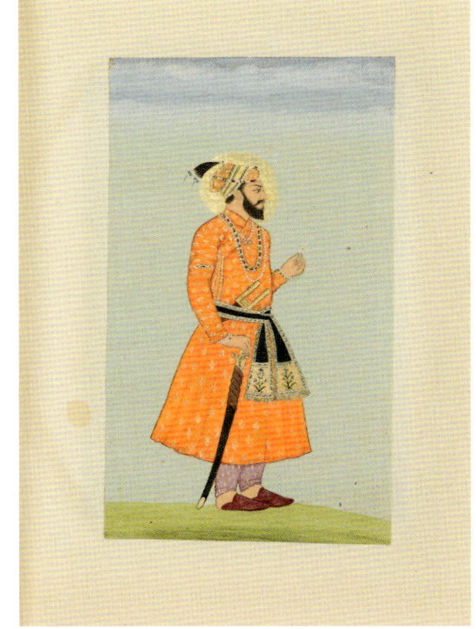

Ca 111/40 (fol. 36)

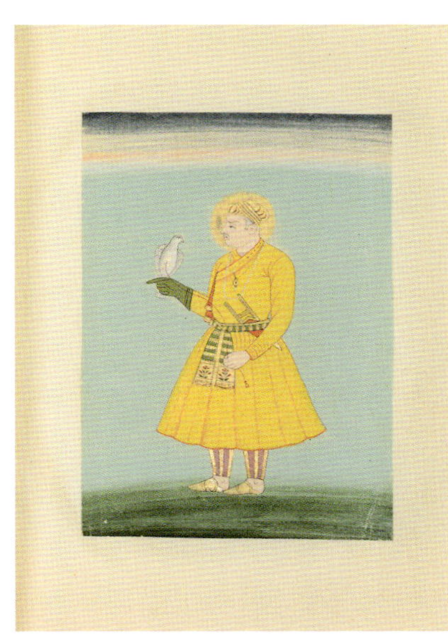

Ca 111/41 (fol. 37)

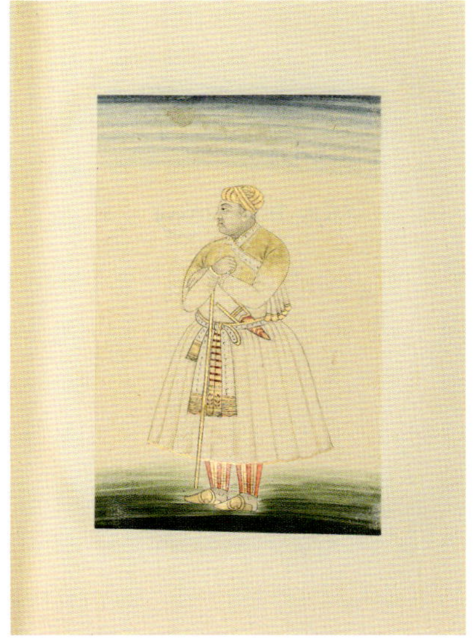

Ca 111/42 (fol. 38)

Ca 111/43 (fol. 39)
Sukh Sīngh
16.6 × 9.9 cm

Ca 111/44 (fol. 40)
Amar Sīngh (1613–1644) [?]
16.7 × 10.4 cm

Ca 111/45 (fol. 41)
Aurangzēb (r. 1658–1707)
17.7 × 10.4 cm

Ca 111/46 (fol. 42)
Shāh Jahān (r. 1628–1658)
18.4 × 10.6 cm

Ca 111/47 (fol. 43)
Shāh Jahān (r. 1628–1658)
16.8 × 11.1 cm

Ca 111/48 (fol. 44)
'Abd al-Ja'far Beg
15.5 × 8.3 cm

Ca 111/49 (fol. 45)
Rānā Amar Sīngh (d. 1620) [?]
16.4 × 10.3 cm

Ca 111/50 (fol. 46)
Tīmūr (r. 1370–1405)
15.8 × 10.2 cm

Ca 111/51 (fol. 47)
Tīmūr (r. 1370–1405)
15.8 × 10.2 cm

Ca 111/52 (fol. 48)
Abū Sa'īd (d. 1469) or
'Omar Shaikh (d. 1494)
17.2 × 10.2 cm

Ca 111/53 (fol. 49)
Abū Sa'īd (d. 1469) or
'Omar Shaikh (d. 1494)
15.9 × 11.6 cm

Ca 111/54 (fol. 50)
Sultān Muḥammad (d. c. 1411)
16.1 × 11.2 cm

Ca 111/55 (fol. 51)
Bābur (r. 1526–1530)
16.3 × 8.6 cm

Ca 111/56 (fol. 52)
Bābur (r. 1526–1530)
16.1 × 9.9 cm

Ca 111/57 (fol. 53)
Mīrān Shāh (d. 1408)
16.3 × 11.7 cm

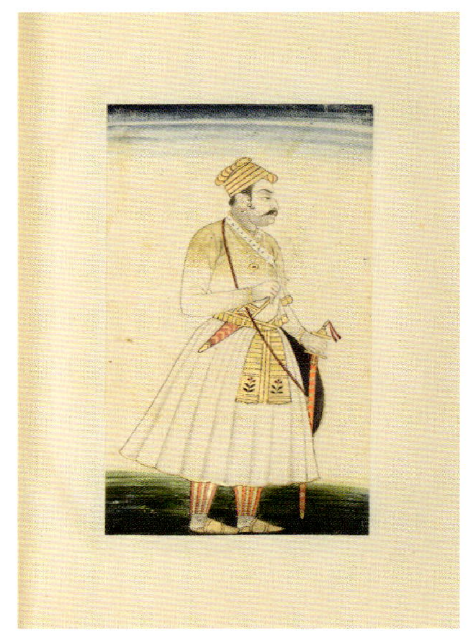
Ca 111/43 (fol. 39)

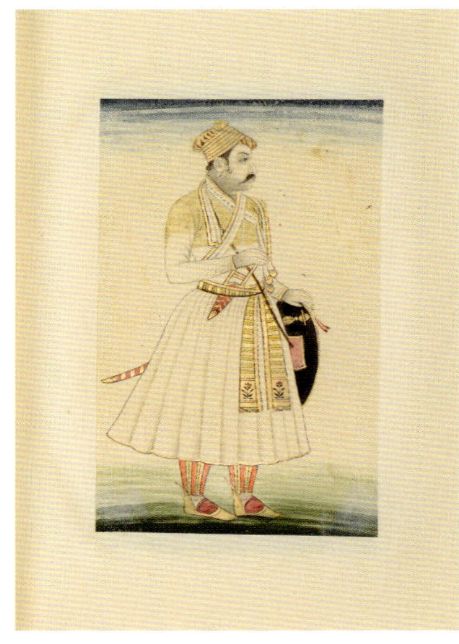
Ca 111/44 (fol. 40)

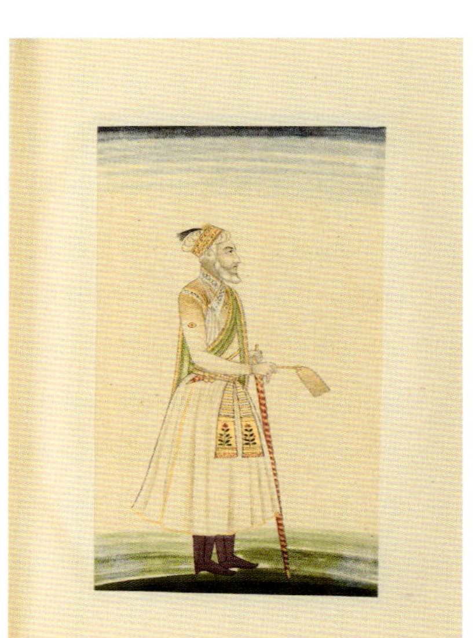
Ca 111/45 (fol. 41)

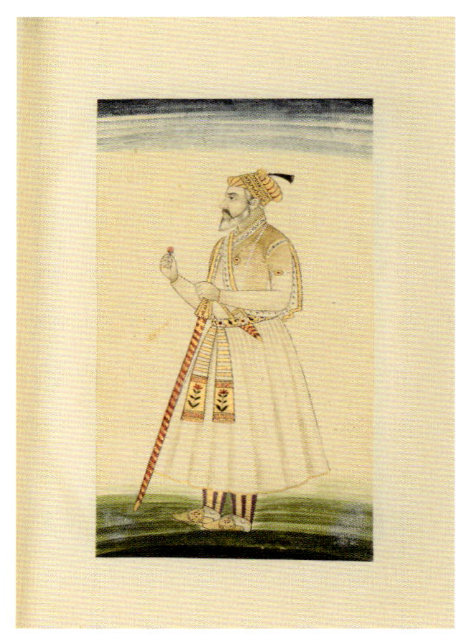
Ca 111/46 (fol. 42)

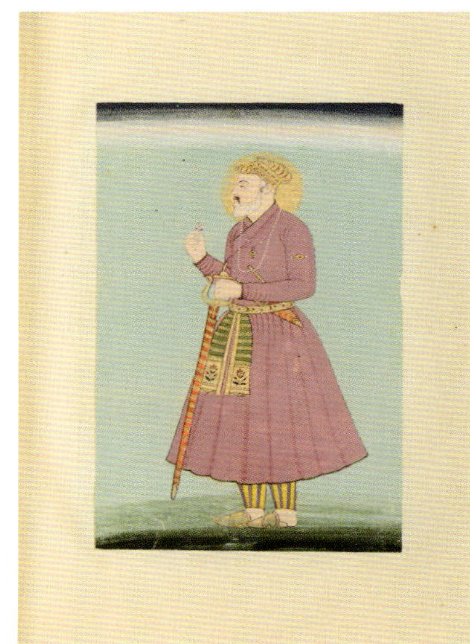
Ca 111/47 (fol. 43)

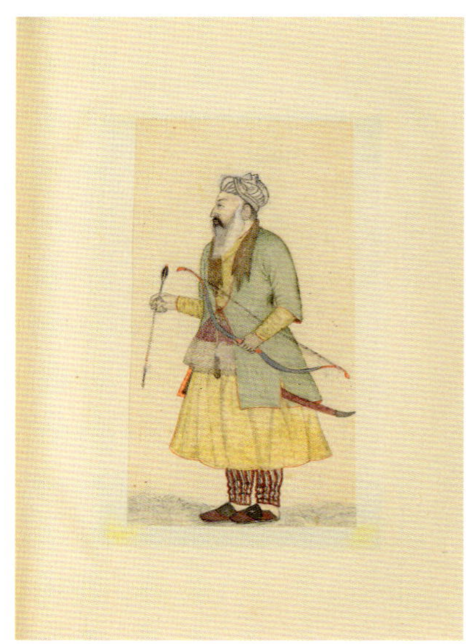
Ca 111/48 (fol. 44)

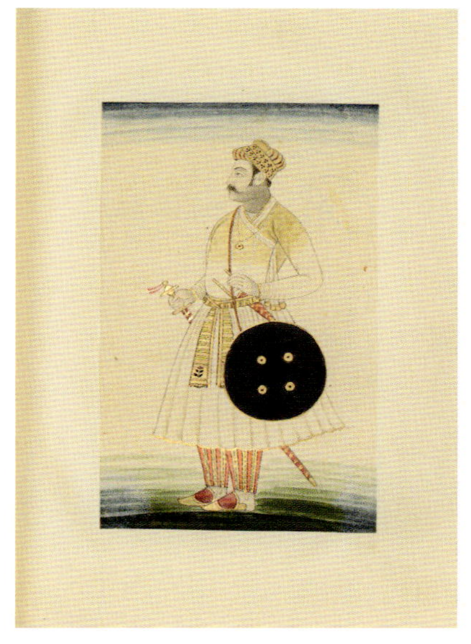
Ca 111/49 (fol. 45)

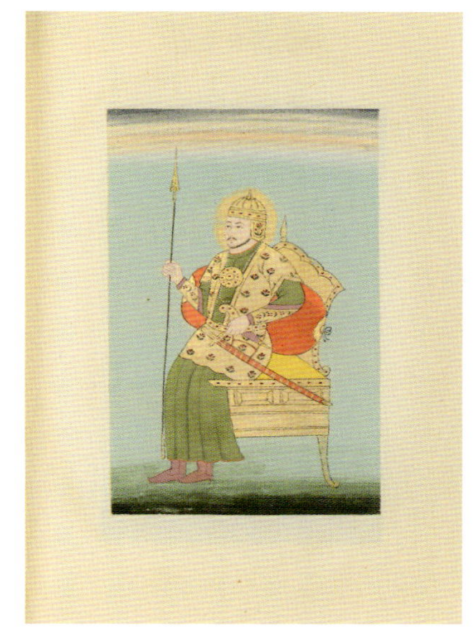
Ca 111/50 (fol. 46)

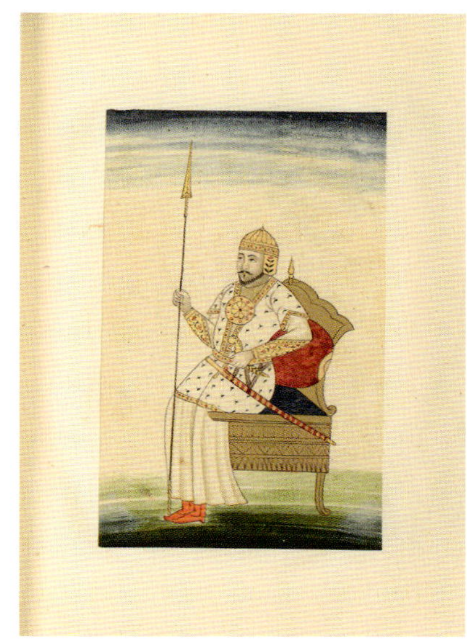
Ca 111/51 (fol. 47)

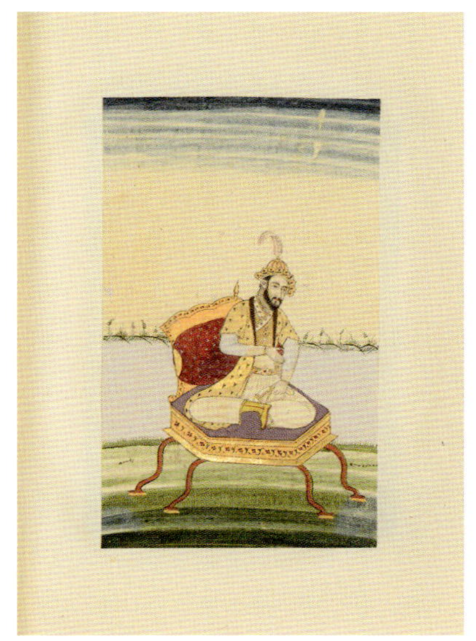
Ca 111/52 (fol. 48)

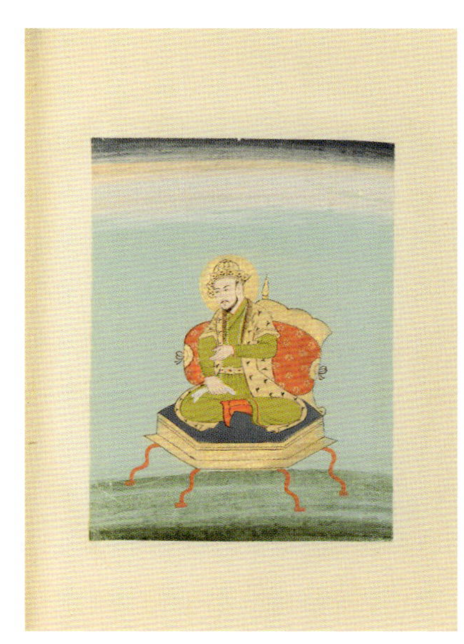
Ca 111/53 (fol. 49)

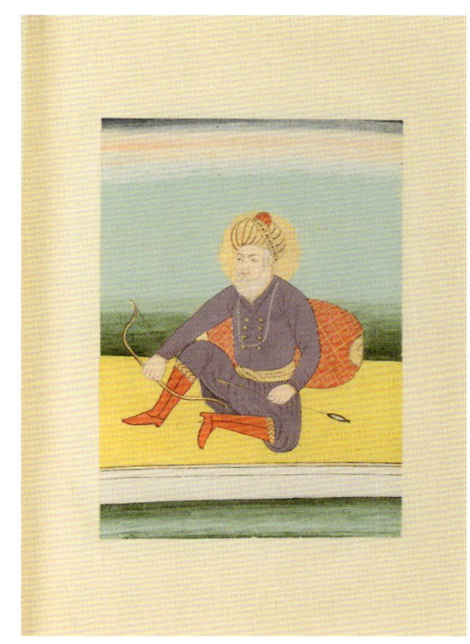
Ca 111/54 (fol. 50)

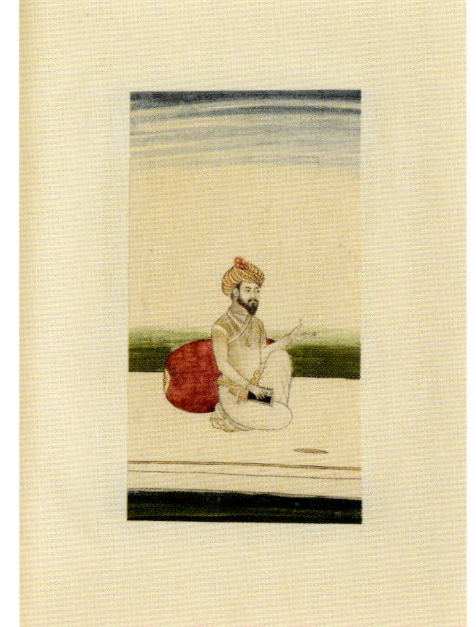
Ca 111/55 (fol. 51)

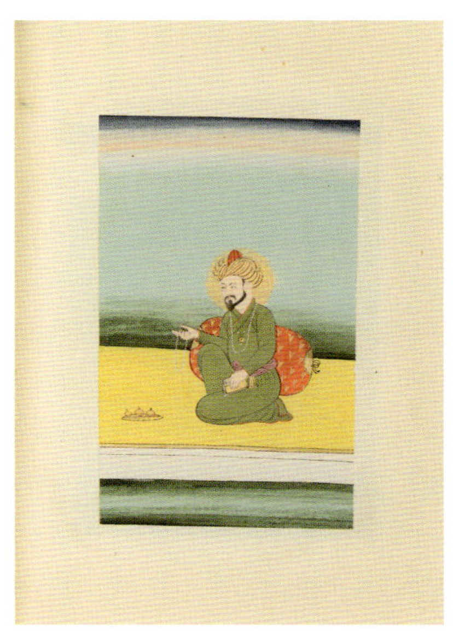
Ca 111/56 (fol. 52)

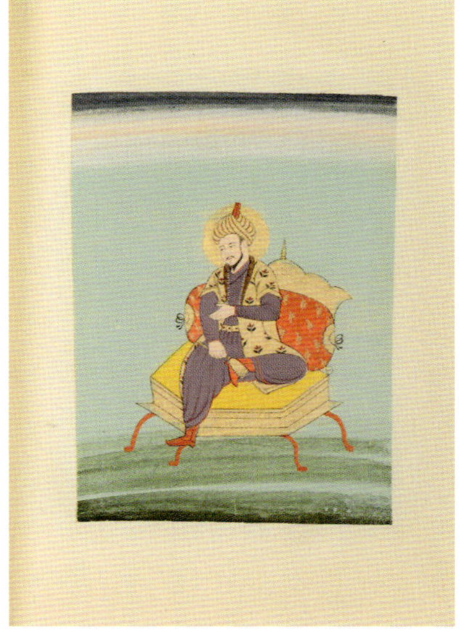
Ca 111/57 (fol. 53)

Ca 111/58 (fol. 54)
Abū Sa'īd (d. 1469) or 'Omar Shaikh (d. 1494)
15.5 × 11.3 cm

Ca 111/59 (fol. 55)
Abū Sa'īd (d. 1469) or 'Omar Shaikh (d. 1494)
17.3 × 11.3 cm

Ca 111/60 (fol. 56)
Sultān Muḥammad (d. c. 1411)
16 × 10.3 cm

Ca 111/61 (fol. 57)
Āzād Khān (1631–1716)
16.2 × 10.2 cm

Ca 111/62 (fol. 58)
Abū Sa'īd (d. 1469) or 'Omar Shaikh (d. 1494)
17.1 × 12.1 cm

Ca 111/63 (fol. 59)
Princess Jahānārā Begum Sāhibā (1614–1681)
23.1 × 17.2 cm

Ca 111/64 (fol. 60)
A Visit to a Shrine
21.9 × 14.4 cm

Ca 111/65 (fol. 61)
A Princess in a Turkish costume
Early 17th century
19.5 × 11.2 cm

Ca 111/66 (fol. 62)
Two ladies in conversation
13.7 × 11 cm

Ca 111/67 (fol. 63)
A lady holding her veil
15.8 × 9.1 cm

Ca 111/68 (fol. 64)
A lady going to worship
14.7 × 10.2 cm

Ca 111/69 (fol. 65)
A girl holding a pān (betel leaf)
13.5 × 7.4 cm

Ca 111/70 (fol. 66)
A female devotee
12 × 8.2 cm (Image, oval)

Ca 111/71 (fol. 67)
A princess (probably Jānī Begum, d. 1705)
Early 17th century
9.3 × 7 cm

Ca 111/72 (fol. 68)
A girl at the window
Early 17th century
3.7 × 3.3 cm

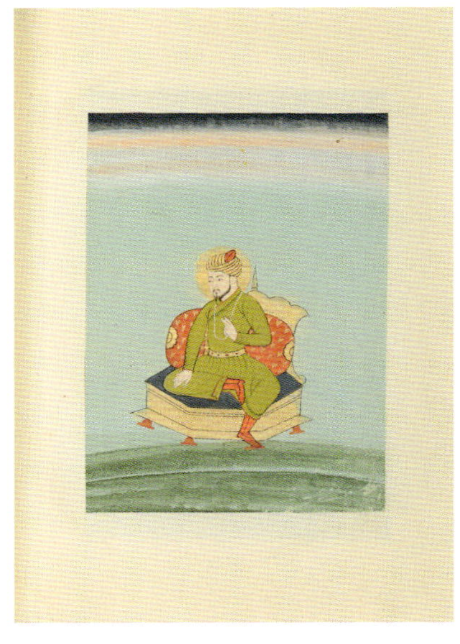
Ca 111/58 (fol. 54)

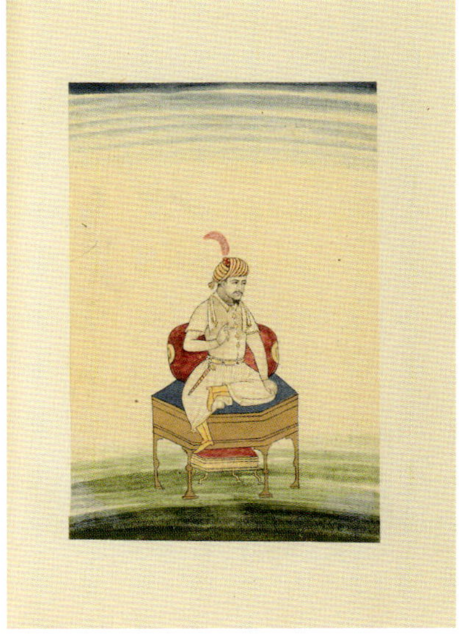
Ca 111/59 (fol. 55)

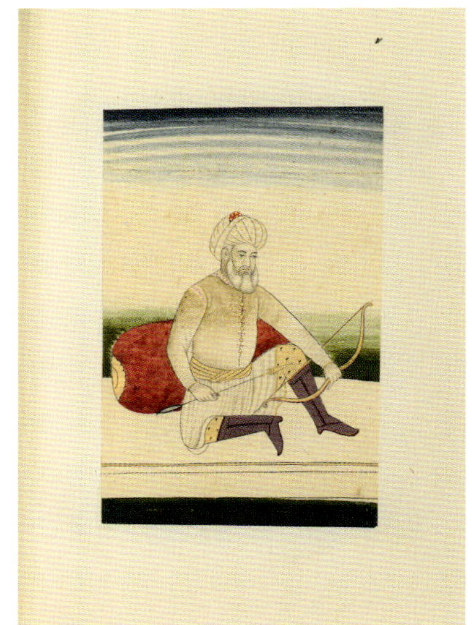
Ca 111/60 (fol. 56)

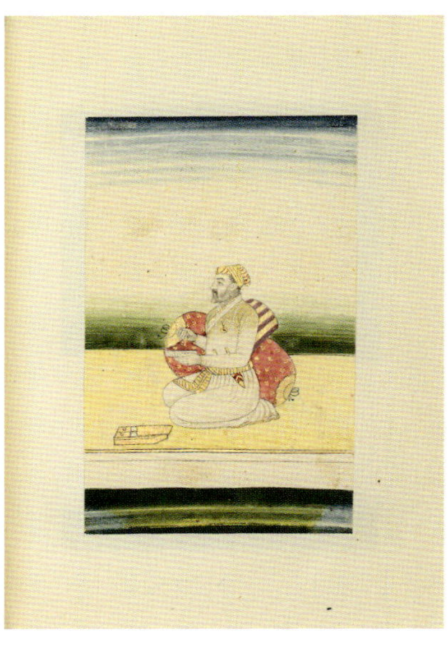
Ca 111/61 (fol. 57)

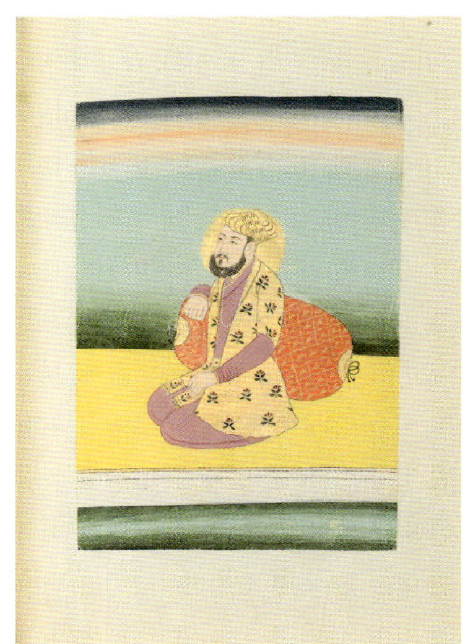
Ca 111/62 (fol. 58)

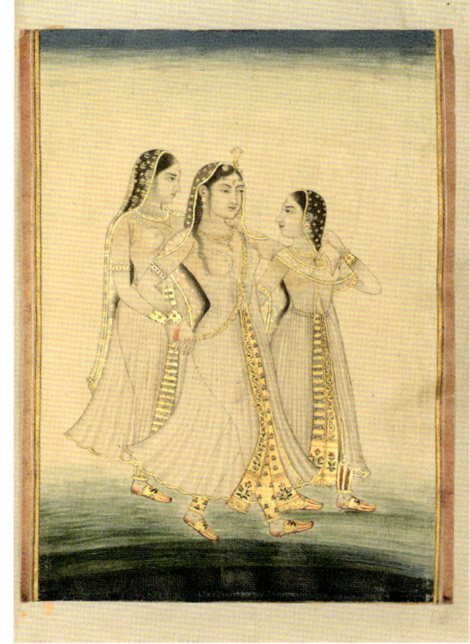
Ca 111/63 (fol. 59)

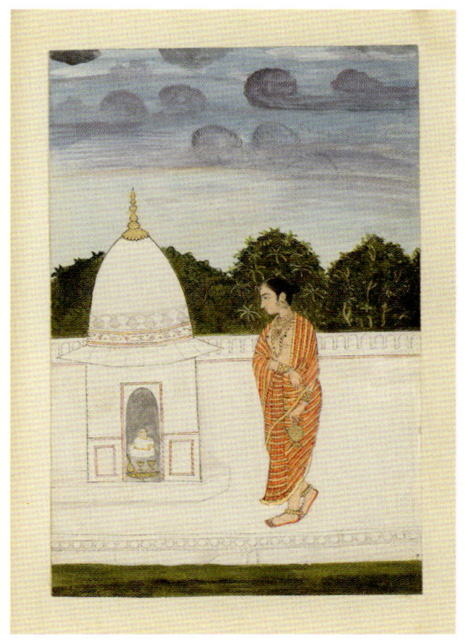
Ca 111/64 (fol. 60)

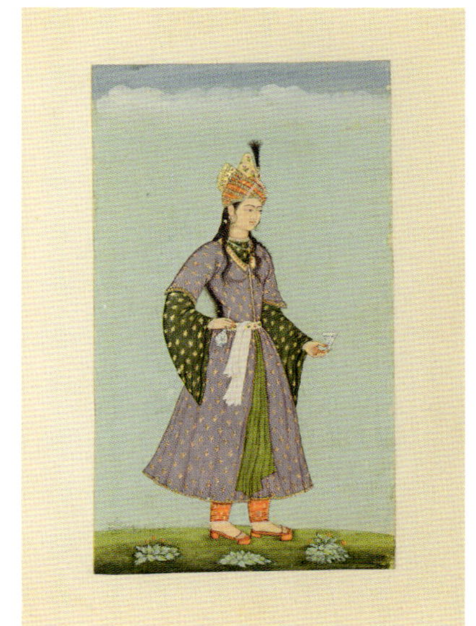
Ca 111/65 (fol. 61)

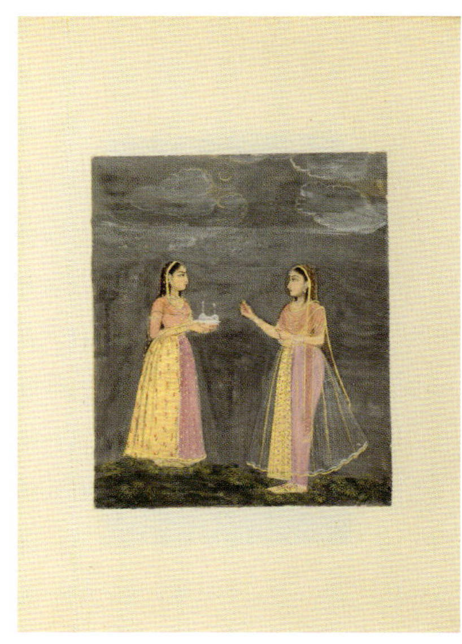
Ca 111/66 (fol. 62)

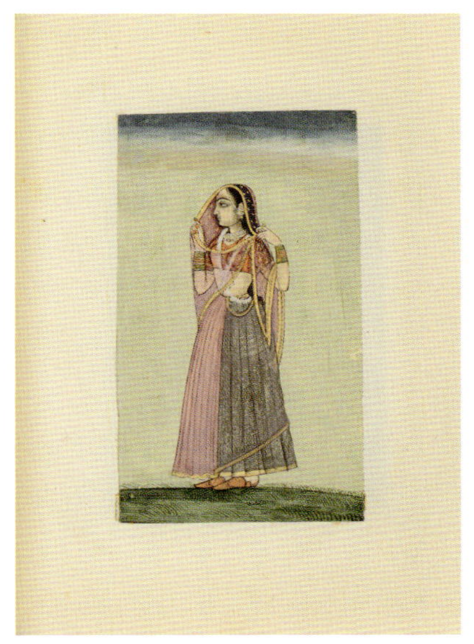
Ca 111/67 (fol. 63)

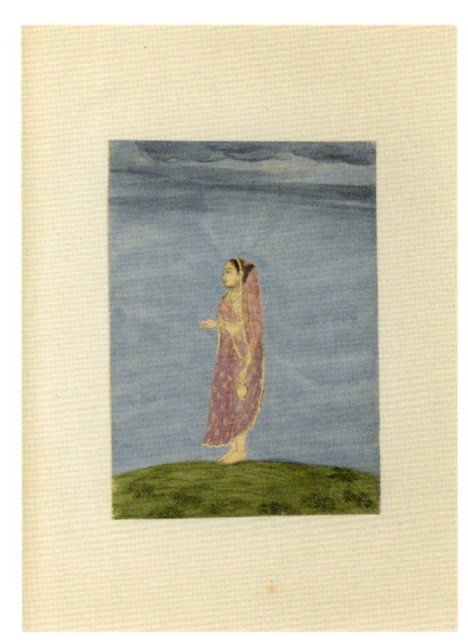
Ca 111/68 (fol. 64)

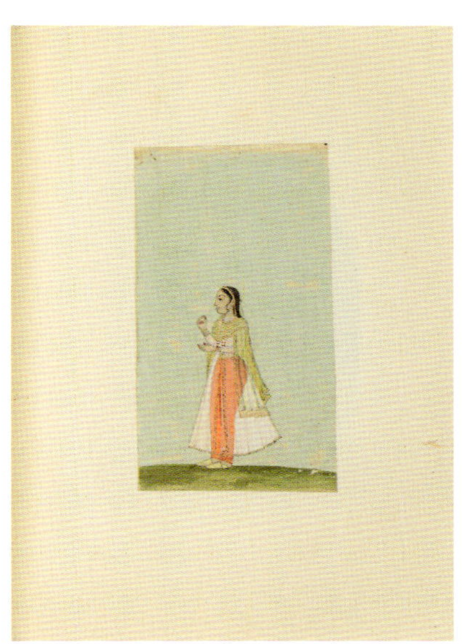
Ca 111/69 (fol. 65)

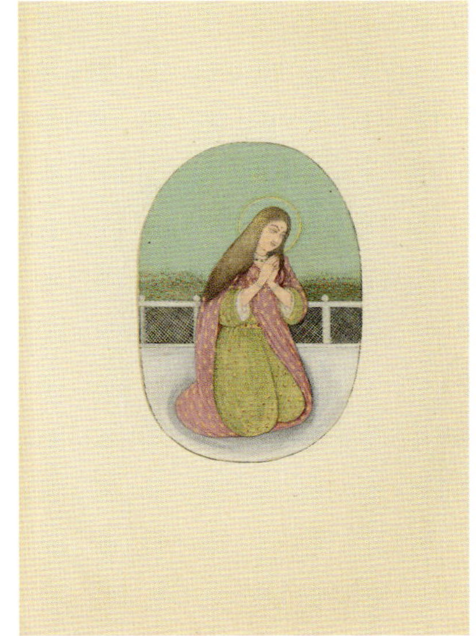
Ca 111/70 (fol. 66)

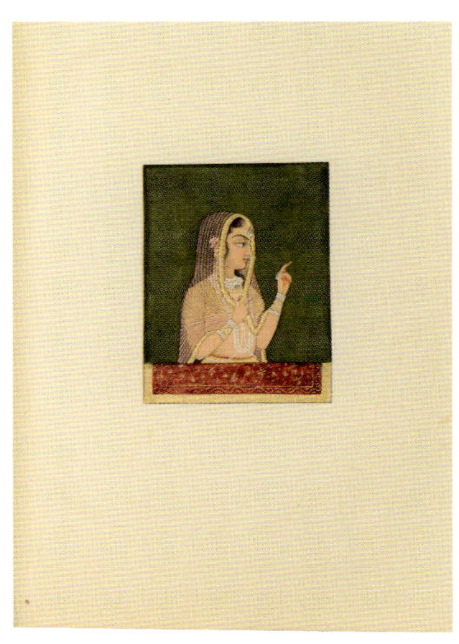
Ca 111/71 (fol. 67)

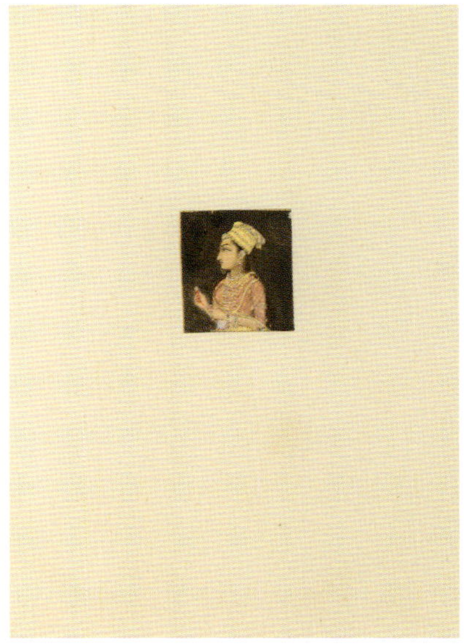
Ca 111/72 (fol. 68)

Cat. 5 | Ca 116

A Wooden Board with Eighteen Medallion Portraits

18 Portraits of Timurid and Mughal Rulers
Deccan, c. 1719
Ink, watercolour and gold,
18 medallions, c. 4.5 × 3.2 cm, on paper,
mounted on a wooden panel
34 × 22.3 × 0.9 cm
Inscribed on mounting paper with
the names of the sitters on labels painted
in silver with black ink in Dutch
References: Dresden 2017, cat. 20, pp. 162–3

Ca 116/1
Tīmūr
(r. 1370–1405)

Ca 116/2
Mīrān Shāh
(c. 1367–1408)

Ca 116/3
Sultān Muḥammad
(d. c. 1411)

Ca 116/4
Abū Sa'īd
(r. c. 1451–1469)

Ca 116/5
'Omar Shaikh
(r. 1469–1494)

Ca 116/6
Bābur
(r. 1526–1530)

Ca 116/7
Humāyūn
(r. 1530–1540, 1555–1556)

Ca 116/8
Akbar
(r. 1556–1605)

Ca 116/9
Jahāngīr
(r. 1605–1627)

Ca 116/10
Shāh Jahān
(r. 1628–1658)

Ca 116/11
Aurangzēb
(r. 1658–1707)

Ca 116/12
Bahādur Shāh I
(r. 1707–1712)

Ca 116/13
Jahāndār Shāh
(r. 1712–1713)

Ca 116/14
Farrukh Sīyar
(r. 1713–1719)

Ca 116/15
Nīkū Sīyar

Ca 116/16
Farkhunda Akhtar
(d. 1712)

Ca 116/17
Rafī' ud-Darajāt
(r. Feb. – June 1719)

Ca 116/18
Rafī' ud-Daula
(Shāh Jahān II.;
r. June – Sept. 1719)

Number 17 in the Heucher Inventory of 1738 lists "18 small miniature portraits of Japanese emperors mounted on a small board."[1] In Ca 112 (cat. 1) and Ca 110 (cat. 2), Heucher refers to representatives of Indian dynasties as "Japanese" as well. The 18 medallion portraits are identified in Dutch on small silver labels painted on European mounting paper.[2] They show the Great Mughals and their dynastic ancestors. Starting with Tīmūr (Ca 116/1) and reaching up to, and including, Akbar (Ca 116/8), these portrait busts are presented in three-quarter profile. Jahāngīr and all subsequent Great Mughals, on the other hand, are shown in full profile. The last ruler portrayed here is Rafī' ud-Daula (Shāh Jahān II) who occupied the throne from June to September 1719 (Ca 116/18). There is no portrait of Farkhunda Akhtar's younger brother, Raushan Akhtar, who eventually succeeded to the throne as Muḥammad Shāh (r. 1719–1748). The compilation, especially in view of the late portraits, suggests a dating immediately before Muḥ ammad Shāh's accession to power in 1719.

Although no precise results to that effect were obtained in the technical analysis, the medallion portraits are quite possibly still today on the same small board on which they were registered in the collection in 1738. The set was apparently combined from several batches and destined for the Dutch market. As evidenced by similar series in Leiden, Amsterdam and Vienna which, in parts, are almost identical in the type and selection of those portrayed, but have larger formats, there were buyers for this kind of portrait series of Mughal rulers in Europe.[3] Other items that can be compared are the set of medallions in Ca 111 (fol. 1–2) and a sheet, lost today, with very similar portraits.[4]

The models for these portrait series, painted in simplified planar form in the Deccan, were Mughal style paintings as well as portraits made in Golconda.[5] PKH

Notes | 1 Heucher Inventory 1738, sig. Cat. 1, p. 156: "18. Kleine Portraits en Migniature von Japanischen Kaysern auf ein Brethgen gezogen". | 2 *1. Temods. / 2. Muran Sjak. / 3. Sultan Inkan / 4. Abukenjed. / 5. Omr Sieg / 6. Babus. / 7. Hemmajoen / 8. Akber. / 9. Jekaangier. / 10. Sjak Jekann / 11. Durengzseel / 12. Bladur Sjak / 13. Jekanja Sjak / 14. Farog Sier. / 15. Necoseer. / 16. Fergondagter / 17. Dauwerbagt / 18. Reffiul Daul[a].* | 3 See Amsterdam, Rijksprentenkabinet, inv. no. NG-2008-60; Leiden, Nationaalmuseum van Wereldculturen, inv. no. RP-T-1996-75; Rome, Academia Nazionale dei Lincei, inv. no. 360-7346 to -7363 as well as Österreichische Nationalbibliothek in Vienna, sig. Cod. Min. 44, fols. 15 and 16. With grateful thanks to Marta Beccerini and Pauline Lunsingh Scheurleer for providing pertinent information. | 4 See cat. 4, pp. 120–1, and pp. 208–9, fig. 3. For the typology, see Weekes 2017, and Lunsingh Scheurleer 2017, pp. 56–7, 59, and 65. | 5 See cat. 1–2.

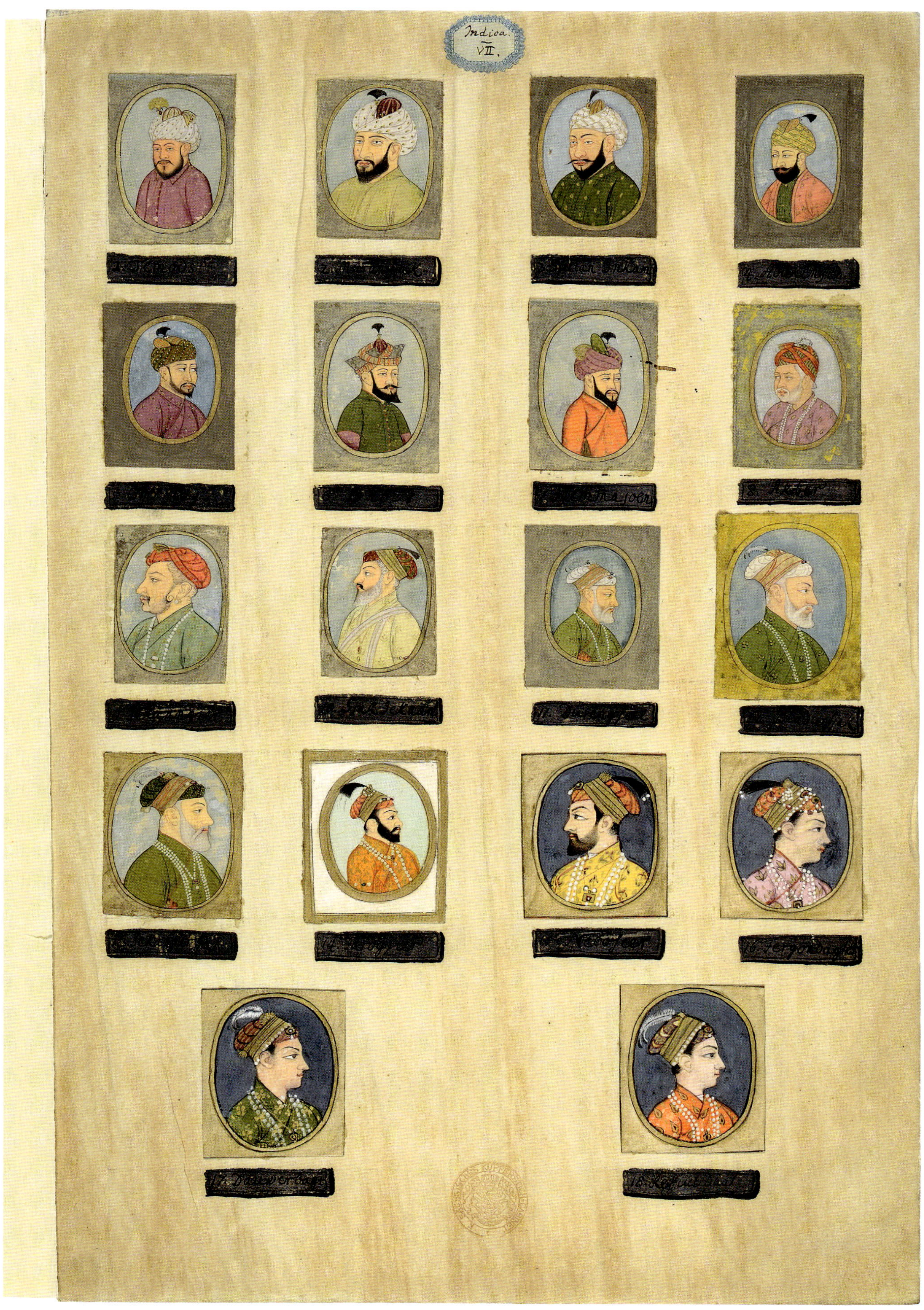

Cat. 5 | Ca 116

Cat. 6 | Ca 125/1 Cat. 7 | Ca 125/2 Two Court Scenes

Cat. 6 | Ca 125/1
Darbār of Aurangzēb
Deccani Mughal, late 17th – early 18th century
Watercolour and gold, 37.2 × 25.7 cm
Inscribed verso in *nasta'līq*: […] 17 Aurang shah Pādshāh

Cat. 7 | Ca 125/2
Shāh Jahān's Morning Audience (jharōka darshan)
Deccani Mughal, late 17th – early 18th century
Watercolour and gold, 35 × 22 cm

Reference: Dresden 2017, cat. 31–2, pp. 174–5

► figs. see pp. 134–5

The 1865 inventory of the Dresden Kupferstich-Kabinett mentions "two precious original drawings from India in bright colours and gold, brought back by the African Scholarly Society which under the government of Augustus the Strong had travelled in these countries for research purposes. The first sheet [Ca 125/2] represents Mughal Emperor Aurangzēb who, together with the noblemen of his empire, attends negotiations. The second sheet [Ca 125/1], represents […] Aurangzēb receiving a Persian delegation whose members wish to place themselves under his protection, bringing gifts and horses."[1]

The "African Scholarly Society" is likely to have been the expedition commissioned by Augustus the Strong in 1731 to gather knowledge and materials for the Royal Collection of Natural History and to bring back exotic animals and plants to Saxony.[2] The expedition under the leadership of Johann Ernst Hebenstreit and Christian Gottlieb Ludwig travelled via Karlsruhe, Strasbourg and other stops in Switzerland to Marseilles, France, from where they crossed over to Sardinia on January 24, reaching Algiers on February 16. For over a year, the explorers toured North Africa with sojourns in and extensive excursions from Algiers, Bona (Annaba), La Cala (El Kala), Tabarka and Tunis. Hebenstreit took some of the group to Bizerte, Tripoli, Lebida and after a crossing to Malta back to Tunis, from where further excursions were undertaken to Gabès and Chott el Jerid in the south. In April 1733 Hebenstreit and Ludwig received news of the king's death. The expedition was cancelled, and on April 17, Hebenstreit set out from Tunis to Marseilles. On June 3, Ludwig returned via Gibraltar and the Channel Islands to Hamburg, from where he travelled back to Dresden with the collections and animals. There is no reason to doubt that the information regarding the origin, handed down with the collection, is correct; the incomplete documents, however, provide no clues as to where Hebenstreit and Ludwig might have purchased the two paintings—the most likely places are the vibrant trading centers of Algiers and Tunis.

At first sight there seems to be no mention of the sheets in the Heucher Inventory which was drawn up soon after the king's death and which accompanied the arrangement and acquisitions of the collection under his successor, King Augustus III. However, it can be assumed that the sheets are the same as the two works listed as number 3, hanging above the cabinet of the Asian collection, the "Bureau XXII. La Chine". Their origin is not indicated, and according to the customs of the time they are not classified as "Indian", but registered as "2 beautiful Chinese paintings—under glass and in a gilt frame".[3] A note probably added by Carl Heinrich von Heineken, who succeeded Heucher in 1746 as museum director, states that they "have been taken out of the glass and wrapped with paper". Apparently, the paintings were again mounted in the nineteenth century and exhibited in the collection rooms in the German pavilion of the Zwinger Palace.[4]

The audience scene mentioned in the inventory in the first place (cat. 7) does, in fact, not represent Aurangzēb but a *darbār* held by his father and predecessor Shāh Jahān (r. 1628–1658).[5] The same scene can be found in the Atlas Van der Hem (fig. 1),[6] and a stylistically very similar version, inserted into a field of rocaille, in the Millionenzimmer at Schönbrunn Castle (fig. 2).[7]

The Persian delegation before Aurangzēb mentioned in the second place (cat. 6) cannot be safely attributed to an historic event. Guests of different garb and complexion, who have obviously come from afar with their retinue, pay a courtesy visit to the emperor and his assembled court. They bring elephants and horses which they offer as

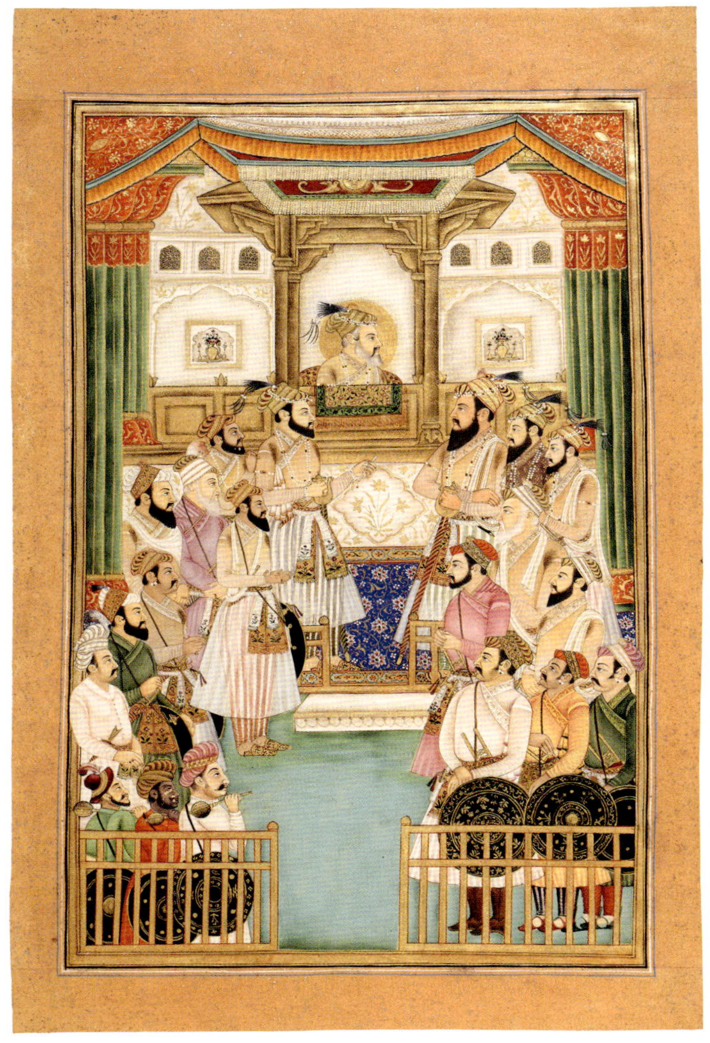

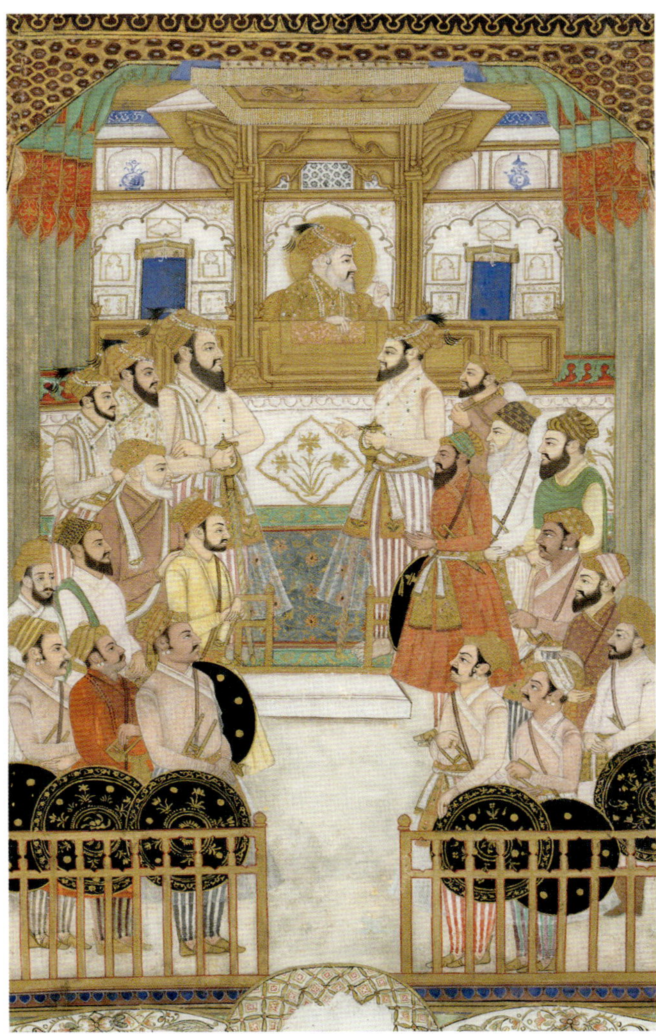

gifts; a petition or message is being read, of which only the first line, "Praise to Allāh",[8] is actually legible. Aurangzēb can be identified by his portrait as well as the inscription on the back, which was discovered during the restoration of the sheet.

The famous representation of his birthday audience in the Green Vault, "Throne of the Great Mughal Aurangzēb"(fig. 2), bears witness to the extent of admiration accorded to Aurangzēb as a mighty Indian potentate in Saxony. Johann Melchior Dinglinger presented the piece, which was completed by his workshop after several years of working, to Augustus the Strong on March 3, 1709—almost precisely two years after the death of Aurangzēb in Ahmednagar on March 2, 1707.[9] In terms of subject matter as well as individual motifs, the lavish goldwork can be compared to the subsequently acquired Indian opaque colour painting in the Kupferstich-Kabinett that is listed in the inventory. Both of these works portray the splendour and power of the Great Mughal's court, also described in travel accounts of the late seventeenth century.[10] PKH

fig. 1
Audience of Shāh Jahān
Separate folio in "Atlas Blaeu-Van der Hem"
Deccani Mughal, c. 1675
Watercolour and gold, 40 × 26.5 cm
Österreichische Nationalbibliothek, Vienna, Map Collection, sig. 389.030-F. K. (40), no. 4

fig. 2
Darbār of Shāh Jahān, court and zenāna scenes (detail)
Deccani Mughal, late 17th century
Watercolour and gold, 93.5 × 55.8 cm
Schönbrunn Castle, Vienna, inv. no. SKB 2610

Notes | 1 Archive of the Staatliche Kunstsammlungen Dresden, Andreas Gottlieb Marius Franke: Catalogue of drawings, sig. Cat. 64 I, p. 406 (translated from the German). | 2 For the Africa expedition, see Grosse 1902; and Weber 1865. Many thanks to Silvia Dolz for providing the compilation of the travel route from her research documents. | 3 Nos. 10, 12 and 18, on the other hand, were listed as "Japanese" or "Tamerlan" (Timurid). | 4 See Dresden 2017, pp. 57–8. | 5 For the portrait of Shāh Jahān, compare Dresden 2017, cat. 21, p. 164. | 6 See Lunsingh Scheurleer 2017, pp. 54–5, fig. 1. | 7 See also Dresden 2017, cat. 87. | 8 With thanks to Mohammed Abdesalam for identifying the text. | 9 See Syndram 2013, p. 7, as well as Syndram 2017. The masterly enamel and goldwork of Dinglinger's workshop exhibits a number of chinoiserie characteristics; the painting of the outside evokes Japanese models. | 10 See Dresden 2017, cat. 90–1.

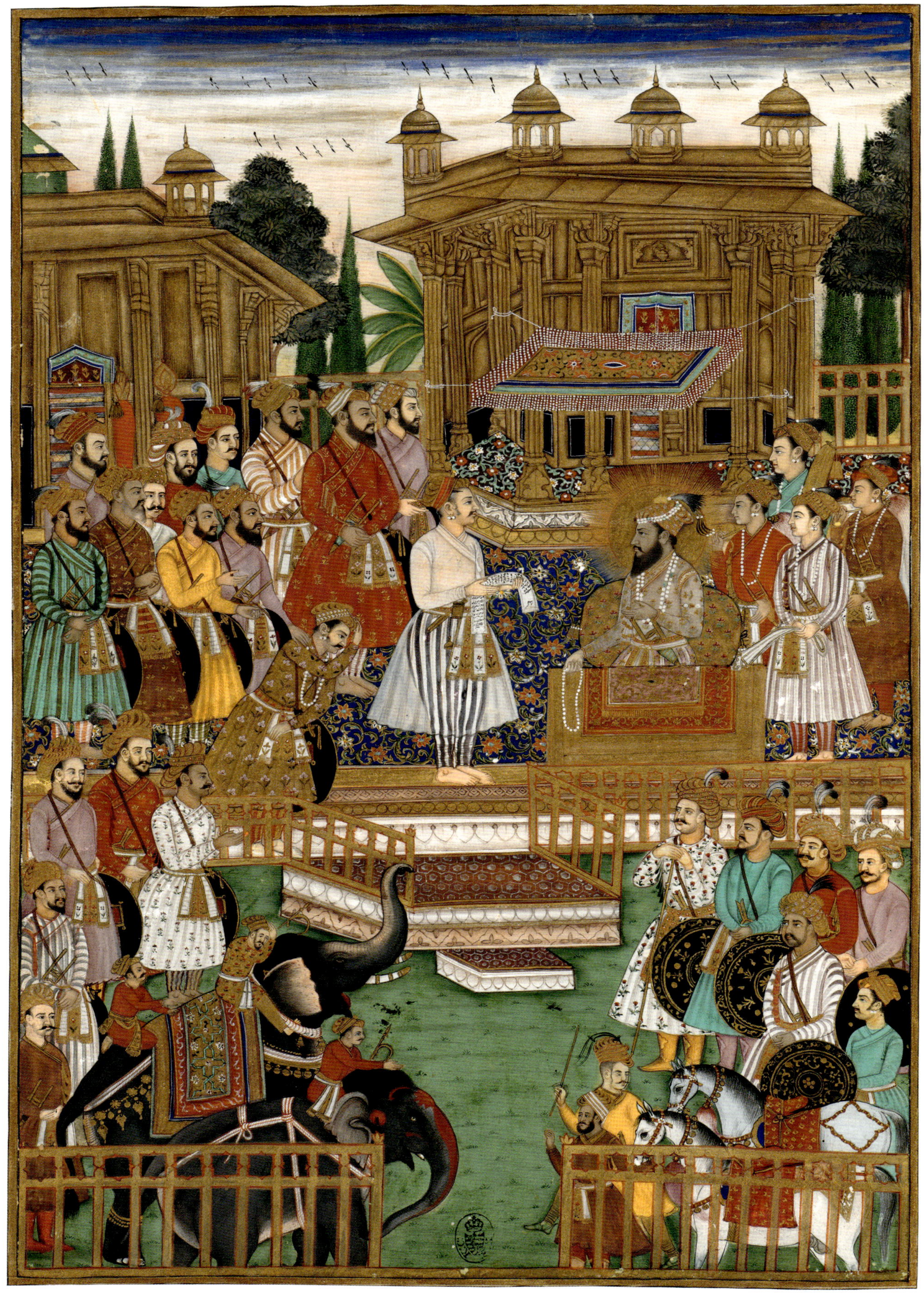

Cat. 6 | Ca 125/1

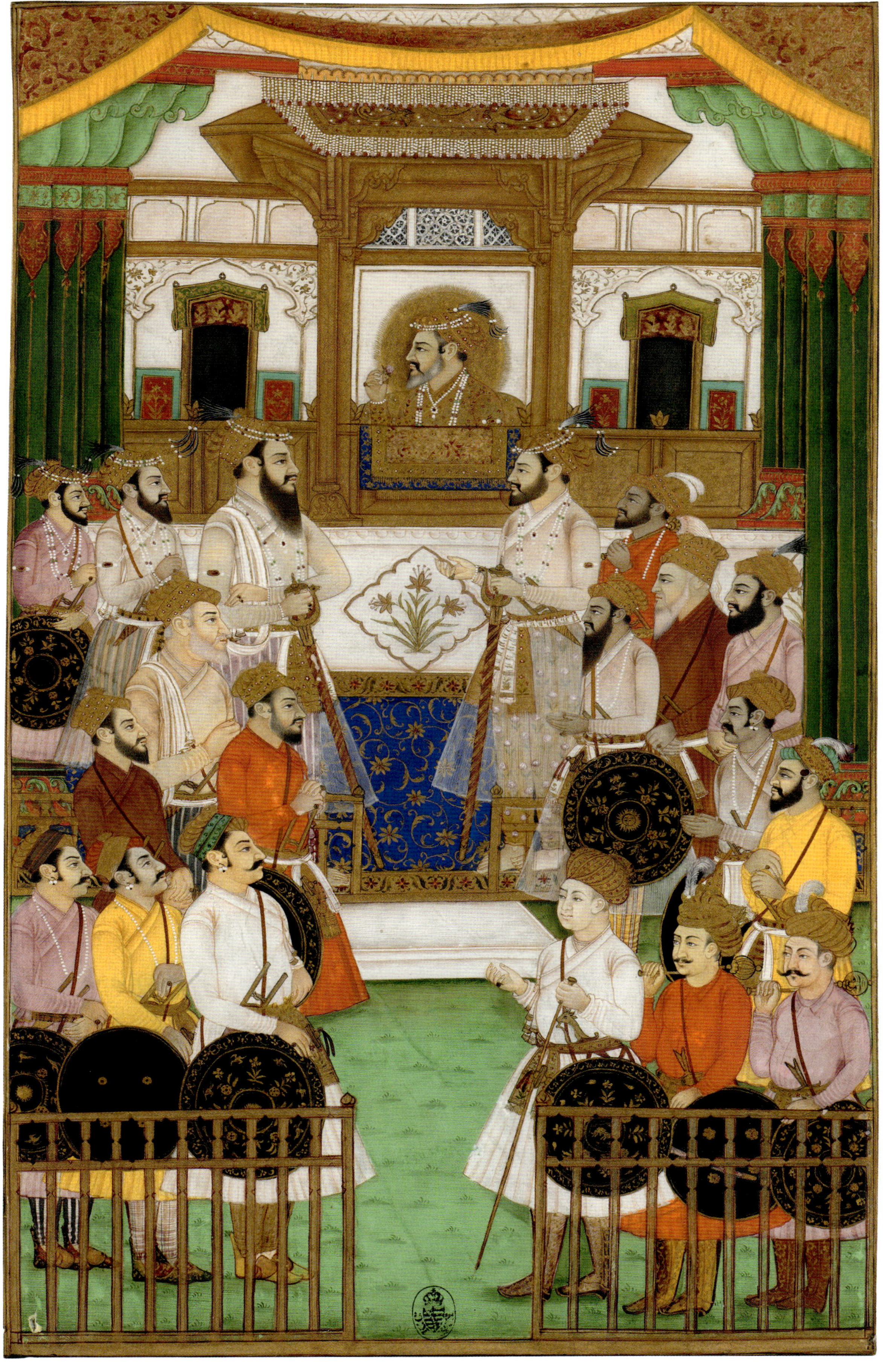

Cat. 7 | Ca 125/2

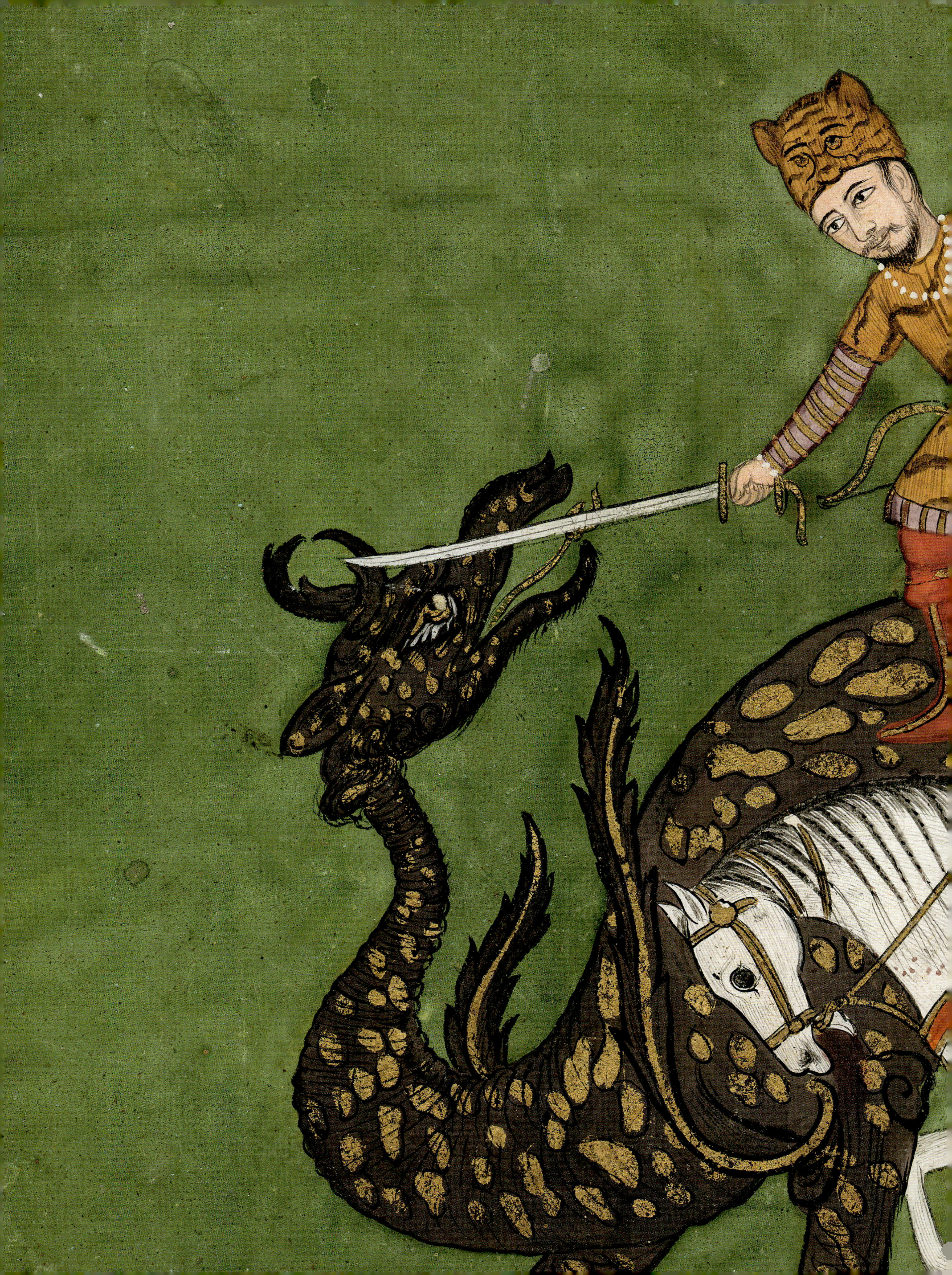

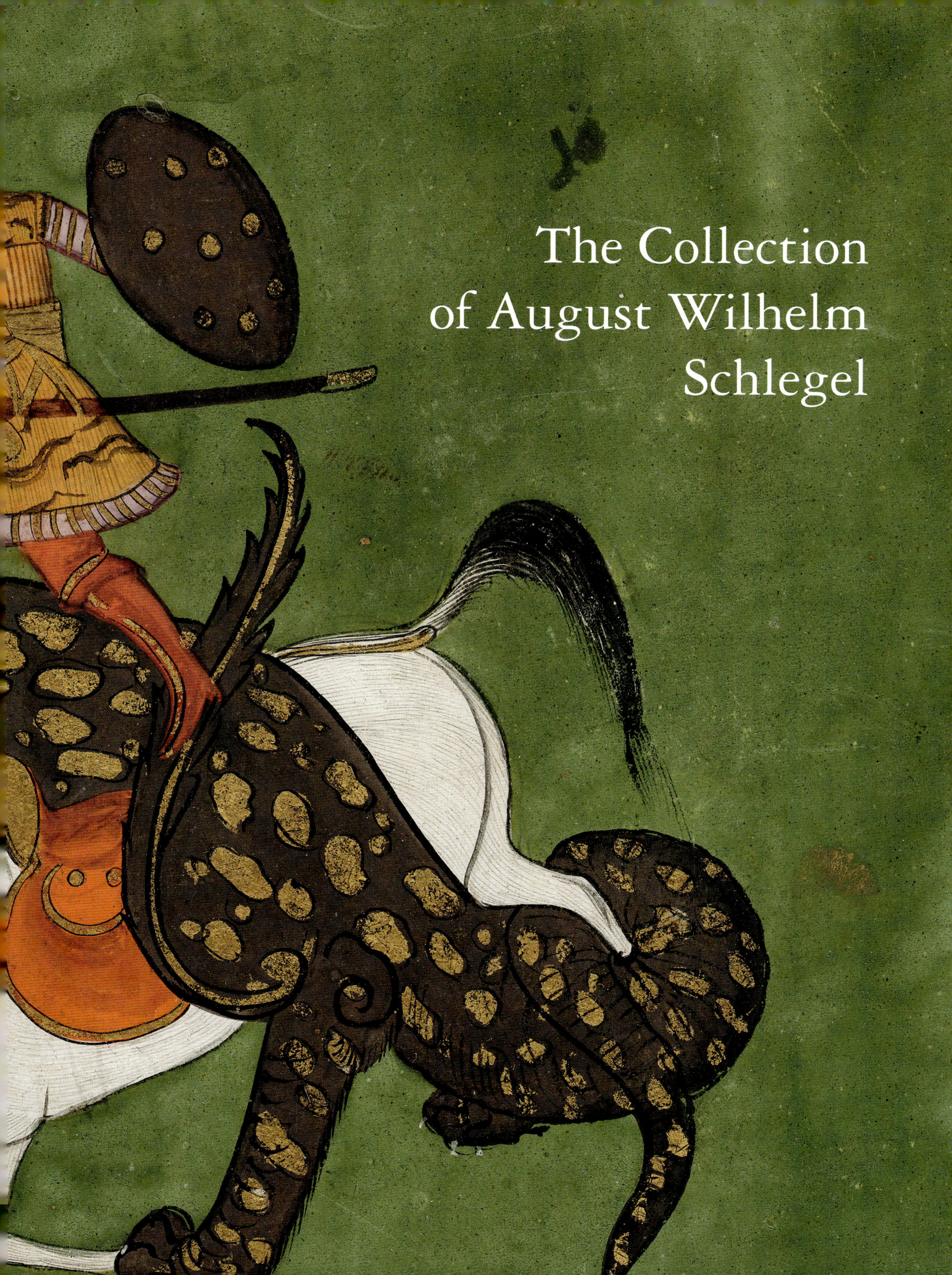
The Collection
of August Wilhelm
Schlegel

Rulers

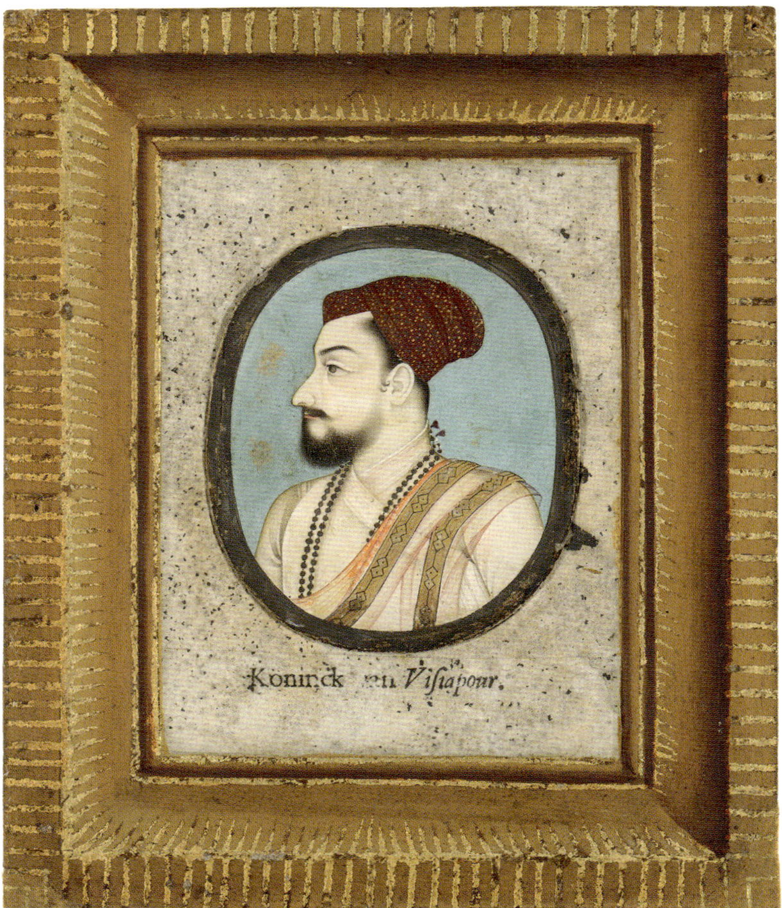

Cat. 8 | Ca 121/7

Cat. 8 | Ca 121/7
Muḥammad ʿĀdil Shāh (r. 1627–1656)
Bijapur (Deccan), mid-17th century
Watercolour, gold, and silver, painted frame 17.2 × 14 cm, image 11.3 × 8.3 cm, medallion 8.1 × 6.8 cm
Inscribed below in Dutch: Koninck von Visiapour (King of Bijapur)
Reference: Dresden 2017, cat. 23, pp. 165–6

Cat. 8 | Muḥammad ʿĀdil Shāh (r. 1627–1656), heir to the Bijapur throne, is shown here in his twenties, with a long, slightly curved nose and a distinctively shaped beard. His portraits are clearly distinct from those of his successor, ʿAlī ʿĀdil Shāh II (r. 1656–1672), who has fuller lips.

In a comparable portrait from the British Museum, Muḥammad ʿĀdil Shāh is depicted with a flower—a well-known symbol of his gentleness—in his right hand and a mango in his left.[1] That work and the present one are representative of portraits of him about 1635.[2] The necklaces, however, differ—that in the British Museum portrait being pearls and the one in Dresden brown beads. Technical study of the pigments used in the Dresden image revealed no signs of discolouration of the white pigments usually used to depict pearls, thus establishing that Muḥammad ʿĀdil Shāh is wearing Hindu *rudrākṣa* beads. This discovery demonstrates his devotion towards Hinduism.

Portraits of Muḥammad in an oval format[3] were produced about 1670 in Hyderabad and Golconda, mostly for a European audience.[4] The present image presumably made its way into a Dutch collection, where it was inscribed.

Court painting at Bijapur ended abruptly in 1686, when the Mughal Emperor Aurangzēb captured the city and its final *sultān*, Sikandar ʿĀdil Shāh, after seventeenth months of warfare. Few paintings from the early period survived after the kingdom's downfall, which was hastened by a terrible famine. Aurangzēb entered the ʿĀdil Shāhī palace and the *asar mahāl* (relic house) and destroyed all paintings drawn in violation of *Qur'ānic* law and all *Shī'a* inscriptions.[5] The Dresden painting, rendered in a loosely Bijapur style, contributes to the study of the changing dynamics within the ateliers and the politics of the kingdom. NB

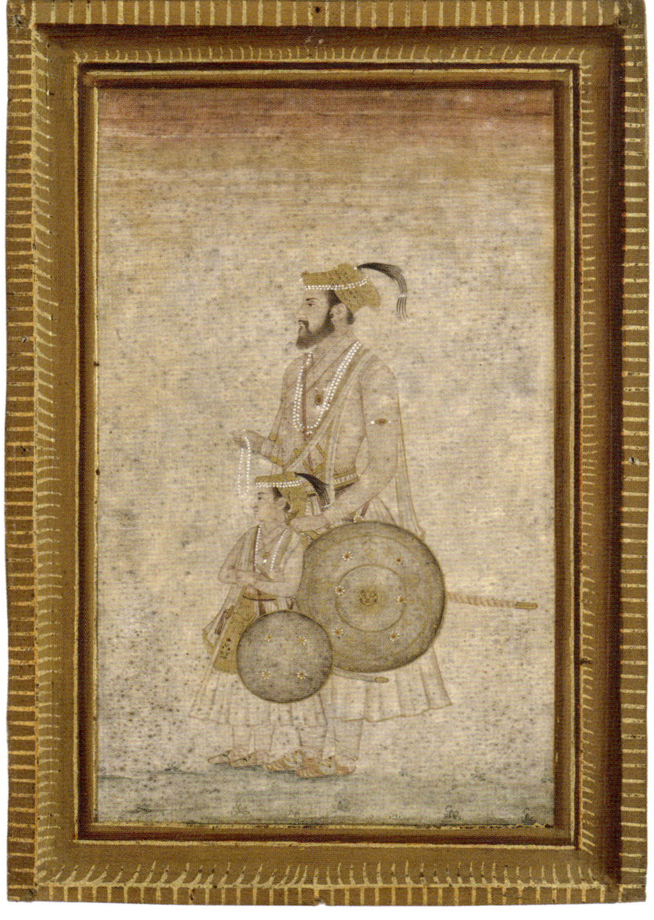

Cat. 9 | Ca 123/1

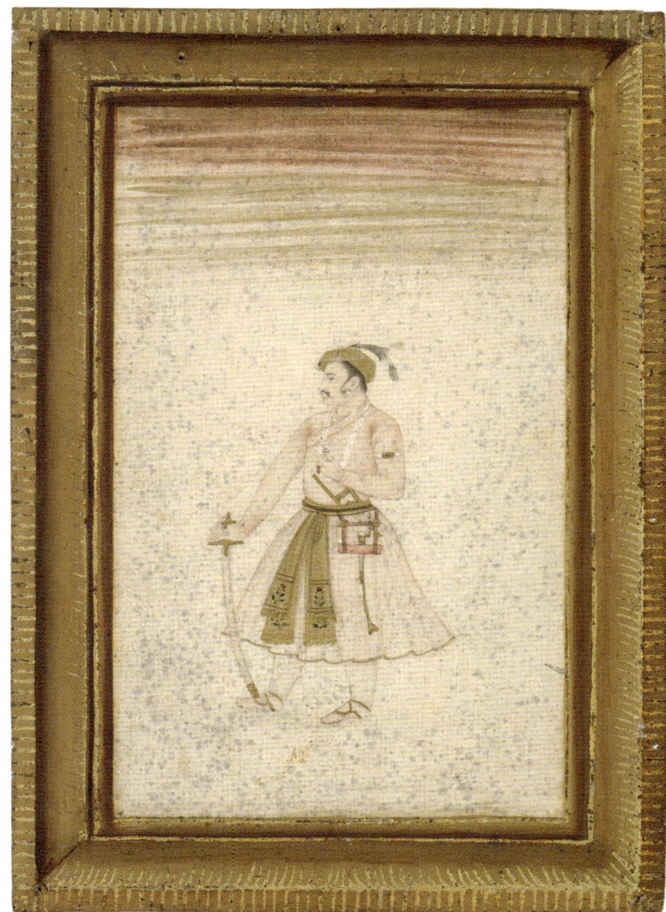

Cat. 10 | Ca 123/4

Cat. 9 | Ca 123/1
Shāh Jahān with young Dārā Shikōh
Mughal, late 17th century
Watercolour and gold, painted frame
28.2 × 19.1 cm, image 22.8 × 13.7 cm
Reference: Dresden 2017, cat. 28, p. 170

Cat. 10 | Ca 123/4
Jahāngīr (r. 1605–1627)
Mughal, late 17th century
Watercolour and gold, painted frame
25.3 × 17.4 cm, image 20.1 × 12.1 cm

Cat. 9 | While paintings produced by modest artists for sale to Europeans and foreign travellers were common, works by court painters occasionally found their way to these buyers as well. This image of Shāh Jahān with his eldest son, Dārā Shikōh (1615–1659), the chosen heir, is one of the finest portraits in the collection.[6] It reflects the tradition of dynastic portraits that began with images of Timurid and Mughal emperors shown with their sons and heirs and became popular during the reign of Shāh Jahān (r. 1628–1658).

This painting is closely comparable to a watercolour miniature embedded in a cartouche with a rich Rococo frame in the Millionenzimmer at Schönbrunn Castle in Vienna.[7] The same in size and format, the Vienna miniature was probably acquired in Amsterdam. The two artworks provide insight into the active art of reproduction of images at the turn of the seventeenth century and the varied quality of the results. NB

Cat. 10 | Executed in a style similar to the dynastic portrait of Shāh Jahān with his eldest son, Dārā Shikōh, and other works from the Schlegel Collection,[8] this miniature of Jahāngīr was made in imitation of a portrait of a Hindu *rājā*. Far from the depictions of Jahāngīr known from imperial manuscripts, he is here recognisable by the pearl earring worn as a sign of devotion towards his spiritual teacher Muʿīn ud-Dīn Chishtī and by his *jāma* tied on the right per Muslim tradition. The leather belt with a moneybag hanging from his waist reflects the influence of Deccani motifs to which the Mughal artist might have been exposed due to the political situation at the turn of the seventeenth century. NB

Cat. 11 | Ca 124/6
Tīmūr (r. 1370–1405)
Deccani Mughal, late 17th–early 18th century
Watercolour and gold, painted frame 23 × 16.4 cm, image 17.9 × 11.4 cm

Cat. 12 | Ca 124/3
Mīrān Shāh (c. 1367–1408)
Deccani Mughal, late 17th–early 18th century
Watercolour and gold, painted frame 23.9 × 18.6 cm, image 18.3 × 13 cm

Cat. 13 | Ca 124/2
Abū Sa'īd (r. 1451–1469) or 'Omar Shaikh (r. 1456–1494)
Deccani Mughal, late 17th–early 18th century
Watercolour and gold, painted frame 23.2 × 17.8 cm, image 17.6 × 12.1 cm

Cat. 14 | Ca 124/1
Humāyūn (r. 1531–1540, 1555–1556)
Deccani Mughal, late 17th–early 18th century
Watercolour and gold, painted frame 23 × 17 cm, image 17.7 × 11.6 cm

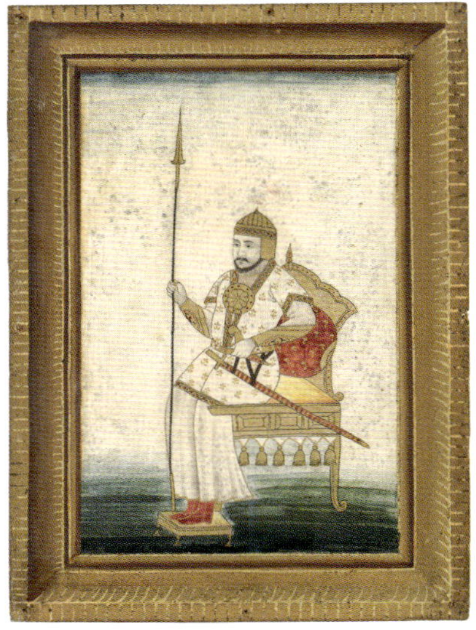
Cat. 11 | Ca 124/6

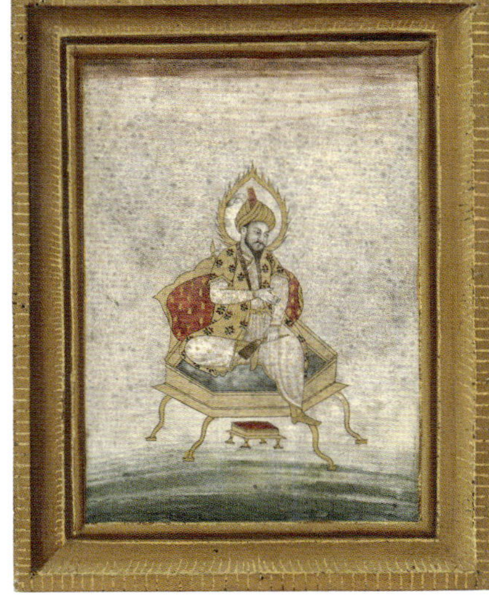
Cat. 12 | Ca 124/3

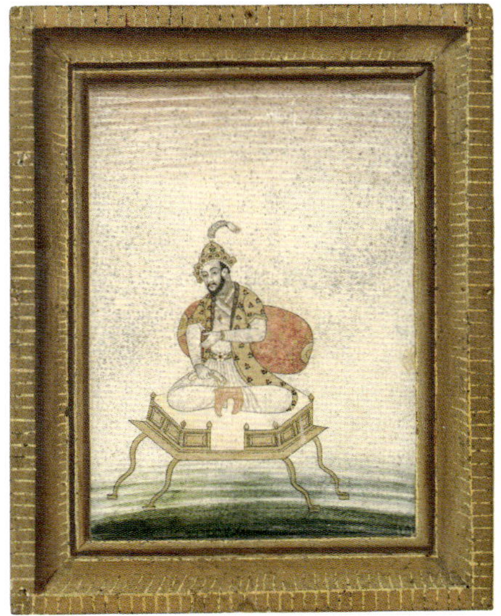
Cat. 13 | Ca 124/2

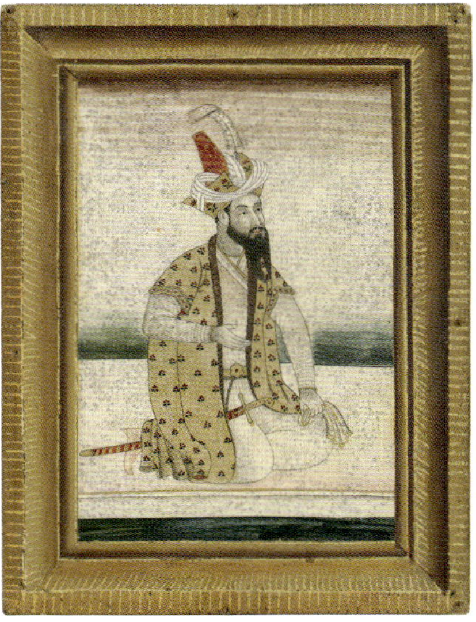
Cat. 14 | Ca 124/1

Cat. 11–9 | Portraits of Mughal rulers and their ancestors up to Tīmūr both legitimised the authority of the reigning emperor. Similar series of portraits were assembled in the late seventeenth or eighteenth century for European clients that supported artists working outside the royal atelier.

The Timurid *sultāns* are shown in three-quarter profile, typical of the representation of Mughal ancestors since the time of Akbar. They wear a helmet and a star-shaped crown like those seen in the *Zafarnāmā* (Victory Letter)[9] and are seated upon a hexagonal throne, a motif associated with Tīmūr's reign. This indicates the artists' concern for using standard characterisations of the figures rather than depicting realistic likenesses. The full-length portraits from Akbar to Aurangzēb, on the other hand, followed models created during the reign of Akbar as individual portraits collected in *muraqqas* (albums).

These portraits, in turn, remind us of the genealogical seal of the Mughal emperors of India, which was one of the most potent symbols of Mughal imperial authority.[10]

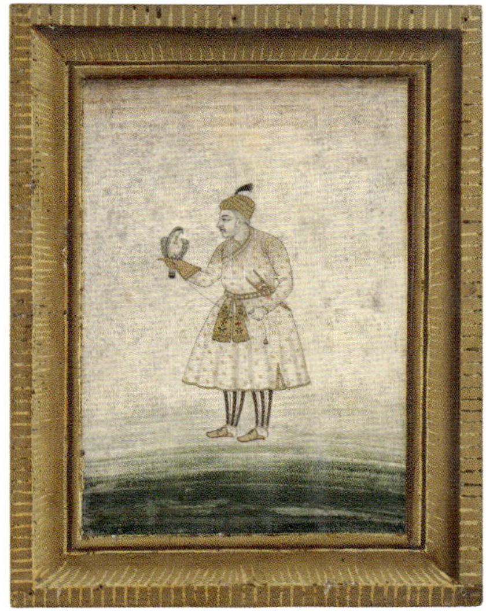

Cat. 15 | Ca 124/5

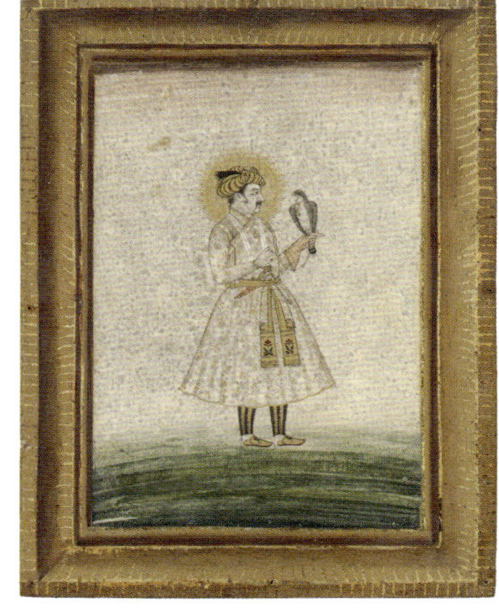

Cat. 16 | Ca 124/4

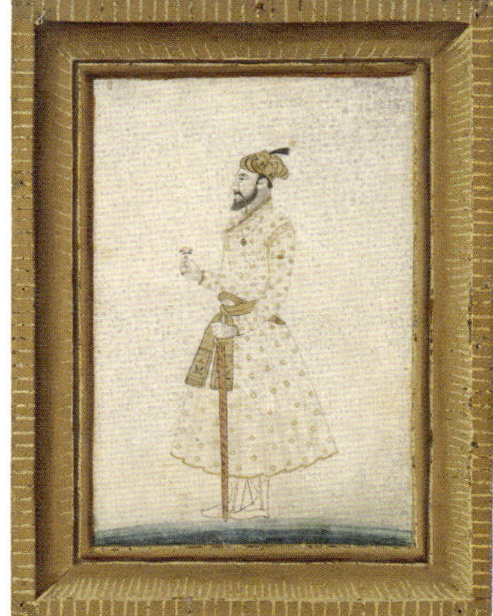

Cat. 17 | Ca 124/8

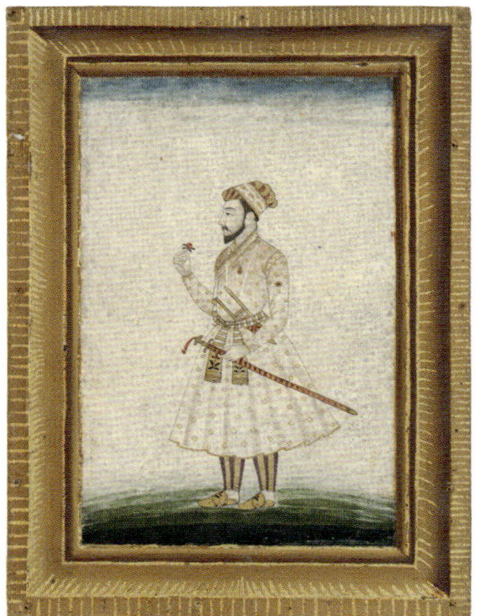

Cat. 18 | Ca 124/7

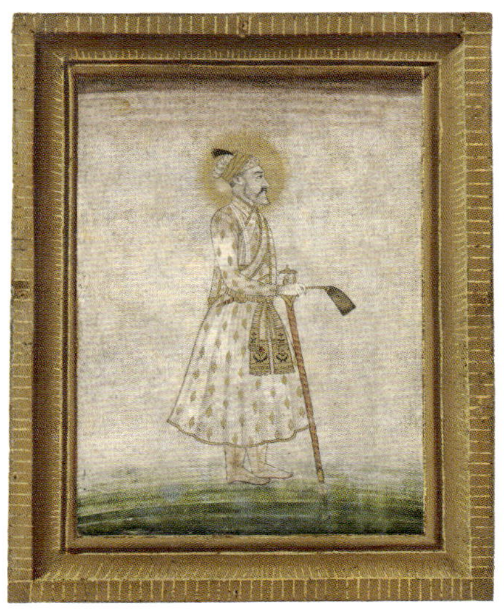

Cat. 19 | Ca 123/7

Cat. 15 | Ca 124/5
Akbar (r. 1556–1605)
Deccani Mughal, late 17th–early 18th century
Watercolour and gold, painted frame 24.1 × 18.4 cm, image 18.4 × 12.7 cm

Cat. 16 | Ca 124/4
Jahāngīr (r. 1605–1627)
Deccani Mughal, late 17th–early 18th century
Watercolour and gold, painted frame 24.1 × 18.6 cm, image 18.5 × 12.8 cm

Cat. 17 | Ca 124/8
Shāh Jahān (r. 1628–1658)
Deccani Mughal, late 17th–early 18th century
Watercolour and gold, painted frame 23.1 × 17 cm, image 17.4 × 15.5 cm

Cat. 18 | Ca 124/7
Murād Bakhsh (1624–1661)
Deccani Mughal, late 17th–early 18th century
Watercolour and gold, painted frame 23.9 × 17.6 cm, image 18.2 × 12 cm

Cat. 19 | Ca 123/7
Aurangzēb (r. 1658–1707)
Deccani Mughal, late 17th–early 18th century
Watercolour and gold, painted frame 23.5 × 18.7 cm, image 18.3 × 13.3 cm

Reference: Dresden 2017, cat. 26a–i, p. 169

The seal of Bābur, founder of the Mughal Empire, dated 1521–1522 bore his name at the centre and the names of his five ancestors up to Tīmūr. It became the prototype for the basic design that remained, with insignificant changes, until the end of Mughal Empire. When subsequent rulers assumed five-fold seals, the number of representations increased, paying close attention to one branch of a family and omitting any mention of short-lived interim rulers. The seal, therefore, became strictly a representation of lineage rather than dynasty. The arrangement of such lineages is seen in the present series. Although some rulers are missing from this set, which was assembled from different sources, it does include a rare representation of Murād Bakhsh, who claimed throne for only seven months in 1657.

Like the *muhr-i muqaddas-i kalan* (Royal Mughal geneological seal) that was safeguarded by the most trusted court official or by the women in the *zenāna*,[11] these sets of images were of extraordinary interest to European travellers and collectors of rarities. NB

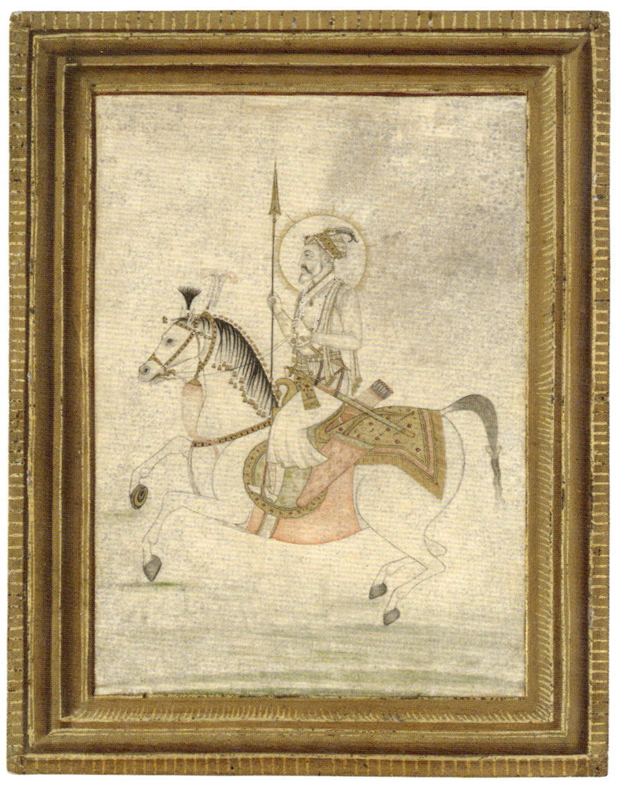

Cat. 20 | Ca 119/5

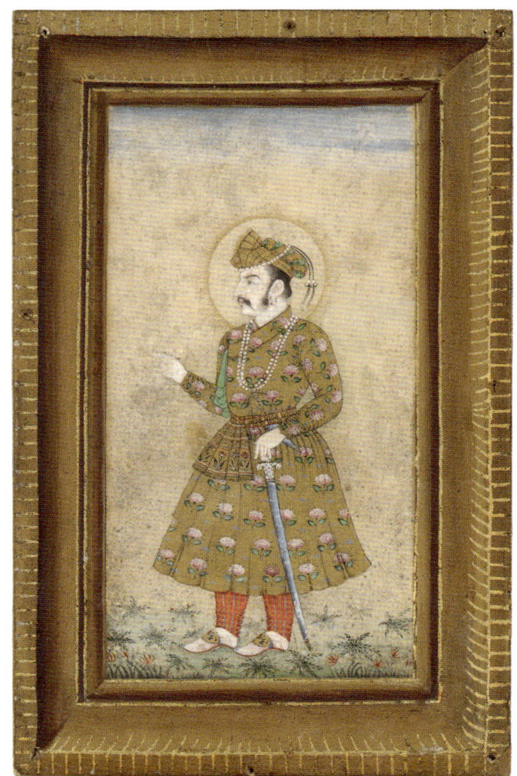

Cat. 21 | Ca 123/8

Cat. 20 | Ca 119/5
Equestrian portrait of Emperor Aurangzēb
Mughal style, late 17th century
Watercolour and gold,
painted frame 32.4 × 24.7 cm,
image 25.8 × 17.8 cm

Cat. 21 | Ca 123/8
Jahāngīr (r. 1605–1627)
Mughal, late 17th century
Watercolour and gold,
painted frame 24.9 × 15.8 cm,
image 18.7 × 9.8 cm
Reference: Dresden 2017,
p. 103, fig. 10a

Cat. 20 | This miniature of Aurangzēb on horseback is the only equestrian portrait in the Schlegel Collection. As in other portraits showing him at the height of his power, Aurangzēb is portrayed with a dark moustache, grey hair, and a beard.[12] Stylistically, the illustration belongs to the full-length portraits of individual Mughal rulers executed in the *nīmqalam* (half-pen) style and presumably from a similar workshop. Early twentieth-century scholars linked this type of Mughal equestrian portrait to European prototypes, whereas later researchers suggested the motif's roots lay in Persia, in accordance with the general tradition of ruler portraits.[13] PKH

Cat. 21 | According to the acclaimed miniature painter Shakir Ali, who specializes in the Mughal style of painting, the most difficult part of composing the face of the Mughal Emperor Jahāngīr was the part between his nose and upper lip—a challenge even for master artists. In such situations, the use of *chārbā* (pounce) was of great help in artist workshops, even though the master artist usually rendered only the outlines of the face.

This image shows Jahāngīr as a young Rājput prince. Jahāngīr was born to a Rājput princess and married to the daughter of Rājā Mān Sīngh. Despite the pearl earrings, the halo, the *jāma* tied on the right side, and the absence of a beard—typical characteristics of the emperor—this image appears to be either a result of an artist's vision of him as a Rājput prince or a product by an immature artist in the absence of a *chārbā.* NB

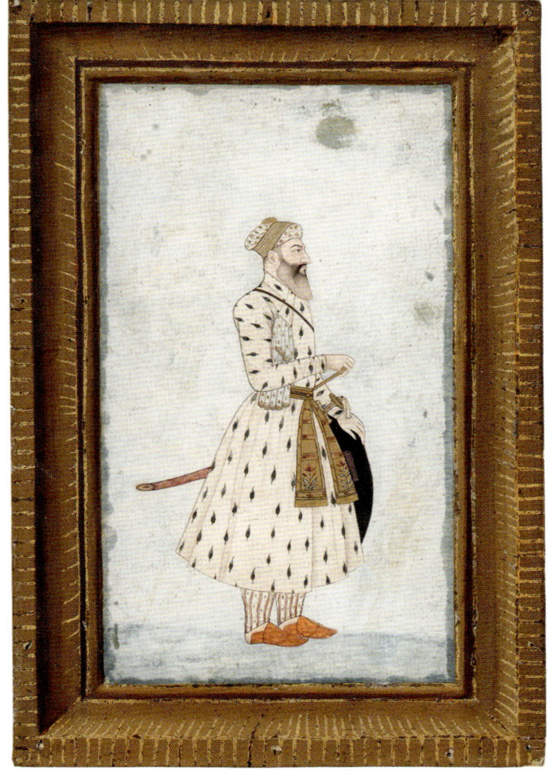

Cat. 22 | Ca 121/3

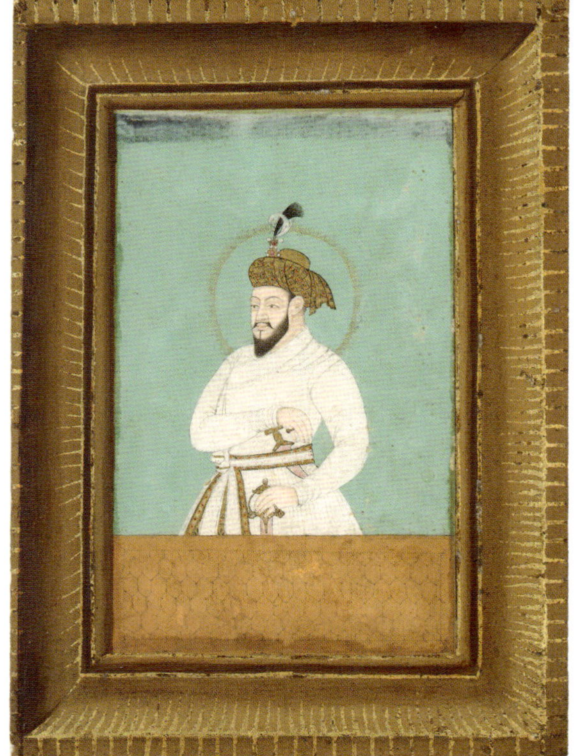

Cat. 23 | Ca 121/10

Cat. 22 | This fine portrait represents an unknown ruler or nobleman, Bahādur Khān Chaghatai, and is comparable to another inscribed portrait of about 1775–1780.[14] In both, he is shown wearing a mid-length *jāma* with a short *paṭkā* (sash) and a sword and shield at his side. As both are the same size, the present work may have been an inspiration for his probably later portrait in drawing and wash in the Johnson album.[15] NB

Cat. 23 | This half-length portrait of a figure standing behind a light brown balustrade decorated with honeycomb patterns within a painted frame[16] probably depicts Bābur, the founder of the Mughal Empire in India, who came from Transoxiana (present-day Uzbekistan) and settled in Agra in 1526.

The imagery in Indian miniature paintings from Golconda such as this one often derives from the royal *darshan* (audience), when the emperor appeared in the *jharōka* (balcony window) at sunrise. Although Humāyūn was the first Mughal emperor to appear in a ceremonial manner by putting a veil over his crown and then raising it to the acclaim of his courtiers who would cry out "Light has shone forth,"[17] Akbar and Jahāngīr presented their divinity in the form of *darshan* and haloed portraits that also embellished their gold coins. These various formulas were standardised by artists in Golconda during the late seventeenth century and used extensively, not only as allegorical symbols but also often as decorative elements in portraits of rulers and nobles.

The aim of the artists was not historical accuracy or capturing the emperor's likeness. They now based their work on frequently reproduced portraits that in turn stemmed from endless repetitions and variations that came to dominate contemporary perception. This portrait of Bābur with his hand resting on his dagger tucked in his *paṭkā* (sash) and wearing a white *jāma* is far removed from his early portraits seen in imperial Mughal manuscripts. The identification of the sitters in these portraits that lack individualisation is, therefore, based on comparable images found in various collections. NB

Cat. 22 | Ca 121/3
Bahādur Khān Chaghatai
Deccani Mughal, late 17th–early 18th century
Watercolour and gold, painted frame 25.7 × 17.3 cm, image 20.3 × 11.7 cm

Cat. 23 | Ca 121/10
Bābur (r. 1526–1530)
Deccan (Golconda), late 17th century
Watercolour and gold, painted frame 17.9 × 12.7 cm, image 12.6 × 7.8 cm
Reference: Dresden 2017, cat. 17, p. 154

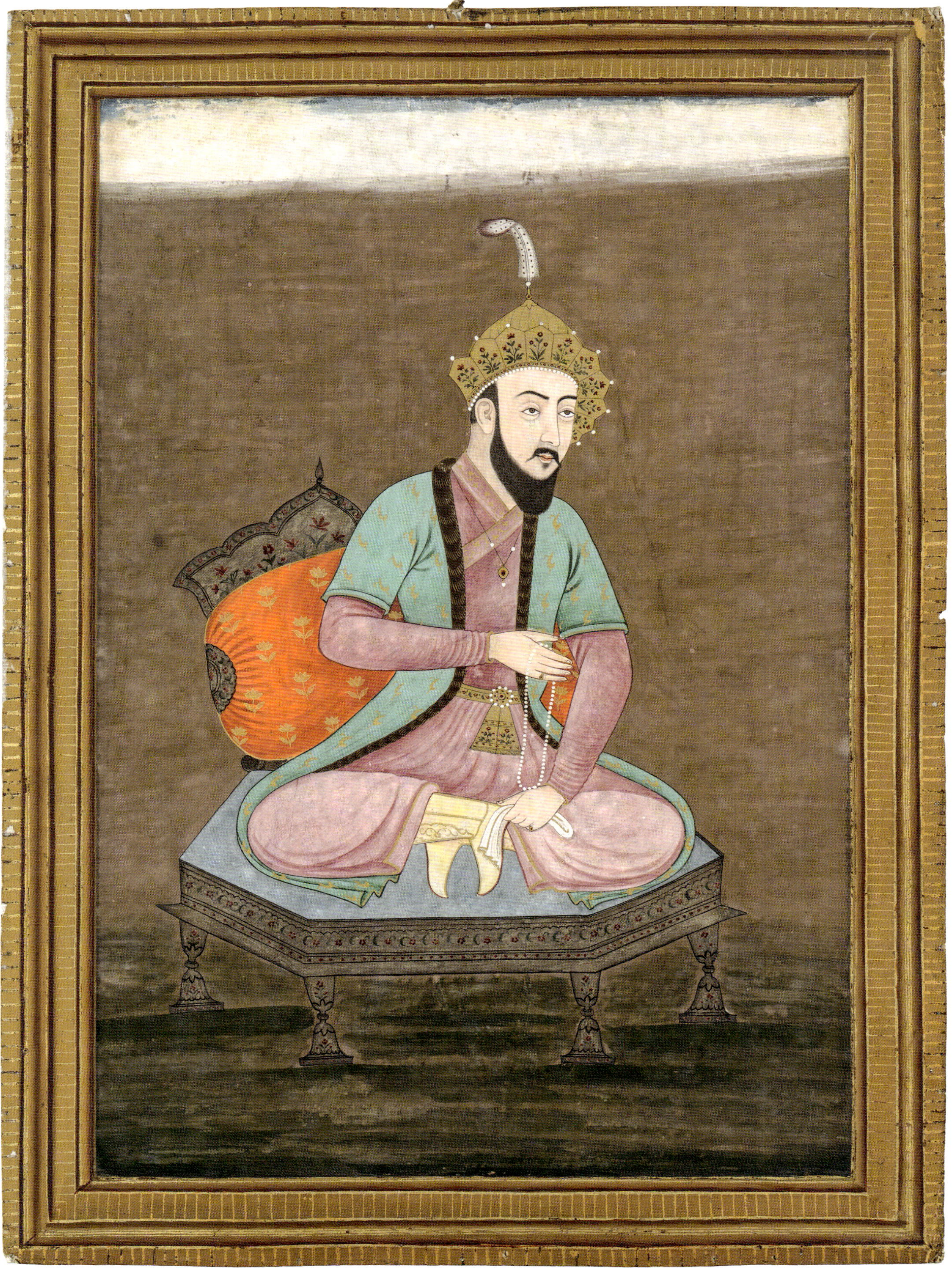

Cat. 24 | Ca 117/3

Cat. 24–9 | Mughal portraiture attained its greatest level of refinement in the sensitive portrayal of individuals during the reign of Emperor Akbar (r. 1556–1605). The predominance of portraits in Mughal painting occurred during the seventeenth century under Jahāngīr and Shāh Jahān and, to a certain extent, Aurangzēb.[18] While the enormous importance of these pictorial series is mostly associated with Mughal ateliers, this portraiture set, strongly influenced by regional Deccani motifs, reflects upon similar practise at local courts in the Deccan.

This set, compiled on the basis of style, size, and composition, probably depicted Mughal rulers from Tīmūr to Aurangzēb. It is defined by the prevailing conditions between artists and clients. After the fall of the kingdoms of Golconda and Bijapur to Aurangzēb's armies in 1686–1687, the Deccani sultanates fell, and the decline of the Mughal Empire during the following decades produced a shift in artistic patronage from rulers to lesser notables and Europeans trading in the area. The depiction of royal ancestors up to Tīmūr, which was typical during Shāh Jahān's reign, though never as single-page images, became a popular staple for artists who gathered in this region from all around the Muslim world.

These artworks, which include large portraits of Mughal rulers, combine the sober realism of Mughal painting with the extravagant taste of the Deccan. Probably large-scale versions of a similar, smaller series found in Leiden[19] and in Dresden (cat. 5, Ca 116), these portraits, with their blue, lilac, and salmon palette, are typical of paintings from the area around Bijapur and Golconda and probably were influenced by locally available pigments.[20] NB

Cat. 24 | Ca 117/3
Abū Sa'īd (r. 1451–1469) or 'Omar Shaikh (r. 1456–1494)
Deccan, late 17th–early 18th century
Watercolour, gold, and silver, painted frame 65.2 × 47.5 cm, image 55.9 × 38.4 cm

► figs. cat. 25–29, see pp. 146–7

Cat. 30 | Though Aurangzēb became increasingly reluctant to be portrayed later in life, the depictions of the last great Mughal emperor usually hark back to the courtly tradition of ruler portraits. Variations of this common type developed in Deccani painting around 1700; they had a different pictorial message and targeted a wider audience, beyond the courtly sphere, interested in the anecdotal. Images such as this miniature from the Schlegel Collection, however, show Aurangzēb as an old and lonely ruler, gaunt and wearing white, having forsaken wordly pleasures and immersing himself in the study of the *Qur'ān*.[21] The elderly Aurangzēb is leaning on his sword as though it were a cane. The green background is coarsely executed, possibly at a later date, and is poorly preserved; the ruler's figure, however, is drawn with great subtlety. PKH

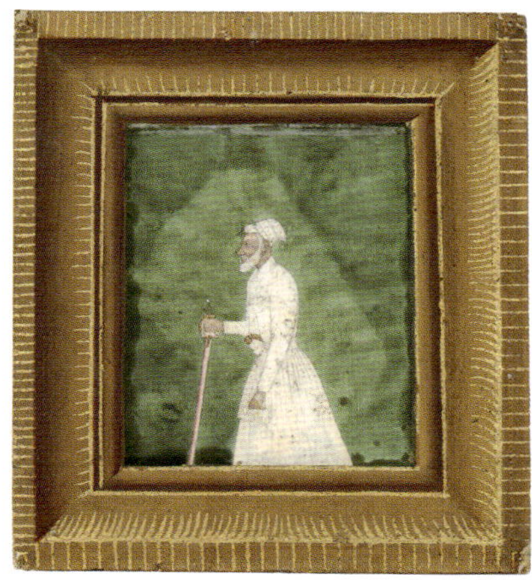

Cat. 30 | Ca 121/9
Aurangzēb (r. 1658–1707)
Deccan, late 17th–early 18th century
Watercolour and gold, painted frame 15.7 × 14 cm, image 9.8 × 8.1 cm
Reference: Dresden 2017, cat. 30, p. 174

Notes | 1 British Museum, London, inv. no. 1937,0410,0.4. See Dresden 2017, p. 166, fig. 24. | 2 The earliest known portraits of Muḥammad 'Ādil Shāh are in the collection of Gursharan and Elvira Sidhu, Seattle, and the Ashmolean Museum of Art and Archaeology, University of Oxford (LI118.54). | 3 Johnson Album in the India Office Library, London. See Falk/Archer 1981, cat. 405–7, pp. 501–2. | 4 Rijksmuseum, Amsterdam, inv. no. 1995-25. | 5 See Zebrowski 1983, pp. 151–2. | 6 Paintings in similar style: cat. 33–7, 46, 50, 51, 53, 54. | 7 Schönbrunn Castle, Vienna, inv. no. SKB 002637. See Strzygowski 1923; and Dresden 2017, cat. 85, p. 220. | 8 Cat. 9. See also cat. 33–7, 50–1, 53–4, 68. | 9 The *Zafarnāmā*, written by Sharaf ud-Dīn 'Alī Yazdī, describes the life and reign of Tīmūr, the founder of the Timurid dynasty; several imperial copies were made during the reigns of Tīmūr's sons and grandsons. The two known illustrated copies of the *Zafarnāmā* are the volume of about 1424 preserved at the British Library, London, and Husain Bāyqarā's 1480 copy, at John Hopkins University, Baltimore. | 10 See Gallop 1999, p. 77. | 11 See ibid., p. 85. | 12 See, for example, cat. 19, Ca 123/7. | 13 See Weber 1982, pp. 52–73. | 14 Johnson Album in the India Office Library, London. See Falk/Archer 1981, cat. 282, p. 443. | 15 See ibid. | 16 Similar portrait formats are seen in the Witsen Album, Rijskmuseum, Amsterdam, inv. no. RP-T 00-3186-1B; Staatliche Museen zu Berlin, Museum für Asiatische Kunst, inv. no. MIK 1 5211 (same size and colour scheme); British Museum, London, inv. no. 1956,1110,0.2; Victoria & Albert Museum, London, inv. no. IS.227-1950; and four folios in the private collection of Amir Mohtashemi, London (unpublished). | 17 Skelton 1988, p. 179. | 18 See Weber 1982, p. 9. | 19 A series of eighteen portrait busts of Mughal emperors and their ancestors from Tīmūr to Aurangzēb and extending as far as Emperor Farrukh Sīyar (r. 1713–1719). Nationaalmuseum van Wereldculturen, Leiden, inv. nos. 360–7346 to 360–7363. | 20 See Zebrowski 1983, p. 155. | 21 See also Prapanna 2017, p. 31, fig. 1.

Cat. 25 | Ca 117/4
Abū Sa'īd (r. 1451–1469) or 'Omar Shaikh (r. 1456–1494)
Deccan, late 17th–early 18th century
Watercolour and gold,
painted frame 65.1 × 46.5 cm,
image 57.1 × 38 cm

Cat. 26 | Ca 117/6
Bābur (r. 1526–1530)
Deccan, late 17th–early 18th century
Watercolour, gold, and silver,
painted frame 65.7 × 47.1 cm,
image 57.1 × 38.6 cm

Cat. 27 | Ca 117/5
Humāyūn (r. 1530–1540, 1555–1556)
Deccan, late 17th–early 18th century
Watercolour, gold, and silver,
painted frame 65.4 × 46.7 cm,
image 56.7 × 37.9 cm

Cat. 28 | Ca 117/1
Shāh Jahān (r. 1628–1658)
Deccan, late 17th–early 18th century
Watercolour and gold, painted frame
63.9 × 47.9 cm, image 54.8 × 38.7 cm

Cat. 29 | Ca 117/2
Aurangzēb (r. 1658–1707)
Deccan, late 17th–early 18th century
Watercolour and gold, painted frame
65.3 × 46.7 cm, image 56.3 × 36.8 cm

Reference: Dresden 2017, cat. 29a–f, pp. 172–3

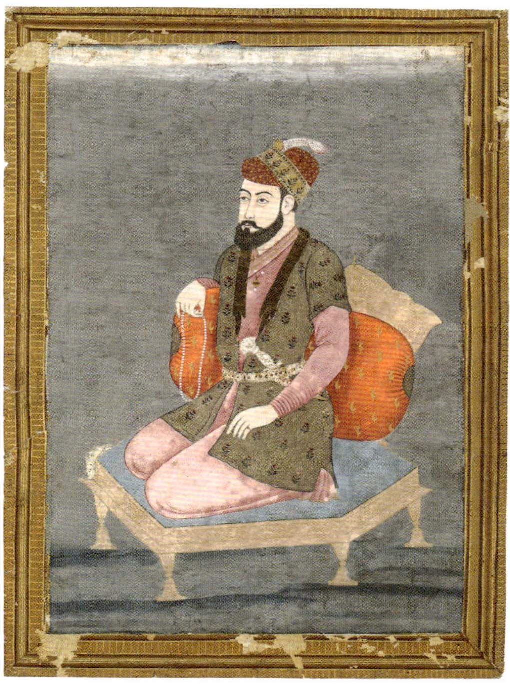

Cat. 25 | Ca 117/4

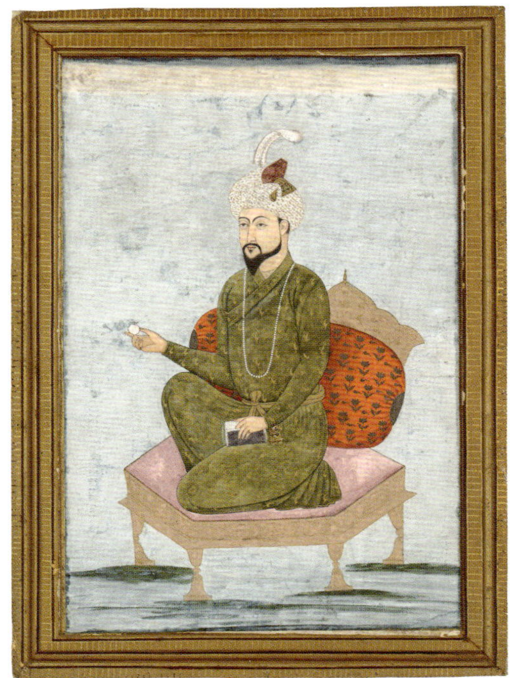

Cat. 26 | Ca 117/6

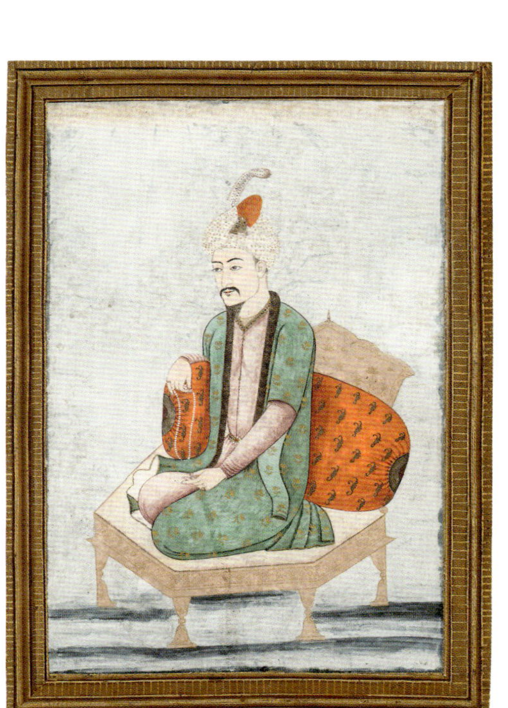

Cat. 27 | Ca 117/5

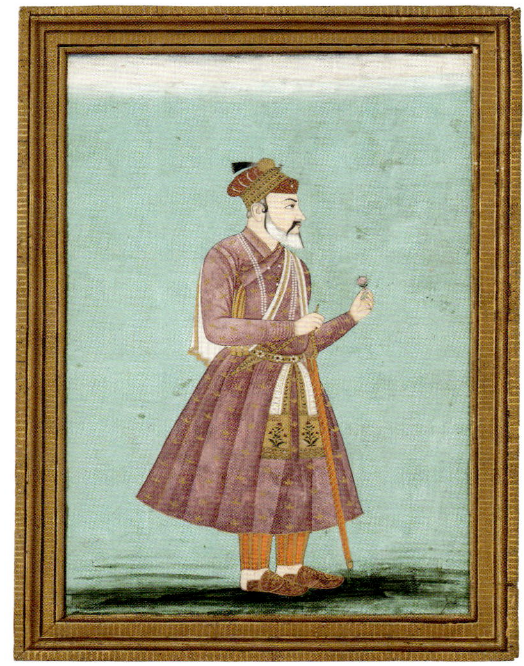

Cat. 28 | Ca 117/1

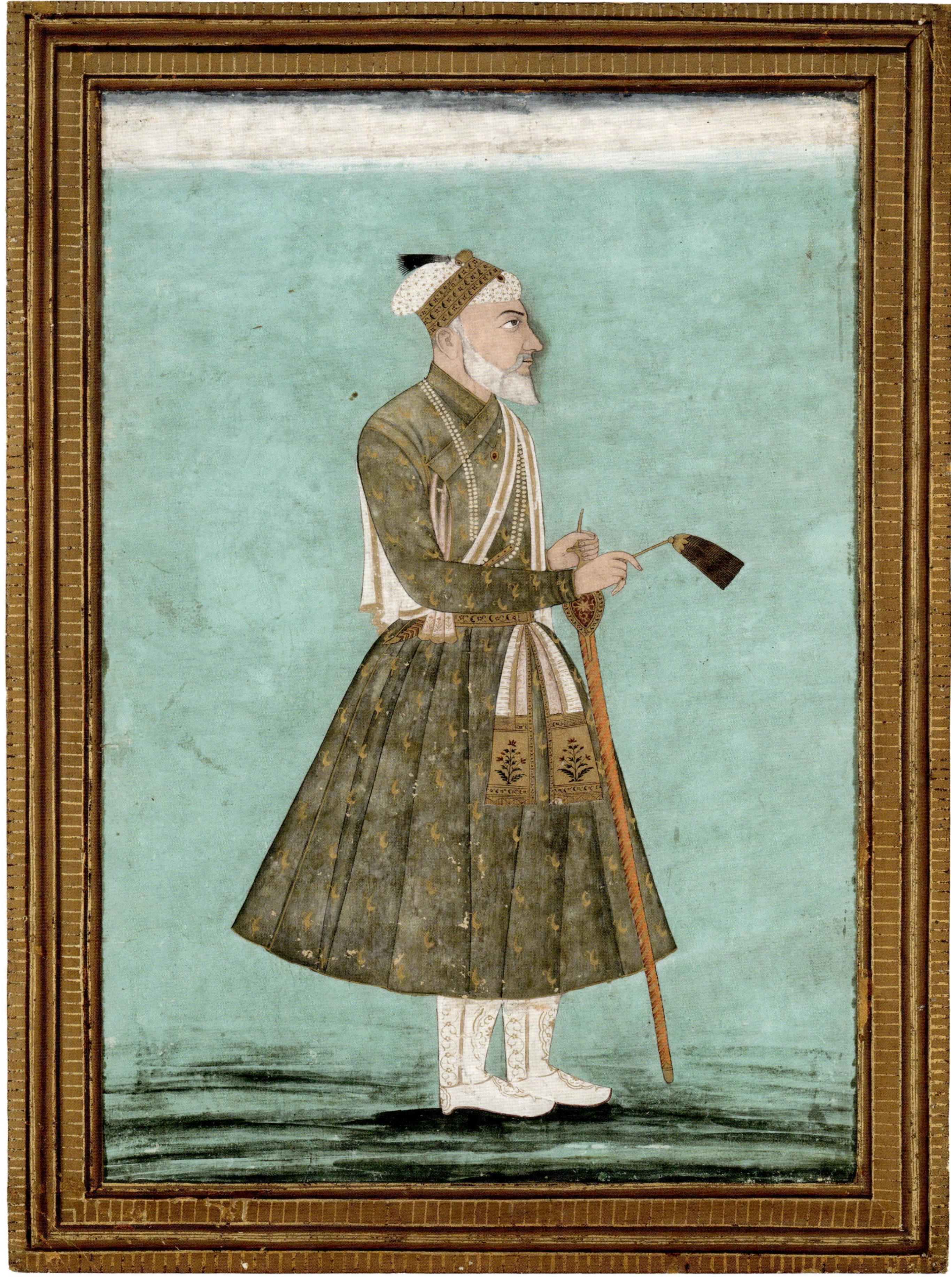

Cat. 29 | Ca 117/2

Noblemen

Cat. 31 | Ca 120/4
A nobleman (Mīrzā Ahmad)
Deccan, early 18th century
Watercolour, gold, and silver,
painted frame 29.9 × 22.6 cm,
image 23.2 × 15.8 cm

Cat. 32 | Ca 121/8
Neknām Khān (d. 1672)
Deccan, late 17th–early 18th century
Watercolour, painted frame
30.1 × 20.7 cm, image 24.4 × 14.8 cm
Reference: Dresden 2017, cat. 34, p. 177

Cat. 31–2 | In the albums compiled in Golconda in the late seventeenth century that include full-length portraits of princes (see cat. 1, Ca 112; and cat. 2, Ca 110), there are several depictions of Mīrzā Ahmad sitting on a chair and of the elderly general Neknām Khān.[1] Both were in the service of Sultān ʿAbdullāh Qutb Shāh (r. 1626–1672). The versions in the Schlegel Collection are also based on the representations in these albums. In cat. 31, Mīrzā Ahmad is seated on a chair; he looks somewhat younger and more robust than he does in the above-mentioned albums and is shown on a balcony with a view of trees.

The painting showing the distinctive features of the white-clad old *wazīr* Neknām Khān (cat. 32) has been done by another artist. Although it is not a standing portrait, the representation recalls the Golconda albums. He is shown in a genre-like setting; the cloud formations in the background clearly show European influence, as does the detailed treatment of the trees and the sky.[2] Neknām Khān is shown sitting on a terrace within a wooden enclosure, holding a glass while smoking a *huqqā*. His sandals and the *huqqā*, standing on a small *cauki*, are placed on the floor. The same composition appears in the "*Description des habits des Persans*" in Chatelain's *Atlas historique*. There the smoking *wazīr* from Golconda appears at the centre of the page[3] along with a number of figures known from Turkish costume books.[4]

A variant of the composition in cat. 32, which differs only in details yet is probably by another hand, can be found in an album that contains Indian miniatures from the collection of the Prince of Liechtenstein.[5]

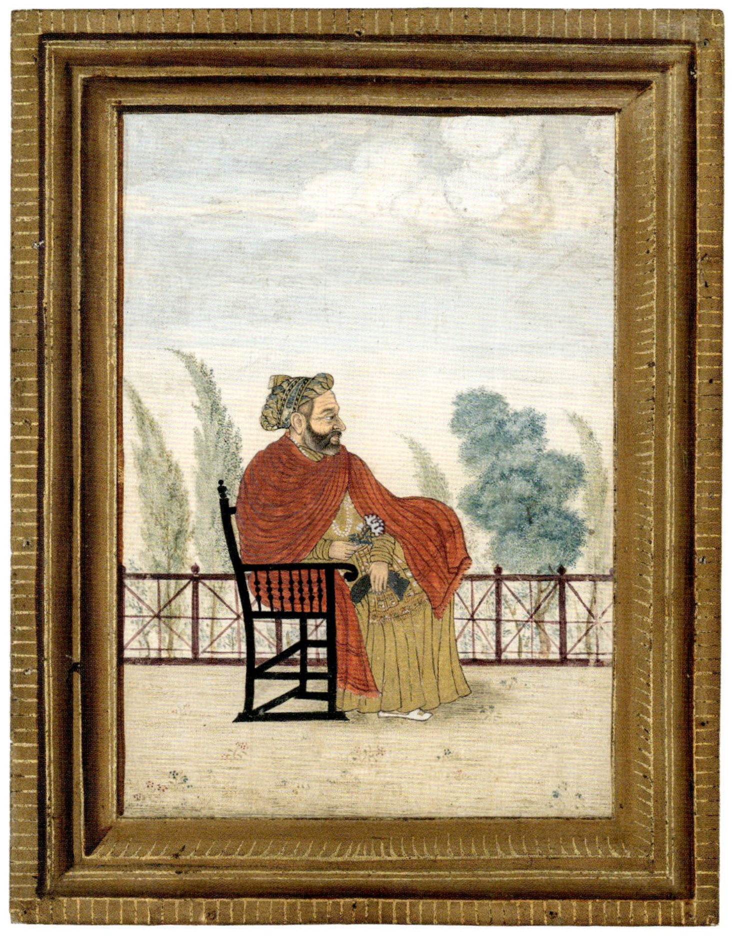

Cat. 31 | Ca 120/4

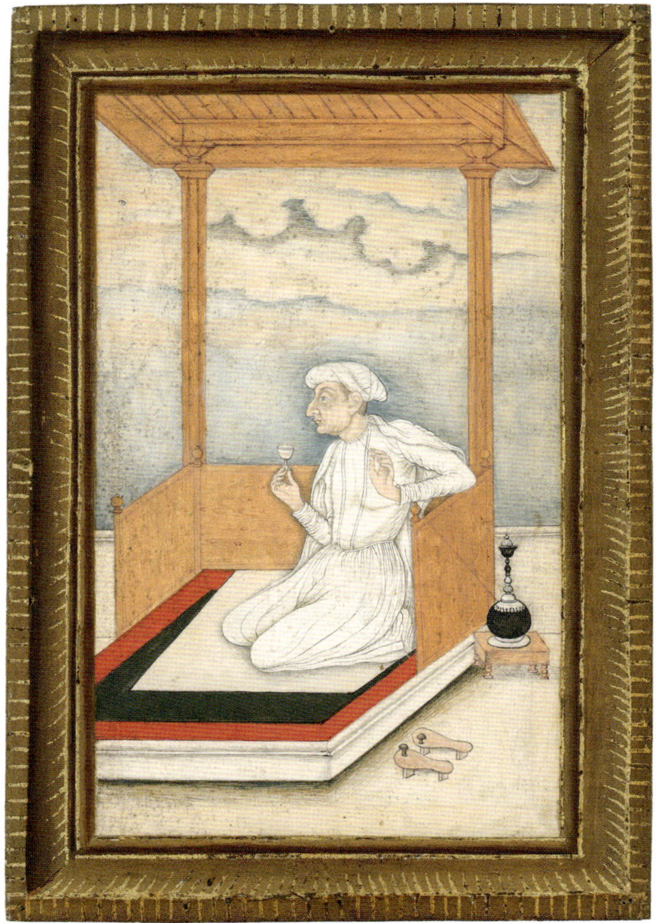

Cat. 32 | Ca 121/8

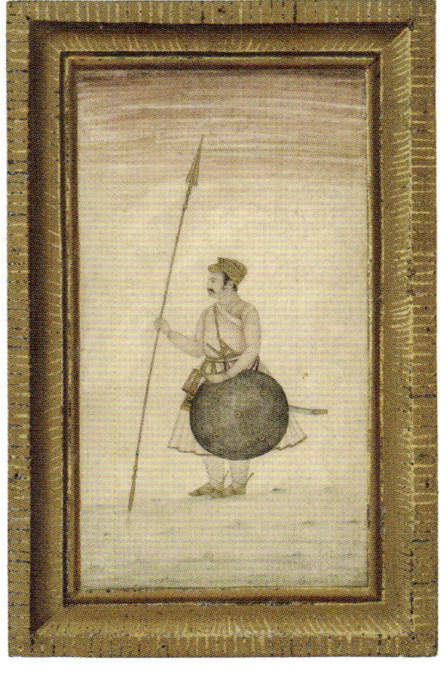

Cat. 33 | Ca 123/2

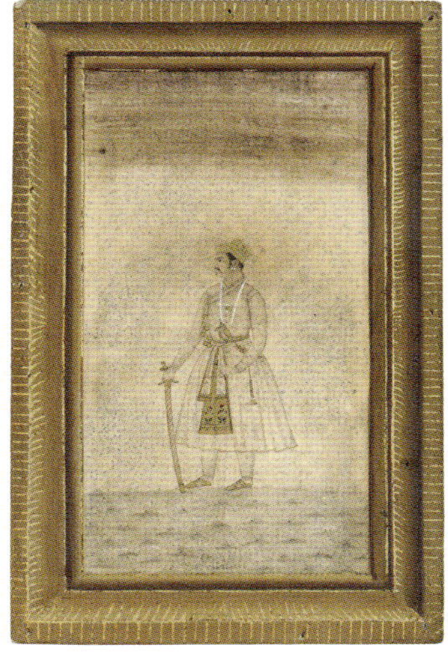

Cat. 34 | Ca 123/5

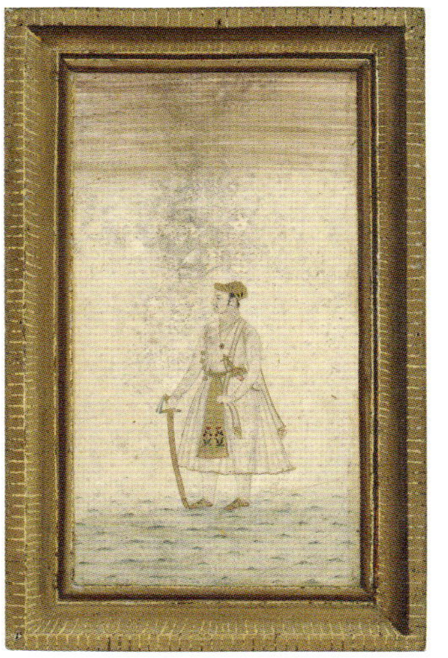

Cat. 35 | Ca 123/6

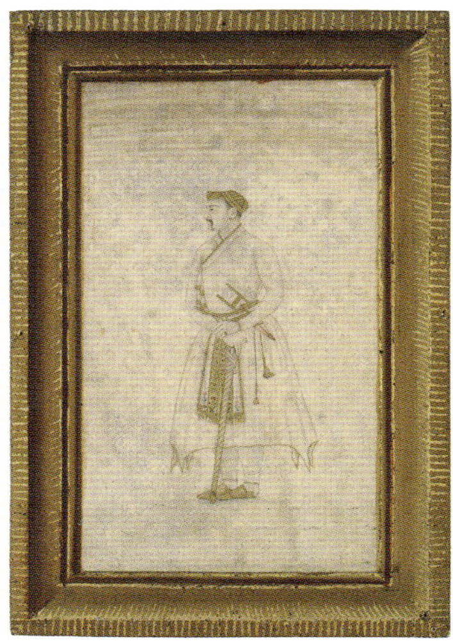

Cat. 36 | Ca 123/3

These two paintings illustrate the development of traditional portrait forms that took place in Golconda about 1700 as a result of the influx of artists and foreign customers. In this milieu, the Mughal style of the Deccan found an expression that was to last well into the eighteenth century.[6] In contrast to the works in the Golconda portrait albums, whose flat surfaces are painted with opaque watercolour, these paintings leave large areas of the paper in reserve and use only a few colours: mostly black ink for contours and hair, red, gold, green, and blue as well as a greyish brown wash for shading.[7] PKH

Cat. 33–7 | A number of portraits of noblemen in the Schlegel holdings are similar in style to paintings in grisaille in the collection.[8] They are characterised by the rigid poses and meticulous technique of Mughal portraiture[9] and demonstrate a sense of refinement in the use of muted colour combinations, handling of the gold accents, and deft treatment of textiles. The selective use of gold to highlight designs on the turban, sash, sword hilt, dagger, shoes, and jewellery contrasts with the nuanced and refined brushwork. This signature style developed during the seventeenth and eighteenth centuries among Indian artists trained in the imperial ateliers but now producing work for local clientele.[10]

The Rājputs dressed in the attire emulating the Mughal style can be distinguished from the other noblemen by their Hindu custom of tying the *jāma* to the left. In the seventeenth century the Rājputs often imitated certain aspects of the Mughals' elegance and refinement for aesthetic and political purposes.

Jai Sīngh,[11] who later became the ruler of Amber (present-day Jaipur), spent his life employed by Mughals in military campaigns and is known to have been present with Emperors Shāh Jahān (r. 1627–1658) and Aurangzēb (r. 1658–1707) on formal occasions such as manuscript presentations.[12] Mān Sīngh,[13] referred to as *farzand* (son) by the Mughal Emperor Akbar (r. 1556–1605),[14] entered imperial service in 1562 and was among the most intimate confidants of the Mughal hierarchy. NB

Cat. 33 | Ca 123/2
A Rājput nobleman (probably Jai Sīngh, d. 1667)
Mughal, late 17th century
Watercolour and gold,
painted frame 26.7 × 16.8 cm,
image 21.3 × 11.4 cm
Reference: Dresden 2017, cat. 27, p. 170

Cat. 34 | Ca 123/5
A nobleman
Mughal, late 17th century
Watercolour and gold,
painted frame 24.7 × 16 cm,
image 19.2 × 10.5 cm

Cat. 35 | Ca 123/6
A nobleman
Mughal, late 17th century
Watercolour and gold,
painted frame 26.8 × 17 cm,
image 21.3 × 11.6 cm

Cat. 36 | Ca 123/3
A Mughal courtier
Mughal, late 17th century
Watercolour and gold,
painted frame 25.3 × 17.4 cm,
image 20.1 × 12.1 cm

Cat. 37 | Ca 123/12
A Rājput nobleman (probably Mān Sīngh I, r. 1589–1614)
Mughal, late 17th century
Watercolour, gold, and silver, painted frame 23.5 × 17.9 cm, image 17.9 × 12.2 cm

Cat. 38 | Ca 123/11
A Rājput nobleman (probably Bhao Sīngh, d. 1678)
Deccani Mughal, late 17th–early 18th century
Watercolour and gold, painted frame 23 × 17.6 cm, image 17.5 × 12 cm

Cat. 39 | Ca 123/10
A nobleman
Deccani Mughal, late 17th–early 18th century
Watercolour and gold, painted frame 23.4 × 17.8 cm, image 18.6 × 12.5 cm

Cat. 38 | Although executed using a few hurried brushstrokes indicating the sky and the ground, similar to other portraits in the Dresden collection,[15] this portrait of a Rājput nobleman is coarser in style. The head, probably made by tracing a *chārbā* (pounce) of a pre-existing Rājput ruler's portrait, is accentuated with detailing in gold in the turban. However, the artist, who may have been junior to the one responsible for the outlining of the face, was less successful in his attempt to draw the rest of the body, giving the sitter a slight bulge at the belly along with stiff folds at the ends of his *jāma*, which flares out from a rather slim waist. NB

Cat. 39 | Depicting a Turkish nobleman, this image is similar in style to the set of portraits beginning with Tīmūr (r. 1370–1405), and ending with Aurangzēb (r. 1658–1707).[16] Illustrated in the Mughal style of single standing figures, this portrait shows a man of Central Asian origin, indicated by the conical metal helmet and the leather boots. His beard, executed in fine single brushstrokes, is long and distinctly shaped in an oblong form. These characteristics are an indication of the transcultural nature of the Mughal courts during the seventeenth and eighteenth centuries. NB

Cat. 40–1 | Except for about four decades (1687–1724), the Deccan maintained its political independence from northern India. After Aurangzēb conquered the Deccan sultanates in the late 1680s, it developed a distinct Islamic culture. The Deccan population was a mix of Indian Muslims and Hindus as well as Turks, Persians, Arabs, and Africans who played a vital role in the socio-political and economic life of various dynasties.[17] The most famous of the Africans are Mālik ʿAmbar (1548–1626) and Bijapur's Ikhlās Khān (d. 1656).

The portrait of an African nobleman depicts a member of the *Siddi* community, which is first documented as settling in western India in 1100. There followed a major influx of *Siddis* between the seventeenth and the nineteenth centuries, when they were enslaved by the Arabs and Portuguese and brought to India.[18] This full-bodied sitter's complexion and facial features suggest he was a member of Golconda's large *Habshī* community,[19] as was Mālik ʿAmbar. Mālik ʿAmbar was the *wazīr* of Ahmadnagar, where he established his own troop of enslaved African soldiers. While the style of the turban

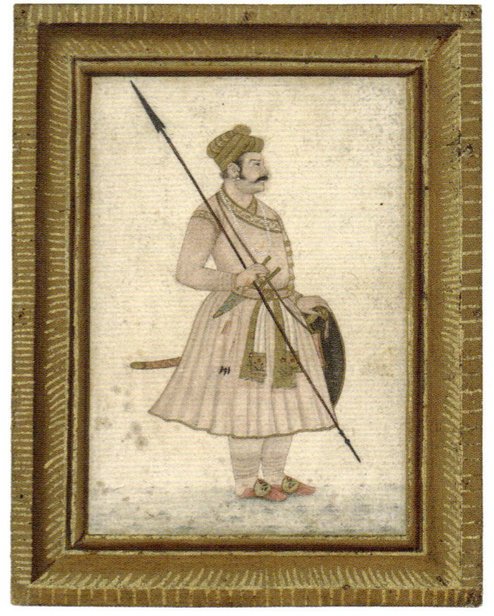

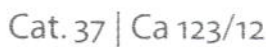
Cat. 37 | Ca 123/12

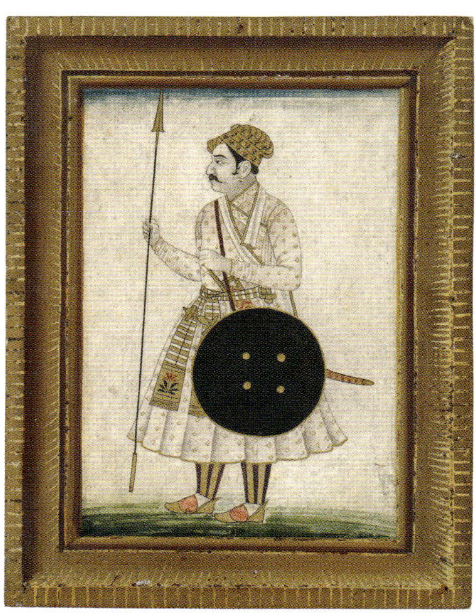

Cat. 38 | Ca 123/11

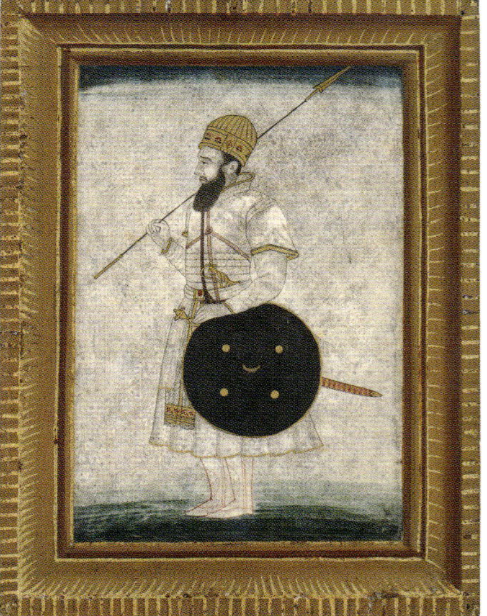

Cat. 39 | Ca 123/10

and the rich green background found in representations of him from the first two decades of the seventeenth century remain here,[20] the eighteenth-century artist replaced the white diaphanous *jāma* with a rather flamboyantly coloured garment. Mālik ʿAmbar sniffs a flower that he holds in his right hand, while his left is closed in a fist, suggestive of power. In earlier portraits, he holds a sword in his left hand.

The portrait of a young Mughal prince seems far from presenting the inner nature of the sitter through the faithful reproduction of his outward appearance. Instead, the portrait defines the status and environment in which early eighteenth-century artists worked. The prince is seen standing with both hands extended in the gesture of *duʿā* (receiving grace), wearing rings and a scarf similar to those worn by the African nobleman. Working from memory of earlier images, the artist failed to capture the distinctive characteristics of any one individual, making a definitive identification of the sitter impossible. NB

Cat. 42 | The golden jacket over a white *jāma* suggests that the subject was Central Asian. He was perhaps a nobleman visiting the Deccan or one who had settled there for economic opportunities. He is holding a Deccani sword and sniffing a flower. NB

Cat. 40 | Ca 121/2
A young Mughal prince
Deccan, late 17th – early 18th century
Watercolour, gold, and silver,
painted frame 26.1 × 16.9 cm,
image 20.5 × 11.2 cm

Cat. 41 | Ca 121/4
An African nobleman (Mālik ʿAmbar ?)
Deccan, late 17th – early 18th century
Watercolour, gold, and silver,
painted frame 27 × 18.2 cm,
image 20.3 × 11.4 cm

Reference: Dresden 2017, cat. 25a–b, pp. 166–7

Cat. 42 | Ca 121/5
A nobleman
Deccan, late 17th – early 18th century
Watercolour and gold,
painted frame 25.7 × 18.4 cm,
image 20.2 × 13 cm

Notes | 1 For Mīrzā Ahmad, see cat. 1, Ca 112/35; and British Museum, London, inv. no. 1974,0617,0.2.12; for Neknām Khān, cat. 1, Ca 112/20, and cat. 2, Ca 110/26. | 2 See Dresden 2017, p. 180, no. 3. | 3 See p. 26, fig. 8. | 4 Similar to the costumes in cat. 3, Ca 114. | 5 See p. 27, fig. 10. | 6 See Losty 2012, p. 62. For works of this type, see Lunsingh Scheurleer 2017. | 7 Portraits executed in this style can be found in albums in Dresden that were acquired earlier as well as in the Schlegel Collection. See cat. 3 and 4. The works in this style in the Österreichische Nationalbibliothek and in the Millionenzimmer at Schönbrunn Castle, Vienna, are particularly comparable to those in Dresden; see Dresden 2017, cat. 85 and 86, pp. 220–1. | 8 See cat. 9, 50–1, 53–4, 68. | 9 See Zebrowski 1983, p. 234. | 10 Cat. 33–4 seem to belong to the same set as cat. 9, Ca 123/1. | 11 See cat. 33. | 12 See Glynn 2000, p. 225. | 13 See cat. 37. | 14 See Glynn 1996, pp. 67–93. | 15 See cat. 11–8. | 16 See cat. 11–8, Ca 124/1–8 and cat. 19, Ca 123/7. | 17 See Zebrowski 1983, p. 9. | 18 See Bhattacharya 1970. | 19 *Habshī* is the Arabic term for Abyssinian, a nationality known today as Ethiopian. *Siddi* (my lord), another Arabic term to identify the group, connotes an elevated status. Although the integration took place much earlier, immigration continued to sustain diasporas throughout Gujarat, Karnatak, Bombay, Goa, and Hyderabad, with about 65,000 Africans living in *Siddi* communities in these regions. | 20 This includes portraits in Museum of Fine Arts, Boston (Arthur Mason Knapp Fund, inv. no. 26.8); Victoria & Albert Museum, London (inv. no. IM. 21-1925); Musée National des Arts Asiatiques-Guimet, Paris (inv. no. 7172); and a portrait titled *African Eunuch* in a private collection; see Michell/Zebrowski 1999, p. 203.

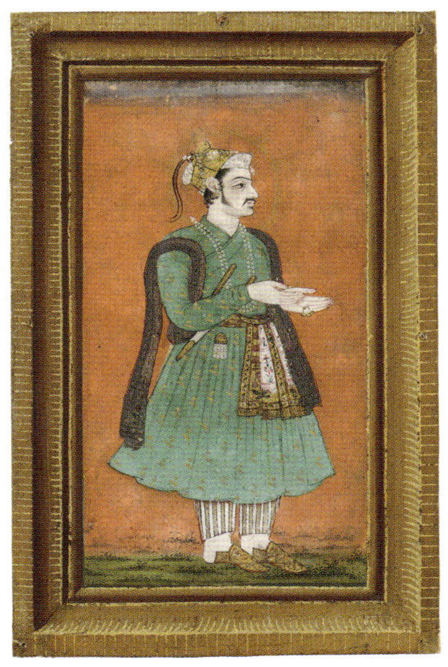

Cat. 40 | Ca 121/2

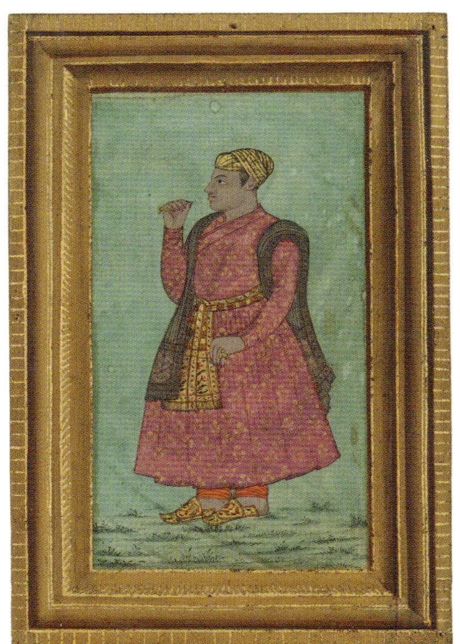

Cat. 41 | Ca 121/4

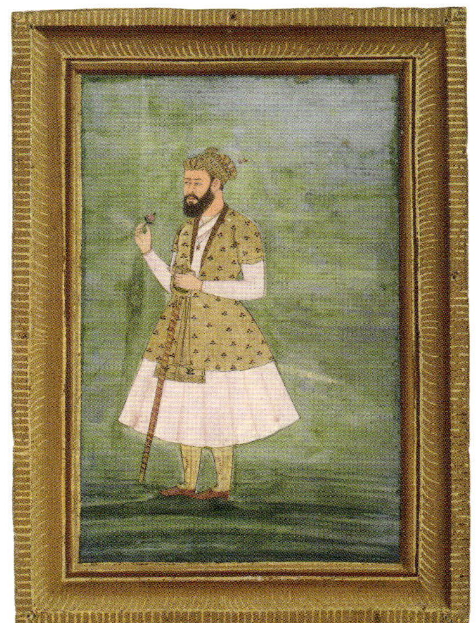

Cat. 42 | Ca 121/5

Court Scenes

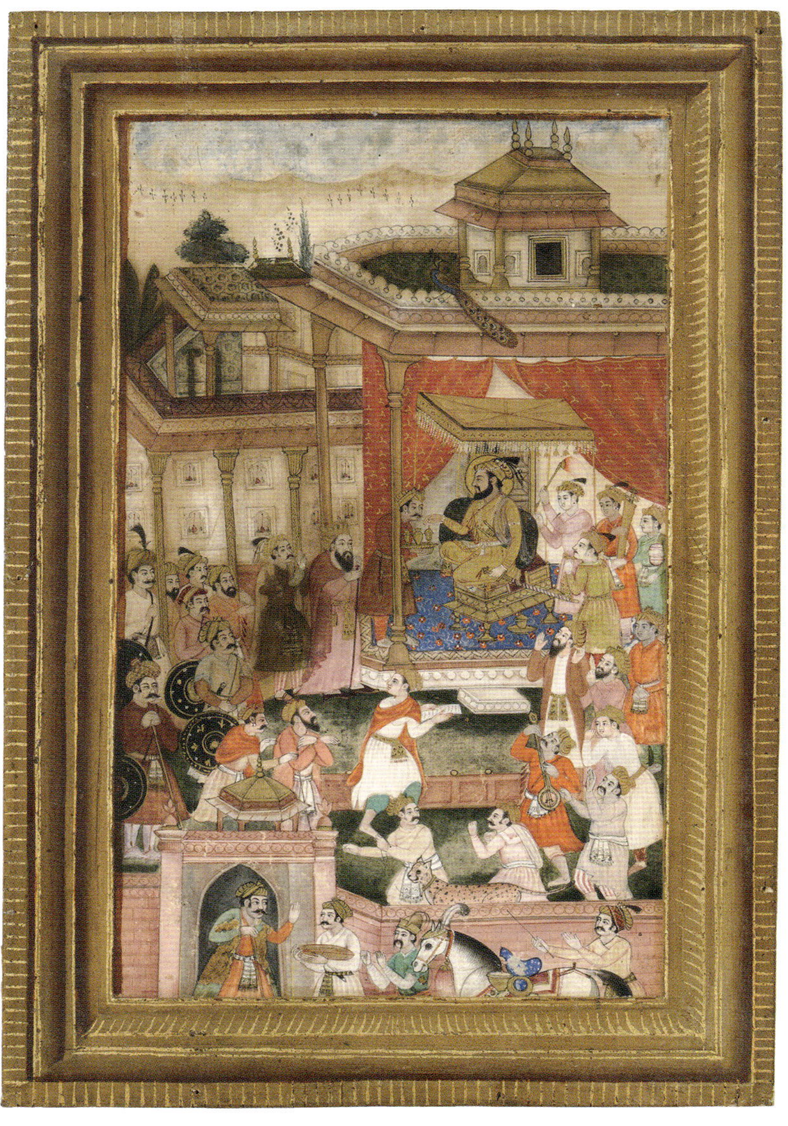

Cat. 43 | Ca 119/3
Darbār of Shāh Jahān
Deccan, Mughal school, late 17th–early 18th century
Watercolour and gold, painted frame 34.3 × 23.4 cm, image 28.1 × 17.6 cm
Reference: Lunsingh Scheurleer 2017, p. 60, fig. 8

Cat. 43 | Representing a famous genre of Mughal painting, this painting shows Shāh Jahān (r. 1628–1658) receiving a visitor—in this case, an ambassador. The emperor, seated on a throne, is shown in profile with a golden halo suggestive of his divine kingship. The audience in the foreground is neatly divided into three tiers according to their status. The *mullāh* (a Muslim learned in Islamic theology and sacred law) stands closest to the emperor. In the second tier are courtiers and ministers, some patiently attending the *darbār* with their hands resting on long sticks while others are more animated as they participate. In the background is a glimpse of the scene outside the palace walls.

Audience scenes were illustrated profusely during Shāh Jahān's reign. There are three known versions, dating about 1675,[1] of scenes in the *Pādshāhnāma*[2] in the Royal Collection at Windsor Castle.[3] The present painting, presumably executed in the early eighteenth century for the European market, is a simplified version of the copies produced in imperial ateliers.

This painting is comparable in style and format to a miniature of Akbar receiving a submissive prince,[4] which in turn is copied after an *Akbarnāma* of about 1604.[5] The only surprising difference in the latter work is that the subject, Shāh Jahān, has been replaced by his grandfather Akbar, while the composition and palette remain the same. Such similarities with noted modifications between these two paintings hint not only towards production in the same workshop but also towards the same audience. NB

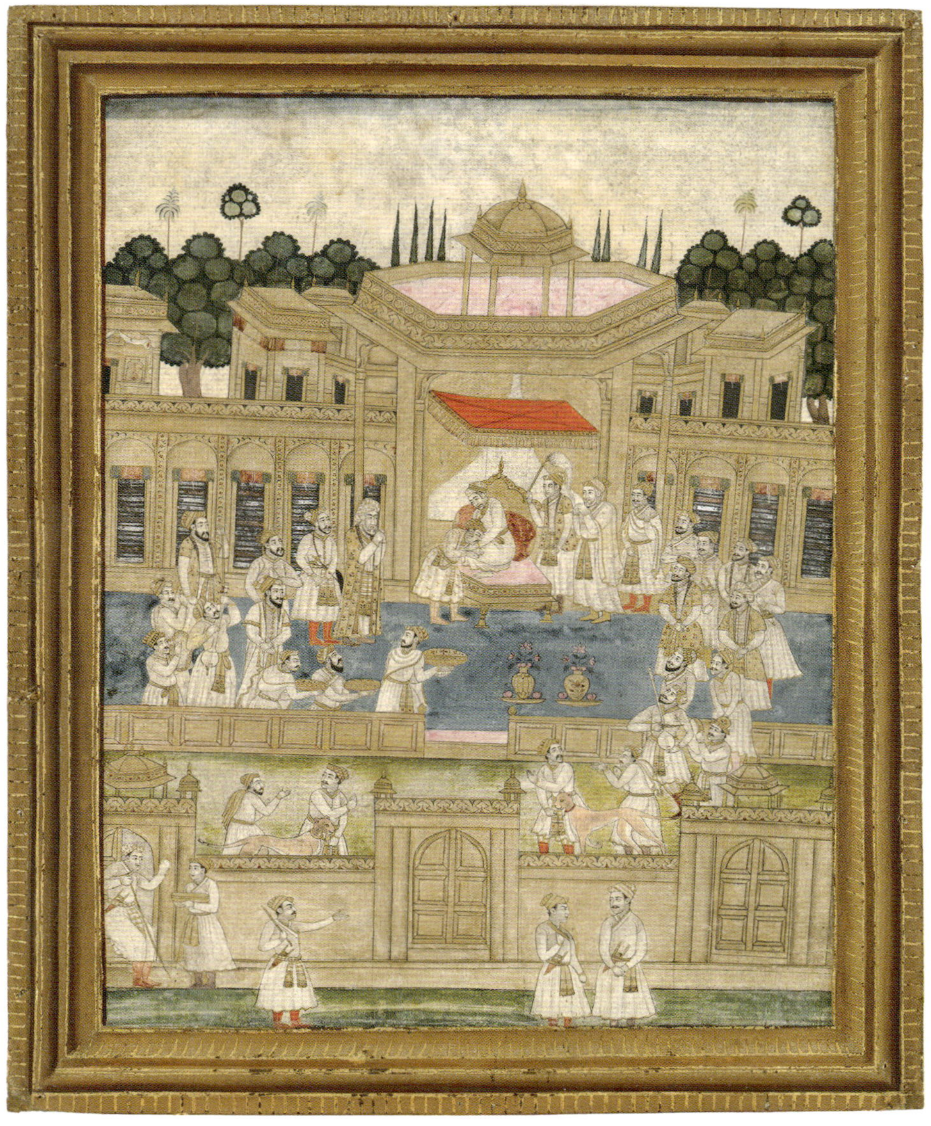

Cat. 44 | Ca 118/1
Darbār of Akbar
Deccani Mughal, early 18th century
Watercolour and gold,
painted frame, 42.3 × 34.4 cm,
image 35.6 × 27.3 cm

Cat. 44 | This *darbār* scene at Akbar's court, probably executed about 1700 in the Deccan, departs a bit more from its precedents than cat. 43. Here, too, there is a tendency towards narrative detail in the description of palace buildings and the throne room, where Akbar's extensive library is shown flanking the canopied throne, along with genre-like scenes set outdoors and on the surrounding palace walls. There are guards patrolling with cheetahs, servants bringing gifts and meals, and musicians playing. The pictorial space, arranged in broad horizontal layers, and the figural vocabulary are simpler, and the colour palette is limited. The schematic representation of the trees in the background is stylistically closer to cat. 45 and cat. 46 and to other paintings from the Schlegel Collection.

The painting probably shows the reconciliation between Akbar and his son, the future Emperor Jahāngīr. This scene, which is illustrated often, appears on a similar sheet from Leiden.[6] The settlement of the dispute, culminating in Jahāngīr's campaign at Agra and the murder of the first minister Abū'l Fazl, was accompanied by Jahāngīr's recognition as legitimate heir to the throne. PKH

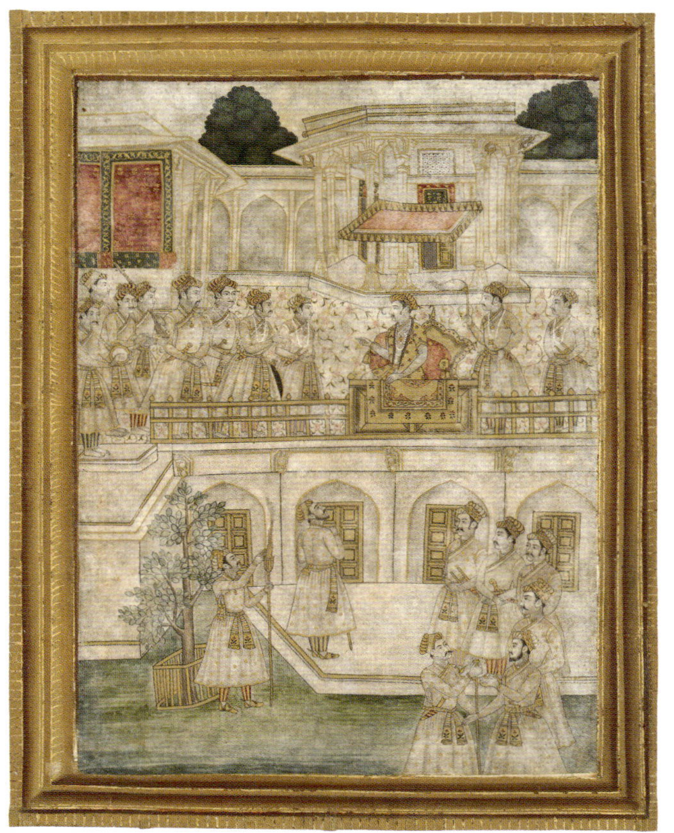

Cat. 45 | Ca 118/3

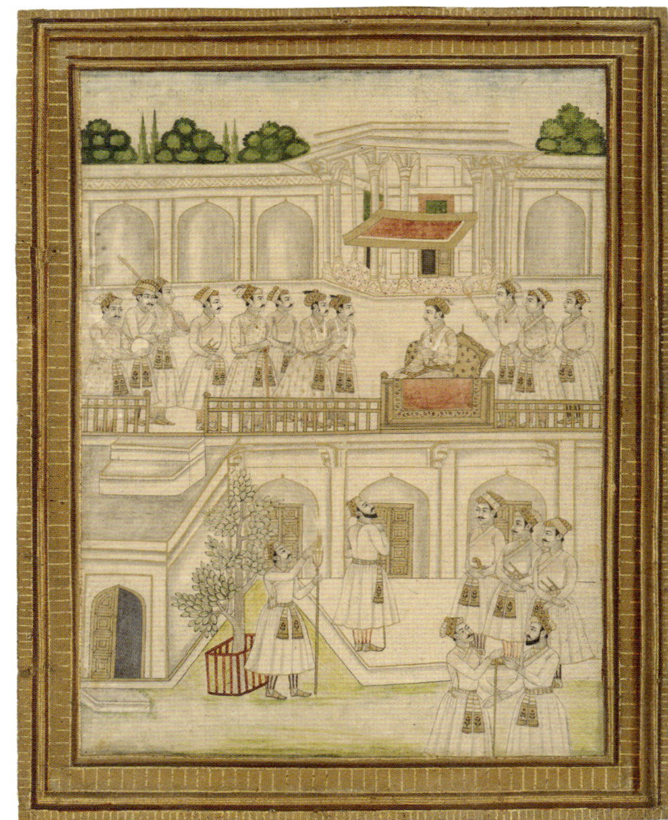

Cat. 46 | Ca 118/4

Cat. 45 | Ca 118/3
Darbār of Jahāngīr (I)
Deccani Mughal, early 18th century
Watercolour and gold,
painted frame 45.1 × 34.7 cm,
image 38.9 × 27.8 cm

Cat. 46 | Ca 118/4
Darbār of Jahāngīr (II)
Deccani Mughal, early 18th century
Watercolour and gold,
painted frame, 46.8 × 36.6 cm,
image 39.6 × 29.3 cm

Reference: Dresden 2017, cat. 55–6, p. 199

Cat. 47 | Ca 119/8
Darbār of Jahāngīr (III)
Deccani Mughal, late 17th–early 18th century
Watercolour and gold,
painted frame 36.6 × 29.2 cm,
image 29.6 × 22.2 cm
Reference: Simon 2017, p. 102, fig. 8a

Cat. 45–6 | The Schlegel Collection includes two *darbār* scenes with Jahāngīr that are almost the same concerning the architecture, the figures, and the arrangements. Some details, however, are different and individual figures have been omitted or added. These variations—compare, for example, the lower right section with the two courtiers and the fenced tree—show that the architectural backgrounds, their similarity notwithstanding, were not made from the same copy and probably also not by the same hand.[7] The complete or partial adaptation of compositions and their variations by precise or free-style copying as documented here was just as widespread as the use of preliminary drawings for tracing (*chārbās*) and workshop templates in which colouring specifications and colour samples could be recorded.[8] It is easy to imagine that these and similar methods of reproducing entire compositions or partly reusing elements of them were employed within a given workshop, and, by way of copying pictures and sketches, shared between different workshops. The adaptation of courtly templates capable of being schematically repeated and used as models was especially popular for *darbār* scenes. PKH

Cat. 47 | This illustration of the audience of Jahāngīr in the *nīmqalam* (half-pen) style is executed in a more sophisticated manner than cat. 45 and cat. 46. The setting is limited to the actual throne area, with courtiers and visitors. The ruler holds a falcon on his hand—a detail usually reserved for full-length portraits. The elaborately carved European throne became fashionable at the Mughal court during Akbar's time. PKH

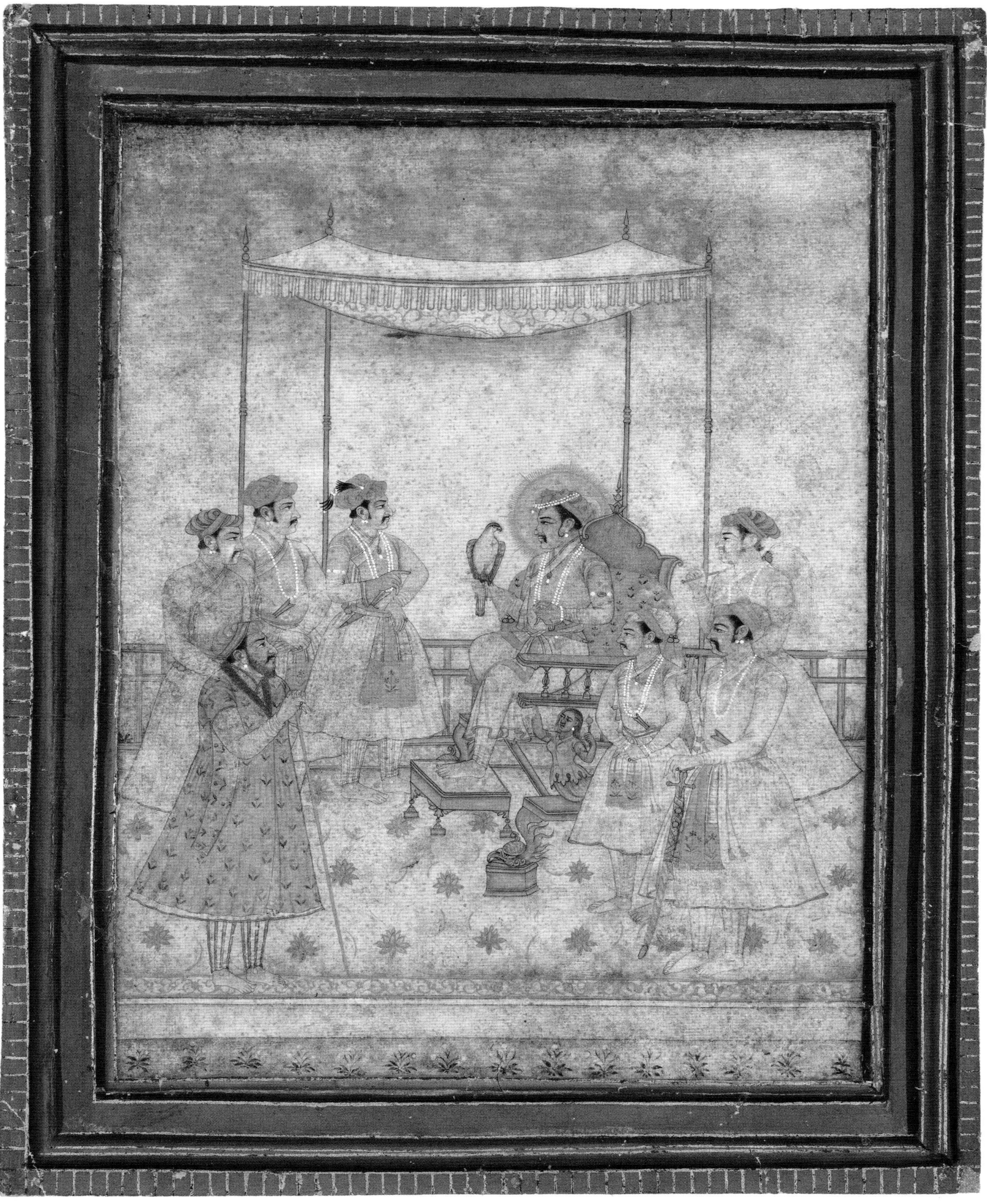

Cat. 47 | Ca 119/8

Cat. 48 | Ca 118/2
Jahāngīr hunting
Deccani Mughal, early 18th century
Watercolour, gold, and silver [?],
painted frame 33.7 × 45.1 cm,
image 26.9 × 37.9 cm
Reference: Dresden 2017,
cat. 33, p. 176

Cat. 49 | Ca 119/9
Shāh Jahān's court in a procession
Deccani Mughal, late 17th–
early 18th century
Watercolour and gold,
painted frame 41.8 × 28.9 cm,
image 35.2 × 22.5 cm
References: Simon 2017, p. 99,
fig. 5a; Frankfurt (Main) 2017,
cat. 129, p. 205

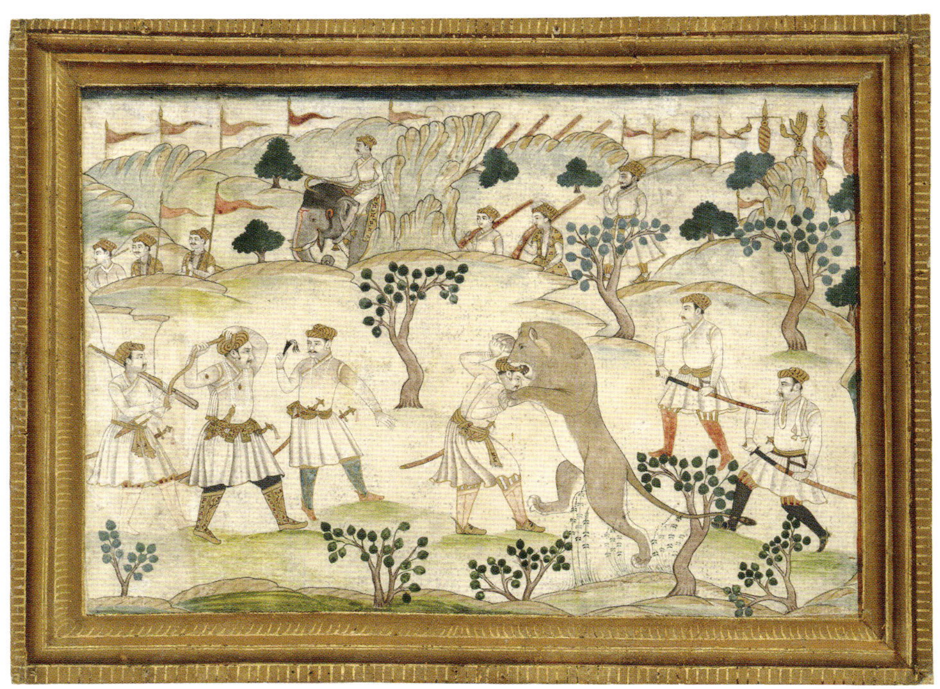

Cat. 48 | Ca 118/2

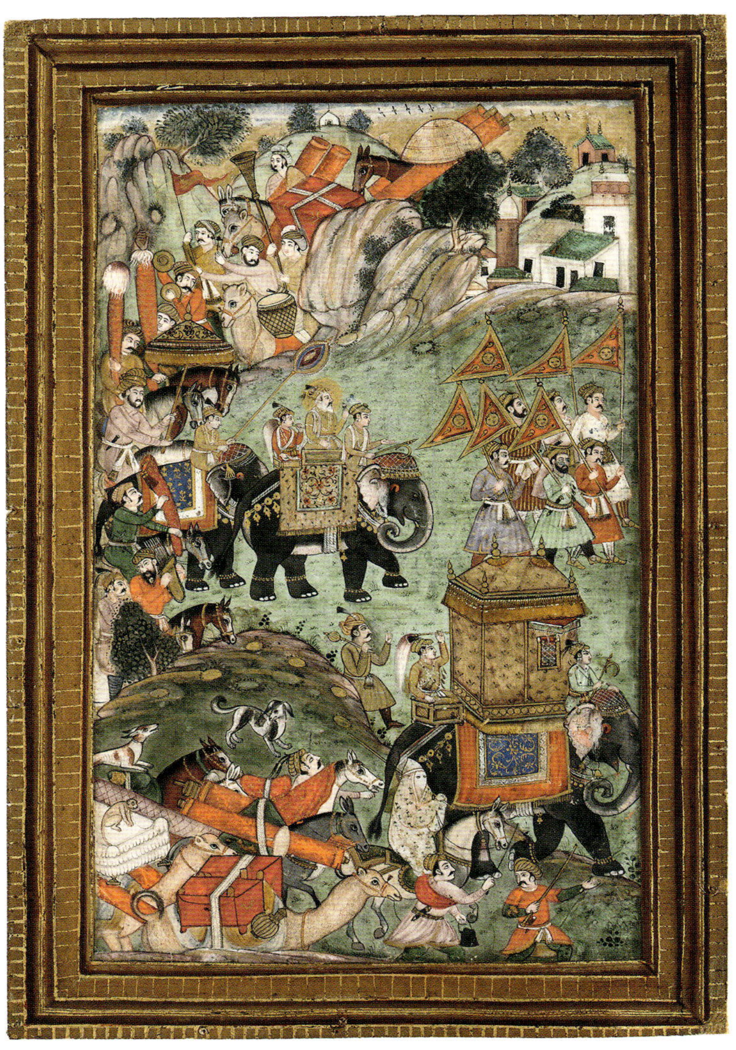

Cat. 49 | Ca 119/9

Cat. 48 | The horizontal composition, arranged in three registers that divide the pictorial space into foreground, middle ground, and background, depicts a lion hunt set in a mountainous landscape.[9] Beyond the distant mountain ranges, the pennants carried by the final group in a long hunting procession stand out—most notably, a standard emblazoned with the hand of Fātima (*ḥamsa* or *Khamsā*), an apotropaic sign.[10] In the middle ground a young Mughal prince, possibly Jahāngīr's son Khurram, is riding through gentle hills in the company of his armed infantry. The largest section of the picture is reserved for the dramatic climax in the foreground. Here a lion is engaged in combat with one of the hunters, while Jahāngīr, at left, is still busy arranging his turban before intervening in the fight. A servant holds the *sarpēch*, the jewellery for his turban.

Hunting scenes were ideally suited for combining representational purposes with drama. They also recalled the imaginary worlds of legendary heroes and the epic tales of fight and victory. The lion hunt offered a stage for the heroic deeds of the Mughal prince and his entourage; at the same time, its exotic motifs were interesting to a European audience familiar with royal hunts.[11]

In the decoration of the Millionenzimmer at Schönbrunn Castle, there is another version of the same scene.[12] Both in size and pose, its protagonists correspond exactly to those in the Dresden miniature, yet they appear in different combinations or positions. The group around Jahāngīr appears above the lion combat. The depiction of trees and landscape also differs. The figures, however, must have been traced from the same template, even though, artistically, the sheet from the Schlegel Collection is simpler. PKH

Cat. 49 | In the long procession coming from a village in the mountains nearby, Shāh Jahān, riding an elephant, is accompanied by members of his household carrying rugs, tents, and crates; servants leading camels and horses; and musicians with kettle drums, cymbals, and a long horn. Six men carrying pennants lead the way. In the second part of the procession, in the foreground, his consort travels on an elephant in a closed howdah with a perforated window. A veiled woman is riding on a horse next to her.

The small-scale composition with its many figures is reminiscent of sixteenth-century Mughal court painting as represented in the *Akbarnāma* in a number of ways such as the format, the pictorial space with a high horizon line, the tiered borders, and the rich narrative. The famous chronicle recorded the career and exploits of Shāh Jahān's grandfather Akbar (1556–1605). Its illustrations achieved exemplary status for subsequent generations of painters and were particularly popular about 1700, when this picture was made.[13]

Similar motifs can be found on a sheet painted with a finer brush in the *nīmqalam* (half-pen) style in an album in the Österreichische Nationalbibliothek.[14] Here, too, Shāh Jahān is depicted riding an elephant at the centre of a courtly procession, preceded by the mahout, followed by a servant with a fly-whisk. This grouping was capable of many variations and could easily be included, with the same or different protagonists, in various compositions.[15] Originally, however, another hero was meant to appear in the Dresden sheet. X-radiography of the work has revealed a horse turned to the left with a rider instead of the Mughal Emperor Shāh Jahān.[16] PKH

Notes | 1 See Duda 1983, p. 291. | 2 See Beach/Koch 1997, nos. 14, 19, 43, 44. | 3 See Lunsingh Scheurleer 2017, p. 60. | 4 Nationaalmuseum van Wereldculturen, Leiden, inv. no. 722-27. See Lunsingh Scheurleer, 2017, p. 60, fig. 7. | 5 See Beach 1981, no. 12b. | 6 Nationaalmuseum van Wereldculturen, Leiden, inv. no. 722-27. See Dresden 2017, p. 60, fig. 7. This painting closely compares to cat. 43. | 7 Although comparison is difficult due to the poor condition of cat. 45 and also because a number of atelier artists might have cooperated in its production, cat. 46 shows a slightly stiffer execution in a number of areas—for example, architectural elements and shadows. | 8 See Lunsingh Scheurleer 2017, cat. 52–4, pp. 196–9. | 9 For the iconography and tradition of hunting representations in Indian painting, see Koch 1998. | 10 See the detail, p. 36, fig. 4. | 11 See Lunsingh Scheurleer 2017. | 12 See Dresden 2017, cat. 86, pp. 220–1. | 13 See Stronge 2002, pp. 58–85. | 14 Sig. Cod. min. 64, no. 65. | 15 See Dresden 2017, p. 59, fig. 6, p. 62, fig. 12. | 16 See p. 37, fig. 5b.

Ascetics

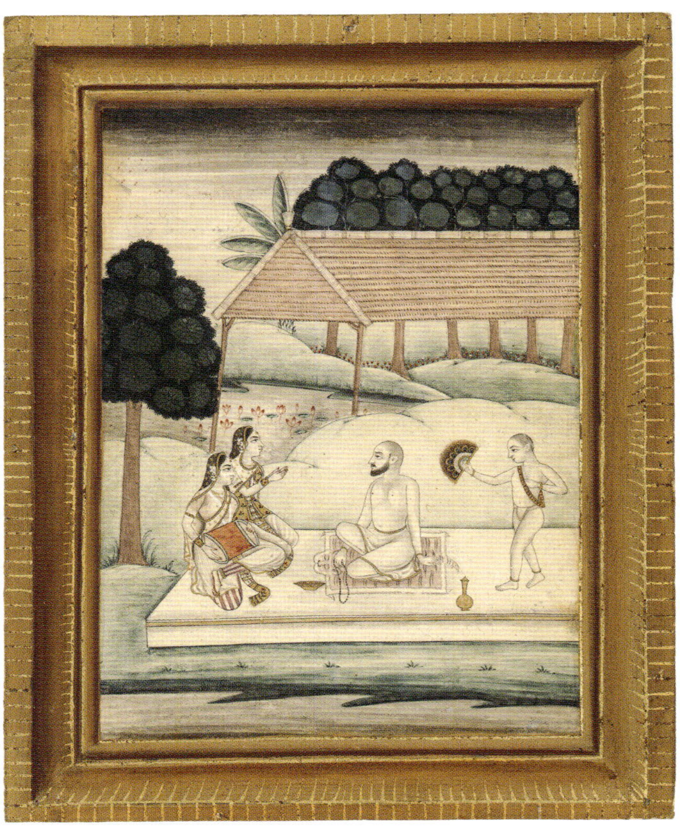

Cat. 50 | Ca 122/6

Cat. 50 | Ca 122/6
Ascetic entertained by musicians (Devagāndhārī rāgiṇī?)
Hyderabad, early 18th century
Watercolour and gold,
painted frame 24.1 × 19.4 cm,
image 18.8 × 13.7 cm

Cat. 51 | Ca 122/5
A female ascetic visited by a lady
Hyderabad, early 18th century
Watercolour and gold,
painted frame 24.1 × 19.4 cm,
image 18.8 × 13.7 cm

Cat. 52 | Ca 122/4
Two ascetics in dialogue
Deccani Mughal, late 17th–
early 18th century
Watercolour and gold,
painted frame 23.7 × 19.7 cm,
image 18 × 14.9 cm

Cat. 50–7 | The Schlegel Collection includes a group of eight sheets related to Hindu themes that deal with ascetics and *yogīs* and form a kind of spiritual counterworld to the splendour of the court. These works continue to reflect the appreciation that the Muslim ruler Akbar had for depictions of monks and hermits. This tradition led to a popular subject in seventeenth- and early eighteenth-century iconography. In many cases, rulers and noblemen were shown visiting a hermitage—a subject not represented in the Schlegel Collection. There are, however, miniatures showing the iconographically related and equally popular motif of women paying respect to a *yogī* or a *yoginī*. The posture of sitting on a pedestal and the inclusion of servants and musicians are elements familiar from courtly representations.

One example is the portrayal of two ascetics, shown by their scriptures to be scholars, seated on a pedestal-like island under a tree, immersed in disputation (cat. 52). The younger beardless figure is sitting cross-legged on a tiger skin while a young servant fans him. Their *rudrākṣa* (prayer beads) and their turbans seem to both imitate and mock the costume of Mughal rulers. The frontal portrait of a *yogī* in meditation (cat. 53) is a simplified version of this theme.

Like the majority of the Schlegel Collection, the portraits of ascetics, originating in Hyderabad and the Deccan, belong thematically and stylistically to the canon that was brought to Europe in the seventeenth and eighteenth centuries via Indian miniatures and copies in printed travelogues. Chatelain's *Atlas historique,* for example, includes portraits of ascetics, among them variants of cat. 50 and 54.[1] Down to precise details, albeit in laterally reversed position, the caricature of two intoxicated fakirs with birds corresponds to the same composition in an engraving in the *Atlas historique*.[2]

Another sheet (cat. 55) shows a gathering of *sādhus*, namely *yogīs* of *nātha saṁpradāya*, a sect of *kanphaṭā yogīs* that was founded by *guru* Matsyendranātha and his

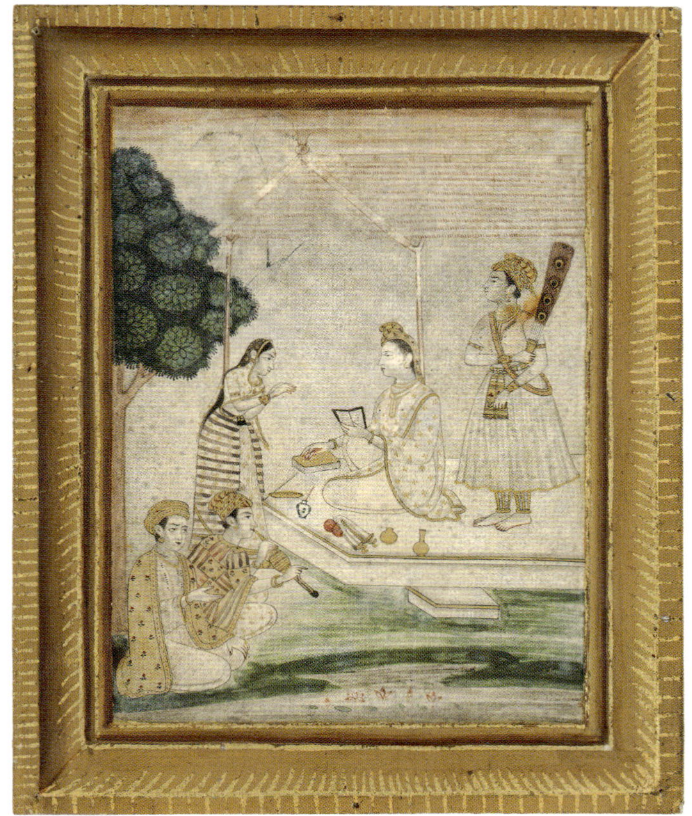

Cat. 51 | Ca 122/5

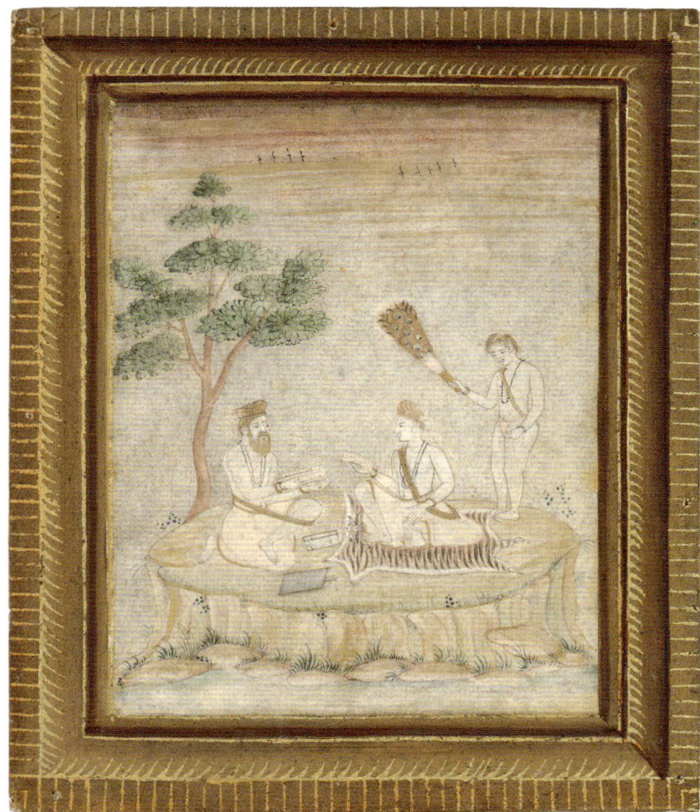

Cat. 52 | Ca 122/4

disciple Gorakhnāth in the ninth century. Matsyendranātha generally is also regarded as the founder of *hatha yoga*.

The *yogīs* have gathered in front of a *nīm* tree,[3] venerated as holy by followers of Lord Śiva. Monks of the *kanphaṭā* sect were either completely naked or wore clothes and turbans made from rags sewn together. They characteristically are shown with long sticks to ward off evil, beggars bowls, necklaces with small wooden amulets, and small hashish pipes. Another distinctive feature are large half-moon-shaped earrings, mostly made of horn and pierced through their earlobes in a special initiation ritual; the sect derives its name, *kanphaṭā* (split earlobes), from these earrings. The light of wisdom was meant to pass through the holes of the earrings and enlighten the *yogī*. The subject matter offered artists a special opportunity to include landscape in their compositions. Ascetics lived in simple small huts far from cities and palaces, as can be seen here in the view of a hilly landscape.

Kanphaṭā yogīs are often accompanied by dogs—a source of provocation to Hindus of higher castes who consider dogs to be unclean. Dogs are shown in this companion role in two Deccani works painted with opaque colours (cat. 56 and 57) that illustrate the extent to which stylistic elements of local schools penetrated Mughal painting. In cat. 56, a *kanphaṭā yogī* visits a group of Shaivite monks with long hair who have gathered in front of their *guru*'s hut. The visitor is sitting on the ground, smoking, his legs tied with a strap to facilitate sitting, his dog lying next to him. In general shape, the pet resembles the dog of the *yogī* sitting under a tree and receiving a woman bringing food in cat. 57. PKH

Notes | 1 See Chatelain 1719, plates 43 and 44. | 2 See Habighorst/Reichart/Sharma 2007, p. 112. | 3 The *nīm* tree is still used as a medicinal plant with a wide range of benefits, especially because of the antiseptic and cholesterol-lowering effect of its seeds and the oil produced from them.

Cat. 53 | Ca 122/11
Yogī
Mughal, late 17th century
Watercolour and gold,
painted frame 28.5 × 19.2 cm,
image 21.7 × 12.5 cm

Cat. 54 | Ca 122/12
Intoxicated faqīrs
Mughal, late 17th century
Watercolour and gold,
painted frame 26 × 21 cm,
image 20.6 × 15.6 cm

Cat. 55 | Ca 119/4
A gathering of Kanphaṭā yogīs
Mughal style,
mid- to late 17th century
Watercolour and gold,
painted frame 36.4 × 27.7 cm,
image 29.7 × 21.3 cm

Cat. 56 | Ca 120/3
A gathering of ascetics
Deccan, 18th century
Watercolour and gold,
painted frame 24.1 × 28.4 cm,
image 16.9 × 21.2 cm

Cat. 57 | Ca 120/10
A Kanphaṭā yogī with a visitor
Deccan, 18th century
Watercolour, gold, and silver,
painted frame 24.2 × 17.9 cm,
image 18.7 × 12.2 cm
References: Dresden 2017,
cat. 44–6, pp. 186–7;
Frankfurt (Main) 2017, cat. 128,
pp. 204–5

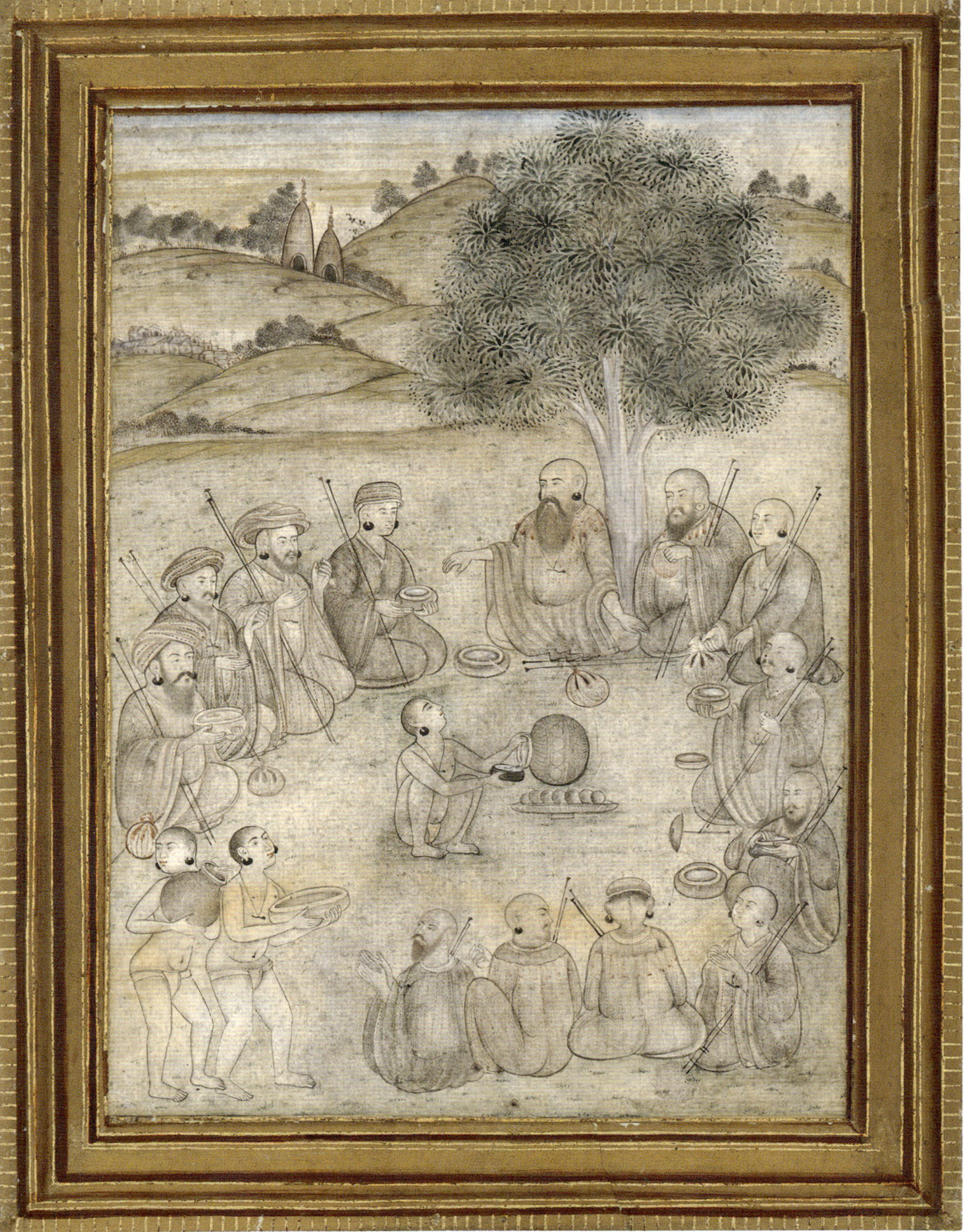

Cat. 55 | Ca 119/4

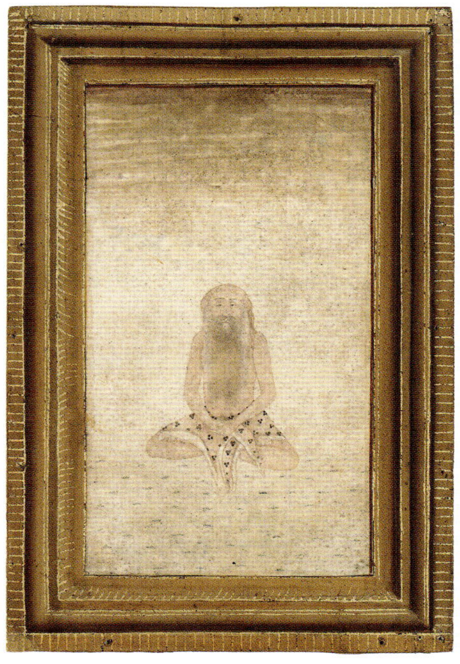

Cat. 53 | Ca 122/11

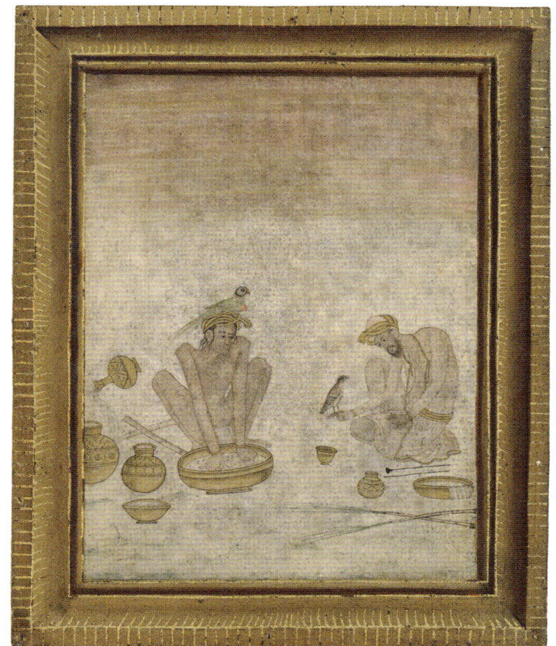

Cat. 54 | Ca 122/12

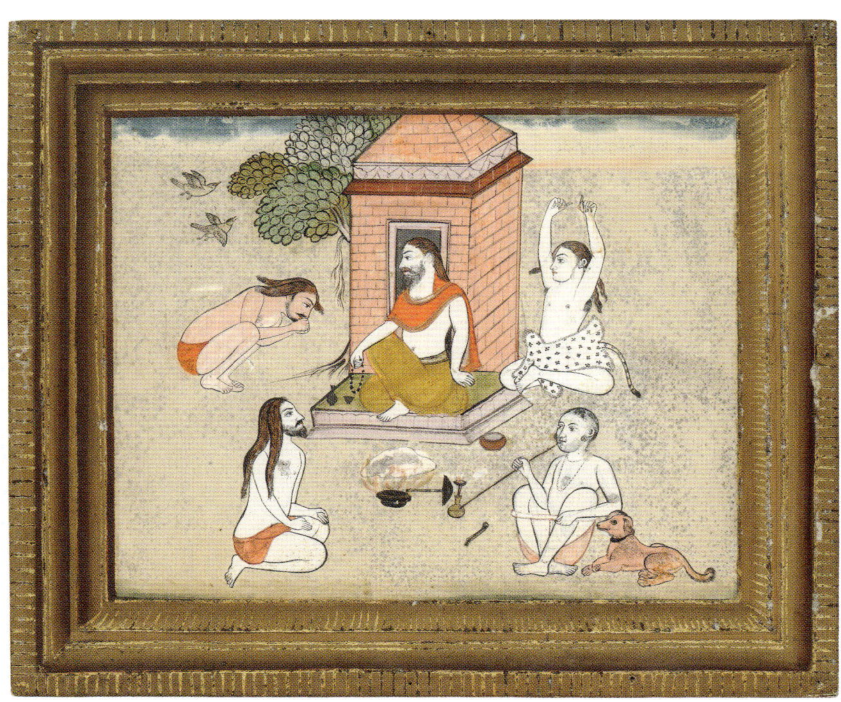

Cat. 56 | Ca 120/3

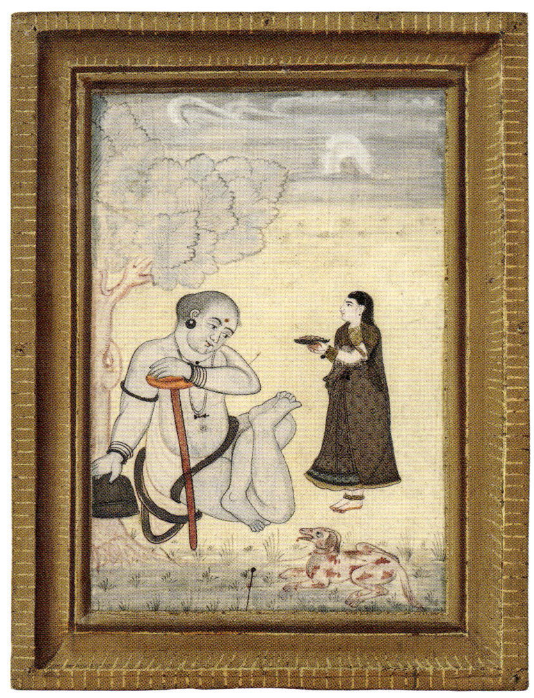

Cat. 57 | Ca 120/10

Cat. 58 | Whereas portraits of rulers and noblemen make up the majority of the earlier collection of Indian paintings at the Dresden Kupferstich-Kabinett listed in the 1738 Heucher Inventory only album Ca 111 (cat. 4) includes a small group of portraits of women. Illustrations of the private sphere, genre scenes, and scenes of lovers, which were particularly popular with European buyers, figure more prominently in the Schlegel Collection.

Many of the women's portraits made in the seventeenth and eighteenth centuries can be traced back to *rāgiṇī* illustrations, the female personification of a musical *rāga*. The Schlegel Collection includes a fairly large number of these images which are, however, so heterogeneous that they cannot be grouped into a single *rāgamālā* set or attributed to a single source.

This portrait of a young woman sitting by the water in a landscape and holding a garland of flowers in both hands (cat. 58) combines motifs from the repertoire associated with the *Gaurī rāgiṇī*. The red and gold of the sky evoke an evening mood, which is also reflected in the associated musical *rāga* which belongs to the *Śrī rāga* series. The detailed landscape in the *Gaurī rāgiṇī* is an essential part of the iconographic programme, as is clear by comparing other representations of the subject in different styles.[1]

The conception of the figure, in its contours and gentle shading; the virtuoso detailing of the forms with delicately iridescent, transparent colours; and the restrained use of gold and white for accentuating jewellery and garments suggest a Mughal school artist, probably no longer active at the court but possibly in the Deccan. The artistic design of the tree and the spatial layout of the landscape background can be directly traced to European models. Under the influence of artists working for Jahāngīr, these models, which were popular well into the eighteenth century, were dispersed in a variety of ways.

It is conceivable that the *Gaurī rāgiṇī* had been preserved in folder 3 of the Schlegel Collection.[2] On a filing card written after 1906, there is a note describing the contents of this folder as "neun Blatt. (eines europäischen Ursprungs?)" (nine sheets, one of which is of European origin?).[3] Another work from the Schlegel Collection that provides a similar panoramatic view is *A Gathering of Kanphaṭā Yogīs* (cat. 55). But, clearly, both are of Indian origin. PKH

Cat. 59 | The Asāfīya dynasty, founded by Nizām ul-Mulk, controlled the Deccan from Hyderabad for more than two centuries, until 1950. Mughal traditions and the ancient Persian culture of the Deccan were preserved by the Nizāms, who continued to patronise miniature painting.[4] Depictions of princesses, *yoginīs,* courtesans, and *rāgiṇīs* became increasingly popular.

Closely related to a *rāgamālā* in the Johnson collection,[5] this lyrical depiction of a Deccan beauty captivates the viewer while retaining a strict profile. She has a slight smile on her face as she sits on a decorated floral carpet conversing with her pet cheetah in the stillness of the night. The vivid white architecture, which contrasts with the surrounding bright colours of the garden flowers and the sky, frames the heroine and her companion. Various elements such as the architecture with its fine niches, the floral environment, the textiles, the jewellery, and the palette of mauve, green, orange, and white indicate Hyderabad as the origin of the miniature. The subject is identified by an inscription in *nasta'līq* at the top left hidden under the paint, discovered during technical analysis of the artwork.[6]

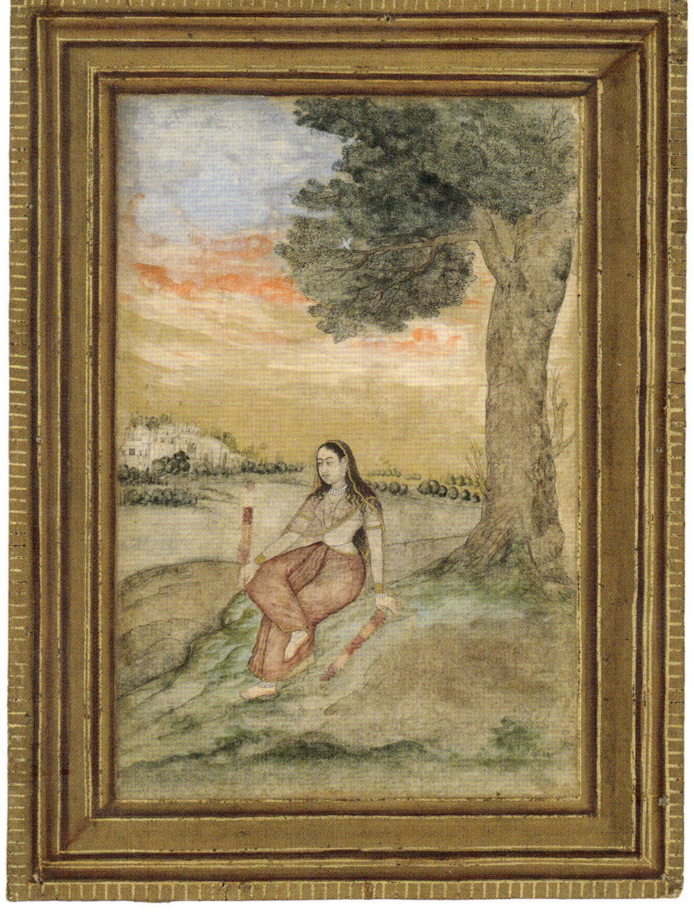

Cat. 58 | Ca 120/11

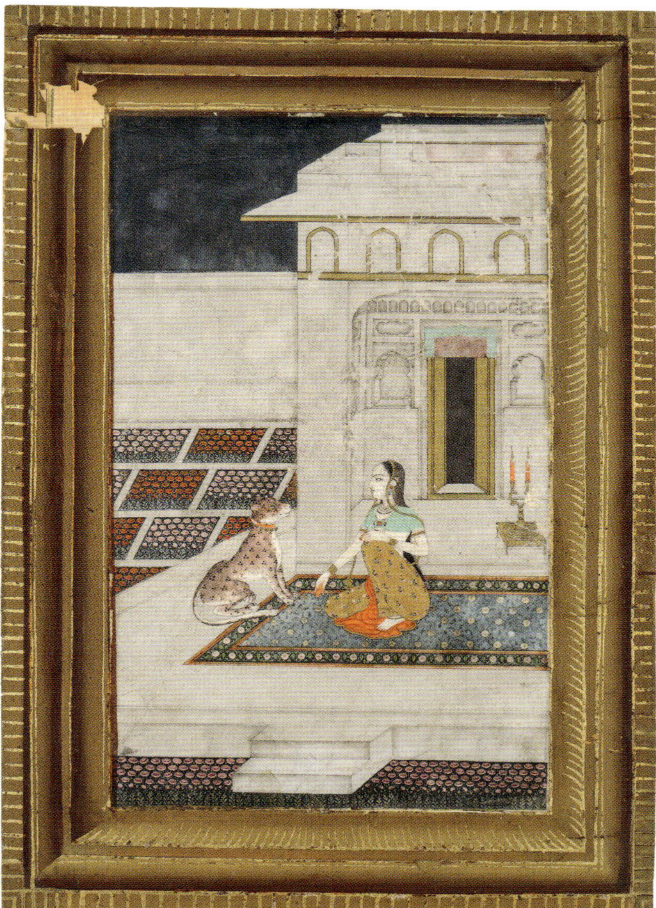

Cat. 59 | Ca 122/14

The idea of associating music with painting is unique to Indian art. Every *rāga* or *rāgiṇī* evokes a human sentiment. The essence of the *rāgas* is based on spiritual, religious, and day-to-day activities transformed into visible form by Indian masters. The connection between Indian art and music, through various *rāgiṇī* representations, fascinated foreign collectors, who often were more interested in literary than artistic expression. NB

Cat. 60 | By the mid-eighteenth century an active provincial Mughal school flourished in Murshidabad, a centre for the Muslim administration of Bengal, Bihar, and Orissa. This painting is reminiscent of works from Murshidabad in other collections[7] as far as motifs such as the dark cumulous clouds, the birds, and the thunderstorm indicated by golden lines in the sky are concerned.

This miniature depicts a *rāgiṇī* in which the *nāyikā* (heroine) is seen sitting on an open palace terrace with three attendants. The grey monsoon clouds that symbolise unrequited love suggest a heavy thunderstorm, while lightning flashes over the dark sky. The artist, however, made an unconventional attempt to lift the mood of the viewer by adding vibrant colours in the heroine's skirt and the rolled-up curtain and by having the third attendant, who holds a peacock feather fan, gaze directly into the viewer's eyes. NB

Cat. 58 | Ca 120/11
Gaurī rāgiṇī
Deccan [?], Mughal style,
late 17th – early 18th century
Watercolour and gold, painted frame
29.8 × 21.7 cm, image 23.4 × 15.1 cm
Reference: Dresden 2017, cat. 6a, pp. 132–4

Cat. 59 | Ca 122/14
Baṅgālī rāgiṇī
Hyderabad, early 18th century
Watercolour and gold, painted frame
28 × 19.5 cm, image 21.3 × 13.1 cm
Inscribed at top left in *nasta'līq*:
he [she] was saying to the Padshāh
[that] last night the Baṅgālī rāgiṇī
[illegible] sar-i man rāg [?]
Reference: Dresden 2017, cat. 41, pp. 182–3

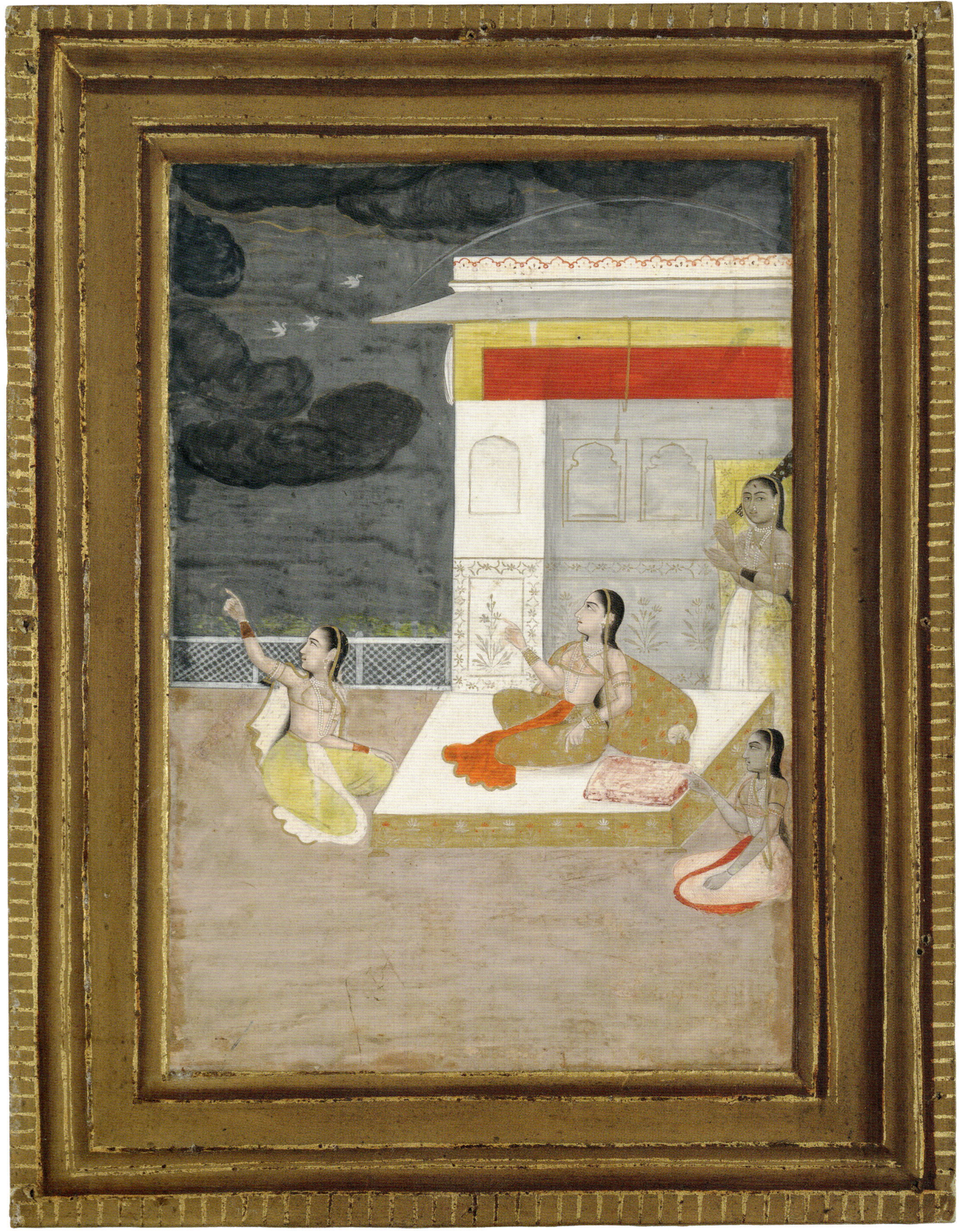

Cat. 60 | Ca 122/13

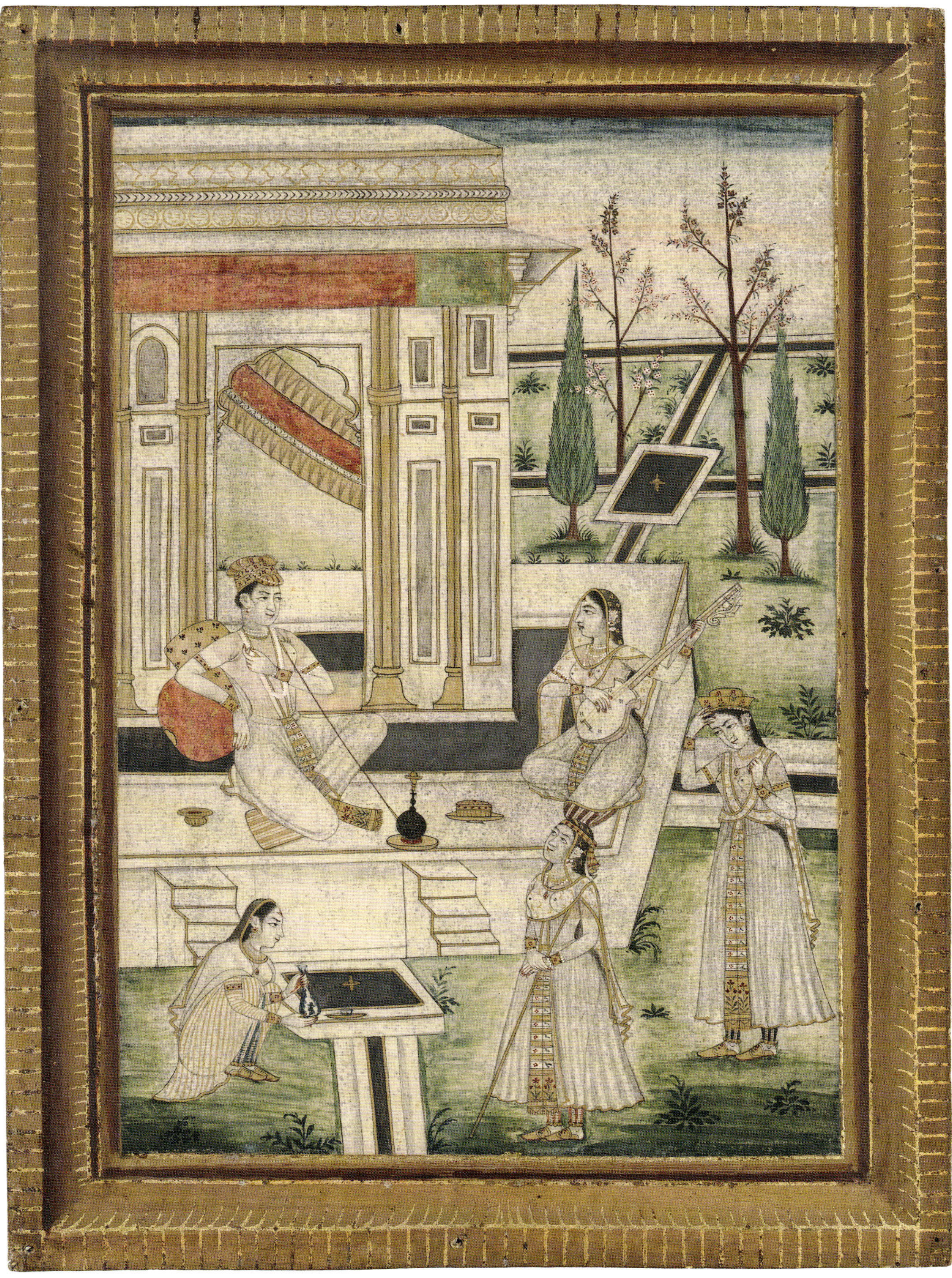

Cat. 61 | Ca 119/7

◄ Cat. 60 | Ca 122/13
Ladies observing lightning in the sky (Madhumādhavī rāgiṇī?)
Murshidabad, 18th century
Watercolour and gold,
painted frame 26.8 × 20.1 cm,
image 20.1 × 13.4 cm
References: Dresden 2017, cat. 42, p. 183; Frankfurt (Main) 2017, cat. 127, p. 203

◄ Cat. 61 | Ca 119/7
Empress Rāzia Sultāna in a courtyard
Hyderabad, early 18th century
Watercolour and gold,
painted frame 32.6 × 24 cm,
image 26.9 × 18.4 cm

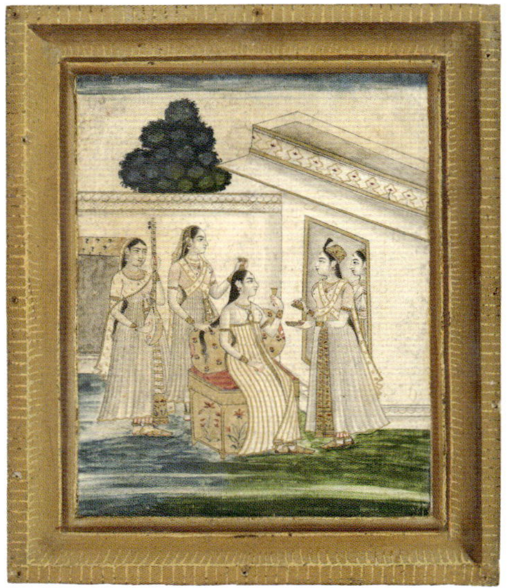
Cat. 62 | Ca 122/3

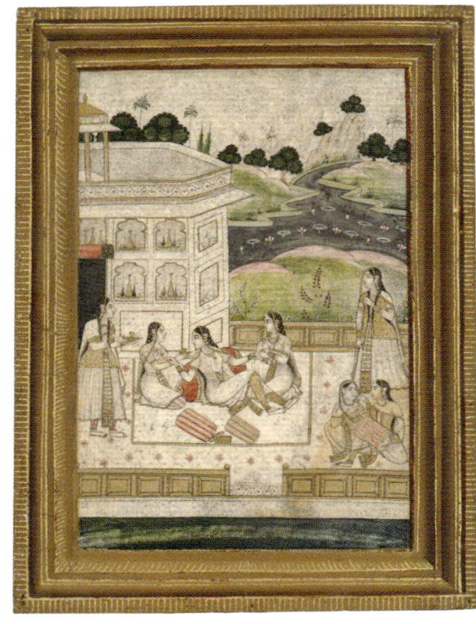
Cat. 63 | Ca 119/6

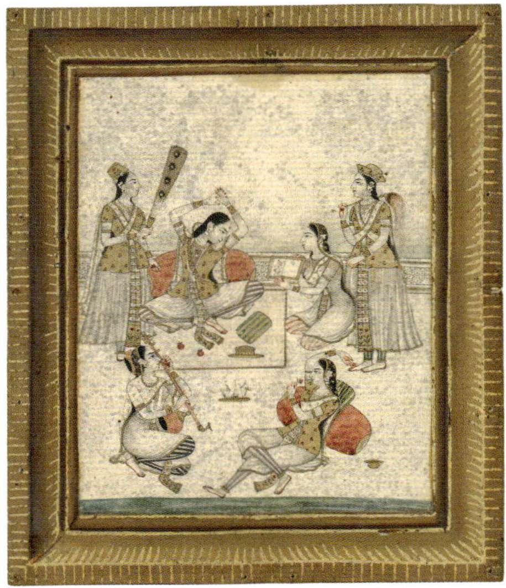
Cat. 64 | Ca 122/9

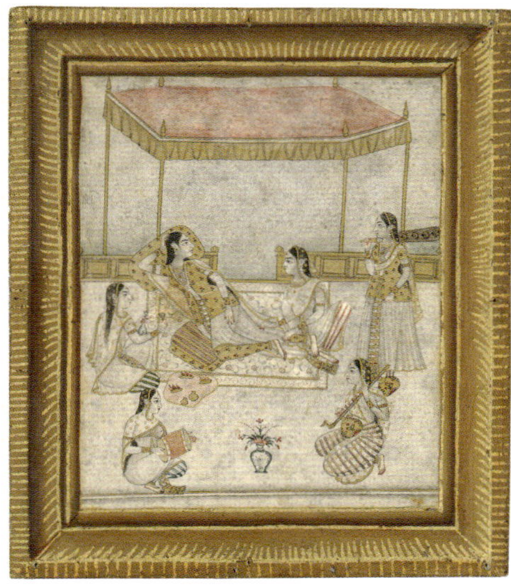
Cat. 65 | Ca 122/10

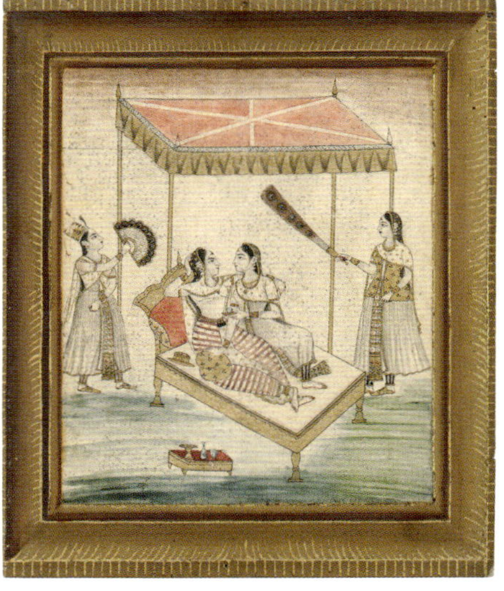
Cat. 66 | Ca 122/8

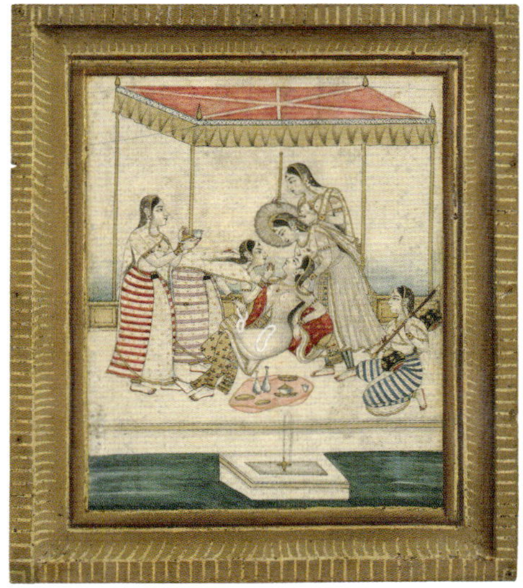
Cat. 67 | Ca 122/7

Cat. 61–7 | A large group of works from the Schlegel Collection, painted in the *nīmqalam* (half-pen) style, shows women in a courtly setting—a subject rarely represented in the part of the Dresden collection compiled during the Baroque period. A miniature of a princess with two female companions (cat. 4, Ca 111/63, fol. 59) is among the sheets later inserted into album Ca 111. An inscription on the verso identifies her as Shāh Jahān's eldest daughter, Jahānārā Sāhibā Begum (1614–1681). Even when they can be explicitly connected with the name of a princess, representations of this type rarely display individualised features and instead usually follow a general type of the idealised woman.

An interesting example in this context is the portrait of the first Muslim *sultāna* of the Mamlūk dynasty, Rāzia Sultāna (r. 1236–1240), preserved in the most comprehensive portrait album in the Dresden collection (cat. 3, Ca 113/130). A portrait similar to the *sultāna* in Ca 113, shown resting on a canopied throne bench, also appears on a sheet from the Schlegel Collection (cat. 61, Ca 119/7), where the ruler is part of a court scene with servants shown on a palace terrace in a garden landscape. This figure is also taken up on a sheet from the Liechtenstein Album that shows the *sultāna* surrounded by servants entertaining her with music and serving wine from Chinese blue-and-white porcelain bottles.[8] Both representations allude to the dual role of the *sultāna* as both a princess surrounded by servants and a ruler ensnared by attendants.

This ruler portrait blends in with similarly composed scenes from the *zenāna* and pictorial narratives based on literary material.[9] The main intention of these works was to visualise feminine grace and beauty using numerous decorative elements as well as courtly or bucolic love. The representation of desire in the image of the patiently waiting or desperate beloved draws on motifs from the *nāyikā*, a tradition allegorising different moods that was handed down in early Sanskrit sources and used in dance, poetry, and painting. It also influenced Mughal painting and was connected with elements of *rāgiṇī* representation. Ca 122/9, for instance, shows the main figure in the position of *Deśavairatī rāgiṇī*. In Europe, these scenes found many customers and were adapted in illustrations of the Baroque period.[10] PKH

Cat. 62 | Ca 122/3
Women in a terrace garden
Hyderabad, early 18th century
Watercolour and gold,
painted frame 23.6 × 19.7 cm,
image 17.9 × 14.2 cm

Cat. 63 | Ca 119/6
Princess and companions
Hyderabad, early 18th century
Watercolour and gold,
painted frame 33.5 × 24.9 cm,
image 26.4 × 17.8 cm

Cat. 64 | Ca 122/9
Ladies in a pavilion (Deśavairatī rāgiṇī?)
Hyderabad, early 18th century
Watercolour and gold,
painted frame 23.5 × 19.5 cm,
image 17.9 × 14 cm

Cat. 65 | Ca 122/10
Princess in despair (Taṅkī rāgiṇī?)
Hyderabad, early 18th century
Watercolour and gold,
painted frame 22.8 × 19.4 cm,
image, 17.6 × 14.1 cm

Cat. 66 | Inv. Ca 122/8
Female lovers in a pavilion
Hyderabad, early 18th century
Watercolour and gold,
painted frame 22.5 × 18.6 cm,
image 17 × 13.4 cm

Cat. 67 | Ca 122/7
Princess with companions in a garden pavilion
Hyderabad, early 18th century
Watercolour and gold,
painted frame 22.4 × 19.2 cm,
image 17 × 13.4 cm

Reference: Dresden 2017, cat. 36–9, pp. 178–80

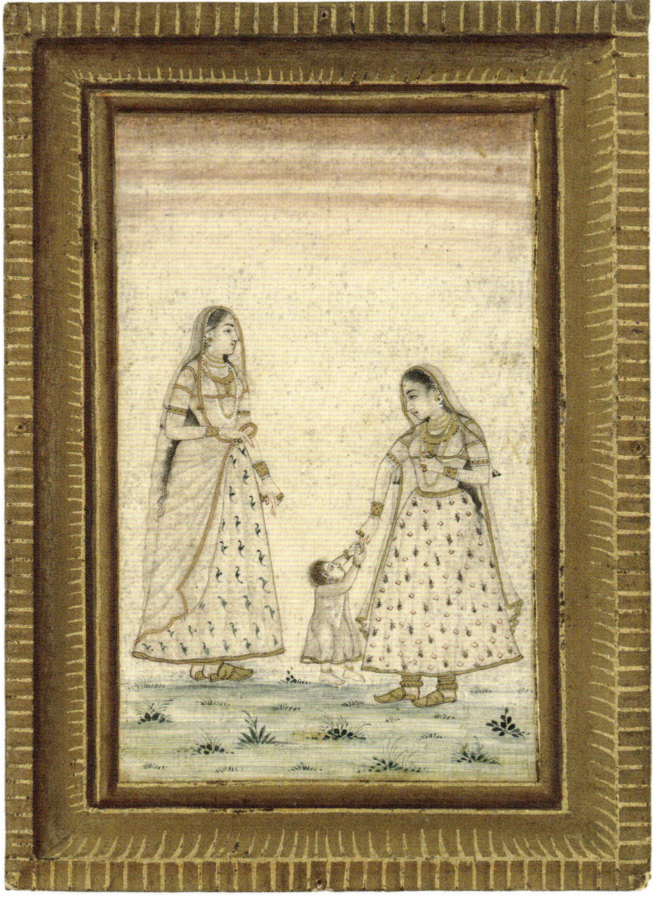

Cat. 68 | Ca 122/1

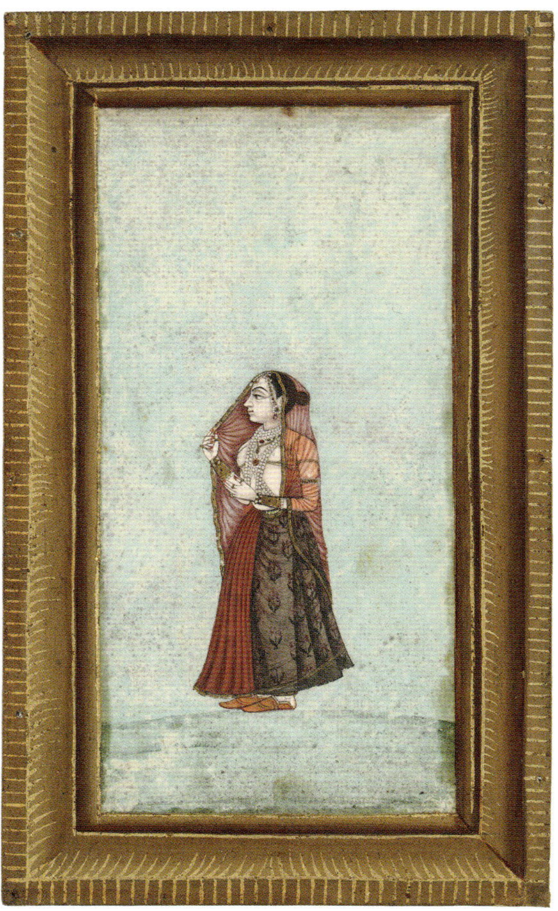

Cat. 69 | Ca 121/1

Cat. 68 | Ca 122/1
Two women with a child
Mughal style, Bijapur, late 17th century
Watercolour and gold,
painted frame 22.8 × 16 cm,
image 17.3 × 10.4 cm

Cat. 69 | Ca 121/1
A princess holding her veil
Murshidabad, 18th century
Watercolour, gold, and silver,
painted frame 26.3 × 15.5 cm,
image 20.6 × 10.2 cm

Cat. 68 | The faces of the subjects here are rendered in Mughal style. The use of a muted palette and brown brushstrokes indicative of sky is seen in other works in the Dresden collection.[11] The women with the ends of their *sārīs* draped over their heads are reminiscent of Bijapuri depictions. This image, with different Mughal and Bijapuri regional motifs, invites the viewer into the intimate space shared by the women, who appear to be in conversation. The child, dressed in a diaphanous dress and a pearl necklace, has certainly captured the attention of the woman who points towards her. NB

Cat. 69 | A woman with 'fish-shaped' eyes (*mīnākṣī*) and lips the colour of the *bimba* fruit stands in profile holding her veil delicately between her fingers. Her jewellery and the fabric of her garment are reminiscent of paintings from the Mughal school in Murshidabad. NB

Cat. 70 | Artists dispersed from the imperial ateliers during the seventeenth and eighteenth centuries found a market in the *bazārs* of towns and cities frequented by traders, merchants, travellers, and other artists trained in various styles. The style and the subject of this painting suggest the hand of a Deccani artist influenced by interaction with North Indian artists who were in turn influenced by Mughal artists. His image reflects the matrimonial alliances between Mughal and Rājput princes and princesses prevalent in India at that time. NB

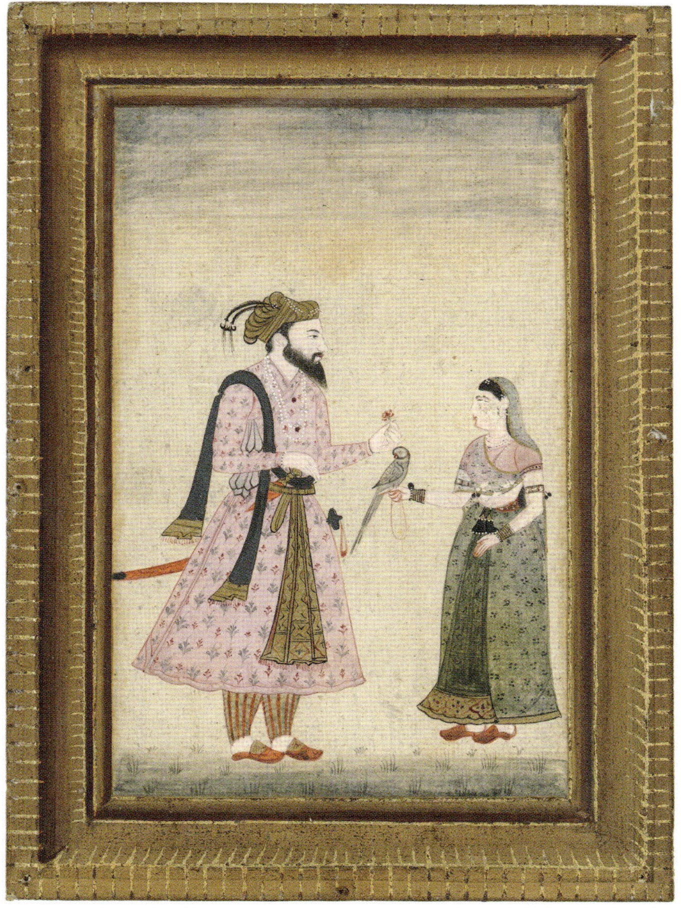

Cat. 70 | Ca 123/9

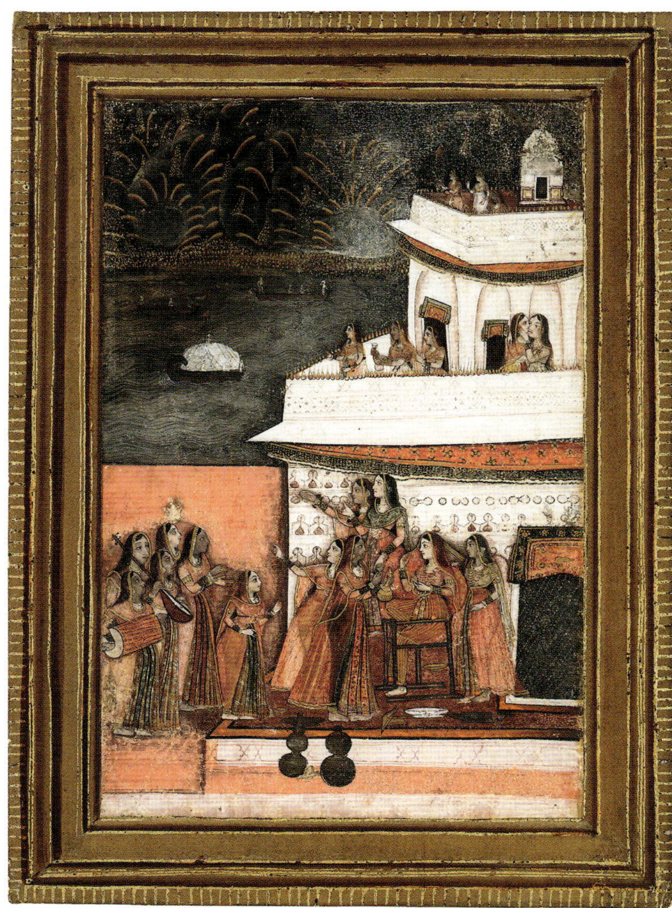

Cat. 71 | Ca 119/2

Cat. 71 | The Awadh (Oudh), located on the northern bank of the Ganges in the region around Faizabad and Lucknow, became one of the most important provinces of the Mughal Empire from 1754 until 1856, when the British conquered it. In 1724 the Mughal Emperor Muḥammad Shāh granted independence to the governor Sa'ādat Khān, and he became the *nawāb* of a newly established state.[12] Although the style of painting initially did not differ significantly from the imperial Mughal style familiar in Delhi, it did change with the growing presence of the British, especially after they had won the Battle of Buxar in 1764. The presence of European adventurers[13] and English portraitists[14] changed the dynamics of paintings styles, with themes that involved both Muslim and Hindu elements. Painting continued to flourish under local patrons[15] as well as within various groups of painters or workshops that emerged around leading artists and continued to pursue their own style. With the collapse of the Mughal Empire in the 1780s, it was no longer difficult for foreigners to acquire and commission manuscripts and paintings, as the imperial and noble families sold their collections through dealers.[16]

This brilliantly illuminated painting depicts *Shab-i Barāt*, held on the eve of the fourteenth day of the month of *sha'bān*. During this holiday, Muslims perform sacrificial rituals on behalf of their ancestors. In this way, the life and destiny of mortals for the coming year will be decided that night.[17]

The lady sitting on a European chair observes the festivities while surrounded by musicians and escorts. The eye is led from the bottom left to the right, up to the palace architecture and to the great clouds of smoke from the burning fireworks, until it finally comes to rest on the gliding river with small, almost illusionary figures on boats. Comparable versions with similar themes can be found in the album *Hindu and Persian Miniatures and Calligraphy* in the British Museum.[18] NB

Cat. 70 | Ca 123/9
Mughal prince with a Rājput princess
Deccani Mughal, late 17th–
early 18th century
Watercolour, gold, and silver,
painted frame 23.6 × 17 cm,
image 18.3 × 11.7 cm

Cat. 71 | Ca 119/2
Shab-i Barāt
Provincial Mughal (Awadh?),
18th century
Watercolour, gold, and silver [?],
painted frame 35.2 × 25.4 cm,
image 28.3 × 18.4 cm
Reference: Dresden 2017, cat. 43, p. 185

Cat. 72 | Ca 119/1
Shāh ʿAbbās with his consort Yakhān Begum [?]
Deccan (Golconda), late 17th–early 18th century
Watercolour and gold,
painted frame 32.1 × 28.5 cm,
image 25.1 × 21.4 cm
Reference: Dresden 2017, cat. 51, p. 194

Cat. 73 | Ca 120/2
Humāyūn with an attendant
Deccan, 18th century
Watercolour, gold, and silver,
painted frame 29.2 × 22.5 cm,
image 22.3 × 15.6 cm

Cat. 72 | During the reign of Shāh ʿAbbās I (r. 1588–1629), one of the most successful rulers of the Safavid dynasty of Iran, the empire reached its political and cultural zenith. Portraits that emerged during this time focused more on depicting ideal characteristics associated with the idea of the semi-divine nature of kings than on physical similarity. Mughal portraits, in contrast, were rendered in a more naturalistic manner.

Here Shāh ʿAbbās sits next to his slender consort Yakhān Begum, who points her finger as if in conversation while smoking a *huqqā*. Shāh ʿAbbās is wearing a Persian style costume with a striped turban and a yellow coat while his bejewelled consort is dressed in plain Persian dress tied with a bright orange waistcloth. The identification as Shāh ʿAbbās is based on facial characteristics such as the unibrow and the drooping moustache, noted by Pietro Della Valle, a Venetian traveller in Iran in 1618: "His mustachios are drooping, this being curiously for reasons of religion, as they say that moustaches which point upwards, as we wear them, show pride, and thus in a certain way they desire to fight with heaven."[19]

During the second half of the seventeenth century, Deccani artists came under the influence of the Iranian style associated with the Safavid painter Shaikh ʿAbbāsī and his sons, ʿAlī Naqī and Muḥammad Taqī.[20] Safavid subjects and motifs continued well into the eighteenth century, and, as seen here, were employed by local artists according to their own conventions. NB

Cat. 73–5 | The presence and influence of North Indian artists in the *kārkhāna* (workshops) in the Deccan can be traced in several works from the Schlegel Collection executed in opaque colours that might have belonged to the same workshop (for example, cat. 73–5, 79–80). These sheets share a similar colour palette and the same kind of detailed treatment of hands, garments, ornaments, flowers, and elements of scenery, even though the figures seem to have been painted by different hands. Persianate representations and genre-like scenes enjoyed particular popularity.

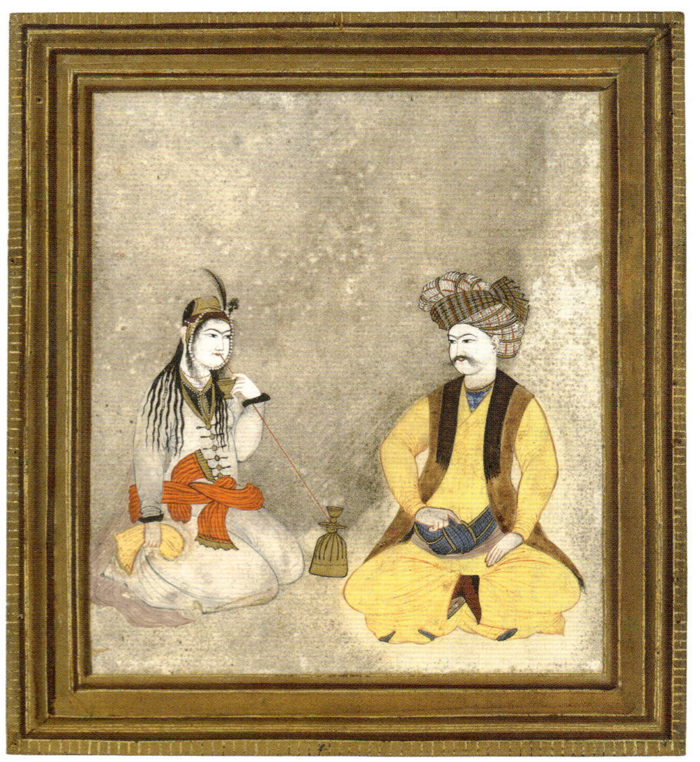

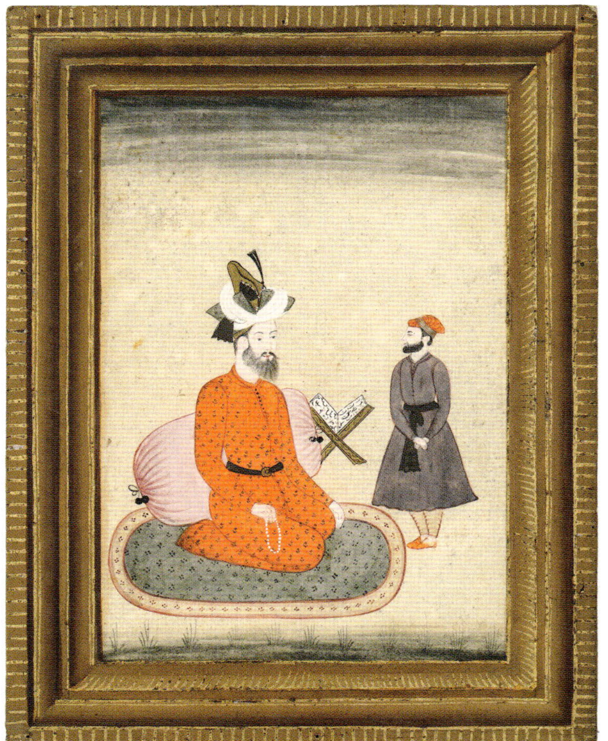

Cat. 72 | Ca 119/1

Cat. 73 | Ca 120/2

One of the paintings shows Humāyūn (r. 1530–1540, 1555–1556) in Safavid costume with a student or servant (cat. 73). A loyal representative of Islam, the ruler is sitting on a carpet and leaning against a pillow, a *Qur'ān* stand with an open book behind him. The comparison with a portrait of the same ruler, executed more in the tradition of Mughal painting (cat. 14, Ca 124/1), clearly shows, in spite of the completely different style, the similarities in the depiction of standardised characteristics that made the ruler recognisable.

Cat. 74 shows a young Safavid prince to whom a servant proffers wine from a blue-and-white Chinese porcelain bottle, while a second holds out a piece of cloth for him. Before him are a water jug and a basin for washing his hands as well as bowls of fruit. Stylistically, the painting is similar to a genre scene with a Hindu woman under a canopy (cat. 75). She is being offered a large carp by a fishmonger. Even though the pictorial motifs do not provide conclusive evidence, the illustration might be associated with the story of *Śakuntalā* as told by Kālidāsa. The German translation by Georg Forster was published in 1791.[21] Kālidāsa's *Abhijñānaśākuntalā* can be traced back to the Hindu epic *Mahābhārata*. One day King Duṣyanta, out hunting in the forest, meets Śakuntalā, the stepdaughter of an ascetic. They fall in love, and Duṣyanta gives Śakuntalā a ring as a token of his feelings, promising to come back and bring her to his palace. When the pregnant Śakuntalā arrives at Duṣyanta's court, the king does not recognise her because the sage Durvāsa had made him forget her. He could have recognised her only if she had shown him the ring he had given her, but she had lost it in a river without noticing. Overcome by despair, she leaves the palace. When a fisherman offers a fish to the royal court, the ring is found in the fish's belly and taken to the king. He regains his memory and fetches his beloved and her child. Herder and Goethe as well as the Schlegel brothers and the German Romantics were captivated by the story, which also inspired Franz Schubert's unfinished opera *Sakontala*. Though a direct reference to the story cannot be stated, it was the atmosphere of this Indian tale that, when taken up in painting, mesmerized Europeans. PKH

Cat. 74 | Ca 120/5
Safavid prince with attendants
Deccan, 18th century
Watercolour, gold, and silver, painted frame 29.4 × 21.4 cm, image 23.4 × 15.6 cm

Cat. 75 | Ca 120/6
Fish seller
Deccan, North Indian style, 18th century
Watercolour, gold, and silver, painted frame 27.4 × 20.9 cm, image 21.9 × 15.4 cm

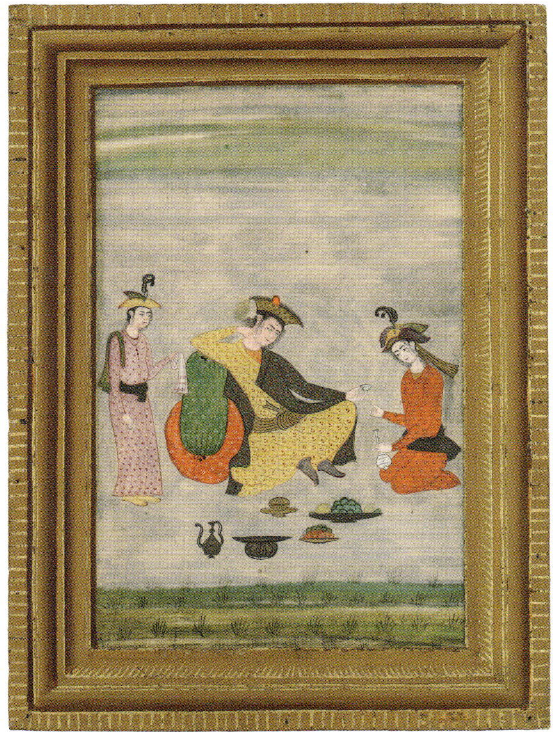

Cat. 74 | Ca 120/5

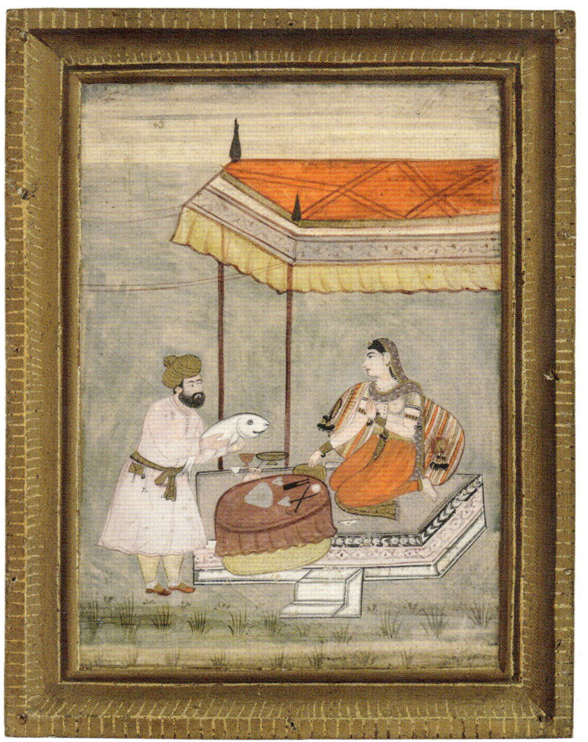

Cat. 75 | Ca 120/6

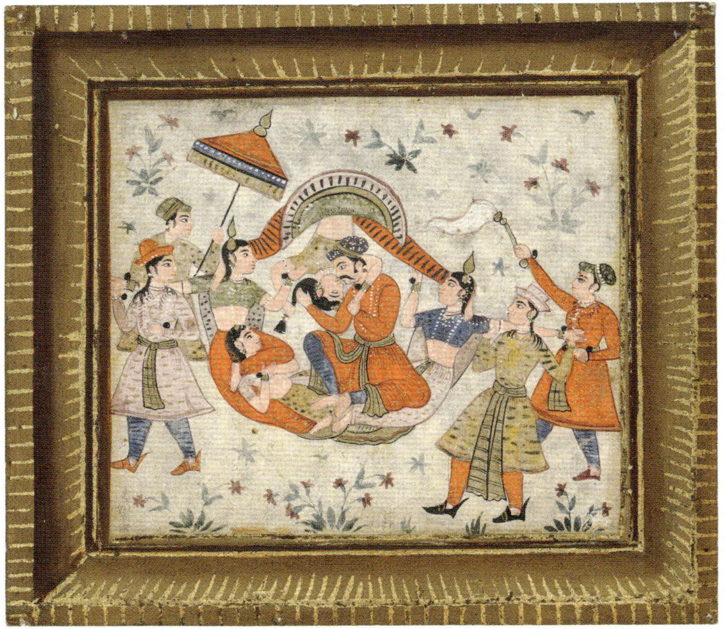

Cat. 76 | Ca 120/1

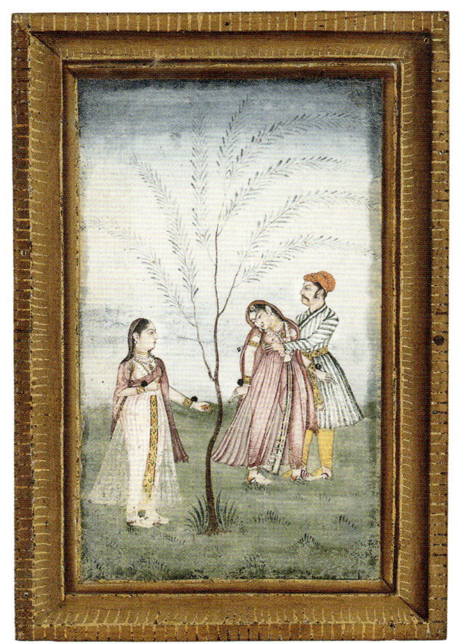

Cat. 77 | Ca 120/9

Cat. 76 | Ca 120/1
Kandarparatha
Deccan, North Indian style, 18th century
Watercolour and gold, painted frame 17.1 × 18.9 cm, image 12.4 × 14.1 cm
Reference: Dresden 2017, cat. 50, p. 194

Cat. 77 | Ca 120/9
Dāruṇa and a girl
Deccan, North Indian style, 18th century
Watercolour and gold, painted frame 26.5 × 18.1 cm, image 21.8 × 12.8 cm

Cat. 78 | Ca 121/6
Portrait of a Deccani nobleman; underdrawing: *Kakubhā rāgiṇī*
Deccan, 18th century
Watercolour and gold, painted frame 26.3 × 18.9 cm, image 20.2 × 13.2 cm
Reference: Simon 2017, p. 98, fig. 3a

Cat. 76 | The painting of a *kandarparatha*—a vehicle composed of human bodies—represents a palanquin of women symbolising love. A prince sits in the midst of this arrangement, surrounded by flowers spread over the areas left in reserve. Such composite figures are known from pre-Islamic animistic cults that were popular in Central Asia.[22] Here, the adaptation of this style, combined with the colourful palette, suggests an attribution to the eighteenth century in northern India. At the turn of the seventeenth century, numerous Turkmen artists had migrated to the Deccan, and, following the collapse of government there, moved farther north. This image is comparable in subject and composition to one formerly in the Liechtenstein Princely Collection, though it varies greatly in style and technique.[23] NB

Cat. 77 | While the melancholy young woman under a weeping willow in the arms of her lover shies away from him, the elderly lady, a *dāruṇa*, persuades her to move closer to him. This natural hesitation of a young damsel who does not let allow the hero near her unless persuaded to unite in love by an experienced and respected advisor is a common theme in painting and poetry in both Hindu and Islamic arts.[24] NB

Cat. 78 | This portrait of a Deccani nobleman holding a flower and wearing a garland of blue flowers contrasting with his crimson *jāma* (robe) is placed against a stark background of light and dark blue. However, it is not the identity of the subject or the fineness of execution that makes this artwork important but the underdrawing in ink that was discovered using infrared reflectography during restoration. Overpainting was a prevalent practice appearing in Persian, Mughal, and Deccani art.

The underdrawing shows a *Kakubhā rāgiṇī* scene of a young woman on a terrace, frightened by a peacock on a pedestal that screams at the lightning (symbol of hope) represented by thin lines (snakes) across the sky.[25] While the conventions of this *rāgiṇī* vary, the theme traditionally shows a lady waiting for her lover. In this case, instead of attendants who, as seen in other illustrations of this *rāgiṇī*, try to console the dismayed *nāyikā*, her only companion is the peacock, which, in an attempt to placate her, only heightens her agony. NB

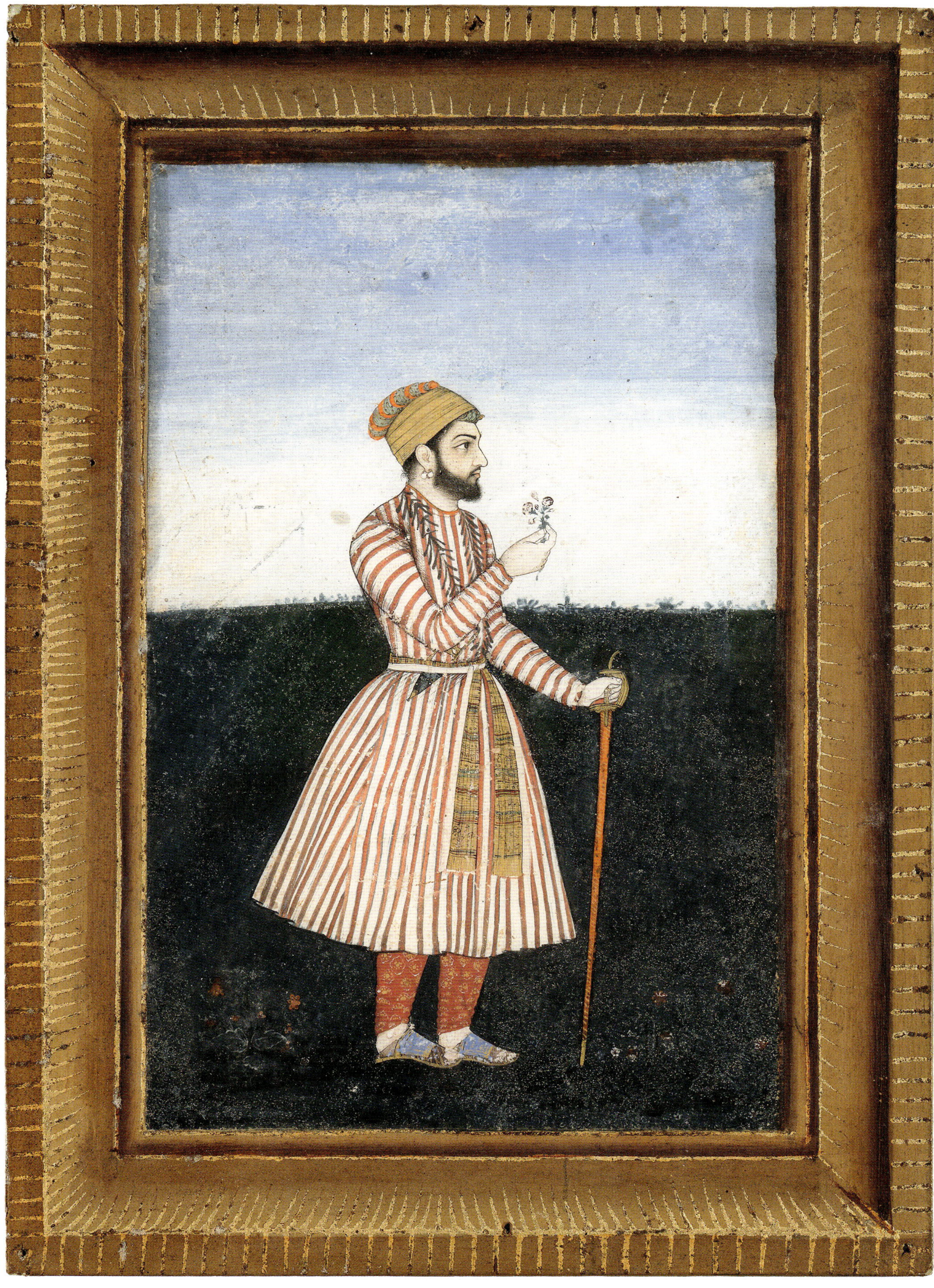

Cat. 78 | Ca 121/6

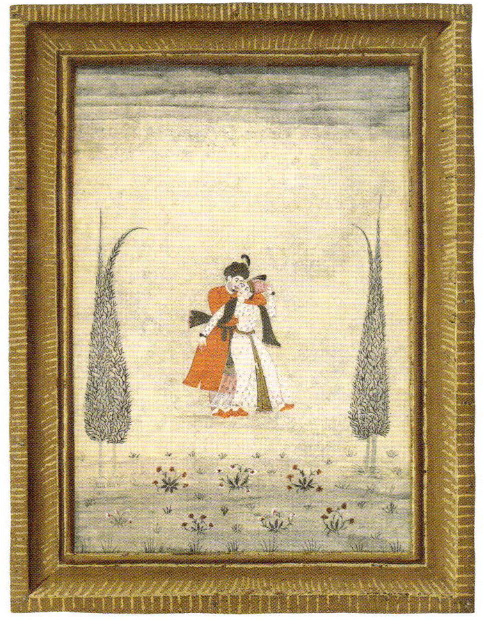

Cat. 79 | Ca 120/8

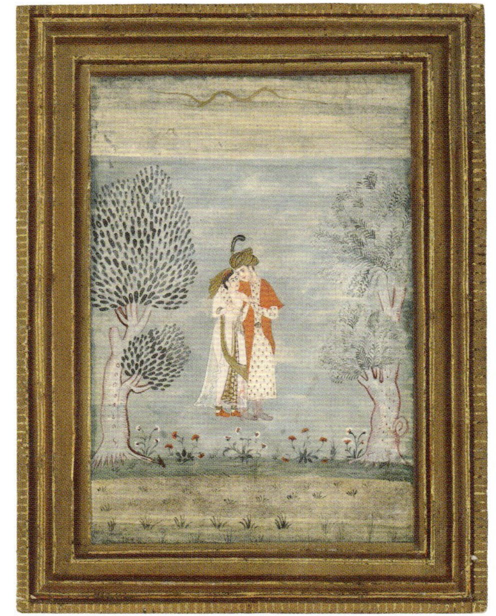

Cat. 80 | Ca 120/7

Cat. 79 | Ca 120/8
Lovers in Persian costume between cypresses
Deccan [?], 18th century
Watercolour, gold, and silver, painted frame 27.8 × 20.5 cm, image 22.2 × 15.1 cm

Cat. 80 | Ca 120/7
Lovers in Persian costume between trees
Deccan [?], 18th century
Watercolour and gold, painted frame 29 × 21.7 cm, image 23 × 15.8 cm

Cat. 81 | Ca 122/15
A couple in a Baṅgāldār-pavilion
Deccan [?], 18th century
Watercolour and gold, painted frame 28 × 19.5 cm, image 21.3 × 13.1 cm

Cat. 79–81 | The portraits of lovers in Persian garments might allude to a literary work such as Kālidāsa's tale *Śakuntalā*.[26] The illustrations, however, are lacking in specifics that their frequent use as a single motif, independently of this model, seems likely.

The Schlegel Collection includes two versions of this composition (cat. 79 and cat. 80). In light of the similarities in the detailing of faces, the Persian robes, the use of opaque colours alternating with watery areas for the background, and the brush drawing of ornaments and plants, both of them may come from the same workshop as cat. 73 and cat. 74. Some of the figures and robes as well as parts of the simplified background motifs are executed according to a pattern and maybe by the same hand. Here it becomes clear how such motifs were distributed by workshop artists and executed in a manufacture-like setting or as the combined product of several painters.

The portrait of lovers meeting on a covered terrace overlooking a river (cat. 81) was probably executed by a different hand than cat. 73 and cat. 74 but is likely to have originated in the Deccan as well. It shows a prince offering wine to his beloved. The stylistic influences and motifs from Mughal painting blended with local styles—a common feature in the eighteenth-century Deccan—makes fixing place and date impossible. PKH

Notes | 1 See, for example, British Museum, London, inv. no. 1920,0917,0.7, URL: http://britishmuseum.org/research/collection_online/collection_object_details.aspx?objectId=232041&partId=1&searchText=1920,0917,0.7&page=1 (3. 12. 2017); and Bibliothèque National de France, Paris, Smith-Lesouëf 231/12, URL: http://archivesetmanuscrits.bnf.fr/ark:/12148/cc950511 (3. 12. 2017). | 2 The collection was preserved in eight folders of varying sizes according to the requirements of the paintings. | 3 The entry refers to "Bestand [inventory] 1 I 1906." As the folders were reorganised several times, the original order is not known. | 4 See Zebrowski 1983, p. 244. | 5 Johnson Album in the India Office Library, London. See Falk/Archer 1981, cat. 426 xxviii, p. 513. | 6 I would like to thank Alasdair Watson, Bodleian Library, Oxford, for reading and translating the inscription. | 7 Similar elements can be found in a *rāgamālā* series that is now distributed among various collections such as the Victoria & Albert Museum, London, inv. no. 1.71-1954; and the Johnson Album in the India Office Library, London. See Falk/Archer 1981, cat. 368 i–vii, pp. 472–4. | 8 See p. 29, fig. 12. | 9 See cat. 62–7, 82. | 10 See Losty 2012, cat. 25/2, pp. 62–3; and Dresden 2017, cat. 35b, p. 178–80. | 11 See cat. 9, 10, 33–7. | 12 See Falk/Archer 1981, p. 135. | 13 Europeans such as Colonel Jean Baptiste Joseph Gentil and Colonel Antoine Louis Henri Polier travelled to the city and became involved in the cultural activities. See ibid. | 14 Tilly Kettle visited Faizabad, capital of Oudh, in 1771–1772. See ibid. | 15 Asaf ud-Daula, son of Shujā' ud-Daula, succeeded him in 1775 and maintained a lavish court culture. | 16 One such collector was Richard Johnson. See Falk/Archer 1981, pp. 14–29. | 17 Ibid., p. 110. | 18 British Museum, London, inv. nos. 1974,0617,0.10.59 and 62. | 19 Kishwar 2012, p. 244. | 20 See Zebrowski 1983, p 166. | 21 See Forster 1791; and Dresden 2017, cat. 97, p. 233. | 22 See Zebrowski 1983, pp. 169–72. | 23 See Losty 2012, p. 71, no. 14. | 24 Another painting with a comparable theme is in the British Museum, London, inv. no. 1955,1008,0.48. | 25 See p. 36, fig. 3b. | 26 See cat. 75.

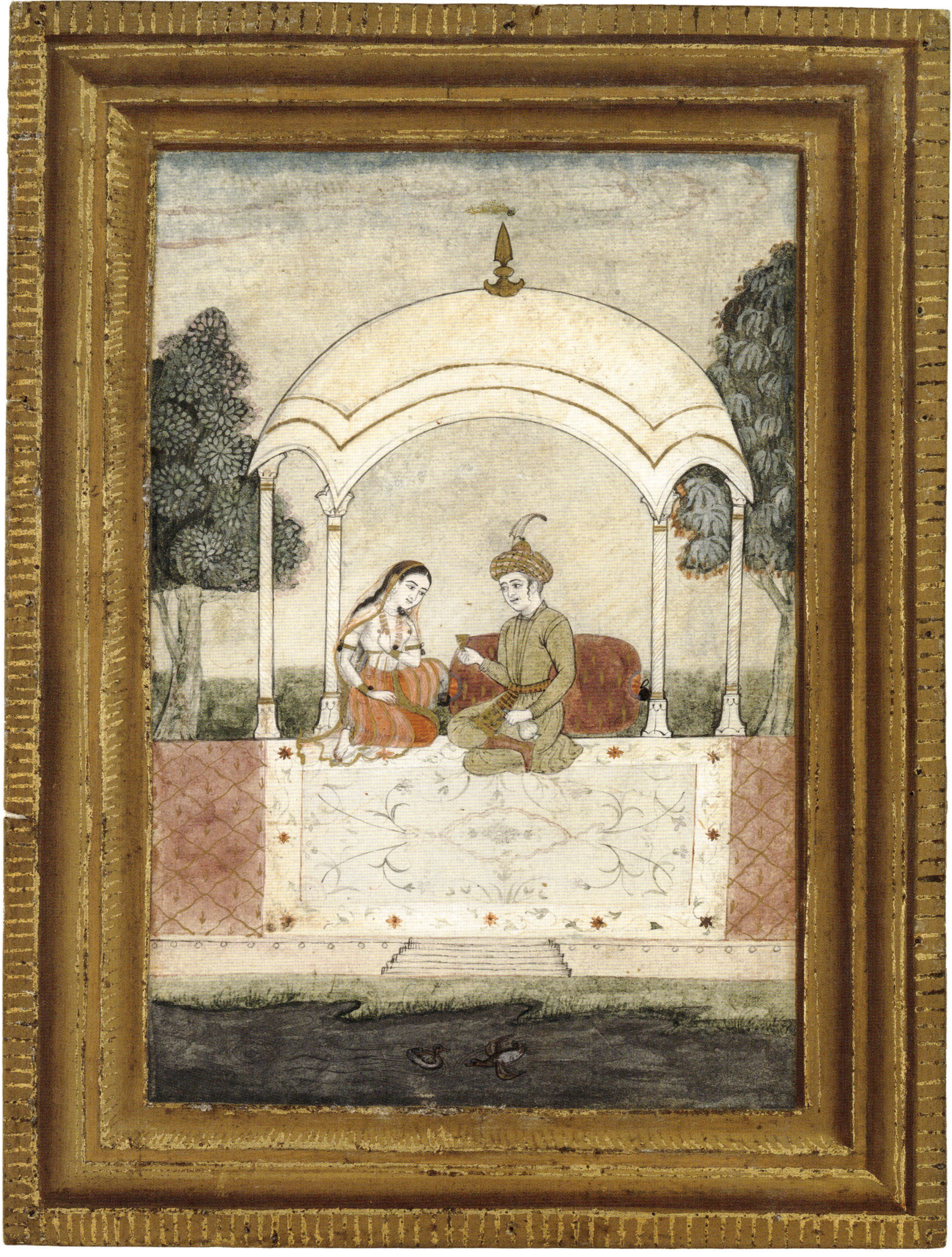

Cat. 81 | Ca 122/15

Epics

Cat. 82 | This sheet—perhaps deliberately left unfinished—belongs stylistically to the softly coloured representations of women in the Schlegel Collection, marked by an abbreviated representation of landscape.[1] At the same time, it is one of the few works from the collection that takes up a story from the Hindu tradition. It shows Kṛṣṇa twice—at left travelling with a yoke of oxen on a road hidden by trees, and at right disguised as a prince watching five shepherdesses bathe from his hiding place in the bushes.[2] In the story, he steals their clothes, forcing each of them to appear naked before him if she wants her robe back. In the pictorial narrative, the young ladies may as yet be unaware of what is going on. Through their various postures, the artist indicates their temperaments and the presentation of their bodies: they either hide behind one another, proudly display themselves while taking off or drying their clothes, strut along while arranging their hair, or act bashfully. As in depictions of the biblical story of Bathsheba bathing, the spectator becomes a fellow observer. PKH

Cat. 83 | In this painting an Iranian artist in the Deccan re-created the image of the "camel fight" from the *Muraqqa ʿ-i Gulshān*[3] and the crouching lion from the 1544–1545 album of Bahrām Mīrzā, brother of Shāh Ṭahmāsp,[4] attributed to the master painter Behzād (1460–1535).[5] Apart from the diverse motifs and styles practised during the seventeenth and eighteenth centuries in the Deccan that are evident in this painting, the fine detailing and decorative corners are equally fascinating. NB

Cat. 82 | Ca 122/2
Kṛṣṇa watching the gopīs bathe
Deccani Mughal (Hyderabad),
late 17th–early 18th century
Watercolour and gold, painted frame,
22.3 × 19.5 cm, image 16.8 × 14.2 cm
References: Dresden 2017, cat. 40, p. 181;
Frankfurt (Main) 2017, cat. 131, p. 207

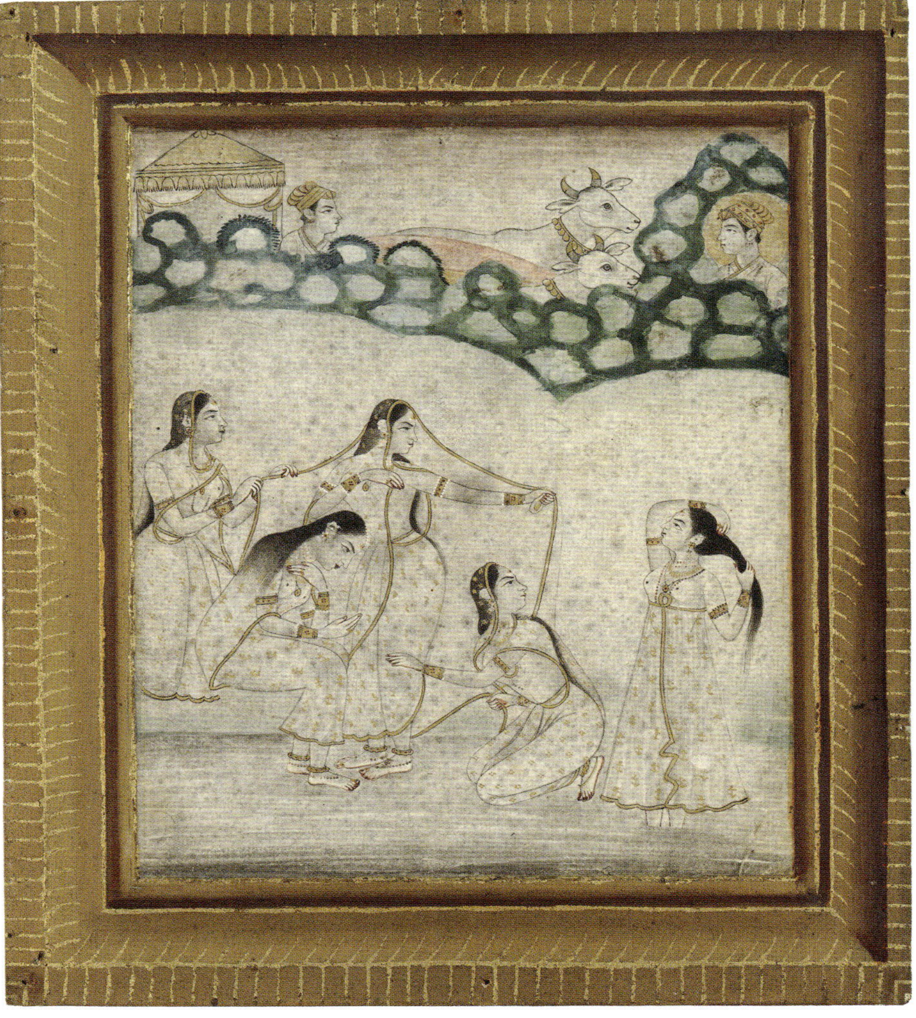

Cat. 82 | Ca 122/2

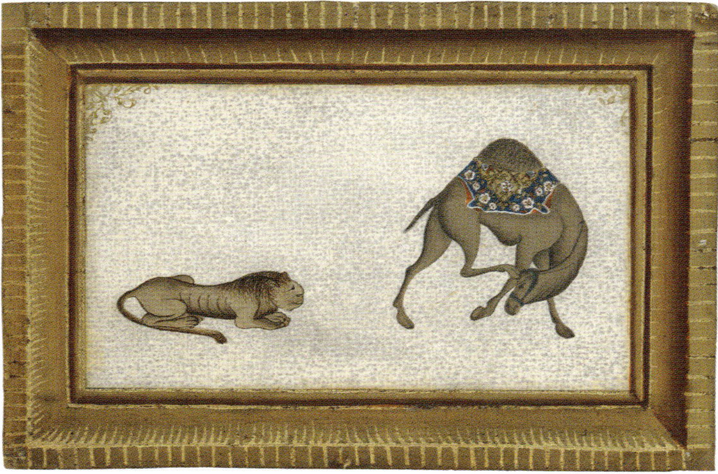

Cat. 83 | Ca 121/13

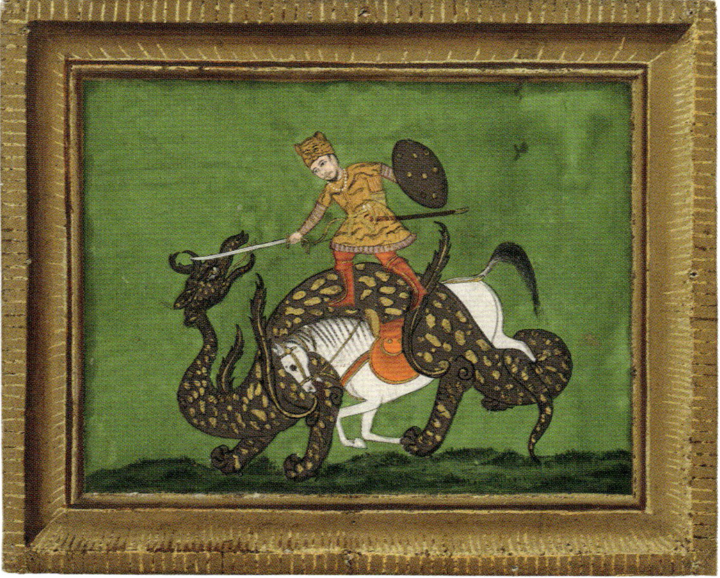

Cat. 84 | Ca 121/11

Cat. 83 | Ca 121/13
Lion and camel
Deccani Mughal, late 17th–
early 18th century
Watercolour and gold,
painted frame 15.9 × 23.6 cm,
image 10.3 × 17.9 cm

Cat. 84 | Ca 121/11
Rustam and Rakhsh fighting a dragon (third labour, Haft-Khān-e Rostam)
Deccan, late 17th–early 18th century
Watercolour and gold,
painted frame 22 × 24.2 cm,
image 15.2 × 19.1 cm
References: Dresden 2017, cat. 48, p. 190–1; Frankfurt (Main) 2017, cat. 130, pp. 106–7

Cat. 84 | The Schlegel Collection includes a small group of works in a simple and rather popular style which, even though possibly from the Deccan, uses Persian themes and models that were often embraced in India.[6] A popular topic was the representation of Rustam defeating the fire-breathing dragon, an episode from the *Shāhnāma* epic which, at its centre, relates the seven adventures of this legendary hero who fought on the side of Iran against Turan.[7] Rustam, who in token of his strength is clad in tiger skin and a bear-skin hat, had fallen asleep near the cave of a mighty dragon whom he had not noticed. Three times did his faithful stallion Rakhsh ("Lighting") warn and wake him. But Rustam, who from where he was lying could not see the dragon, got annoyed and rebuked his horse. Only when being woken up for the third time—almost too late, for the dragon was already attacking him—did Rustam become aware of his danger. He drew his sword, and engaged in fierce battle. Rustam was saved only because of the support of Rakhsh who daringly bit the huge animal.[8] This dramatic climax is shown in the Dresden painting. Rustam is identified by wearing a predator's skin and cap. Compared to the miniature preserved in the Bodleian Library in Oxford, which presents nearly the same constellation of figures, the simplicity of the Dresden version becomes obvious.[9] PKH

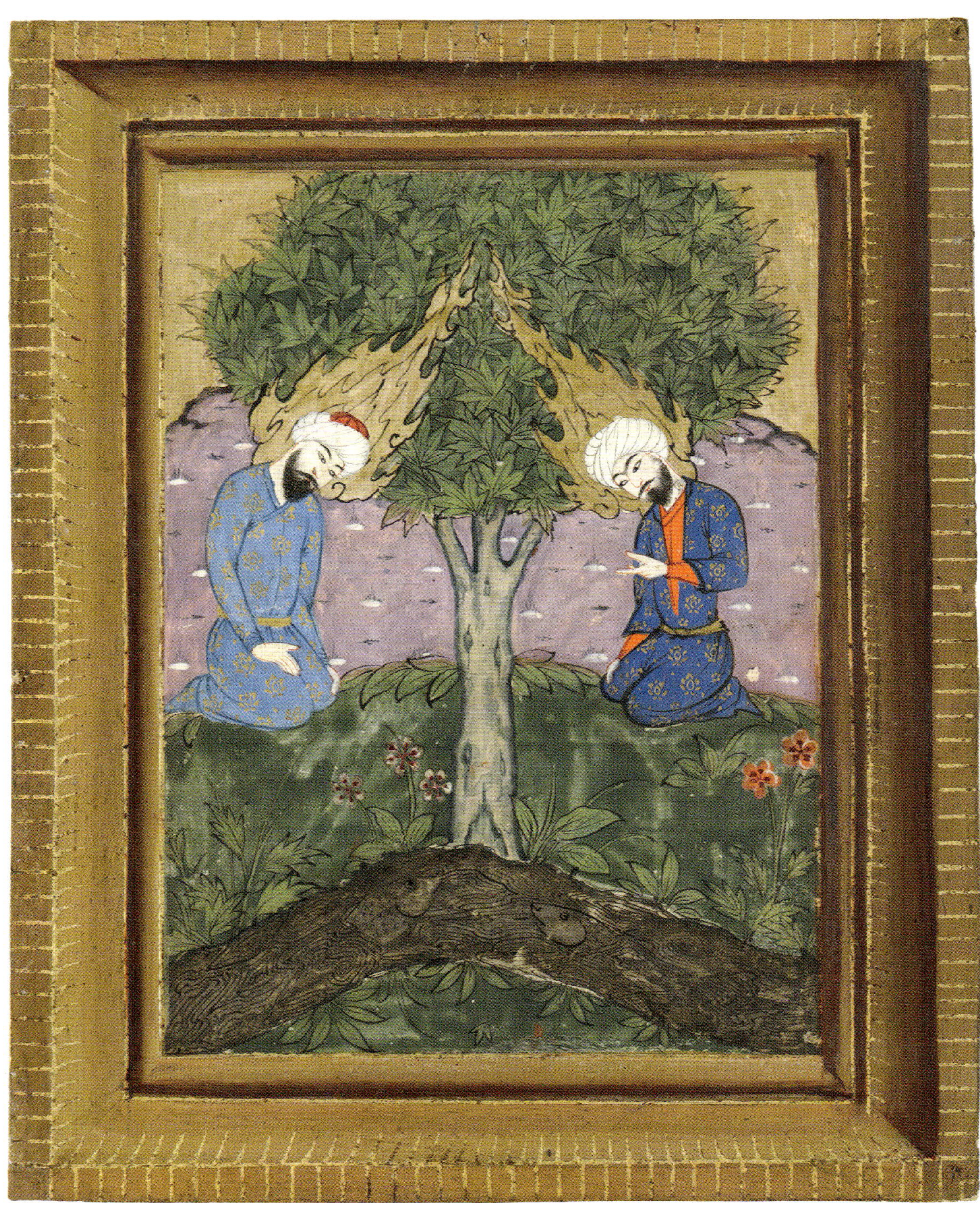

Cat. 85 | Ca 121/12

Cat. 85 | Ca 121/12
Khiẓr and Moses
Deccan, late 17th – early 18th century
Watercolour, gold, and silver,
painted frame 22.3 × 17.7 cm,
image 16.7 × 12.2 cm
Inscribed verso in *nasta'liq*
(see note 13)
Reference: Dresden 2017,
cat. 47, p. 188

Cat. 85 | The painting, which is thematically and stylistically related to Persian illustrations, probably originated in the Deccan.[10] The portrait of two prophets kneeling by the bank of a river, their heads surrounded by a nimbus of golden flame, falls into line with the pictorial tradition of an episode from the *Alexander Romance* in which Jewish and Islamic traditions are merged.[11] In search of the source of the water of life, Alexander and his retinue pass Khiẓr and Elias without noticing them. The two prophets have come together in a cave close to this source. The painting only shows the two holy men under a tree by the water; their gestures suggest that they are immersed in scholarly dialogue.

The technical examination of the miniature revealed an inscription on the verso which proves that the men shown are not Khiẕr and Elias, but Khiẕr and Moses.[12] The source of this text, which has not been reliably identified, can be traced back to a Sura in the *Qur'ān* (*The Cave*, Sura 18, verse 60–82), which relates the encounter of the two men:[13] Moses was travelling with his servant to the place where the seas flow together. They are about to settle down for a rest, when the servant remembers he has forgotten the dried fish which they wanted to eat on a rock; so he returns to get them, but the fish had come to life again and swam away. After hearing that, also Moses goes back to the place. There he encounters the "holy man" Khiẕr (also called "the Green"). Moses desires to partake of Khiẕr's wisdom, and Khiẕr takes him along, and puts him on the test three times, thus demonstrating to Moses his ignorance and lack of patience.

The Dresden painting shows the two men in dialogue. It is characterized by its clear contours[14] and the discreet internal detailing of foliage and water, executed with a keen sense for decorative effect. The solemn character and holiness of the scene is emphasised by the symmetrical and very simple composition as well as the few colour values (with shades of red cautiously accentuated), but especially by the rich use of silver (for the river) and gold (for the light of the sky and the blazing nimbi). Contrary to Western principles of perspective, the golden flames have been placed in front of the foliage. The figure on the right, with the gesture of a teacher, is probably Khiẕr; Moses, on the left, is listening intently. In the background, one might recognise the rock on which the fish were forgotten; and in the foreground, the river in which they swim after coming back to life.

The Persian text on the verso, written in non-calligraphic manuscript style, gives a slightly more elaborate account of the story, compared to the *Qur'ān*. Khiẕr asks Moses what he desires to learn, also inquiring what he might have forgotten. Moses refers to Joshua, his companion, who is alleged to have forgotten bread and two fishes. Khiẕr instantly knows what happened next: Allāh has involved himself and given the fish back its life. Moses is surprised and realises: the Almighty has created the fish and given us food. The fishes came out of the water to return there alive.

A part of the text, not visible in infrared light, was revealed only by X-ray fluorescence analysis,[15] as it was written in gold – thus creating a similarity to the destinctive depiction of light in the painting itself using gold in the sky and the nimbi of flames. Regrettably this short section containing as honorary title of Allāh "Excellency" is hardly legible. Venturing an interpretation, it might be referring to the light of knowledge the text is aiming on. PKH

Notes | 1 See cat. 61–7. There are similar trees in cat. 44–6, 48, 50, 51, 62, 63. On the workshops using this motif, see Lunsingh Scheurleer 2017, p. 58–61. | 2 I would like to thank Dipanwita Donde for help identifying the scene. See similar compositions in the Victoria & Albert Museum, London, inv. no. 132-13-1885, and in an album in the Bodleian Library, University of Oxford, MS Ouseley Add. 166/fol. 10a. Both have descriptive titles that mention a prince instead of Kṛṣṇa and show a main group of only three women, perhaps a princess with her attendants, according to a related scene from the story of Prince Khusrau watching Shirīn bathe, handed down by the poet Nizāmī Ganjavī (1141–1209). | 3 Adamova 2004, p. 12. | 4 Roxburgh 2000, pp. 119–46. | 5 Comparative information kindly provided by Dipanwita Donde. | 6 For a summary of the influence of Persian painting on the Deccan and relevant literature, see Galloway London n. d., p. 28, no. 11. See also cat. 72–5, and 85. | 7 See cat. 86. | 8 Ferdausi 2010, pp. 79–82. | 9 Inv. no. MS Douce or.a.1.f 26b; see also Topsfield 2008, p. 66, no. 29. With many thanks to Friederike Weis for pointing out this work. | 10 For the influence of Persian painting in the Deccan, see Losty 2016, cat. 11, p. 28. | 11 See the folio of the Walters Art Museum, inv. no. W.607.258B, dated around 1800; URL: http://art.thewalters.org/detail/81253 (30. 1. 2017). | 12 See Dresden 2017, p. 101. | 13 Parts of the text are difficult to decipher. The transcription reads as follows: [1] ba cha āmadah-ī va az kujā āmadāh-ī? Mūsá ʿalayhi al-salām guft: man ba justan-i tu āmadah-am [2] Khiẕr guft: agar…Mūsá guft: tu rā salām kunam va …biyāmūzam [3] Khiẕr guft: ay Mūsá! nūrīst ba tu āmadah va khudāy taʿālā bā tu sukhan guft [4] az man cha āmūzī? guft… [5] Khiẕr guft: inna[?] fidā[?] nisyān[?] haḏa[?] [6] guft…chand… nān nayāft māhī nayāft. yūshaʿ guft… [7] Khiẕr tabassum kard va guft: qul iḥyāhā…allāh [8] taʿālā…Mūsá taʿajjub kard. māhiyān paydā [9] shudand va guftand: mā rā khudāy taʿālā zindah gardānīd [10] aknūn mā rā bikhur ki ravā dārīm. pas har du māhī bīrūn āmadand. With thanks to Anna Martin for the transcription and explanation of the text, and to Mohamed Abdesalam for additional information. | 14 In the Persian manner of painting, mainly the flesh tones are often rendered in red. | 15 This text was discovered in transmitted light and most of it could be identified when scanned with infrared light (RFA). See the essay of Olaf Simon, p. 38–9.

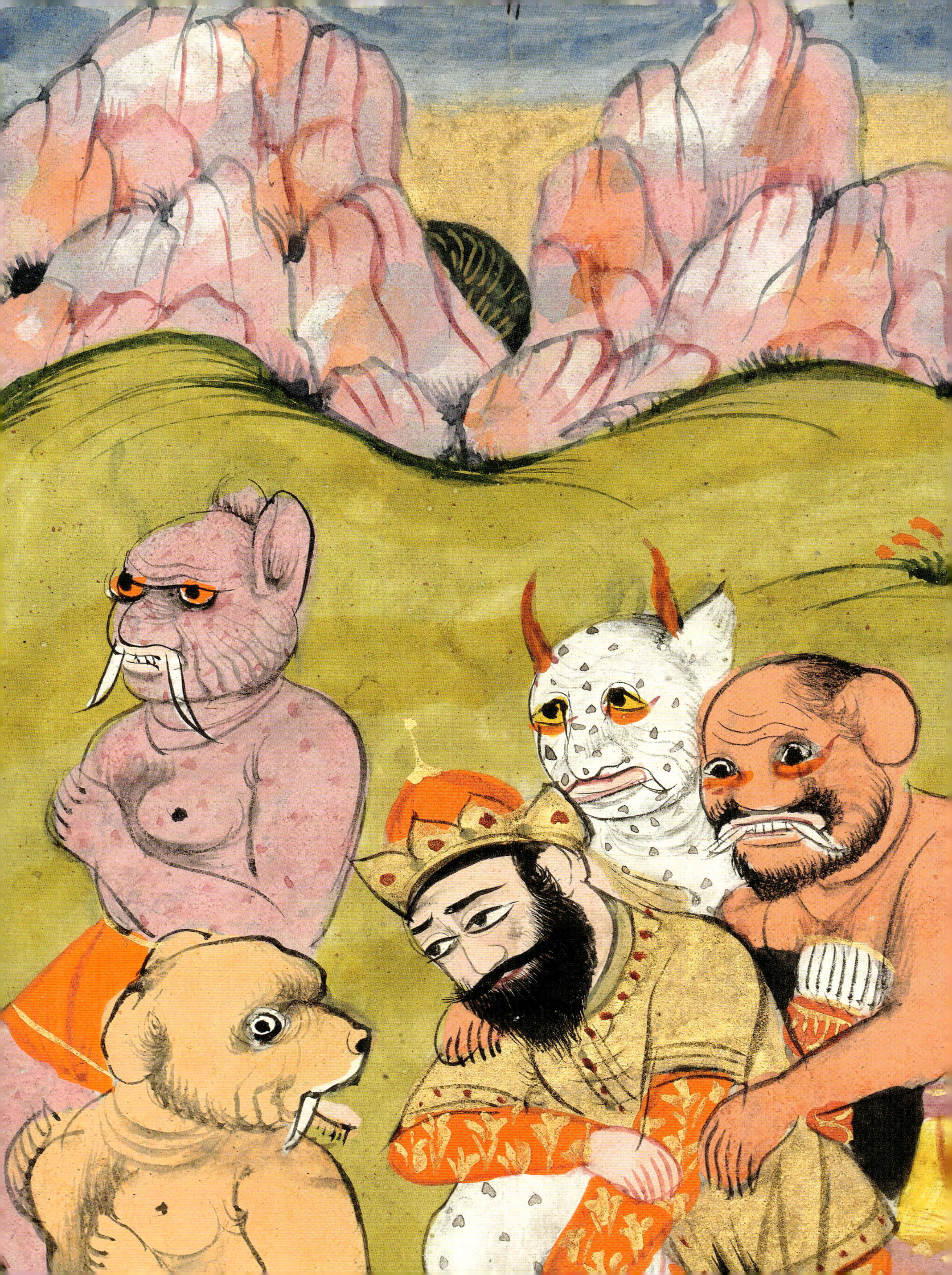

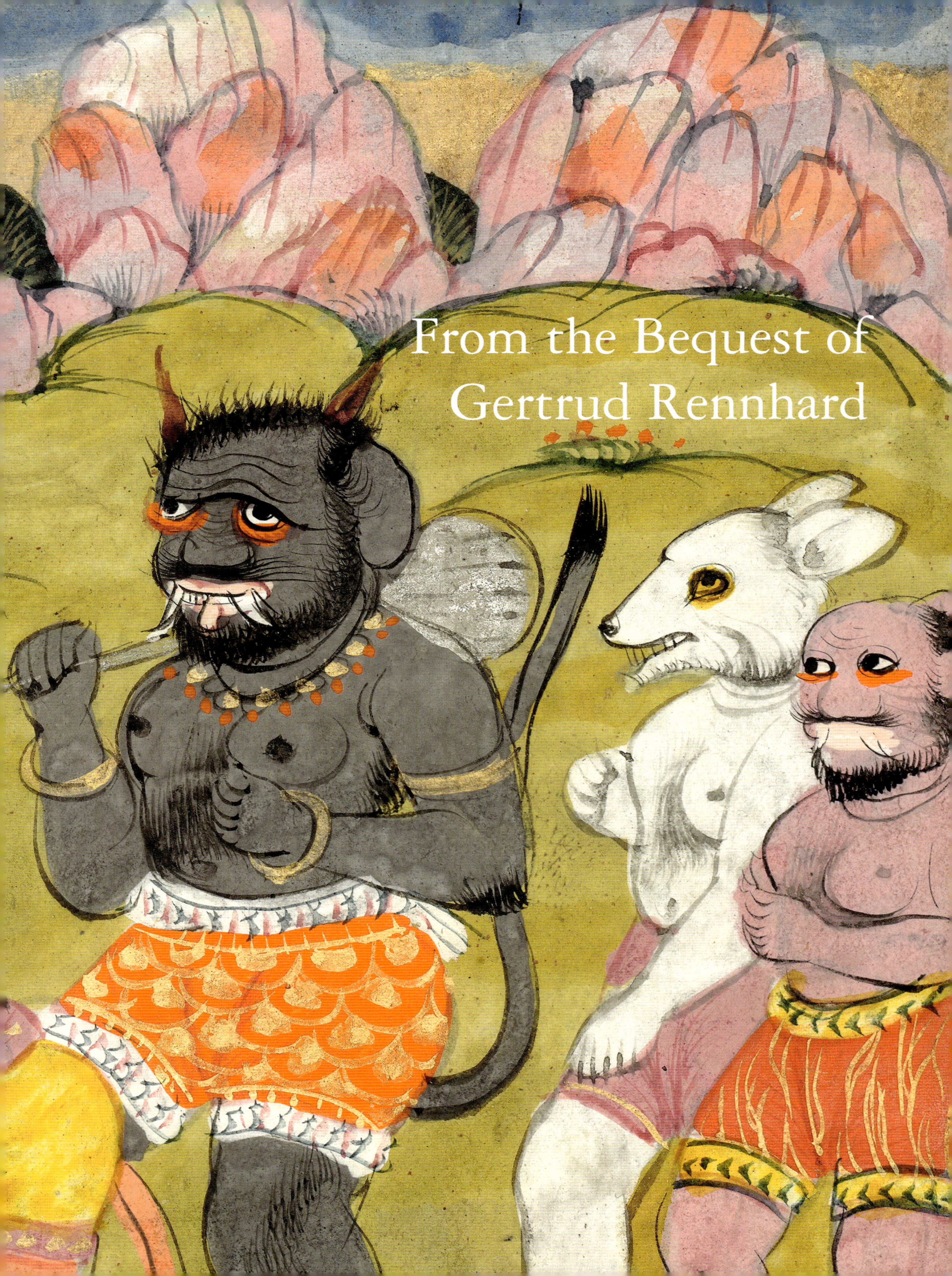

From the Bequest of Gertrud Rennhard

Cat. 86 | Ca 2017-1

An Early Nineteenth-Century Copy of the *Shāhnāma*

Ca 2017-1/1 (p. 1)
Front page with ornamental head (*'unvān*) and invocation *basmala*

Cat. 86 | Ca 2017-1
Illustrated manuscript of the *Shāhnāma* by Firdausī, written 976–1010
brown leather binding (modern), gold-embossed margin, 29.5 × 20 × 7.6 cm
Mughal India, 18th century; calligraphy *nasta'līq*, black ink; headings in red ink; golden and bluish black borders; added in the same calligrapher's hand are parts of the Iranian epic *Humāy and Humāyūn* by Khvājū Kermānī, written in 1331, beginning of text missing; ornamental headpiece (*'unvān*) in lapis lazuli and gold, inscribed with the *basmala* (invocation of God).
Illustrations in the northern Indian style, probably Kashmir, late 18th–early 19th century (before 1814), 96 illustrations of the *Shāhnāma* and 4 illustrations of *Humāy and Humāyūn*, 24 large and small areas left blank for illustrations; watercolour, gold, and silver
Donation by Roland Steffan and Hans-Jörg Schwabl, Dresden, from the estate of Gertrud Rennhard, Küsnacht, Canton of Zurich

The Iranian *Shāhnāma* (The Book of Kings) is among the most complex ethical, mythological, and historical lyric poems of world literature, to be considered alongside with Homer's *Iliad* and *Odyssey*, the Indian *Mahābhārata*, the Tibetan *Gesar* saga, and Dante's *Divine Comedy*. It is divided into fifty chapters, each devoted to one Iranian king, and has between 55,000 and 66,000 verses (there are several different versions). It took the author, Abū'l-Qāsim Firdausī, thirty-five years to complete the epic, in 1010. Firdausī took over from Abū-Mansūr Daqiqī, who died after completing only the first few chapters.

The first part covers the mythical age. It relates history from the first man, Keyumars, who became the first king, until the great king Kay Khusrau and the conflict between Iran and Turan. The hero of these battles is Rustam, born in Zabulistan (present-day Zabul in southern Afghanistan).

The second phase deals with the heroic age. It briefly mentions Garshāsp and his son Narimān, under whom the doctrine of Zarathustra is spread. The battle against Turan and its ruler Afrāsiyāb, begun by Rustam, is won by the hero Isfandiyār, the grandson of Luhrāsp. After heroic battles against evil forces and sinister predators, Isfandiyār is sent by his father to capture the ruler Rustam. However, Rustam shoots the hero in the eye with the feather of a Sīmurgh.

Part three deals with the historical age. It begins with Darab and Dārā, known to the Greeks as Darius, and his war against Alexander the Great. His victory and succession as Shāh of Iran culminated in the fall of his nation to this ruler from the West. Little is said about the history of the Parthians, but a selection of stories, legends, and romances from the Sasanian period is included. The epic ends with the Arab invasion of Iran and the death of the last Sasanian ruler, Yazdigerd III (r. 632–51), who was killed at Marv.

The work exerted a profound impact during the Mongol and Timurid periods (1222–1506) as well as under the last monarchs of the Qājār and Pahlavī dynasties in the nineteenth and twentieth centuries. This ongoing fascination is surprising, for the epic, which was composed in the early days of the Islamisation of Iran, deals exclusively with the pre-Islamic history of the country and its great kings and heroes. Firdausī dedicated the epic to Sultān Maḥmūd-i Ġaznavī (971–1030), who was of Turkish descent and initially did not like it, perhaps because of his own literary naivety. The Sunni ruler also may have disliked Firdausī's *Shī'a* leanings, which were not in favour in Iran at the time. A central motif of the *Shāhnāma* is the conflict between the rulers of Iran (roughly present-day Iran and Afghanistan) and those of Turan (Central Asia), which had for centuries been settled and dominated by Turks.

The epic deals with this conflict at all levels, political as well as ethical, and offers a wide range of interpretations of the role of the key figures. On the one hand, Firdausī depicts Iranian heroic virtues and superhuman strength in a manner that might be seen as "nationalistic." On the other hand, the poet tempers this exaggeration with the reality that the early Turanian kings belonged to the same Iranian dynasty. Only one ruler on the Turanian throne, who is deceived by the devil, is of Arabic origin: Żaḥḥāk, out of whose shoulders grow man-eating snakes. It is this very Żaḥḥāk who subjugates Iran and becomes one of its great kings. Also included among the great kings is Alexander the Great, known by his Eastern name, Iskandar or Sikandar. According to the ancient Iranian religion of Zoroastrianism, Alexander is condemned for vanquishing Darius III and looting Persepolis. But Firdausī has Alexander mourn the murder of Darius as unjustified; he relates his succession in accordance with Hellenistic tradition and

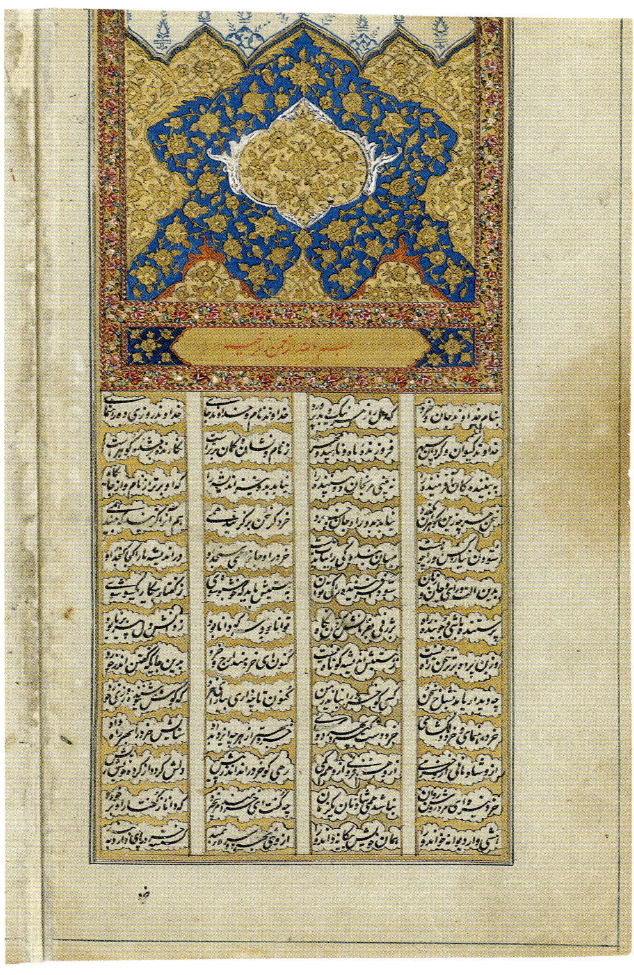

Ca 2017-1/1 (p. 1)

includes Alexander's heroic deeds among those of the Iranian heroes. Some of the kings and heroes are described, warts and all, in a way so human that readers might recognise themselves in these characters. In satire, Firdausī also immortalises his own experiences with Sultān Maḥmūd-i Ġaznavī and the poor remuneration he received. This, too, has contributed to the author's role as a sceptic facing an autocrat's overwhelming power and to his status as a role model in the eyes of some Iranian writers.

The Hellenistic rulers were impressed by the persuasive power of Iran's royal ideology. The ceremonies of the Iranian court were highly appreciated by some of the caliphs and undoubtedly by Iran's Mongolian Il-Khān dynasty (1256–1340). The literati in Herat in the circle of Prince Bāysunqur (d. 1432/33) undertook a slight revision of the *Shāhnāma*, to which he added a new introduction. Some of the interpolated verses, Arabicised terminology, and Islamic orientation have been traced back to this version by the most recent editor of the epic, Djalal Khaleghi-Motlagh.

Interest in the work during the Timurid period had an impact on the Mughals. The Mughal emperors were descendants of Tīmūr, and they held Iran's literary heritage in high esteem. In addition to the Turkic languages, Iranian was one of the languages spoken at court. A large number of manuscripts of the *Shāhnāma* were copied during the heyday of imperial rule under Akbar (r. 1556–1605), and it continued to be copied until the beginning of the reign of Aurangzēb (r. 1658–1707). Manuscripts with numerous textual errors and misspelled names, produced especially during the period of decline between the late eighteenth and mid-nineteenth century, are indicative of the epic's dissemination among the less educated, though affluent, population. The selection of illustrations for many of these late manuscripts contributed to the popularity of the work.

Ca 2017-1/2 (p. 7)
The court of King Gayūmars

The Dresden manuscript dates to the late Mughal period and probably originates from the North Indian province of Kashmir.[1] The text is not dated, and the high quality of the calligraphy suggests a wealthy client or a professional writer hoping to attract wealthy customers.[2] There are many places where areas of various sizes were left blank for illustrations and ornamental headings.[3] Following an old tradition, the illustrations are always accompanied by at least two lines of text; here they are on the top and the bottom of each page. The calligrapher's text is framed by margins and subdivided into four columns by another hand. The same person might have added the red headings that occur in almost all the early chapters but less often in the second half of the book. Most of the spaces left blank for illustrations and the numerous textual gaps of varying lengths appear in the last third of the manuscript—evidence that it is incomplete. If the manuscript had been finished, these lacunae would have been filled in and the cycle of illustrations completed.

The manuscript's design is indicative of its recipients in the Mughal Empire. The main chapters of the epic following the courts of fifty Iranian kings are not particularly emphasised; some are omitted in the chapter headings. The manuscript begins with the rhymed epic. Missing is one of the two prose introductions, either by the author or the editor Bāysunqur, that usually begin the Iranian versions. Richly illuminated headings (*'unvān*) can be found in the early chapters, near the middle of the book (no. 64, p. 634) and in the chapters that deal with Luhrasp's accession to the throne (no. 72, p. 759), which, since late Timurid times, has been considered the central episode of the epic. Accordingly, one would expect another illumination at the end of the epic, though it is missing here as are a number of other illustrations. The second *'unvān* roughly marks the centre of the projected series of illustrations. It shows the Iranian hero Bīzhan killing the Turanian Humān in a duel, then, clad in his victim's armour, sneaking through enemy lines (no. 65, p. 654).

The Iranian kings were somewhat neglected by the illustrators; they are represented on their thrones or in action in only twenty-three scenes. On the other hand, there are twenty-six illustrations that emphasise the heroic achievements of Rustam. Most of the remaining forty-seven illustrations show the exploits and military achievements of other Iranian heroes. There are fourteen illustrations showing women as protagonists, two of them as witches (no. 30, p. 195 and no. 77, p. 826) and two as rulers (no. 83, p. 914 and no. 87, p. 953). This is a greater number of illustrations of women compared to other pre-Islamic Iranian representations.

The Iranian love epic *Humāy and Humāyūn* by Khvājū Kermānī (1290–1349 or 1352)[4] begins on page 1391, right in the middle of the preface.This text, by the same calligrapher, was also left unfinished. CPH

Notes | 1 The Mughal Indian series of richly illustrated manuscripts might be based on the model of a work with a similarly extensive cycle and a similar selection: The British Library, London, MS Add. 5600, Rieu II 536; Titley 1977, no. 105, Mughal period, early seventeenth century, 90 illustrations. | 2 A note inscribed on the left endpaper of the volume mentions the son of Dīvān Sardār Mohkam Chand (d. 1814), First Minister of Mahārājā Ranjīt Sīngh, the first Sikh ruler of Punjab (b. 1780, r. 1797–1839), as the owner of this manuscript: "This (book) belong(s) to [added and corrected later] / Sardar Maharaj Chand Kumari / S /o [son of] / Sardar Mokham Chand Sahib Kumari / Rais azam [illegible, crossed out], Amritsar [written earlier and by a different hand than the first line]." During the First Anglo-Sikh War (1845–1846), between the Sikh empire of Punjab and the East India Company, the *Shāhnāma* manuscript might have been plundered by the English. More than 120 years later, at the end of the 1960s, the book was purchased by Gertrud Rennhard in Delhi. A note inserted in the book on a piece of paper dating from this time states: "Written for: / Diwan Mokham Chand / Courtier of Maharaja Ranjit Singh / Ruler of Punjab 1797–1839 / Diwan Mokham Chand enjoyed the title of Sardar Maharaj, from the Sikh Court. / Sardar Maharaj Mokham Chand was a powerful Courtier and General of Sikh Court. / Indo-Persian style, by Kashmiri Artist / Names of painter and transcriber not known definitely. The most popular writer of those days in the Sikh Court at Lahore was Pandit-Tota Ram. It is believed that this is his work. / It is possible that the book has been written and prepared earlier and presented to Sardar Maharad ['d' crossed out] Mohkam Chand by some one." | 3 Manuscripts such as these are not uncommon; see e. g. The British Library, London, inv. no. A.18804, 1719, with 97 illustrations; see Titley 1977, p. 46, no. 112; see also Staatsbibliothek Berlin, ms. Minutoli 134, with 94 illustrations, dated Kashmir 1245H/1830 (Steiner et al. 1971, no. 73); New York Public Library, ms. Spencer, Indo-Pers. 13, with 93 miniatures, c. 1815–1820 (Schmitz 1992, no. III.4, p. 169–175). | 4 See De Bruijn 2009; and Bürgel 1990.

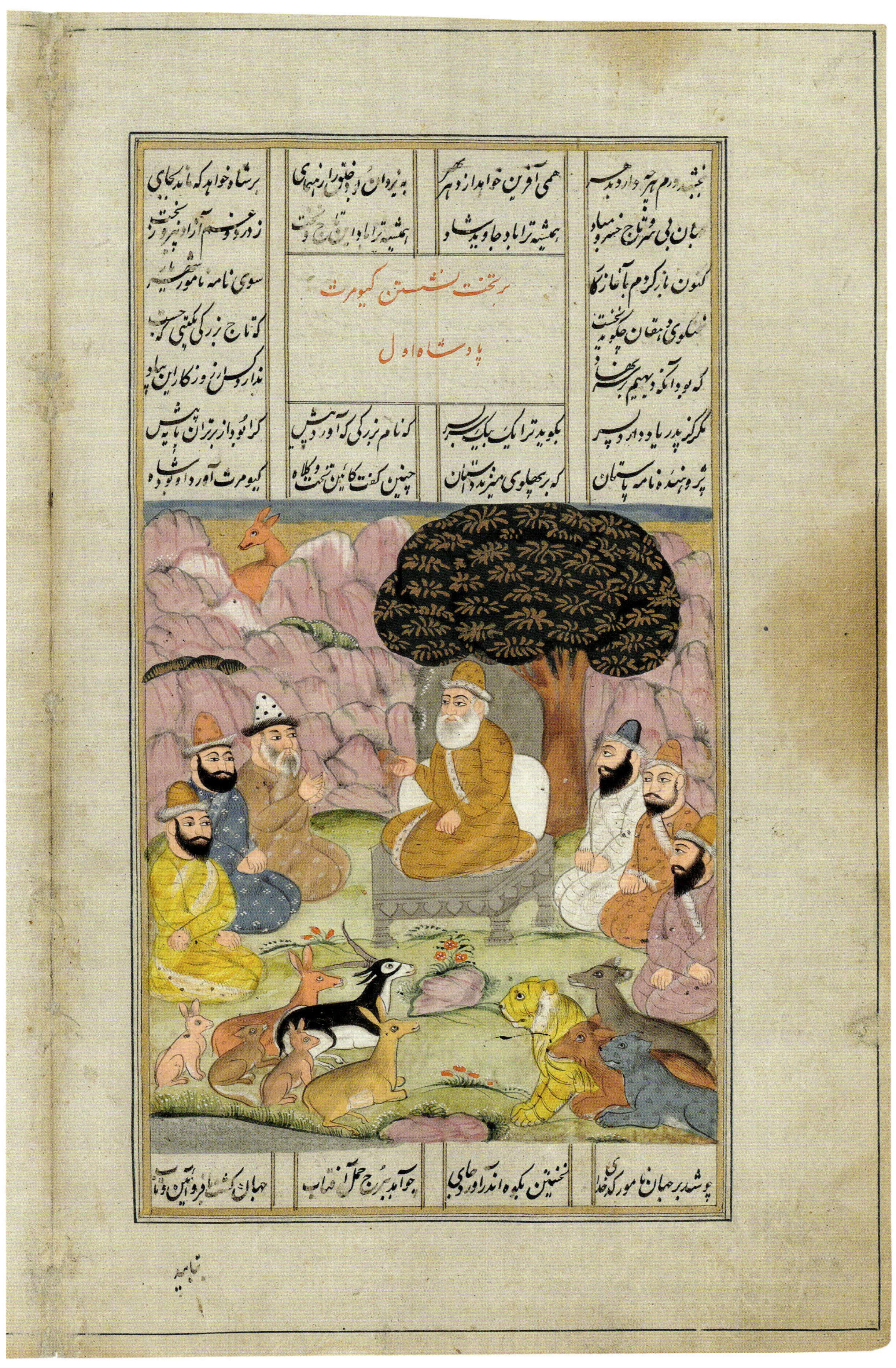

Ca 2017-1/2 (p. 7)

Ca 2017-1/3 (p. 12)
The Black Dīv Khazarvān fights Siyāmak, son of Gayūmars

Ca 2017-1/4 (p. 15)
The court of Jamshīd

Ca 2017-1/5 (p. 17)
Jamshīd in conversation (probably Żaḥḥāk and his father)
in front: Satan (Iblīs) comes to Prince Żaḥḥāk

Ca 2017-1/6 (p. 19)
Page with floral ornaments

Ca 2017-1/7 (p. 20)
Satan tells Żaḥḥāk to feed the snakes with human brains

Ca 2017-1/8 (p. 29)
Page with floral ornaments

Ca 2017-1/9 (p. 30)
The Feast of Farīdūn and Kāveh

Ca 2017-1/10 (p. 33)
Farīdūn and his two consorts

Ca 2017-1/11 (p. 38)
Farīdūn locks up Żaḥḥāk in a mountain cave

Ca 2017-1/12 (p. 52)
Tūr decapitates his brother Īraj

Ca 2017-1/13 (p. 57)
Farīdūn tests his sons Salm and Tūr

Ca 2017-1/14 (p. 64)
Manuchehr kills Tūr in battle

Ca 2017-1/15 (p. 75)
Sām fetches his son Zāl from Bird Sīmurgh's care

Ca 2017-1/16 (p. 76)
Astrologers reading Zāl's horoscope before King Manuchehr, Sām, Zāl, and Qarān

Ca 2017-1/17 (p. 88)
Zāl secretly meets Rūdāba

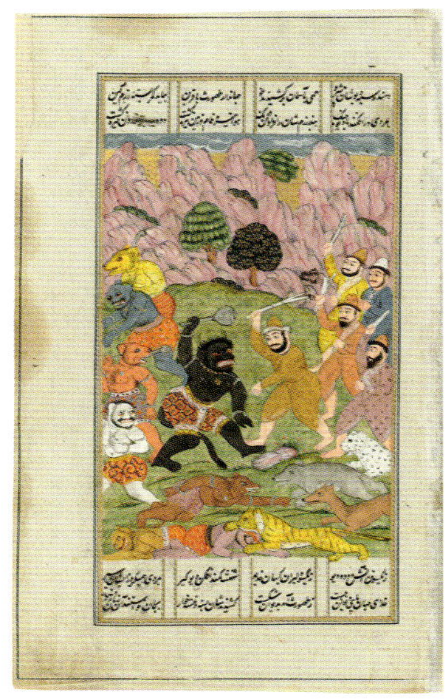

Ca 2017-1/3 (p. 12)

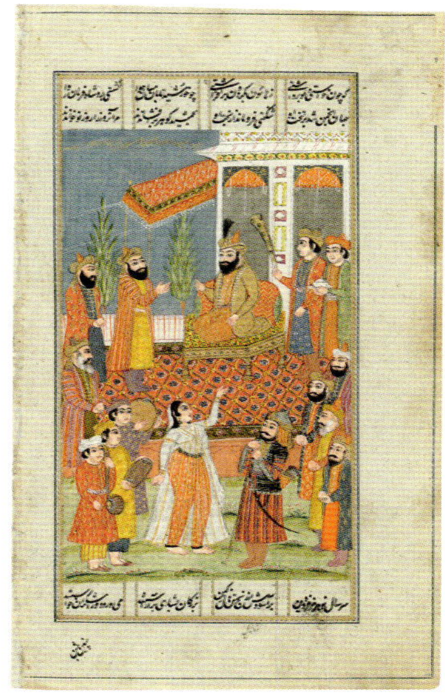

Ca 2017-1/4 (p. 15)

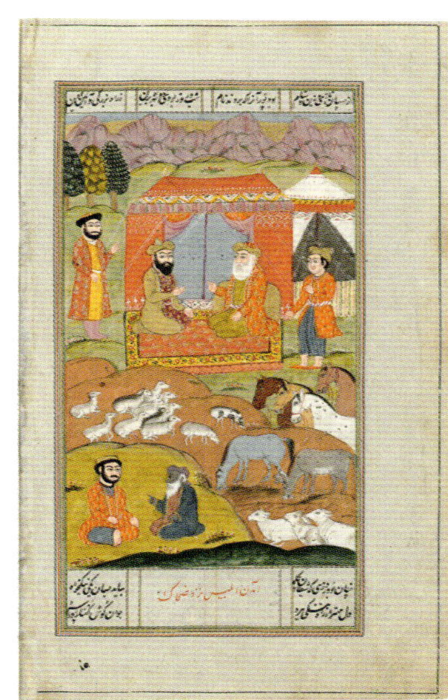

Ca 2017-1/5 (p. 17)

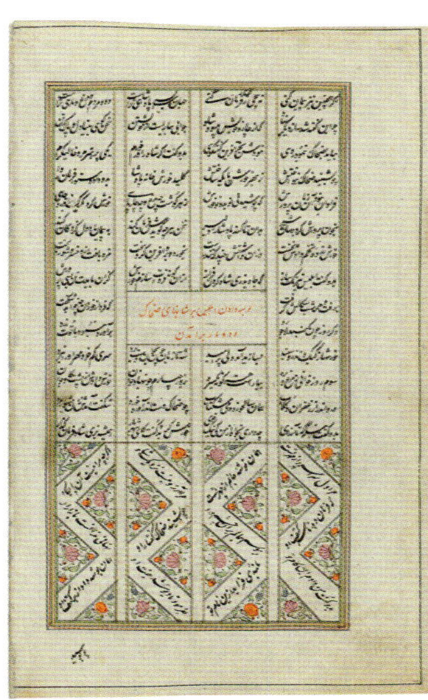

Ca 2017-1/6 (p. 19)

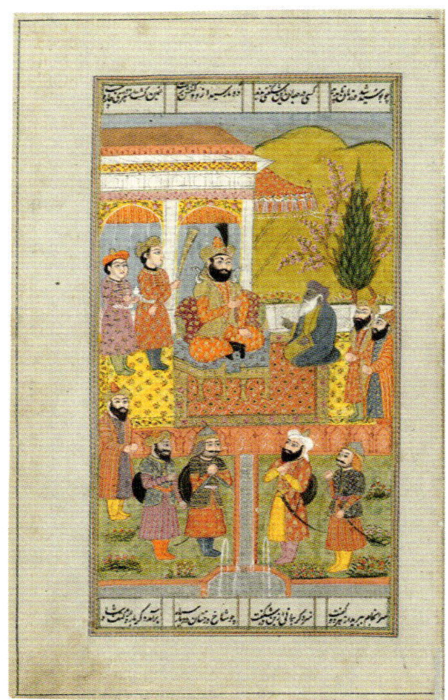

Ca 2017-1/7 (p. 20)

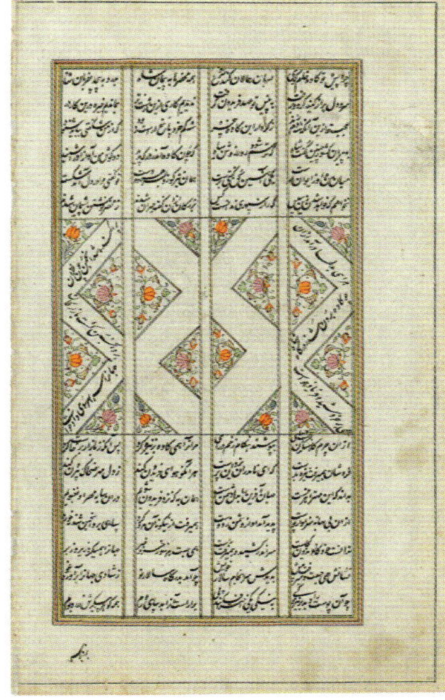

Ca 2017-1/8 (p. 29)

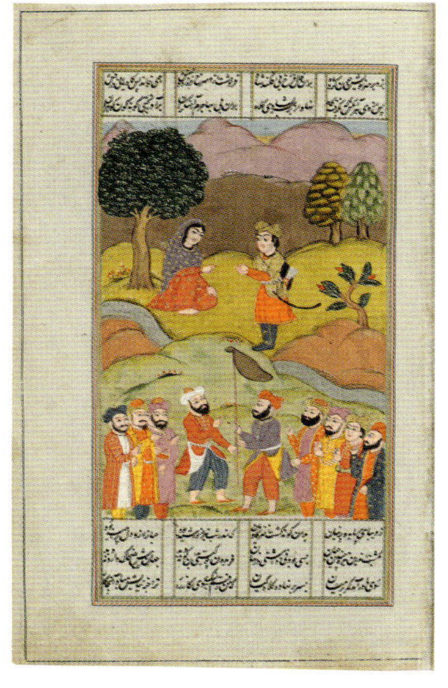
Ca 2017-1/9 (p. 30)

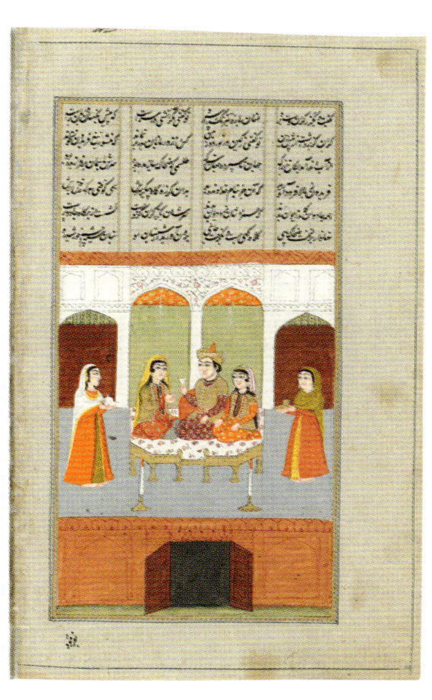
Ca 2017-1/10 (p. 33)

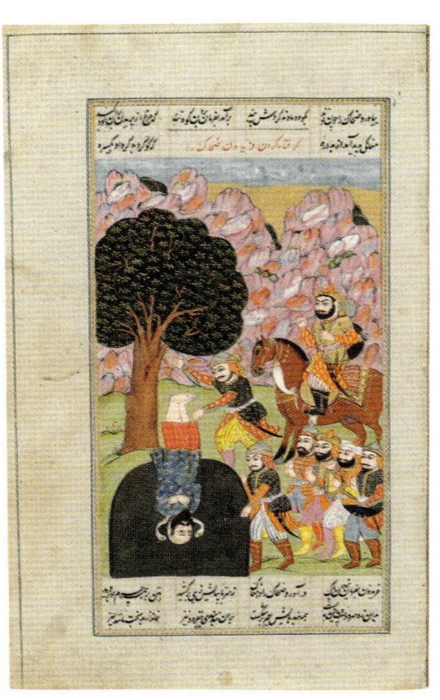
Ca 2017-1/11 (p. 38)

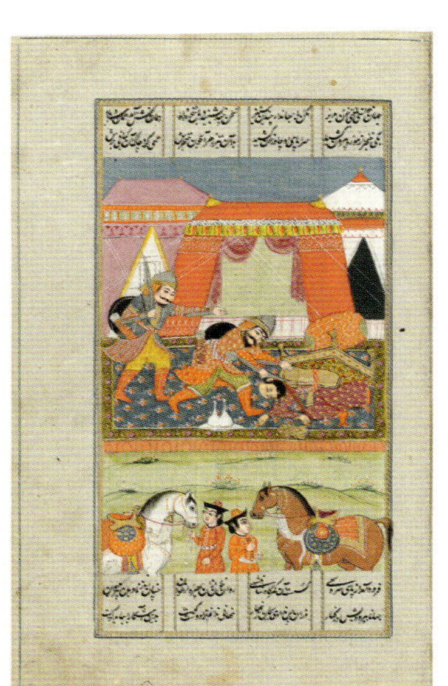
Ca 2017-1/12 (p. 52)

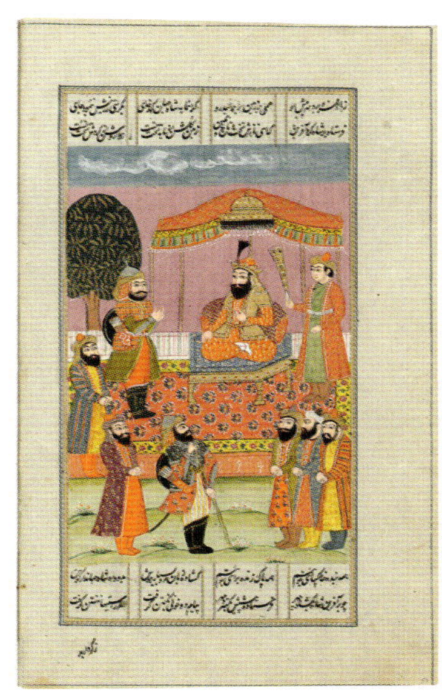
Ca 2017-1/13 (p. 57)

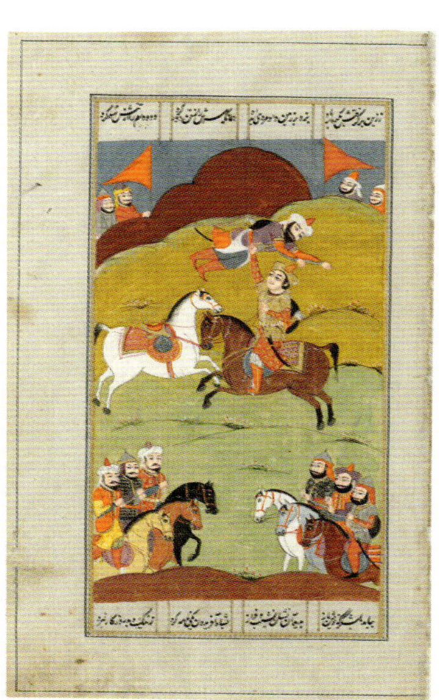
Ca 2017-1/14 (p. 64)

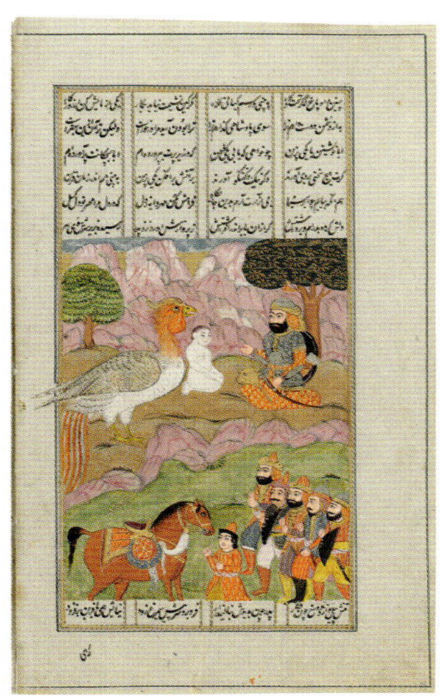
Ca 2017-1/15 (p. 75)

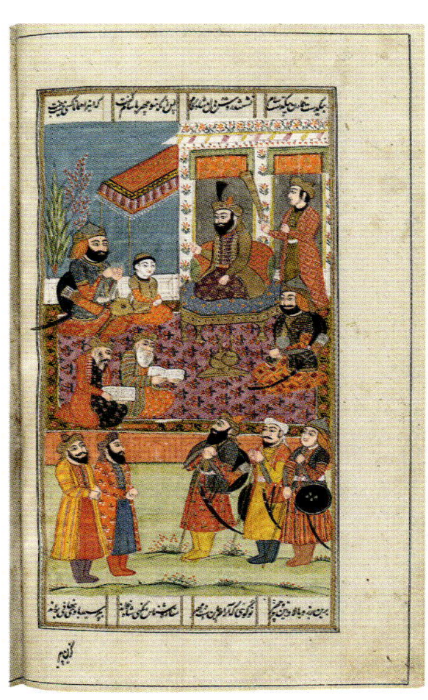
Ca 2017-1/16 (p. 76)

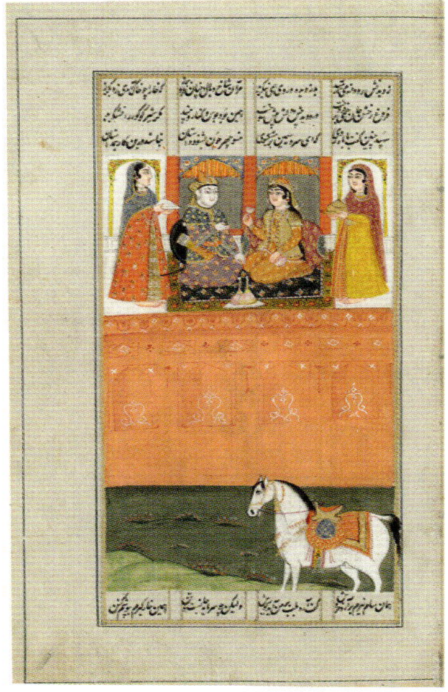
Ca 2017-1/17 (p. 88)

Ca 2017-1/18 (p. 95)
King Mihrāb hears of his daughter Rūdāba's folly

Ca 2017-1/19 (p. 118)
The birth of Rustam and the advice of the Bird Sīmurgh to Zāl

Ca 2017-1/20 (p. 123)
The boy Rustam slays Zāl's white elephant with his mace

Ca 2017-1/21 (p. 126)
Rustam takes revenge for his ancestors in Fort Dizhbār

Ca 2017-1/22 (p. 134)
Rustam fights Tuvurg

Ca 2017-1/23 (p. 143)
Rustam fights a dragon

Ca 2017-1/24(p. 170)
Zāl captures wild horses for Rustam; Rustam lassoes Rakhsh

Ca 2017-1/25 (p. 174)
The Great King Kay Qūbād I at court

Ca 2017-1/26 (p. 176)
Rustam lifts King Afrāsiyāb of Turan by the belt

Ca 2017-1/27 (p. 186)
An army of Dīvs capture Kay Kāvūs and his retinue

Ca 2017-1/28 (p. 189)
Rustam's first labour: His horse Rakhsh slays a lion

Ca 2017-1/29 (p. 193)
Rustam's third labour: He and his horse slay a dragon

Ca 2017-1/30 (p. 195)
Rustam's fourth labour: He cleaves a witch in half

Ca 2017-1/31 (p. 197)
Rustam's fifth labour: The capture of the Demon Aulad

Ca 2017-1/32 (p. 199)
Rustam's sixth labour: He slays the Dīv Arzhang

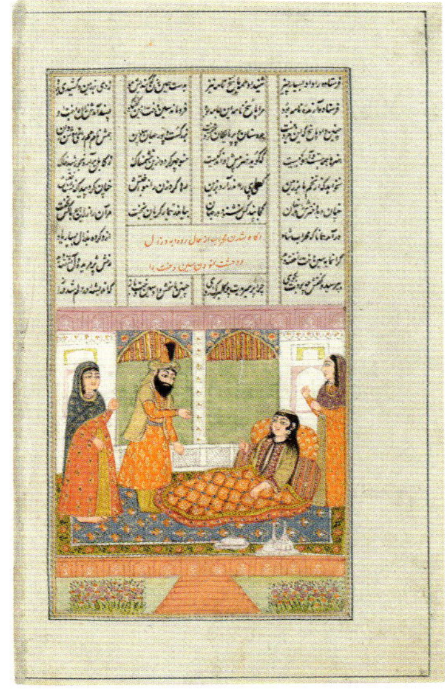

Ca 2017-1/18 (p. 95)

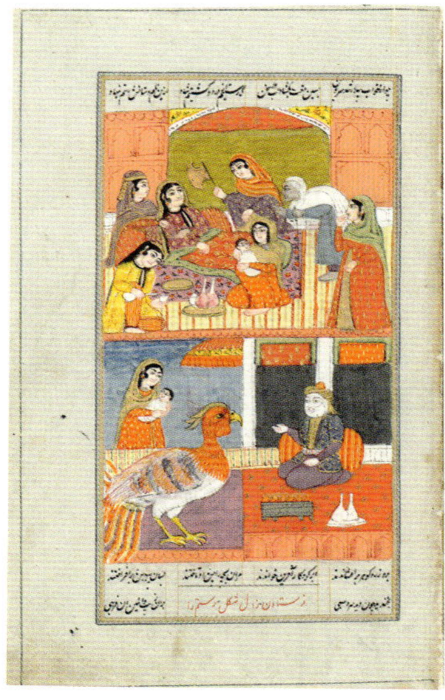

Ca 2017-1/19 (p. 118)

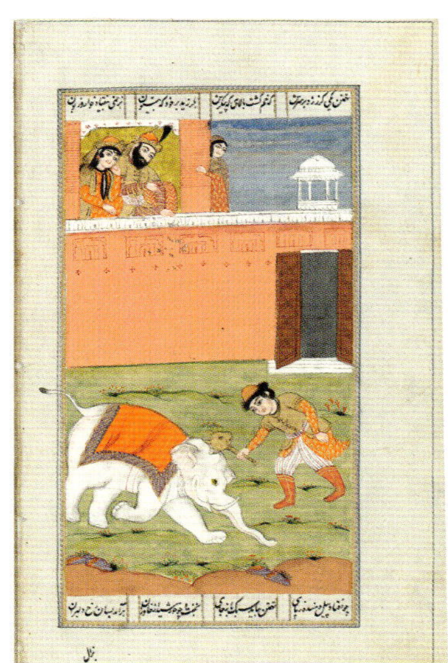

Ca 2017-1/20 (p. 123)

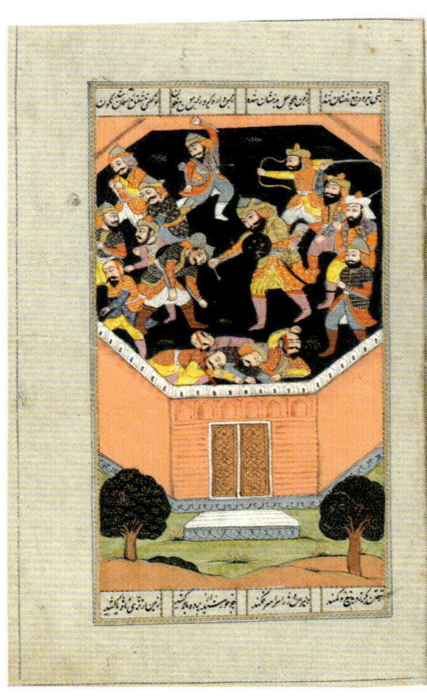

Ca 2017-1/21 (p. 126)

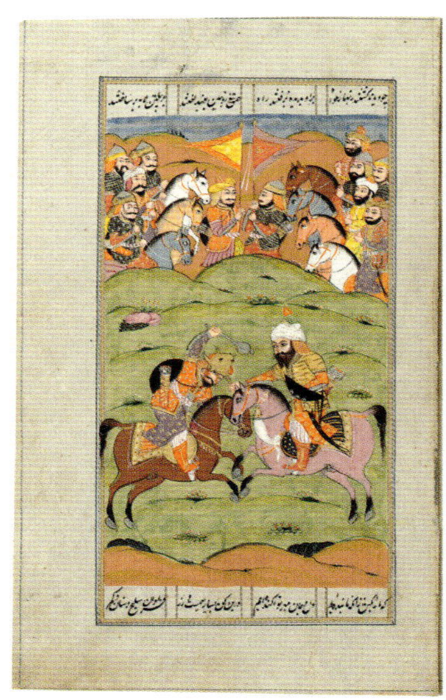

Ca 2017-1/22 (p. 134)

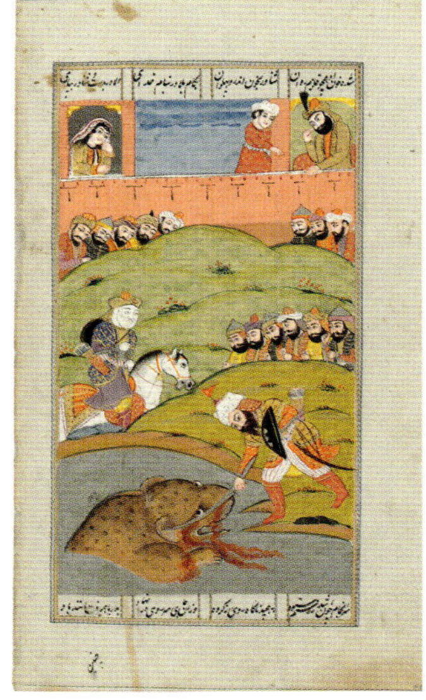

Ca 2017-1/23 (p. 143)

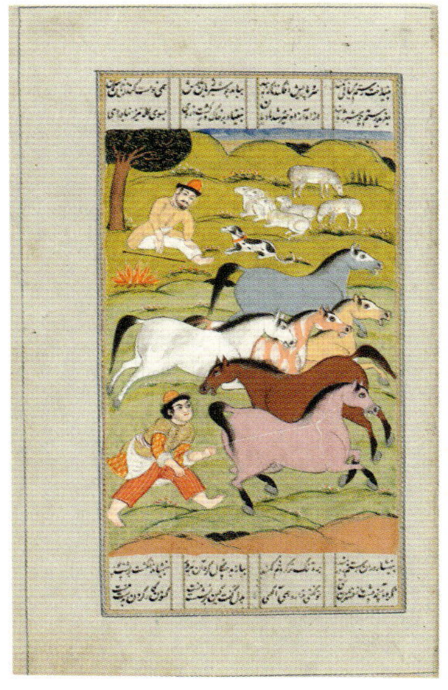
Ca 2017-1/24(p. 170)

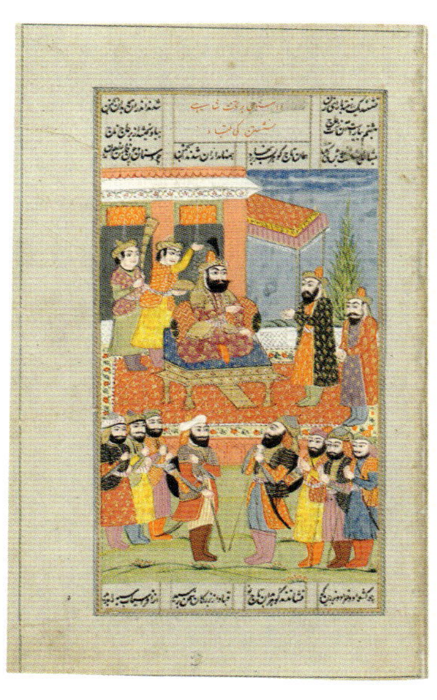
Ca 2017-1/25 (p. 174)

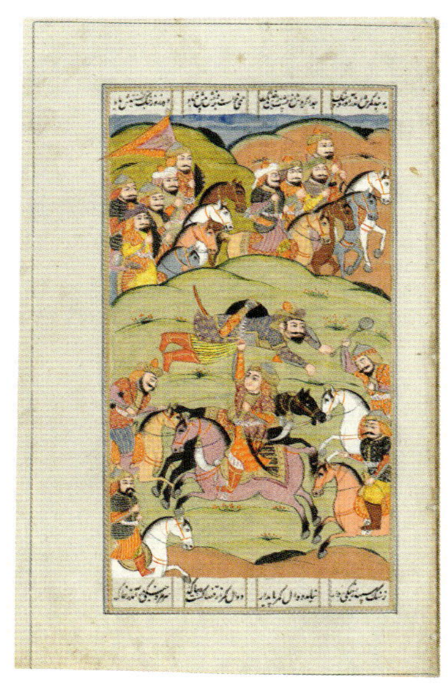
Ca 2017-1/26 (p. 176)

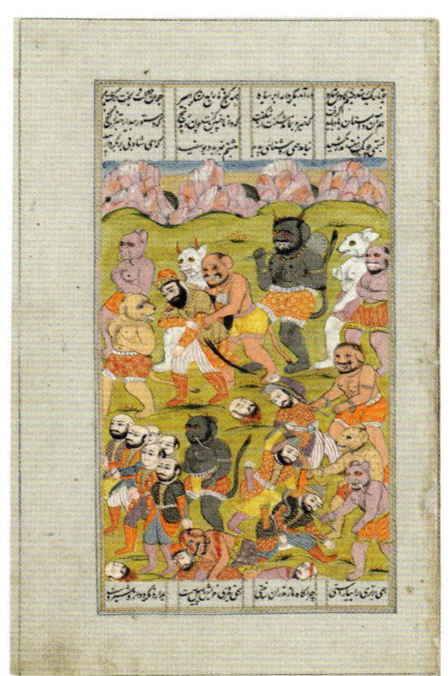
Ca 2017-1/27 (p. 186)

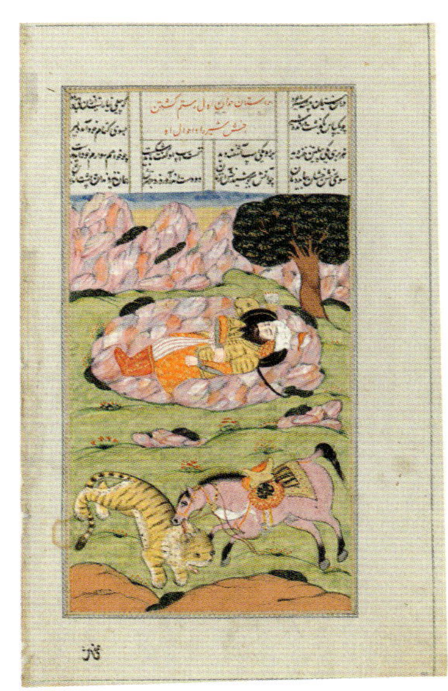
Ca 2017-1/28 (p. 189)

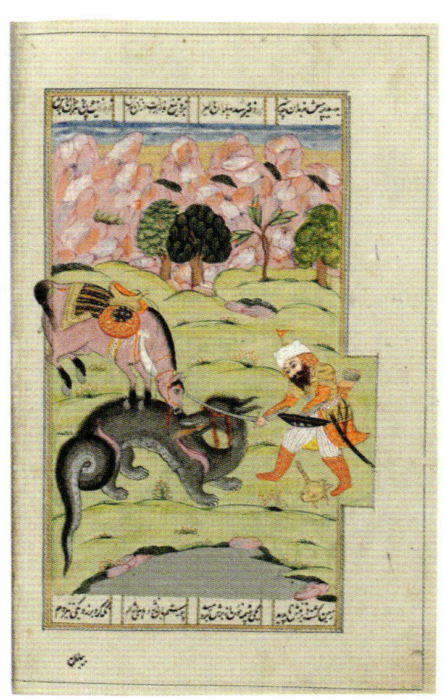
Ca 2017-1/29 (p. 193)

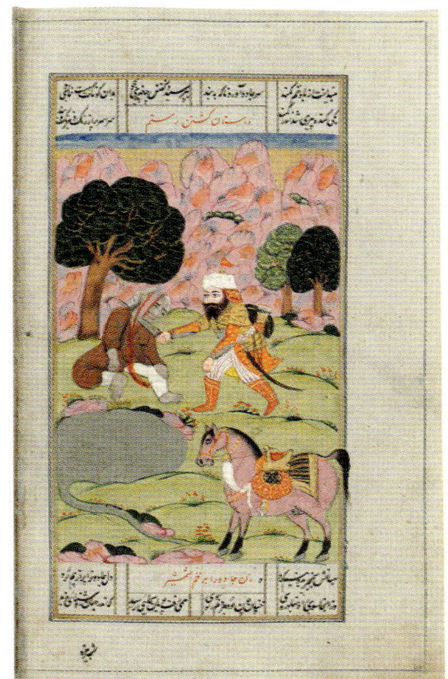
Ca 2017-1/30 (p. 195)

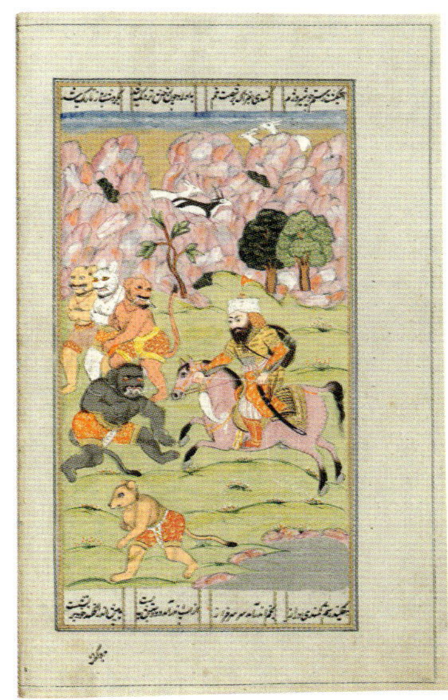
Ca 2017-1/31 (p. 197)

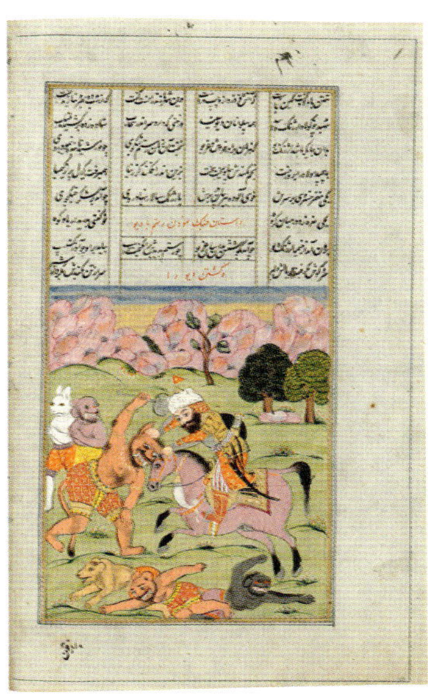
Ca 2017-1/32 (p. 199)

Ca 2017-1/33 (p. 202)
Rustam's seventh labour: He kills the White Dīv in his cave

Ca 2017-1/34 (p. 210)
Rustam travels to Māzandarān bringing the Dīv King to Kay Kāvūs for trial

Ca 2017-1/35 (p. 223)
Kay Kāvūs tries to ascend to the sky

Ca 2017-1/36 (p. 232)
Tahmīna visits Rustam at night

Ca 2017-1/37 (p. 246)
Rustam in council with the Great King Kay Kāvūs

Ca 2017-1/38 (p. 253)
On the second day Suhrāb gains the upper hand over Rustam

Ca 2017-1/39 (p. 256)
On the third day Rustam kills Suhrāb and recognizes him as his son

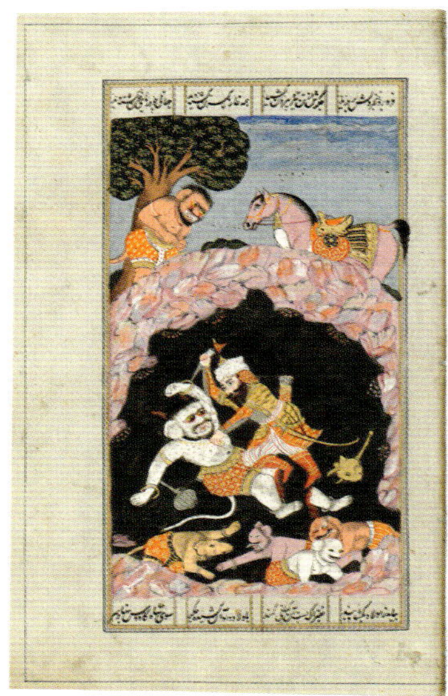

Ca 2017-1/33 (p. 202)

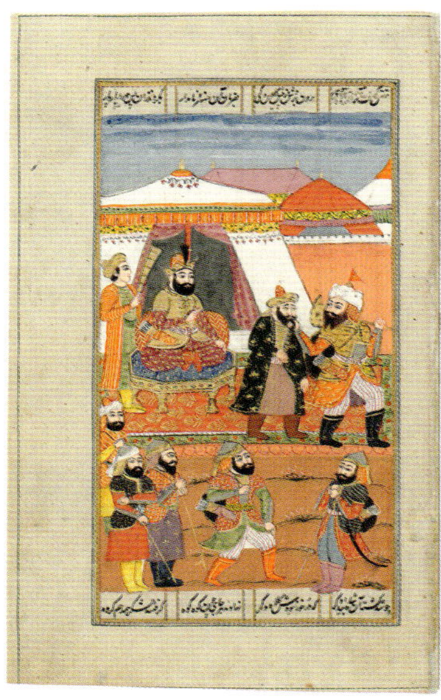

Ca 2017-1/34 (p. 210)

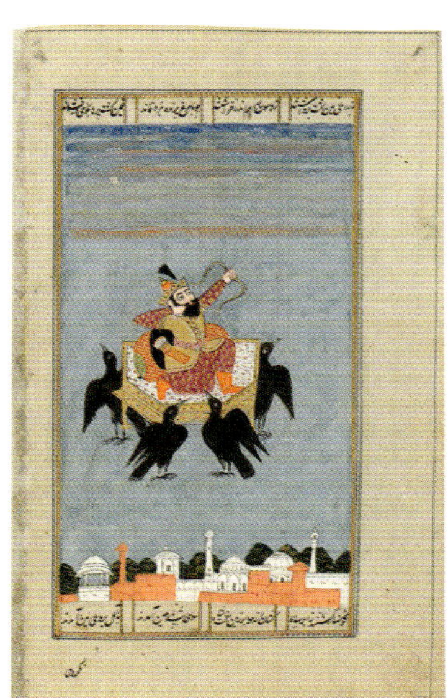

Ca 2017-1/35 (p. 223)

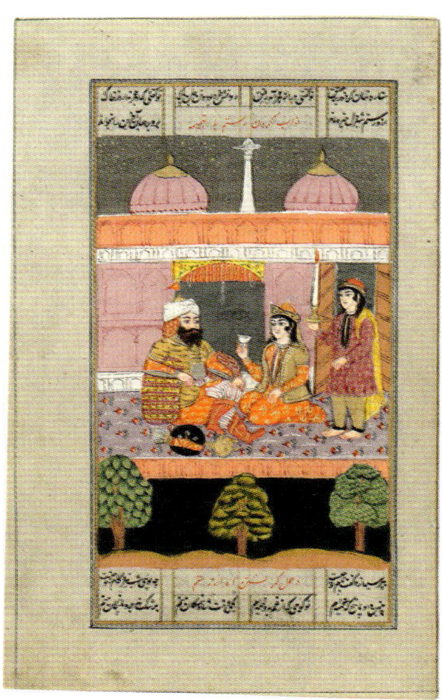

Ca 2017-1/36 (p. 232)

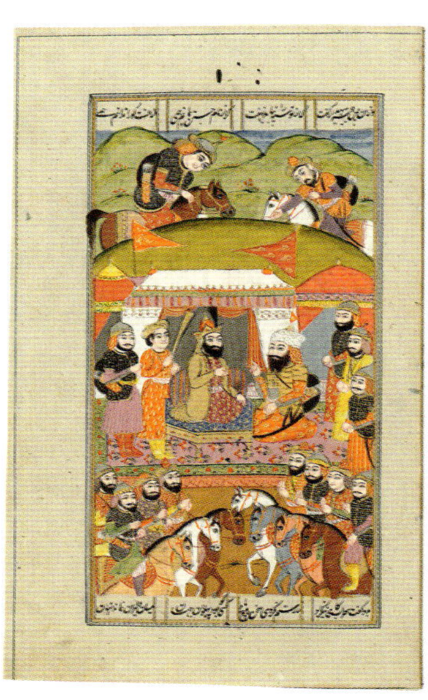

Ca 2017-1/37 (p. 246)

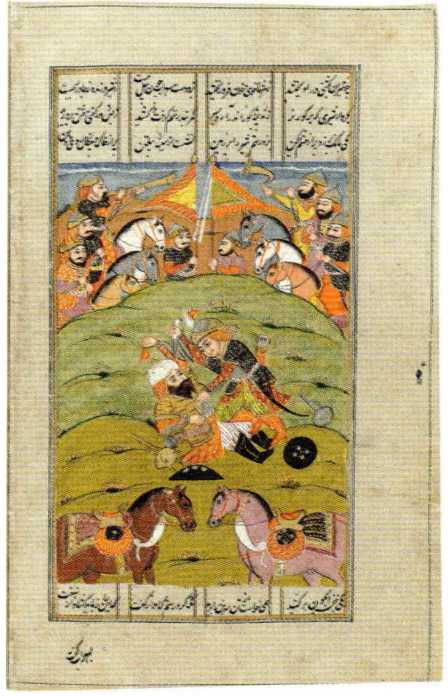

Ca 2017-1/38 (p. 253)

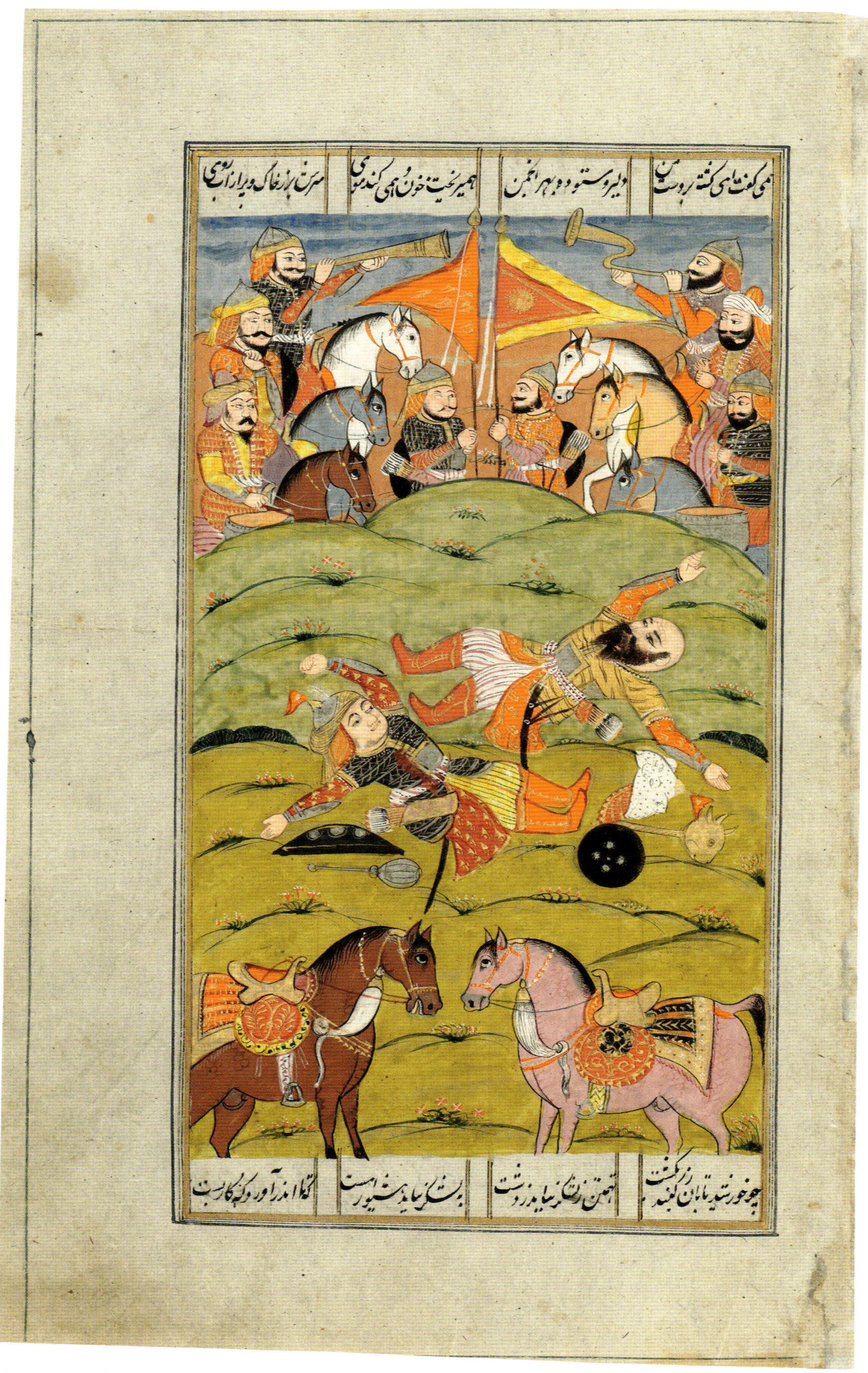

Ca 2017-1/39 (p. 256)

Ca 2017-1/40 (p. 271)
Meeting of Sudābeh and Siyāvush

Ca 2017-1/41 (p. 275)
The fire ordeal of Siyāvush

Ca 2017-1/42 (p. 284)
Siyāvush and Garsīvaz

Ca 2017-1/43 (p. 298)
Afrāsiyāb and Siyāvush in the hunting field

Ca 2017-1/44 (p. 308)
Siyāvush marries Farīgīs, the daughter of Afrāsiyāb

Ca 2017-1/45 (p. 322)
Guruy and Damor execute the innocent Siyāvush

Ca 2017-1/46 (p. 333)
Surkha is condemned by Rustam and executed by Zavāra to avenge Siyāvush

Ca 2017-1/47 (p. 340)
Rustam brings loot from Turan to Zabulistan

Ca 2017-1/48 (p. 343)
Pūlādvand lifts the Iranian heroes Gīv and Tūs out of their saddles

Ca 2017-1/49 (p. 352)
Gīv visits a temple

Ca 2017-1/50 (p. 361)
Gīv captures the hero Pīrān from Turan

Ca 2017-1/51 (p. 367)
Kay Khusrau and Rustam welcomed by Kay Kāvūs

Ca 2017-1/52 (p. 397)
Bīzhan fights against Gīv

Ca 2017-1/53 (p. 420)
Tūs and Rustam prepare the Iranian army for the battle with the Turanians

Ca 2017-1/54 (p. 435)
Pīrān meets the Khāqān of China

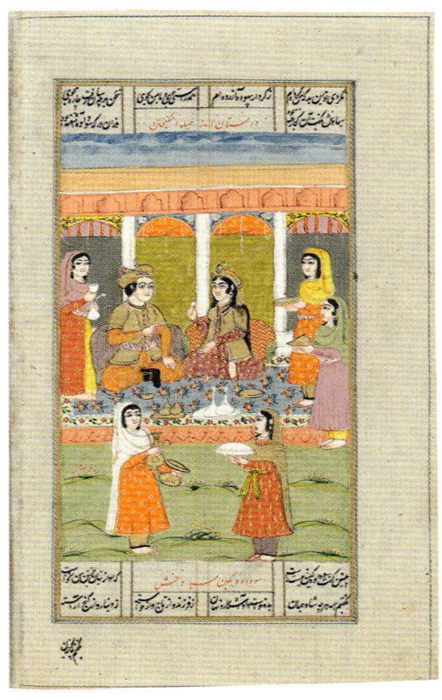
Ca 2017-1/40 (p. 271)

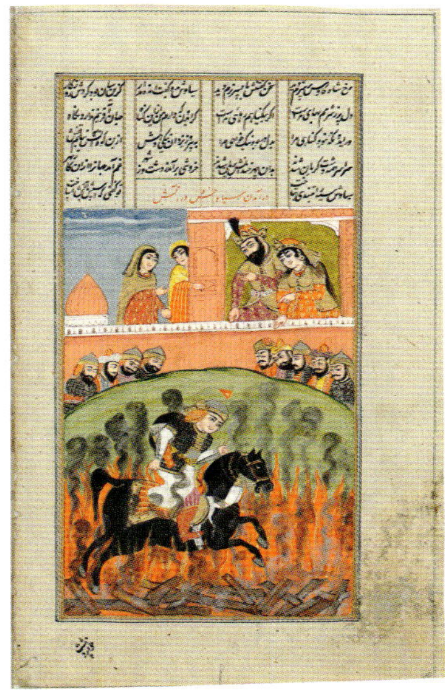
Ca 2017-1/41 (p. 275)

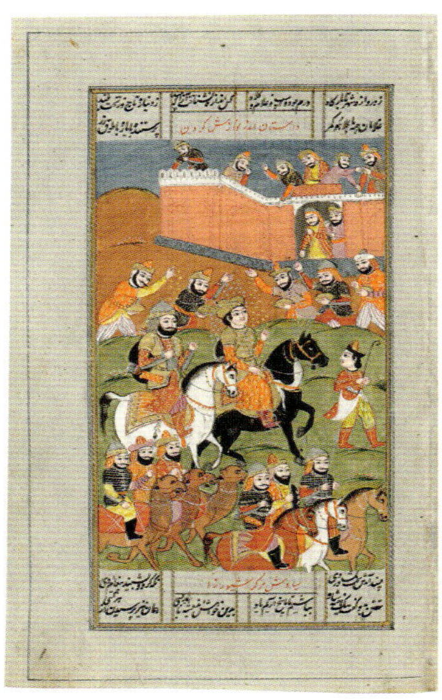
Ca 2017-1/42 (p. 284)

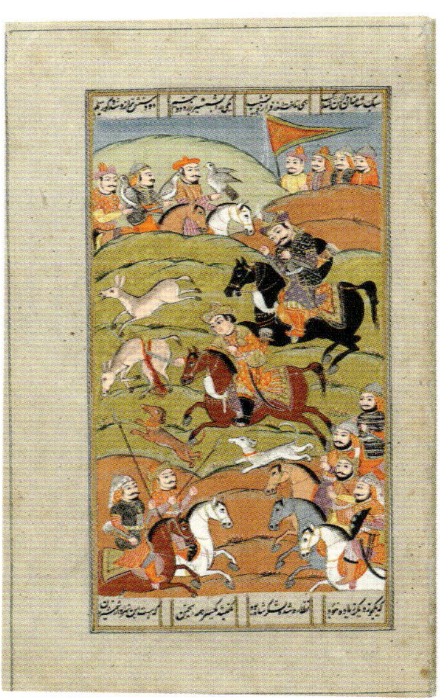
Ca 2017-1/43 (p. 298)

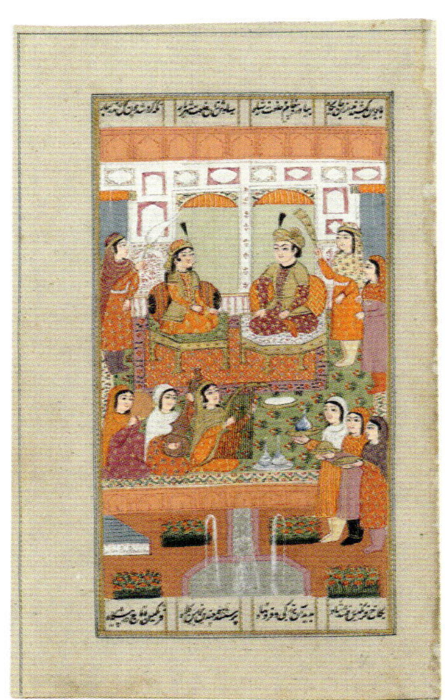
Ca 2017-1/44 (p. 308)

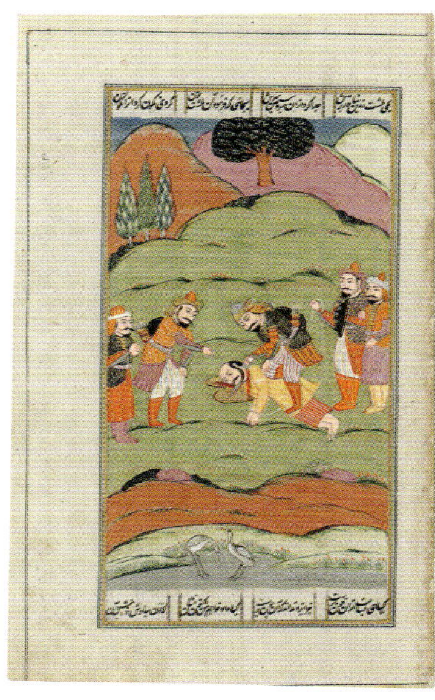
Ca 2017-1/45 (p. 322)

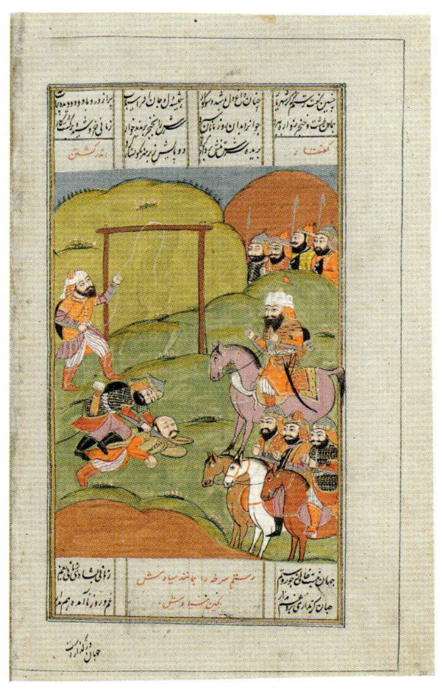

Ca 2017-1/46 (p. 333)

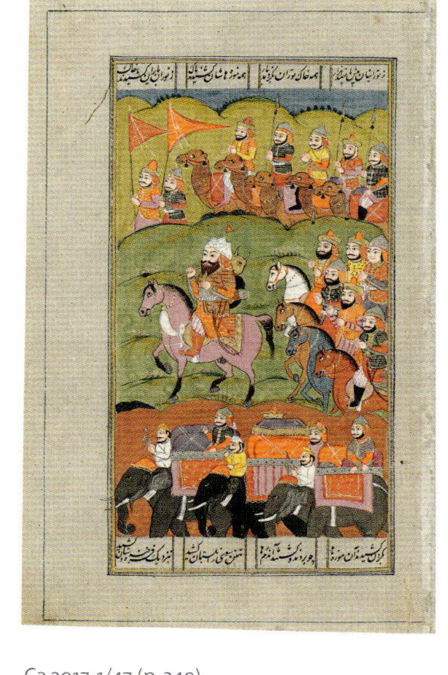

Ca 2017-1/47 (p. 340)

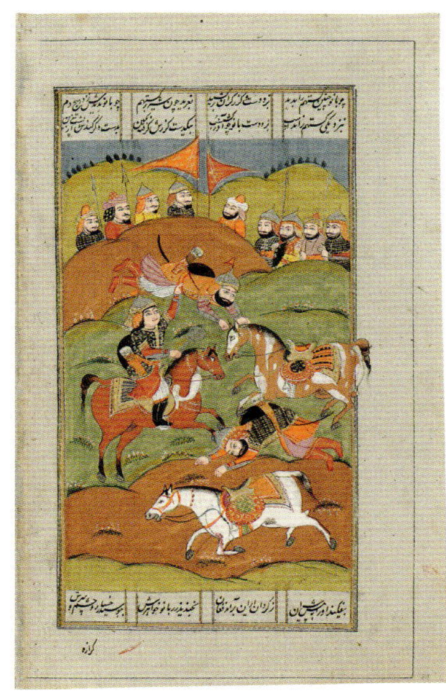

Ca 2017-1/48 (p. 343)

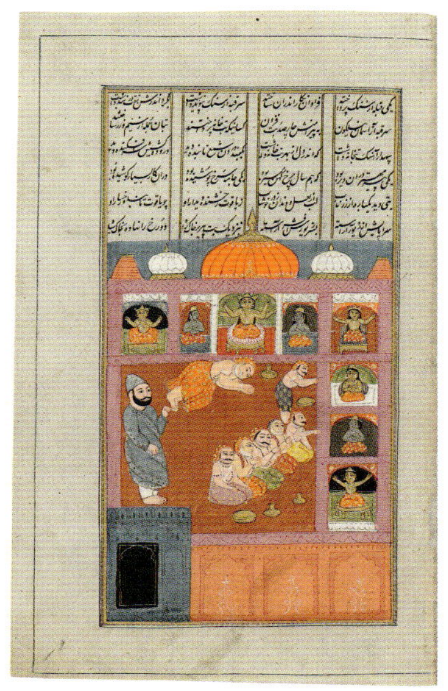

Ca 2017-1/49 (p. 352)

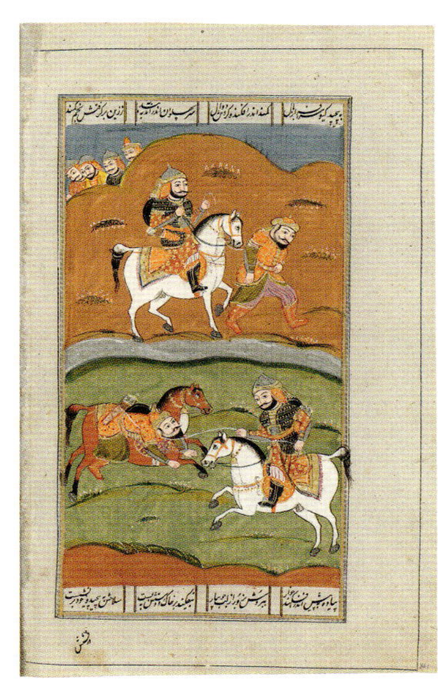

Ca 2017-1/50 (p. 361)

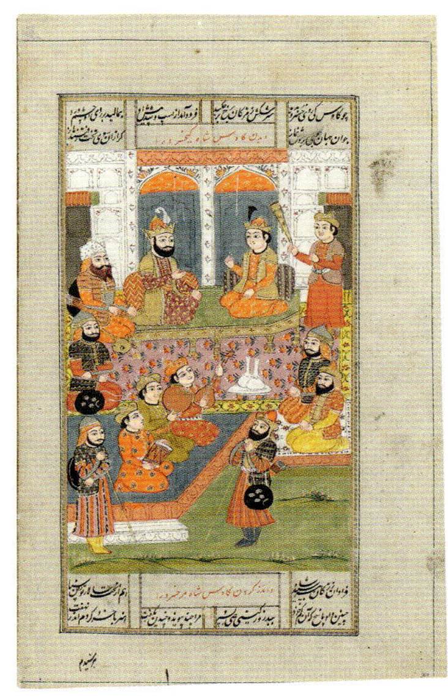

Ca 2017-1/51 (p. 367)

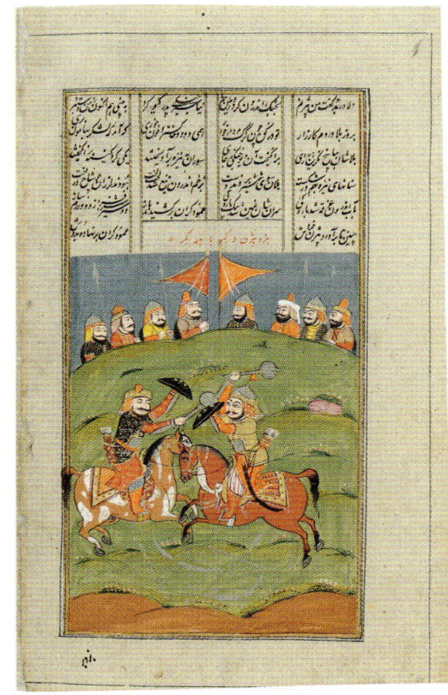

Ca 2017-1/52 (p. 397)

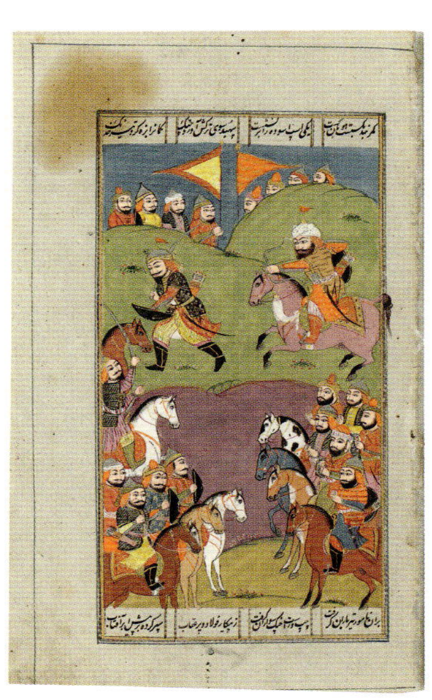

Ca 2017-1/53 (p. 420)

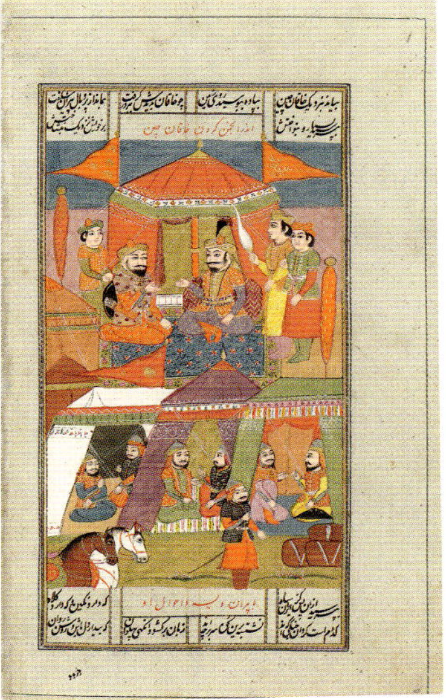

Ca 2017-1/54 (p. 435)

Ca 2017-1/55 (p. 450)
Rustam unhorses Kāmūs from Kushān in battle

Ca 2017-1/56 (p. 469)
In combat Rustam pulls the Khāqān of China from his elephant with a rope

Ca 2017-1/57 (p. 485)
Rustam defeats Pūlādvand

Ca 2017-1/58 (p. 490)
Dīv Akvān hurls Rustam into the sea

Ca 2017-1/59 (p. 501)
Bīzhan and Manīzha

Ca 2017-1/60 (p. 508)
Manīzha is tied up and Bīzhan is captured in a pit

Ca 2017-1/61 (p. 528)
Rustam pulls Bīzhan out of the pit

Ca 2017-1/62 (p. 546)
Tūs and Farīburz set out with the Iranian army against Turan

Ca 2017-1/63 (p. 557)
Rustam kills Barzū in duel

Ca 2017-1/64 (p. 634)
Page with ornamental chapter head (ʻunvān)

Ca 2017-1/65 (p. 654)
Bīzhan stabs Humān in single combat

Ca 2017-1/66 (p. 673)
Battle of Gīv against Lahhāk and Farshīdvard

Ca 2017-1/67 (p. 685)
The eleventh combat: Gūdarz versus Pīrān

Ca 2017-1/68 (p. 696)
Gustaham slays Lahhāk and Farshīdvard

Ca 2017-1/69 (p. 717)
Afrāsiyāb learns of the killing of Humān and Pīrān and the defeat of the Turanians

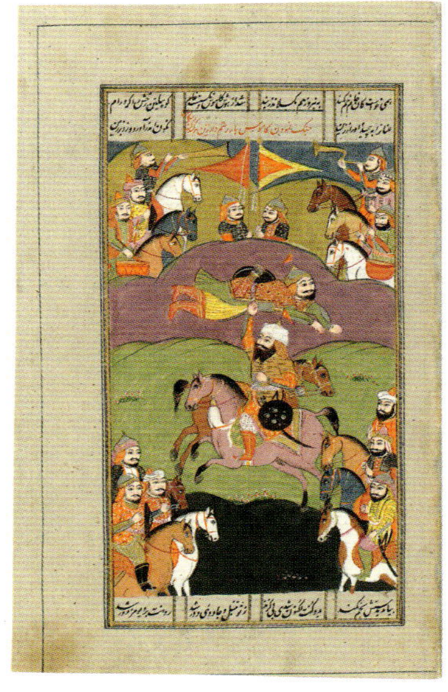
Ca 2017-1/55 (p. 450)

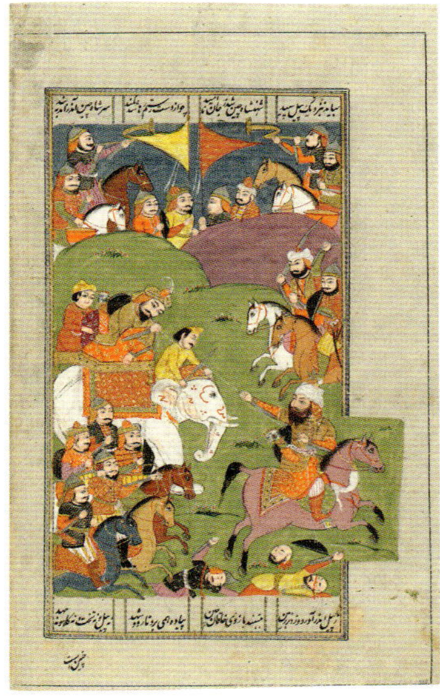
Ca 2017-1/56 (p. 469)

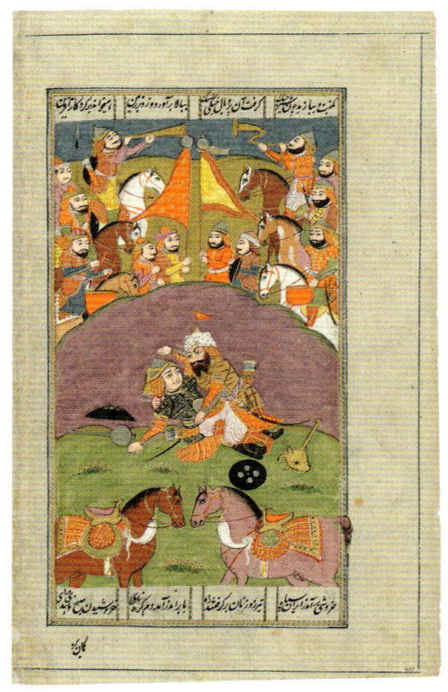
Ca 2017-1/57 (p. 485)

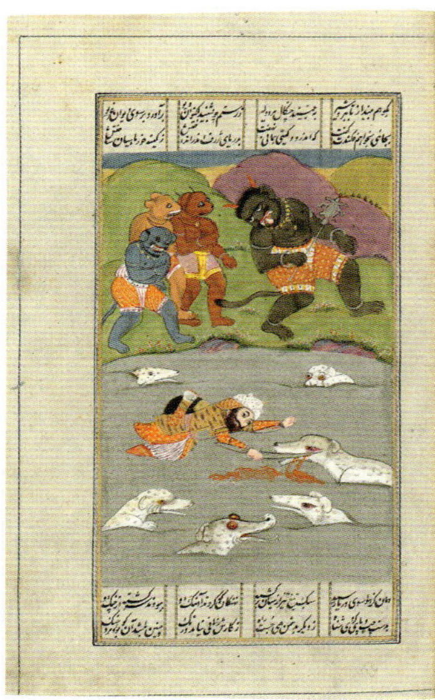
Ca 2017-1/58 (p. 490)

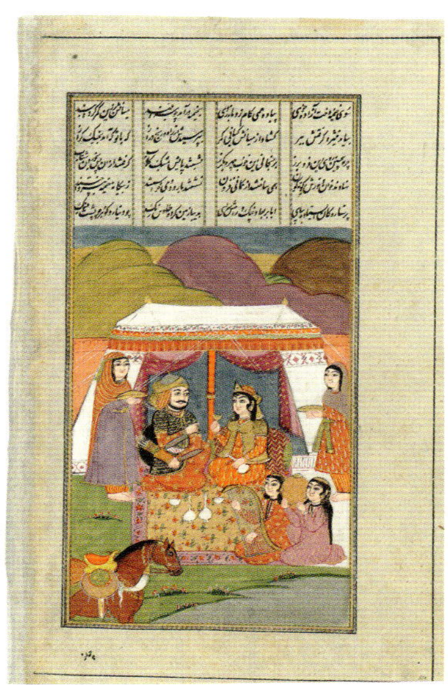
Ca 2017-1/59 (p. 501)

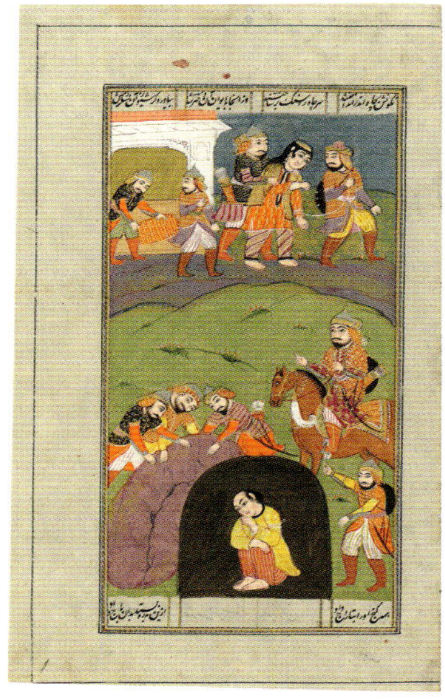
Ca 2017-1/60 (p. 508)

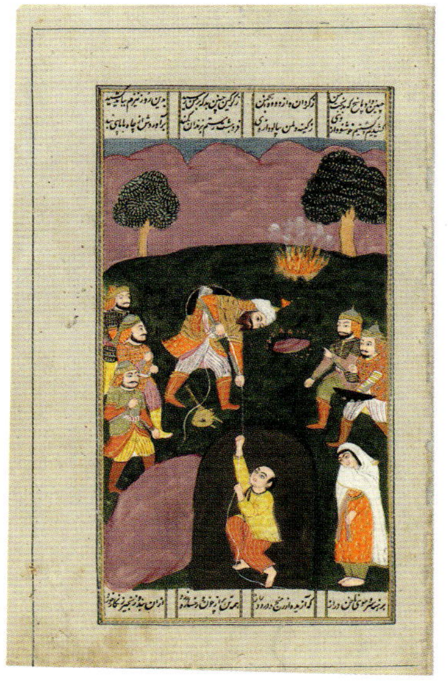
Ca 2017-1/61 (p. 528)

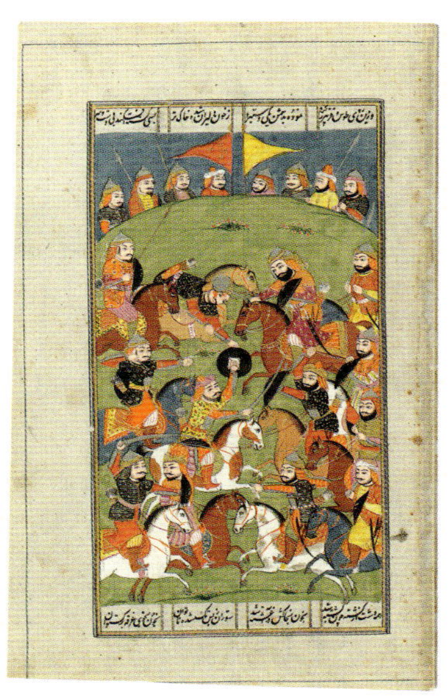
Ca 2017-1/62 (p. 546)

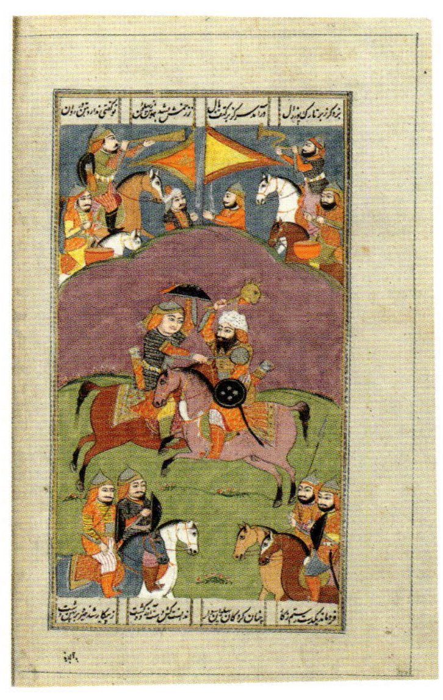
Ca 2017-1/63 (p. 557)

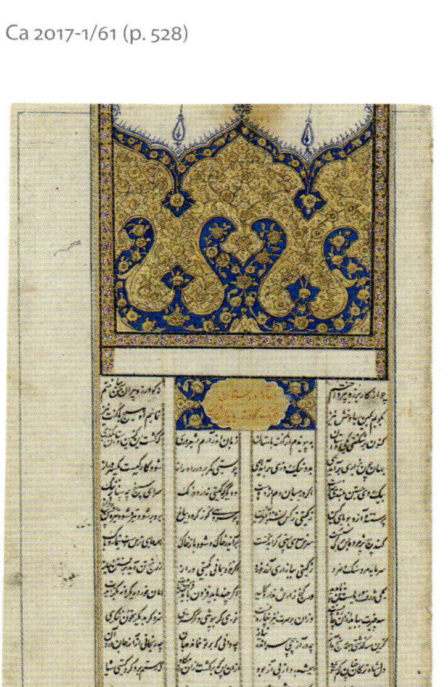
Ca 2017-1/64 (p. 634)

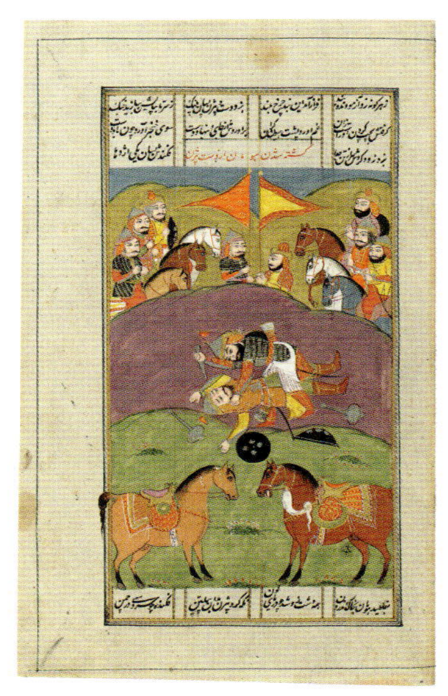
Ca 2017-1/65 (p. 654)

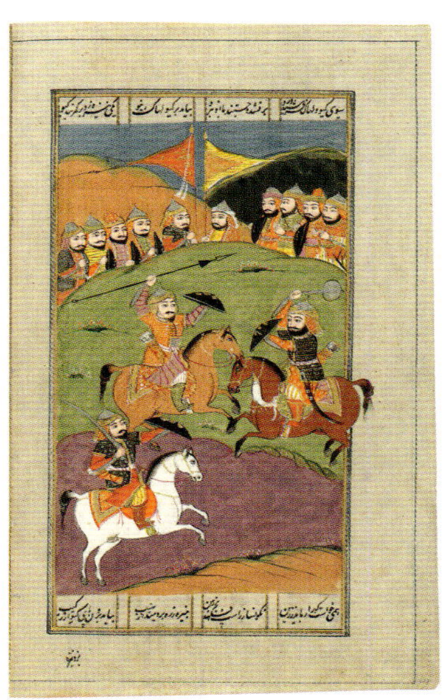
Ca 2017-1/66 (p. 673)

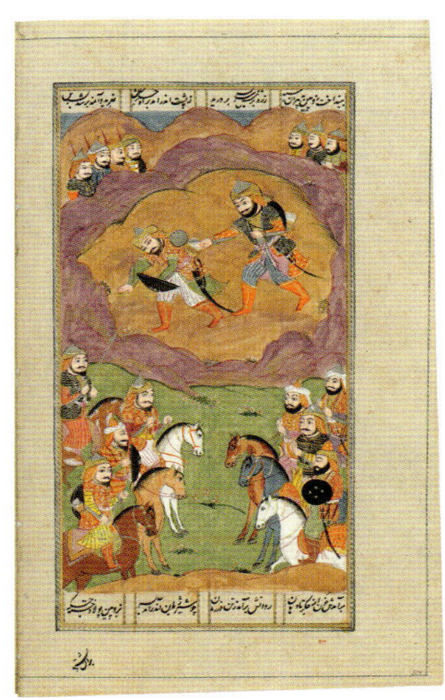
Ca 2017-1/67 (p. 685)

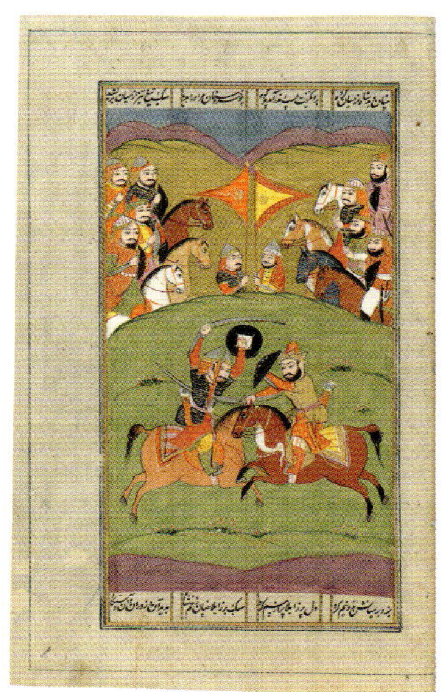
Ca 2017-1/68 (p. 696)

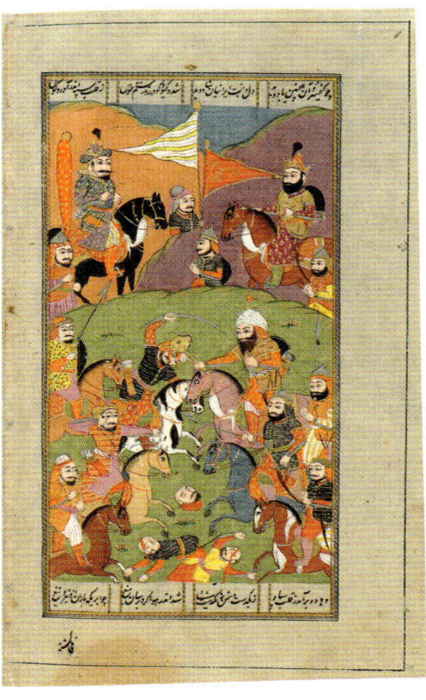
Ca 2017-1/69 (p. 717)

Ca 2017-1/70 (p. 735)
Kay Khusrau slays Afrāsiyāb in revenge of his father Siyāvush

Ca 2017-1/71 (p. 747)
Kay Khusrau and Gūdarz

Ca 2017-1/72 (p. 759)
Page with ornamental chapter head ('unvān), middle of the epic

Ca 2017-1/73 (p. 803)
The death of Luhrāsp by Kuhram in a battle against the forces of Arjāsp

Ca 2017-1/74 (p. 819)
Isfandiyār's first labour: He slays two wolves

Ca 2017-1/75 (p. 821)
Isfandiyār's second labour: He slays the lions

Ca 2017-1/76 (p. 823)
Isfandiyār's third labour: He slays the dragon

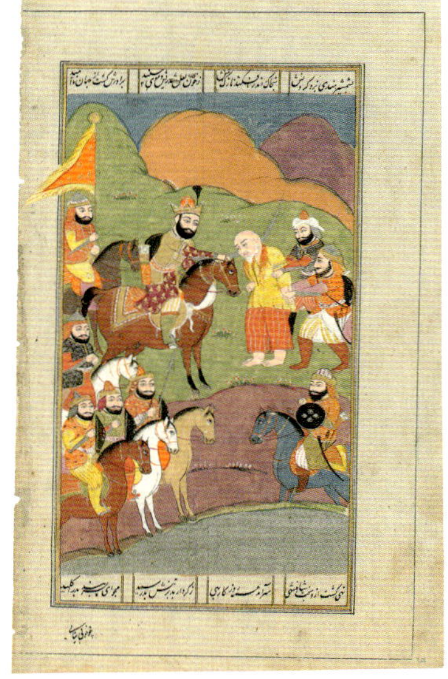
Ca 2017-1/70 (p. 735)

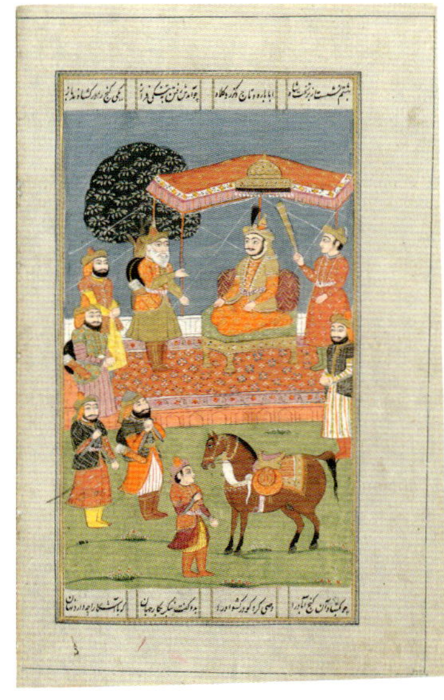
Ca 2017-1/71 (p. 747)

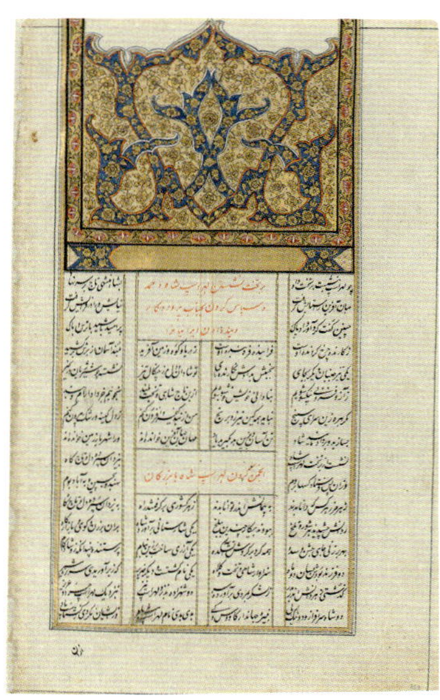
Ca 2017-1/72 (p. 759)

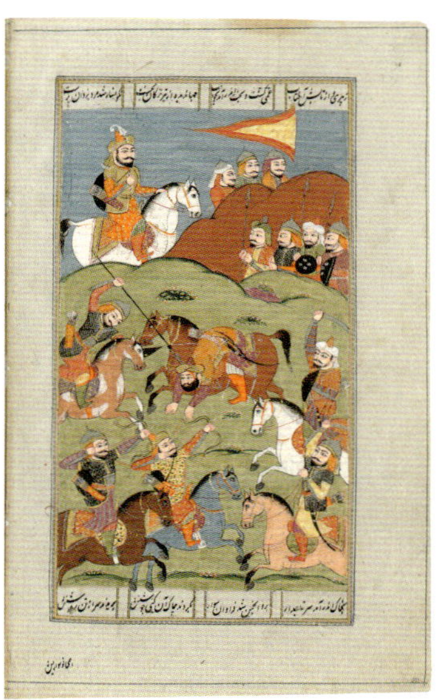
Ca 2017-1/73 (p. 803)

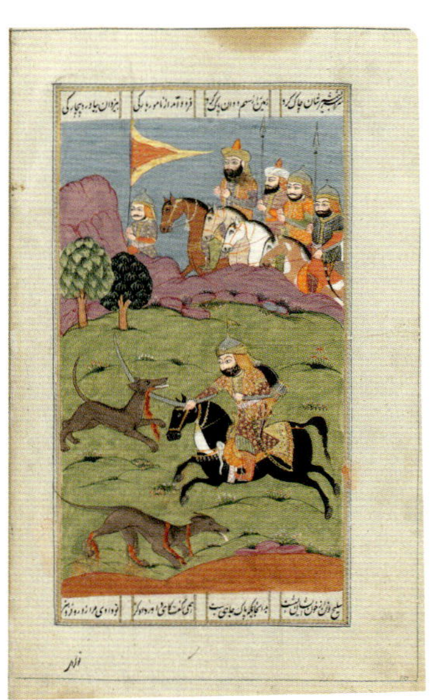
Ca 2017-1/74 (p. 819)

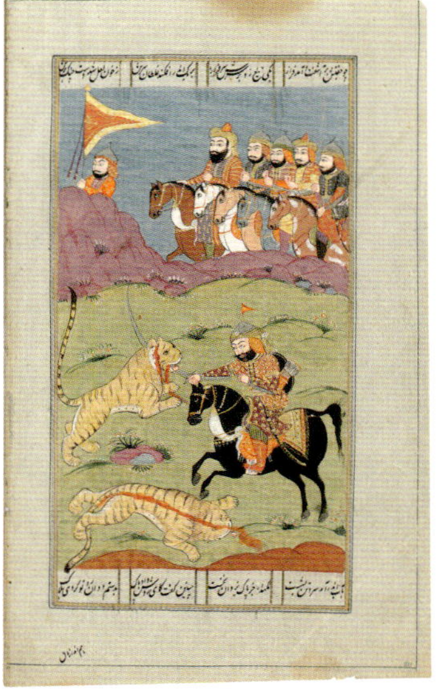
Ca 2017-1/75 (p. 821)

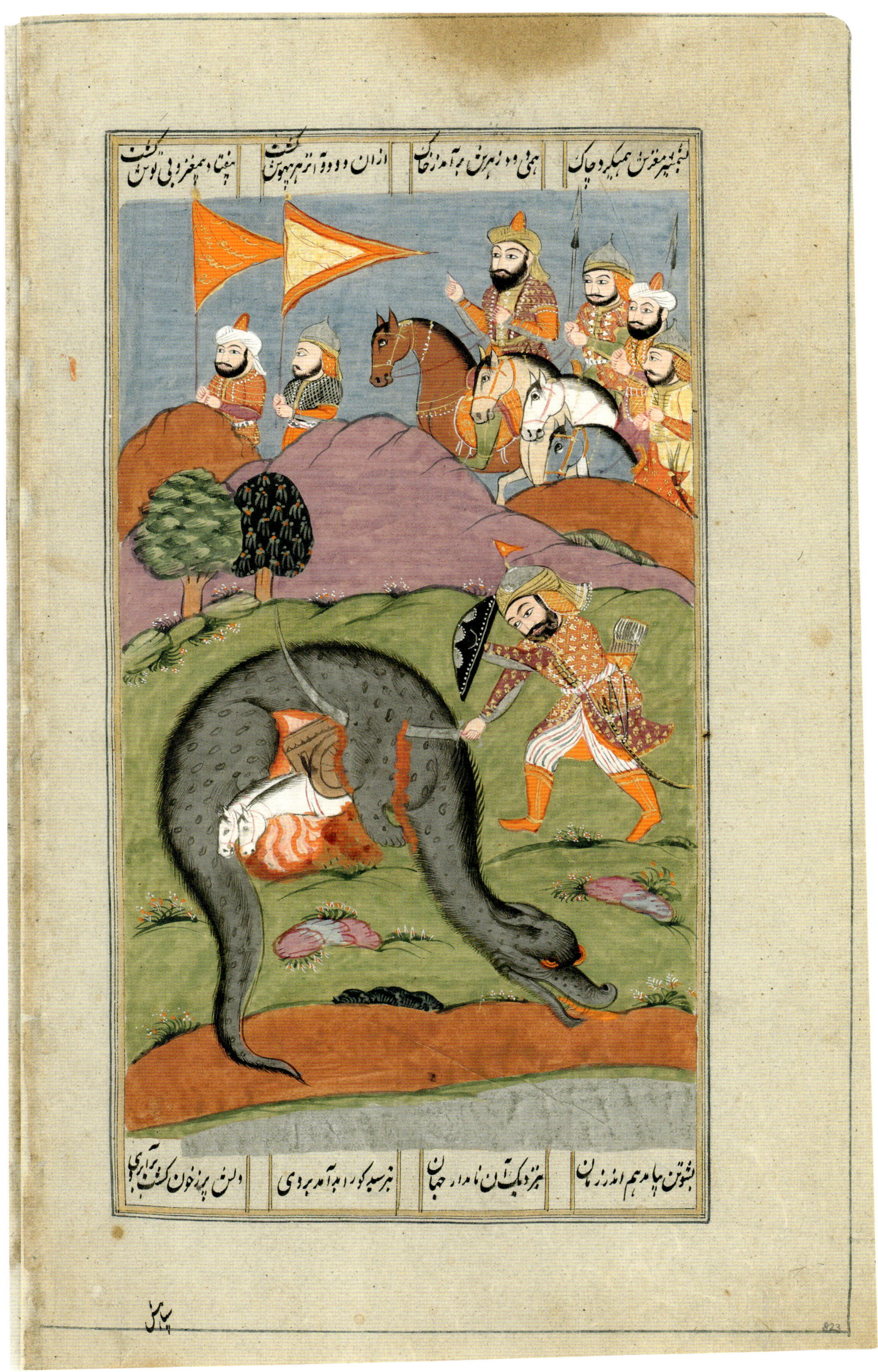

Ca 2017-1/76 (p. 823)

Ca 2017-1/77 (p. 826)
Isfandiyār's fourth labour:
He slays the sorceress

Ca 2017-1/78 (p. 832)
Prayer of the Irānians before
their campaign against Turan

Ca 2017-1/79 (p. 845)
Isfandiyār sets Turan on fire and
executes Kohram and Andarīmān

Ca 2017-1/80 (p. 884)
Rustam shoots Isfandiyār in the eyes

Ca 2017-1/81 (p. 898)
Rustam avenges his own impending
death by killing his half-brother Shagād

Ca 2017-1/82 (p. 905)
The execution of Farāmarẓ by Bahman

Ca 2017-1/83 (p. 914)
Bahman's daughter enthrones (Hu)māy
by order of her father

Ca 2017-1/84 (p. 927)
Iskandar attends the dying Dārā,
King of Persia

Ca 2017-1/85 (p. 934)
Mihrān predicts Iskandar's arrival
to the Indian King Kayd(āvar)

Ca 2017-1/86 (p. 946)
Iskandar slays Kayd(āvar) and
conquers Hind (India)

Ca 2017-1/87 (p. 953)
Queen Qaydāfa recognizes Iskandar
through a portrait she had received
earlier

Ca 2017-1/88 (p. 962)
The campaign of Iskandar in Abyssinia

Ca 2017-1/89 (p. 995)
King Ardashīr's victory over Bahman

Ca 2017-1/90 (p. 1007)
Ardashīr recognizes his son Shāpūr I
during a Polo match

Ca 2017-1/91 (p. 1049)
Bahrām Gūr hunting

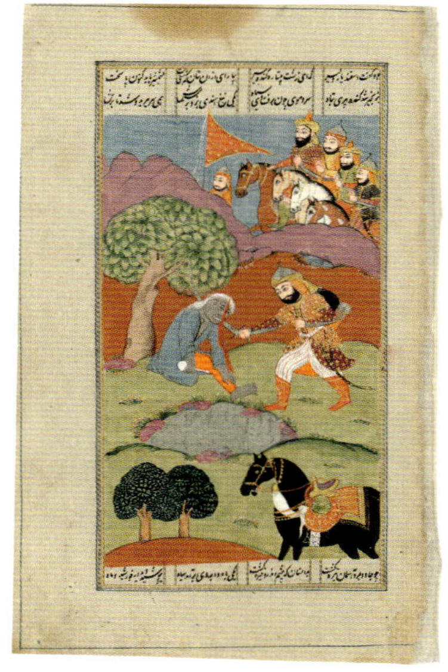

Ca 2017-1/77 (p. 826)

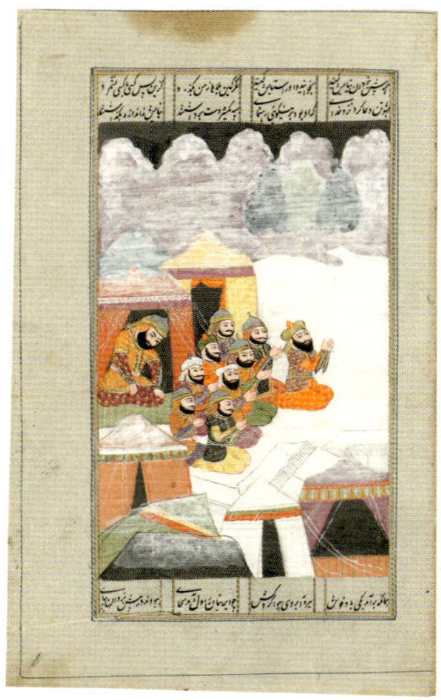

Ca 2017-1/78(p. 832)

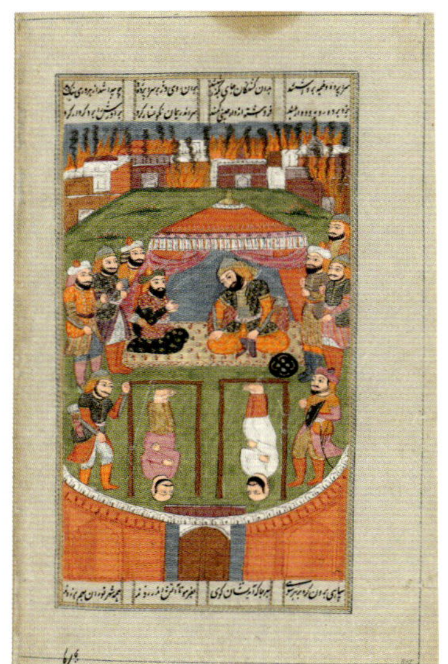

Ca 2017-1/79 (p. 845)

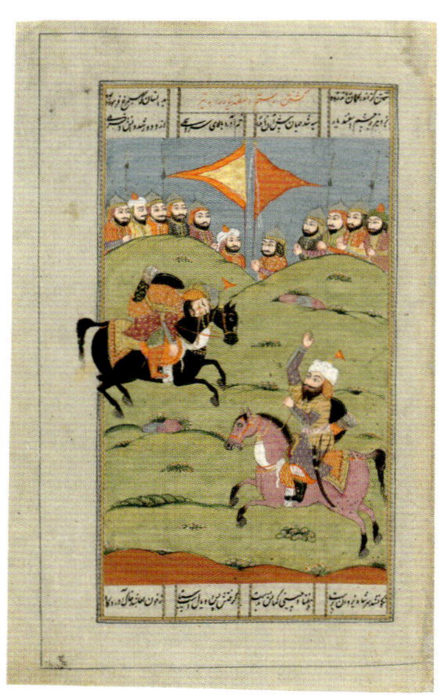

Ca 2017-1/80 (p. 884)

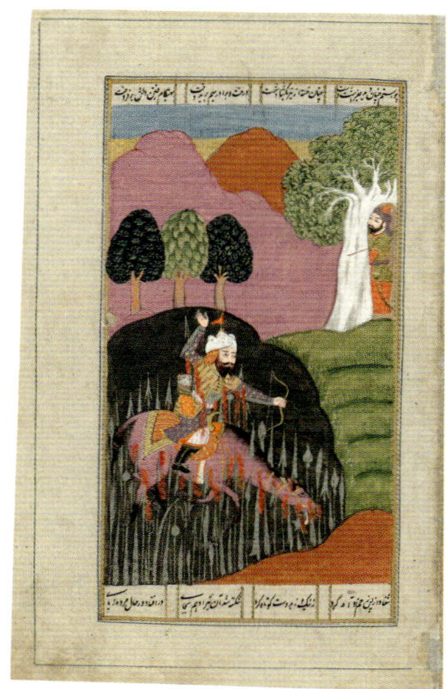

Ca 2017-1/81 (p. 898)

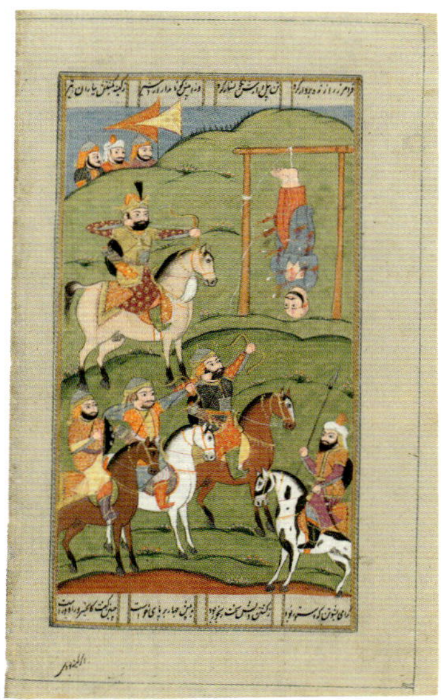

Ca 2017-1/82 (p. 905)

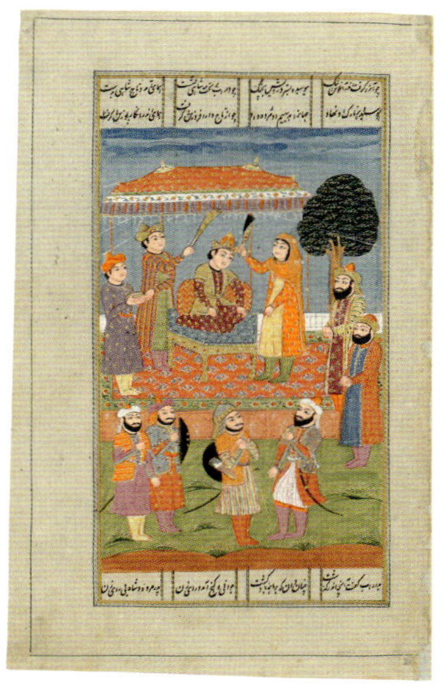
Ca 2017-1/83 (p. 914)

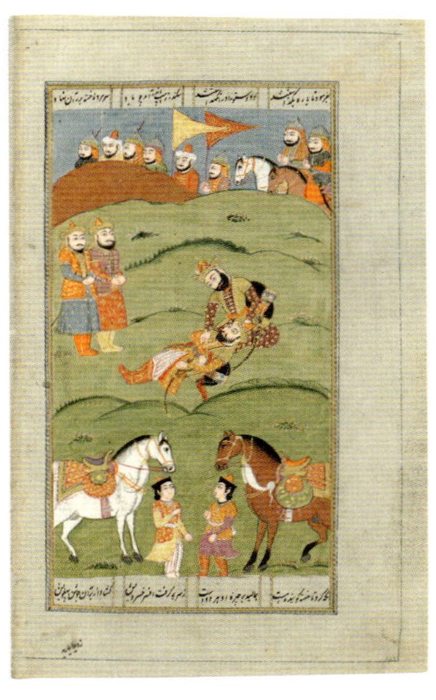
Ca 2017-1/84 (p. 927)

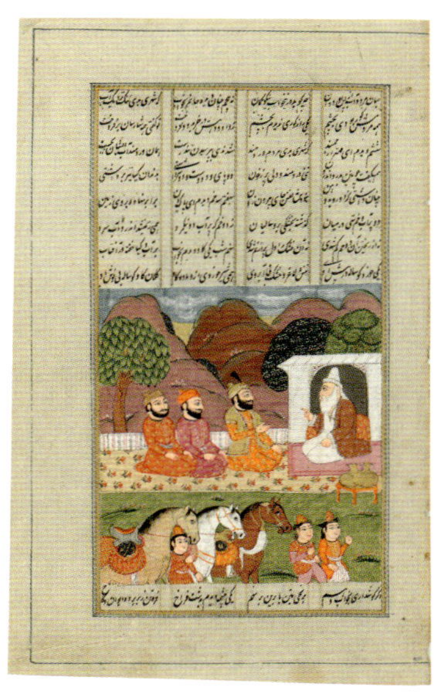
Ca 2017-1/85 (p. 934)

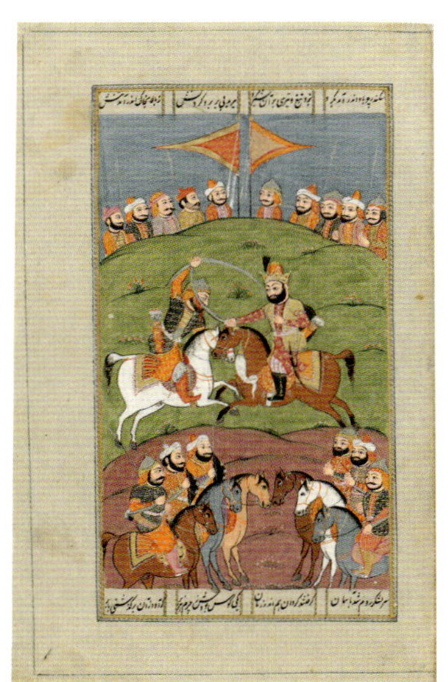
Ca 2017-1/86 (p. 946)

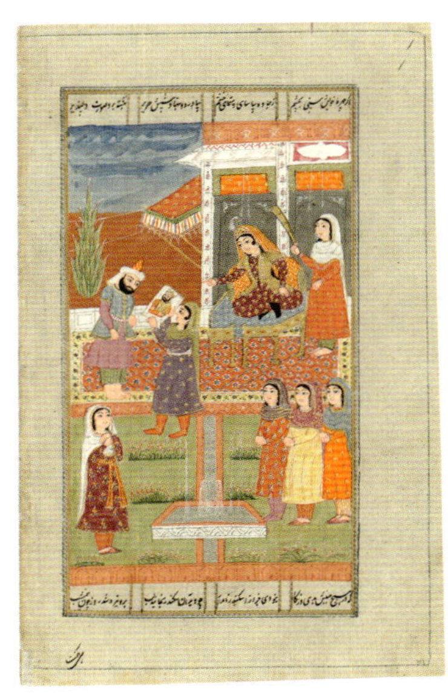
Ca 2017-1/87 (p. 953)

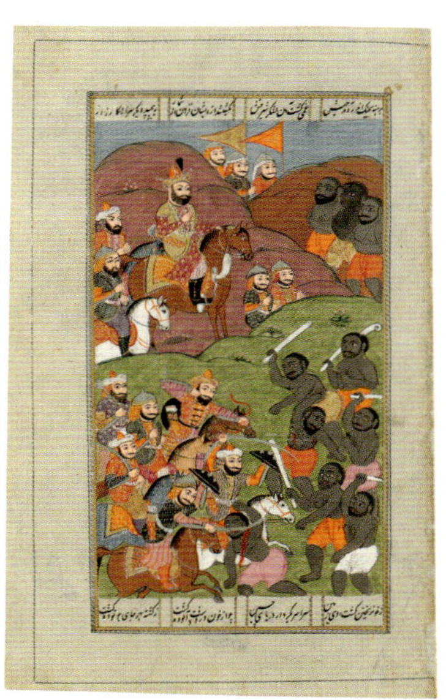
Ca 2017-1/88 (p. 962)

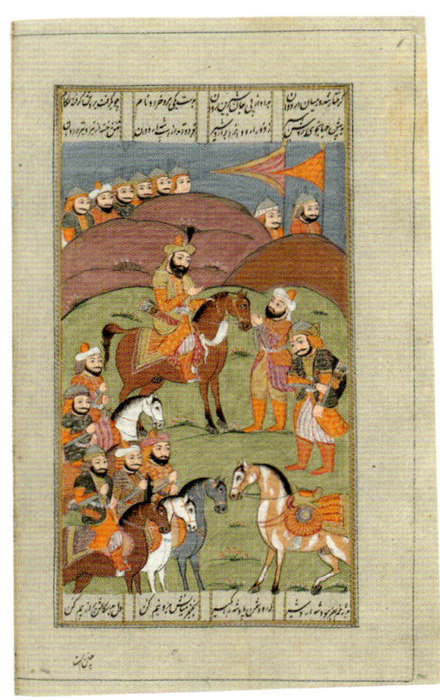
Ca 2017-1/89 (p. 995)

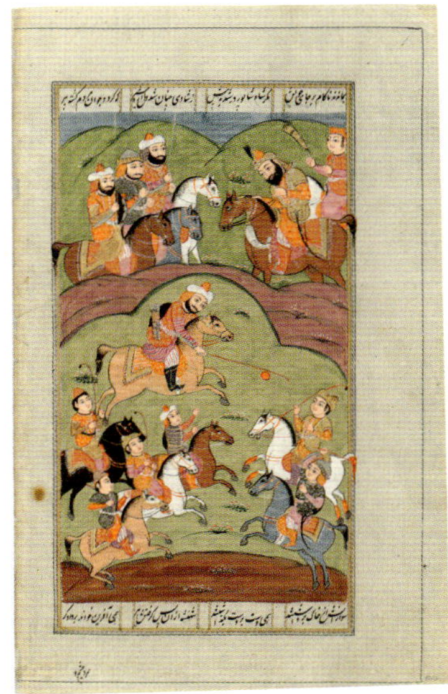
Ca 2017-1/90 (p. 1007)

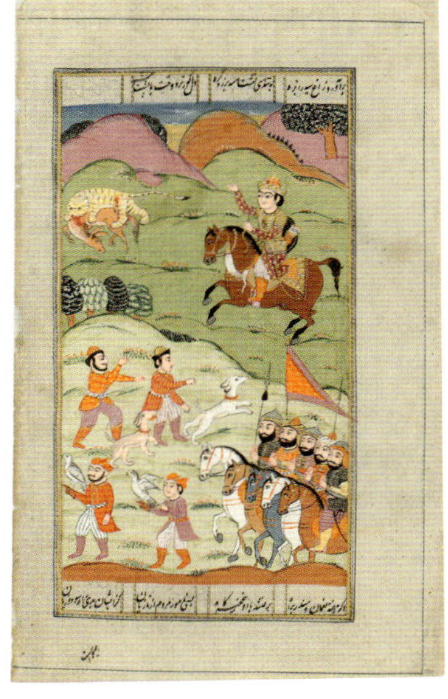
Ca 2017-1/91 (p. 1049)

Ca 2017-1/92 (p. 1082)
Bahrām Gūr kills two lions

Ca 2017-1/93 (p. 1112)
The king of India, Shangal, sends Bahrām Gūr to slay a dragon

Ca 2017-1/94 (p. 1121)
King Yazdigerd nominates his son Hurmuzd as crown prince

Ca 2017-1/95 (p. 1132)
Shāpūr II captures Sūfarāy and leads him before the Great King Qūbād I

Ca 2017-1/96 (p. 1142)
(A)nūshīrvān speaks at his accession to the throne

Ca 2017-1/97 (p. 1157)
(A)nūshīrvān defeats the Romans in a battle

Ca 2017-1/98 (p. 1203)
(Hu)māy ascends the throne instead of his brother [?]

Ca 2017-1/99 (p. 1214)
(A)nūshīrvān and the envoy of the Indian King muse upon a game of chess

Ca 2017-1/100 (p. 1265)
Battle between Bahrām Chūbīn(a)and Sāveh Shāh

Ca 2017-1/101 (p. 1323)
Envoys before Khusrau Parvīz

Ca 2017-1/102 (p. 1327)
Khusrau Parvīz's charge against the usurper Bahrām Chūbīn(a)

Ca 2017-1/103 (p. 1401)
Khusrau Parvīz arranges the murder of Bahrām Chūbīn(a)

Ca 2017-1/104 (p. 1405)
Bahrām Chūbīn(a) and his sister Gurdiya plan to slay the Khāqān's brother Tuvurg

Ca 2017-1/105 (p. 1412)
Bahrām Chūbīn(a)receives Tuvurg at court

Ca 2017-1/106 (p. 1416)
Gurdiya kills Tuvurg after she convinces him to meet her in seclusion

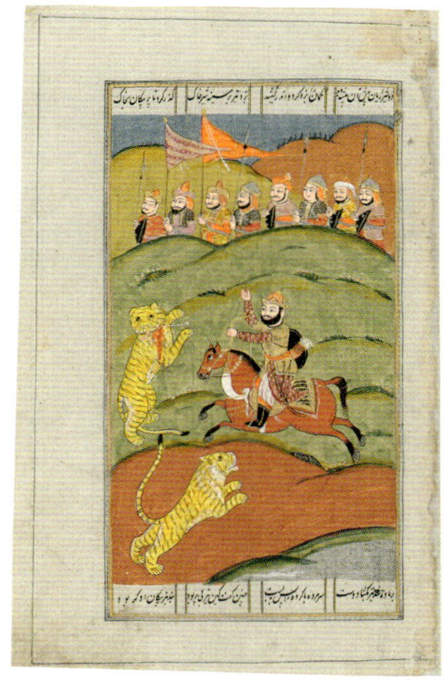
Ca 2017-1/92 (p. 1082)

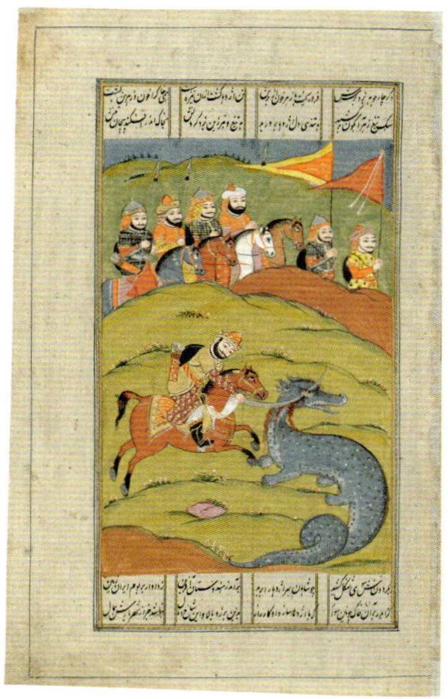
Ca 2017-1/93 (p. 1112)

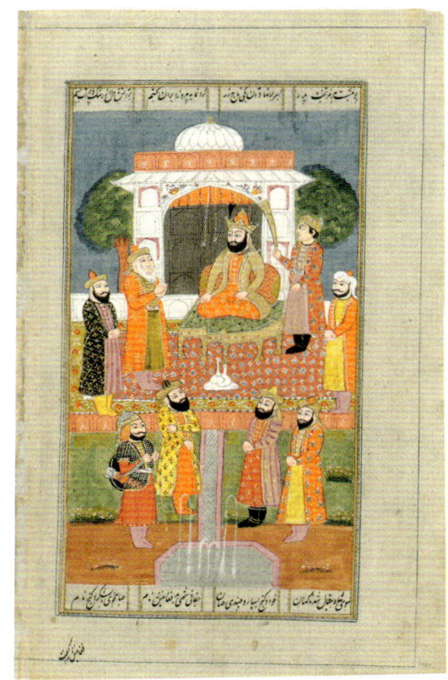
Ca 2017-1/94 (p. 1121)

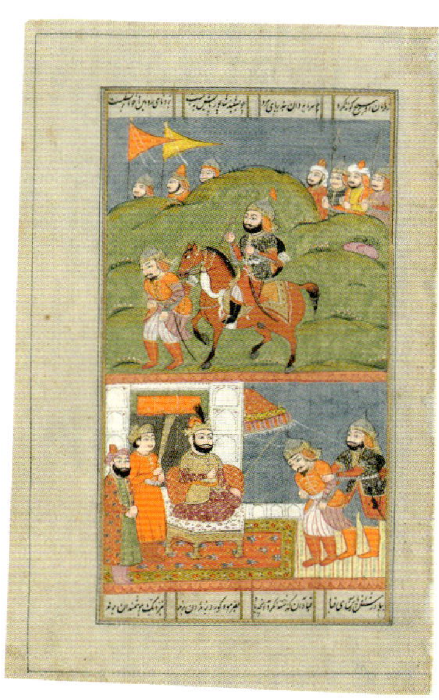
Ca 2017-1/95 (p. 1132)

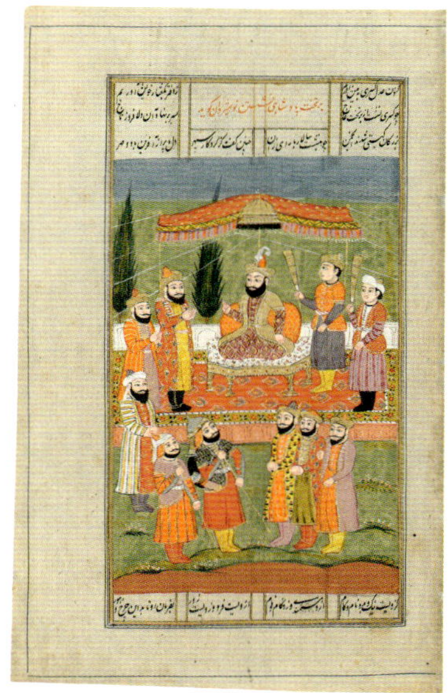
Ca 2017-1/96 (p. 1142)

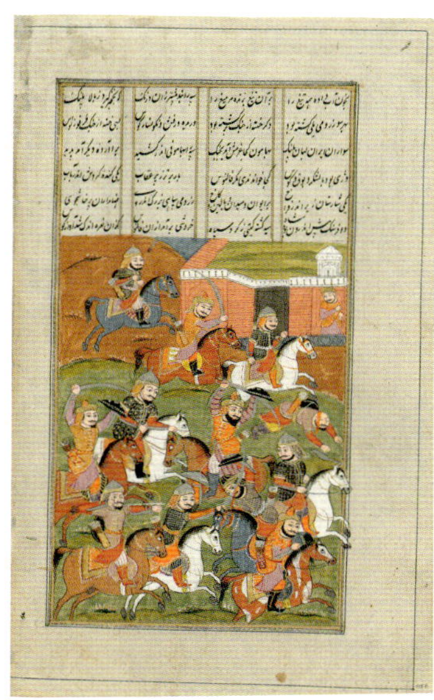
Ca 2017-1/97 (p. 1157)

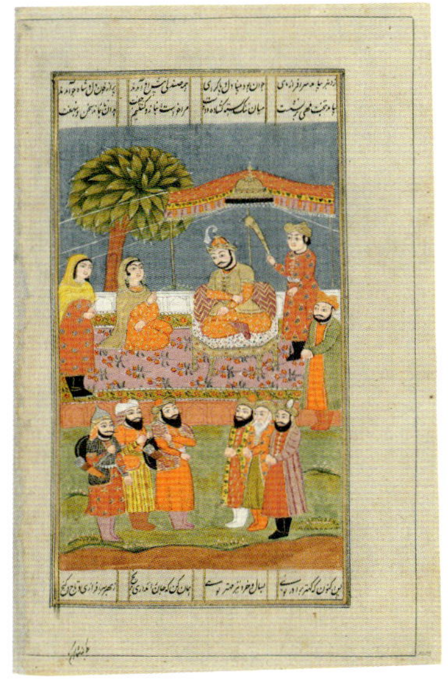

Ca 2017-1/98 (p. 1203)

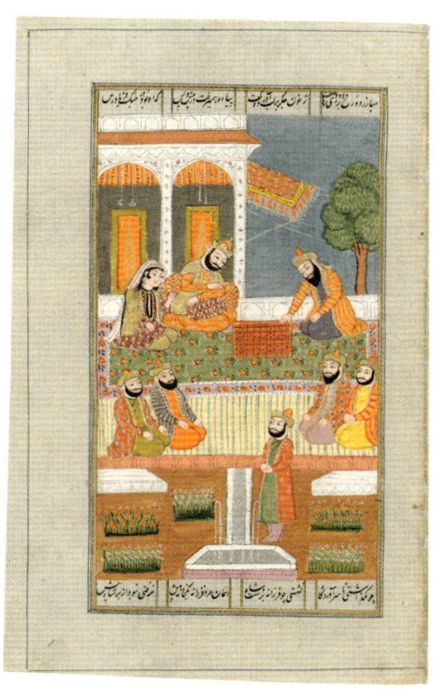

Ca 2017-1/99 (p. 1214)

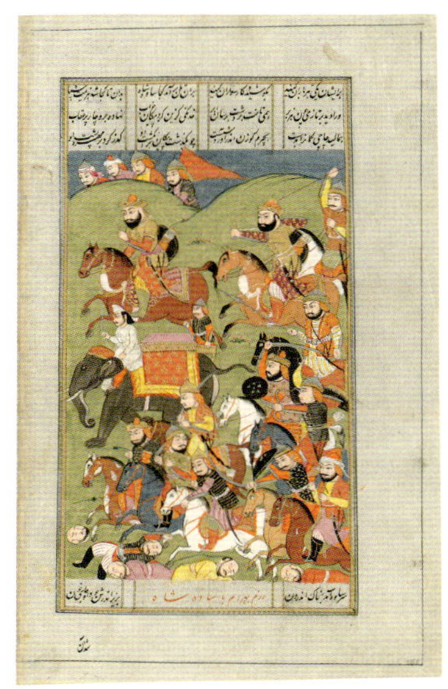

Ca 2017-1/100 (p. 1265)

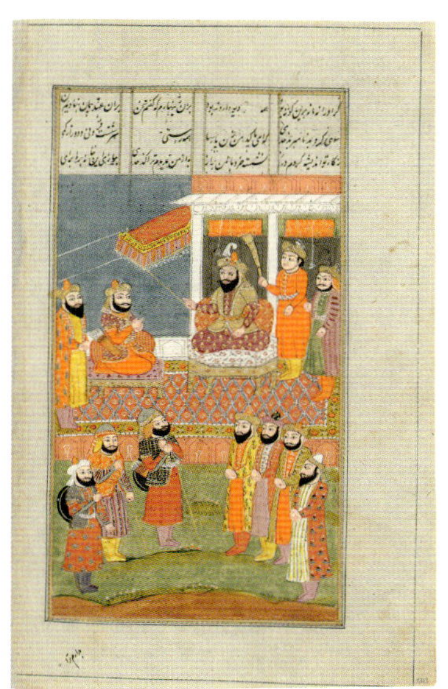

Ca 2017-1/101 (p. 1323)

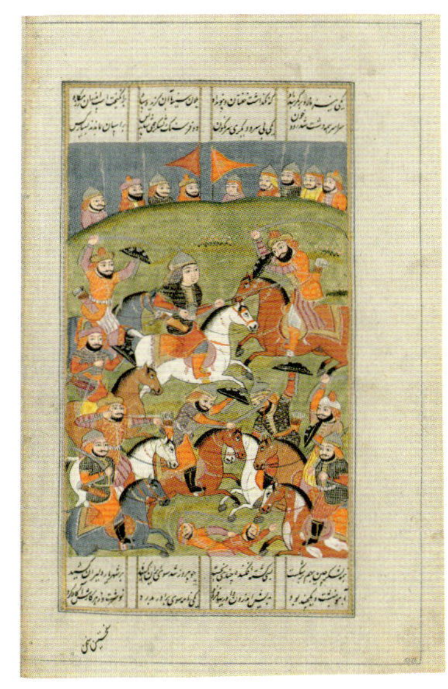

Ca 2017-1/102 (p. 1327)

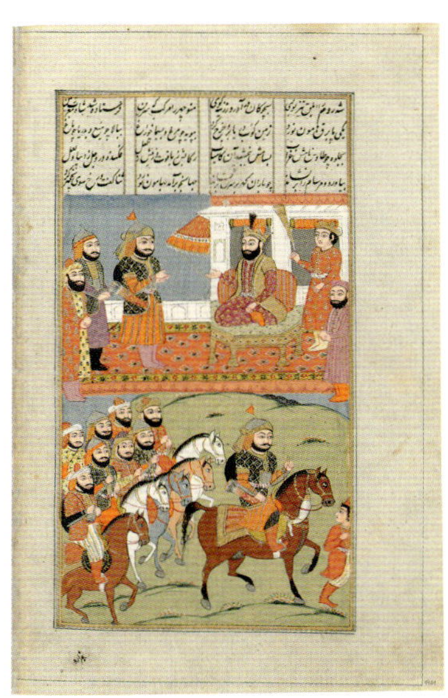

Ca 2017-1/103 (p. 1401)

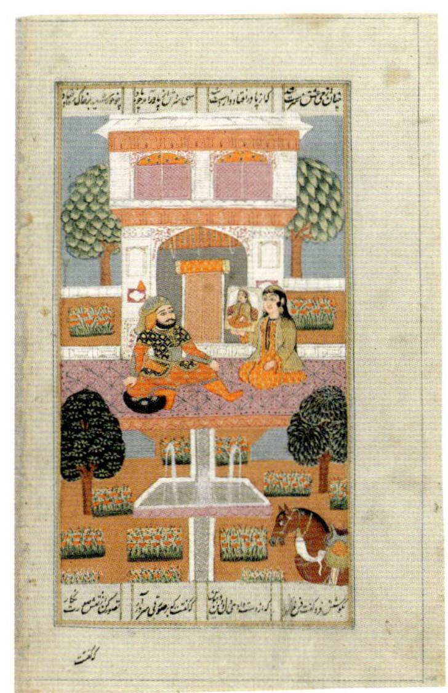

Ca 2017-1/104 (p. 1405)

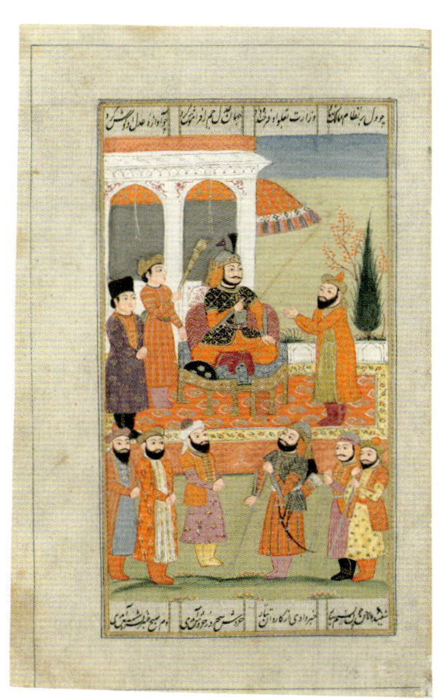

Ca 2017-1/105 (p. 1412)

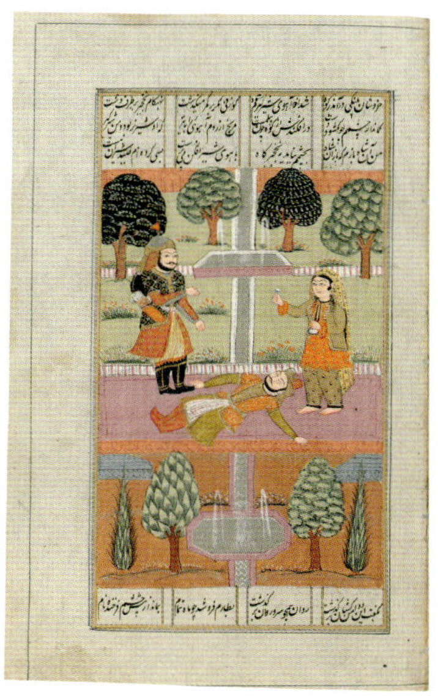

Ca 2017-1/106 (p. 1416)

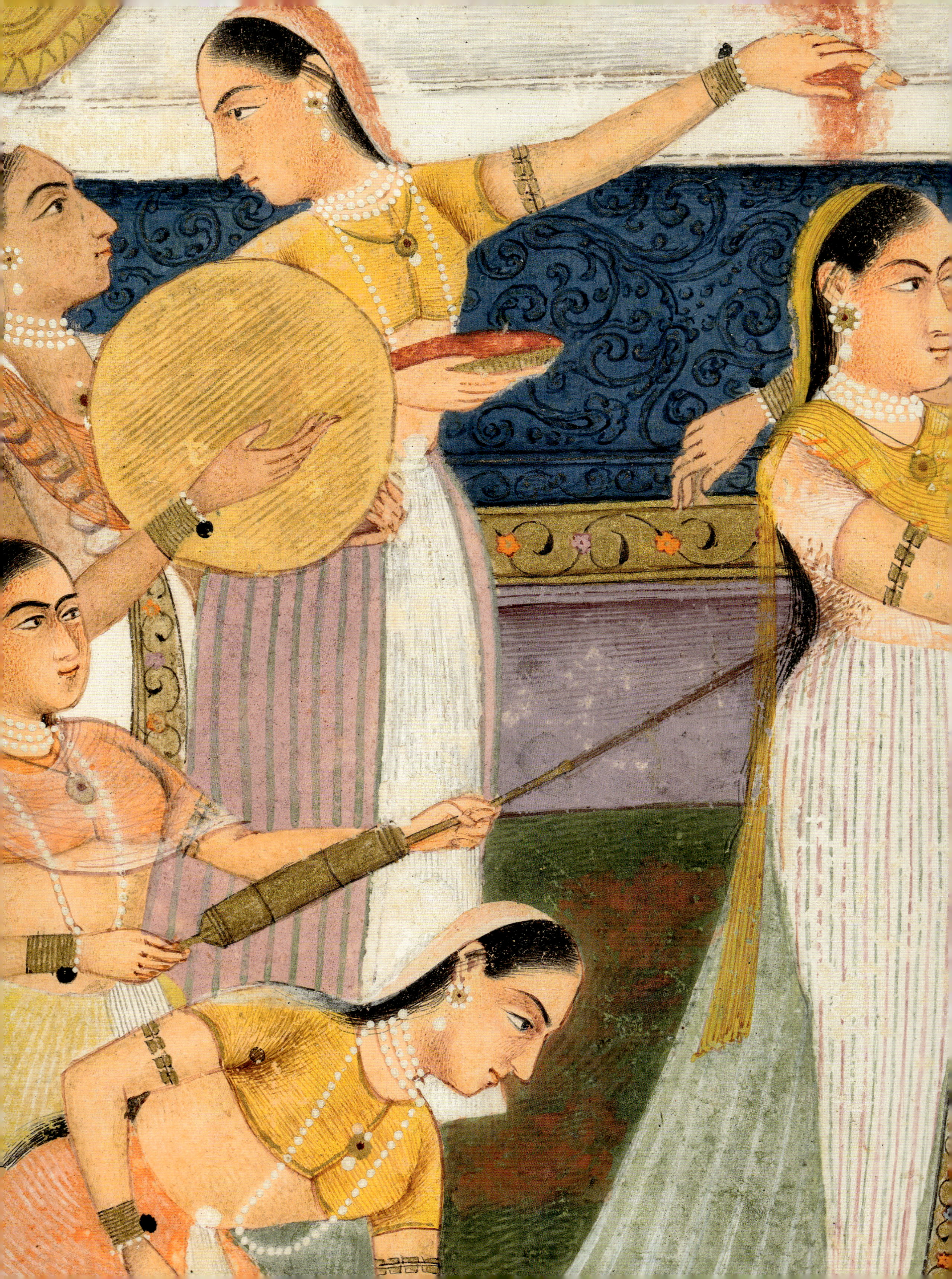

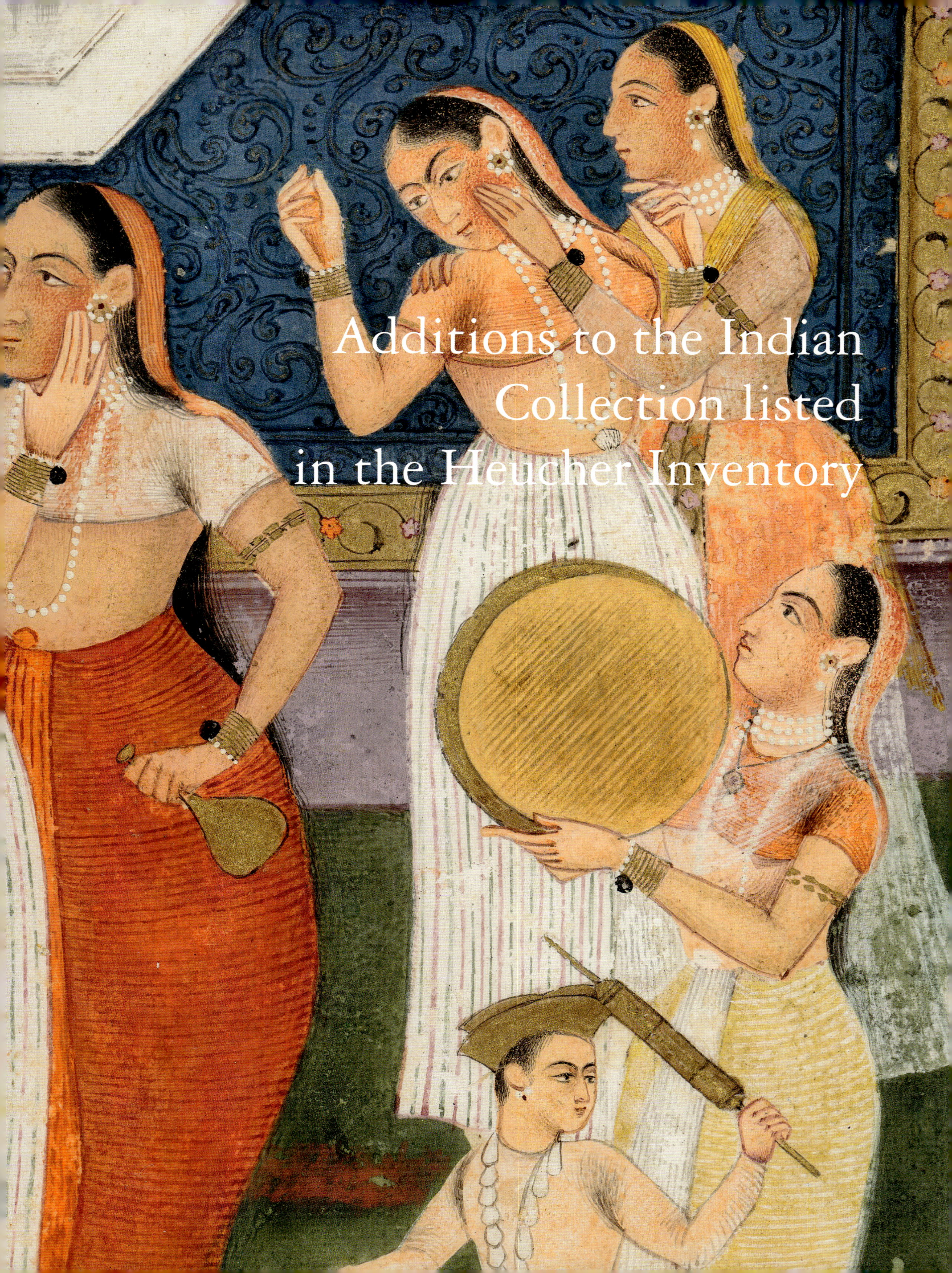

Additions to the Indian Collection listed in the Heucher Inventory

Cat. 87 | Ca 160 Three Indian Paintings from an Album of Various Motifs

Album with various Asiatica
Japanese, Indian, Chinese and European representations of animals, plants, folk costumes and genre scenes, after 1689, before 1738
Album with 82 sheets, white parchment cover, 61 sheets with 76 drawings in watercolour and 30 texts, bleed of 6 removed pages with Chinese woodcuts, 79 blank pages, 41 × 51 × 4.5 cm
Reference: Dresden 2017, cat. 5, pp. 130–1

fig. 1
Ca 160/14
The main hall of the Kiyomizu-dera temple in Kyoto, first of a series of four sheets
Japan, late 17th century
Watercolour, 33.6 × 46.8 cm

The present volume brings together a wide variety of sets and single sheets which may have been found after a large part of the Asiatica had been sorted and compiled in scrapbook-albums, probably some time around 1700. Amongst other treasures, it features four opaquely-painted views of the Kiyomizu-dera temple in Kyoto (the *Otowasan Kiyomizudera*), built in 1633 and still preserved today, with everyday scenes from the lives of pilgrims and visitors (fols. 14–6, 18). The series starts with a view of the main hall with the terrace built on tall stilts and the broad staircase leading to the waterfall (fol. 14, fig. 1).[1] Other works pasted into the album include three Chinese watercolours (fols. 5–7) which, apparently, had been part of a different volume before. Originally, there were six Chinese woodcuts which neither stylistically nor thematically matched the album's watercolours (fols. 8–13).

The majority of the album consists of a description of the plants, animals and persons of Batavia (Jakarta), with illustrations partly related and partly assigned incorrectly during the compilation of the volume.[2] The text is written in two different handwritings and divided into individual pages belonging together in terms of content.

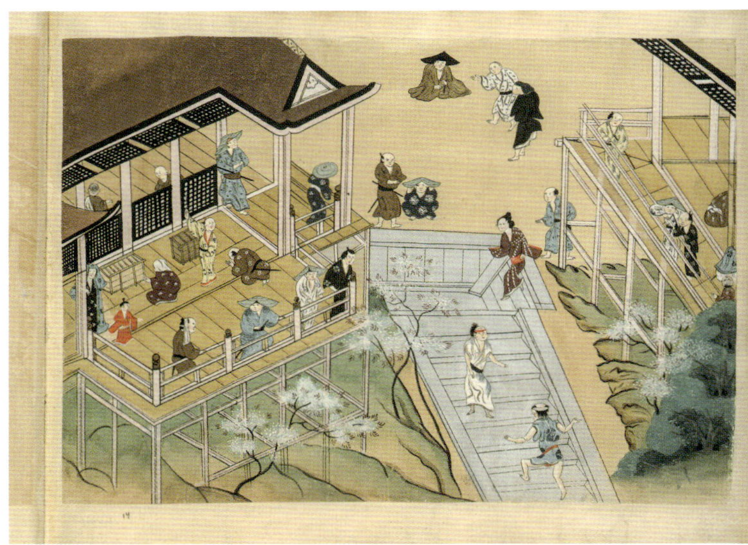

Ca 160/14

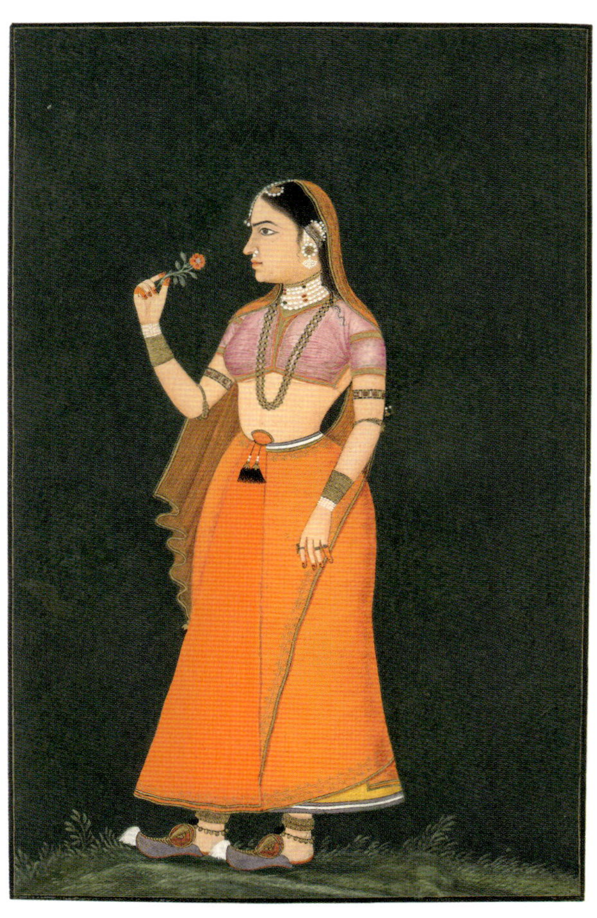

Ca 160/1

The written entries offer some clues as to the author and the context of origin: the report relates the experiences of a German Protestant traveller enlisted as a soldier in the service of the Dutch East India Company in Batavia. The author's reflections, on the other hand, provide some evidence for dating the text and, thus, the album. Accordingly, the text was written when the author returned from Batavia—in any case after 1689, possibly in 1703.

The first page of the volume, the apparently European representation of a Japanese samurai warrior, is followed by three Indian paintings: the portrait of an elegant lady, a representation of the goddess Devī, here accompanied by the monkey-god Hanumān, and a scene of the spring festival, celebrated by the Hindus in parts of India and called "Holī" in northern India. Women and a child in a courtly ambience are shown here with paint sprays which they use to spray each other with paint.[3] The three Indian works still need to be identified stylistically, but can presumably be attributed to North Indian painting, which separates them not only from the other works in the portfolio but also from the Kabinett's entire India collection and its predominantly Mughal and Deccani style works. CB/PKH

Notes | 1 Hempel 1995, p. 17. | 2 A detailed description of the volume is being prepared by Cordula Bischoff and Anita Xiaoming Wang for the scholarly inventory catalogue of the Chinese and chinoiserie artefacts of the Kupferstich-Kabinett (publication expected in 2021). | 3 A representation from the so-called "Minto album", which is iconographically comparable, is evidence that the *Holī* festival had also arrived at the court of Mughal Emperor Jahāngīr, whose mother was a Hindu (*Jahāngīr celebrating the festival of Holī*, attributed to Govardhan, c. 1635, Chester Beatty Library, Dublin, sig. In 07A.4a).

Cat. 87 | Ca 160/2
Lady holding a blossom
North Indian style, late 17th – early 18th century
Watercolour and gold, 27 × 17.2 cm

Cat. 87 | Ca 160/3
The eight-armed goddess Devī enthroned on a lotus seat with the monkey-god Hanumān holding her umbrella, and a worshipper
North India, late 17th – early 18th century
Watercolour, 16.7 × 12.1 cm

Cat. 87 | Ca 160/4
Women celebrating the festival of *Holī*
North Indian style, late 17th – early 18th century
Watercolour and gold, 17.9 × 12.6 cm

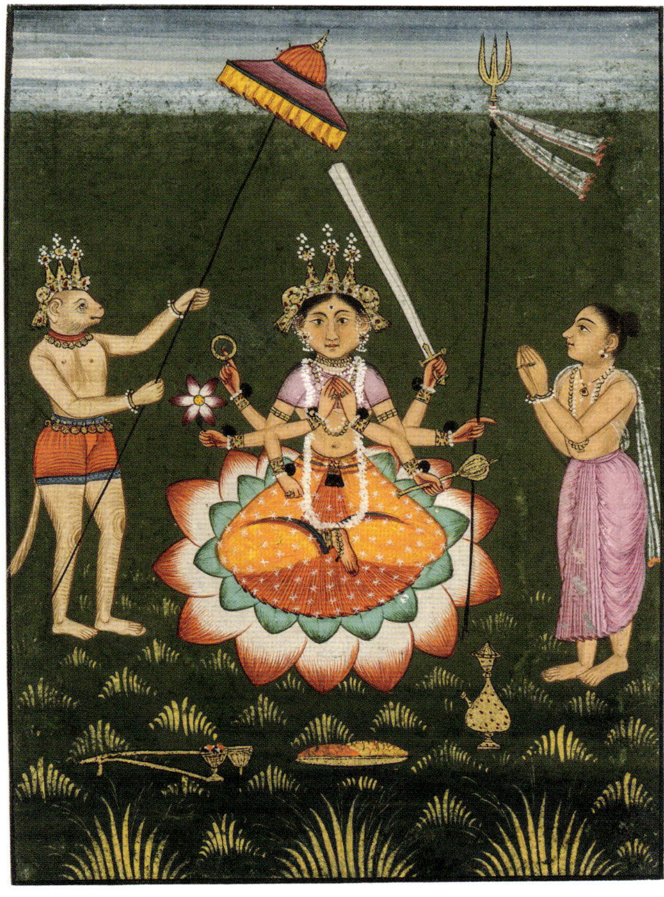

Ca 160/2

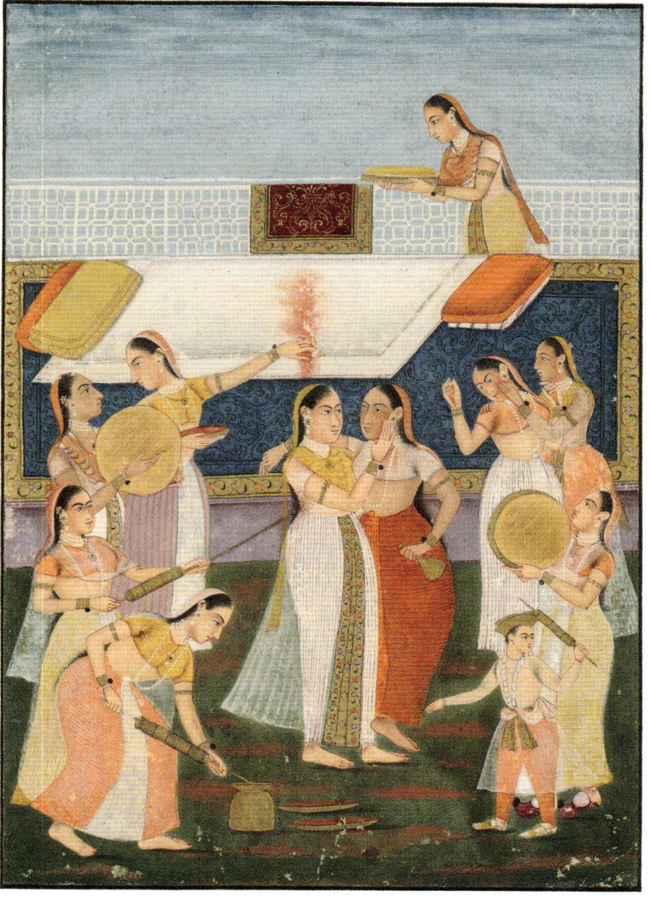

Ca 160/3

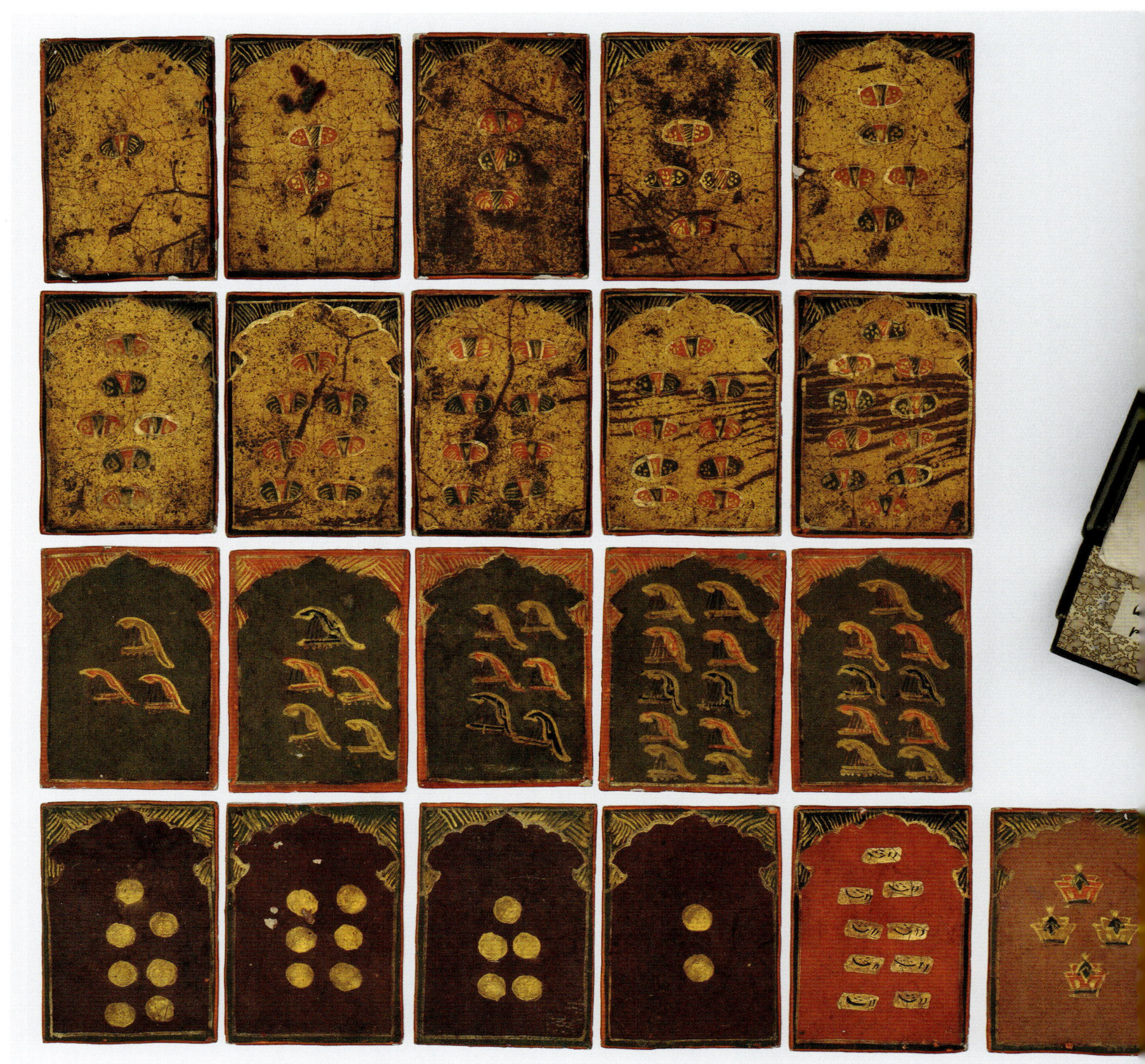

fig. 1 | cat. 88 | Ca 127
21 Playing cards from a Mughal *ganjīfa* pack
Deccan [?], early 18th century
Painted and lacquered cards,
each 6.7 × 4.8 cm
Reference: Dresden 2017, cat. 77, p. 210

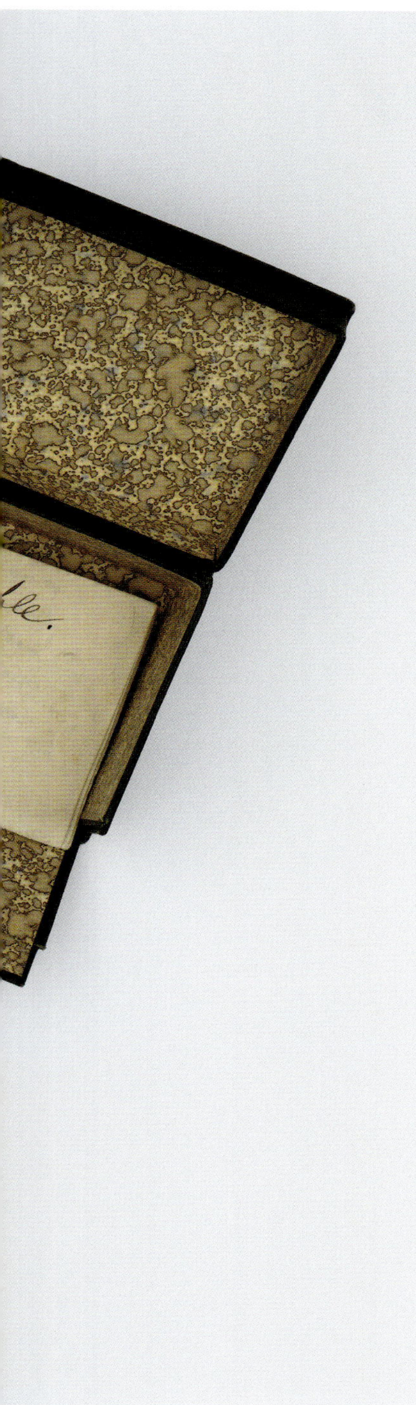

Cat. 88 | Ca 127
An Incomplete Set of *Ganjīfa* Cards

Playing cards and card games which had developed in the Islamic world, particularly Iran, also reached India by the early sixteenth century. According to his court historian Abū'l Fazl, the Mughal Emperor Akbar (r. 1556–1605) himself took a hand in modifying the composition of the *ganjīfa* (playing card) pack. In the standard 96-card Mughal *ganjīfa*, the eight suits of twelve cards symbolically reflect different aspects of court life.

The previously unpublished 21 numeral cards from the Dresden Kupferstich-Kabinett belong to a Mughal *ganjīfa* set. They were part of Nicolaas Witsen's collection, sold in 1728, and were mentioned in 1738 in the inventory of the Dresden royal collection under the heading "La Chine".[1]

As the third oldest documented Indian playing cards which have entered a European collection, they are of much historic interest. The only earlier instances are an incomplete set of 74 cards inventoried in the Danish royal Kunstkammer in 1674,[2] and two sets of *ganjīfa* cards donated in 1726 to the Cambridge University Library by the Reverend George Lewis, who had been chaplain to the East India Company at Madras from 1692 to 1714.[3] Like these three sets, the present pack most likely originated in the Deccan region, which had increasingly come under Mughal domination and cultural influence during the seventeenth century. These painted cards show some rapidity and unevenness in their execution. They were perhaps intended either for a minor member of the nobility or a patron of the merchant or other social class.

Unfortunately no figurative court cards from this pack have survived, i. e. the king (*mīr*) and minister (*wazīr*) cards which head each of the eight suits are missing. The *ghulām* (servant) suit, which would also show human figures, is absent too. Five of the eight suits are represented, including all ten numeral cards for the *qimash* (cushion) suit, with its characteristic yellow ground under the usual cusped arch surround. The *tāj* (crown) 4 card shows four double-stepped crowns rising to a crest, against a light brown ground. The five *chang* (harp) cards (3, 5–6, 9–10) have a dark green ground, the four *surkh* (gold coin) cards (2, 5–7) a dark brown ground, and the *barāt* (document) 9 card a red ground. The backs of the cards are orange-red with a yellow marginal line and narrow blue border; most but not all bear a red Dresden state collection stamp as well.

The cards are now stored in a box presumably from the late nineteenth century, with a descriptive note written by F. Max Uhle, who worked as a curator at the Dresden Museum für Völkerkunde in the 1880s (later distinguishing himself as an archaeologist of South America). AT

Notes | 1 Amsterdam 1728, p. 11, no. 11 ("Een Chineese Almanach") and Heucher Inventory 1738, sig. Cat. 1, p. 157, no. 30 ("1 Chinesischer Almanach., n. 11", with a marginal note, possibly added as an explanation by Carl Heinrich von Heineken before 1763: [no.] 30. "sind kleine holtzerne laquierte täffelgen n. 16." ([these] are small lacquered wooden tablets / no. 16). The designation as "Chinese almanac" still remains to be clarified. | 2 Mikkelsen/Lundbaek 1980, pp. 128–130; London 1982, no. 76; Hopewell 2006, fig. 2. I am grateful to Revd Jeff Hopewell for his comments on the present cards. | 3 Leyden 1982, p. 42.

Cat. 89 | Ca 115 An Album of Thirteen Medallion Portraits

fig. 1 | Ca 115
Front Cover

Album with thirteen medallion portraits in Indian habit
European [?], c. 1700
Album with a simple cover of thick grey-blue rag paper, inside pages of laid paper, thread-stitching, decorated front and back endpaper, pasted down on the inside cover, 19 fols., 18.9 × 1.4 × 1.3 cm
Reference: Dresden 2017, p. 224–5, cat. 89

fig. 2 | Ca 115
Front endpaper

The booklet which is filed, according to collection notes, under "Indica VIII" and entitled "Japanesische Mignatur-Portraits" (Japanese Miniature Portraits)—the title is identical with number 32 of the 1738 Heucher Inventory—contains 13 medallion portraits on paper. These portraits are made by different artists and conform to the type of Indian painted medallion portraits. However, the play of light and shade as well as the brushwork bespeak a European authorship or influence.

Remarkably, the cover is decorated with pasted paper strips, flowers cut from decorative paper and Japanese seals (fig. 1). The portraits are centrally fitted into round or oval medallions, each of which has a background of uniform colour; eleven sheets were then pasted, with a coloured support slightly larger, onto hexagonal bronze varnish paper[1] which was also used for the decoration of cover and endpaper (fig. 2) as well as, interestingly, in a completely different context, namely as support paper for a genealogical arrangement of portraits of Mughal emperors (fig. 3).[2]

The persons portrayed are represented alternatively in three-quarter profile, full profile or almost *en face*. Their physiognomies differ from each other and are not always clearly identifiable; most of them are depicted with turbans, some are apparently Europeans (number 3) or Africans (number 2). Although the German title (probably attrib-

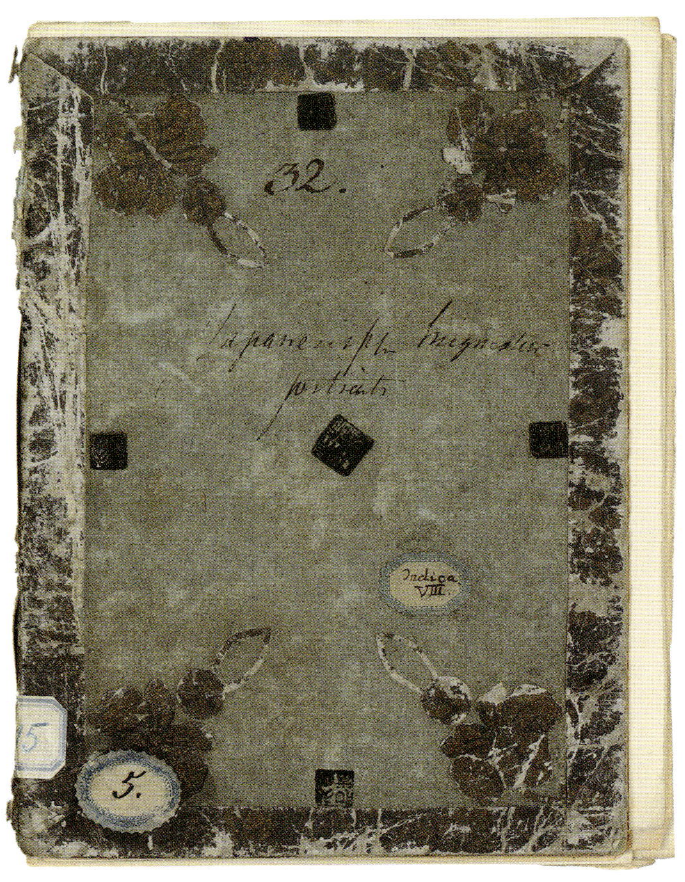

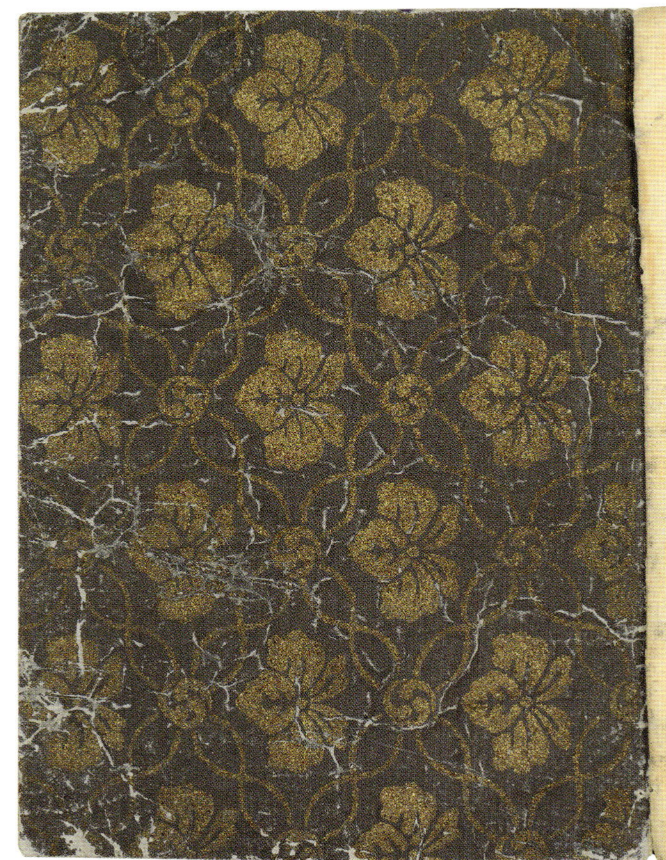

uted to the set when it became part of the Dresden collection) and the French inscriptions suggest that the persons portrayed are members of the Japanese court, most of the thirteen men are dressed in Indian-Oriental style, wearing turbans of a simple, yet finely patterned (striped, plaid or floral) cloth, and a *jāma* fastened to the right; some wear pearl earrings or a long chain. Number 12, the "Catechist at Court Impododaica", wears a black jacket over the *jāma* and a Jesuit's hat, while number 13, according to the inscription, represents a monk from the Japanese order of "bonzes" without headgear and wearing a plain habit.

The portraits differ from each other in terms of size, edging line and style of painting. Numbers 4 and 6, 5 and 13, 8 and 9, as well as 10 and 11 might each form a pair from a set. Number 1, which is a little smaller and, in contrast to the rest of the portraits, mounted on a larger rectangular piece of brocade paper, is very delicately painted; number 2, the portrait of an African-looking young man, on the other hand, was pasted into the album without such a support and is painted in a more desultory way. It seems likely, then, that the medallions were not painted for this book but compiled from a disparate stock of various sets originally larger in size.

On the left-hand sides of the sheets, high-ranking personalities and guests of the Japanese court, their rank and, as the case may be, their annual income are specified in French. These specifications appear to have been compiled from contemporary sources, including Arnoldus Montanus's *Gedenkwaerdige gesantschappen der Oost-Indische Maetschappy in't Vereenigde Nederland, aen de kaisaren van Japan*, published in Amsterdam in 1669.[3]

The related illustrations are not in Montanus's richly-illustrated volume but seem to have been included here without direct reference to such a source. The result is a kind of pseudo-historical document, whose goal and function have not yet been identified. The portraits, although no exact matches have been found, correspond in type to a printed portrait series of representatives from the Indian court in Valentijn's *Beschryving van Groot Djava*.[4] A painted equivalent can be found in an album formerly in the Liechtenstein Princely Collections.[5] The medallion, which represents a person called "Ontadono"[6] mentioned under number 5 and painted in a slightly looser brush style, might in turn be compared with a series of six painted medallion portraits today preserved in the Leiden Nationaalmuseum van Wereldculturen.[7] These portraits feature small Japanese seals, clipped fragments from printed works as well as letters and words in ink, incorporated like a seal, which have not yet been fully decrypted and whose significance for the given context remains unclear. Not only a correspondence with the seals used on the cover of Ca 115 emerges here; in photos taken with transmitted light it became clear that similar names and seals are used on the backs of several of the Dresden sheets in Ca 115 (fig. 4).[8]

This small booklet of portraits thus leaves us with a number of puzzles. Once again, however, it serves as evidence of the close connection between the Dresden "Indica" and other European collections as well as the importance of the Dutch and, possibly, French markets for this context. PKH

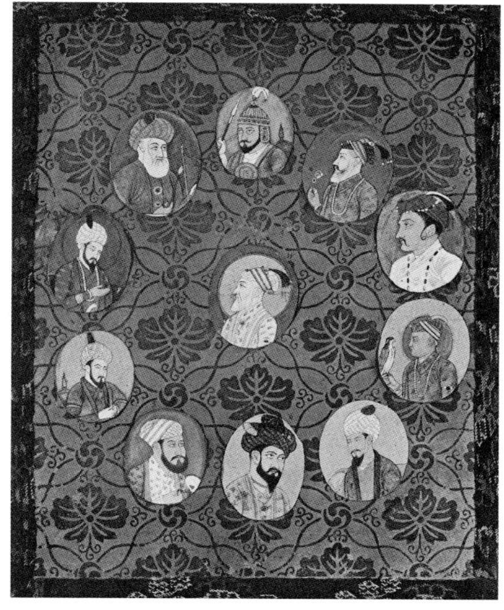

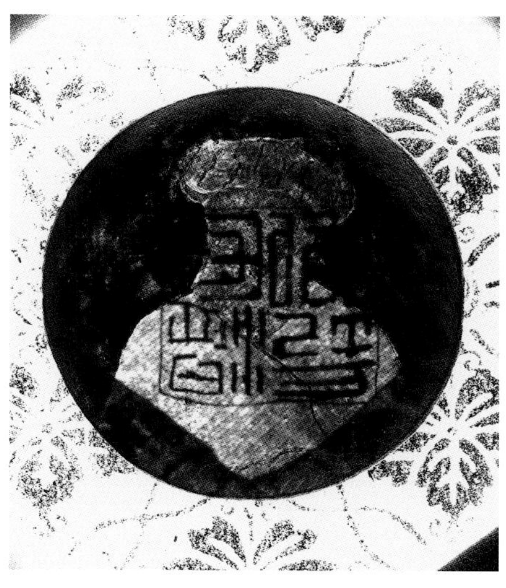

fig. 3
A set of eleven medallion portraits of the Grand Mughals
Deccani Mughal, early 18th century
Watercolour and gold, 30.7 × 24.5 cm
Present location unknown
Reproduced from Rouffaer 1906, pl. II

fig. 4 | Ca 115/4
Hoÿno Oÿdonno
Verso Japanese seal made visible using transmitted light

Notes | 1 Bronze varnish papers were exclusively manufactured in the early eighteenth century using a letterpress-printing technique with wooden moulds and ink made of bronze varnish mixture. Thanks to Nedim Sönmez for pointing out this special technique. The floral design is modelled on a blue bell tree (paulownia) leaf which also served as a Japanese clan badge and still today appears in the Japanese government's coat of arms. | 2 See Dresden 2017, p. 57, fig. 3 and p. 59. | 3 Montanus 1669, p. 65. | 4 Valentijn 1726, unpaginated. | 5 See p. 28, fig. 11; and Losty 2012, p. 64, no. 26. | 6 Montanus 1669, p. 65. | 7 Inv. no. E8-1 to 6. With thanks to Pauline Lunsingh Scheurleer for her initiative and the joint research in Leiden. | 8 Thus on Ca 115/2, 3 and 4—for technical reasons it was not possible to screen all the sheets. Many thanks to Carsten Wintermann and Olaf Simon for taking the photographs, and to Pauline Lunsingh Scheurleer and Anita Xiaouming Wang for related research and clues for the identification.

Ca 115/1

1 L'Empereur du Japon Cabacundono qui si/gnifie Souveram Seigneur du Japon, et apres il rejeta ce nom, comme les autres; il pret celui de Taycosama c'est a dire Grand Empereur.
Sa table, et ses concubines, luÿ coutant par an 4 000 000. Livres; la garde 10. ton. d'or Les grands, la cour, la malice tous les ans coutant, 29345 ton. d'or.
(1 The Japanese Emperor Cabacundono, considered the sovereign of Japan, after rejecting this title as well as others, adopted the name Tycosama, which means "great ruler". His table and his concubines cost him 4,000,000 pounds a year; the guards 10,000 tons of gold, the noblemen, the court, the jesters, 29,345 tons of gold per year.)

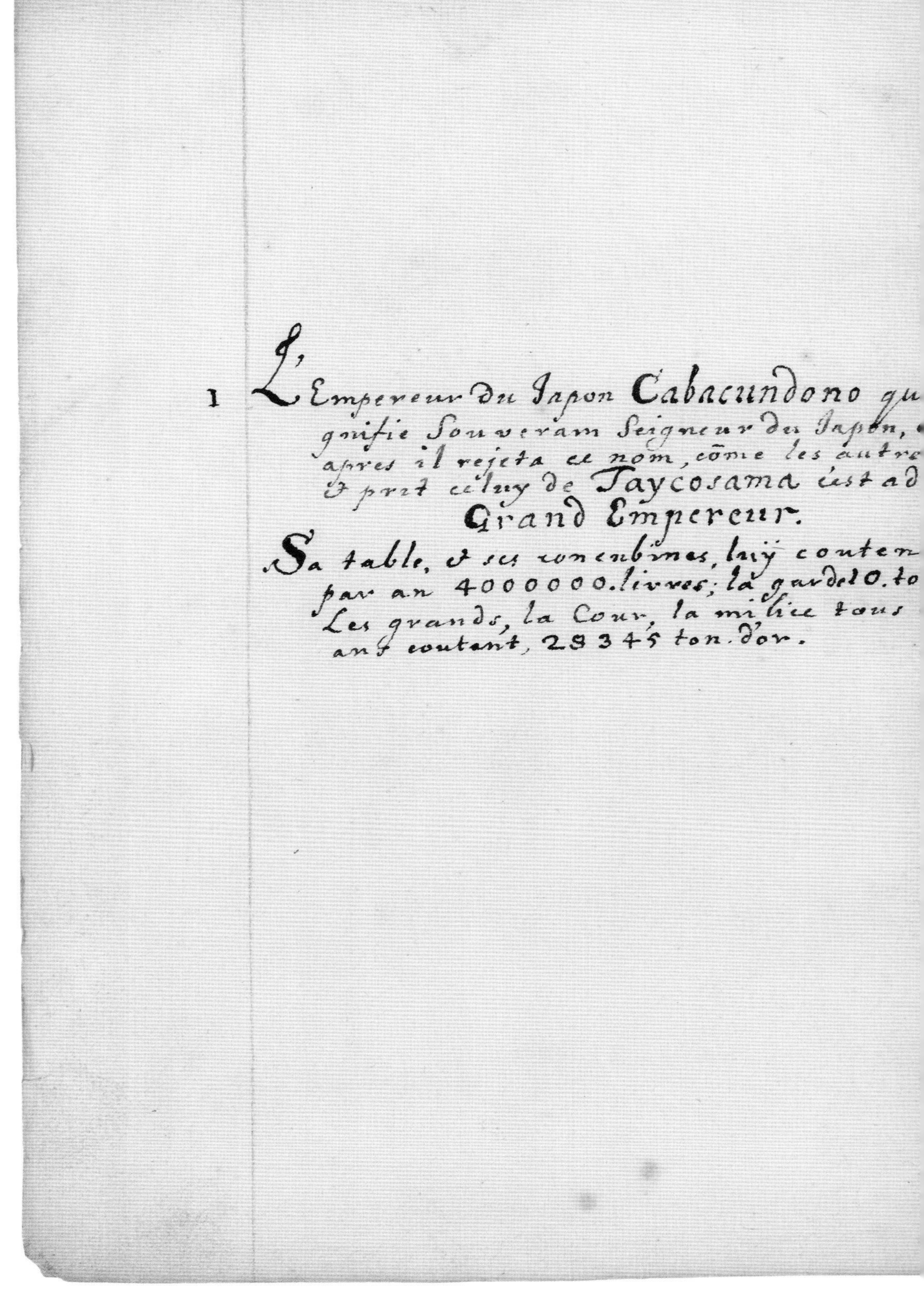

1 L'Empereur du Japon Cabacundono qu
gnifie Souveram Seigneur du Japon, e
apres il rejeta ce nom, cōme les autre
& pret celuy de Taycosama cest a d
Grand Empereur.
Sa table, & ses concubines, luÿ couten
par an 4000000. livres; la garde 10. to
Les grands, la Cour, la milice tous
ans coutant, 29345 ton. d'or.

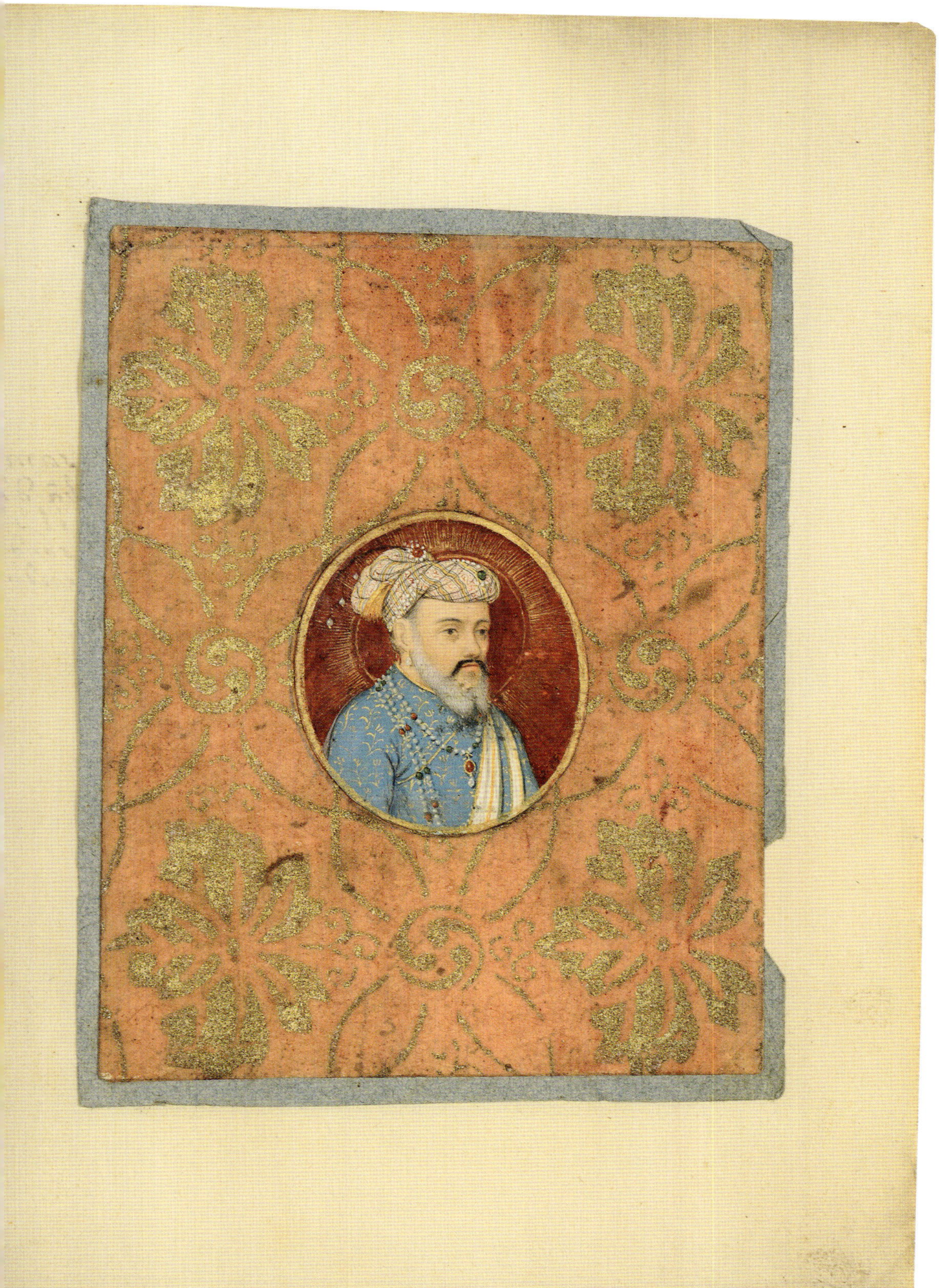

Ca 115/2

2 L'unique fils de l'Empereur Toxogunsama signifie bien aime; il porte le rubā d'or masif; la marque de sa qualite; il s'entretient magnifiquement du tresor de son Pere, ayant la liberte de prendre autant quil a besoing.
(2. The only son of ruler Toyogunsama is very popular; he wears the golden ribbon in token of his qualities; he draws generously on his father's treasures, taking the liberty to avail himself of whatever he needs.)

Ca 115/3

3 Le principal favorit de l'Empereur Onogoschio signifie plaisant, il est comme le second fils de l'Empereur, tant il est aime et tire du Tresor 300 000 francs par an.
(3. The emperor's first favourite, Onogoshio, is considered to be very pleasant; to the emperor, who loves him dearly, he is like a second son; he takes 300,000 francs a year from the treasures.)

Ca 115/4

4 Le premier President au Conseil d'Estat, Hoÿno Oÿdonno signifie sage et fidel; tire chaque année du Tresor de L'Empereur 15. ton. d'or.
(4. The states council's first president, Hoÿno Oÿdonno, is considered prudent and faithful; he receives 15 tons of gold from the emperor's treasures every year.)

Ca 115/5

5 Grand Chancelier de la Cour Sackay Ontadon/no Nongay Sinadōno signifie prompt et diligent dans sa charge, tire du Tresor de L'Empereur 10. ton d'or par an.
(5. The grand chancellor of the court, Sackay Ontadonno Nongay Sinadōno, who is said to be very quick and diligent in following his duties, receives 10 tons of gold from the emperor's treasures.)

Ca 115/6

6 Grand Secretaire de la Chambre de 'Empereur Qu[?]a Jamma Sammon signifie qui se taise quand il faut, tire du Tresor de l'Empereur chaque anée 5. ton. d'or
(6. The secretary of the imperial chamber, Qu[?]a Jamma Sammon, is said to remain silent when it is required; he receives 5 tons of gold from the emperor's treasures.)

Ca 115/7

7 Grand Tresorier de la Cour de L'Empereur Pochicinnemondonne signifie recevoir et doner il tire vintieme sous de ce qui recoive et done.
(7. The grand-treasurer of the imperial court, Pochicinnemondonne, is considered to be someone who takes and gives; he receives the twentieth part of what is given and taken [the revenues].)

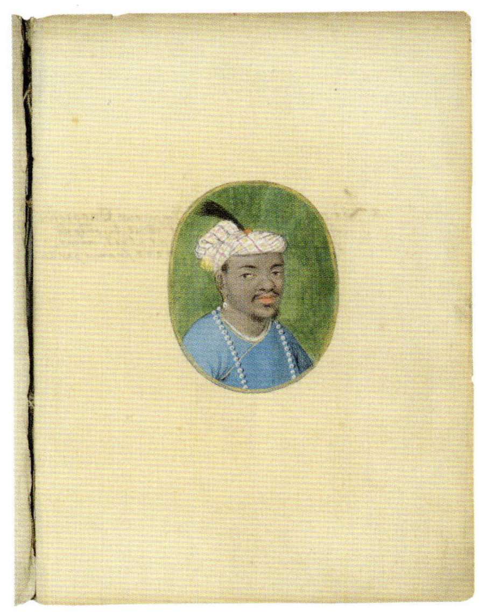
Ca 115/2

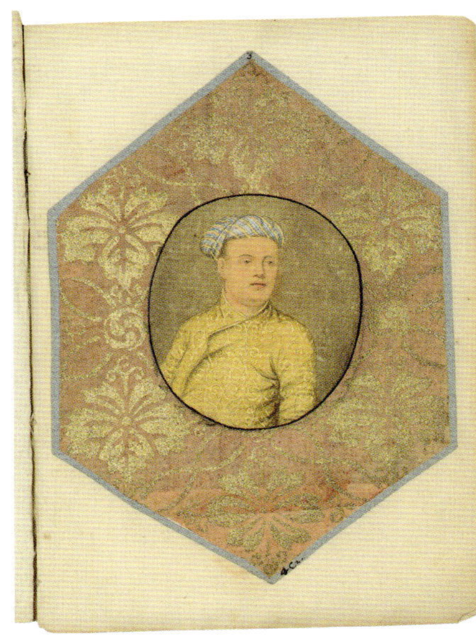
Ca 115/3

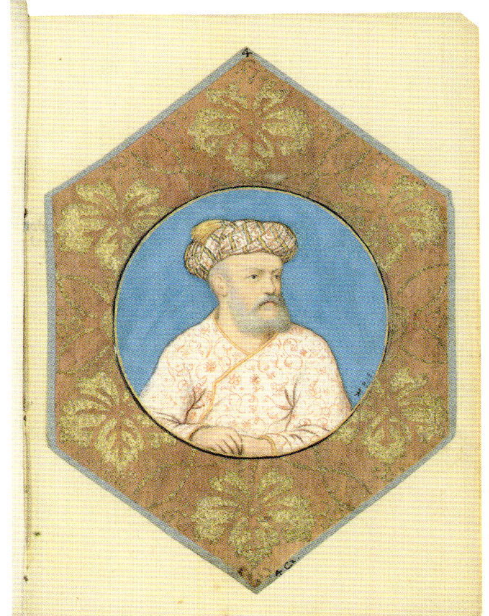
Ca 115/4

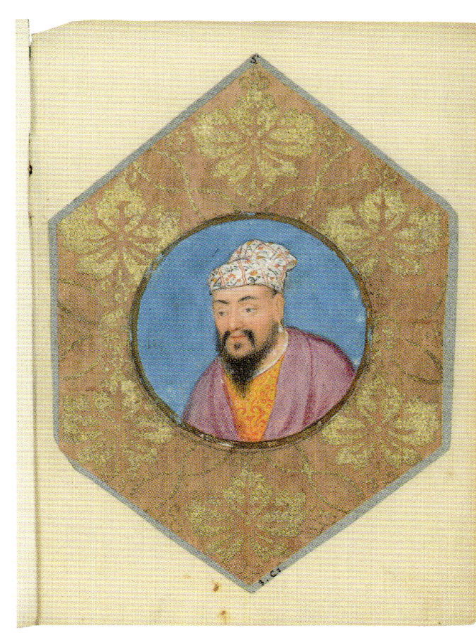
Ca 115/5

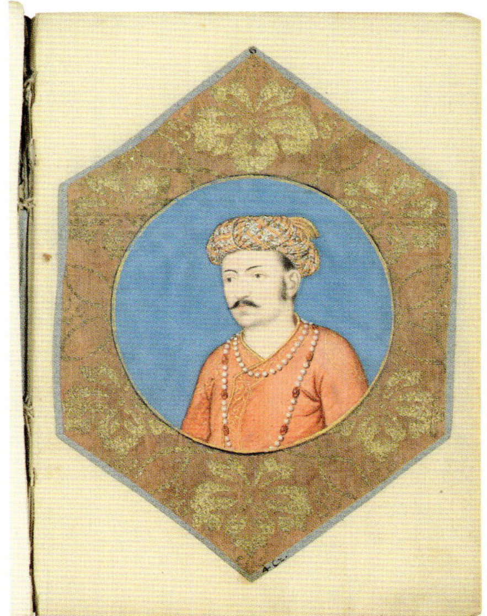
Ca 115/6

Ca 115/7

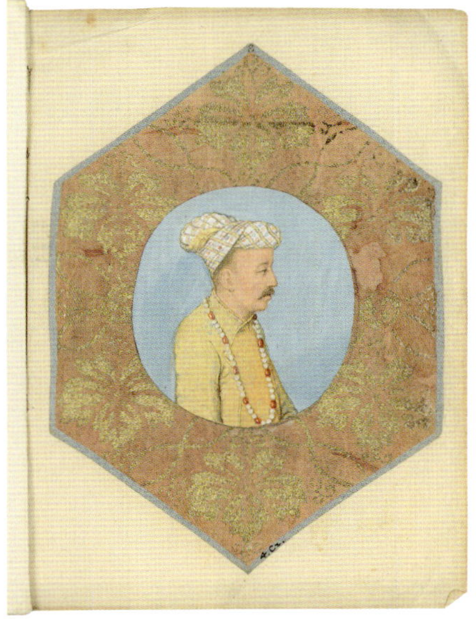

Ca 115/8

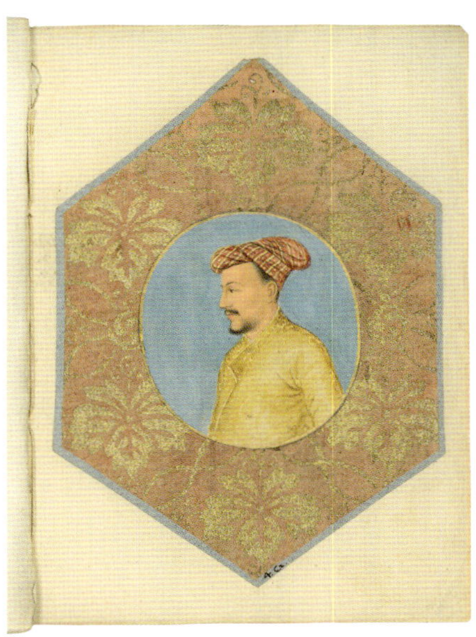

Ca 115/9

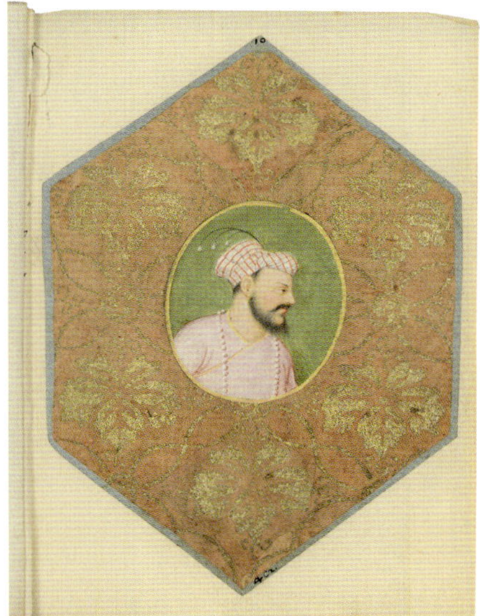

Ca 115/10

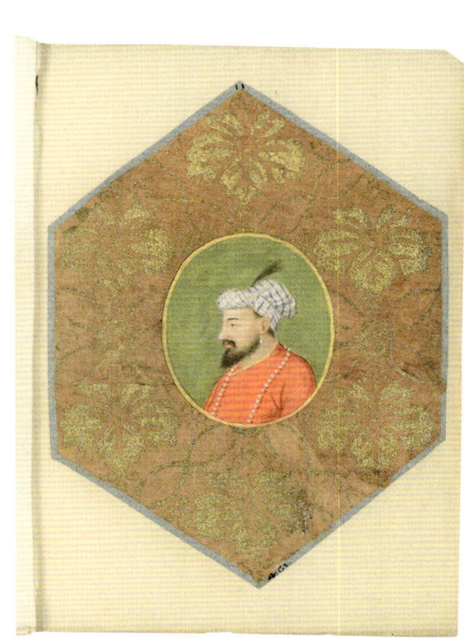

Ca 115/11

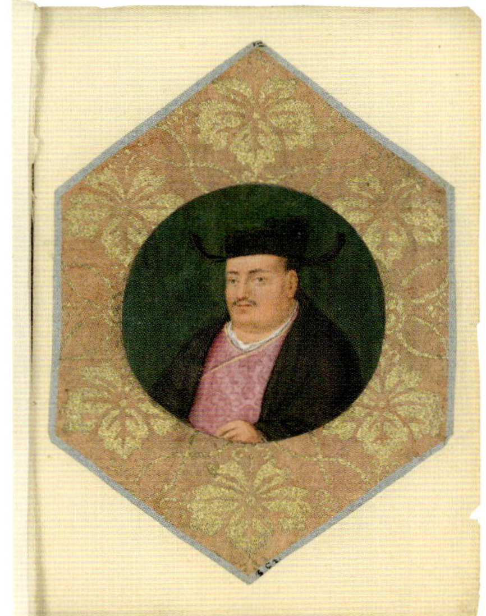

Ca 115/12

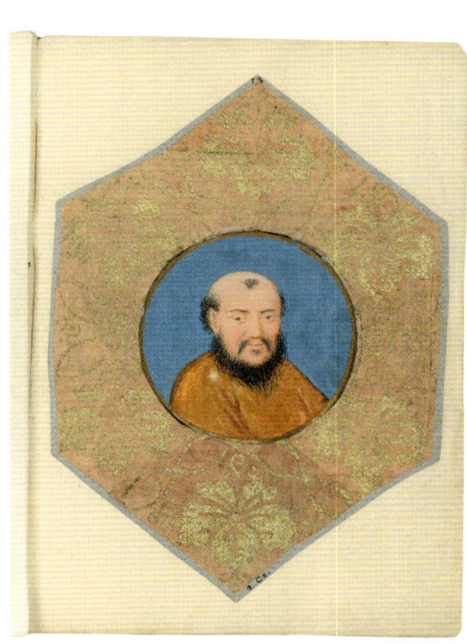

Ca 115/13

Ca 115/8

8 Admiral de la flote de L'Empereur d. Japon Auve Jamma Onckerodonne signifie com/batter le vent et l'ennemi. tire la cinqui/eme part du butin et du Tresor 6. ton d'or

(8. The navy's grand admiral, Auve Jamma Onckerodonne, is said to face the wind and beat the enemy, he receives a fifth from the booty and 6 tons of gold from the treasures.)

Ca 115/9

9 General de la garde de l'Empereur Mÿnagauwa Chinamowanÿ signifie, l'un des Dieux, est mon Maistre. Il tire chaque anée du Tresor 300 000. francs sans autres accidens qui sont innombrables

(9. The general of the imperial guard, Mÿnagauwa Chinamowanÿ, is a god, and he is my lord; he receives 300,000 francs every year from the treasures, not to mention innumerable other opportunities.)

Ca 115/10

10 Quienmonsama, Gouverneur du grand Jedo capitale ville de l'Emire. il prenn[überschrieben „d"]e de tout, ce qu'on aport dans la ville, quin/sieme part et tire du Tresor 5. ton d'or

(10. Quienmonsama, governor of the great imperial city of Jedo, takes the fifth part of whatever is brought into the city and 5 tons of gold from the treasures.)

Ca 115/11

11 Pochicennemondonne, Gouverneur du Palais de L'Empereur a Mïaco, ville Imperiale et de fort grande estendue, il tire du Tresor par an 500 000 francs.

(11. Pochicennemondonne, governor of the imperial palace at Miaco, an imperial city covering a vast area, receives 500,000 francs from the treasures per year.)

Ca 115/12

12 Impododaica, Cathechise, de la cour, qui ne prenne aucun gage, mais il est en/tre tenue magnifiquement, par l'or/dre de L'Empereur

(12. The court's catechist, Impododaica, receives no wagesbut is amazingly well cared for.)

Ca 115/13

13 Bonzes L'un des Moÿnes de Japons, Jaloux extremement aux Chrestians, ily a 5 sorts de Moynes a Japon, aussy bien que des religieuses, avec grandes re/venues, mais ceux la vivent da la seule charite.

(13. Bonzes, one of the Japanese monk orders, is extremely jealous of the Christians; there are five monastic orders in Japan as well as nuns with substantial income, but the others survive on charity alone.)

Cat. 90 | Ca 114, Ca 114a

The *Album Amicorum* of Elector Augustus

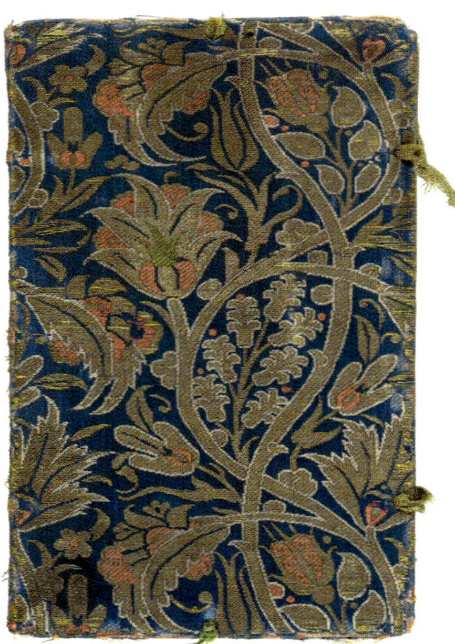

Fig. 1 | Ca 114
Cover, left

Album amicorum **of Elector Augustus**
Ottoman, c. 1582
Book with 264 fols., cover (Turkish?) brocade (silk) coated, 21.4 × 13.2 × 5 cm, 192 Turkish decorative papers, 44 fols. vacat, 28 fols. with illustrations of traditional Turkish costumes bound into it, European hand, watercolour, 20.5 × 13.2 cm
An attached booklet, 22.5 × 14.9 × 0.3 cm, with seven illustrations of traditional costumes, watercolour, 22.5 × 14.9 cm
Reference: Dresden 2017, cat. 3, pp. 125–7

The Dresden Kupferstich-Kabinett harbours one of the major testimonies of the history of decorated paper made in Istanbul.[1] Initially stored together with its Chinese collection, it was later classified among the "Indica". An entry which very likely refers to this book lists "Miscellaneous Turkish papers, bound into a book"[2] as number 174 of the 1587 inventory of the Dresden chamber. Dated to the early 1580s because of its decorated papers and watermarks, the album is named according to its function and after the person who commissioned it, *Album amicorum of Elector Augustus* (Stammbuch Kurfürst Augusts). Its decorated papers were pages intended for writing but were never used for this purpose.[3] In addition to the colourful papers, the volume contains 28 illustrations of traditional costumes. The papers used are predominantly from northern Italian mills and carry watermarks used between approximately 1570 and 1590.[4] Both the "Turkish papers" and the costume illustrations must have been imported as loose sheets from Istanbul around the end of 1581 or 1582.

In 1581, David Ungnad Freiherr von Sonneck, ambassador to the Sublime Porte from 1573 to 1578, wrote to Elector Augustus of Saxony, advising him to have his painter provide himself with "beautiful Turkish paper" and to make drawings of Turkish costumes.[5]

Ungnad might have come across this "Turkish paper" during his first diplomatic mission to Istanbul in 1572 or, as the case may be, during his tenure as ambassador. His interest in this paper is evidenced in the diary of Stephan Gerlach, the legation preacher and chaplain who accompanied Ungnad to Istanbul. In his diary entry on January 17, 1574, Gerlach writes that Ungnad had a small prayer book sent to his bride through the agency of the former Venetian envoy, describing it as made "of the finest Persian paper with all kinds of gold, silver and other colours" and containing a portrait made by Mr. Albrecht as well as illustrations of the finest locations, palaces and gates in Constantinople.[6]

The *album amicorum* of Baron Stephan von Haymb zu Reichenau, available in the manuscript collection of Det Kongelige Bibliotek in Copenhagen, shows some similarities to the specimen extant in Dresden.[7] Haymb zu Reichenau was on diplomatic mission in Istanbul in 1575–1576, where he might have met David Ungnad in the German House. It was probably in the same bindery that the content of the two books, originally dispatched in the form of loose sheets from Istanbul to Vienna, was bound with brocade fabrics from Istanbul (fig. 1).[8]

Silhouette paper, an Ottoman decoration method paper developed around 1560, is especially well represented in the *Album amicorum of Elector Augustus*. Patterns cut out from parchment with sharp knives were soaked with colours. Usually, these patterns were arranged on one half of a paper that had been treated with alum—so as to frame the space provided for the writing. Then the other half of the paper was folded over the first. The colours of the leather pattern were transferred by softly pressing the two paper halves onto one another. The first examples of this method are two manuscripts from 1566.[9] Some of the characteristics of silhouette technique, such as its four-stage process and the use of negative as well as positive templates, can be gleaned from the Dresden *album amicorum*.

The album, however, features only a few marbled papers—the marbling technique reached Istanbul only at the beginning of the 1580s. Marbled papers (*ebru*) from before 1581 were either brought from Persia or manufactured by Persian masters in Istanbul.[10]

In addition to decorative papers, the *Album amicorum of Elector Augustus* contains 28 illustrations of costumes. Like coloured papers also pictures of costumes were very popular at the time as easy-to-carry exotic gifts: "[...] particularly toward the end of the 16th century, such small-format albums were almost mass-produced for the many visitors from abroad who came to Istanbul with foreign legations and were only allowed, or willing, to move within a limited space."[11] Other than the "Turkish papers" of the album, which are among the most beautiful of those manufactured in Istanbul, not all of the costume illustrations can be considered masterpieces. It is not known whether they are the work of the painter mentioned in Ungnad's letter to Elector Augustus;[12] presumably, they were drawn from costume books available in the library of the German House.

On the other hand, six of the seven costume illustrations attached to the Dresden album,[13] in terms of quality, stand comparison with the drawings in the "Turkish Costume Book of Lambert de Vos".[14] It was commissioned in 1574 by Karel Rijm who worked in Istanbul between 1571 and 1574. Ungnad, who came to Istanbul during the same year, must have pursued the progress of the artist's work in the German House. Another work that he brought with him from Istanbul is the so-called "Book of Turks" (*Türkenbuch*) with accounts of the Ottomans' way of life and of the seraglio. Zacharias Wehme made a copy of it for Elector Augustus.[15] NS

Notes | 1 Translations from Turkish: Taner Uysal, DaF lecturer, Ege University, Izmir, University of Foreign Languages. | 2 Syndram/Minning 2010, no. 174 on fol. 184v/194v; Melzer 2010, p. 16. The term "Turkish paper"(*Türkisch Papier*) is used here for the first time. Initially, it was applied to all coloured papers produced in Istanbul, such as silhouette paper, marbled paper, sprinkled paper, dribbled paper and tree-root marbled paper; as an exclusive designation of *ebru* marbled paper it was only used since the first half of the seventeenth century. See also Sönmez 2016. | 3 The so-called *Stammbücher* or *albae amicorum* were a kind of prefiguration of autograph and friendship books. They were bound volumes commonly used between the sixteenth and the middle of the nineteenth century in German-speaking countries and, more generally, in Protestant Europe. Clerics, scholars, and artists, as well as kings and nobles used them when traveling and filled their pages with drawings of coats of arms, illustrations and sayings. The "Turkish papers" were first included in albums of travellers visiting Istanbul. Another example of an unused *Stammbuch* is the "Costume Book" that is part of the art collection of the Veste Coburg (sig. Hz12). | 4 Among its 264 folios, the volume contains 37 sheets of silhouette paper, 9 sheets of one-sided marbled paper, 40 sheets of one-sided sprinkled paper, 19 sheets of double sided sprinkled paper (produced by means of a template or lattice work placed on the paper), 13 sheets of dribbled marbled paper (produced by inclining the sheet during the colouring process), as well as 74 monochrome and 44 non-coloured paper. | 5 Sächsisches Staatsarchiv, Hauptstaatsarchiv Dresden, sig. 10024, Geheimer Rat (Geheimes Archiv), loc. 8302/01, Viertes Buch, Grafen- und Herrensachen, 1578–1581, fol. 412a: "Es wäre woll nit vnratsam, da er ain gueten maller, von Euer Chur: gde: zuegeordent. mit sich hat. Der khöndte sich mit türggischem schönem Pappir, in was groß daselb Euer Chur: gde: habens woltens, zur notdurft versehen, vnnd darinnen alberait ain anfang machen, sich mit abmallung der türggischen trachten zuüeben, doch müsset er damit zuvorsten für-gehen, in der gehaim die Sachen halten [...]." | 6 See Gerlach 1674, p. 47: "Den 17. hat mein Gn. Herr / D. U. durch des alten Venedischen Gesandten des Bajoli Sohn / seiner Braut ein schön Gebet-Büchlein geschickt / welches von schönem Persianischen Papyr / allerley von Gold / Silber und andern Farben / durch Jeremiam / unfers Herren Hoffmeiters Dienern / geschrieben gewesen. Auff dẽ I. Blat war er / der Hr. Von M. Albrechten des Hn. Rymen Mahlern / gar künstlich abconterfäyet / wie auch die Stadt Constantinopel mit allẽ ihre vornehmsteẽ Porten / Palästen und Säulen." | 7 Inv. no. Kvarto Thott 1279. | 8 The precious fabrics might be leftover bits from the production of clothes, and either given to the envoys as presents or which they purchased and brought with them. A faulty editorial addendum in Dresden 2017, p. 126, specifies Venice as a potential production site for the binding of the volume. The more likely place, however, is Vienna. | 9 Muhibbi Diwan, Topkapı Museum Library, TSK R. 738 mük. and Yahya Efendi Taşlıcalı, Şah-u Geda Diwan, Manuscript Library of Amasya, inv. BAo 2134. | 10 One of the first examples from the early phase of Turkish *ebru* is the *Album amicorum* of Ringler, Württembergische Landesbibliothek, Stuttgart, Codex hist. 80 no. 5. | 11 Stichel 1991, p. 32. | 12 In the years around 1900, illustrations of costumes, due to the similarity of the figures and the correspondence to the type pursued, were often ascribed to Melchior Lorch (1527–1594); see the hand-written note on the slipcase of the volume: "This volume, which privy councilor Gurlitt considers to be very precious, includes drawings by Melchior Lorck [...] H[ans] W. S[inger], October 28, 1909". | 13 Ca 114a. The final, stylistically different sheet shows an African and was added later; the 1738 Heucher Inventory only lists six enclosed sheets (p. 157, no. 31). | 14 Bremen, Staats- und Universitätsbibliothek Bremen, Codex Ms. or. 9. | 15 Inv. no. Ca 169. Copy of the lost Book of Turks. For more detailed information, see Schnitzer 1995.

Ca 114
Selection of 37 fols.
showing 28 Turkish costumes,
9 decorative papers including sheets
of silhouette paper (fols. 9, 15),
one-sided marbled paper (fols. 8, 74),
one-sided sprinkled paper (fols. 53, 209),
dribbled marbled paper (fols. 27, 193),
monochrome coloured paper (fol. 51)

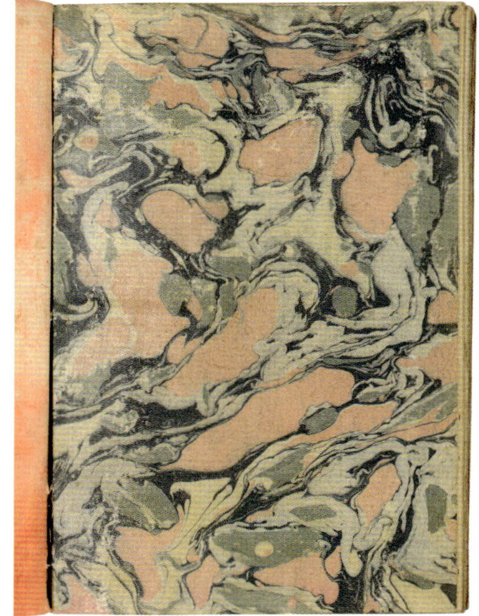
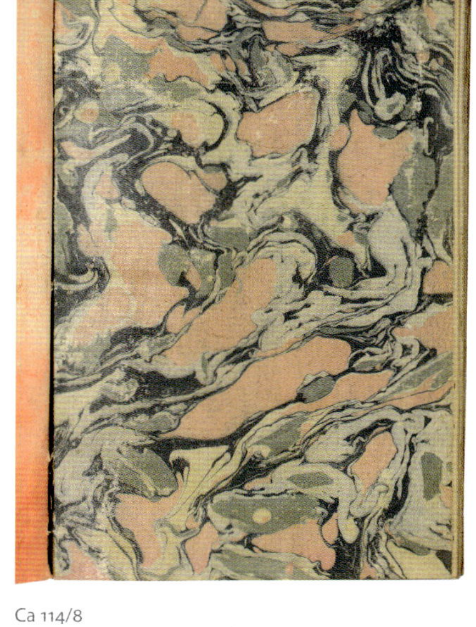

Ca 114/8

Ca 114/9

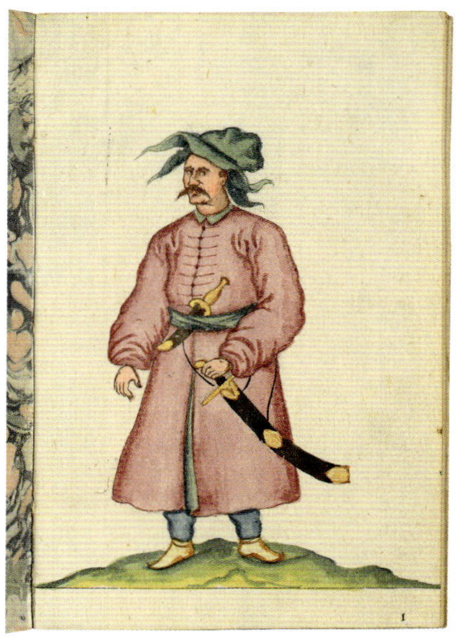

Ca 114/12

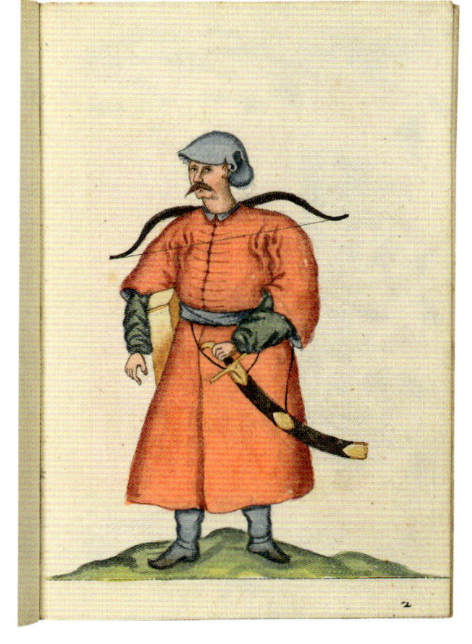

Ca 114/14

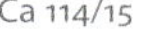

Ca 114/15

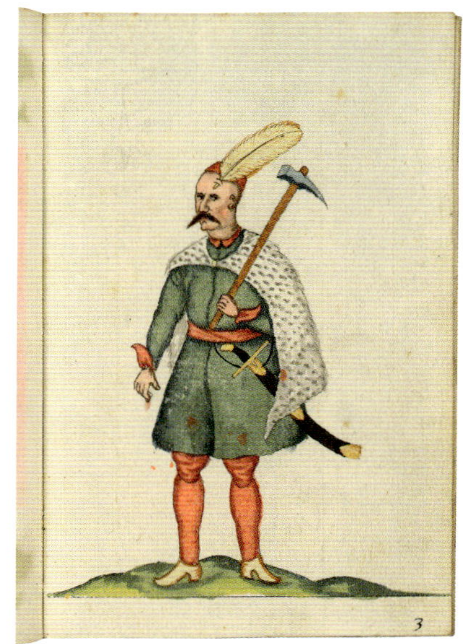

Ca 114/16

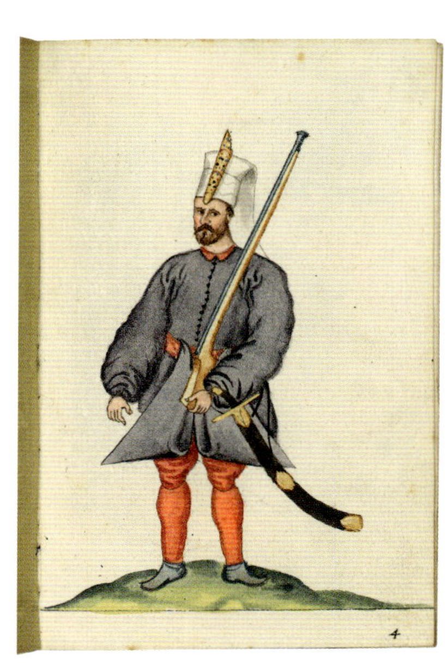
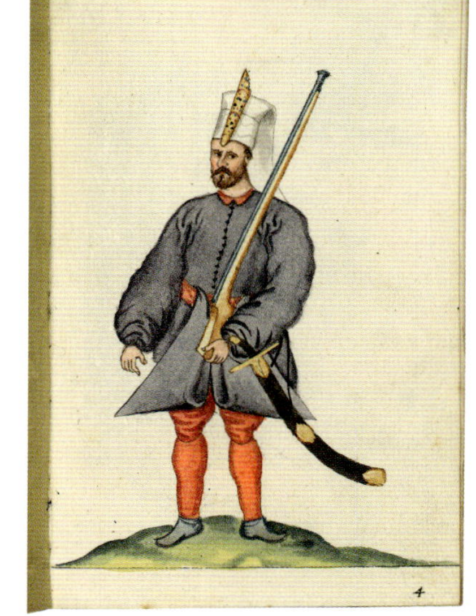

Ca 114/19

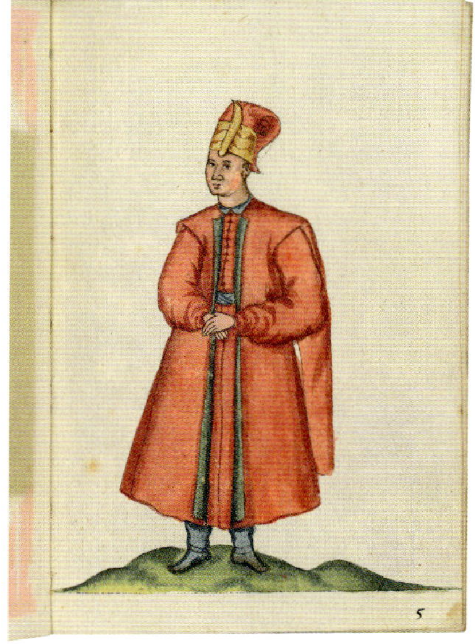

Ca 114/21

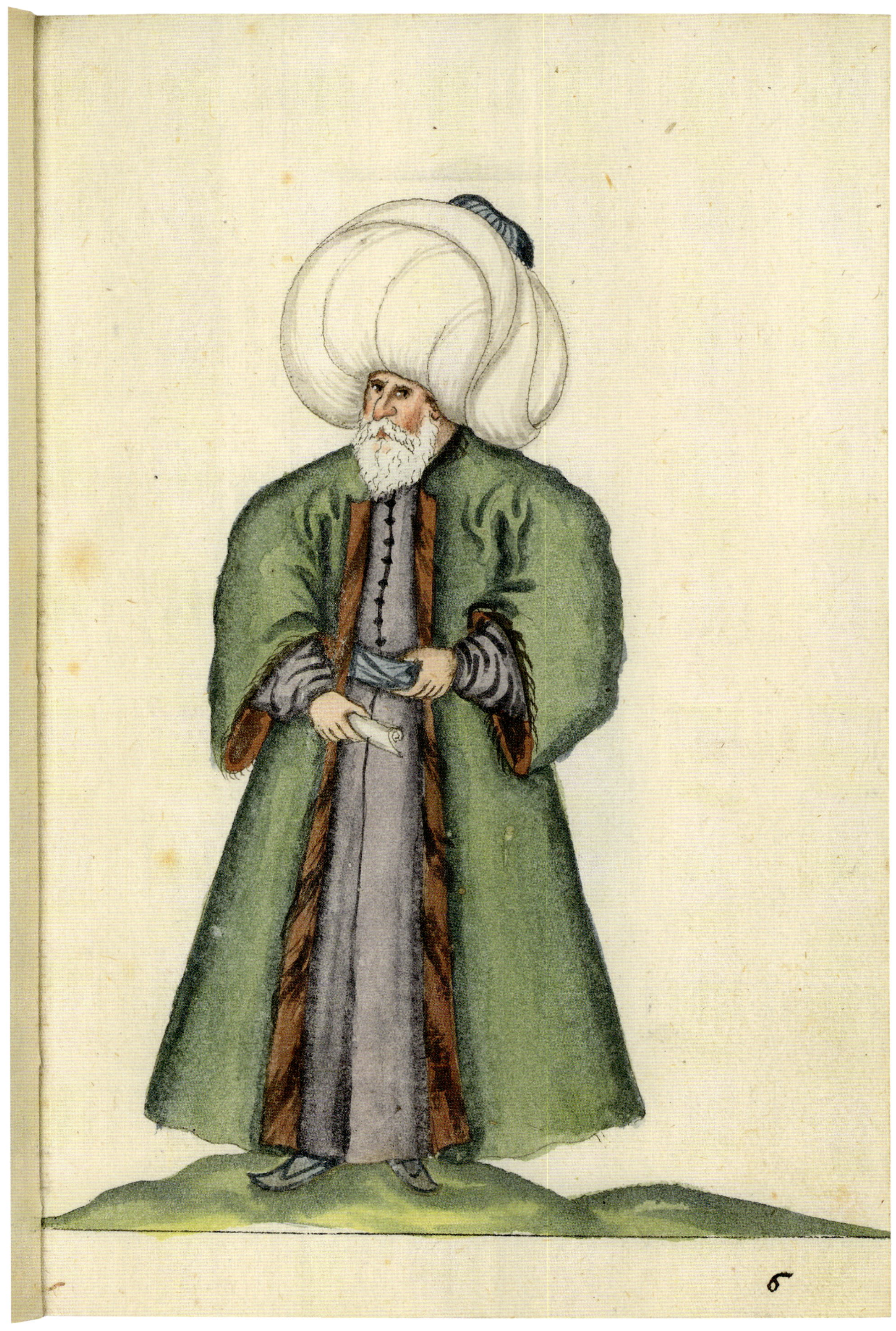

Ca 114/23

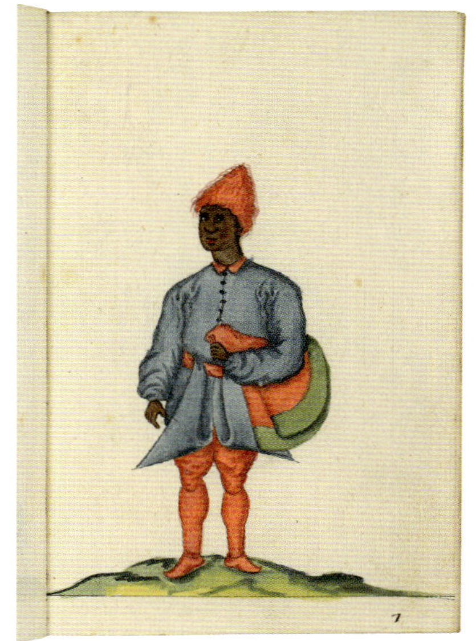

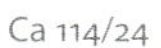

Ca 114/24

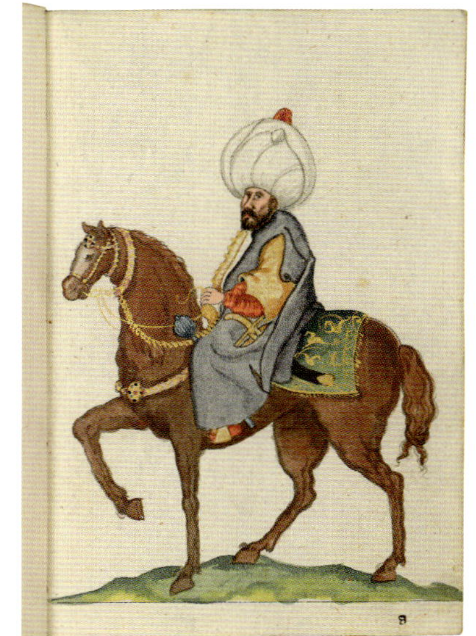

Ca 114/26

Ca 114/27

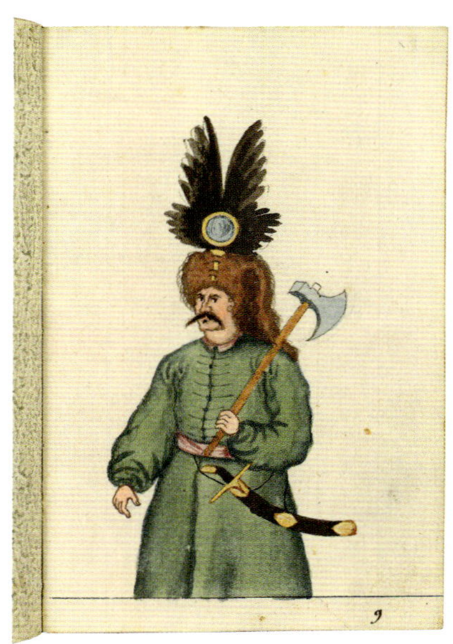

Ca 114/28

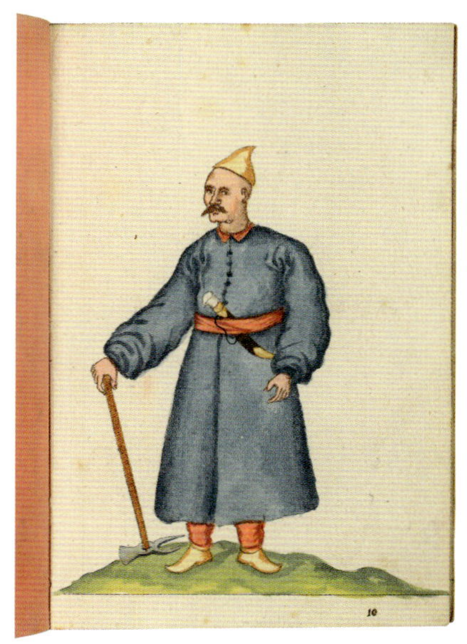

Ca 114/30

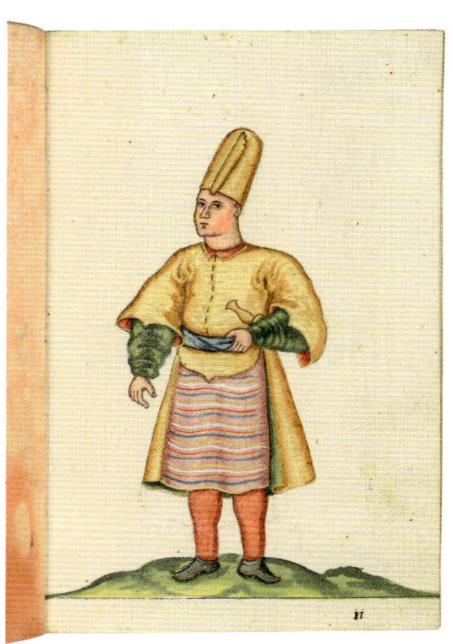

Ca 114/33

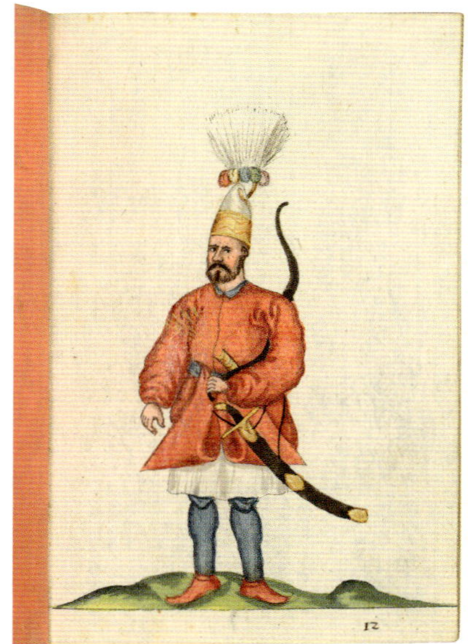

Ca 114/35

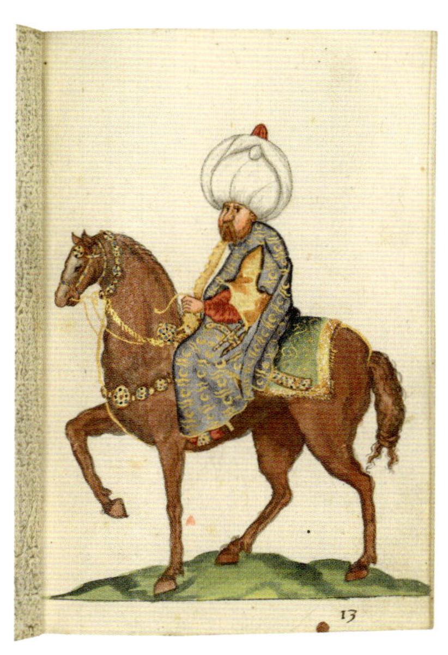

Ca 114/37

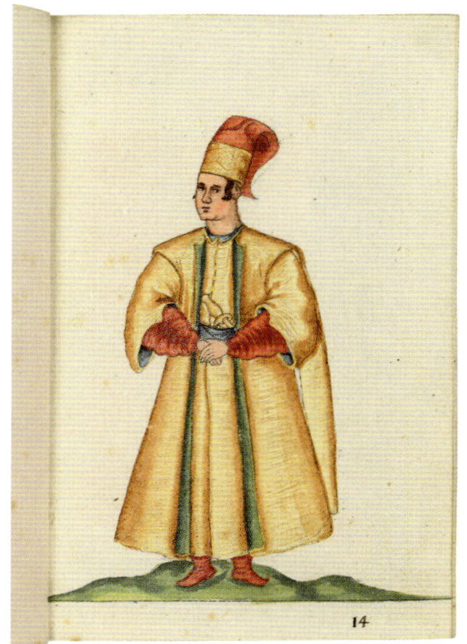

Ca 114/39

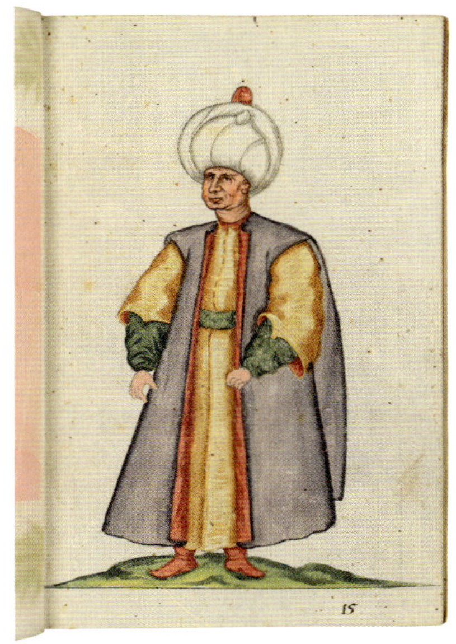

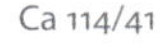
Ca 114/41

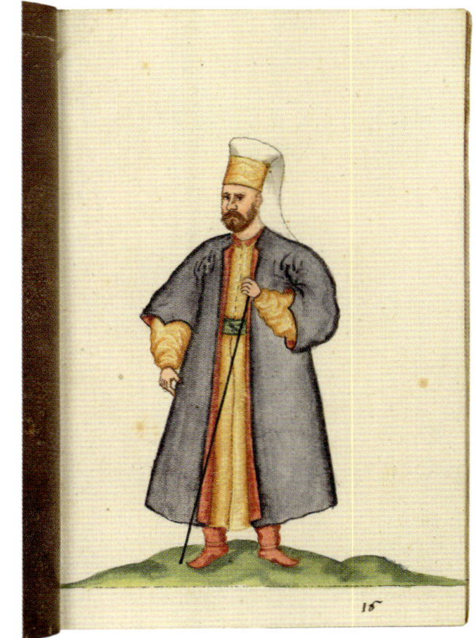

Ca 114/43

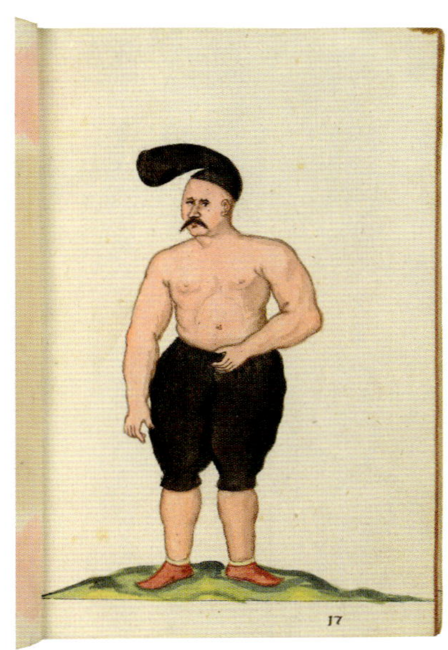

Ca 114/50

Ca 114/51

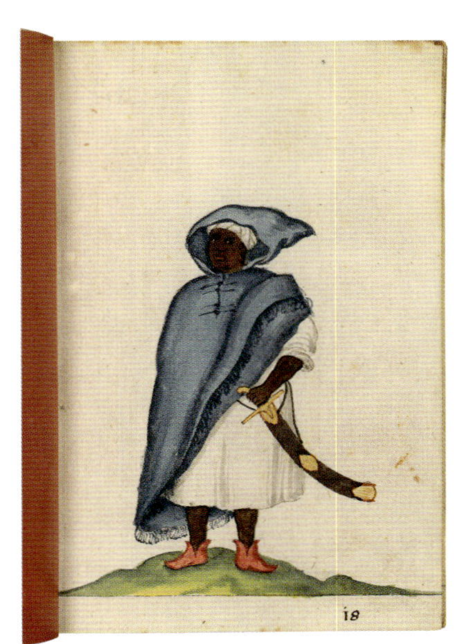

Ca 114/52

Ca 114/53

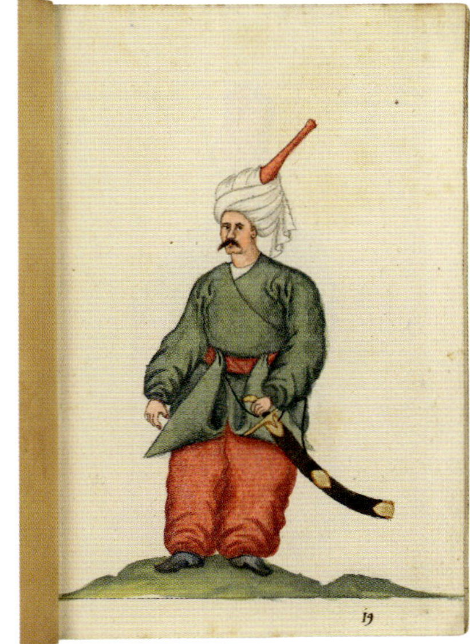

Ca 114/54

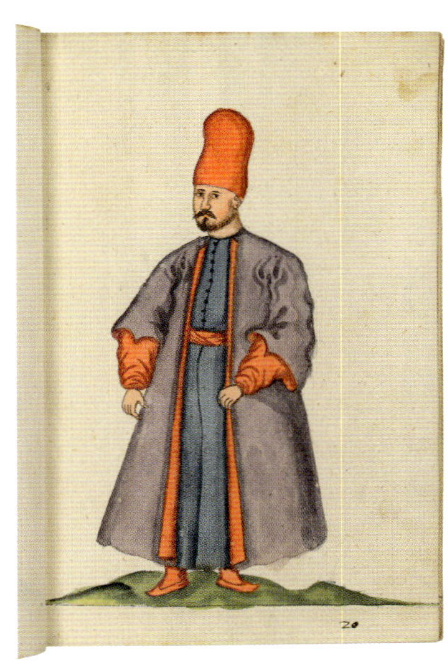

Ca 114/55

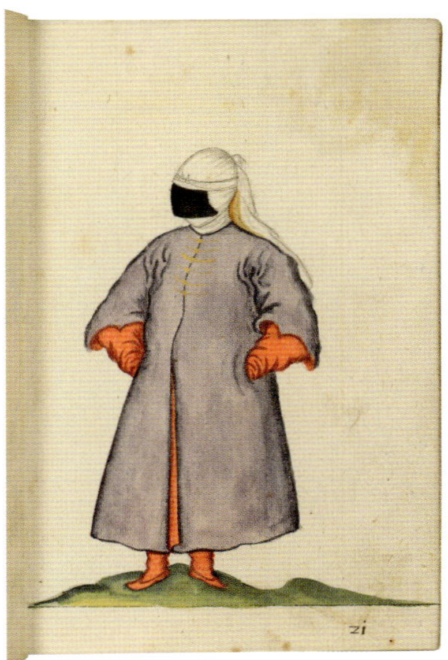

Ca 114/61

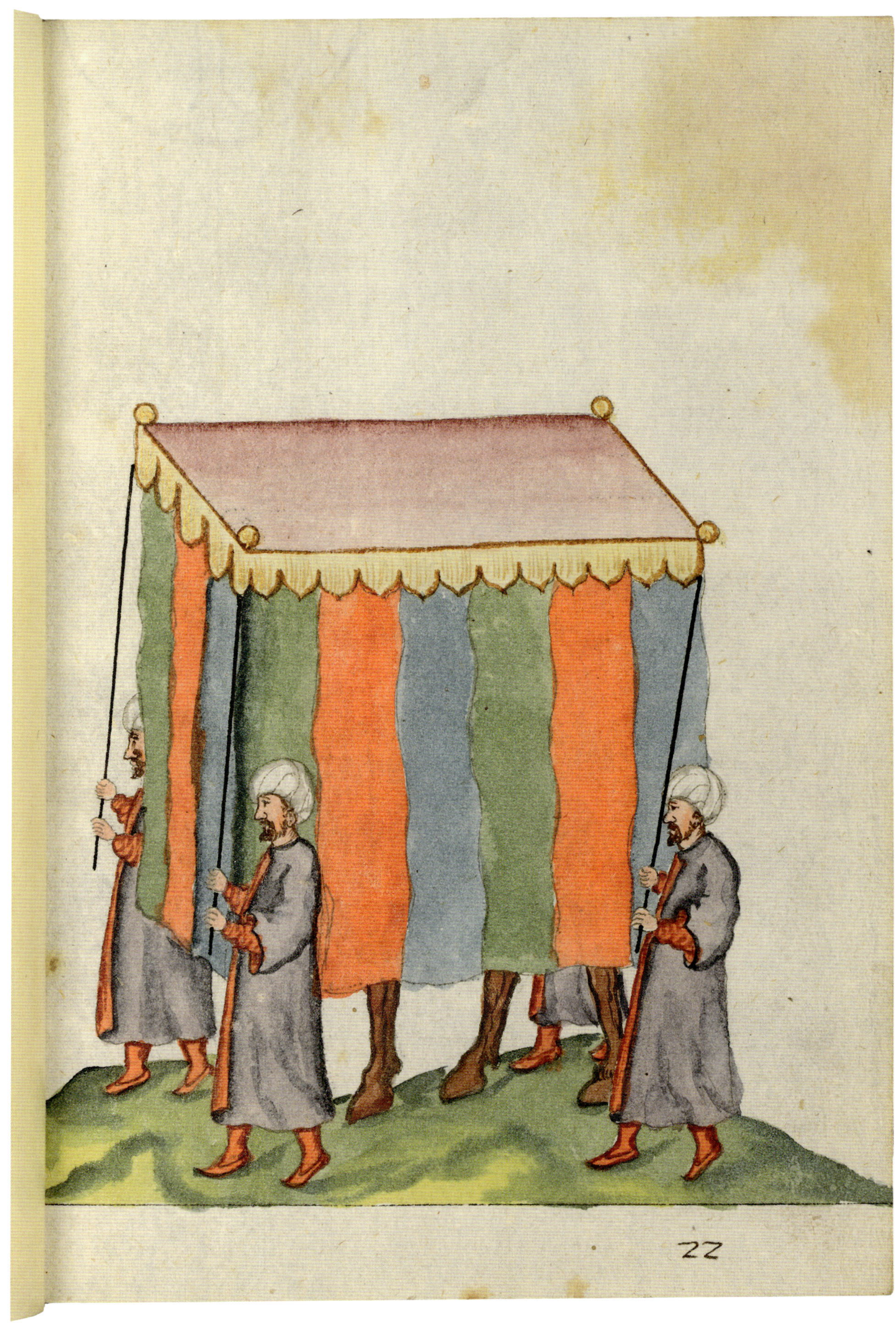

Ca 114/63

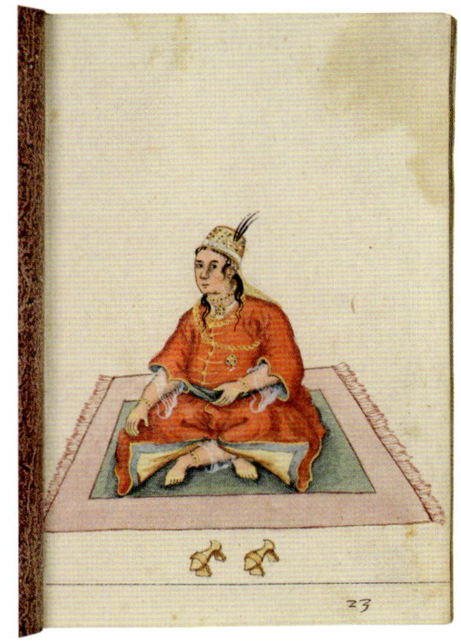

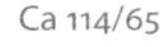
Ca 114/65

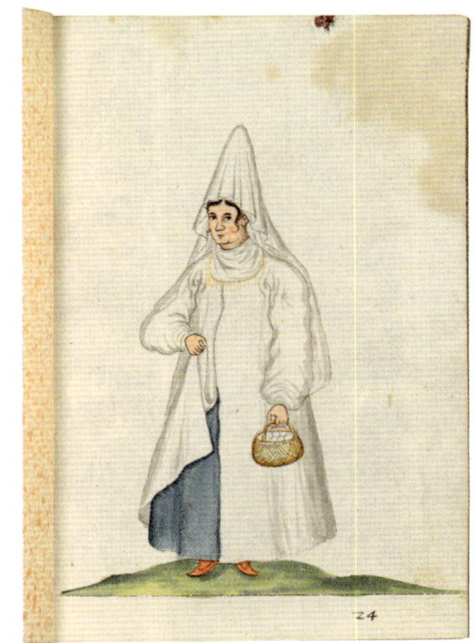

Ca 114/68

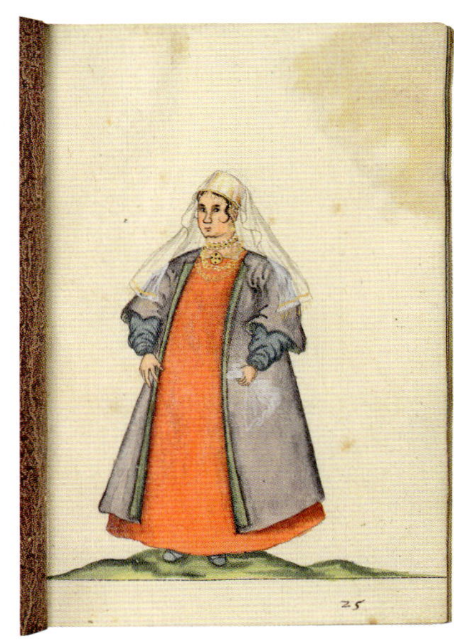

Ca 114/70

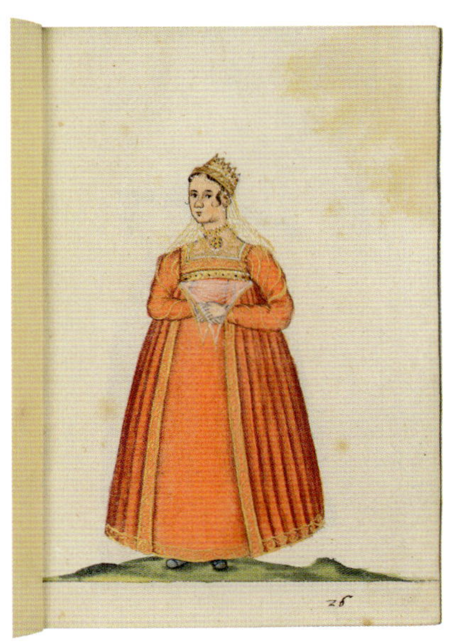

Ca 114/72

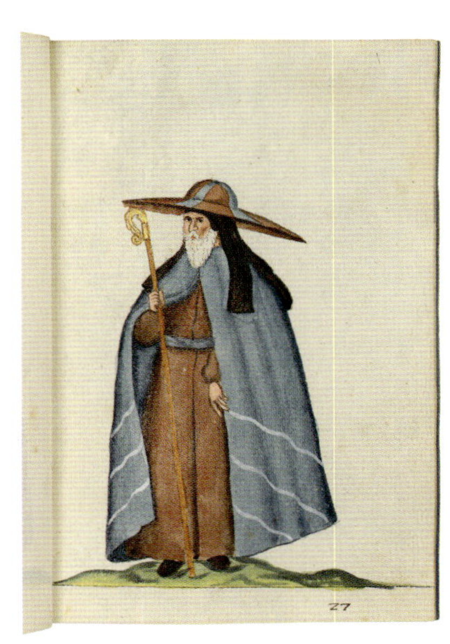

Ca 114/73

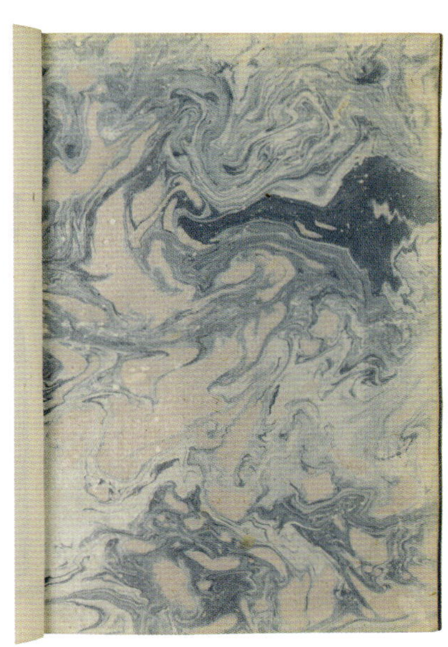

Ca 114/74

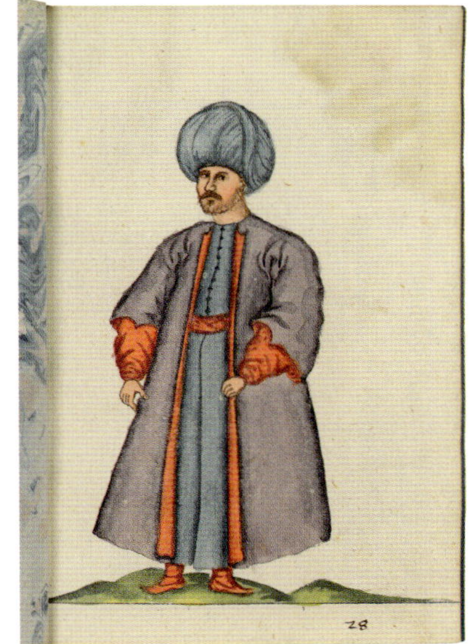

Ca 114/76

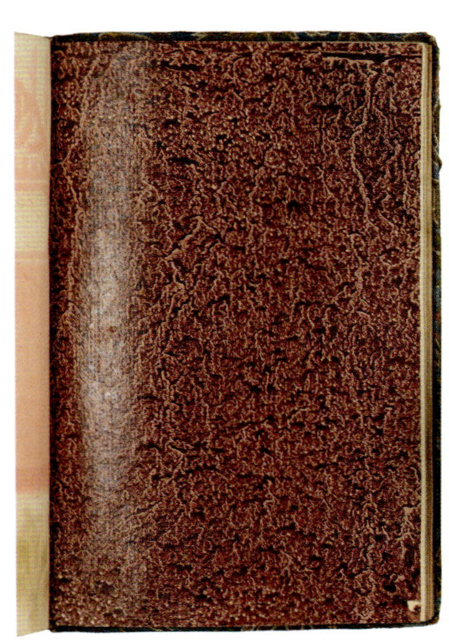

Ca 114/193

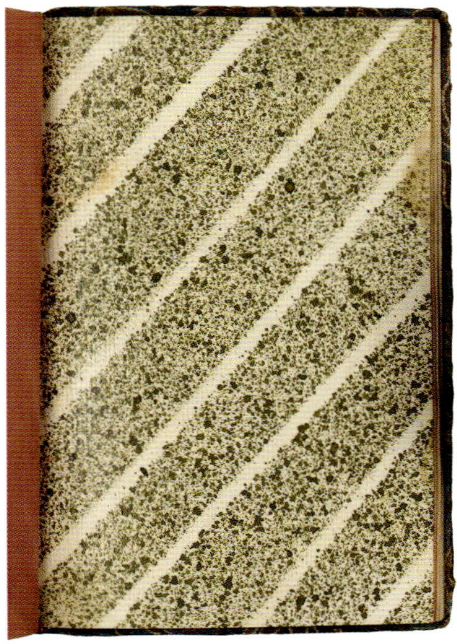

Ca 114/209

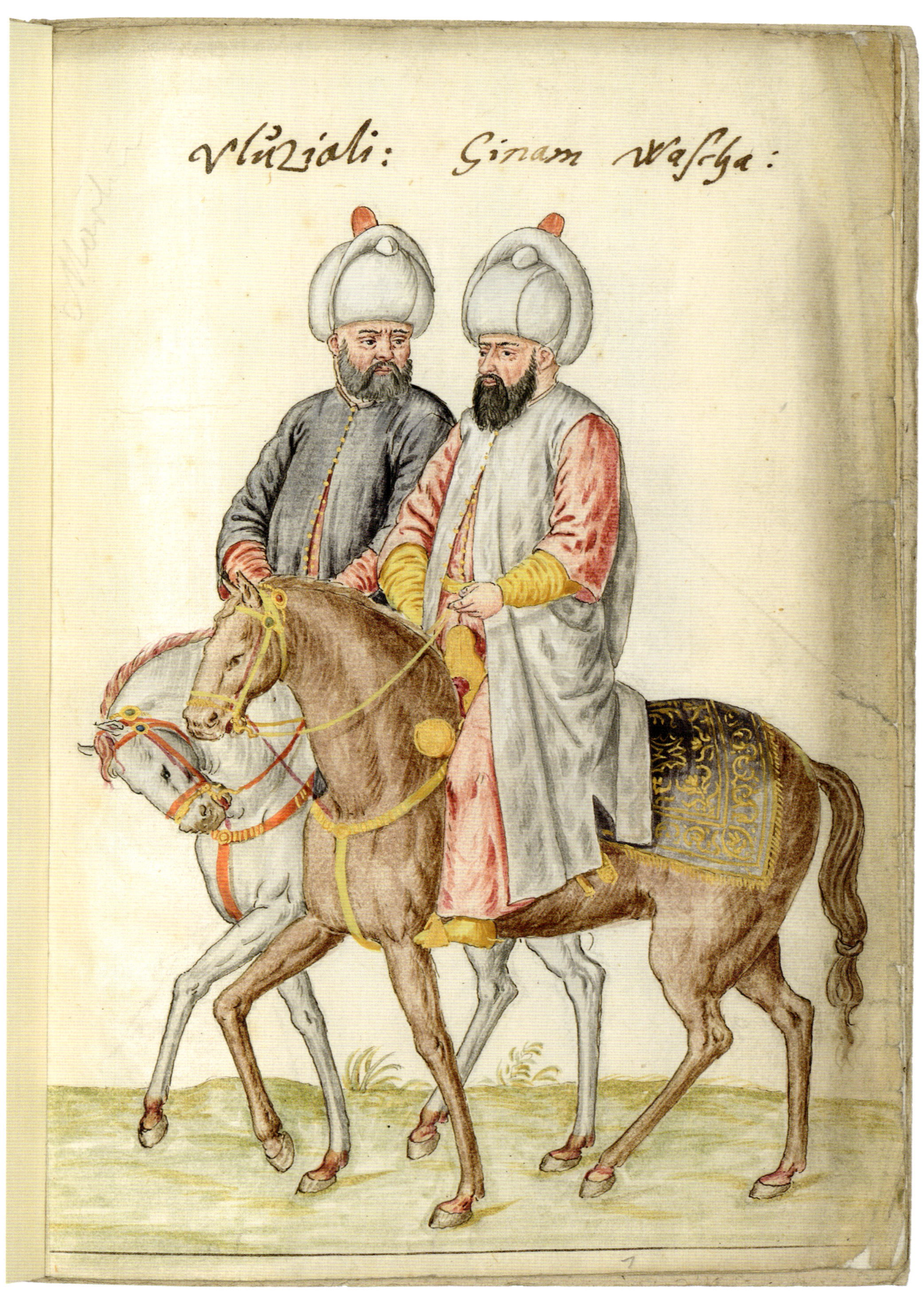

Ca 114 a/1

Ca 114 a
6 fols. showing Turkish costumes and one smaller sheet, attached later, showing an African figurine (fol. 7)

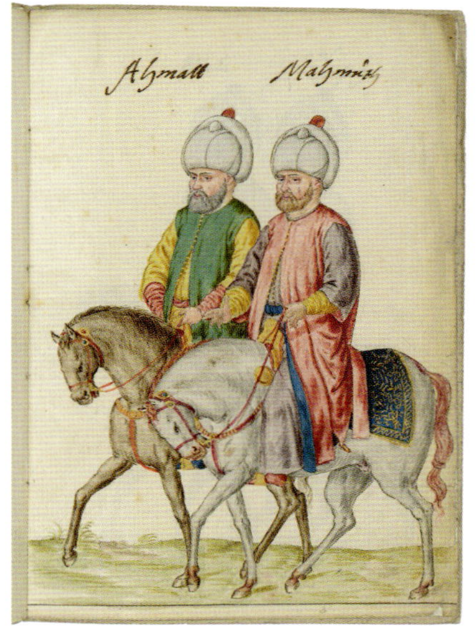

Ca 114 a/2

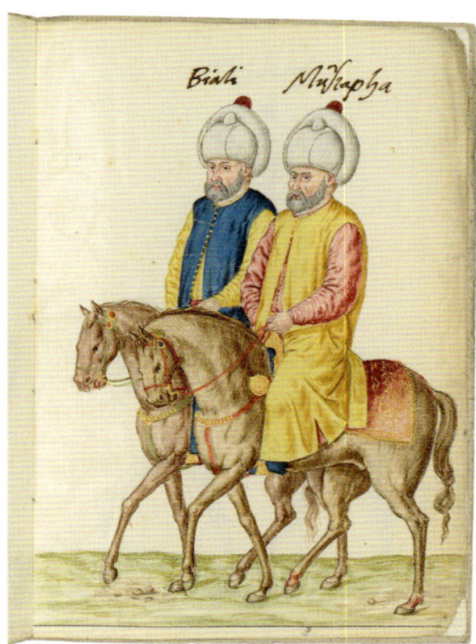

Ca 114 a/3

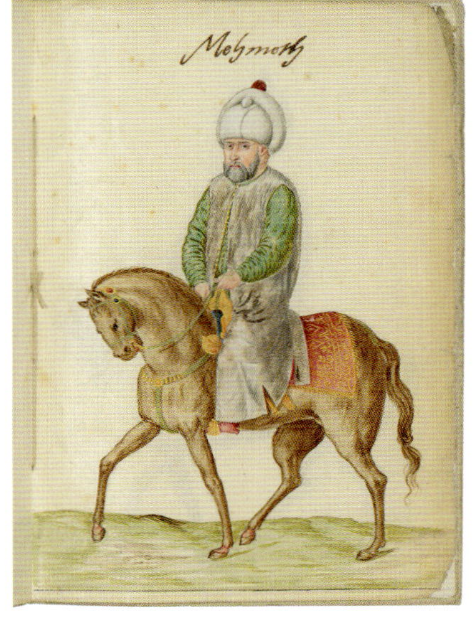

Ca 114 a/4

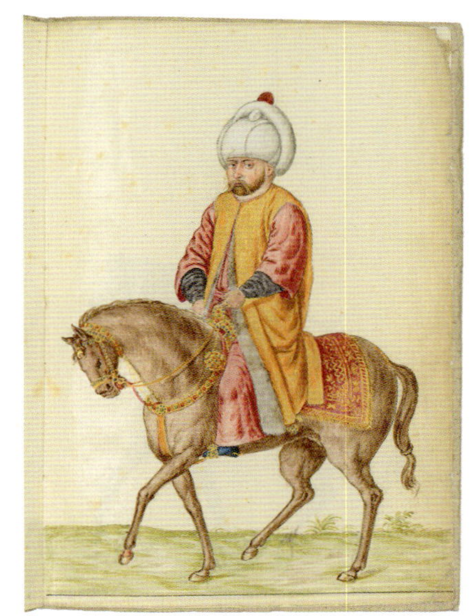

Ca 114 a/5

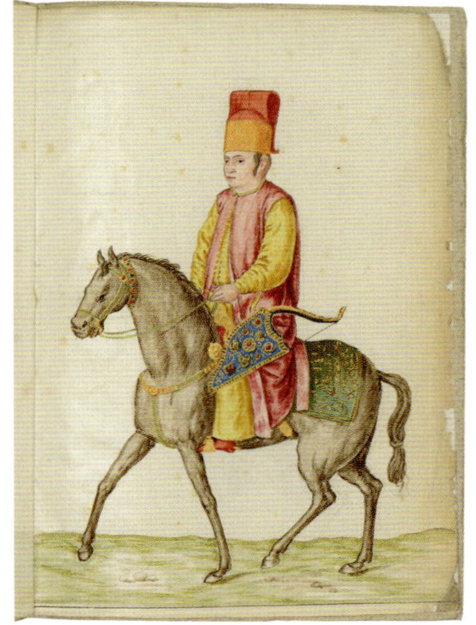

Ca 114 a/6

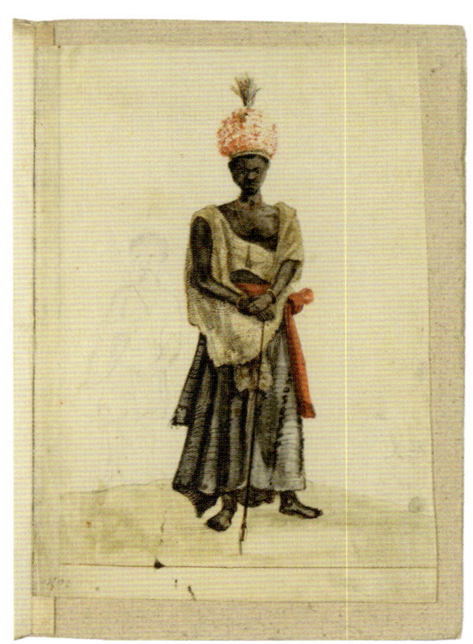

Ca 114 a/7

Cat. 91 | Ca 126 Fifteen Costumed Figures from Constantinople

Booklet with 15 costumed figures from Constantinople
Ottoman, late 17th / early 18th century
Album with 30 fols., 30 × 20.4 × 0.7 cm,
15 drawings on European paper,
watercolour, 16.9 to 19.1 cm × 10 to 11.5 cm
Reference: Dresden 2017, cat. 4, pp. 128–9

Several volumes with Turkish motifs, such as David Ungnad's "Book of Turks",[1] were kept in the so-called Turkish Chamber at the Dresden Court, whereas the *Album Amicorum of Elector Augustus* (cat. 90), acquired in 1582, was stored in the "Bureau XXII. La Chine" – only in the nineteenth century, when the collection was divided into "Sinica" and "Indica", it was classified as belonging to the latter.[2] A small booklet with "15. Blat Trachten zu Constantinopel" (15 sheets of Constantinople costumes) (fig. 1),[3] acquired in 1728 at the auctioning of the Nicolaas Witsen collection, belongs in the same category as the entries in the Heucher Inventory, here listed as "Indica V". In the early twentieth century, this booklet, together with two Indian court scenes (cat. 6–7, Ca 125) and an Indian card game (cat. 88, Ca 127),[4] was entered into the inventory of Indian works, where it came last, following the lot of Indian paintings from the Schlegel Collection (cat. 8–85, Ca 117 to Ca 124).

It is conceivable that the sheets are from one of the Constantinople *bazārs*. It appears, however, that such works, together with Indian miniatures, were sold as commodities via the Netherlands and then ended up in the same collections. Likewise, there are three similar sheets with costume drawings in the collectors' albums acquired in

Fig. 1
Front cover

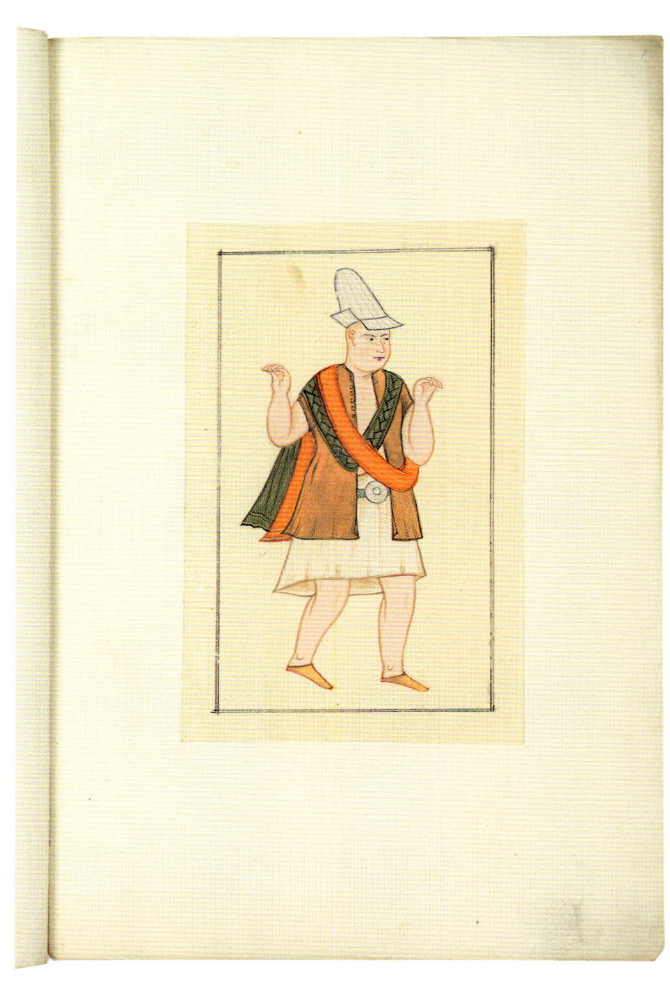

Ca 126/1

1762 by the Vienna court library—there, too, they have been added to the collection of Indian miniatures.[5]

The wish to compile illustrations of costumes from all over the world for royal collections undoubtedly has to do with the idea of courtly representation and festivals. The illustrations of folk costumes from Constantinople with the representation of local types and trades as here mainly Muslim *Sūfīs*, mendicants, and derwishes are, however, also evidence of a simple interest in the quaint and exotic. Some of the figures—like Ca 126/1, 11, 14, or 15—have traits verging on the caricature. The red book with its typical Persian décor, which he holds in his hand, is similar to the covers used for manuscripts and miniature albums in Turkish and Persian countries, but also in India. They can be found on Indian portrait albums from Golconda that were made around 1700, for example on the covers of albums extant in Dresden and Paris[6] as well as in the representations in these albums. PKH

Notes | 1 Ca 169, see Dresden 2017, p. 127, note 13. | 2 This is reflected in the labelling of the volumes from the former "La Chine" cabinet and the nineteenth-century inventories (see Franke Inventory 1865, sig. Cat. 64 I, fol. 391–2). In the late nineteenth century, small labels with a decorative blue edge, which specified these entries, were added, and the numbering used for "Indica" and "Sinica" was adopted for the collection's newly created file cards. The Indian portrait albums were given numbers I to IV in the "Indica" collection. | 3 Heucher Inventory 1738, sig. Cat. 1, p. 157, no. 27; see Amsterdam 1728, in the auction catalogue, p. 12, no. R. | 4 In the Heucher Inventory, the two court scenes Ca 125, cat. 6–7, are listed as "Chinese" (Heucher Inventory 1738, p. 155, no. 3: "2 beautiful Chinese paintings"). In view of the addendum, "1. Chinesischer Almanach n. 11" (1 Chinese almanac), the card game (ibid., p. 157, no. 30) can be identified as the playing cards acquired at the Witsen auction (Amsterdam 1728, p. 11, no. 11). | 5 Österreichische Nationalbibliothek, Vienna, sig. Cod. Min. 44, fol. 24. For comparable objects in the British Museum, London, and in the Biblioteka Narodowa, Warsaw, see Collaço 2017. | 6 See, for example, cat. 1, fig. 1–2; and cat. 1, Ca 112/36.

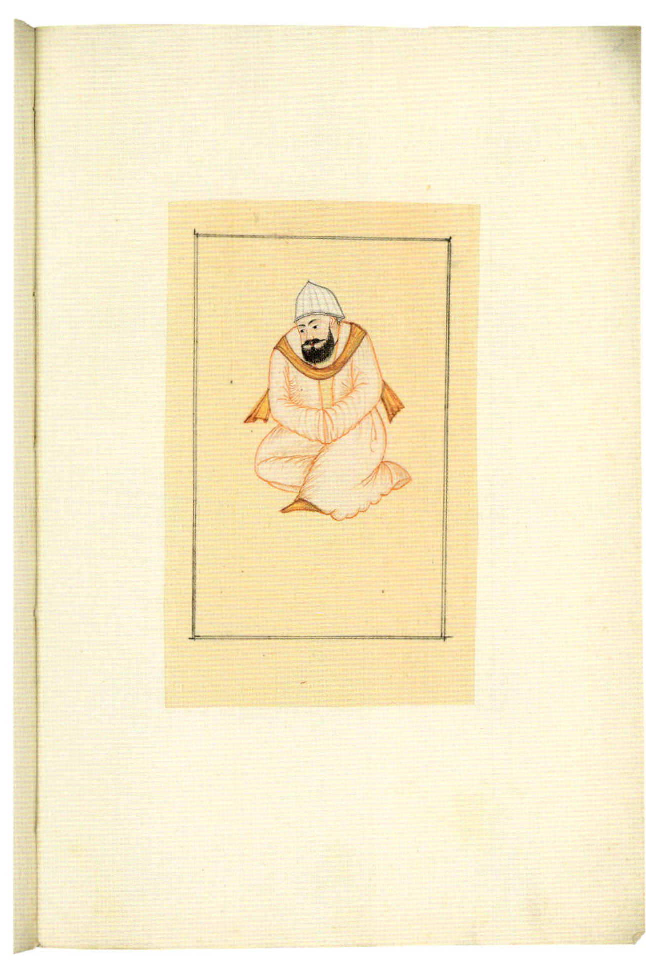

Ca 126/2

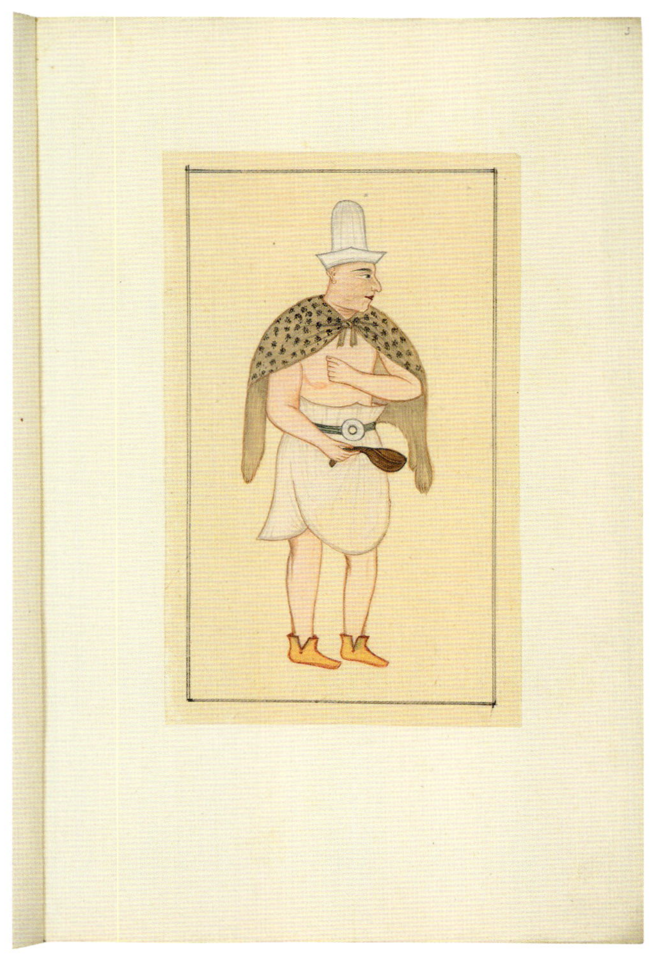

Ca 126/3

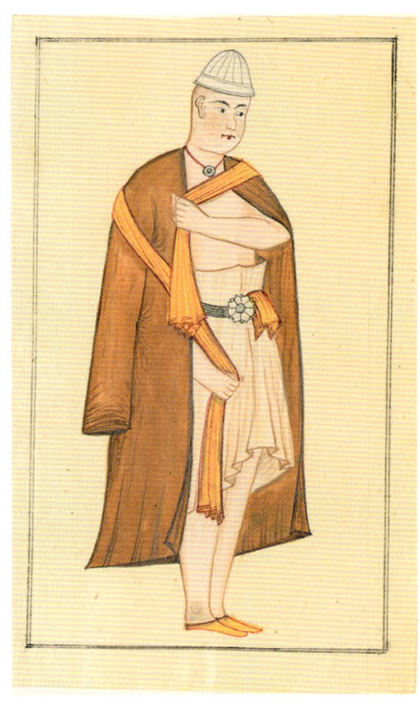
Ca 126/4

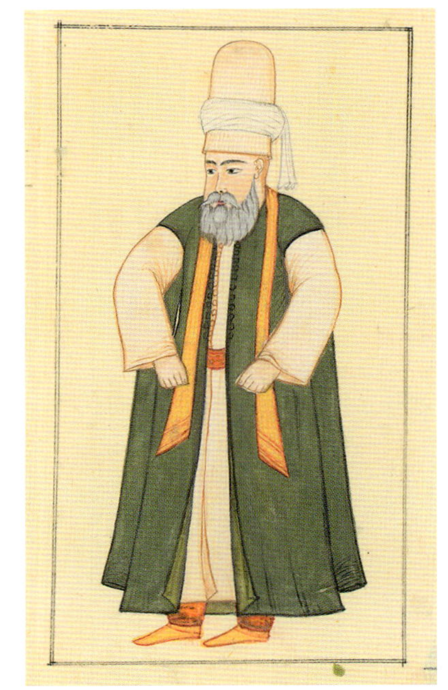
Ca 126/5

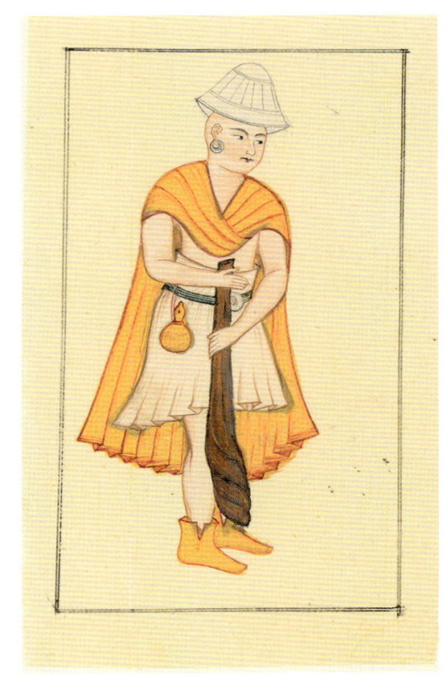
Ca 126/6

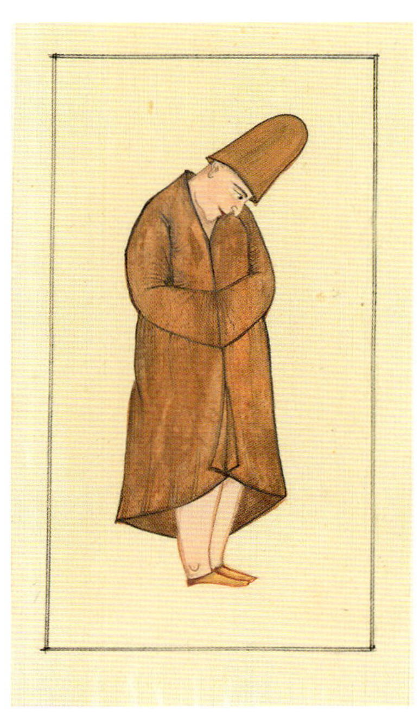
Ca 126/7

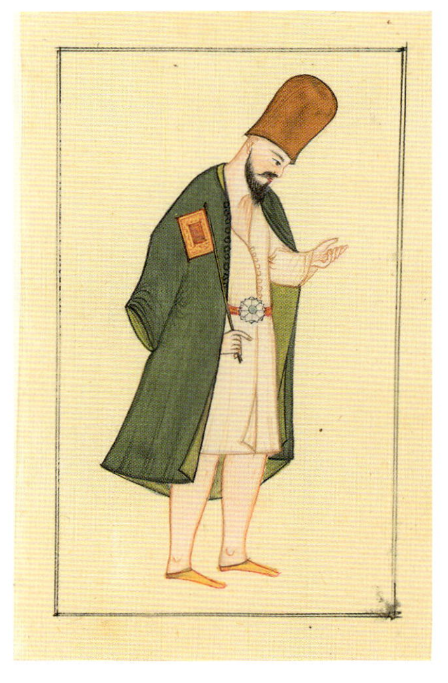
Ca 126/8

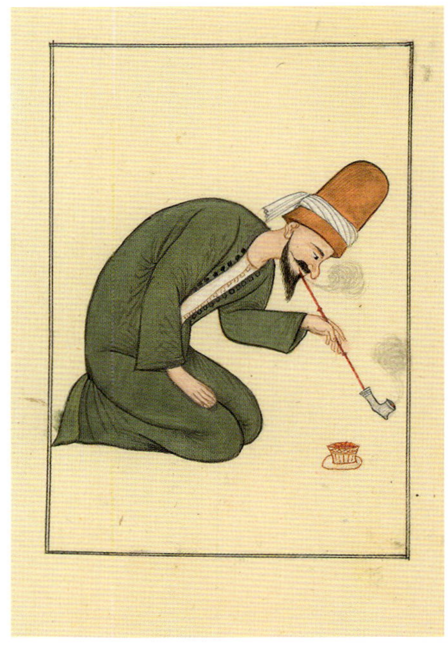
Ca 126/9

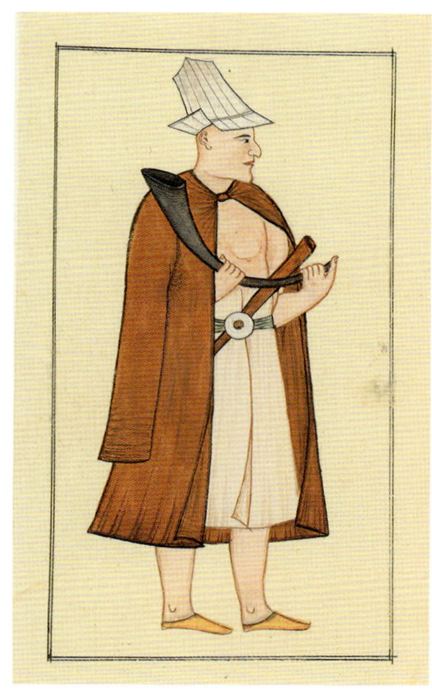
Ca 126/10

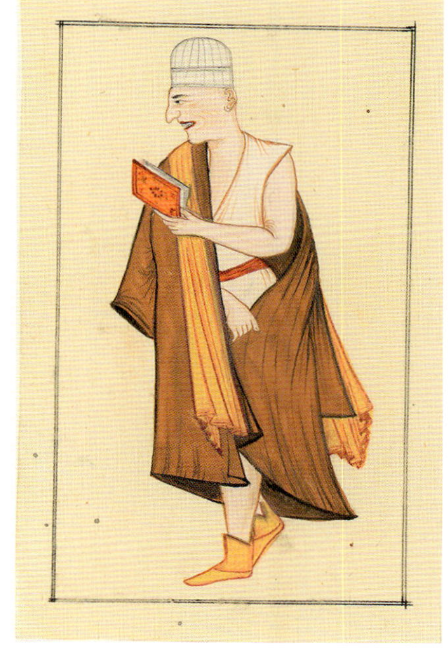
Ca 126/11

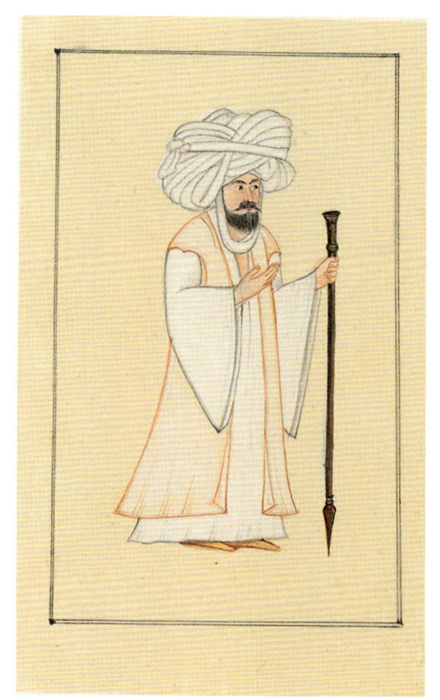
Ca 126/12

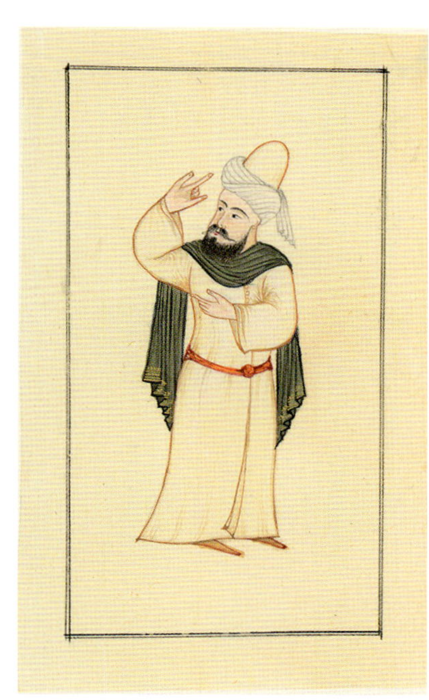
Ca 126/13

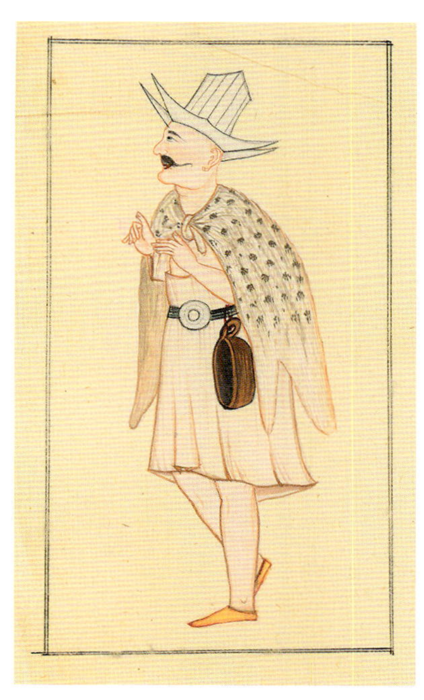
Ca 126/14

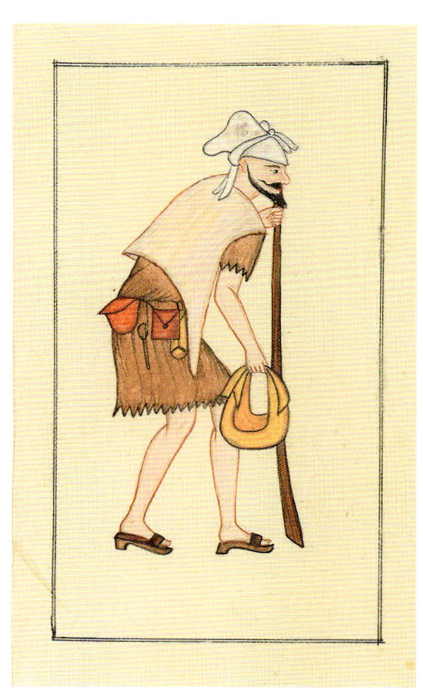
Ca 126/15

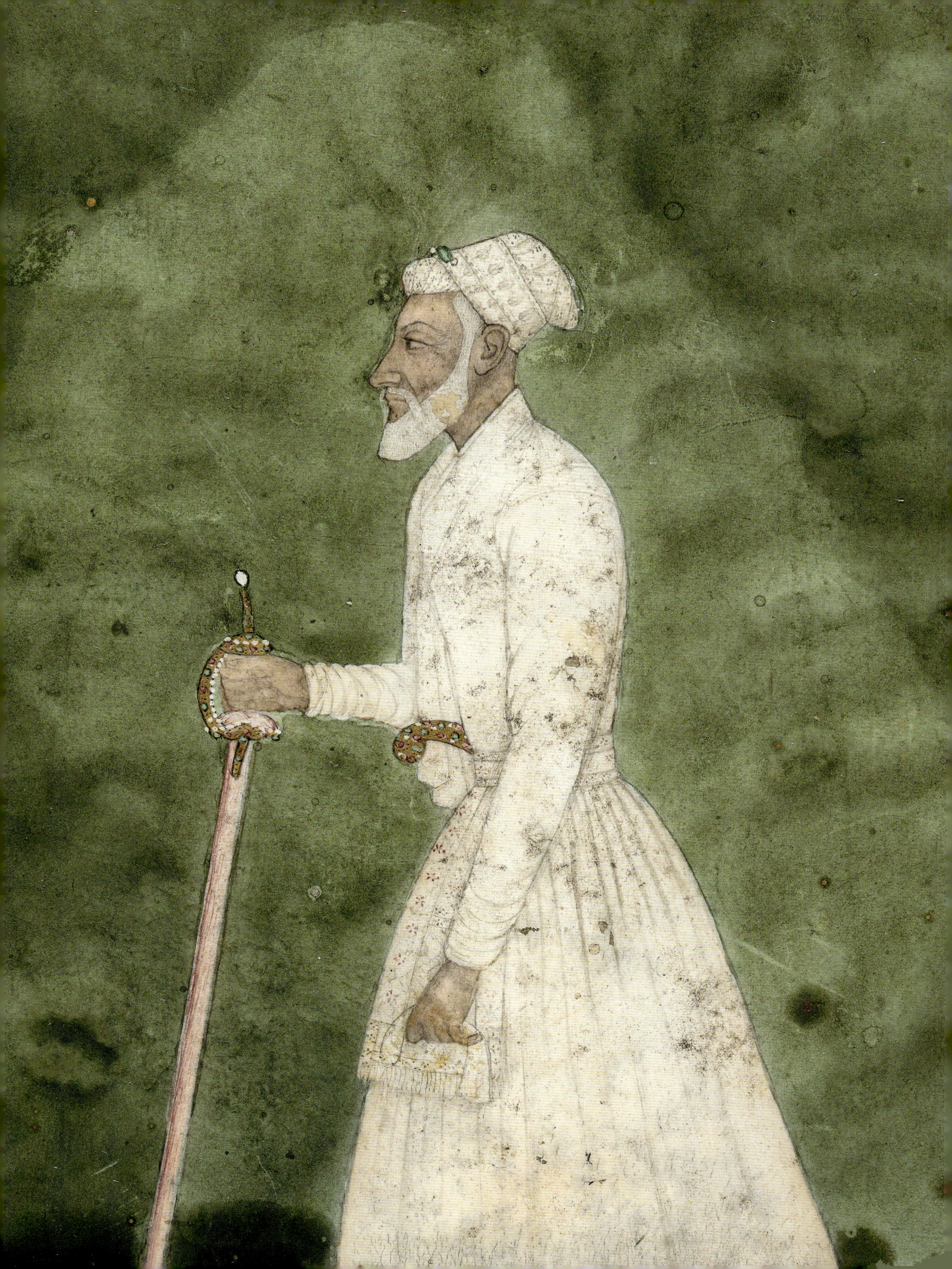

Appendices

Map of India

Karte
von
VORDER INDIEN
1829.
Himalaya Gipfel
1 Kedar Kanta
2 Bunderpuch
3 Sri Kanta
4 Kedarnath
5 Bhadrinath
6 Saliantor
7 Gosaingsthan
8 Salpu
HOCHASIEN
KLEIN TIBET
GROSS TIBET
TURKESTAN
ARABISCHES MEER
MEERBUSEN VON BENGALEN
INDISCHER OCEAN
I.CEYLON
I.SUMATRA
Gr Andaman
Andaman Inseln
Nicobarische Inseln
Laksha Dwipa oder Lakediven
Malaya Dwipa oder Malediven
Adschmer
Calcutta
Madras
Bombai
Hyderabad
Delhi
Lahore
Kabul
Kandahar
Multan
Tranquebar
Seringapatam
Golf von Cambaja
Gest. von E. Rolbe.

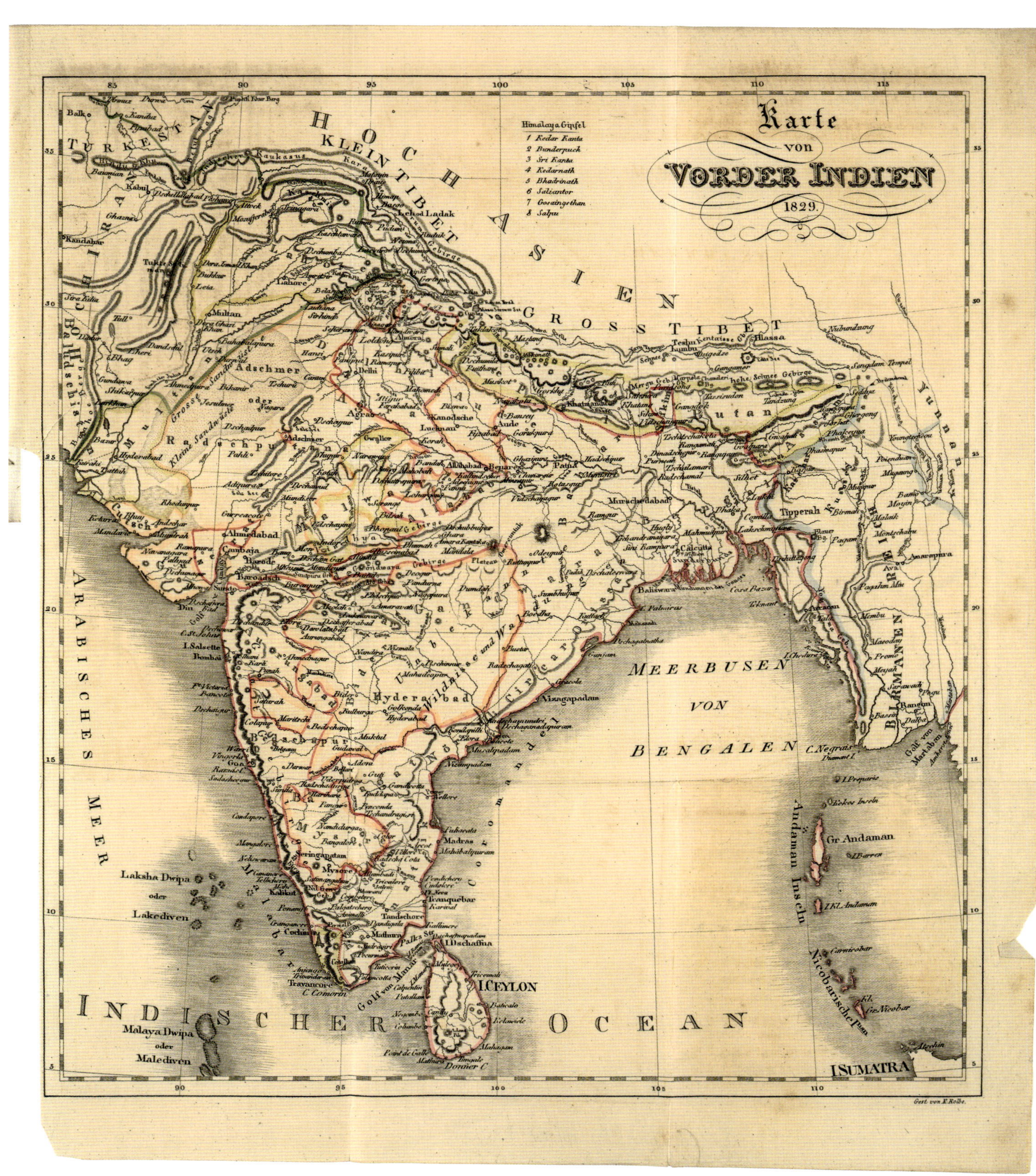

Dynastic Chronology

◄ fig. 1
Map of India, 1829
engraved by Karl Kolbe (1792–1849)
From *Berliner Kalender auf das Gemein-Jahr 1829*
Illustration to the essays by Carl Ritter, *Landeskunde von Indien (Geography of India)* and August Wilhelm Schlegel, *Indien in seinen Hauptbeziehungen (India's main relationships)*

The Timurids (r. 1370–1506)	Tīmūr	r. 1370–1405
	Khalīl Sultān	r. 1405–1409
	Shāh Rukh	r. 1409–1447
	Ulūgh Beg	r. 1447–1449
	'Abd al-Latīf	r. 1449–1450
	'Abd Allāh Mīrzā ('Abdullāh Mīrzā)	r. 1450–1451
	Abū Sa'īd	r. 1451–1469
	Sultān Husain Bāyqarā	r. 1469–1506
The Safavids (r. 1501–1722)	Ismā'īl I	r. 1501–1524
	Ṭahmāsp (Ṭahmāseb) I	r. 1524–1576
	Ismā'īl II	r. 1576–1577
	Muḥammad Khudabanda	r. 1578–1588
	'Abbās I	r. 1588–1629
	Safī I	r. 1629–1642
	'Abbās II	r. 1642–1666
	Sulaimān (Safī II)	r. 1666–1694
	Sultān Husain	r. 1694–1722
The Great Mughals (r. 1526–1707)	Bābur	r. 1526–1530
	Humāyūn	r. 1530–1540 and 1555–1556
	Akbar	r. 1556–1605
	Jahāngīr (Prince Salīm)	r. 1605–1627
	Shāh Jahān (Prince Khurram)	r. 1628–1658
	Aurangzēb ('Ālamgīr I)	r. 1658–1707
The Later Mughals (r. 1707–1858)	Bahādur Shāh I (Prince Mu'azzam)	r. 1707–1712
	Jahāndār Shāh	r. 1712–1713
	Farrukh Sīyar	r. 1713–1719
	Muḥammad Shāh (Raushan Akhtar)	r. 1719–1748
	Ahmad Shāh	r. 1748–1754
	'Ālamgīr II	r. 1754–1759
	Shāh 'Ālam II	r. 1759–1806
	Akbar II	r. 1806–1837
	Bahādur Shāh II	r. 1837–1858
The 'Ādil Shāhīs of Bijapur (r. 1490–1686)	Yusūf	r. 1490–1510
	Ismā'īl	r. 1510–1534
	Mallū	r. 1534–1535
	Ibrāhīm I	r. 1535–1558
	'Alī I	r. 1558–1580
	Ibrāhīm II	r. 1580–1627
	Muḥammad	r. 1627–1656
	'Alī II	r. 1656–1672
	Sikandar	r. 1672–1686
The Qutb Shāhīs of Golconda (r. 1496–1687)	Sultān Qūlī	r. 1496–1543
	Jamshīd	r. 1543–1550
	Subhan	r. 1550
	Ibrāhīm	r. 1550–1580
	Muḥammad Qūlī	r. 1580–1612
	Muḥammad	r. 1612–1626
	'Abdullāh	r. 1626–1672
	Abū'l Hasan	r. 1672–1687

Biographies

Short Biographies of Persons indicated in the Index with an asterisk (*)

Shāh **'Abbās I (1571–1629; r. 1588–1629)** Shāh 'Abbās I was the fifth ruler of the Safavid dynasty in Iran (1501–1722), which was in contact with the Mughals in India and often served as a source of inspiration for Mughal art and architecture. Under his rule, Iran reached its greatest territorial expansion.[1] In 1598 Isfahan was made the new capital, which saw the increased production of manuscripts such as the *Shāhnāma* that became an important demonstration of imperial patronage and ideology.[2]

Shāh **'Abbās II (1632–1666; r. 1642–1666)** Sultān Muḥammad Mīrzā, the seventh ruler of the Safavid dynasty in Iran, reigned as Shāh 'Abbās II. He took an active interest in governance and worked towards the consolidation of the Iranian Empire. His reign was marked by a significant increase in the activities of the western trading companies and consistent struggle with the Mughals, who aimed to conquer Kandahar in order to prove their hereditary descent from Tīmūr (r. 1370–1405).[3]

'Abd al-Ja'far Beg ('Abd al-Jabbār Beg) 'Abd al-Ja'far Beg (Servant of the Powerful) was a *wazīr* of the seventh king, 'Abdullāh Qutb Shāh (r. 1626–1672), of the Qutb Shāhī dynasty of Golconda (1496–1687).[4]

Mullāh **'Abd al-Samad** Mullāh 'Abd al-Samad was the secretary of the 'Abdullāh Qutb Shāh (r. 1626–1672).[5]

Mullāh **'Abdul Mali** Mullāh 'Abdul Mali was a spiritual guide to a king of the Qutb Shāhī dynasty of Golconda (1496–1687).

'Abdullāh Qutb Shāh (1614–1672; r. 1626–1672) 'Abdullāh Qutb Shāh was proclaimed seventh ruler of Golconda after his father's death. He continued to maintain diplomatic relations with Iran and evoked the Shāh's name during his Friday sermon at Golconda.[6] The Mughals considered this practice, along with the recitation of the names of the Twelve *Shī'a Imāms*, a sin. It was thus only a matter of time until 'Abdullāh was forced to sign the Deed of Submission to the Mughals in 1636.[7] Painting during the time of 'Abdullāh came in contact with foreign elements and spread the popularity of European themes such as the Virgin and Child and the Holy Family.[8]

'Alā' ud-Dīn (Shāh Alauddin; śāha alāvadīna; r. 1445–1451) Shāh 'Alā' ud-Dīn was the final ruler of the Sayyid dynasty in India (1414–1451).

'Alā' ud-Dīn 'Omar Khiljī (r. 1296–1316) Shāh 'Alā' ud-Dīn was the second ruler of the Khiljī dynasty in India (1290–1320).

'Alī 'Ādil Shāh II (1638–1672; r. 1656–1672) Upon the death of his father, 'Alī 'Ādil Shāh II succeeded to the throne as the eighth ruler of the 'Ādil Shāhī dynasty of Bijapur (1490–1686), an Indo-Islamic kingdom in the Deccan. The decline of the mighty Bijapur sultanate that began with his predecessor continued during his reign, marked by attacks mounted by the Hindu warrior Śivājī (r. 1674–1680).[9]

Azīm ush-Shān (1664–1712) 'Azīm ush-Shān, the second son of Bahādur Shāh I (r. 1707–1712), was appointed viceroy of Bengal, Bihar, and Orissa by his grandfather Aurangzēb. Upon his father's death, 'Azīm announced himself emperor of the Mughal dynasty and minted coins in his name. In spite of having the support of the court, he was soon challenged by his brother Jahāndār Shāh. In the war of succession, Jahāndār Shāh (r. 1712–1713) emerged victorious.

Abū Sa'īd (r. c. 1451–1469) After Shāh Rukh's death, Abū Sa'īd (d. 1469), grandson of Mīrān Shāh, claimed the throne of Samarkand. With him, the Timurid Empire entered a new phase of disintegration whilst the line of Mīrān Shāh continued to play a prominent role in what remained.

Abū'l Hasan Qutb Shāh (1600–1687; r. 1672–1687) Abū'l Hasan Qutb Shāh was the eighth and last *sultān* of the Qutb Shāhī dynasty of Golconda (1496–1687). A great patron of the arts and follower of the famous saint Shāh Rājū, he was nicknamed Tānā Shāh (King of Taste). After the fall of Bijapur in 1686, the Mughal army was free to concentrate on Hyderabad and ultimately captured Golconda the following year. Tānā Shāh's defeat marked the end of the Qutb Shāhī dynasty and the beginning of the Nizām dynasty under the control of the Mughals in Hyderabad. The arts had flourished under Qutb Shāhī rulers, and the tradition continued into the early eighteenth century under the Mughals.[9]

Ahmad Khān Ahmad Khān was probably a *wazīr* to a king of the Qutb Shāhī dynasty of Golconda (1496–1687).

Akbar (1542–1605; r. 1556–1605) Akbar succeeded his father, Humāyūn, as Mughal ruler at the age of thirteen under the guidance of regent Bairām Khān, Humāyūn's friend and general, whom he dismissed in 1560, taking over the administration himself. Akbar's rule was aimed at establishing a strong administration, expansion, and liberal social policies. Questioning the Muslim religious establishment, Akbar abolished *sharī'a*, a practice of collecting taxes from Hindu pilgrims, in 1563, and *jizya*, an annual tax imposed on the property of non-Muslims, in 1579. He also celebrated the Hindu festival of light, Diwāli. Despite his inability to read or write, Akbar exerted a spectacular influence on literature and the visual arts. Various manuscripts were illustrated during his reign such as the *Tūtīnāma* (Tales of a Parrot), *Hamzanāma* (Stories of the Adventures of Hamza), *Razmnāma* (Book of Wars), and *Akbarnāma,* his biography compiled by his friend Abū'l Fazl.[10]

Māhārāna **Amar Sīngh I (1559–1620)** Amar Sīngh I, the Māhārāna of Mewar, was the eldest son of Māhārāna Pratāp.

Amar Sīngh (1613–1644) Rāo Amar Sīngh Rāthor was the eldest son of Gaj Sīngh, the Māhārāna of Marwar. Achieving high esteem for his valour and might, he was a courtier at Shāh Jahān's court and served as the governor of Nagaur.[12]

Muḥammad **Amīn Khān Turānī (d. 1721)** Muḥammad Amīn Khān, son of Muḥammad Sa'īd Mīr Jumla, an important politician at the Deccani and Mughal courts, served as prime minister of Golconda during the reign of 'Abdullāh Qutb Shāh (r. 1626–1672). Both Amīn and his father shifted their political allegiance and left Golconda to serve the Mughal Emperor Shāh Jahān (r. 1628–1658).

Aurangzēb (1618–1707; r. 1658–1707) Upon Shāh Jahān's death, his four sons commenced a struggle for the throne. Aurangzēb emerged victorious, crowning himself emperor with the title 'Ālamgīr (World Seizer). Akbar's ideology, which had already begun changing during Shāh Jahān's rule, saw a full transformation under Aurangzēb, who devoted seven years to learning the *Qur'ān*. Royal patronage of manuscripts and book illustration declined during his rule, and artists often went to other courts and cities in search of work. The writing of the chronicles of his reign, the *'Ālamgīrnāma,* was brought to a halt in his tenth regnal year. He was considered a vigorous ruler for half a century, but the empire declined rapidly after his death, ultimately coming under the control of the British East India Company in 1858.[13]

Āzād Khān (1631–1716) Āzād Khān was a favourite of Emperor Shāh Jahān. In 1670 he became deputy *wazīr* to Aurangzēb and full *wazīr* in 1676, retaining the office until the end of Aurangzēb's reign. He was regarded as a kind and sympathetic figure that was closely related to the imperial family.[14]

Muḥammad **A'zam Shāh (1653–1707; r. 1707)** Muḥammad A'zam Shāh was the eldest son of the sixth Mughal emperor, Aurangzēb (r. 1658–1707), and his consort Dilras Bānū Begum, a Safavid princess. Emperor Aurangzēb's death initiated a war of succession among his sons for control of the Deccan. A'zam ascended the Mughal throne less than one month after Aurangzēb's death but was soon challenged by his brother Mu'azzam, who then ascended the throne as Bahādur Shāh I (r. 1707–1712).[15]

Bābur (1483–1530; r. Farghana 1494; Kabul 1504; Delhi 1526–1530) The Mughals were descendants of the Timurids and shared a cultural legacy similar to the Turko-Mongol rulers of Central Asia. Zahīr ud-Dīn Muḥammad was born in 1483 in Farghana, a region of Central Asia, during the dissipation of the Timurid Empire. He inherited the throne as an eleven year old and later established the Mughal Empire in India.[16]

Bahādur Shāh I (1643–1712; r. 1707–1712) Prince Mu'azzam, later known as Bahādur Shāh, became the seventh ruler of the Mughal dynasty in India (1526–1858). He was born in Burhanpur in the Deccan, the second son of Aurangzēb (r. 1658–1707), governor of the Deccan. Mu'azzam rebelled against Aurangzēb in 1670 and 1680 in an attempt to claim the throne but was dissuaded by his mother. When Aurangzēb died without appointing an heir, Mu'azzam, then governor of Kabul, was quick to take charge after defeating his brothers and other contenders to the throne. He ascended the Mughal throne at age sixty-three on June 19, 1707, with the title Bahādur Shāh I.

Bhao Sīngh (d. 1678) Bhao Sīngh, a *wazīr* of Aurangzēb, was the *rāo* (*rājā*) of Bundi (r. 1658–1678). He defeated Atmarām Gaur of Sheopur, who had attacked Bundi at the instigation of Aurangzēb in 1660, and became the governor of Aurangabad under Prince Mu'azzam.[17]

Chatra Sal Rāo (d. 1658) Chatra Sal Rāo was a Rājput prince, who died in the war between Prince Dārā and Aurangzēb in 1658.[18]

Daniyāl (1572–1604) Daniyāl was a son of the Mughal Emperor Akbar (r. 1556–1605). He served as the viceroy of the Deccan from 1601 to 1604.[19] His mother was a cousin of Akbar's first wife from Amber. While Akbar had seven wives, Daniyāl had nine. Like his father, Daniyāl was notorious for his appetite for worldly pleasures. Both Daniyāl and his brother Murād succumbed to alcoholism and predeceased their father. His lineage ended when Shāh Jahān killed Daniyāl's sons during a battle against Shāhryar for the throne of the Mughal kingdom.[20]

Dārā Shikōh (1615–1659) Dārā Shikōh, the heir apparent, was the first son of Shāh Jahān's with his favorite wife, Mumtāz-i Mahāl, and was granted the title *Shāhzāda-e Buland Iqbāl* (Prince of High Fortune). He was forty-three when the war of succession began. When news of Shāh Jahān's illness reached his younger brother Aurangzēb in the Deccan, Aurangzēb carefully planned a joint action with his brother Murād to dispose of Dārā and his fourth brother, Shujā' (d. 1661), leading to his successful victory over Dārā in the battle of Samugarh.[21] A great patron of the arts and literature, Dārā is credited with the translation of about forty Upaniṣads from Sanskrit into Persian.[22]

Diler Khān (d. 1683) In traveller and writer Nicolao Manucci's (1638–1717) accounts of the Mughals,[23] Aurangzēb ordered Diler Khān to succeed Bahādur Khān in 1678 in conducting the war against the Marātha warrior Śivājī. He died at Aurangabad.

Farkhunda Akhtar (d. 1712) Farkhunda Akhtar was the brother of Muḥammad Shāh (r. 1719–1748), the tenth ruler of the Mughal dynasty in India.

Farrukh Sīyar (r. 1713–1719) Farrukh Sīyar was the grandson of Bahādur Shāh I (r. 1707–1712) from his son 'Azīm ush-Shān. After the deposition of Farrukh Sīyar, several puppet rulers controlled the Mughal Empire for brief periods of time until Muḥammad Shāh (r. 1719–1748) was put on the throne.[24]

Fath Jang Khān (Ghāzi ud-Dīn) Fath Jang Khān served as a chief *wazīr* during the reign of the Mughal Emperor Aurangzēb (r. 1658–1707).[25] A Sunni Turk, son of Qilich Khān, he, together with Safshikan Khān, played a prominent role in the battles preceding the fall of Bijapur (1685–1686). He was made the *sūbadār* (governor) of Gujarat province during the reign of the Mughal Emperor Bahādur Shāh I (r. 1707–1712).

Fīrōz Shāh Sūrī (r. 1554) Fīrōz Shāh was the third ruler of the Sūr dynasty in India (1540–1555).

Sultān **Fīrōz Shāh Tughluq (r. 1351–1388)** Fīrōz Shāh Tughluq was the fourth ruler of the Tughluq dynasty in India (1320–1414).

Gaj Sīngh (1595–1638; r. 1618–1638) Rājā Gaj Sīngh was the ruler of Marwar. He succeeded his father, Suraj Sīngh, whose sister was a wife of Jahāngīr and the mother of Shāh Jahān. Upon his death, he was succeeded by his son Jaswanth Sīngh; while his other son, Amar Sīngh, was killed by order of Shāh Jahān in 1644.[26]

Sultān **Ghiyās ud-Dīn Balban (r. 1266–1286)** Sultān Ghiyās ud-Dīn was the ninth *sultān* of the Mamlūk dynasty in India (1206–1290). He was a former slave and a son-in-law of Sultān Nāsir ud-Dīn Mahmūd.

Shāh **Ghiyās ud-Dīn Tughluq I (r. 1320–1325)** Shāh Ghiyās ud-Dīn was the founder and first ruler of the Tughluq (also Tughlaq or Tughluk) dynasty in India (1320–1414). The Tughluq was a Muslim dynasty of Turkic origin that ruled the Delhi sultanate in medieval India. Its reign began in Delhi in 1320, when Shāh Ghiyās ud-Dīn assumed the throne with the title Ghiyās ud-Dīn Tughluq.

Hasan Khān Hasan Khān was a *wazīr* to a king of the Qutb Shāhī dynasty of Golconda (1496–1687). Mīr Jumla (1591–1663), who was known for his civil and military administration, sent Hasan Khān to Pegu in Myanmar to begin commercial relations with its ruler.[27]

Humāyūn (1508–1556; r. 1530–1540, 1555–1556) Humāyūn, Bābur's eldest son, became ruler and encountered massive difficulties in his efforts to retain and expand his father's conquests in India. Conflicts with the Pashtun rebel Shēr Shāh Sūrī (r. 1540–1545) ended with Humāyūn fleeing to Agra and then to Lahore in 1540. There, Humāyūn employed two Safavid artists, Mīr Sayyid 'Alī and 'Abd al-Samad, as well as other artists from the Safavidi court in Tabriz who later played a crucial role in the development of painting under the Mughals. Poor administration and famine had weakened Sūr's control in India, and Humāyūn, after his exile in Iran, successfully restored the Mughal rule in India by 1555.[28]

Husain Shāh Husain Shāh was probably a *wazīr* to a king of the Qutb Shāhī dynasty of Golconda (1496–1687).

Ibn-i Khātūn (Shaikh Muḥammad Khātūn, Muḥammad Ibn-i Khātūn) Muḥammad Ibn-i Khātūn was the prime minister to Sultān 'Abdullāh Qutb Shāh (r. 1626–1672) of Golconda. Ibn-i Khātūn was permitted to sit beside 'Abdullāh's throne in 1629.[29]

Shāh **Ibrāhīm Lōdī (r. 1517–1526)** Shāh Ibrāhīm was the third and final ruler of the Lōdī dynasty in India (1451–1526).

Ibrāhīm Shāh Sūrī (r. 1555) Ibrāhīm Shāh was the fifth ruler of the Sūr dynasty in India (1540–1555).

Ikhlās Khān (d. 1656) Ikhlās Khān, an Abyssinian, was commander-in-chief and minister of finances under Sultān Ibrāhīm ʿĀdil Shāh II (r. 1580–1627) and continued serving under Muḥammad ʿĀdil Shāh II (r. 1627–1656) of the ʿĀdil Shāhī dynasty of Bijapur (1490–1686).[30]

Ja'far Khān (d. 1670) Ja'far Khān, son of Sādiq Khān (Mīr Bakhsh) and son-in-law of Asaf Khān, was made *wazīr* under Aurangzēb in 1664. As per Mannuci's account, he was friendly towards Christians.[31] He was the most famous Mughal scholar and the first secretary and minister of state.

Jahāndār Shāh (1661–1713; r. 1712–1713) Jahāndār Shāh was the son of Bahādur Shāh I (r. 1707–1712), the seventh emperor of the Mughal dynasty (1526–1857). Upon the death of Bahādur Shāh I, wars of succession took place among his sons—Jahāndār Shāh, ʿAzīm ush-Shān, Rafī' ush-Shān, and Jahān Shāh—all of whom were in Lahore. Jahāndār emerged victorious with the support of Zū'lfiqār Khān. During Jahāndār's rule, the Mughal Empire and army experienced huge losses. Farrukh Sīyar (r. 1713–1719), son of his late cousin ʿAzīm, raised an army against him in Bengal and won. Jahāndār Shāh was imprisoned in Delhi and put to death on February 11, 1713, on Farrukh Sīyar's orders.[32]

Jahāngīr (1569–1627; r. 1605–1627) In 1600 Akbar's son Salīm rebelled against his father and became the Mughal Emperor Jahāngīr (World Seizer). Religious tolerance continued to remain a feature of Jahāngīr's court. While the new universal religion *Dīn-i Ilāhī*, announced in 1582, pronounced the ruler as divine, Jahāngīr's relationship to his nobles was more akin to that of a *Sūfī* master and his disciples than an emperor and his subjects.[33] While Jahāngīr spent his adult life addicted to opium, which ultimately led to his death, his legacy centres on his role as a patron and connoisseur of great works of art.[34] The most substantial manuscript undertaken by the royal atelier during his reign was the *Jahāngīrnāma* (or *Tuzuk-i Jahāngīrī*), a memoir that covers his first seventeen years as emperor.[35]

Jalāl ud-Dīn Fīrōz Shāh Khiljī (r. 1290–1296) Jalāl ud-Dīn was the first ruler of the Khiljī dynasty in India (1290–1320). The Khiljī was a Muslim dynasty of Turkic origin, long settled in present-day Afghanistan, which ruled large parts of South Asia.

Janamejaya III A legendary figure, Janamejaya III succeeded his father, Parikṣit, as the king of Hastinapura, with its capital at Indraprastha (present-day Delhi). According to ancient historical tradition, the *Mahābhārata* was recited by Vaiśampāyana, pupil of Vyāsa, to Janamejaya at the *sarpasattra* (snake sacrifice).

Rājā **Karan Sīngh (d. 1666/67)**[36] Rājā Karan Sīngh, the ruler of Bikaner, also served as a *wazīr* of Aurangzēb (r. 1658–1707). Upon Aurangzēb's succession he refused to appear before the new Mughal emperor, insisting that he could not act against the precedents set by his ancestors. Aurangzēb finally agreed but ordered him to proceed towards the Deccan to fight against the rising Marātha warrior Śivājī.[37]

Khayrāt Khān (d. 1655) Khayrāt Khān was an ambassador, promoted to the rank of a minister during the reign of Sultān ʿAbdullāh Qutb Shāh (r. 1626–1672), the seventh *sultān* of the Qutb Shāhī dynasty of Golconda (1496–1687). Several gardens close to the Mūsā Burj in the Golconda Fort are credited to Khayrāt Khān. His grave is in the old city of Hyderabad near the Gaulipūra Gate.

Khusrau (1587–1622) Khusrau, the eldest son of Jahāngīr (r. 1605–1627), challenged his father for control of the Mughal Empire following the death of his grandfather Akbar (1556–1605). After his father's death, Khusrau and his brothers Parvīz, Khurram, and Shahriyār fought for control, with Khurram ultimately seizing the throne.[38]

Mādanna Paṇḍit (d. 1685) Mādanna Paṇḍit, a Brahmin, was one of the most important ministers of Abū'l Hasan Qutb Shāh (r. 1672–1687), the eighth Shāh of the Golconda dynasty (1496–1687). Mādanna and his brother Ākannā began their careers in Hyderabad in the service of Sayyid Muzaffar during the reign of ʿAbdullāh Qutb Shāh (r. 1626–1672). Mādanna and Ākannā rose to prominence in the sultanate of Golconda between 1674 and 1685, and dominated affairs of state in Golconda towards the end of their lives.[39]

Sultān **Mahmūd Ghaznavī (971–1030; r. 998–1001, ʿAmīr of Ghazna; r. 1002–1030, Sultān of Ghazna)** Sultān Mahmūd Ghaznavī was the most prominent ruler of the Ghaznavid Empire. In 1001 he invaded parts of India as well as present-day Afghanistan and Pakistan. Eventually he conquered Nagarkot-Kangra, Thanesar, Kanauj, and Gwalior. Although he did not settle in India, he supressed revolt against the empire by adapting strict policies against Hindus.

Mān Sīngh I (1589–1614) Rājā Mān Sīngh was the ruler of Amber and one of Akbar's close companions.[40] He was a member of the circle the emperor called the *nauratan* (nine jewels). He joined Akbar's court in 1562, when Akbar married the eldest daughter of Rājā Bihār Māl of Amber, who had adopted Mān Sīngh. Closeness between the Muslim monarch and his Hindu subject was such that Akbar referred to him as *farzand* (son).[41] He was appointed governor of Bihar and later of Bengal. Under Jahāngīr, he served in the Deccan, where he died.[42]

Mīr Jumla II (1591–1663) Mīr Muḥammad Sa'īd Ardistānī, popularly known as Mīr Jumla II was born to a poor oil merchant in Isfahan. He escaped the difficult conditions in Persia and in the 1630s began working as a clerk to a diamond merchant in business with Golconda. In 1635–1636 he became the *Sar-i Daftar Shāhī* (keeper of royal records) during the reign of ʿAbdullāh Qutb Shāh (r. 1626–1672) and his zeal and loyalty gained him unrivalled authority in affairs of state. In 1643 he was appointed minister general. He served the *sultān* until 1653, and he joined the service of the Mughals in 1658, when Aurangzēb persuaded Shāh Jahān to petition for him.[43]

Mīrān Shāh (c. 1367–1408) Mīrān Shāh was the third son of Tīmūr. In the battle for succession following Tīmūr's death, his youngest son, Shāh Rukh (d. 1447), took control of Transoxiana and the Timurid capital, Samarkand.[44] Supported by the *amīrs*, he eliminated any contenders to the throne and installed his sons rather than Tīmūr's. The complex political history of the Timurid Empire is seen in Indian miniature paintings via the exploits of the sons of Tīmūr and the line of Mīrān Shāh until the beginning of the reign of Bābur, the first Mughal emperor of India.[45]

Shāh **Mīrzā** Shāh Mīrzā was the nephew of Sayyid Muzzafar. He served as military commander at the time of the eighth king, ʿAbū'l Hasan Qutb Shāh (r. 1672–1687), of the Qutb Shāhī dynasty of Golconda (1496–1687) and also as military leader of Karnatak until he was overthrown in 1673 and died under house arrest.[46]

Mīrzā Ahmad A nobleman from Mekka, Mīrzā Ahmad married Bara Sāhib, the eldest daughter of Sultān ʿAbdullāh Qutb Shāh (r. 1626–1672) of the Golconda dynasty.[47] He was one of the mightiest nobles of the state and was honoured with the title *A'in al-Mulk*. Later, he was confined and removed because of the growing threat posed by his power. He and his wife were poisoned to death by order of Sultān ʿAbdullāh Shāh.[48]

Mīrzā Nāsir Mīrzā Nāsir was a *wazīr* to a king of the Qutb Shāhī dynasty of Golconda (1496–1687).

Shāh **Mubārak (r. 1421–1434)** Shāh Mubārak, a man of great vision, was the son of Khīzr Khān, the founder of the Sayyid dynasty in India (1414–1451).

Sultān **Muḥammad (d. c. 1411)** Sultān Muḥammad was a son of Mīrān Shāh (c. 1367–1408) and a grandson of Tīmūr (r. 1370–1405).

Sultān **Muḥammad Tughluq** The name Sultān Muḥammad is mentioned on a number of paintings (see cat. 3). It could refer to the second, third, sixth, or final *sultān* of the Tughluq dynasty in India (1320–1414).

Muḥammad ʿĀdil Shāh (r. 1627–1656) Muḥammad ʿĀdil Shāh succeeded his father as the seventh ruler of Bijapur, ascending the throne at the age of sixteen. Under his rule, Bijapur reached its maximum territorial expansion to the south, yet his triumph was not complete, as along with these successes came a major threat from the Marāthas and the Mughals.[49]

Sayyid **Muḥammad ʿAlī** Sayyid Muḥammad ʿAlī was probably the son of the late chancellor to the one of the Qutb Shāhī rulers of Golconda.[50]

Muḥammad Ibrāhīm (d. 1688/89) Muḥammad Ibrāhīm began his career as a military commander in Karnatak and then became commander general of the cavalry.[51] He held the Qutb Shāhī title of *Khalīlullāh Khān* during the rule of Abū'l Hasan (r. 1672–1687). In October 1685 he sided with the Mughals during the siege of Hyderabad by Shāh ʿĀlam. He was appointed commander-in-chief during the war with Aurangzēb (r. 1658–1707) and given the title Mahābat Khān. His nickname was Qimar-bash, the gambler.[52]

Muḥammad Khān (ʿAdlī) ʿĀdil Shāh Sūrī (r. 1554–1555) Muḥammad Khān ʿĀdil was the fourth ruler of the Sūr dynasty in India (1540–1555).

Sultān **Muḥammad Qūlī Shāh (1565–1612; r. 1580–1612)** Muḥammad Qūlī succeeded Ibrāhīm Qutb Shāh and moved the capital from Golconda to Hyderabad, where he built the famous Chār Minār Gate (Four Towers) in 1591–1592. A great patron of the arts and himself a poet, Muḥammad Qūlī reigned for thirty-two years, dying at the age of forty-eight and leaving his nephew Sultān Muḥammad (r. 1612–1626), the next emperor of the Qutb Shāhī dynasty, to deal with the increasing Mughal threat with the settlement of Mughal Prince Khurram in Burhanpur.[53]

Shāhzāda **Muḥammad Sultān (Sultānjī, 1639–1676)** Shāhzāda Muḥammad Sultān was the eldest son of the Mughal Emperor Aurangzēb with his second wife, Nawāb Bāi, and the elder brother of Bahādur Shāh I (r. 1707–1712).[54] In 1636 ʿAbdullāh Qutb Shāh (r. 1626–1672), the *sultān* of Golconda, signed the Deed of Submission to the Mughals and married his daughter to Muḥammad Sultān. It was decided that upon ʿAbdullāh's death his son-in-law Muḥammad Sultān would succeed him.[55] However, when it was time to choose the next *sultān*, ʿAbdullāh chose Abū'l Hasan Qutb Shāh (r. 1672–1687), the husband of his youngest daughter, to succeed him. Muḥammad Sultān was imprisoned by his own father for joining forces with his uncle, Shāh Shujāʿ.

Murād Bakhsh (1624–1661) Murād Bakhsh, the youngest son of Shāh Jahān (r. 1628–1658), was born at Rohtas and was the vice regent of Malwa and Gujarat during his father's lifetime. He was the brother of the crown prince Dārā Shikōh, Shujāʿ, and Aurangzēb. At age thirty-three, in an attempt to take over, he crowned himself in Gujarat. He captured the fort and treasure of Surat and set out for Delhi. But by this time, the ailing Shāh Jahān had recovered. Aurangzēb, more cautious, allied with Murād in secret against his eldest brother, Dārā. Dārā was defeated by Shāh Jahān at Samugarh in 1659. To Murād's surprise, he was repaid with another conspiracy against him. Murād was imprisoned at Gwalior Fort, where he stood trial for murdering the former dīwān ʿAlī Naqī and was sentenced to death in 1661.[56]

Mūsā Khān Mūsā Khān was made the commander of Karnatak one month before the end of the reign of the seventh ruler, Sultān ʿAbdullāh Qutb Shāh (r. 1626–1672), of the Qutb Shāhī dynasty of Golconda (1496–1687).[57] In collaboration with Sayyid Muzaffar, Mūsā Khān planned the fall of Mīrzā Ahmad and succeeded in convincing Abū'l Hasan (r. 1672–1687), the next ruler of Golconda, to have him arrested. Mūsā Khān was given the title *Khānkhānān* (doyen of the nobles).[58]

Sultān **Nāsir ud-Dīn Mahmūd (r. 1246–1266)** Nāsir ud-Dīn was the eighth *sultān* of the Mamlūk dynasty in India (1206–1290). He was the son of Īltutmish.

Neknām Khān (d. 1672) Neknām Khān, a eunuch, was a *wazīr* of Sultān ʿAbdullāh Qutb Shāh (r. 1626–1672), the seventh *sultān* of the Qutb Shāhī dynasty of Golconda (1496–1687), and served as the commander-in-chief of Karnatak.[59] His original Persian name was Rizā Qūlī. A great scholar, poet, and administrator, he was one of the most accomplished generals and prime ministers of ʿAbdullāh Qutb Shāh and died a month before him. He was honoured with a burial in the royal cemetery in Golconda, and a village was assigned to maintain his mausoleum.

Nīkū Sīyar Nīkū Sīyar claimed the Mughal throne of India in 1719 but did not rule. He was the grandson of Aurangzēb.

ʿOmar Shaikh (1456; r. 1469–1494) ʿOmar Shaikh succeeded his father, Abū Saʿīd, and ruled Farghana from Andijan. His wife Qutluq Nikār Khānum, a descendant of Ghengis Khān, was the mother of his son Zahīr ud-Dīn Muḥammad, who ruled as Bābur (r. 1526–1530).

Parikṣit II A legendary character, Parikṣit II, the successor of King Yudhiṣṭhira, was the grandson of Arjuna and Subhadrā and the son of Abhimañju and his wife, Uttarā.

Parvīz (1589–1626) Muḥammad Parvīz Mīrzā was the second son of Mughal Emperor Jahāngīr. In 1609 he was appointed governor of Khandesh and Berar. He married a sister of Gaj Sīngh, the ruler of Mewar, in 1624 and a daughter of Sulaimān Shikōh in 1654/55. Believed to have been an alcoholic, he had neither the talent nor the inclination for military pursuits. Parvīz was succeeded by his brother Khurram.

Prabhāvatī (Rāṇī Padmāvatī, d. 1303) Prabhāvatī, popularly known as Rāṇī Padminī was a legendary queen of Chitor, the wife of King Rāwal Ratan Sīngh (r. 1302–3), and the daughter of the contemporary Siṅhala king. Although no mentions of her are found in Amīr Khusrau's (1253–1325) accounts, an epic poem written by Mālik Muḥammad Jayasī in 1540 describes Prabhāvatī as an exceptionally beautiful princess who married a Rājput ruler of Chitor and committed *jōhar* (self-immolation by jumping into a flaming pyre) to protect her honour when Chitor was siezed in 1303 by ʿAlāʾ ud-Din Khiljī, the *sultān* of Delhi (r. 1296–1316), who had heard of her great beauty.

Prithvīrāj Chauhān III (Rāi Pithora, r. 1178–1192) Prithvīrāj Chauhān III, popularly known as Rājā Pithora was a king of the Chauhān dynasty. The last celebrated ruler of Delhi, Prithvīrāj defeated Muḥammad Ghōrī in the first battle of Tarain, in 1191. However, he was defeated, captured, and killed in 1192 in another battle with the Ghorids.

Mīrzā **Qilich Khān (Ghāzi Qilich Khān)** Ghāzi Qilich Khān, a son of Shaikh Mīr Ismāʿīl Siddīqī (ʿĀlam Shaikh Siddīqī), was also known as Qilich Khān, a title given to him by Emperor Shāh Jahān. He became a *nawāb* under Emperor Aurangzēb. He was the father of Ghāzi ud-Dīn Khān Fīrūz Jang (Fath Jang Khān), also a Mughal general, and the grandfather of Nizām ul-Mulk Qamar ud-Dīn Khān, Asaf Jāh I of Hyderabad.[60]

Sultān **Qutb ud-Dīn Aibak (r. 1206–1210)** Qutb ud-Dīn was the founder and first *sultān* of the Mamlūk dynasty in India (1206–1290).

Qutb ud-Dīn Mubārak Shāh (r. 1316–1320) Qutb ud-Dīn was the fourth and last ruler of the Khiljī dynasty in India (1290–1320).

Rafīʾ ud-Darajāt (r. Feb.–June 1719) Rafīʾ ud-Darajāt was youngest son of Rafīʾ ush-Shān. He and his brother, Rafīʾ ud-Daula, both claimed the Mughal throne in India after the reign of Farrukh Sīyar but ruled for only a few months until Muḥammad Shāh (r. 1719–1748) took over.

Rafī' ud-Daula (Shāh Jahān II, r. June–Sept. 1719) Rafī' ud-Daula was the brother of Rafī' ud-Darajāt.

Rājā Todar Māl (d. 1589) Rājā Todar Māl was a minister and general of Akbar.[61] He was responsible for land revenue reforms and for conquering of the Rājput forts of Chitor in 1568 and Ranthambor in 1573.[62]

Rāṇā **Rāj Sīngh I (1629–1680; r. 1652–1680)** Rāj Sīngh I of Mewar, father of Jai Sīngh (d. 1667), was considered the leader of the Hindus during Aurangzēb's rule, and he refuted many of the king's policies and orders that would have destroyed Hindu practice. His portrait cannot easily be distinguished from that of Rām Sīngh (d. 1658).[63]

Shāh **Rājū (Hazrat Sayyid Shāh Razi ud-Dīn, Hazrat Shāh Rājū Qattal)** Shāh Rājū of Gulbarga was the *pīr* (spiritual guide) of Sultān Abū'l Hasan (r. 1672–1687), the last *sultān* of the Qutb Shāhī dynasty of Golconda (1496–1687).[64] A teacher and a *Sūfī* saint, he renamed the *sultān*, Tānī Shāh (benevolent ruler) before he was even a contender for the throne. The *sultān* spent eight years as his (Shāh Rājū's) pupil at the shrine of Gēsūdarāz.[65]

Rām Sīngh Rautela (d. 1658) Rām Sīngh Rautela fought on the side of Dārā Shikōh, son of Shāh Jahān, during the war for succession among the emperor's sons and was finally killed by Murād Bakhsh during the battle of Samugarh. His portrait might be taken for that of Rāj Sīngh I.[66]

Mullāh **Rauhā** Portraits of Mullāh Rauhā are similar to those seen in many sets of Deccani and Mughal princes and notables assembled in the late seventeenth century for European—mostly Dutch and English use. His appearance in these sets opposite Mīrzā Ahmad, a high-ranking official in the court of Sultān 'Abdullāh Qutb Shāh (r. 1626–1672) of the Golconda dynasty, allows us to connect him to the Golconda court.

Rāzia Sultāna (Rāziyyat ud-Dīn, r. 1236–1240) Rāzia Sultāna was the fifth *sultāna* of the Mamlūk dynasty in India (1206–1290). She was the daughter of Īltutmish.

Sultān **Rukn ud-Dīn (r. 1236)** Sultān Rukn ud-Dīn was the fourth *sultān* of the Mamlūk dynasty in India (1206–1290).

Mullāh **Sādullāh** Mullāh Sādullāh was the *ustād* (teacher) of the seventh king, 'Abdullāh Qutb Shāh (r. 1626–1672), of the Qutb Shāhī dynasty of Golconda (1496–1687).[67]

Sādullāh Khān (1589–1656) Sādullāh Khān, a man of great wisdom, was a prince from Punjab who became a *wazīr* under Shāh Jahān. He died at Shahjahanabad. His mansion is said to have been standing opposite the Royal palace (between the end of the Faiz Bazār and the Delhi Gate of the palace fort) that was later presented to the Mu'azzam Khān, Mīr Jumla.[68]

Shāh **Safī II (Sulaimān, 1647–1694; r. 1666 and 1694)** After Shāh 'Abbās II's death, his eldest son, Safī Mīrzā, ascended as the eighth ruler of Iran with the title Shāh Safī II. In 1668 a second coronation was held and the Shāh was renamed Sulaimān. While the harem remained his primary interest, one redeeming feature of his rule was his patronage of the art of painting.[69]

Safshikan Khān Safshikan Khān was a *wazīr* of Aurangzēb (r. 1658–1707). A *Shī'a* Persian, he fought in the war against the last Nizām Shāh in 1630, besieged Bir, and took part in the siege of Bijapur in 1685–1686, with Fath Jang Khān playing a prominent role. In 1687 he served as chief of artillery during the siege of Golconda.[70]

Sultān **Sahab ud-Dīn Ghōrī (1149; r. 1173–1202)** Sahab ud-Dīn Ghōrī laid the foundation for the Muslim kingdom in India with the establishment of a Delhi-based Muslim kingdom that stretched over large parts of India for 320 years. Five dynasties ruled over this Delhi sultanate: the Mamlūk dynasty (1206–1290); the Khiljī dynasty (1290–1320); the Tughluq dynasty (1320–1414); the Sayyid dynasty (1414–1451); and the Afghan Lōdī dynasty (1451–1526). The Lōdī dynasty was superceded by the Mughal dynasty.

Salīm (Islām) Shāh Sūrī (r. 1545–1554) Salīm (Islām) Shāh was the second ruler of the Sūr dynasty in India (1540–1555). He succeeded his father as Jalāl Khān and later took the title of Islām Shāh Sūrī.

Muḥammad **Sayyid Muzzafar** Sayyid Muzzafar, the uncle of Shāh Mīrzā, was the *peshwā* (commander-in-chief) at the time of the eighth king, 'Abū'l Hasan Qutb Shāh (r. 1672–1687), of the Qutb Shāhī dynasty of Golconda (1496–1687).[71] In 1643 he was one of the officers in charge of Karnatak after its successful domination by Mīr Muḥammad Jumla. In 1673 he was overthrown by Mādanna Paṇḍit and imprisoned. In 1679 he was released by a Mughal ambassador and died about the age of ninety.

Shāh Jahān (1594–1666; r. 1628–1658) After Jahāngīr's death, his four sons were candidates for succession: the blind Khusrau, Parvīz, Khurram, and Shahriyār. After securing his position in 1628, prince Khurram, now Shāh Jahān (Emperor of the World), established his capital at Agra. During his reign Mughal power and wealth reached an apogee. His sense of Mughal grandeur found creative expression in monumental building projects. His first commissioned work, the Peacock Throne (1635), set the tone for a new era of ceremonial display, followed by the Tāj Mahāl, built in the memory of his beloved wife Mumtāz-i Mahāl. That year Shāh Jahān also commissioned the *Pādshāhnāma*, an illustrated history of his reign, its victories, and its court ceremonies. He was deposed by his own son Aurangzēb and imprisoned in his own fort at Agra.

Shāhriyār (1605–1628; r. Nov 1627–Jan 1628) Shāhriyār was the fifth and youngest son of the Mughal Emperor Jahāngīr (r. 1605–1627). Upon Jahāngīr's death, Shāhriyār assumed the regnal title at Lahore, where he seized the royal treasure and secured troops and supporters. In the war of succession, Shāhriyār was captured and blinded and finally killed following orders from Shāh Jahān, thus bringing his short reign to an end.[72]

Sultān **Shams ud-Dīn Īltutmish (r. 1211–1236)** Shams ud-Dīn was the third *sultān* of the Mamlūk dynasty in India (1206–1290). He was the son-in-law of Qutb ud-Dīn Aibak.

Sharzah Khān (Sayyid Makhdūm) Sayyid[73] Makhdūm Sharzah Khān was a Golconda general who invaded the Mughal territory in 1665. He was an opponent of Bahlōl Khān and later joined the Mughals under the name Rustam Khān. He was caught by the Marāthas in 1690.[74] Initially pushed aside by Sayyid Muzzafar and Mādanna Paṇḍit, he rose to power again after the death of the latter.[75]

Shēr Shāh Sūrī (r. 1540–1545) Shēr Shāh was the founder of the Sūr Empire in North India, with its capital at Delhi. Shēr Shāh belonged to the Sūr tribe from Afghanistan that ruled the Sūrī Empire from 1540 until they were defeated in 1555 by the Mughals.

Shihāb ud-Daula Masūd (r. 1030–1041) Shihāb ud-Daula Masūd was the fifth *sultān* of the Ghaznavid Empire (977–1186).

Shāh **Shujā' (1616–1661)** Shāh Shujā', the second son of Shāh Jahān (r. 1628–1658) and Mumtāz-i Mahāl, was born in Ajmer. From 1632 to 1634 he was military commander in the Deccan against the last Nizām Shāh and Shāhjī Bhonsle, father of Śivājī, and was appointed by his father as the *sūbadār* (governor) of Bengal. Shujā', like his two brothers, lost to Aurangzēb in the war of succession at the Battle of Khajwa in 1659. He fled to Arakan in 1661 and disappeared.[76]

Shāh **Sikandar Lōdī (r. 1489–1517)** Shāh Sikandar was the second ruler of the Lōdī dynasty in India (1451–1526). He succeeded his father, Bahlōl Lōdī (r. 1451–1489), who was the founder of the dynasty.

Sikandar Shāh Sūrī (r. 1555) Sikandar Shāh was the sixth and final ruler of the Sūr dynasty in India (1540–1555).

Śivājī (Chattrāpati Śivājī Mahārāj, 1628–1680; r. 1674–1680) Śivājī was the founder of the Marātha Empire (1674–1818) in India. Śivājī was born to Shājī and Jijabāi. His reign was marked by civic rule as well as military and administrative organization. He introduced guerrilla warfare methods. He was considered a hero of the Hindus and the initiator of the idea of an independent India.[77]

Tīmūr (Tīmūr-i Lenk, Tīmūr Gurgān, 1336–1405; r. 1370–1405) The warlord Tīmūr or Tamerlane, born in Transoxiana, invaded northern India in 1398, culminating in the sack of Delhi. In 1404 his empire extended from Delhi to the borders of Mongolia in Central Asia and to Moscow, Asia Minor, and Baghdad. He died on his way to conquer China.[78] The artistic production, court culture, religious scholarship, and administration of the Timurids exercised great influence on the Ottomans, Safavids, and Mughals.[79]

Yudhiṣṭhira In the Hindu epic the *Mahābhārata,* Yudhiṣṭhira is the eldest of the Pāṇḍavas, a Candravaṁśa Kuru branch of the ancient Vedic Āryans of India descending primarily from the legendary vedic king Pururava (also known as Puru), who lived in the fourteenth century b.c.
NB

Notes | 1 Berlia 2017, p. 108. | 2 Kishwar 2012, pp. 226–45. | 3 Kandahar was annexed by Bābur (r. 1526–1530) and was then lost to the Persians under his son Humāyūn's rule. The struggle continued for generations as the Mughals regained Kandahar in 1595 only to lose it again, this time permanently to the troops of 'Abbās II in 1649. Preparations to launch a campaign against India had just been begun by the Shāh when he died at the age of thirty-three in autumn 1666. See Roemer 1986, pp. 288–304; and Berlia 2017, pp. 108, 115 n. 10. | 4 Goetz 1958, p. 42. | 5 Ibid., p. 42. See also Lunsingh Scheurleer 1996, p. 235. | 6 Berlia 2017, p. 114. See also Sherwani 1973, p. 464. | 7 Berlia 2017, p. 114. See also Michell/Zebrowski 1999, pp. 17–8. | 8 Ibid., p. 191. | 9 Ibid., p. 115. | 10 Ibid. 2017, p. 111. | 11 Berlia 2017, p. 114. | 12 Irvine 1965–1967, p. 208. | 13 Berlia 2017, p. 112. | 14 Irvine 1965–1967, p. 21. | 15 Richards 1993, p. 253. See also Michell/Zebrowski 1999, p. 19. | 16 Berlia 2017, p. 109. See also Roemer 1986, pp. 42–147. | 17 Irvine 1965–1967, p. 402. | 18 Ibid., p. 275. | 19 Richards 1993, p. 55. | 20 Ibid., 1993, p. 55. | 21 Goetz 1958, p. 35. | 22 Glynn, 2000 pp. 238–9. | 23 Irvine 1965–1967, p. 230. For the date of war with Śivājī, see ibid. p. 410. | 24 Richards 1993, pp. 258–72. | 25 As indicated on a folio in the British Museum, London, inv. no. 1974,0617,0.2.32. | 26 Irvine 1965–1967, p. 208. | 27 Sarkar 1979, p. 84. | 28 Berlia 2017, p. 109. | 29 Michell/Zebrowski 1999, pp. 196–9. The portrait of Ibn-i Khātūn in the Dresden inscribed portraits is comparable to the sitter in a painting titled *Darbar of Sultān 'Abdullāh Qutb Shāh as a youth*, Golconda and dated c. 1630 and *Procession of Sultān 'Abdullāh Qutb Shāh riding an elephant*, Golconda, dated c. 1650. | 30 Michell/Zebrowski 1999, p. 14. | 31 Irvine 1965–1967, pp. 156–8. | 32 Richards 1993, p. 261. | 33 Berlia 2017, p. 111. | 34 Wright 2008, p. 17. | 35 Falk/Archer 1981, p. 57. | 36 *Maasir al-Umara* 2, pp. 287, 289. | 37 Irvine 1965–1967, pp. 22–3. | 38 Berlia 2017, p. 112. | 39 Aiyangar 1931, pp. 91–142. | 40 Goetz 1925, p. 242. | 41 Glynn 2000, p. 231. | 42 Goetz 1958, p. 38. | 43 Sarkar 1979, pp. 10–158. | 44 Binbas 2014, p. 277. | 45 Berlia 2017, p. 115, no. 2. | 46 Goetz 1958, p. 43. | 47 Goetz 1958, p. 42. | 48 Lunsingh Scheurleer 1996, p. 234. | 49 Berlia 2017, p. 113. | 50 As indicated on a folio in the British Museum, London, inv. no. 1974,0617,0.2.40. | 51 Goetz 1958, p. 43–4. | 52 Irvine 1965–1967, p. 288. See also *Maasir al-Umara* 3, p. 627. | 53 Berlia 2017, p. 114. | 54 Ibid., p. 36. | 55 Irvine 1965–1967, p. 225. | 56 Richards 1993, pp. 158–62. | 57 Goetz 1958, pp. 42–3. | 58 Ibid. | 59 Lunsingh Scheurleer 1996, p. 234. | 60 Goetz 1958, p. 37. | 61 Stronge 2002, pp. 71–5. | 62 Stein 1998, pp. 175, 196. | 63 Irvine 1965–1967, p. 236. | 64 Lunsingh Scheurleer 1996, p. 235. | 65 Goetz 1958, p. 42. | 66 Irvine 1965–1967, p. 257. | 67 Goetz 1958, p. 42. Mullāh Sādullāh's (Ca 112/28, inscribed in *nasta'līq*) representation in various other portrait albums in Europe finds different inscriptions. In Witsen Album, Rijksmuseum, Amsterdam, inv. no. RP-T-00-3186-31 the same person/portrait is inscribed in Dutch as *Mola Taifour, leermeester [ustād] van Sultan Abdullah* and in the British Museum, London, inv. no. 1974 6- 17 04/33 as Mulla Semi. | 68 Irvine 1965–1967, pp. 210, 238. | 69 Roemer 1986, pp. 304–10. | 70 Goetz 1958, p. 37. | 71 Lunsingh Scheurleer 1996, p. 234. | 72 Richards 1993, p. 113. | 73 On the Sayyids, see Khalidi 2004, pp. 329–52. | 74 Goetz 1958, p. 39. | 75 Ibid., p. 44. | 76 Ibid., p. 35. | 77 Berlia 2017, p. 115. | 78 Manz 1998, p. 36. | 79 Wright 2008, p. 13.

Glossary

A'in-i Akbarī Book about the reign of Emperor Akbar written by Abū'l Fazl i 'Ālamī

Añjali mudra Hindu greeting with joined palms in front of the chest showing respect

Arjuna Third prince of Pāṇḍava, hero of the *Mahābhārata,* the one to whom Kṛṣṇa addresses the *Bhagavadgītā*

āsana Yoga posture. A common yoga āsana is *padmāsana* (lotus pose)

asar mahāl Relic house at 'Ādil Shāhī Palace

aśoka *Saraca indica.* A tree revered in Buddhism and important in Hinduism. Because Sītā was confined in an *aśoka* grove, the species acquired the significance of constancy and purity

Asuras Mythological demons or demigods

Avatāra Incarnation of Viṣṇu

Awādh, Oudh Mughal province and kingdom (1818–1856)

bādshāh, pādshāh "Great King"; figure on Indian playing card; title of Mughal rulers

bazār Marketplace

Bengal East India and Bangladesh; Mughal province

Berār Former sultanate in the Deccan

Bhagavadgītā Sanskrit scripture that is part of the *Mahābhārata*; consists of a dialogue between Kṛṣṇa and Arjuna before a battle

Bhāgavata-Purāṇa Religious writings and legends about Viṣṇu and Kṛṣṇa

bhakta Hindu devotee

bhakti One of several spiritual paths to liberation in Hinduism, bhakti refers to devotional worship of god; branch of yoga

Bharata Half-brother of Rāmā

bībī Muslim lady; figure on Indian playing card

Bidār City and former sultanate in the Deccan

Bihār Indian federal state; Mughal province

Bīkāner City and former principality in Rajasthan

Brahma God of creation in the Hindu trinity

cakra Wheel, sun symbol, Viṣṇu's discus. When referring to the human body, cakras are the six circles running up the spinal cord believed to be centres of power

chakdar jāma Early Mughal style tunic with long sleeves and four long points on the hem

chārbā Pounce

chatri Architectural term referring to a canopy of pavilion

chauri Fly whisk made of horse or yak hair; badge of honour worn by nobles

cholī Short bodice worn by women

darbār Audience of the emperor and his nobles generally held in a hall built especially for the purpose

darshan, darśana Ceremony of viewing an important person. Mughal emperors gave *darshan* daily in which they appeared to the people from a palace window; audience of a deity

dāruṇa Elderly female chaperone

darwīsh In Persian sources, a Sūfī. When anglicized to "dervish," refers to a Sūfī who stresses ecstasy over knowledge, even at the risk of violating Islamic Law

Deccan, Dakkhin Large plateau covering most of central and southern India

devanāgarī Script used for writing Sanskrit and Prakrit as well as contemporary Hindi and Marathi

Devī Hindu goddess

dhotī Garment worn by Hindu men consisting of a piece of cloth draped around the body and between the legs

dīwān First minister; royal counsel

dopatta, dupatta Long scarf worn by women to cover head and shoulders

du'ā Literally, "call out" or "summon"; gesture of receiving grace

faqīr Wandering Muslim mendicant who subsists on alms. Term used by Bījāpūri Sūfīs of all types when referring to themselves, doubtless because of the word's literal meaning ("a poor man"). Poverty was held as an ideal by even the most worldly Sūfīs

farmān Written command issued by the court and bearing the Royal seal

Fatehpūr City founded by Akbar; district in Uttar Pradesh

gaddī Throne

ganjīfa Indian card game; probably of Persian origin

gopī Cowgirl, milkmaid; female devotee of Kṛṣṇa

guru Hindu spiritual guide or religious teacher

ḥamsa, Khamsā Hand of Fātima used as an amulet

Holī Hindu festival of spring

jāma Tunic with long sleeves and a long skirt, typically worn at the Mughal court; fastened on the left side by Hindus and on the right by Muslims

jharōka Cloth; multifoil arch; balcony window

jizya Poll tax levied on non-Muslims

kandarparatha Vehicle composed of human bodies

Kanphaṭā Yogic follower of Gorakhnāth, recognizable by large round earrings

kārkhāna Factory; workshop; painting atelier

katār Wedge-shaped Rājput dagger

khwāja Title of respect for man of distinction, especially a deceased saint

liṅga Phallic emblem; a symbol of Śiva that devotees carry with them at all times, usually around the neck

mansabdār Mughal official in government administration who might also have civil or ceremonial court duties

mantra Word or phrase repeated because of its spiritual power

mīnākṣī Literally, the one with "fish-shaped" eyes; *avatāra* of the goddess Pārvatī

mīr Prince, king; highest court card in *ganjīfa*

morchal Fan made of peacock feathers

mudrā Hand gesture, important in religious worship, drama, dance, sculpture, and painting

muhr-i muqaddas-i kalan Royal Mughal genealogical seal

mujaddid Reformer or redeemer prophesied by Islām

mullāh A Muslim learned in Islamic theology and sacred law

muraqqa' Album consisting of calligraphy and/or painting

nasta'līq Arab script popular in Persia and India

nawāb Governor

nāyikā Heroine; female lover

nīmqalam Literally, "half pen"; an artistic technique using light tinted wash

padma White lotus; colour sign in Indian playing cards

pān Betel leaf; heart in Indian playing cards

paṭkā Belt or sash worn over the *jāma*

peshwā Ruler of the Marāthas

pīr Literally, „elder." Master Sūfi, teacher of the Sūfi Way

pūjā Any form of veneration before Hindu deities; in Muslim hagiographies, idol worship

rāga Musical mode conveying an emotion

rāgamālā String of *rāgas*; figurative depiction of musical moods; a treatise on music, including pictures illustrating the subjects appropriate to the various modes

rāgiṇī Female personification of a *rāga*

rājā King; court card in Indian playing cards

rudrākṣa Seed traditionally used to form Hindu *mālā* or prayer beads

śaktī Female energy of a god

sanyāsi Hindu man who abandons all worldly connections and lives as a mendicant

sardār Courtier; gentleman

sha'bān Eighth month of the Islamic calendar

Śrī Honorific salutation; name of goddess Lakṣmī

ustād Teacher; master; expert

vajra Thunderbolt; attribute of god Indra

Vedas Ancient Hindu scriptures

vīṇā String instrument; attribute of goddess Saraswatī

Viṣṇu Highest divinity of Hindu trinity

wazīr Minister; high official; governor; second highest piece in chess and *ganjīfa*

yogī; yoginī One who practices yoga, a philosophical path to spiritual liberation and union with the divine

zamīndār Kannadiga or Telugu chieftain in the sub-Tungabhadra Karnatak; landholder

zenāna Women's quarters of the palace

Compiled by Neha Berlia and Désirée Noffke, with thanks to Roland Steffan.

References: Falk/Archer 1981; Leach 1986; Beach/Koch 1997; Desai 2002.

Table of Inscriptions Found in Ca III*

	Persons and Titles	Inscribed verso in *nasta'līq*	Inscribed verso in *devanāgarī*	Inscribed verso in Dutch
Ca III/13 (fol. 9)	Shāh Jahān (r. 1628–1658)	*Shāhzādah Sulṭān Khurram valad-i Jahāngīr* Pādshāh (... Son of Emperor Jahāngīr)	*Khurram Jahāngīr kā Betā* (Khurram, son of Jahāngīr)	*de koning gorem soon van koning Jehaengier* (King Khurram, son of king Jahāngīr)
Ca III/14 (fol. 10)	Parvīz (1589–1626)	*Sulṭān* [?] *Parvīz valad-i Jahāngīr Pādshāh* (... Parvīz, son of Emperor Jahāngīr)	*Parvez Jahāngīr kā Betā* (Parvīz, son of Jahāngīr)	*de prins pervoes soon van den* [...] (Prince Parvīz, son of ...)
Ca III/15 (fol. 11)	Khusrau (1587–1622) [?]	*A*[?]*mīr sulṭān valad-i Jahāngīr Pādshāh* (Sultān Amīr, son of Emperor Jahāngīr)	*Sultān Jahāngīr kā Betā* (Son of Sultān Jahāngīr)	*de prins seer soltaan, soon van Jehaengier* (Prince Shēr Sultān, son of Jahāngīr)
Ca III/16 (fol. 12)	'Azīm ush-Shān (1664–1712)			*asiem esjaen soon van Badursjah* ('Azīm ush-Shān, son of Bahādur Shāh I)
Ca III/17 (fol. 13)	Rājā Todar Māl (d. 1589)	[...] *Māl* [...] *vazīr-i Pādšāh* (... Māl ..., wazīr of Emperor Akbar)		*den raje todermel vesier van den koning acber* (Rājā Todar Māl, *wazīr* of king Akbar)
Ca III/18 (fol. 14)	Sultān Muḥammad (d. c. 1411)		*Mīrān Shāh*	
Ca III/19 (fol. 15)	Shahriyār (r. Nov 1627 – Jan 1628) [?]	*Shāhzādah Shahriyār valad-i Akbar Pādshāh* (Prince Shahriyār, son of Emperor Akbar)	*Shahryār Akbar kā Betā* (Shahriyār, son of Akbar)	*de prins sejaer soon van acber* (Prince Shahriyār, son of Akbar)
Ca III/20 (fol. 16)	Shāh Shujā' (1616–1661)	*Shāh Shujā' valad-i Shāh Jahān Pādšāh-i Bangālah, ṣūbah-dār* [...] (Shāh Shujā', son of Shāh Jahān, Sūbadār of Bengal)	*Sujā Shāh Jahān kā Betā* (Shujā' Shāh, son of Shāh Jahān)	[...] *l sjah souza soon van Sjahjehaen* (... l Shāh Shujā', son of Shāh Jahān)
Ca III/21 (fol. 17)	Daniyāl (1572–1604)	*Shāhzādah Dān*[...] *Shāh valad-i Akbar shāh* (Prince Dan ..., son of Akbar Shāh)	[...] *Shāh Ackbar kā Betā* (... Shāh, son of Akbar)	*de prins daensjah soon van ackberboed* [...] (Prince Daniyāl, son of Akbar ...)
Ca III/22 (fol. 18)	Muḥammad A'zam Shāh (r. 1707)	*Muḥammad A'ẓam Shāh*		
Ca III/24 (fol. 20)	Murād Bakhsh (1624–1661)	*Shāhzādah Murād Shāh valad-i Shāh Jahān Pādshāh* [?] (Prince Murād Shāh, son of Emperor Shāh Jahān [?])	[...]*urad Shāh Betā Shāh Jahān kā* (...urad Shāh, son of Shāh Jahān)	den prins moeradsjah soon Sjahjehaen (Prince Murād Shāh, son of Shāh Jahān)
Ca III/27 (fol. 23)	Rāṇā Rāj Sīngh I (r. 1652–1680) / Ram Sīngh (d. 1658)		[...] *Shāh*	
Ca III/28 (fol. 24)	Gaj Sīngh (r. 1618–1638)	Geh Sing (Gaj [?] Sīngh)		*Gedsing* (Gaj [?] Sīngh)
Ca III/29 (fol. 25)	Diler Khān (d. 1683)	*Dalīr Khān*		*Den amerau Dellelichan* (umarā Diler [?] Khān)
Ca III/30 (fol. 26)	Chatra Sal Rāo (d. 1658)	*Chattar Singh* (Chatra Sal [?])		*Fedter Sing* (Fateh [?] Sīngh)
Ca III/31 (fol. 27)	Vīr [?] Sīngh	*Vīr Singh* (Vīr Sīngh)		*Wiersing* (Vīr Sīngh)
Ca III/32 (fol. 28)	Jahāngīr (r. 1605–1627)	*Jahāngīr*	*Jāngir* [...] (Jahāngīr)	
Ca III/33 (fol. 29)	Sādullāh Khān (1589–1656)	*Savād-Allāh Khān* (Sādullāh Khān)		*Den amerau sadullechan* (umarā Sādullāh Khān)
Ca III/35 (fol. 31)	Sūr Sīngh	*Ṣūrat* [?] *Singh* (Sūr [?] Sīngh)		Foered sing (Sūr [?] Sīngh)
Ca III/36 (fol. 32)	Ja'far Khān (d. 1670)	*Ja'far Khān*	...	*Zafferchan* (Ja'far Khān)
Ca III/37 (fol. 33)	Akbar (r. 1556–1605)	*Akbar Pādshāh* (Emperor Akbar)	*Akbar 8* (Akbar, the 8th)	

	Persons and Titles	Inscribed verso in *nasta'līq*	Inscribed verso in *devanāgarī*	Inscribed verso in Dutch
Ca III/38 (fol. 34)	Bahādur Shāh I (r. 1707–1712)		*12 Bahādur Shāh* (Bahādur Shāh, the 12th)	
Ca III/39 (fol. 35)	Aurangzēb (r. 1658–1707)	*Awrangzīb*		*den koning ouranseeb* (The king Aurangzēb)
Ca III/40 (fol. 36)	Dārā Shikōh (1615–1659)	*Dārā Shikūh*		*Dara sickou*
Ca III/42 (fol. 38)	Mān Sīngh I (r. 1589–1614) [?]	*Rājah Mān Singh*		*Radja manetsing*
Ca III/43 (fol. 39)	Sukh Sīngh	*Sukhah Singh*	*S[...] Sīngh*	*Sockeng*
Ca III/44 (fol. 40)	Amar Sīngh (1613–1644) [?]	*Amir Singh* [?]		*ammersing*
Ca III/45 (fol. 41)	Aurangzēb (r. 1658–1707)	*Awrangzīb*	*Aurangzēb*	
Ca III/46 (fol. 42)	Shāh Jahān (r. 1628–1658)	*Shāh Jahān*	*Shāh 10* (The 10th Shāh)	
Ca III/47 (fol. 43)	Shāh Jahān (r. 1628–1658)	*Shāh Jahān*	*Shāh Jahān*	*sia Jehaan den 10 koning* (Shāh Jahān, the 10th king)
Ca III/48 (fol. 44)	'Abd al-Ja'far Beg	*Arshad Bayg* (Arshad [?] Beg)		
Ca III/49 (fol. 45)	Rāṇā Amar Sīngh (d. 1620) [?]	*Rānā Amir [?]*		*Rana Amer Sing*
Ca III/50 (fol. 46)	Tīmūr (r. 1370–1405)	*Taymūr Pādshāh* (Emperor Tīmūr)	...	*Teammerlaan de 1e koning* (Tamerlane, the 1st king)
Ca III/51 (fol. 47)	Tīmūr (r. 1370–1405)	*Taymūr Pādshāh* (Emperor Tīmūr)	*Tīmar* [...] *1* (Tīmūr ..., the 1st)	
Ca III/52 (fol. 48)	Abū Sa'īd (d. 1469) or 'Omar Shaikh (d. 1494)	*Sulṭān Muḥammad*	*Abū Sa'īd* [cut across] *3 Sultān Muḥamad*	
Ca III/55 (fol. 51)	Bābur (r. 1526–1530)	*Bābur*	*Bābur 5* (Bābur, the 5th)	
Ca III/56 (fol. 52)	Bābur (r. 1526–1530)	*Bābur Shāh*	[...]*h* (... h)	
Ca III/58 (fol. 54)	Abū Sa'īd (d. 1469) or 'Omar Shaikh (d. 1494)	*Humāyūn*		
Ca III/59 (fol. 55)	Abū Sa'īd (d. 1469) or 'Omar Shaikh (d. 1494)	*Humāyūn*	*Humāyūn 7* Humāyūn, the 7th	
Ca III/60 (fol. 56)	Sultān Muḥammad (d. c. 1411)	*Abū Sa'īd*	*Abū Sa'īd 4* Abū Sa'īd, the 4th	
Ca III/61 (fol. 57)	Āzād Khān (1631–1716)	*Asad Khān*		*Den heer assedchan* (Lord Asad Khān)
Ca III/63 (fol. 59)	Princess Jahānārā Begum Sāhibā (1614–1681)		*Begum Sāhi* (Sāhibā Begum)	
Ca III/67 (fol. 63)	A lady holding her veil			*Rapt* [...] *d*[...]*ul*

Compiled by Neha Berlia with thanks to Roland Steffan, Anna Martin and Negar Kavoosi.

* These inscriptions can be seen via transmitted light on the verso of the folios pasted in cat. 4, Ca III.

Concordance of Eleven Portrait Sets in European Collections

Among the albums of Indian paintings in the Dresden Kupferstich-Kabinett, Ca 110, Ca 111, Ca 112, and the set on Ca 116 contain portraits of the Timurids, Safavids, Mughals, ʿĀdil Shāhīs, and Qutb Shāhīs as well as of their prominent officers and noblemen. The table below shows how these four albums compare to one another and to other eight albums: three at the British Museum, London (London BM);[1] two at the Bibliothèque Nationale de France, Paris, Département des Manuscrits (Paris BnF);[2] two at the Rijksmuseum, Amsterdam,[3] and two at the Österreichische Nationalbibliothek, Vienna.[4]

Establishing legitimacy to rule was of the utmost importance to dynasties for millennia.[5] Through the practice of reinforcing the prestige of the dynasty by recording the features of its rulers and their ancestors, the artists documented their lineage and, in turn, their right to rule. This idea of sacred kingship, dominated by the memory of Tīmūr and his successors and by the rulers of Safavid Iran, continued to influence the formation of the identity of the divine rulers of Mughal India (1526–1857) and of the rulers of the Golconda and Bijapur dynasties in the Deccan, as often portrayed together in these albums. A careful study of the eighty-four personalities painstakingly identified through earlier portraits, inscriptions, or iconography often reveals more than what meets the eye. Similar representations and groupings in various Indian miniature portrait albums, many with similar formats and subjects and not too far apart in dating, demonstrates the nature of demand and the interest of the patron and artists, both in India and abroad. The dispersal of artists that began with the accession of Aurangzēb in 1658 and continued when he conquered the sultanates of the Deccan, Bijapur, and Golconda in 1686 and 1687, respectively, drained the creative energies of the painters, who now produced works to be sold at the market to earn a living. The owner of such an album would, however, gain the aura of the great kings of the distant lands about which they were so curious. The table reflects this change in the purpose and meaning of Indian artworks at the turn of the century as they now became objects to be collected and admired by European travelers, patrons, and connoisseurs. NB

Notes | 1 "Effigies regum et satrapum persiae, Persian Portraits, Etc. and Portraits of Indian Princes", inv. nos. 1974,0617,0.4, 1974,0617,0.2, and 1974 6-17 011. | 2 Smith-Lesouëf Album 232 and 233. | 3 Witsen Album and Canter Visscher Album, inv. nos. RP-T-00-3186 and NG-2008-60, respectively. | 4 Sig. Cod. Min. 44 and 64. | 5 Berlia 2017, p. 115.

Persons	Dresden Ca 112 (fols. 1–49)	Dresden Ca 110 (fols. 1–39)	Dresden Ca 111 no. 1–72 (fols. 1–68)	Dresden Ca 116 (fols. 1–18)	London, BM 1974,0617,0.4 (fols. 1–51)	London, BM 1974,0617,0.2 (fols. 1–67)	London, BM 1974,0617,0.11 (fols. 1–26)	Paris, BnF S.-L 232 (fols. 1v–29v)	Paris, BnF S.-L 233 (fols. 1v–25r)	Amsterdam, Rijksmuseum, RP-T-00-3186 (fols. 1A–47)	Amsterdam, Rijksmuseum, NG-2008-60 (fols. 00–30)	Vienna, ÖNB Cod. Min. 64 (fols. 1–66)	Vienna, ÖNB Cod. Min. 44 no. 1-49 (fols. 1–24)
Shāh ʿAbbās I (r. 1588–1629)	1					4			22r				
Shāh ʿAbbās II (r. 1642–1666)	2[1]				2[2]	2		23v	1v				
Safī II (r. 1666–1694)	3[3]				1[4]	1		24v	2r	47			
The bow bearer of Shāh ʿAbbās	4					57			2v				
ʿAlī ʿĀdil Shāh II (r. 1656–1672)	5	39			27	56	13		4v	41			
Mullāh 'Abdul Mali	6				30	55		28v[5]	5r				
Ikhlās Khān (d. 1656)	7	37			26	54		26v	5v	42[6]			
Muḥammad ʿĀdil Shāh (r. 1627–1656)	8	38			28	53	14	25v	6r	40			
Mūsā Khān	9	31			44	52		17v	7v	26			
Ahmad Khān	10				50	3 51			8r				
Husain Shāh	11				51	50		15v[7]	6v				
Hasan Khān	12	27			49	48			7r				

Persons	Dresden Ca 112 (fols. 1–49)	Dresden Ca 110 (fols. 1–39)	Dresden Ca 111 no. 1–72 (fols. 1–68)	Dresden Ca 116 (fols. 1–18)	London, BM 1974,0617,0.4 (fols. 1–51)	London, BM 1974,0617,0.2 (fols. 1–67)	London, BM 1974,0617,0.11 (fols. 1–26)	Paris, BnF S.-L 232 (fols. 1v–29v)	Paris, BnF S.-L 233 (fols. 1v–25r)	Amsterdam, Rijksmuseum, RP-T-00-3186 (fols. 1A-47)	Amsterdam, Rijksmuseum, NG-2008-60 (fols. 00–30)	Vienna, ÖNB Cod. Min. 64 (fols. 1–66)	Vienna, ÖNB Cod. Min. 44 no. 1-49 (fols. 1–24)
Sharzah Khān	13				48	49	26		11v	45[8]		6	
Mīrzā Nāsir	14	32			38	46			12r				
Shāh Rājū	15					47	22		22v	30		7	
Abū'l Hasan Qutb Shāh (r. 1672–1687)	16	33			35 43	20[9] 45	21	18v 27v	3r	23		1 14	
Mullāh ʿAbd al-Samad	17	29			41	44	19		8v	32			
Sayyid Muḥammad ʿAlī	18				42	40[10]			9r				
Khayrāt Khān (d. 1655)	19				47	41			9v				
Neknām Khān (d. 1672)	20	26			40	42[11]	17	29v	11r	25			
ʿAbd al-Jaʿfar Beg	21	25 30	48 (fol. 44)		45	43	20		12v	34		4	
Shāh Mīrzā	22	28			39	39	18		13r	27		3	
Muḥammad Sayyid Muzzafar	23	21			37	38	16	14v	13v	28		2	
ʿAbdullāh Qutb Shāh (r. 1626–1672)	24	22			33	7 37	15	13v	14r	22		16[12]	
ʿAbdullāh Qutb Shāh (r. 1626–1672)	25	18			32	36			14v				
Ibn-i Khātūn	26	19			31	34			15r				
Sultān Muḥammad Qūlī Shāh (r. 1580–1612)	27				29	35		12v[13]	15v	20		8	
Mullāh Sādullāh	28	20			34	33			16r	31[14]			
Fath Jang Khān	29	16			20	6 32	11		16v	2			
Bhao Sīngh (d. 1678)	30	11			13	30			17r	13			
Mīrzā Qilich Khān	31	10			18	31			17v	15			
Safshikan Khān	32	17			15	29			18r	18			
Mān Sīngh I (r. 1589–1614)	33	14	42 (fol. 38)		17[15]	28			18v	14			
Karan Sīngh (d. 1666/1667)	34	15			16	27			19r	16			
Mīrzā Ahmad	35	23			36	12 26		16v	19v	24		5	
Mullāh Rauhā	36	24				25			20r				
Muḥammad Amīn Khān Turānī (d. 1721)	37	12			14 23	24	10	11v	20v	[16]			
Mīr Jumla II (1591–1663)	38	13			11 24	23	9	10v	21r				
Muḥammad Sultān (1639–1676)	39	8			9 22	22	8	8v	21v	10			
Bahādur Shāh I (r. 1707–1712)	40	9	12 (fol. 8) 25 (fol. 21) 38 (fol. 34)	12	12 21	19		9v	3v	11			24 (fol. 16)
Aurangzēb (r. 1658–1707)	41	6	11 (fol. 8) 39 (fol. 35) 45 (fol. 41)	11	10 19	9 18	7	5v[17]		6	7 11	10	2 21 (fol. 15) 23 (fol. 15)

Persons	Dresden Ca 112 (fols. 1–49)	Dresden Ca 110 (fols. 1–39)	Dresden Ca 111 no. 1–72 (fols. 1–68)	Dresden Ca 116 (fols. 1–18)	London, BM 1974,0617,0.4 (fols. 1–51)	London, BM 1974,0617,0.2 (fols. 1–67)	London, BM 1974,0617,0.11 (fols. 1–26)	Paris, BnF S.-L 232 (fols. 1v–29v)	Paris, BnF S.-L 233 (fols. 1v–25r)	Amsterdam, Rijksmuseum, RP-T-00-3186 (fols. 1A-47)	Amsterdam, Rijksmuseum, NG-2008-60 (fols. 00–30)	Vienna, ÖNB Cod. Min. 64 (fols. 1–66)	Vienna, ÖNB Cod. Min. 44 no. 1-49 (fols. 1–24)
Murād Bakhsh (1624–1661)	42	5	24 (fol. 20)		7	15	6	6v[18]	23r	7			15 (fol. 12)[19]
Shāh Jahān (r. 1628–1658)	43	3	10 (fol. 8) 13 (fol. 9) 46 (fol. 42) 47 (fol. 43)	10	8	14	3	3v	23v	5	10 12	15	27 (fol. 16) 30 (fol. 17)
Dārā Shikōh (1615–1659)	44[20]	4	40 (fol. 36)		3	17	4	4v	24r	8			
Shāh Shujā‘ (1616–1661)	44[21]	7	20 (fol. 16)		5		5	7v[22]		9			
Jahāngīr (r. 1605–1627)	45	2	9 (fol. 8) 32 (fol. 28) 34 (fol. 30) 41 (fol. 37)	9	6	8 16	2	2v	24v	4	9	12	14 (fol. 11) 28 (fol. 16)
Akbar (r. 1556–1605)	46	1	8 (fol. 8) 37 (fol. 33)	8	4	13	1	1v	25r	3	8 15	13	6 25 (fol. 16)
Muḥammad Ibrāhīm (d. 1688/1689)		34			46	5	24	21v		29			
Mādanna Paṇḍit (d. 1685)		35					23	19v		37			
Śivājī (r. 1674–1680)		36					12	20v		46			
Tīmūr (r. 1370–1405)			1 (fol. 7) 50 (fol. 46) 51 (fol. 47)	1						1B	1		
Mīrān Shāh (c. 1367–1408)			2 (fol. 7) 57 (fol. 53)	2							2 13		
Sultān Muḥammad (d. c. 1411)			3 (fol. 7) 18 (fol. 14) 54 (fol. 50) 60 (fol. 56)	3									8
Abū Sa'īd (r. c. 1451–1469) / ‘Omar Shaikh (r. 1469–1494)[23]			4 (fol. 7) 5 (fol. 7) 52 (fol. 48) 53 (fol. 49) 58 (fol. 54) 59 (fol. 55) 62 (fol. 58)	4 5							4 5		1 12 (fol. 10) 13 (fol. 11) 32 (fol. 17)
Bābur (r. 1526–1530)			6 (fol. 7) 55 (fol. 51) 56 (fol. 52)	6					4r	1A	6		9 (fol. 9)
Humāyūn (r. 1530–1540, 1555–1556)			7 (fol. 8)	7						12	3		4 10 (fol. 9) 29 (fol. 16)
Parvīz (1589–1626)			14 (fol. 10)								16		
Khusrau (1587–1622)			15 (fol. 11)										
‘Azīm ush-Shān (1664–1712)			16 (fol. 12)										
Rājā Todar Māl (d. 1589)			17 (fol. 13)										
Shahriyār (r. Nov 1627 – Jan 1628)			19 (fol. 15)										
Daniyāl (1572–1604)			21 (fol. 17)										
Muḥammad A'zam Shāh (r. 1707)			22 (fol. 18) 26 (fol. 22)										16 (fol. 12)[24]

Persons	Dresden Ca 112 (fols. 1–49)	Dresden Ca 110 (fols. 1–39)	Dresden Ca 111 no. 1–72 (fols. 1–68)	Dresden Ca 116 (fols. 1–18)	London, BM 1974,0617,0.4 (fols. 1–51)	London, BM 1974,0617,0.2 (fols. 1–67)	London, BM 1974,0617,0.11 (fols. 1–26)	Paris, BnF S.-L 232 (fols. 1v–29v)	Paris, BnF S.-L 233 (fols. 1v–25r)	Amsterdam, Rijksmuseum, RP-T-00-3186 (fols. 1A-47)	Amsterdam, Rijksmuseum, NG-2008-60 (fols. 00–30)	Vienna, ÖNB Cod. Min. 64 (fols. 1–66)	Vienna, ÖNB Cod. Min. 44 no. 1-49 (fols. 1–24)
Jahāndār Shāh (r. 1712–1713)			23 (fol. 19)	13									26 (fol. 16)
Rājā Sīngh (r. 1652–1680) / Rām Sīngh (d. 1658)			27 (fol. 23)										
Gaj Sīngh (r. 1618–1638)			28 (fol. 24)										
Diler Khān (d. 1683)			29 (fol. 25)										
Chatra Sal Rāo (d. 1658)			30 (fol. 26)										
Vīr [?] Sīngh			31 (fol. 27)										
Sādullāh Khān (1589–1656)			33 (fol. 29)										
Sūr Sīngh			35 (fol. 31)										
Ja'far Khān (d. 1670)			36 (fol. 32)										
Sukh Sīngh			43 (fol. 39)										
Amar Sīngh (1613–1644)			44 (fol. 40)										
Rāṇā Amar Sīngh (d. 1620)			49 (fol. 45)										
Āzād Khān (1631–1716)			61 (fol. 57)										
Farrukh Sīyar (r. 1713–1719)				14							14		
Nīkū Sīyar				15									
Farkhunda Akhtar (d. 1712)				16									3
Rafī' ud-Daula (r. June–Sept 1719)				17									5
Rafī' ud-Darajāt (r. Feb–June 1719)				18									7

Notes | 1 Inscribed in *nasta'līq* (incorrectly): *Shāh Sulaimān*. The image actually represents Shāh 'Abbās II, whose name is inscribed on the following image (Ca 112/3). | 2 This image (along with the British Museum, London, inv. no. 1974,0617,0.2.2 and Smith-Lesouëf 232/23v) is correctly inscribed in *nasta'līq: Shāh 'Abbās II / Great 'Abbās*. In other albums e. g. Ca 112/2 a version of the same image is inscribed (incorrectly): *Shāh Sulaimān*. | 3 Inscribed in *nasta'līq* (incorrectly): *Shāh Abbās*. The image represents Shāh Sulaimān, whose name is inscribed on the previous image (Ca 112/2). | 4 This image (along with Smith-Lesouëf 232/24v, Rijksmuseum, Amsterdam, inv. no. RP-T-00-3186-47 and British Museum, London, inv. no. 1974,0617,0.2.1 is correctly attributed to Sulaimān. | 5 Inscribed in *nasta'līq* (incorrectly*): Sayyid Muzzafar*. | 6 Inscribed in Dutch (incorrectly): *Khawas Khan*. The image is similar to Ca 112/7, hence attributed to Ikhlās Khān. | 7 Probably Husain Shāh. | 8 Another image in the same album (fol. 35) is inscribed *Sayyid Makhdūm*. However, along with the difficulty of understanding the reason for the repetition of representation of the same person (especially a minister), which is rather not popular as studied from various other albums, the characteristics of this image too is very different from other known images of Sayyid Makhdūm Sharzah Khān. | 9 Inscribed in *nasta'līq* (incorrectly): *Kām Bakhsh* (probably referring to the son of Aurangzēb). The other image of Abū'l Hasan (fol. 45) in the same album is inscribed: *Sultān 'Abū'l Hasan Qutb Shāh, present king of Golconda*. Inscriptions with such extended information contribute to date these albums. For this reason this album is to be dated before 1687. | 10 The image is inscribed in *nasta'līq: Sayyid 'Alī, son of Sayyid Muzaffar, the late chancellor to the king of Golconda*. His father was the chancellor until 1673, before being overthrown by Mādanna Paṇḍit. So the album must have been made after this. | 11 The image is inscribed in *nasta'līq: Necknam (sic) Khān A eunuch general to the late king of Golconda. Both died about one time with late king*. This informs about the date of death of Neknām Khān, c. d. 1672. | 12 This image seems to represent 'Abdullāh Qutb Shāh. | 13 Inscribed in *nasta'līq* (incorrectly*): Sultān Muḥammad, Father of 'Abdullāh*. The image represents Muḥammad Qūlī, who is the father of Sultān Muḥammad. | 14 Inscribed in Dutch: *Mulla Tayfur, leraar (ustād) van Sultan Abdullah*. In a similar representation in Dresden, Ca 112/28, the image is inscribed in *nasta'līq: Mullāh Sādullāh* and in the British Museum, London, inv. no. 1974 6- 17 04/33 it is inscribed: *Mullāh Semi*. | 15 Inscribed in *nasta'līq: Rām Sīngh*. But the image is very similar to the British Museum, London, inv. no. 1974,0617,0.2.28, listed there as Mān Sīngh. | 16 Rijksmuseum, Amsterdam, inv. no. RP-T-00-3186.33 image is inscribed *Muḥammad Amīn*, but the sitters representation does not match the Dresden Ca 112 and Ca 110 as well as other known collections (as indicated in the list). Hence, one might assume it to be another instance of incorrect inscription. | 17 Incorrectly inscribed in Dutch: *Shah Shuja, son of Shah Jahan*. The distinction between the younger models of the sons of the emperors is often found with wrong inscription. Especially when distinguishing between the four sons of Shāh Jahān, Dārā Shikōh, Shāh Shujā', Murād Bakhsh and Aurangzēb. | 18 Incorrect inscription. See note 17. | 19 The portrait on the left is Murād Bakhsh. | 20 The portrait on the left is Dārā Shikōh. | 21 The portrait on the right is Shāh Shujā'. | 22 Incorrect inscription. See note 17. | 23 The distinction between the two sitters Abū Sa'īd (r. c. 1451–1469)/'Omar Shaikh (r. 1469–1494) is not yet established. Therefore, all the images with inscriptions of either have been listed together. | 24 The portrait on the right is Muḥammad A'zam Shāh.

Concordance of Three Portrait Sets in Dresden, London, and Oxford

A survey of the ruling families represented in the Indian portrait albums in Dresden (Ca 113), London (MS. Ind. Misc. d. 3) and Oxford (I. M. 9-1912)

The tradition of book making at the Muslim courts included histories—ancient and recent—and literary texts and poetry written in calligraphy with compilations often intended to legitimize the rule of a particular king.[1] Although by 1500 Hindu kings, warriors, and priests had lost their battle with the powerful imperial system that had begun infiltrating during the early thirteenth century, their memory survived in the minds of the Mughals long after Bābur (r. 1526–1530) made his first move towards north India, where he laid the foundations of the Mughal Empire (1526–1858) following his victory at Panipat in 1526 against Ibrāhīm Lōdī (r. 1517–1526). Politics became infused with such memories, which often made it acceptable for a ruler to remain religiously tolerant towards his varied subjects and, in the process, accept their histories as if they were his own in order to secure a place in the line of succession of a particular region. Album Ca 113 follows a formula similar to the one adopted by the Mughals in whose palaces the original set of miniature portraits of the successive sovereigns of *Hindustan* was once kept.[2]

Ca 113 contains 179 portraits of Indian kings and queens from legendary times until the Mughal Emperor Aurangzēb (r. 1658–1707). A similar list of sitters with the length of their reign is found in the manuscript *Khulasāt-at-Tawārīkh*, which was written in the fortieth year of Aurangzēb's reign.[3] The writer provides a narrative of all of Delhi's *rājās* and *sultāns* from Yudhiṣṭhira until the period when this book was written. The subject matter of the book can be divided into the geography of India during the reign of Aurangzēb; the history of the *rājās* from Yudhiṣṭhira to Prithvīrāj Chauhān (r. 1178–1192); and the history of the Muslim emperors until Aurangzēb.[4] The portraits in the album represent only the last two categories. A similar list indicating the twenty-three different families of rulers from India comprising the same sitters along with the length of their reign is also found in a letter of 1726 from Antonio Vallisnieri to P. D. Piercaterino Zeno.[5]

A chronology of the Indian kings up to Muslim rulers appears online[6] and is based on the 1939 publication *Satyartha Prakash* by Swami Dayananda Saraswati, who based his information on a Sanskrit book published in 1726. Along with the grouping of families, this list, quoted below, provides additional notes about each family.[7] NB

Ca 113/1–30[8]
Famiglia di Judister [Yudhiṣṭhira]
"About 30 rulers belonging to the House of Yudhiṣṭhira ruled Indraprastha collectively for 1,770 years, 11 months and 10 days ..."

Ca 113/31–44
Famiglia di Vistau [Viśhrava?]
"The Prime Minister Vishrava killed his Emperor Kshemaka[9] and began to rule himself in his place. Fourteen emperors belonged to his House who ruled collectively in Indraprastha for 500 years, 3 months, and 17 days ..."

Ca 113/45–60
Famiglia di Serpariz [Sarpa?]
"The Prime Minister Viramaha[10] killed his Emperor Virasalasena and began to reign in his place. Sixteen Emperors of his House ruled (in Indraprastha) collectively for 445 years, 5 months and 3 days ..."

Ca 113/61–9
Famiglia di Dander [Dhanadhara?]
"King Dhanadhara of Prayaag (Allahabad) killed Emperor A'dityaketu[11] of Maghda and began to reign in his place. Nine kings of his House ruled for 374 years, 11 months and 26 days ..."

Ca 113/70–1
Famiglia di Secuan [Sakvant?]
"Samanta Mahapal killed the Emperor Rajapala and reigned for 14 years. Raja Vikrammaditya of Avantika (Ujjain) invaded his territory and put the Emperor Mahanpala to death. He reigned for 93 years."

Ca 113/72–87
Famiglia di Sunder [Sundarapāla Yogi?]
"He was killed by a minster of King Shalivahana called Samudrapala Yogi of Paithana who began to reign in Raja Vikramaditya's time. Sixteen kings of his House ruled collectively for 372 years, 4 months and 27 days ..."

Ca 113/88–97
Famiglia di Maluq Chan [Malikcandra?]
"Vikramapala led an expedition against Malukh Chand Bohara, King of the West (India), and fought a battle with him in an open field and was killed at the hand of Malukh Chand who began to reign Indraprastha (Delhi). Ten kings of his house ruled collectively for 191 years, 1 month and 16 days ..."

Ca 113/98–100
Famiglia di Arberam [Harivarma Yogi?]
"Queen Padmavati (wife of Govind Chand) died childless. All her ministers unanimously plaved Hari Prem Vairagee to rule in his name. Four kings[12] of his House ruled collectively for 50 years and 21 days."

Ca 113/101–113
Famiglia di Manat [Mahānāth Yogi?]
"Raja Mahabahu[13] abdicated his throne and went to live in a forest, in order to engage himself in Divine contemplation. A'dhi Sena, King of Bengal, having heard this, came to Indraprastha and took possession of the capital and began to reign there. Twelve kings of his House ruled in Indraprastha for 151 years, 11months, 2 days."

Ca 113/114–9
Famiglia di Dip. Seng. [Dīpasiṁha?]
"Damodra Sena oppressed his nobles very much. One of them, called Dipa Singh, revolted against him and got the army to join him. He slew the Raja in a battle and began to reign himself. There were 6 kings of his dynasty who collectively ruled for 107 years, 6 months and 22 days ..."

Ca 113/120–124[14]
Famiglia di Atti Mal [Haṭhīmala?]
"Raja Jivan Singh, for some reason, sent all his army to the North. Prithvi Raj Chauhan, King of Vairat, on hearing this, marched against him, killed him in a battle and began to reign* in Indraprastha. There were 5 kings of his dynasty who collectively ruled for 86 years and 20 days ..."

These descriptions end with the beginning of Muslim rule in India. However, Vallisnieri's list with family groupings continues (without notes) below:

Ca 113/125[15]–132
Famiglia di Sueb Din [Sahab ud-Dīn Ghōrī]

Ca 113/133–6
Famiglia di Userira [Husain]

Ca 113/137–140
Famiglia di Sames Din [Shams ud-Dīn]

Ca 113/141–3
Famiglia di Sames Din [Shams ud-Dīn][16]

Ca 113/144–8
Famiglia di Pirrosa [Fīrōz Shāh]

Ca 113/149
Famiglia

Ca 113/150–1
Famiglia

Ca 113/152–4
Famiglia

Ca 113/155–6
Famiglia

Ca 113/157–179
Famiglia di Tamerlan [Tīmūr][17]

Concordance with comparison between the inscriptions (inscribed on verso in *nāgarī*) and images (likeness of the sitter) of Ca 113 to Victoria & Albert Museum, London (V&A), inv. no. IM9-1912 and Bodleian Library, Oxford (BL), MS. Ind. Misc. d. 3.

** (double asterisk): same image
** (asterisk): similar image
? probably

Dresden Ca 113 (cat. 3) (fols. 1–179)			BL MS. Ind. Misc. d. 3 (fols. 1–178)		V&A I.M. 9-1912 (fols. 1–177)	
inv. no.		**inscribed (verso)**	**corresponding name on fol.**	**corresponding image on fol.**	**corresponding name on fol.**	**corresponding image on fol.**
Ca 113/1	Rājā Yudhiṣṭhira	rājā judhiṣṭara	1**	1	1**	1
Ca 113/2	Parikṣit II	parīchata	2	3	2**	2
Ca 113/3	Janamejaya III	janmejaya	3	22	3*	3
Ca 113/4	Aśvatthāman	asvamedhā	4*	4	4*	4
Ca 113/5		rājā ādhīna	5	19	–	5
Ca 113/6		mañjalāpa	6*	6	6**	6
Ca 113/7		chatraratha	7	62	9	7
Ca 113/8		dīpapāla	8	7	10	8
Ca 113/9		ugrasaina	9**	9	7	9
Ca 113/10		sūrasaina	10	8	8	10
Ca 113/11		śrīpata	11	–	–	11
Ca 113/12		anajaya	12	5	–	–
Ca 113/13		rājā sarajaga	13	14	–	13
Ca 113/14		suṣitapāla	14	–	–	14
Ca 113/15		harada-urāma	15	53	[illegible]	15
Ca 113/16		sūrajaratha	16*	16	14	16
Ca 113/17		lokapāla	17*	17	–	17
Ca 113/18	Rājā Śāntanu	rājā sutana	18	–	–	18
Ca 113/19		mādhavasaina	19	15	–	19
Ca 113/20		subhabhañjana	20	18	–	20
Ca 113/21	Bhīṣma	bhīṣama	21	27	22	21
Ca 113/22	Bharata	bhartha	22	9	20	22
Ca 113/23		rājā pūrana	23	13	21	23
Ca 113/24		rājā adalī	24	23	–	24
Ca 113/25		rājā dhannīdhara	25	–	25*	25
Ca 113/26		ḍhaṇḍhapāla	26	–	39	26
Ca 113/27		rājā durvalarāi	27	38	–	27
Ca 113/28		sīrīnāga	28*	28	–	28
Ca 113/29		rājā ṣema	29	12	–	29
Ca 113/30		laṣamana	30	–	–	30
Ca 113/31		visnusaravā	31	26	31**	31
Ca 113/32		sūrajasaina	32**	32	32**	32
Ca 113/33		vīrasāha	33*	33	33*	33
Ca 113/34		tavaisāha	34*	34	34	–
Ca 113/35		vīrajīta	35*	35	–	35
Ca 113/36		duratha	36*	36	–	36
Ca 113/37		siddhapāla	37*	37	37**	37

Dresden Ca 113 (cat. 3) (fols. 1–179)			BL MS. Ind. Misc. d. 3 (fols. 1–178)		V&A I.M. 9-1912 (fols. 1–177)	
inv. no.		**inscribed (verso)**	**corresponding name on fol.**	**corresponding image on fol.**	**corresponding name on fol.**	**corresponding image on fol.**
Ca 113/38		rājā punīta	38	31	–	38
Ca 113/39		rājā vijai	39	38	46	39
Ca 113/40		amarajodha	40*	40	–	40
Ca 113/41		amīpāla	41*	41	–	41
Ca 113/42		rājā sarohī	42*	42	–	42
Ca 113/43		rājā padāratha	43*	43	–	43
Ca 113/44		paravalasaina	44*	44	–	44
Ca 113/45		rājā sarapā	45*	45	-	–
Ca 113/46		rājā jurātasuṣa	46	21	–	46
Ca 113/47		saraghana	47	46	–	47
Ca 113/48		dhanapata	48*	48	–	48
Ca 113/49		mahāvala	49	39	45?	–
Ca 113/50		sātadatta	50*	50	–	50
Ca 113/51		chatrasaina	folio missing		47	51
Ca 113/52		suṣadāna [?]	52*	52	–	52
Ca 113/53		jātavala	53	49	–	53
Ca 113/54		rājā mahālaṣa	54*	54	–	–
Ca 113/55		kālagana	55**	55	–	55
Ca 113/56		sarabharā	56	–	–	56
Ca 113/57		jīvanasaina	57	56	62	57
Ca 113/58		harajaga	58*	58	61	58
Ca 113/59		vīrasaina	59*	59	–	59
Ca 113/60		udhanta	60	71	–	60
Ca 113/61		rājā dhadhara	61	60	57	61
Ca 113/62		rājā sainadhuja	62	47	58	62
Ca 113/63		venīgaṅgārājā	63**	63	59	63
Ca 113/64		rājā mahājodhā	64*	64	60	64
Ca 113/65		haranātha	65**	65	61	65
Ca 113/66		jīvanarāi	66**	66	62	70
Ca 113/67		udaisaina	67**	67	63?	67
Ca 113/68		ananda jala	68*	68	64	68
Ca 113/69		rājapāla	69	75	65	69
Ca 113/70		rājā sakavanta	70*	70	66	–
Ca 113/71	Rājā Vikramāditya I/II	rājā vikramājīta / vīra vikramājīta	71	62	70	71
Ca 113/72		sundarapāla jogī	72**	72	71	72
Ca 113/73		chatrapāla	73	–	72	73
Ca 113/74		sālabāhana	74	–	73	74
Ca 113/75		hasapāla jogī	75	–	74	75
Ca 113/76		suṣapāla	76	73	75	76
Ca 113/77	Śūrapāla I/II	subhapāla	77	–	76	77
Ca 113/78		gaṅgapāla	78	81	77	78

Dresden Ca 113 (cat. 3) (fols. 1–179)			BL MS. Ind. Misc. d. 3 (fols. 1–178)		V&A I.M. 9-1912 (fols. 1–177)	
inv. no.		**inscribed (verso)**	**corresponding name on fol.**	**corresponding image on fol.**	**corresponding name on fol.**	**corresponding image on fol.**
Ca 113/79	Govindapāla (Gopāla)	govindapāla	79	93	78	79
Ca 113/80		amrāpāla	80	–	–	80
Ca 113/81		valīpāla	81	90	80	81
Ca 113/82	Mahīpalā I/II	mahīpāla	82	94	81	–
Ca 113/83		harapāla	83	–	79	83
Ca 113/84		bhīmapāla	–	–	83	84
Ca 113/85	Madanapāla	madanapāla	folio missing		84	–
Ca 113/86		karmapāla	86	–	85	86
Ca 113/87	Vigrahapāla I/II/III	bikramapāla	87	–	86	–
Ca 113/88		malūkacanda	88**	88	87	88
Ca 113/89	Vikramacandra	vikramacanda	89**	89	88	89
Ca 113/90		kātalacanda	90	99	–	90
Ca 113/91		rāmacanda	91	103	90	91
Ca 113/92		dhanīcanda	92**	92	91	92
Ca 113/93	Kalyānacandra	kalyānaca(n)da	93	102	89	93
Ca 113/94		bhīmacanda	94*	94	93	94
Ca 113/95	Laḍahacandra	lohacanda	95**	95	94	95
Ca 113/96	Govindacandra	govi(n)daca(n)da	96**	96	92	96
Ca 113/97	Rāṇī Prabhāvatī	rānī parabhāvatī	97*	97	128**	128
Ca 113/98		haravarama jogī	98	–	96	–
Ca 113/99		govindavarama jogī	99	–	97	99
Ca 113/100	Gopālavarma	gopālavarama	100	–	98	–
Ca 113/101		mahānātha j(o)g(ī)	101	–	99	100
Ca 113/102		rājā mahīsena vaṅgālī	102**	102	100	102
Ca 113/103	Vallālasena	vilāvalasaina	103**	103	101	–
Ca 113/104		raghūsaina	104	105	102	103
Ca 113/105		mādhos(ai)na	105*	105	103	–
Ca 113/106		sūrasaina	106*	106	104	105
Ca 113/107		bhīmasaina	107*	107	105	106
Ca 113/108		kātagasaina	108*	108	106	107
Ca 113/109		harīsaina	109	–	107	108
Ca 113/110		ṣemasaina	110*	110	108	109
Ca 113/111		narāinasaina	111	113	109	110
Ca 113/112	Lakṣmaṇasena	laṣamīsaina	112*	112	110	111
Ca 113/113		damodarasaina	113	–	111	112
Ca 113/114		dīpasiṅgha	114**	114	112	113
Ca 113/115		rājā anasi(n)gha	115*	115	113	–
Ca 113/116		rājāsi(ṅ)gha	116	91	114	–
Ca 113/117	Vīra Narasiṁha	vīrasiṅgha	117	–	115	–
Ca 113/118	Harihara I/II	harasiṅgha	118	98	116	–
Ca 113/119		jīvanasiṅgha	119	–	117	–

Dresden Ca 113 (cat. 3) (fols. 1–179)			BL MS. Ind. Misc. d. 3 (fols. 1–178)		V&A I.M. 9-1912 (fols. 1–177)	
inv. no.		**inscribed (verso)**	**corresponding name on fol.**	**corresponding image on fol.**	**corresponding name on fol.**	**corresponding image on fol.**
Ca 113/120	Prithvīrāj Chauhān III (Rāi Pithora)	rājā pithaura	120	117	122?	119
Ca 113/121		haṭhīmala	121		–	120
Ca 113/122		durjanamadanna	122	118	119	121
Ca 113/123		udaimadanna	123	122	120	122
Ca 113/124		lachīmadanna	124	–	121	123
Ca 113/125	Sultān Sahab ud-Dīn Ghōrī	sulatāna sahāvadī gorī	125**	125	124**	124
Ca 113/126	Sultān Rukn ud-Dīn	sulatāna rukanudī	126**	126	125**	125
Ca 113/127	Sultān Shams ud-Dīn Īltutmish	sulatāna samsuddī	127**	127	126**	126
Ca 113/128	Sultān Qutb ud-Dīn Aibak	sulatāna kutabadī	130	128	129	127
Ca 113/129		sulatāna sahāvadī	128	130	127	129
Ca 113/130	Rāzia Sultāna (Bībī Rāje)	vīvī rāje	129**	129	128**	128
Ca 113/131	Sultān Nāsir ud-Dīn Mahmūd	sulatāna nas(ī)radīna	131**	131	130**	130
Ca 113/132	Sultān Ghiyās ud-Dīn Balban	sulatāna gayāsudīna	132**	132	131**	131
Ca 113/133	Shāh Husain	śāha hus(ai)na	133**	133	132**	132
Ca 113/134	Jalāl ud-Dīn Fīrōz Shāh Khiljī	śāha jalāladīna	134**	134	133**	133
Ca 113/135		śāha duladula	135**	135	134**	134
Ca 113/136	Shāh Sanjar	śāha ṣañjara	136*	136	135**	135
Ca 113/137	Shams ud-Dīn	samasudīna	137**	137	136**	136
Ca 113/138	Shāh Alā ud-Dīn 'Omar Khiljī	śāha alāvadīna	138*	138	137**	137
Ca 113/139	Qutb ud-Dīn Mubārak Shāh	kutavadīna	139	–	138	138
Ca 113/140	Shāh Ghiyās ud-Dīn Tughluq I	śāha gayāsudīna	140**	140	139**	139
Ca 113/141		śāha saramasta	141**	141	140**	140
Ca 113/142		śāha ṣālaka	142	–	141	141
Ca 113/143		śāha mahammada alāvadīna	143*	143	142**	142
Ca 113/144	Sultān Fīrōz Shāh Tughluq	sulatāna perośāha	144*	144	143**	143
Ca 113/145	Sultān Muḥammad Tughluq [?]	sulatāna mahammada	145**	145	144**	144
Ca 113/146	Sultān Ahmad (Mahmūd) Bayqarā	sulatāna ahamadavāīpāva	146*	146	145**	145
Ca 113/147		kutabaśāha	147	156	146**	146
Ca 113/148		lākanaśāha	148	147	147**	147
Ca 113/149		nūrasāha gorī	149	148	148**	148
Ca 113/150		... [illegible] jāumapati	150**	150	149**	149
Ca 113/151	Sultān Mahmūd Ghaznavī	sulatāna mahamūda gajanavī	151	149	150**	150

Dresden Ca 113 (cat. 3) (fols. 1–179)			**BL MS. Ind. Misc. d. 3 (fols. 1–178)**		**V&A I.M. 9-1912 (fols. 1–177)**	
inv. no.		**inscribed (verso)**	**corresponding name on fol.**	**corresponding image on fol.**	**corresponding name on fol.**	**corresponding image on fol.**
Ca 113/152	Shihāb ud-Daula Masūd	(ś)āha maulā	152	151	151**	151
Ca 113/153		śāha ṭoḍā	153	152	152	152
Ca 113/154	Shāh Mubārak	sāha muvāraka	154	153	153**	153
Ca 113/155		madhūsāha	155**	155	–	171
Ca 113/156		sulatāna hamī sāha	156	154	171	154
Ca 113/157	Tīmūr	taimūra	157**	157	–	155
Ca 113/158	Shāh Muḥammad	śāha mahammada	–	171	155?	–
Ca 113/159	Sultān Muḥammad	sulatāna mahammada	158	161	–	157
Ca 113/160	Abū Sa'īd	abū saida	159	160	164	159
Ca 113/161	Mīrān Shāh	mīrā saida	160	158	163	156?
Ca 113/162	'Omar Shaikh	umara śāha	161	159	165	158
Ca 113/163	Shāh Alā ud-Dīn	śāha alāvadīna	162	163	156	160
Ca 113/164	Shāh Husain Bayqarā	śāha husaina	163	173	157	–
Ca 113/165		śāha … [illegible]	–	139	–	138
Ca 113/166	Shāh Sikandar Lōdī	śāha sikandara	165**	165	160	162
Ca 113/167	Shāh Ibrāhīm Lōdī	śāha ibarāhīma	166	164	161	164
Ca 113/168	Bābur	bābara	167**	167	168**	168
Ca 113/169	Shēr Shāh Sūrī	serasāha	168**	168	169**	169
Ca 113/170	Salīm (Islām) Shāh Sūrī	salemasāha	169**	169	170**	170
Ca 113/171	Fīrōz Shāh Sūrī	saro sāha sakā	170**	170	172**	172
Ca 113/172	Muḥammad Khān ('Adlī) 'Ādil Shāh Sūrī	mahamada ṣāna adalī	171	162	166	163
Ca 113/173	Ibrahīm Shāh Sūrī	śāha ibarāhīma	172	166	167**	167
Ca 113/174	Sikandar Shāh Sūrī	śāha sikandara	173	172	–	161
Ca 113/175	Humāyūn	humāūn	174**	174	173**	173
Ca 113/176	Akbar	akavara	175**	175	174**	174
Ca 113/177	Jahāngīr	jahāgira	176**	176	175**	175
Ca 113/178	Shāh Jahān	sāhi jahā	177**	177	176**	176
Ca 113/179	Aurangzēb	auragajeba	178**	178	177**	177

Notes | 1 Gylnn 2000, p. 223. | 2 John Cleland to "Mr. Everard, F. Br N. Coll, Lalivurd to ef. Librarian by Mr. Mayo Fall of [illegible] Noss College," 1760, sig. Ms. Ind. misc. d. 3, Bodleian, p. 2. | 3 Bhandari 1918, pp. ii–v. | 4 Ibid., p. iv. | 5 Vallisnieri 1726, pp. 337–76 (see titles below in italics); also see cat. 3. | 6 See pp. 321–8, in URL: www.aryasamaj.org/newsite/Light_Of_Truth.pdf (25. 11. 2017). | 7 Listed are 124 Hindu rulers under different families that ruled in Indraprastha (modern Delhi) for a total number of 4, 157 years, 9 months, and 14 days. The individual terms of rule differ slightly in different sources. | 8 Corresponding names in Dresden Ca 113 folios. | 9 Instead of the 30th ruler, the 29th ruler in both Ca 113 and Vallisnieri's list there are *rājā ṣema* and *Sema* [sic] respectively. | 10 Instead of the Viramaha, the 45th ruler in both Ca 113 and Vallisnieri's list there are *rājā sarapā* and *Sarpa* respectively. | 11 Instead of the Adityaketu, the 60th ruler in both Ca 113 and Vallisnieri's list there are *udhanta* and *Udhant* respectively. | 12 In Vallisnieri's list only 3 kings of his house ruled followed by the house of Mahanath Jogi. | 13 Rājā Mahabahu (*rājā mahīsena vaṅgālī* [?]) appears as the next ruler after *mahānātha j(o)g(ī)* in Ca 113 and Vallisnieri's list and is not considered as the first member of the family. | 14 In Vallisnieri's list, no. 120 is a family with only one ruler (listed as *Famiglia*) and 121–4 as the *Famiglia di Atti Mal* [Haṭhīmala]. | 15 A similar image [a pencil drawing] of the famous Persian poet Shams ud-Dīn (b. c. 1325/26–c. 1390), known as *Hāfiẓ*, is found in the collection of Richard Johnson (1753–1807), published in Robinson 2007, p. 41. | 16 In Vallisnieri's notes, this family is also called *Shams ud-Din* while in Dresden Ca 113/141 the person is *śāha saramasta*. | 17 In Ca 113, fols. 163–7 and 169–74, are not descendants of Tīmūr. However, their grouping under one family might be due to the relation between these houses. The same can be said for the presence of Bengal rulers (fols. 137, 143, and 156) in the above list who have been sometimes put into false houses, perhaps serving more as a timeline rather than an entirely correct division between families.

Pigment and Dye Analysis

Measuring Methods (see chart)

Indian paintings from the Dresden Kupferstich-Kabinett were analysed using visible spectrophotometry (1), X-ray fluorescence analysis (2), and Raman spectroscopy (3) to obtain information about the colourants. The main red pigments are red lead, red ochre, and cinnabar. Pink-coloured areas contain white lead and red lac dye. Most of the green areas contain the same copper chloride pigment, probably atacamite. Some drawings contain mixtures of indigo with a yellow pigment. Smalt, indigo, and lapis lazuli were used as blue pigments; the yellow areas contain orpiment as well as an organic dye, probably Indian yellow.

Visible spectrophotometry is a convenient tool for classification of coloured materials.[1] The investigations were performed with colour spectrometer SPM 100 (Gretag-Imaging AG, Regensdorf, Switzerland), which measures the reflection of visible light (380–730 nm). The characteristic reflectance spectrum was then measured and stored. By comparing this specific spectrum with a database, it was possible to identify most of the colourants, both organic and inorganic. The method is unsuitable for the differentiation of copper green pigments.

X-ray fluorescence represents one of the most suitable methods for obtaining qualitative and semi-quantitative information on a great diversity of materials. The analyses were carried out with a handheld X-ray fluorescence spectrometer TRACER III-SD (Bruker Nano GmbH) with an interaction spot of about 1 cm. All measurements were conducted with a low-power rhodium tube; excitation parameters were, respectively, 15 kV and 55 μA for the determination of light elements and 40 kV and 15 μA for the detection of heavy elements.

Raman spectroscopy is a convenient tool for the investigation of pigments and minerals.[2] The Raman spectrometer (Renishaw inVia) has been specially adapted for the study of objects in the cultural heritage field. Instead of a microscope, it is equipped with a fiber optic probe (FOP) connected to lasers (200 mW, 532 nm and 300 mW, 785 nm). The probe is connected to a camera to position the object and to a CCD camera for signal registration. Measurements were carried out in the spectral range 100 to 3,600 cm^{-1}, with a spectral resolution of 4 cm^{-1} and different exposure times. OH

Notes | 1 See Fuchs 1988. | 2 See Clark 1995.

Comparison of Different XRF Devices for Pigment Analysis

A wide variety of techniques is used to investigate art objects. The most important requirement for the investigation of unique objects is the use of techniques that are non-destructive or need only minimal sampling. Following Lahanier,[1] the ideal procedure should also be fast, universal, versatile, sensitive, and multi-elemental.[2] X-ray fluorescence analysis (XRF) satisfies all these requirements and has been in the service of studies in the field of cultural heritage for many years. This essay focuses on XRF and presents two high-resolution scanning devices specifically developed for application in the field of cultural heritage.

XRF provides information on the elemental composition of an object and relies on the study of characteristic patterns of X-ray emissions from atoms irradiated with high-energy X-rays. When the external excitation beam interacts with an atom within the sample, an electron is ejected from the atom's inner shell, creating a vacancy. In the next step, another electron from an outer shell fills the vacancy. The energy of the emitted X-ray fluorescence is characteristic for a certain element, whereas the signal intensity allows one to determine the amount of the element in the sample. However, it should be noted that XRF is not well suited for the study of organic materials containing mainly carbon, nitrogen, hydrogen, and oxygen since these elements cannot be detected using this technique. XRF is one of the most suitable methods to extract qualitative and semi-quantitative information on the elemental composition of various materials containing elements heavier than sodium. This technique benefits from the availability of a variety of transportable instruments ranging from single-spot measurements to high-resolution scanning equipment.

Both μ-XRF scanners use an air-cooled low-power X-ray tube, poly-capillary X-ray optics, and an electrothermally cooled X-flash detector. The first one, ArtTAX (Bruker Nano GmbH), has a measuring spot of 70 μm diameter. The movable probe is operated by XYZ motors that allow for spot measurements as well as line and small area scans. This instrument is used for a semi-quantitative analysis of iron gall inks, pigments, minerals, glass, etc.[3] The imaging spectrometer Jet Stream (M6, Bruker Nano GmbH) has a variable measuring spot size of 75–850 μm diameter. The movable probe is mounted on a large frame, allowing for the mapping of surfaces up to 60 × 80 cm. Quick mapping facility and variable spatial resolution of the Jet make it the best choice for the initial investigation. Among these areas of interest we usually find touch-ups (*pentimenti*), damaged areas, and traces of previous conservation actions. Sometimes one discovers underdrawing (if it was not in carbon) or overpainting.[4] The "on-the-fly" modus of operation that allows obtaining elemental maps in a reasonable time results in the slight lowering of the spatial resolution. Therefore, we use the slow but extremely precise line scanner Artax for ink or pigment comparisons. To do so we have translated the measured intensities into concentrations using validated quantification routines. Our fingerprint model developed more than a decade ago for the studies of iron gall inks can be successfully applied to the comparison of contaminated pigments and metals.[5] For cat. 83, Ca 121/13, semi-quantitative XRF analysis reveals identical gold paint applied to corner and saddle decoration that differs from that on the frame (fig. 1). IR/OH

Notes | 1 See Lahanier et al. 1986. | 2 See Mantler/Schreiner 2000. | 3 See Bronk et al. 2001. | 4 See cat. 78, Ca 121/6, p. 36, figs. 3a and b. | 5 See Hahn et al. 2004.

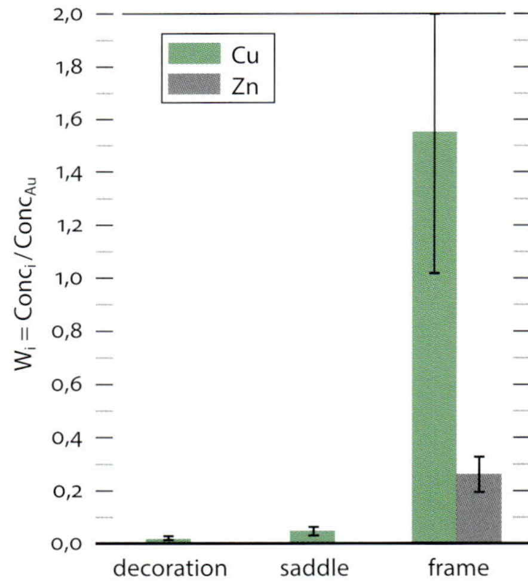

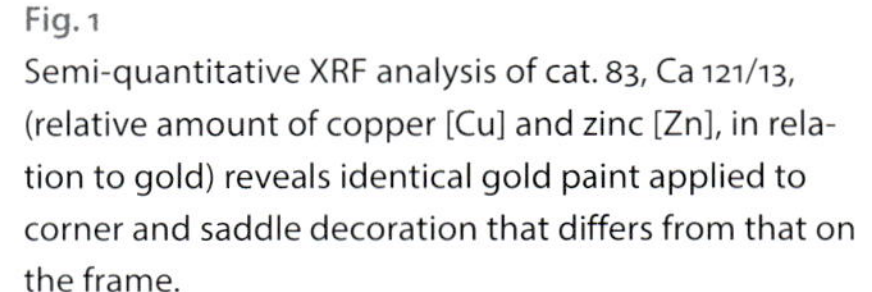

Fig. 1
Semi-quantitative XRF analysis of cat. 83, Ca 121/13, (relative amount of copper [Cu] and zinc [Zn], in relation to gold) reveals identical gold paint applied to corner and saddle decoration that differs from that on the frame.

	red	yellow / brown	green	blue	violet	white
Ca 110/20[1, 2]	lac dye, red ochre	yellow, brown ochre	copper green pigment (atacamite)	smalt	–	white lead
Ca 110/22[1]	lac dye, red ochre, red lead	Indian yellow	copper green pigment	smalt	indigo + lac dye	not analysed [n. a.]
Ca 111/18[1, 2]	lac dye, red ochre, red lead	–	copper green pigment (atacamite), indigo + organic yellow pigment	indigo	–	white lead
Ca 111/28[2]	n. a.	n. a.	n. a.	n. a.	–	calcite, white lead, traces of Hg
Ca 111/30[1, 2]	lac dye	–	indigo + yellow pigment	indigo		calcite, white lead, traces of Hg
Ca 111/31[2]	n. a.	n. a.	n. a.	n. a.		calcite, white lead
Ca 111/48 (fol. 44)[1]	lac dye, red ochre, red lead	Indian yellow	indigo + yellow	indigo	–	n. a.
Ca 111/50 (fol. 46)[1]	cinnabar, red ochre	Indian yellow	copper green pigment, indigo + yellow pigment	indigo	lac dye + indigo	n. a.
Ca 111/51 (fol. 47)[1]	lac dye, red lead, red ochre	yellow ochre	indigo + yellow pigment	indigo	–	n. a.
Ca 111/52 (fol. 48)[1]	lac dye, cinnabar	Indian yellow	indigo + yellow pigment	indigo	lac dye + indigo	n. a.
Ca 111/54 (fol. 50)[1]	cinnabar, red lead	Indian yellow	copper green pigment, indigo + yellow pigment	indigo	lac dye + indigo	n. a.
Ca 111/60 (fol. 56)[1]	lac dye, red ochre	–	indigo + yellow pigment	indigo	lac dye, indigo	n. a.
Ca 111/64 (fol. 60)[1]	lac dye, red ochre, red lead	–	indigo, yellow pigment	indigo	lac dye, indigo	n. a.
Ca 111/65 (fol. 61)[1]	lac dye, red lead	–	copper green pigment, indigo, yellow pigment	indigo	lac dye, indigo	n. a.
Ca 111/70 (fol. 66)[1]	lac dye, red ochre, red lead	–	copper green pigment, indigo, yellow pigment	indigo	–	n. a.
Ca 111/71 (fol. 67)[1]	lac dye , red ochre, red lead	–	indigo + yellow pigment	indigo	–	n. a.
Ca 112/9[1,2]	lac dye, red ochre, red lead	Indian yellow	copper green pigment (atacamite)	smalt	–	n. a.
Ca 112/14[1]	n. a.	n. a.	n. a.	lapis lazuli	–	n. a.
Ca 112/23[1,2]	lac dye, red lead,	yellow ochre	copper green pigment (atacamite)	indigo	–	n. a.
Ca 112/24[1]	lac dye, red lead (cinnabar)	–	copper green pigment, smalt + yellow pigment	smalt, indigo	lac dye + indigo	n. a.
Ca 112/28[1,2]	lac dye, red lead	yellow ochre	copper green pigment (atacamite)	smalt		n. a.
Ca 112/43[1]	lac dye, red lead, red ochre	–	indigo + yellow pigment	smalt	lac dye + indigo	n. a.
Ca 112/46[1, 2]	red lead, lac dye	–	copper green pigment (atacamite)	smalt	–	white lead
Ca 113/177[2]	n. a.	n. a.	n. a.	n. a.	–	calcite, white lead
Ca 114/22[1, 2]	cinnabar, brazilwood	orpiment	indigo, orpiment	indigo		white lead

	red	yellow / brown	green	blue	violet	white
Ca 114/37 (no. 13)[1]	cinnabar, madder	–	indigo, yellow pigment	indigo	–	n. a.
Ca 114a/2[1]	cinnabar, madder	orpiment?	copper green pigment, smalt, yellow pigment	azurite	indigo and red	n. a.
Ca 115/6[1,2]	red ochre, cinnabar	–	–	azurite	–	white lead
Ca 115/7[2]	n. a.	organic dye	copper green pigment (atacamite)	–	–	white lead
Ca 116[1,2]	cinnabar, lac dye, brazilwood	organic dye	indigo + yellow pigment	indigo	–	white lead
Ca 117/1[1]	lac dye, red lead	–	copper green pigment	–	–	n. a.
Ca 118/1[1]	lac dye, cinnabar (red lead)	–	indigo + yellow pigment	indigo	–	n. a.
Ca 119/2[1]	cinnabar, red lead	Indian yellow	–	indigo	–	n. a.
Ca 119/4[1]	–	–	indigo + yellow pigment	?	–	n. a.
Ca 119/7[1]	lac dye, red ochre	–	indigo + yellow pigment	indigo	–	n. a.
Ca 119/9[1]	lac dye, red ochre, red lead, cinnabar	–	copper green pigment	lapis lazuli	lac dye + indigo	n. a.
Ca 120/11[1]	lac dye, red ochre, red lead	–	copper green pigment, indigo + yellow pigment	lapis lazuli	–	n. a.
Ca 121/1[1]	red lead, red ochre	–	indigo + yellow pigment (orpigment)	–	lac dye + indigo	n. a.
Ca 121/12[1]	red lead, cinnabar	–	indigo + yellow pigment (orpigment)	lapis lazuli	lac dye + indigo	n. a.
Ca 121/13[1]	–	yellow ochre	–	–	–	n. a.
Ca 124/2[1]	lac dye?	–	indigo + yellow pigment	–	–	n. a.
Ca 124/3[1]	lac dye, red ochre	–	indigo + yellow pigment	indigo	–	n. a.
Ca 126/5[1]	red ochre, cinnabar, (red lead)	yellow ochre	indigo + yellow pigment	–	–	n. a.
Ca 124/6[1]	lac dye	Indian yellow	indigo + yellow pigment	indigo	–	n. a.
Ca 124/7[1]	lac dye	–	indigo + yellow pigment	–	–	n. a.
Ca 125/1[1, 3]	lac dye, red ochre, cinnabar, red lead	organic yellow pigment	atacamite	lapis lazuli	–	n. a.
Ca 125/2[1]	lac dye, red ochre, cinnabar, red lead	organic yellow pigment	copper green pigment	lapis lazuli	–	n. a.

Inventory Numbers and Catalogue Numbers

Inventory Numbers	Catalogue Numbers
Ca 110	2
Ca 111	4
Ca 112	1
Ca 113	3
Ca 114	90
Ca 115	89
Ca 116	5
Ca 117/1	28
Ca 117/2	29
Ca 117/3	24
Ca 117/4	25
Ca 117/5	27
Ca 117/6	26
Ca 118/1	44
Ca 118/2	48
Ca 118/3	45
Ca 118/4	46
Ca 119/1	72
Ca 119/2	71
Ca 119/3	43
Ca 119/4	55
Ca 119/5	20
Ca 119/6	63
Ca 119/7	61
Ca 119/8	47
Ca 119/9	49
Ca 120/1	76
Ca 120/2	73
Ca 120/3	56
Ca 120/4	31
Ca 120/5	74
Ca 120/6	75
Ca 120/7	80
Ca 120/8	79

Inventory Numbers	Catalogue Numbers
Ca 120/9	77
Ca 120/10	57
Ca 120/11	58
Ca 121/1	69
Ca 121/2	40
Ca 121/3	22
Ca 121/4	41
Ca 121/5	42
Ca 121/6	78
Ca 121/7	8
Ca 121/8	32
Ca 121/9	30
Ca 121/10	23
Ca 121/11	84
Ca 121/12	85
Ca 121/13	83
Ca 122/1	68
Ca 122/2	82
Ca 122/3	62
Ca 122/4	52
Ca 122/5	51
Ca 122/6	50
Ca 122/7	67
Ca 122/8	66
Ca 122/9	64
Ca 122/10	65
Ca 122/11	53
Ca 122/12	54
Ca 122/13	60
Ca 122/14	59
Ca 122/15	81
Ca 123/1	9
Ca 123/2	33
Ca 123/3	36

Inventory Numbers	Catalogue Numbers
Ca 123/4	10
Ca 123/5	34
Ca 123/6	35
Ca 123/7	19
Ca 123/8	21
Ca 123/9	70
Ca 123/10	39
Ca 123/11	38
Ca 123/12	37
Ca 124/1	14
Ca 124/2	13
Ca 124/3	12
Ca 124/4	16
Ca 124/5	15
Ca 124/6	11
Ca 124/7	18
Ca 124/8	17
Ca 125/1	6
Ca 125/2	7
Ca 126	91
Ca 127	88
Ca 160	87
Ca 2017/1	86

Bibliography

Adamova 2004 Adel T. Adamova, 'The Iconography of A Camel Fight', transl. by J. M. Rogers, in *Muqarnas*, vol. 21 (*Essays in Honour of J. M. Rogers*), 2004, pp. 1–14

Agrawal 1984 Om Prakash Agrawal, *Conservation of Manuscripts and Paintings of South East Asia*, London 1984

Amsterdam 1728 Nicolaas Witsen, *Catalogus van een Heerlyk Kabinet met oost-indische en andere konstwerken* [...] *naargelaten door* [...] *Mr. Nicolaas Witzen* [...]. *De Verkoopinge zal geschieden door de Makelaars Dirk van Hage, Vincent Posthumus, Pieter Kerkhoven en Jan Lempjes* [...] *den 30 Maart 1728. en volgende dagen* [...] *tot Amsteldam* [...], Amsterdam 1728

Beach 1978 Milo Cleveland Beach, *The Grand Mogul. Imperial Painting in India 1600–1660*, Williamstown, Massachusetts, 1978

Beach 1981 Milo Cleveland Beach, *The Imperial Image: paintings for the Mughal court*, Freer Gallery of Art, Smithsonian Institution, Washington, D. C. 1981

Beach/Goswamy/Fischer 2011 Milo Cleveland Beach, Brijinder Nath Goswamy and Eberhard Fischer, *Masters of Indian Painting*, 2 vols., Zurich 2011

Beach/Koch 1997 Milo Cleveland Beach and Ebba Koch, *King of the World. The Padshahnama, an Imperial Mughal Manuscript from the Royal Library, Windsor Castle* (with new translation by Wheeler Thackston), London 1997

Berlia 2017 Neha Berlia, 'From Timur to the Marathas Dynasties of India as Represented in late 17th to early 18th century Portrait Albums in European Collections', in Dresden 2017, pp. 106–15

Bernier 1670–1671 François Bernier, *Histoire de la dernière révolution des états du Grand Mogol, Evenements particuliers, ou cequi s'est passé de plus considerable après la guerre pendant cinq ans, ou environ, dans les états du Grand Mogol*, 2 vols., Paris 1670–1671

Bernier 1699 François Bernier, *Voyage dans les États du Grand Mogol*, Amsterdam 1699

Bhattacharya 1970 D. K. Bhattacharya, 'Indians of African Origin', in *Cahiers d'Études Africaines*, vol. 10, no. 40, 1970, pp. 579–82

Brauer 1993 Ursula Brauer, *Isaac von Sinclair. Eine Biographie*, Stuttgart 1993

Brilliant 1991 Richard Brilliant, *Portraiture. Between Transience and Eternity*, London 1991

Bronk et al. 2001 Heike Bronk, Stefan Röhrs, Aniouar Bjeoumikhov, Norbert Langhoff, Günther Schmalz, Reiner Wedell, Hans-Eberhard Gorny, Andreas Herold, and Ulrich Waldschläger, 'ArtTAX – A new mobile spectrometer for energy dispersive micro X-ray fluorescence spectrometry on art and archaeological objects', in *Fresenius' Journal of Analytical Chemistry*, vol. 371, 2001, pp. 307–16

Brown 1975 Percy Brown, *Indian Painting under the Mughals A. D. 1550 to A. D. 1750*, New York (1924) 1975

De Bruin 1737 Cornelis De Bruin [Cornelius le Bruyn], *Travels into Muscovy, Persia, and part of the East- Indies, Containing, an accurate description of whatever is most remarkable in those countries, and embellished with above 320 copper plates*, 2 vols., London 1737

De Bruijn 2009 Johannes T. P. de Bruijn, 'Kvāju Kermāni', in *Encyclopædia Iranica*, URL: www.iranicaonline.org/articles/kvaju-kerman-poet-and-mystic, 2009 (27. 11. 2016).

Bürgel 1990 Johann Christoph Bürgel, 'Humāy and Humāyūn: a Medieval Persian Romance', in *Proceedings of the First European Conference of Iranian Studies Held in Turin, September 7th–11th, 1987. By the Societas Iranologica Europaea: Part 1: Old and Middle Iranian Studies*, vol. 2, Rom 1990, pp. 347–57

Campan 1823 *Memoirs of the private life of Marie Antoinette, Queen of France and Navarre. To which are added, Recollections, sketches, and anecdotes, illustrative of the reigns of Louis XIV. Louis XV. and Louis XVI. by Madame Campan*, Philadelphia 1823

Chandra 1949 Moti Chandra, *The Technique of Mughal Painting*, Lucknow 1949

Chandra 1999 Satish Chandra: *Medieval India: From Sultanat to the Mughals*, Delhi 1999

Chatelain 1719 Henri Abraham Chatelain, *Atlas Historique, Ou Nouvelle Introduction A l'Histoire, à la Chronologie & à la Géographie Ancienne & Moderne, Tome 5, Qui comprend l'Asie en général & en particulier, l'Assyrie, l'Armenie, la Georgie, la Turquie Asiatique, la Terre-sainte, l'Arabie, la Perse, la Tartarie, les Etats du Grand Mogol, les Indes Orientales, la Chine, le Japon, & le Roïaume de Siam*, ed. by L'Honoré & Châtelain, Amsterdam 1719.

Chézy 1830 Antoine-Léonard de Chézy (ed.), *La reconnaissance de Sacountala*, Paris 1830

Churchill 1935 William Algeron Churchill, *Watermarks in papers in Holland, England, France etc. in the XVII and XVIII centuries and their interconnection*, Amsterdam 1935

Clark 1995 Robin J. H. Clark, 'Raman Microscopy: Application to the Identification of Pigments on Medieval Manuscripts', in *Chemical Society Reviews*, vol. 3, 1995, pp. 187–96

Collaço 2017 Gwendolyn Collaço, 'Dressing a City's Demeanour: Ottoman Costume Albums and the Portrayal of Urban Identity in the Early Seventeenth Century', in *Textile History*, 48 (2), November 2017, pp. 248–67, URL: www.tandfonline.com/doi/full/10.1080/00404969.2017.1369331?scroll=top&needAccess=true, 2017 (17. 11. 2017)

Czapla/Schankweiler 2012 Ralf Georg Czapla and Franca Victoria Schankweiler (eds.), *"Meine liebe Marie" – "Werthester Herr Professor". Der Briefwechsel zwischen August Wilhelm von Schlegel und seiner Bonner Haushälterin Maria Löbel*, Historisch-kritische Ausgabe, Bonn 2012

Dapper 1668 Olfert Dapper, *Naukeurige Beschrijvinge Der Afrikaensche Gewesten Van Egypten, Barbaryen, Libyen, Biledulgerid, Negroslant, Guinea, Ethiopiën, Abyssinie: Vertoont In de Benamingen, Grenspalen, Steden, Revieren, gewassen, Dieren, Zeeden, Drachten, Talen, Rijkdommen, Godsdiensten en Heerschappyen*, ed. by Jacob van Meurs, Amsterdam 1668

Dapper 1672 Olfert Dapper, *Asia, of naukeurige beschryving van Het Rijk des Grooten Mogols, En een groot gedeelte van Indien: Behelsende De Landschappen van Kandahar, Kabul, Multan, Haikan, Bukkar, Send of Diu, Jeffelmeer, Attak, Peniab, Kaximir, Jangapore,Dely, Mando, Malva, Chitor, Utrad, Zuratte of Kambaye, Chandisch, Narvar, Gwaliar, Indostan, Sanbat, Bakar, Nagrakat, Dekan en Visiapour, Beneffenseen volkone Beschryving van geheel Persie, Georgie, Mengrelie en andere Gebuur-gewesten. In de Benamingen, Grens-palen, Steden, Gewaffen, Dieren, Zeden der inwoonders, Drachten, Bestiering en Gods-dienst, Verciert door gaensmet verscheide Afbeeldgen in Koopergesneden*, ed. by Jacob van Meurs, Amsterdam 1672.

Das Gupta 1979 Asin Das Gupta, *Indian Merchants and the Decline of Surat c. 1700–1750*, Wiesbaden 1979

Del Bonta 2002 Robert J. Del Bonta, 'Late or faux Mughal Painting. A Question of Intent', in Barbara Schmitz (ed.), *After the Great Mughals. Painting in Delhi and the Regional Courts in the 18th and 19th Centuries*, vol. 53, no. 4, Bombay 2002, pp. 150–165

Dresden 2000 *Eine gute Figur machen. Kostüm und Fest am Dresdner Hof*, ed. by Claudia Schnitzer and Petra Hölscher, exh. cat. Staatliche Kunstsammlungen Dresden, Kupferstich-Kabinett (10. 9.–3. 12. 2000), Dresden 2000

Dresden 2013 Bernhard Maaz (ed.), *Das Kupferstich-Kabinett Dresden*, Berlin/München 2013

Dresden 2017 Monica Juneja and Petra Kuhlmann-Hodick (eds.) *Miniatur-Geschichten. Indische Malerei im Kupferstich-Kabinett*, exh. cat. Staatliche Kunstsammlungen Dresden, Kupferstich-Kabinett (3. 5. – 5. 6. 2017), Dresden 2017

Dresden/Bonn 1995 *Im Lichte des Halbmonds. Das Abendland und der türkische Orient*, exh. cat. Staatliche Kunstsammlungen Dresden, ed. by Holger Schuckelt and Claudia Schnitzer, Albertinum, Dresden (20. 8. – 12. 11. 1995), Kunst- und Ausstellungshalle der Bundesrepublik Deutschland, Bonn (15. 12. 1995 – 17. 3. 1996), Dresden/Bonn 1995

Duda 1983 Dorothea Duda, 'Islamische Handschriften I: Persische Handschriften', in *Veröffentlichungen der Kommission für Schrift- und Buchwesen des Mittelalters*, serie I: *Die illuminierten Handschriften und Inkunabeln der Österreichischen Nationalbibliothek* (Fortsetzung des beschreibenden Verzeichnisses der illuminierten Handschriften der Nationalbibliothek) vol. 4, (= Denkschriften der philosophisch-historischen Klasse 167), 2 vols., Vienna 1983

Duda 1984 Dorothea Duda, 'Das Millionenzimmer im Schloß Schönbrunn', in *Texte – Noten – Bilder. Neuerwerbungen. Restaurierungen. Konservierungen 1977–1983*, exh. cat. Österreichische Nationalbibliothek Wien, Vienna 1984

Duda 1991 Dorothea Duda, 'Das Forschungsvorhaben "Schönbrunner Millionenzimmer"', in *Österreichische Zeitschrift für Kunst und Denkmalpflege*, vol. XLV, 1991, pp. 30–40

Duda 1997 Dorothea Duda, 'Die Kaiserin und der Großmogul. Untersuchungen zu den Miniaturen des Millionenzimmers im Schloss Schönbrunn', in Karin K. Troschke (ed.), *Malerei auf Papier und Pergament in dem Prunkräumen des Schlosses*, Vienna 1997, pp. 33–55

Enzinger 1967 Moriz Enzinger, 'Die Malerin Auguste von Buttlar und ihre Grillparzer-Bildnisse', in *Jahrbuch der Grillparzer-Gesellschaft*, vol. 3, 1967, pp. 11–69

Fabbri 1991 Beatrice Buscaroli Fabbri, *Carlo Cignani: Affreschi, dipinti, disegni*, Bologna 1991

Falk/Archer 1981 Toby Falk and Mildred Archer, *Indian Miniatures in the India Office Library*, London et al. 1981

Ferdausi 2010 Abū'l-Qāsem Ferdausi, *Schāhnāme. Die Rostam-Legenden*, transl. and ed. by Jürgen Ehlers, Stuttgart 2010

Fisch 1986 Jörg Fisch, *Hollands Ruhm in Asien. François Valentyns Vision des niederländischen Imperiums im 18. Jahrhundert*, Stuttgart 1986

Forberg 2015 Corinna Forberg, *Die Rezeption indischer Miniaturen in der europäischen Kunst des 17. und 18. Jahrhunderts*, Petersberg 2015

Forster 1791 *Sakontala oder der entscheidende Ring, ein indisches Schauspiel von Kalidas*, transl. and comm. by Georg Forster, Mainz/Leipzig 1791

Forster 1963 Georg Forster, *Kleine Schriften zu Kunst und Literatur. Sakontala*, ed. by Gerhard Steiner, Berlin 1963

Foster 1921 William Foster (ed.), *Early Travels in India, 1583–1619*, London/Kolkata 1921

Frankfurt (Main) 2017 Claudia Bamberg and Cornelia Ilbrig (eds.), *Aufbruch ins romantische Universum. August Wilhelm Schlegel*, exh. cat. Frankfurter Goethe-Haus, Freies Deutsches Hochstift – Frankfurter Goethe-Museum, Frankfurt (Main) et al. 2017

Fuchs 1988 Robert Fuchs, 'Farbmittel in der mittelalterlichen Buchmalerei – Untersuchungen zur Konservierung geschädigter Handschriften', in *Praxis der Naturwissenschaften. Chemie*, vol. 37, 8, 1988, pp. 20–9

Gallop 1999 Annabel Teh Gallop, 'The Genealogical Seal of the Mughal Emperors of India', in *Journal of the Royal Asiatic Society*, vol. 3, no. 9, Cambridge 1999, pp. 77–140

Gerlach 1674 Samuel Gerlach, *Stephen Gerlachs deß Aeltern Tage-Buch, der von zween glorwürdigsten Römischen Käysern, Maximiliano und Rudolpho beyderseits den Andern dieses Nahmens, höchstseeligster Gedächtnüß, an die Ottomannische Pforte zu Constantinopel abgefertigten, und durch den wohlgebohrnen Herrn Hn. David Ungnad* [...] *mit würcklicher Erhalt- und Verlängerung deß Friedens, zwischen dem Ottomanischen und Römischen Käyserthum* [...] *glücklichst-vollbrachter Gesandtschafft*, Frankfurt (Main) 1674

Glynn 1996 Catherine Glynn, Evidence of Royal Painting for the Amber Court, in Artibus Asiae, vol. 56, no. 1/2, 1996, pp. 67–93

Glynn 2000 Catherine Glynn, 'A Rājasthānī Princely Album: Rājput Patronage of Mughal-Style Painting', in *Artibus Asiae*, vol. 60, no. 2, Arthur M. Sackler Gallery, Washington, D. C. 2000, pp. 222–64

Goetz 1925 Hermann Goetz, Indische Historische Porträts, in Asia Major, vol. 2 1925, pp. 227–50

Goetz 1958 Hermann Goetz, *The Indian and Persian Miniature Paintings in the Rijksprentenkabinet (Rijksmuseum)*, Amsterdam 1958

Gothart/Strobel 2010 York-Gothart Mix and Jochen Strobel (eds.), *Der Europäer August Wilhelm Schlegel. Romantischer Kulturtransfer – romantische Wissenswelten*, Berlin/New York 2010 (= Quellen und Forschungen zur Literatur- und Kulturgeschichte 62)

Grosse 1902 Martin Grosse, 'Die beiden Afrikaforscher Johann Ernst Hebenstreit und Christian Gottlieb Ludwig, ihr Leben und ihre Reise', in *Mitteilungen des Vereins für Erdkunde zu Leipzig 1901*, Leipzig 1902, pp. 1–87

Habighorst 2006 Ludwig V. Habighorst, *Moghul Ragamala. Gemalte indische Tonfolgen und Dichtung des Kshemakarna*, Coblenz 2006

Habighorst/Reichart/Sharma 2007 Ludwig V. Habighorst, Peter A. Reichart, Vijay Sharma, *Genuss und Rausch. Betel, Tabak, Wein und Rauschdrogen in indischen Miniaturen*, Coblenz 2007

Hahn et al. 2004 Oliver Hahn, Wolfgang Malzer, Birgit Kanngießer, and Burkhard Beckhoff, 'Characterization of Iron Gall Inks in Historical Manuscripts using X-Ray Fluorescence Spectrometry', in *X-Ray Spectrometry*, vol. 33, 4, 2004, pp. 234–9

Hahn/Rabin 2017 Oliver Hahn and Ira Rabin, 'Röntgenfluoreszenzanalyse als bildgebendes Verfahren – die Visualisierung von Materialität', in *N.i.Ke – Schriftenreihe*, vol. 1, 2017, pp. 66–71

Haidar/Sardar 2015 Navina Najat Haider and Marika Sardar, *Sultans of Deccan India, 500–1700: Opulence and Fantasy*, New York 2015

Haldane 1983 Duncan Haldane, *Islamic Bookbindings in the Victoria and Albert Museum*, London 1983

Hanneder 2017 Jürgen Hanneder, 'August Wilhelm Schlegel als Indienforscher', in Dresden 2017, pp. 87–93

Heawood 1950 Edward Heawood, *Watermarks, mainly of the 17th and 18th centuries*, Hilversum 1950

Heberle 1845 *Katalog der von Aug. Wilh. von Schlegel* [...] *nachgelassenen Büchersammlung: welche Montag, d. 1. Dezember 1845* [...] *bei J. M. Heberle in Bonn öffentl. versteigert* [...] *wird*, Bonn 1845

Hempel 1995 Rose Hempel, *Ukiyo-e, Meisterwerke des Japanischen Holzschnittes aus dem Kupferstichkabinett Dresden*, Dresden 1995

Ho 2013 Gitta Ho, 'Buttlar, Augusta von', in Bénédicte Savoy and France Nerlich (eds.), *Pariser Lehrjahre. Ein Lexikon zur Ausbildung deutscher Maler in der französischen Hauptstadt*, vol. 1: 1793–1843, Berlin et al. 2013, pp. 39–41.

Hopewell 2006 Jeff Hopewell, 'Ganjifa: India's contribution to the world of playing cards', in Andrew Topsfield (ed.), *The Art of Play: Board and card games of India*, Bombay 2006

Huntington 1984 Susan L. Huntington, *The 'Pāla-Sena' Schools of Sculpture*, Leiden 1984

Hurel 2010 Roselyne Hurel, *Miniatures & peintures indiennes: collection du département des estampes et de la photographie de la Bibliothèque nationale de France*, vol. 1, Paris 2010

Huschens 2000 Franz-Josef Huschens, *Die orientalischen Handschriften der Universitäts- und Landesbibliothek Bonn, ein Verzeichnis unter besonderer Berücksichtigung der Provenienzen und der Bestandsgeschichte*, Bonn 2000

Hutton 2005 Deborah S. Hutton, 'Carved in Stone: The Codification of a Visual Identity for the Indo-Islamic Sultanate of Bijapur', in *Archives of Asian Art* 55, Honolulu 2005, pp. 65–78

Hutton 2006 Deborah S. Hutton, *Art of the Court of Bijapur*, Bloomington 2006

Irblich Zwischenbericht Schönbrunn (n. y.) Eva Irblich, *Das Unternehmen der Konservierung und wissenschaftliche Bearbeitung der indischen Miniaturen des Millionenzimmers von Schloß Schönbrunn* (status report), manuscript n. y.

Irvine 1965–1967 William Irvine (transl./ed.), *Storia do Mogor or Mogul India, 1653–1708* (by Niccolao Manucci), 4 vols., Kolkata (1907) 1965–1967

Jaffer 1999 Amin Jaffer, 'Tipú Sultán, Warren Hastings and Queen Charlotte: The Mythology and Typology of Anglo-Indian Ivory Furniture', in *The Burlington Magazine*, vol. 141, no. 1154, May 1999, pp. 271–81

Jahangirnama 1999 *The Jahangirnama. Memoirs of Jahangir Emperor of India*, ed. and transl. by Wheeler M. Thackston [1624], New York 1999

Jones 1789 *Sakontalá; or, The Fatal Ring: an Indian Drama*, transl. by William Jones, Kolkata 1789

Juneja 2017 Monica Juneja, 'Sehen, Begehren, Sammeln. Ästhetische Wahrnehmungen in den frühmodernen Bildkulturen Südasiens', in Dresden 2017, pp. 21–9

Khalidi 2004 Khalidi, Omar, 'Sayyids of Hadhramaut in early Modern India', in *Asia Journal of Social Science*, vol. 32, 2004, pp. 329–52

Kircher 1667 Athanasius Kircher, *China monumentis qua sacris qua profanis, nec non variis naturae & artis spectaculis, aliarumque rerum memorabilium argumentis,* Antwerpen/Amsterdam 1967

Kishwar 2012 Rizvi Kishwar, 'The Suggestive Portrait of Shah 'Abbas: Prayer and Likeness in a Safavid "Shahnama"', in *The Art Bulletin*, vol. 94, no. 2, 2012, pp. 226–50

Koch 2004 Ebba Koch, 'The "Moghuleries" of the Millionenzimmer, Schönbrunn Palace, Vienna', in *Arts of Mughal India. Studies in Honour of Robert Skelton*, ed. by Rosemary Crill, London/Ahmedabad 2004, pp. 153–67

Kruijtzer 2002 Gijs Kruijtzer, 'Madanna, Akkanna and the Brahmin Revolution: A Study of Mentality, Group Behaviour and Personality in Seventeenth-Century India', in *Journal of the Economic and Social History of the Orient,* vol. 45, no. 2, 2002, pp. 231–67

Kruijtzer 2010 Gijs Kruijtzer, 'Pomp before Disgrace: A Dutchman Commissions, Two Golconda Miniatures on the Eve of the Mughal Conquest', in *Journal of the David Collection*, vol. 3, 2010, Copenhagen, pp. 160–82

Kuhlmann-Hodick 2017 Petra Kuhlmann-Hodick, 'Berührungspunkte. Werke indischer Malerei im Dresdner Kupferstich-Kabinett', in Dresden 2017, pp. 13–9

Kurz 1967 Otto Kurz, 'A Volume of Indian Miniatures and Drawings', in *Journal of the Warburg and Courtauld Institutes*, vol. 30, 1967, pp. 251–71

Lahanier et al. 1986 Christian Lahanier, Georges Amsel, Christian Heitz, Michel Menu, and Hellmuth H. Andersen, 'International workshop devoted to ion beam analysis in the arts and archaeology', in *Nuclear Instruments and methods. Section B: Beam Interactions with Materials and Atoms*, 14, 1986, pp. 1–168

Leach 1986 Linda York Leach, *Indian Miniature Paintings and Drawings. The Cleveland Museum of Art. Catalogue for Oriental Art, Part One*, Ohio 1986

Leach 1995 Linda York Leach, *Mughal and Other Indian Paintings in the Chester Beatty Library*, London 1995

Leach 1998 Linda York Leach, *Paintings from India. The Nasser R. Khalili Collection of Islamic Art*, London/Oxford 1998

Les Indiens ou Tipou Sultan 1788 *Les Indiens ou Tipou-Sultan, fils d'Ayder-Aly, etc., avec quelques particularités sur ce prince, ses ambassadeurs en France, sur l'audience qui leur a été donnée par sa Majesté Louis XVI à Versailles le 10 aôut 1788; précédées du précis d'une partie de l'administration de M. Hastings, etc* [...], Paris/London 1788

Leyden 1982 Rudolf van Leyden, *Ganjifa: The playing cards of India*, exh. cat. Victoria & Albert Museum, London 1982

Lightbown 1969 Ronald W. Lightbown, 'Oriental Art and the Orient in Late Renaissance and Baroque Italy', in *Journal of the Warburg and Courtauld Institutes*, vol. 32, 1969, pp. 228–79

London 1982 *The Indian Heritage: Court Life and Arts under Mughal rule*, exh. cat. Victoria & Albert Museum, London 1982

Losty 2012 Jeremiah P. Losty, *The Divine and the Profane. Gods, Kings and Merchants in Indian Art*, ed. by Francesca Galloway, London 2012

Losty 2013 Jeremiah P. Losty, 'The Carpet at the Window: A European Motif in the Mughal Jharokha Portrait', in *Indian Painting: Essays in honour of B. N. Goswamy*, eds. Mahesh Sharma and Padma Kaimal, Ahmedabad 2013, pp. 52–64

Losty 2016 Jeremiah P. Losty, *Court Paintings from Persia and India 1500–1900*, ed. by Francesca Galloway, London 2016

Losty/Roy 2012 Jeremiah P. Losty and Malini Roy, *Mughal India: art, culture and empire: manuscripts and paintings in the British Library,* London 2012

Lunsingh Scheurleer 1996 Pauline Lunsingh Scheurleer, 'Het Witsenalbum: zeventiende-eeuwse Indiase portretten op bestelling', in *Bulletin van het Rijksmuseum*, vol. 44, no. 3, 1996, pp. 167–254 [English summary: The Witsen Album: 17th century Indian portraits to order, pp. 266–70]

Lunsingh Scheurleer 2016 Pauline Lunsingh Scheurleer, 'The Indian miniatures of the Canter Visscher Album', in *Bulletin of the Rijksmuseum*, vol. 64, 2016, no. 3, pp. 195–244

Lunsingh Scheurleer 2017 Pauline Lunsingh Scheurleer, 'Indian Miniatures for Europe. The Dutch Market in the 17th and 18th Centuries', in Dresden 2017, pp. 55–67

Lunsingh Scheurleer/Kruijtzer 2005 Pauline Lunsingh Scheurleer and Gijs Kruijtzer, 'Camping with the Mughal Emperor. A Golkonda Artist Portrays a Dutch Ambassador in 1689', in *Arts of Asia*, vol. 35, no. 3, May/June 2005, pp. 48–60

Maāthir-ul-umarā 1979 *The Maāthir-ul-umarā, being biographies of the Muḥammadan and Hindu officers of the Timurid sovereigns of India from 1500 to about 1780* A.D transl. by H. Beveridge and Baini Prashad, 2 pts. in 3 vols., 2nd edn, Patna 1979

Mantler/Schreiner 2000 Michael Mantler and Manfred Schreiner, 'X-Ray fluorescence spectrometry in art and archaeology', in *X-Ray Spectrometry*, vol. 29, 1, 2000, pp. 3–17

Melzer 2010 Christien Melzer, *Von der Kunstkammer zum Kupferstich-Kabinett. Zur Frühgeschichte des Graphiksammelns in Dresden (1560–1738)*, Hildesheim et al. 2010

Menzhausen 1965 Joachim Menzhausen, *Am Hofe des Großmoguls. Der Hofstaat zu Delhi am Geburtstage des Grossmoguls Aurang-Zeb*, Munich 1965

Michell/Zebrowski 1999 George Michell and Mark Zebrowski, 'Architecture and Art of the Deccan Sultanates', in *The New Cambridge History of India*, vol. 1, no. 7, Cambridge 1999

Mikkelsen/Lundbaek 1980 Bente Dam-Mikkelsen and Torben Lundbaek, *Ethnographic objects in the Royal Danish Kunstkammer 1650–1800*, Copenhagen 1980

Montanus 1669 *Arnoldus Montanus, Gedenkwaerdige gesantschappen der Oost-Indische Maetschappy in't Vereenigde Nederland, aen de kaisaren van Japan: vervaetende wonderlijke voorvallen op de togt der Nederlandsche gesanten: beschryving van de dorpen, sterkten, steden, landschappen, tempels, gods-diensten, dragten [...] vereeuwde en nieuwe oorlogs-daeden der Japanners: verçiert met een groot getal afbeeldsels in Japan geteikent: getrokken uit de geschriften en reis-aentekeningen derzelve gesanten*, vol. 1, ed. by Jacob van Meurs, Amsterdam 1669

Ohri 2001 Vishwa Chander Ohri, *The Technique of Pahari Painting – An inquiry into aspects of materials, methods and history*, New Delhi 2001

Paulin 2016 Roger Paulin, *August Wilhelm Schlegel. Cosmopolitan of Art and Poetry*, Cambridge 2016

Paulin 2017 Roger Paulin, 'August Wilhelm Schlegel und Indien', in Dresden 2017, pp. 77–85

Pertsch 1888 Wilhelm Pertsch, *Verzeichniss der Persischen Handschriften. Die Handschriften-Verzeichnisse der Königlichen Bibliotheken*, ed. by Georg Heinrich Pertz, vol. 4, Berlin 1888

Peters 1994 Marion Peters, 'From the study of Nicolaes Witsen (1641–1717). His life with books and manuscripts', in *Lias. Sources and documents relating to the early modern history of ideas*, 21/1, Löwen et al. 1994, pp. 1–49

Peters 2010 Marion Peters, *De wijze koopman. Het wereldwijde onderzoek van Nicolaes Witsen (1641– 1717), burgemeester en VOC-bewindhebber van Amsterdam*, Amsterdam 2010 [Transl.: "Mercator Sapiens. The Worldwide Investigations of Nicolaes Witsen, Amsterdam Mayor and Board member of the East India Company"]

Prapanna 2017 Vandana Prapanna, 'The Collections of the Chhatrapati Shivaji Maharaj Vastu Sangrahalaya', in Dresden 2017, pp. 31–7

Randhawa 1960 Mohinder Singh Randhawa, *Kangra Paintings of Bhagavata Purana*, Delhi 1960

Rice 2011 Vael Rice, *The Emperor's Eye and the Painter's Brush: The Rise of the Mughal Court Artist, c. 1546–1627*, PhD thesis, University of Pennsylvania, Philadelphia 2011

Richards 1993 John F. Richards, 'The Mughal Empire', in *The New Cambridge History of India*, vol. 1, no. 5, Cambridge 1995

Ritter 1828/29 Carl Ritter, 'Landeskunde von Indien (zur Erklärung der Karte)', pl. 1 in *Berliner Kalender auf das Gemein-Jahr 1829*, ed. by Königlich-Preussische Kalender-Deputation, Berlin 1828, pp. 87–210, pt. 2 in *Berliner Kalender auf das Gemein-Jahr 1830*, ed. by Königlich-Preussische Kalender-Deputation, Berlin 1829, pp. 1–204 and pp. 364–80 (commented by Carl Ritter and August Wilhelm Schlegel)

Rizvi 1975 Sajjad A. Rizvi, *Religious and Intellectual History of the Muslims in Akbar's Reign*, New Delhi 1975

Robinson 1972 Basil William Robinson, 'Shāh 'Abbās and the Mughal Ambassador Khān 'Ālam: The Pictorial Record.', in *The Burlington Magazine*, vol. 114, no. 827, 1972, pp. 58–63

Robinson 2007 Francis Robinson, *The Mughal Emperors and the Islamic Dynasties of India, Iran and Central Asia, 1206–1925*, London 2007

Rocher/Rocher 2012 Rosane Rocher and Ludo Rocher, *The Making of Western Indology. Henry Thomas Colebrooke and the East India Company*, London/New York 2012

Roemer 1986 Hans Robert Roemer, 'The Successors of Timur', in *The Cambridge History of Iran, The Timurid and Safavid Periods*, vol. 6, eds. Peter Jackson and Laurence Lockhart, Cambridge 1986, pp. 98–146

Rogers/Beveridge 1909 *Tuzuk-i-Jahangiri or Memoire of Jahangir*, transl. by Alexander Rogers and ed. by Henry Beveridge, London 1909

Roxburgh 2000 David J. Roxburgh, *Kamal al-Din Bihzad and Authorship in Persianate Painting*, in *Muqarnas*, vol. 17, 2000, pp. 119–46

Roxburgh 2005 David J. Roxburgh, *The Persian Album 1400–1600. From Dispersal to Collection*, New Haven 2005

Sarkar 1925 Jadunath Sarkar, *Anecdotes of Aurangzib* (English translation of Ahkam-I-Alamgiri ascribed to Hamid-ud-din Khan Bahadur) with a Life of Aurangzib and historical notes, 2nd edn, Kolkata 1925

Sarkar 1979 Jadunath N. Sarkar, *The Life of Mir Jumla–The General of Aurangzeb*, New Delhi/Allahabad 1979

Schimmel/Welch 1983 Annemarie Schimmel and Stuart Cary Welch, *Anvari's Divan: A Pocket Book for Akbar: a Dīvān of Auh. aduddin Anvari, copied for the Mughal emperor Jalaluddin Akbar (r. 1556–1605) at Lahore in A.H. 996/A.D. 1588 now in the Fogg Art Museum of Harvard University*, New York 1983

Schlegel Bhagavad-Gita 1823 August Wilhelm Schlegel, *Bhagavad-Gita, id est thespesion melos sive almi Krishnae et Arjunae colloquium de rebus divinis, Bharateae episcodium*, Bonn 1823

Schlegel Briefe 1890 *Friedrich Schlegels Briefe an seinen Bruder August Wilhelm*, ed. by Oskar Walzel, Berlin 1890

Schlegel Briefe 1930 *Briefe von und an August Wilhelm Schlegel*, 2 vols., ed. by Josef Körner, Zurich/Leipzig/Vienna 1930, vol. 1: Die Texte, vol. 2: Die Erläuterungen

Schlegel/Colebrooke 2013 *Founders of Western Indology. August Wilhelm von Schlegel and Henry Thomas Colebrooke in Correspondence 1820–1837*, ed. by Rosane Rocher and Ludo Rocher, Wiesbaden 2013, Wiesbaden 2013, (= Abhandlungen für die Kunde des Morgenlandes 84)

Schlegel Hauptbeziehungen 1/1828 A. W. von Schlegel, 'Indien in seinen Hauptbeziehungen. Erster Jahrgang. Einleitung. Über die Zunahme und den gegenwärtigen Stand unserer Kenntnisse von Indien. Erste Abtheilung bis auf Vasco de Gama', in *Berliner Kalender auf das Gemein-Jahr 1829*, ed. by Königlich-Preussische Kalender-Deputation, Berlin 1828, pp. 1–86

Schlegel Hauptbeziehungen 2/1830 A. W. von Schlegel, 'Indien in seinen Hauptbeziehungen. Dritter und letzter Jahrgang. Einleitung. Über die Zunahme und den gegenwärtigen Stand unserer Kenntnisse von Indien. Zweite Abtheilung. Von Vasco de Gama bis auf die neueste Zeit', in *Berliner Kalender auf das Gemein-Jahr 1831*, ed. by Königlich-Preussische Kalender-Deputation, Berlin 1830, pp. 3–160

Schlegel Hitopadesas 1829 *Hitopadesas id est institutio salutaris* [...], ed. by August Wilhelm Schlegel and Christian Lassen, Bonn 1829

Schlegel Indische Bibliothek 1820–1830 *Indische Bibliothek. Eine Zeitschrift von August Wilhelm von Schlegel*, 3 vols., Bonn, vol. 1: 1820/1823–1830; vol. 2: 1824/1827, vol. 3 (booklet 1): 1830

Schlegel/Lassen 1914 *Briefwechsel A. W. von Schlegel, Christian Lassen*, ed. by Willibald Kirfel, Bonn 1914

Schlegel Œuvres 1846 *Les Mille et une nuits. Receuil de contes originairement indiens, Œuvres de M. Auguste-Guillaume de Schlegel écrites en français*, ed. by Eduard Böcking, Leipzig 1846, vol. 3.

Schlegel Ramayana 1829 August Wilhelm Schlegel, *Ramayana id est carmen epicum de Ramae rebus gestis poetae antiquissimi Valmicis opus*, Bonn 1829

Schlegel Werke 1846–1848 *August Wilhelm von Schlegel's sämmtliche Werke*, ed. by Eduard Böcking, 16 vols., Leipzig 1846–1848

Schmitz 1992 Barbara Schmitz, *Islamic Manuscripts in The New York Public Library*, New York/ Oxford 1992, pp. 169–75

Schnitzer 1995 Claudia Schnitzer, 'Ein "Spionagebericht in Bildern" aus Istanbul. Das Ungnadsche Türkenbuch und seine Kopie von Zacharias Wehme', in *Dresdener Kunstblätter* vol. 39, 1995, pp. 98–105

Schnitzer 2000 Claudia Schnitzer, '"in angenehmster Ordnung". Die Gründung des Dresdner Kupferstich-Kabinetts als höfische Vorlagen- und Dokumentationssammlung', in Dresden 2000, pp. 12–29

Schnitzer 2010 Claudia Schnitzer, 'Zwischen "Auszierung der Wände" und "Stufengang der Kupferstechkunst". Grafik-Dauerausstellungen im Dresdener Kupferstich-Kabinett von 1728 bis 1882 und ihre Bezüge zu Klebeband, Sammlungsrecueil und Tafelmontage', in *Jahrbuch der Staatlichen Kunstsammlungen Dresden,* 2010, pp. 50–61

Seyller 1999 John Seyller, 'Workshop and Patron in Mughal India: The Freer Ramayana and Other Illustrated Manuscripts of 'Abd al-Rahim', in *Artibus Asia/Supplementum* 42, Zurich 1999

Seyller 2013 John Seyller, 'Five Folios from the Jahangir Album', in *God is Beautiful and Loves Beauty: The Object in Islamic Art and Culture*, ed. by Sheila Blair and Jonathan Bloom, New Haven/London 2013, pp. 300–39

Sherwani/Joshi 1973/74 Haroon Khan Sherwani and Purshottam Mahadeo Joshi, *History of Medieval Deccan (1295–1724)*, 2 vols., Hyderabad 1973/74, vol. 1: *Mainly Political and Military Aspects,* vol. 2: *Mainly Cultural Aspects*

Simon 2017 Olaf Simon, '"… wie du hier sehen kannst". Kunsttechnologische Untersuchungen und Restaurierung der indischen Bestände des Dresdner Kupferstich-Kabinetts', in Dresden 2017, pp. 95–105

Skelton 1988 Robert Skelton, 'Arts of the Book: Sultanate and Mughal India', in *Islamic Art in the Keir Collection*, ed. by B.W. Robinson, London 1988

Sönmez 2016 Nedim Sönmez, 'Türkische Papiere in europäischen Stammbüchern des 16. Jahrhunderts. Mit zwei Beispielen aus der Württembergischen Landesbibliothek: Stammbuch Georg Ringler und Stammbuch Johannes Weckherlin', in *Alter Ego. Amitiés et réseaux du XVIe au XXIe siècle/Alter Ego. Freundschaften und Netzwerke vom 16. bis zum 21. Jahrhundert*, ed. by Kerstin Losert and Aude Therstappen, exh. cat. Bibliothèque Nationale et Universitaire de Strabourg, Württembergische Landesbibliothek Stuttgart, Stuttgart 2016, pp. 156–77

Sotheby's London 1976 *Catalogue of fine oriental miniatures, manuscripts and Qajar paintings,* Sotheby's 13 and 14 April 1976, catalogue 267, London 1976

Steiner et al. 1971 Franz Steiner, Ivan Stchoukine, Barbara Flemming, and Paul Luft (eds.), *Illuminierte islamische Handschriften* (Verzeichnis der orientalischen Handschriften in Deutschland, XVI), Wiesbaden 1971

Stichel 1991 Rudolf H. W. Stichel, 'Das Bremer Album und seine Stellung innerhalb der orientalischen Trachtenbücher', in Hans-Albrecht Koch (ed.), *Das Kostümbuch des Lambert de Vos*, commentary vol., Graz 1991

Stronge 2002 Susan Stronge, *Painting for the Mughal Emperor – the art of the book, 1560–1660*, Victoria & Albert Museum, London 2002

Strzygowski 1923 Josef Strzygowski, *Die indischen Miniaturen im Schlosse Schönbrunn*, Vienna 1923

Subrahmanyam 2012 Sanjay Subrahmanyam, *Courtly Encounters – Translating Courtliness and Violence in Early Modern Eurasia*, Cambridge/ London 2012

Subrahmanyam 2017 Sanjay Subrahmanyam, *Europe's India. Words, People, Empires 1500–1800*, Cambridge 2017

Syndram 2013 Dirk Syndram, *Der Thron des Großmoguls im Grünen Gewölbe zu Dresden*, Leipzig 2013

Syndram 2017 Dirk Syndram, 'Der "Thron des Großmoguls". Ein königlicher Traum vom Fernen Osten', in Dresden 2017, pp. 69–75

Syndram/Minning 2010 Dirk Syndram and Martina Minning (eds.), *Die kurfürstlich-sächsische Kunstkammer in Dresden. Das Inventar von 1587*, rev. by Jochen Vötsch, Dresden 2010

Tavernier 1676 Jean Baptiste Tavernier, *Les six voyages de Jean-Baptiste Tavernier, écuyer baron d'Aubonne, qu'il a fait en Turquie, en Perse, et aux Indes, pendant l'espace de quaranteans, & par toutes les routes que l'on peut tenir: accompagnez d'observations particulieres sur la qualité, la religion, le gouvernement, les coutumes & le commerce de chaque païs; avec les figures, le poids, & la valeur de monnoyes qui y ont court*, eds. Gervais Clouzier and Claude Barbin, Paris 1676

Tavernier 1681 Johann Baptist Tavernier, *Freyherr von Aubonne – Vierzig-Jährige Reise-Beschreibung*, vol. 2, Nuremberg 1681

Tavernier 1925 Johann Baptist Tavernier, *Travels in India by Jean-Baptiste Tavernier, Baron of Aubonne,* ed. and transl. by Valentine Ball and William Crooke, 2 vols., 2nd edn, London 1925

Titley 1977 Norah M. Titley, *Miniatures from Persian Manuscripts* […] *in the British Library and the British Museum*, London 1977

Topsfield 1984/85 Andrew Topsfield, 'Ketelaar's embassy and the Farangi theme in the art of Udaipur', in *Oriental Art* new serie 30, 1984/85, pp. 350–67

Topsfield 2008 Andrew Topsfield, *Paintings from Mughal India*, Oxford 2008

Tzoref-Ashkenazi 2009 Chen Tzoref-Ashkenazi, *Der romantische Mythos vom Ursprung der Deutschen. Friedrich Schlegels Suche nach der indogermanischen Verbindung,* Schriftenreihe des Minerva Instituts für deutsche Geschichte der Universität Tel Aviv 29, Göttingen 2009

Valentijn 1724–1726 François Valentijn, *Oud en Nieuw Oost-Indiën, vervattende Een Naaukeurige en Uitvoerige Verhandelinge van Nederlands Mogentheyd in die Gewesten, benevens Eene wydluftige Beschryvinge der Moluccos, Amboina, Banda, Timor, en Solor, Java, en alle de Eylanden onder dezelve Landbestieringen behoorende; het Nederlands Comptoir op Suratte, en de Levens der Groote Mogols; als ook Een Keuryke Verhandeling van 't wezentlykste datmen behoort te weten van Choromandel, Pegu, Arracan, Bengale, Mocha, Persien, Malacca, Sumatra, Ceylon, Malabar, Celebes of Macassar, China, Japan, Tayouanof Formosa, Tonkin, Cambodia, Siam, Borneo, Bali, Kaap der Goede Hoop en van Mauritius. Te zamen dus behelzende niet alleen eene zeer nette Beschryving van alles, wat Nederlands Oost-Indiën betreft, maarook 't voornaamste date eenigzins tot eenige andere Europeërs, in die Gewesten, betrekking heeft. Met meer dan thien honderd en vyftig Prentver beeldingen verrykt. Alles zeer naaukeurig, in opzigt van de Landen, Steden, Sterkten, Zeden der Volken, Boomen, Gewasschen, Land- en Zeèdieren, met alle* *het Wereldyke en Kerkelyke, van d' Oudste tyden af tot nu toeal daar voorgevallen, beschreven, en met veele zeer nette daar toe vereyschte Kaarten op geheldert door François Valentijn, Onlangs Bedienaar des Goddelijken Woords in Amboina, Banda, enz. in vyfdeelen*, 8 vols., ed. by Joannes van Braam and Gerard onder de Linden, Dordrecht/Amsterdam 1724–1726

Vallisnieri 1722 Antonio Vallisnieri, 'Catalogo di alcune rarità, che il Sig. Abate Co. Giovannantonio Baldini ha riportate da' suoi viaggi, venute principalmente dall'Indie e dalla Cina; indiritto al P. D. Piercaterino Zeno C. R. S. dal Sig. Antonio Vallisnieri, pubblico primario Professore di medicina teorica nello studio di Padova, con lettera data di Padova il dì terzo di novembre, 1719', in *Giornale de' Letterati d'Italia* vol. 33, no. 2, 1722, pp. 118–48

Vallisnieri 1726 Antonio Vallisnieri, 'Altra Lettera del Signor Antonio Vallisnieri al Padre D. Piercaterino Zeno, C. R. S. con cui mandagli il Catalogo de' Re del Mogol, i ritratti de' quali serbansi nel ricco museo del Co. Ab. Giovannantonio Baldini.', in *Supplementi al Giornale de' Letterati d'Italia*, no. 3, 1726, pp. 337–76

Van Gelder 1997 Roelof van Gelder, *Het Oost-Indisch avontuur: Duitsers in dienst van de VOC (1600–1800)*, Nijmegen 1997

Vogel 1937 Jean Philippe Vogel, *Journaal van Ketelaar's Hofreis naar den Groot Mogol te Lahore 1711–1713*, The Hague 1937

Weber 1853 Albrecht Weber, *Verzeichniss der Sanskrit-Handschriften. Die Handschriften-Verzeichnisse der Königlichen Bibliotheken*, ed. by Georg Heinrich Pertz, vol. 1, Berlin 1853

Weber 1865 Karl Weber, 'Eine sächsische Expedition nach Afrika. 1731 fl.', in *Archiv für die sächsische Geschichte*, vol. 3, Leipzig 1865, pp. 3–50

Weber 1982 Rolf Weber, *Porträts und historische Darstellungen in der Miniaturensammlung des Museums für Indische Kunst Berlin*, Berlin 1982

Weekes 2017 Ursula Weekes, 'Medallion Portraits in India and Europe', in Dresden 2017, pp. 47–53

Welch 1974 Anthony Welch, 'Painting and Patronage under Shah 'Abbas I', in *Studies on Isfahan: Proceedings of the Isfahan Colloquium*, pt. 2, Special issue, *Iranina Studies* 7, nos. 3–4 (Summer autumn 1974): 458–507

Welch 1976 Stuart Cary Welch, *Indian Drawings and Painted Sketches 16th through 19th centuries*, New York 1976

Welch 1978 Stuart Cary Welch, *Persische Buchmalerei aus fünf königlichen Handschriften des sechzehnten Jahrhunderts,* Munich 1978

Wright 2008 Elaine Julia Wright, *Muraqqa': Imperial Mughal Albums from the Chester Beatty Library, Dublin*, with contributions by Susan Stronge et al., exh. cat. Arthur M. Sackler Gallery, Smithsonian Institution, Washington, D. C. et al., Alexandria, Virginia 2008

Zebrowski 1983 Mark Zebrowski, *Deccani Painting*, London/Berkeley 1983

Zürich 2010 John Seyller (ed.), Konrad Seitz, *Mughal and Deccani paintings: Eva and Konrad Seitz collection of Indian miniatures,* exh. cat. Museum Rietberg, Zurich 2010

Index of Names

* For names with asterisk see biographies pp. 234–9.

Names in *italics* refer to inscriptions naming yet unidentifiable persons in cat. 3, Ca 113, and cat. 4, Ca 111.

A

B

Abbreviations

c.	circa
cat.	catalogue (catalogue number/ catalogue numbers)
cf.	confer (refer to)
d.	died
ed.	Edited
e. g.	exempli gratia (for example)
et al.	et alii/et aliae/et alia (and others)
etc.	et cetera
fig./figs.	Figure/figures
fol./fols.	folio/folios
i. e.	id est (that is)
ibid.	ibidem (in that very place)
inv. no.	inventory number
n. a.	not analysed
no./nos	number/numbers
p./pp.	page/pages
pl.	plate
r.	ruled
sig.	signature
transl.	translation, translated by
vol./vols.	volume/volumes

Photographic Credits

Bibliothèque Nationale de France, Paris, Département des Manuscrits | pp. 47, 50, 65 (l)

Bodleian Library Oxford | p. 87

Bundesanstalt für Materialforschung und -prüfung (BAM), Berlin | Ira Rabin/Oliver Hahn | p. 39 (r)

Courtesy of Francesca Galloway, London, and Sam Fogg, London | pp. 25 (l), 27 (r), 28, 29

Courtesy of The Trustees of the British Museum, London | pp. 24, 65 (r)

Grünes Gewölbe, Staatliche Kunstsammlungen Dresden | Jürgen Karpinski p. 23 (b)

Kerstin Riße, Dresden | p. 37 (r)

Kupferstich-Kabinett, Staatliche Kunstsammlungen Dresden | Herbert Boswank pp. 6–7, 20, 134–5, 180–1, 183–201, 206–7
| Andreas Diesend | pp. 2–5, 8–15, 22, 25 (r), 27 (l), 35 (l), 36 (m), 37 (l), 38, 39 (l), 40 (tr), 40 (br), 41 (ml), 41 (r), 42–3, 119 (l), 136–78, 182, 202–5, 228, 230
| Carsten Wintermann | pp. 34, 35 (r), 36 (l), 36 (r), 39 (m), 40 (tl, bl), 41 (l, mr), 46, 48–9, 52–63, 64, 66–85, 90–116, 120–31, 208–27

Nationaalmuseum for Wereldculturen, Leiden | p. 117

Österreichische Nationalbibliothek, Vienna | p. 133 (l)

Sächsische Landesbibliothek – Staats- und Universitätsbibliothek Dresden | pp. 23 (t), 26, 119 (r), 230

Schloß Schönbrunn Kultur- und Betriebsges.m.b.h, Vienna | pp. 118, 133 (r)

Victoria & Albert Museum, London | p. 86

Details

p. 2: cat. 6 | Ca 125/1

p. 4–5: cat. 85 | Ca 121/12

p. 6–7: cat. 86 | Ca 2017-1/21 (p. 126)

p. 8–9: cat. 76 | Ca 120/1

p. 10–1: cat. 60 | Ca 122/13

p. 12–3: cat. 64 | Ca 122/9

p. 43–4: cat. 1 | Ca 112/1

p. 136–7: cat. 84 | Ca 121/11

p. 180–1: cat. 86 | Ca 2017-1/27 (p. 186)

p. 203–4: cat. 87 | Ca 160/4

p. 228: cat. 30 | Ca 121/9

p. 271–2: cat. 86 | Ca 2017-1/1 (p. 1)

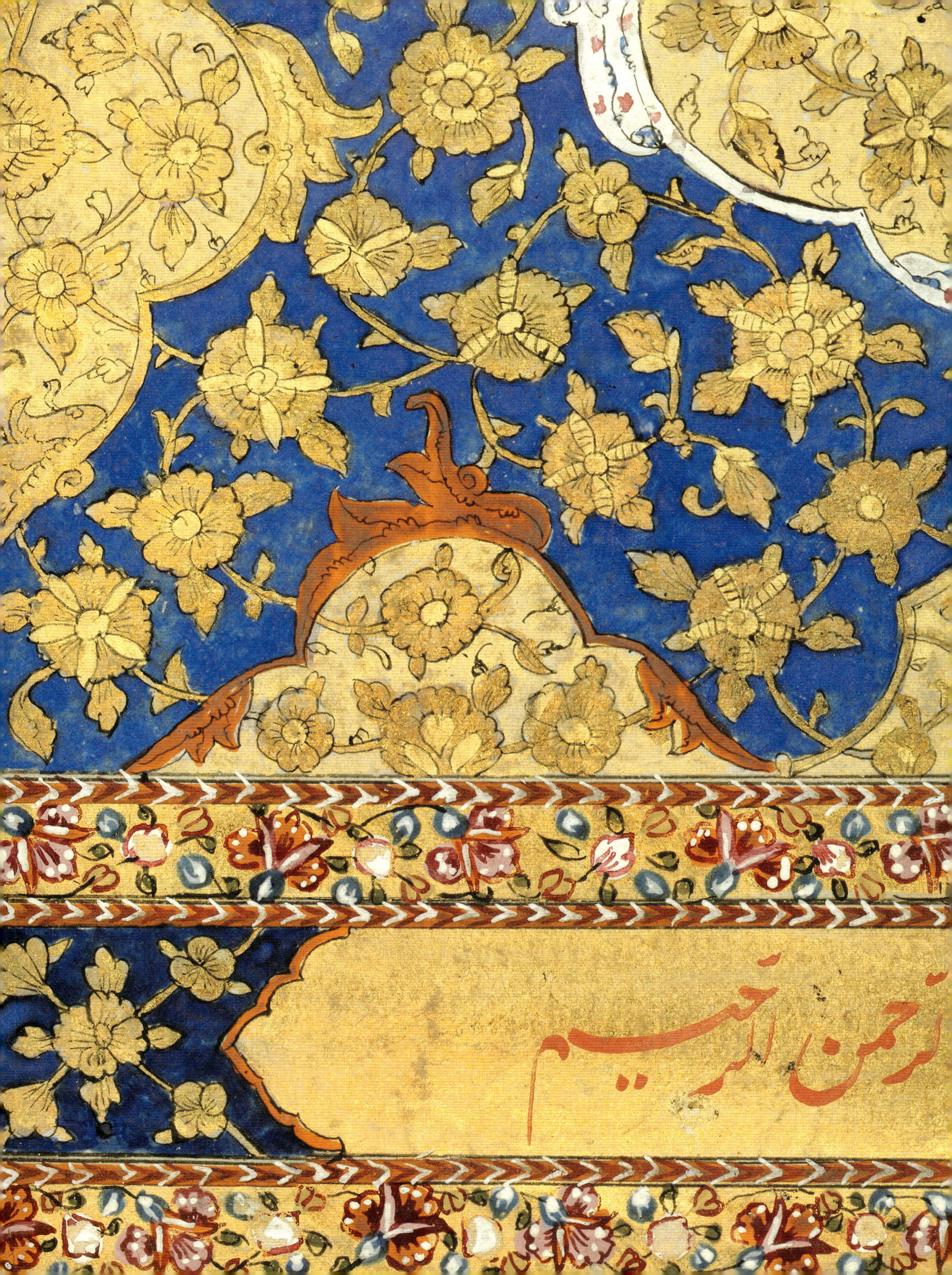
رحمن الرحيم

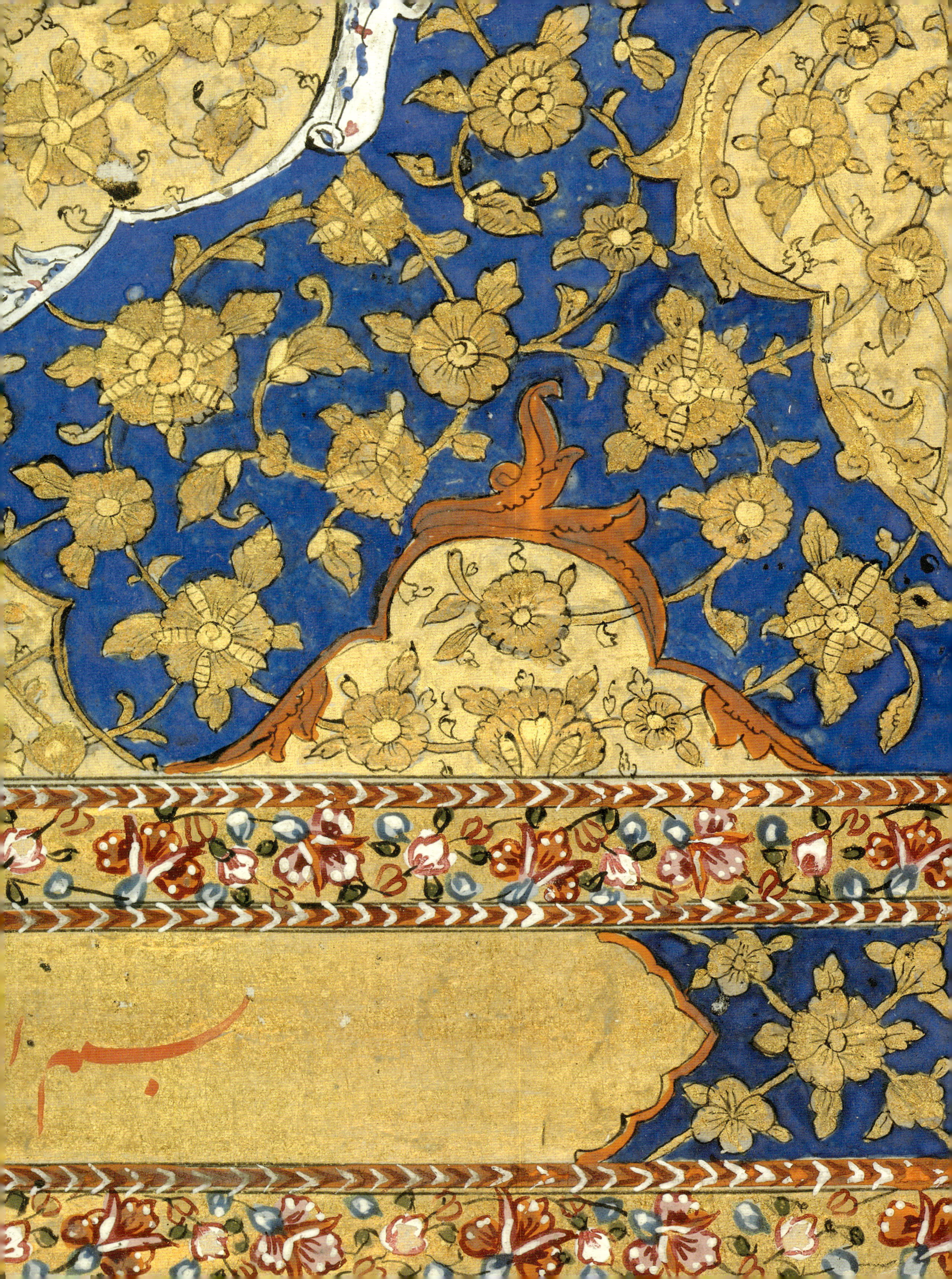
بسم

Indian Paintings

The collection of the Dresden Kupferstich-Kabinett

Edited by
Staatliche Kunstsammlungen Dresden
Petra Kuhlmann-Hodick

Co-edited by
Neha Berlia

Copyediting
Pamela Barr
Roland Steffan (Indian cultural history, terms and names)
with the assistance of Désirée Noffke

Design
Joachim Steuerer, Sandstein Verlag

Typesetting and reprography
Gudrun Diesel, Jana Neumann, Sandstein Verlag

Origination and printing
FINIDR, s. r. o., Český Těšín

The Deutsche Nationalbibliothek catalogues this publication in the German National Bibliography; detailed bibliographic information can be found online https://dnd.ddb.de.

www.sandstein-verlag.de
ISBN 978-3-95498-272-1

Research Project
"Europe · World"

Director General
Marion Ackermann

Director Kupferstich-Kabinett
Stephanie Buck

Managing Director
Dirk Burghardt

Head of the Department of Scientific Research and Cooperation
Gilbert Lupfer

In collaboration with

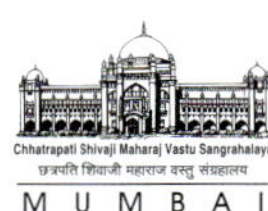

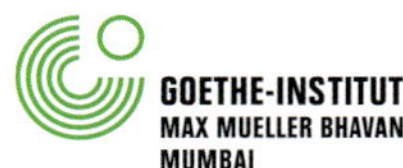

Supported by
Museum & Research Foundation GmbH, Dresden

This publication was realised with the generous support of

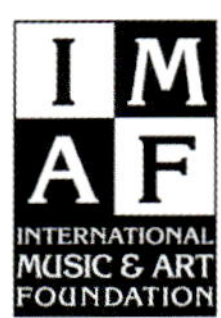

Francesca Galloway Ltd, London
Sam Fogg, London

Gefördert durch

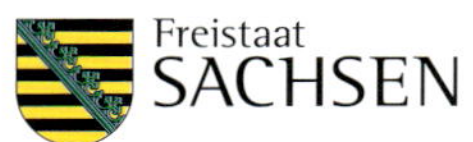

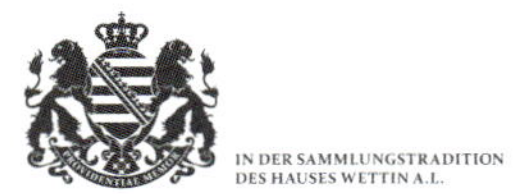

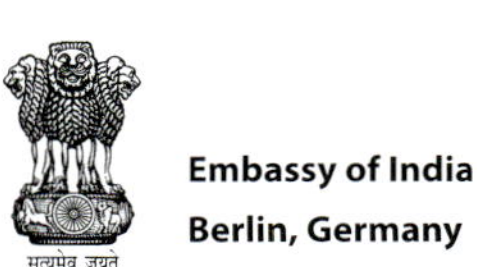

STAATLICHE
KUNSTSAMMLUNGEN
DRESDEN